Egypt: Portrait of A President, 1971-1981

Ghali Shoukri

U S. Distribution

Lawrence Hill & Co.,
520 Riverside Avenue, Conn. 06880, U.S.A.

Egypt: Portrait of A President, 1971-1981

The Counter-Revolution in Egypt
Sadat's Road to Jerusalem

Ghali Shoukri

Zed Press, 57 Caledonian Road, London N1 9DN

Egypt: Portrait of a President was first
published in Arabic; then in French by Le
Sycomore, 102 Boulevard Beaumarchais,
75011 Paris in 1979; and in English — with
a new Preface by the author — by Zed Press,
57 Caledonian Road, London N1 9DN in
December 1981.

Copyright © Ghali Shoukri, 1978, 1981
Translation Copyright © Zed Press, 1981

Typeset by Lyn Caldwell, Margaret Cole, and
Donald Typesetters
Copyedited by Anna Gourlay
Cover visual by George Bahgoury
Cover design by Jan Brown
Proofread by Penelope Fryxell and Anna
Gourlay
Printed by Krips Repro, Holland

**British Library Cataloguing in Publication
Data**

Shoukri, Ghali
    Egypt: portrait of a President
    1. Sadat, Anwar el- 2. Egypt — Politics
    and government—1970- 3. Egypt —
    History—1952-
    I. Title
    962'.054   DT107.85

    ISBN Hb 0 86232 062 3
           Pb 0 86232 072 0

Contents

Murder of the President

Who killed Sadat? That was the first question asked by the West.

Would the 'democratic regime' in Egypt change after Sadat? That was the second question; and the third was:

What future is there for 'peace' in the Middle East after Sadat?

I

The West answered the first question itself saying that Sadat's killer was 'Islamic fanaticism', strongly influenced by the phenomenon of Khomeini. That answer is a clear revelation of the West's ignorance, despite the extensive attention during the past eight years — or since the 1973 October War — directed towards Egypt, Islam, Khomeini and Sadat, through propaganda or by the mass media and universities, and the strategic research organizations.

Perhaps the question itself was wrong; perhaps we should first ask how and why, before asking who killed Sadat. Sadat was killed on 6 October 1981, exactly eight years after the Egyptian Army had fought to reclaim Sinai from the Israeli occupation. That day — the 6th of October 1973 — is unforgettable in the history of the Egyptian Armed Forces. The choice of that particular date, eight years after, to kill Sadat, surely has historical, social and cultural significance for those who killed him.

What does history say about the period between the proclamation of the War and Sadat's killing? What does it mean in the mind and soul of the Egyptian soldier and young officer? Or to the worker, the employee and the peasant, after the Army and the military colleges became open and free for the middle and even poorest classes during the era of Gamal Abdel Nasser?

History says that the occupied lands have not yet been liberated; the Palestinians have not regained their independent state; the Syrians, our partners in war, have not got back the Golan Heights. As for Egypt, she reclaimed some unfortified parts of Sinai, but still lacks sovereignty there . . . and American military bases have replaced the Israelis.

History also tells how Israel, under cover of the Egyptian 'peace', isolated Egypt from her Arab identity, an isolation that has even reached the lengths of an undeclared war between two neighbouring Arab countries: Egypt and Libya.

Another point is the high cost of that peace which really never took on substance. Prices of basic foods increased rapidly and continuously, so that the middle classes — let alone the lower classes — could not afford to keep pace with them. Inflation increased to the extent that one Egyptian £ was worth one U.S. dollar in the official exchange markets. Over two million people were unemployed and emigrants to Arab and Western capitals reached a total of five million. Debts to the I.M.F. and Western banks exceeded 24 billion dollars by 1981, and the crime rate in Egypt was the third highest in the world with the percentage of crimes increasing even in the last five years, while deficits in the balance of payments grew higher year by year.

All that, while a very small sector of society — the newly rich — enjoyed exceptional leisure and economic openings with the West; getting whatever they wanted from the boutiques of Cairo and Alexandria — exhibiting the latest fashions and fancies of Dior, Cardin, Saint Laurent and Ricci, in their brightly lighted windows, and even displaying these exciting Parisian scenes to the people at large by means of television.

And Egypt, which never knew religious fanaticism — Islamic or Christian — throughout her history, in the face of these rapid changes in society, economy and culture, realised that the end of war did not mean liberation, or leisure and abundance, but the flaying of the Arab identity from the depths of the Egyptian people. Egypt realised that the main outcome of the War was to force the Western way of life on her people; this in a poor country where this new mode of living led only to more poverty and lack of progress. No wonder Egypt was faced with a deepthroated demand for economic, social and cultural change. A demand manifested in peacefully directed means: from students' demonstrations to workers' barricades, strikes by the working class and by the professional unions, and an attempt to unify the organised groups into one national democratic front drawing support from the right, the centre and the left.

Meantime, the Armed Forces were not removed from what was happening in the Egyptian streets; as I have said, most of the young officers and soldiers were the sons of this disintegrating society. In addition, the Armed Forces were a national organization born initially with the beginning of Muhammad Ali Pasha's (1805-40) era, and had played a cardinal role in the State, in facing the Ottoman Empire and the other Western Empires. That Egyptian army was behind the officer Orabi Pasha in 1881 fighting the Khedive Tewfiq and demanding a Parliament, a Constitution and democracy. It was that army which changed the face of Egypt during the leadership of Abdel Nasser (1952-70) and in direct battles with the occupying forces in Suez in 1956.

Accordingly, we can assume that this army is a continuation of the people in the street in Egypt, caring about the increasing anxieties and tragedies of the populace, and at the same time, this army is the hero of the partial victories of 1973, from which not liberation and abundance was obtained, but new demands for war in the depths of Africa (Zaire), and a threat to an Arab neighbour (Libya). All this was completely new to the ideology and tradition of the Egyptian Armed Forces. Hence, the Egyptian army realised, as did civilians, the bitterness of the fruits of war; those who benefited were only the lucky few — export and import agents, representatives of the foreign companies, and their cronies. Thus, what was stirring in Egyptian society, stirred too within the body of the army, and so organised groups were born inside the Armed Forces — which is not a new phenomenon. The Orabi Revolution, a century ago, was an organised military revolution, a continuation of the National Party that was founded then. The Nasser Revolution, 30 years ago, was also an organised military revolution, gathering into one national front young officers from right, left and centre groups.

Since 1970, when Sadat took over Egypt, he sought to establish his own secret organisations inside and outside the army. He started by encouraging the Muslim Brotherhood and freeing those who had been imprisoned in Nasser's time. He began training extremist Islamic groups, in order to confront the Marxists, Liberals and Nasserists among the university youths. It is interesting to reflect that investigations into religious conflicts between Muslims and Christians in the last ten years (1972-81) always led to an unknown person. Also, what is called the religious conflict between Muslims and Copts, has been unknown in Egypt since the 1919 Revolution, except during the last ten years. The explanation is that Sadat's security forces were under the supervision of his Deputy Mubarak in the last few years, and that security regime deliberately created those events to divert people's minds from their real problems. Confirming that are two events: first, in 1972, during the students' movement, one student stabbed his colleague, and in the investigation later admitted to being a member of an organisation led by Muhammad Ismail, a high Egyptian official, now governor of Assiout. Ismail had told the students and other members of his organisation that their enemies were three: Communists, Christians and Jews. The second incident happened in the middle of 1981, when the bloody confrontation took place between Muslims and Christians in the Zaweia Hamra quarter in one of Cairo's popular areas. The inhabitants of that area arrested some people who were burning, destroying and shooting in the streets, but the police set them free because they were in fact from the secret service.

Sadat called himself 'the believing President', and his country 'the country of science and belief'. He included a statement in the Egyptian Constitution that 'Islam is the only source of legislation'. And he gave educational programmes and information centres an opportunity to spread Islamic culture. Sadat established the Raddeh Law Project to which the Church, headed by Pope Chenouda III had objected. This is the law condemning anyone to death who for overriding social circumstances reconverts to Christianity after adopting Islam. That law was abolished but Sadat never forgot the Pope's objection to it. He even forbade the Copts from visiting Jerusalem as long as it was occupied by Israel. And he ordered the Pope's removal, even though the Coptic Pope's appointment is not made in accordance with civil law, since he is chosen by the Christians and the Holy Spirit. Sadat even arrested priests and bishops, which had never happened before in modern Egyptian history.

In short, Sadat tried to stir up dissension between all the people. What amazed foreigners was when Sadat wanted to attack the religious headquarters of the Copts, and he tried to weaken their influence by saying that he was a Muslim President in a Muslim country, thus tacitly giving the green light for their slaughter. But the exact opposite happened; religious dissension died down immediately. This was because Egyptians felt that their country was in danger: one match could light a religious fire in the state.

For all that, Islamic fanaticism is innocent of Sadat's blood because it does not exist. The Islamic groups that he patronized were not, nor ever will be the owner of the long arm in the Egyptian streets or in the Armed Forces. What did happen was simply that Sadat had slammed shut all doors to change in the face of peaceful, democratic dialogue which is one of the basic components of Egyptian society. The national opposition of progressive and democratic Egypt was patient for ten years, and the Armed Forces for eight years after the War of 1973. But patience has its limits, and when Sadat began his campaign to arrest all the opposition – a month before his death, he condemned himself to death. The opposition had reached a high degree of organisation and coordination. On the eve of the arrests, Sadat himself said that it was a matter of life or death, and by arresting 5,000 important national leaders, he chose the easy way – death.

Death was the Egyptian people's verdict on the whole regime and not just the person of Sadat. Violence came in the execution of that decision, as a reaction to the extreme violence of the regime in repressing the opposition. It was the fruit of ten years of slow accumulations. It was carried out by an Egyptian officer on 6th October 1981, a symbol of the victorious Army's revenge and a reminder to people that the Armed Forces are the legal offspring of the Egyptian people.

It was not an assassination, but an execution, not of Sadat but of the system. The religious extremists were not responsible for this condemnation, but the Egyptian people, with their national progressive democratic opposition, were. The motivating factors were the national Arab identity that Sadat's regime wanted to wrest from them, and the way of life inflicted upon a poor nation that does not want to increase its poverty.

That is my answer to the West's first and wrong question.

But what of the question of democracy? Was Sadat's regime democratic? Westerners understand the democratic system as a system attached to the West, and it is true that Sadat's system was and still is tied to the West. Yet the truth is that it never was a democratic system. The West began a fairminded campaign against the Sadat dictatorship several weeks before his execution, because of the 1,500 arrests that he made among Egypt's national and cultural leaders, but it quickly lost its memory when the first bullet was fired at Sadat. In moments of historic decisiveness, the West supports its man and agent no matter if he is a dictator.

Sadat was a dictator not only in the last month prior to his execution, but throughout his reign and he left a dictatorial regime which will not change with Mubarak. The series of statutes issued from 1971 to 1981 under such innocuous titles as 'national unity and social peace', 'shame', and 'the suspicion', were radical intrusions on the essentials of democracy, and are not comparable with any laws except those of Hitler, Mussolini, Franco and Salazar. Not even one article exists in the Egyptian press that raises a voice against the Camp David Treaties, because no one who objects has the right to write, or to express himself through the radio or television. The President commanded complete authority and did not recognize any democratic constitution. He it was who created the title of General Socialist Prosecutor in an unsocialist country, in order to abolish the usual judicial obligations, and to establish exceptional military and political justice conferring the right to detain any person on trivial charges without trial and for several years.

That regime will not be changed by President Mubarak who, instead of freeing those detained, added thousands more to them, and has not abolished martial law and the state of emergency — as if Egypt were in a state of war; and, instead of complying with the usual electoral procedures that take 60 days, he finished the job in a week!

The execution — not of Sadat but of the regime — still stands; its significance was and still is death to dictatorship, to Camp David, to poverty and to the continued absence of progress.

Coming to the third question asked in the West, on the future of peace in the Middle East: if ignorance was the source of the first two questions then the source of the third is illusion.

The peace treaty between Egypt, Israel and America did not establish peace in the Middle East, but opened the doors to war for one simple reason — the Palestinian problem. This is the main component of the conflict in the Middle East, and unless that problem is solved, there will never be peace in the region. The Camp David treaties proved their failure, and the talks about Palestinian autonomy reached a dead end. That fact was immediately reflected in several new wars, the most dangerous of which was the Lebanese War. Israel took advantage of the Egyptian peace treaty to enter the south of Lebanon and strike at Beirut, and later to reach out to attack the nuclear power plant in Baghdad. Egypt and Sudan take refuge under the American umbrella, and threaten Libya and Chad. Thus the question is: where is peace?

There is no peace in Egypt where war is now declared between the people and the regime. There will never be any settlement until the whole regime collapses. And there can be no peace in the Middle East while the declared war between Israel and all the Arabs extends its range day after day.

There is no peace, either, to be gained from isolating Egypt from the Arabs, because it is impossible for a nation to be torn from its identity, and because it is impossible to impose a Western life-style on a society struggling with poverty, and, lastly, because it is impossible to impose military bases in countries where they are not wanted, so that one occupation is exchanged for another.

And because it is impossible for Israel, America and the rest of the West to kill the Palestinian People.

Ghali Shoukri
20 October 1981

Preface

From the very beginning of the Arab League, Egypt had been at the head of a movement, which, in the view of some British writers, could operate only on a regional basis: an amplified substitute for the 'brown dominion' of which T.E. Lawrence had dreamed. Nasser's harsh insistence on his rights, his wide popular support, the enthusiasm he aroused in the whole Arab world, gave this artificial background new life and reality, especially after the nationalisation of Suez. International capitalism, its local allies — both individuals and groups — and its cultural correspondents, who were not the least active, ignored this fact all through Nasser's period in power.

More recently the oil revolt, if we may call it that, made imperialism's last attempts at stabilisation precarious, or at least costly. Israel was a foothold for the West in the Middle Eastern camp, and perceived as a challenge by the Arab world: a bridgehead and a stumbling-block — if we may be allowed these contradictory metaphors — Israel was and is both at once. Meanwhile, the Arab movement, spurred on by Nasser and too, by Libya, Algeria etc., had become a synonym for progressive and definite views. The Palestinians had become its vanguard; their exploits may have been considered dangerously extremist, but, as a symbol, never rejected.

It was this conjuration, political, social and semantic at one and the same time, which culminated in Sadat's visit to Jerusalem.

Imagine, between 1871 and 1914, a President of the Third Republic of France meeting the German Emperor at Strasbourg, and you will have some idea of the violent feelings engendered by this counter-symbol, so to speak, with which Sadat was crushing the Arabian dream and its counterparts in reality. Of course, measured discussion with an adversary, and positive compromise, have indisputable value. But they could not compensate in kind for the price Egypt was paying in abandoning the Arabs' last diplomatic weapon: refusal to recognize Israel *de jure,* without substantial concessions on the part of the adversary. For how can they ever use this weapon in future, knowing that the President of the largest Arab state has been to Jerusalem and spoken before the Knesset?

The demobilisation on the Egyptian side which followed, broke the alliance — whether it was a good or a bad thing — which had united all these States for 30 years, in reality or in appearance only. We can understand the weariness and resentment of a country that had given of its best to the Arab cause for a whole generation — which was more than most had done. Was that a reason for breaking the political and ideological — and even sentimental - bonds which Egypt herself had forged all through that period? More abruptly still, she gave up her own style of expression. *Mutatis mutandis,* the visit to Jerusalem can be considered the reverse of the nationalisation of the Canal. It was, in fact, anti-Suez.

The success or failure of this attempt, a suspiciously bold poker move, does not of course depend on its reception by the other Arab states, which are more divided than ever. It depends on its concrete results, or their absence. Without real gains, it would simply look like an appalling swindle. Obviously, when Sadat went to Jerusalem it was not Israel he had in mind, but America. Opinion polls in the United States immediately showed that his calculation was a plausible one — but not sufficiently so to be decisive. It was to be expected that the pressure of the Zionist lobby in the United States would prevent President Carter suggesting the indispensable concessions to Israel. He could not do so. He did not even want to. Sadat's initiative has had to come down to the most inglorious bargainings.

Whether intentionally or not, Egypt — or at least its rulers — has resound-ingly broken the Arab front which it had kept alive since the end of the Second World War, and of which Nasser and his followers had, in the 60s, worked out the theory and the practical application. This retreat, even though it suited many conservative opinions, is nonetheless a terrible blow to a cause of Arab politics, which for a generation had coincided with progress-ive thought in the region. Doubtless the supporters of Egyptian nationalism could point to the Revolution of 1919, which, for the first time in the Third World, had brought a parliamentary democracy into power. But it is no detriment to the merits of Zaghlul — on the contrary to emphasise the moti-vation of his movement, patriotic even more than reformist. And can it be the same in the atmosphere of compromise, of defeatism masked by pseudo-realism, and of Westernism at all costs, in which Sadat moves? No, indeed not.

For reasons which apply to Egypt, just as they do to Arabs in general and to the world at large, the restoration and progress of a collective identity, in Egypt or anywhere else, cannot be divorced from a struggle for the restoration of the Palestinian people. That does not mean that we have to opt for an unrealistic intransigence. Nasser made that clear by his support for Resolution 242 of the Security Council. But that means that the visit to Jerusalem, with whatever verbal demands it may have been matched, offered Egypt the means for healthy realism and for an honourable compromise. Despite its size and its past claims on the admiration of the Arabs and the esteem of the world, Egypt, as long as this situation lasts, can only be an encumbrance to herself and to her friends.

To maintain a negative view, however, even a provisory one, would be to show a strange forgetfulness of the nature of the Egyptian people, its long political experience, and its formidable intensity of life. This book by Ghali Shoukri,

an Egyptian essayist and critic of international repute, illustrates the com-
plexity, the fertile variety, the moral, social and political courage of this great
body, which made its entry into contemporary history almost two centuries
ago — under conditions we remember well.

It is true that the course it followed alternated in a curious way between
phases of acceleration and of inertia; the Revolution of 1919 was followed by
cumbersome debates, and the glory of Nasserism might well have emerged into
events other than the Six Day War and the talks at Camp David. However
that may be, the vital energy of this great people remains intact through all
trials. Egypt is always losing but has never lost. And amid the complexities,
sometimes very gloomy, which Ghali Shoukri analyses, we will find not only
the factors leading to a counter-revolution, but also indications of potential
new upheavals. Everyone who reads these pages will appreciate not only the
wealth of documentary evidence, but their healthy, constructive optimism.
It is a history of Egypt, and a history seen from within which is offered to us,
with all its disappointments and promises of renewal.

The break-up of one form of Arabism, that which has occupied the history
of the last three decades — a form typified, alas, by the confusion of plans
and by rivalries between States and governments — must in fact give rise to
indispensable revisions. The Arabs, since gaining independence, have lingered
halfway between the chauvinistic pursuit of their own particular interests and
the utopia of unification. If they learn their lesson from the present failure,
they should abandon a policy which is risky on both the ideal and the practical
level, and replace it by a strategy which gives to each its rightful place. They
should go beyond state socialism and nationalism, which have often led them
into blind alleys, they should build between them, by means of broad
coalitions of people, what we might call their pre-unity.

The reconciliation between the two branches of the Ba'ath, which has
recently begun to take shape, could be one of the premises of such a movement. An Arab entity, unitary and plural, going from the Persian Gulf to the
Mediterranean would be of ample consequence to repair the tragic breach
that, as I have already mentioned, rended the front. In its turn, instead of
tearing itself to pieces over the Western Sahara, the Maghreb should make its
tripartite, interdependent entity into a reality. With the Nile Valley and the
Arab Peninsula, three great blocs would thus come to birth, and would play
a decisive part in world politics. By re-establishing their relations with the
Iranians, the Turks and the Africans, or rather building them on new foundations, the Arabs themselves could liberate the Afro-Asian dimension which,
up to now, has been inexcusably lacking, a fact which cannot be forgotten
despite all their professions of faith. Thus they would cease to appear, despite
their denials, as the poor relations (billionaires though they may be) of a
liberal or socialist West. If they re-established themselves on the true foundations of their identity, they could also propose to the other dwellers on the
same shores a new system of relationships, an organisation, which even by
their own Mediterranean dimension would restore the equilibrium of the
Afro-Asian dimension which they have so long neglected and repressed in

3

their history. And these dimensions, Afro-Asian and Mediterranean, blend together in Palestine.

Jacques Berque

Introduction: Towards a Sociology of Counter-Revolution

I

'Every country which has experienced revolution has seen the revolutionaries on one side facing the reformists and future traitors on the other.' These words by Regis Debray[1] summarise his experience as a young European fascinated by the revolutionary 'troubles' of the under-developed countries, in this case Latin America, exacerbated by a successful birth (Cuba — Castro) or a cruel abortion (Bolivia — Che). What interests us in this conclusion is that Debray, as a young European in the second half of the 20th Century, has on two occasions gone beyond direct and tangible reality. The first time was when he abandoned the potential struggle in his own country, where internationalist participation is possible, to go, drawn by an irresistible force, into the forests of Latin America. The second time was when he abandoned his profession of journalist and his middle-class social environment to enter the ranks of the 'armed struggle' and suffer the consequences in an arduous life. Experience led him to a twofold return to base: to his country and to his profession, to write memoirs and novels; he says he is no longer prepared to commit or incite others to commit murder in the name of revolution or of other slogans.

It is not important whether Regis Debray was right or wrong at the beginning, the middle or the end of his experience. Nor is it important whether his case is an individual one that cannot serve as an example, or whether it is a general phenomenon from which the beginning and end can be used to draw a conclusion. What matters is rather the complex context which led him to say: 'every country which has experienced revolution has seen the revolutionaries on one side facing the reformists and future traitors on the other.' This theoretical generalisation coming from a young man who had not yet reached full intellectual maturity, and politically was almost in a state of confusion, is completely confirmed by both the present and the past. What is perhaps lacking is the specific, something which Debray could not provide from his experience, which is nearer to that of an adventurer than to that of a revolutionary.

However, this specific quality in Western thought and experience can be traced from one extreme to another, beginning with Engels' *L'Allemagne:*

5

la revolution et la contre-revolution, which consists of articles published in the middle of last century, and going on to Herbert Marcuse's *La Revolte et la contre-revolution.* Marcuse could have added 'American' to his title, for the book deals essentially with the phenomenon of the 'new left' in the United States and, implicitly, in Western Europe at the beginning of the 1970s, the golden age of the youth of the 60s. Engels, the philosopher who helped to form the basic principles of Marxism, deals very concisely with risings in Germany, Austria, France, Poland and Czechoslovakia. But, of necessity, he goes into more detail about Germany, and the rest is mentioned only in support or because of relationships with Germany. The general background of the book is 'Europe in the 19th Century'; the substance of it is Germany. That is a methodological point which we should keep in mind while sorting out the general from the particular in this important classic. We find confirmation of this point when we read the beginning of his article on the June rising in Paris:

> From the beginning of April 1848, the revolutionary torrent was stemmed over the whole European continent by the alliance which the classes of society which had benefited from the first victory at once formed with the losing side. In France, small businessmen and the Republican fraction of the middle class formed a coalition with the monarchist middle class against the proletariat; in Germany and Italy, the victorious bourgeoisie had hastened to obtain the support of the feudal nobility, the official bureaucracy and the army against the mass of the people and small traders. Soon the conservative and counter-revolutionary parties in coalition had the upper hand again. In England, a premature and badly prepared demonstration (10th April) turned into a complete and decisive defeat for the popular party. In France, two similar movements (16th April and 15th May) also failed. In Italy, King Bomba regained his authority at one stroke, on May 15th. In Germany, the different bourgeois governments, newly set up, and their constituent assemblies, consolidated their position; and although that eventful day May 15th saw a popular victory in Vienna, it was an event of secondary importance.[2]

The general conclusions we can draw from times and places so qualitatively different from our own may be the following: a regional victory sometimes leads to a coalition of classes on a wider scale than the regional boundaries between the forces of the revolution which the victory is supposed to consolidate. On the other hand, the overthrown reactionary parties could always reappear under their former or new names. In addition, popular movements that are badly calculated, organised or directed, can lead to a long-lasting defeat, while the new reactionary regime devotes itself to strong legislative institutions whatever the number of governments may be:

Let us go back to Engels' article:

When combats followed one after the other for several days with an exacerbation unexampled in the history of modern civil wars but without any apparent advantage to one side or the other, then it became obvious to all that this was the great decisive battle, which, if the insurrection was victorious, would inundate the whole continent with renewed revolutions, or, if it was crushed, would lead to the re-establishment, at least temporarily, of the counter-revolutionary regime. The proletariat of Paris was beaten, decimated, crushed, with such force that even today they have not yet recovered from the blow. And immediately, from one end of Europe to the other, the conservatives and counter-revolutionaries, old and new, raised their heads, with an arrogance which showed how well they understood the importance of the event. Everywhere the press was harried, the right of assembly and association blocked; the slightest incident in any little provincial town served as a pretext for disarming the people and declaring a state of siege.

There too the general principles are clear and easy to see; when regional civil war does not reach a standard at which matters can be settled militarily by the forces of revolution, that means that it will be repressed with incomparable violence, for if it succeeds, other uprisings threaten to break out over a wider area than the one which is already inflamed. In the case of defeat, the blood of the conquered is drunk to the last drop by all the forces of counter-revolution in the widest possible area. At once total war is declared on the slightest of democratic freedoms, beginning with war against the freedom of the press and of assembly and demonstration.

If we change the expression 'proletariat' in Engels' book for the term 'historical bloc' in Gramsci and later Garaudy, or that of 'youth' in Marcuse, we shall find the thread linking the classic Engels to Marcuse, whether or not we agree on the general content or in details. Marcuse, at the beginning of the first chapter ('la Gauche sous le contre revolution') of his book writes: 'The Western world has reached a new stage of development: to defend itself, the capitalist system must at present organise counter-revolution within and outside its frontiers. In its extreme manifestations it has recourse to the horrors of the Nazi regime.'[3] The author then gives some examples from the developing countries where veritable massacres have been committed, exterminating populations considered to be communist, or in revolt against governments subject to the imperialist nations. In other regions persecution is spreading; torture has become a habitual instrument of interrogation in every, or almost every, country in the world. Counter-revolution is largely preventive in general; in the Western world it is exclusively so. Here, there is no recent revolution to crush, nor even one in prospect. It is, nevertheless, the fear of revolution that unites the interests and links the various phases and forms of counter-revolution. It covers the whole range, from parliamentary democracy to open dictatorship, taking in the police state on the way.

Although Marcuse mainly treats the problem of the West, the new left and the United States, and unlike Engels he replaces the working class (which for him is ranged with the middle class) by new revolutionary forces — youth in general and students in particular — Marcuse adds to Engels two fundamental truths: the internationalism of counter-revolution which has been irrefutably proved by the last years of this decade; and internationalism ensured either by total co-ordination of information services and police forces throughout the West to suppress what is called 'international terrorism', or by co-ordination between different armies to suppress what is claimed to be interference in African affairs. The second truth is the preventive aspect of counter-revolution. This, by definition, is not a reaction; it precedes action. Consequently, its essence is premeditated aggression; it gives an exaggerated report of the size of the revolutionary forces in order to quickly abort the foetus before it grows and is born.

Despite the time lapse between Engels' period and that of Marcuse, despite the contrast between the two views of the problem of revolution, the experience of the German revolution awakens in the mind memories of the Spartacists' programme, in which:

> All bourgeois resistance must be systematically crushed, with an iron fist and an unshakeable will. We must answer the violence of counter-revolution with counter-violence, revolutionary violence on the part of the whole proletariat. Similarly we have to meet the traps and tricks of the bourgeoisie with the clarity of our global purpose, by arousing the working masses and disarming the property-owning classes. We must reply to the blocking manoeuvres of the bourgeoisie in Parliament by intense activity of popular organisations in the factories and in the army. We must reply to the intense and multiple sources of power of bourgeois society with the strength which has reached its highest level of concentration, cohesion and intensity, the strength of all toiling masses.[4]

That is where we find the specific quality of German revolutionary experience, and similarly the specific quality of the French experience clearly explained by Marx in *18 Brumaire* when he is dealing with the nature of social, economic and political power, and with its institutional expression:

> This executive power, with the gigantic bureaucratic and military organisation it possesses, with its immense State hierarchy, with its half-million civil servants and its half-million soldiers — this parasitic institution, encircling the body of French society and choking its pores, developed at the time of the absolute monarchy and with the decline of feudalism which it helped to complete. . . . The first revolution developed centralism; but it also extended the dimensions and the competence of the central power and its representatives. Napoleon brought this machine to a state of perfection. Legitimate royalty and the July monarchy added nothing but even more division of labour. The

parliamentary republic, in its struggle against the revolution, was compelled to consolidate the powers of the government and centralise it while strengthening repressive measures. All the revolutions perfected the State machine instead of destroying it. The parties which alternately rivalled with each other for power thought that taking possession of this great edifice was the principal spoils of the victor.

The characteristic suggested by the programme of the Spartacists during the revolution and counter-revolution in Germany, as well as that which emerges from Marx's analysis of revolution and counter-revolution in France, are only the other facet of the method used both by Engels more than a century ago, and Marcuse in the sixth decade of this century. The general considerations we have been able to obtain have a context in time (last century) and in space (the West), which are fundamentally different from the time and space of our backward world, which we euphemistically call 'developing countries' or, simplistically, the 'Third World'. Here, let it be said in passing, lies the importance of the saying of the French social historian Jacques Berque: 'There are no under-developed countries; there are countries that are under-analysed and under-loved.'

However, as there is no opposition between Engels' generalisations and Marx's specifications, we must not create opposition between the generalisations of Marcuse, Mendel, Garaudy or Bettelheim, and the specific light which can be thrown by the various practical applications on our under-developed reality, although the State, the supreme power, the feudal system, the Church, the army and the bourgeoisie have given the West an economic, social, political and cultural 'context' qualitatively different from the paths followed by the under-developed world in our modern era. In a word, the general considerations we can draw from modern writings on revolution and counter-revolution can be useful so long as we do not touch on the specific aspects of our so-called Third World; *a fortiori,* we shall have to avoid the mistakes resulting in the West from the incorrect application of a generality to a definite case, like the very strange error which we can find in a text by Lenin on the Paris Commune.

Lenin was, above all, the man who was not impeded by the classic background of Marx's definitions; at the same time he was Russian to the core and an innovating Marxist in practical matters. He even added important modifications to the theory, when he realised that the weakest and most backward link in the capitalist chain could bring about revolution, thus opposing the prediction of Marx. But he still opposed Trotsky, theoretically and practically, when he affirmed that revolution could break out in a single country surrounded by others where revolutions were not expected. However, this same man wrote:

After the *coup d'etat,* which ended the 1848 revolution, France fell under the yoke of the Napoleonic regime for eighteen years. This regime led the country to economic ruin and also to national humiliation. The proletariat rising against the old regime accomplished two tasks, one national and the other social: liberating France from the German invasion and the workers from capitalism. The reconciliation of these two ends constitutes the great originality of the Commune.

Up to this point Lenin's diagnosis needs nothing to make it convincing. But he goes on: 'The bourgeoisie then formed a government for national defence under which the proletariat had to fight for national independence. In reality it was a government for national betrayal which saw its mission in the struggle against the proletariat of Paris.' Here too, there is no argument against the diagnosis. But this statement introduces the following conclusion: 'But the proletariat, blinded by its patriotic illusions, did not perceive it.' No one knows where Lenin got this information from. Awareness is one thing, objective reality another. Becoming aware of a factor or a phenomenon does not necessarily imply that you follow or avoid an action, or that you adopt a different attitude; revolution would turn into vulgar experimentalism, which Lenin himself condemned so strongly. But to continue with his text:

> The patriotic idea goes back to the great French Revolution of the 18th Century; it dominated the minds of the socialists of the Commune. Blanqui, for example, an undoubted revolutionary and a staunch supporter of socialism, could not find a more appropriate name for his paper than the bourgeois cry: *La Patrie en Danger!* The reconciliation of contradictory aims − patriotism and socialism − was the fatal mistake of the French socialists.[5]

This thought may perhaps also have been inherent in Stalin's attitude to Nazism at the conclusion of the German-Soviet Pact. But the German invasion soon proved the weakness of such an idea; for the Fatherland and socialism were the Soviet State united in war, just as the Fatherland and democracy were the Western State united. In fact Lenin's analysis contains a double error; it has had its influence on socialist movements in the Third World for a certain time. The first aspect of the error was to separate patriotism from the social content; for even if the bourgeoisie demolished the alliance after the realisation of national independence by weakening the forces of social transformation, that in no way means that the aim is to effect this transformation, even at the expense of the homeland. The second aspect of the error lies in the fact of considering every defeat, every fall, as the downfall of the forces of revolution in the matter of planning, execution or the choice of moment. Such criteria for analysis and evaluation would lead us to condemn any rising, any initiative, on the pretext that it lacks awareness or maturity. Such criteria often lead to their opposite, that is to say, long-lasting submission to hostile rule and a gradual division of the forces of the people. Defeat is not a synonym of downfall, for often an external factor intervenes to an extent which is hard to calculate, and cancels an event which was originally ripe for taking place.

However that may be, the general and the particular in classical and modern Marxist literature confront us with an intersection which acts as a check when we have to analyse a specific problem different from those arising in a Western context either last century or in modern times. These intersections can be defined in the following way:

As a whole, Marxist analyses of counter-revolution are very far from constituting a sociology; they fit rather into a purely political context. Despite the exactitude of the lessons we can draw from the general method, their particular tactics add nothing of importance to contemporary revolutionary awareness of national experience in the Third World, except the fact of basing oneself on an experience, and trying to discover its internal laws in the context of the method chosen by the investigator into modern cultural sociology.

In the course of the last quarter century, power in the Arab countries was not based on structures known in Europe of the last century and in the West in general in modern times. It is no more or less than a very complex mixture of the remains of archaic traditions, Western colonial repression, and the modern education of a few social strata after the Second World War.

The feudal system in Egypt, and certain other Arab countries, has never been, either economically or socially, anything like the European feudal system; similarly, tribes, castes, nomad and Bedouin society have never been the exact equivalent of certain situations in Europe. And though the long periods of obscurantism have prevented any evolution of the class system, any scientific invention, or the appearance of any industrial proletariat, that does not mean that revolution in our countries has to be a reproduction of the periods of the Renaissance, the Enlightenment and the liberal, socialist and technological revolutions in the West. Revolution in our countries cannot follow the same economic, social or cultural paths, and the same can be said of counter-revolution. All this makes us different from the West, not only in the basis for development but also, and more especially, in strategic planning. To catch up with the West in the fields of modernisation and revolution is not what is wanted; neither is it possible to follow it, as the forces of counter-revolution would wish.

The part played by the Church in Europe is fundamentally different from that of Islam and Eastern Christianity in Arab countries. The complete fusion between 'life below' and 'life beyond' in medieval Catholicism, thanks to the Inquisition and ecclesiastical-feudal society, differs in many ways from the climate — autocratic and theocratic at the same time — which many countries of the Muslim world have known and still know today. For this reason, contrary to what certain Western thinkers believe, as well as their disciples among Arab thinkers, the Islamic institution is not an obstacle to evolution, quite simply because there is no institution bearing that name. On the other hand, there are ideological institutions of different social strata and classes which could make a double-edged weapon of a political or religious doctrine. For example, in the war of Algerian Liberation and in the Lebanese war, Islam played a different part from that which it played in other

Arab countries. We could say the same thing of Christianity, and even of bourgeois liberal democracy and of Marxism.

There is no possible comparison between European militarism of the time of the French Revolution in France, Germany or Russia, and modern militarism in the Third World. The Egyptian army, for example, by its birth more than a century and a half ago in the time of Muhammad Ali (1769-1849), by its evolution from about a century ago at the time of the Orabian revolution, and finally by the direction it has been taking for more than a quarter of a century, is a national institution.

Whether, formerly, in different social environments, certain people agreed or not in considering nationalism and social transformation as two sides of one coin, today we cannot fail to agree on this truth, especially after the Second World War and the decline of colonialism, and after the colonised nations have achieved national independence. Economic independence and political independence, that is to say liberation and development, are today two objective conditions for the completion of national independence. Experience proves that to make a concession on one of the two necessarily implies the abandonment of the other. So it is no longer possible for the (national) bourgeoisie to refrain from making an essential modification at the very heart of the social structure. Nor is it possible for revolutionary forces to refrain from active participation in the defence of the frontiers.

The particular characteristic of European history, from the dawn of the Renaissance to the present day, consists of a series of historico-social developments in the form of almost complementary cycles. This is a characteristic completely different from modern Arab history, from the national awakening at the beginning of the last century up to today. The imbrications of decline and rebirth, of foreign repression and internal tyranny, of the remains of the traditional legacy and the wind of modernism, of theories and practice, have led to networks of social forces, the result of which has been to slow down the rhythm of their development; thus we have seen the phenomenon of the co-existence of rebirth and decline in matters intellectual, and revolution and counter-revolution in matters social, economic and political.

II

For all the reasons just indicated, it is essential to make a distinction between the sociology of counter-revolution and the sociology of imperialism. We can make this distinction on the basis of Anouar Abd Al-Malik's study, included in his very substantial book, *La dialectique sociale.*[6] The sociology of imperialism gives us the international dimension of the sociology of counter-revolution in the Third World. This dimension sometimes plays an influential part within Europe, as is the case in Greece, Turkey and Cyprus; all these regions are situated not far from the Middle East; this is a factor we have to include in any analysis. In reality the very essence of this distinction is methodological, as the comparison holds not for what has been but for what could be. This tendency is clear in one of the most important works of Jacques Berque.[7]

In this light we can modify the position of a paradox which embarrasses the social historian dealing with modern Egyptian thought; at the time of the defeat, Doctor Louis Awad (1915-) published his important work: *Tarikh Al-Fikr Al-Misri Al Hadith (History of Modern Egyptian Thought)* on the period of the Nahda, the Renaissance. The 70s, that is to say the time of the victory according to the terminology of the present Egyptian government, correspond to what Egyptian thinkers call the period of decadence. Doubtless the 'motive' remains at the level of importance of what has been written; for Louis Awad meant that the defeat was transitory, that it was not inherent in the Egyptian people nor in its history. The others, faced with the 'victory' have wondered: What is the importance of a military victory where there is intellectual decadence? Each of these two groups is right and wrong at the same time. For rebirth and decline in the history of modern Egypt are one and the same phenomenon. Both the people and the government in power have shared responsibility for rebirth and decline. The secular residues of repression and ignorance, and false information in the Machiavellian style, can lead nations into error. On its side, power — what it represents in the way of social forces, and the background against which the elements of their progress are acting — can, at the level of means of production and their relationships, bring about higher rates of progress. The contrary is also true; a regime hostile to the tide of history can bring the renaissance to a halt and send it on a long retrograde course. A victory, a defeat, whether military or economic, is never the fruit of purely technological activity. It always has its social precursors, its cultural context and its consequences for progress and civilisation. Thus, every socio-cultural analysis of the last decade of Egyptian thought should take into account everything that goes to make up what is specifically Egyptian.

For example, in our research on counter-revolution, we should consider all the following characteristics: The fall of a regime does not automatically mean the fall of a culture; in the same way the rebirth of the regime in power is not synonymous with cultural rebirth. The history of Egypt has known more than one fall and more than one rebirth in a single period; sometimes the rebirth went hand in hand with the regime, sometimes across it. Often the cultural facade contradicted cultural production, at other times it reflected it faithfully, either at the will of the government or without any particular directive. The institutional expressions of politics, that is to say the parties, were not always a cultural representation of the level of thought and awareness, and often there have been paradoxes. For example, the intellectuals of the aristocratic elite supported democracy of expression, and venerated reason; while the leaders of the majority often bowed before the ignorance of the public, which led them to take up false or openly hostile positions with respect to liberty of expression, reason and conscience. From Rifaah Al-Tahtawi (1801-1873) to Muhammad Abdah (1849-1905), through the two first renaissances, from the time of Muhammad Ali to the revolution of Orabi, Egyptian thought was dominated by intellectual Manichaeism. It aspired, but without having the elements it needed, to reconcile authenticity and contemporaneity, the legacy of tradition and modernisation, Islam and modern civilisation. This attempt has since been one of the characteristics of modern Arab thought in general, and Egyptian in particular. Two distinct tendencies resulted or were derived from it: a pragmatism going as far as to suggest that one can enjoy the products of a civilisation without approaching the thought that produced it; a partial and fragmentary philosophy that can go so far as to deny its own conviction at any given stage. This was the case with Muhammad Abduh's condemnation of the revolution of Orabi, and Ali Abd Ar-Raziq (1888-1966) forbidding the republication of his own book *Al-Islam wa Usul Al-Hukm (Islam and the foundations of power)* (1925) (despite the disappearance of the reasons for forbidding it), the drawing back of Taha Hussein (1889-1973) who suppressed the most important chapter of his book *Fi El-Chi r Al-Gahili (On Anti-Islamic Poetry)* (1926) and finally, half a century later, twenty years after the revolution of 1952, Tawfid Al-Hakim's denial of the Nasser movement of which he was the spiritual father. In 1974 Tawfiq Al-Hakim wrote a booklet entitled *Audat Al Wa y (The return of conscience)*.

This Manichaeism is not based on abstract thought; it is a socio-cultural formulation of the lower middle class, the formation of which is linked with foreign monopolies and with the simultaneous development of the proletarian classes and the upper middle class. This led of necessity to a sort of duality of thought and conduct between the yields of production and social values. The divorce between thought and action dominated the course of culture and politics, not only in the life of intellectuals and politicians, but also in that of the people and the supreme power.

One positive aspect consists in the fact that objective conditions of the national liberation have taken up the subjective constituents of social liberation; that is why the crisis, which extended throughout all the years of the Nasser revolution and all the years of the counter-revolution, has on the one hand covered all the social forces in the first phase, and on the other hand put the different sides concerned into an embarrassing situation.

Starting from these facts, we must examine closely what has been said on the subject of the decadence accompanying the whole period of the present Egyptian regime from the October War under the sign of victory, to the visit to Israel in November 1977 under the sign of defeat. Are we to consider this the decadence of Egypt or of its reason?

The important works written by Egyptian thinkers living in France at the beginning of Nasser's time, pre-eminent among which is *Egypt: Military Society,* followed by *Egypt under Nasser* by Hassan Riad, and *The Class Struggle in Egypt* by Mahmud Hussein, express no particular enthusiasm for Nasser's government; they do not, however, mention any decadence of reason in this period, although two of these authors suffered torture and imprisonment for more than five years, and another two chose exile — even more painful than prison and torture. How did it happen, then, that five of the greatest men within the confines of Egypt, belonging to different trends and generations, could agree on the decadence of thought in Egypt? Let us read them first:

Zaki Nagib-Mahmud, who professes positivist philosophy, and is at present a writer at *Al-Ahram,* wrote that thinkers in our country 'cannot find the way to reach their aim, for there are obstacles and blocks represented by intellectual rigidity in the authorities as well as in a large section of the public.'[8] In his opinion, the difficult situation of the thinker in the Third World in general lies in the ambiguity of his picture of the future. He has before him two models of development: the capitalist model and the Marxist-socialist model; he would like to find a third formula which he can apply. The Third World is not yet fixed. That is why the thinker does not express himself clearly and directly. 'And when they transmit to the public their vision of the society of the future, they will not let themselves transmit all their thought for fear of shocking the reactionary section of society; they cross it out and alter it to make it acceptable to public opinion.' One of the most serious consequences, he says, is the fact that 'up to the present we have not formed a genuine Arab line of thought with respect to the problems of our times.' Zaki Nagib-Mahmud rejects the two dominant tendencies in Arab thought, the trend towards the West and the traditionalist trend. In his view, to follow the West does not solve the problems which concern us, or those of our development. The Salafite trend:

> contradicts itself completely every instant. The Salafites demand a return to a religious tradition through means of communication which were not available to our ancestors. They write, they publish their conservative ideas in newspapers and magazines which our ancestors never knew. And they have recourse to all the modern methods. If they are really serious they should do without all the means offered to them by modern times.

The author describes the situation of thought in our country:

> This alien call, hostile to evolution, uttered by these eager partisans of the past, makes me feel that I am constantly living a horrible nightmare or a drama of the absurd. The partisans of the tradition of 'piety' demand that the thief's hand should be cut off, that an adulterer should be stoned, and that other sanctions should be applied that completely contradict the spirit of our times. I should like to ask a question of the partisans of this strange call: 'Who is going to cut off the thief's hand? The doctor who has sworn an oath to protect and save human beings? Or the butcher?' We are struck down by paralysis of thought, and I say quite frankly: today we are less free to express our ideas than we were a century ago . . . The condemnation of thought, any thought, is a commonplace today.

Latifa Az-Zayyat, professor of literature and left-wing writer, writes under the title *Arab reason struck with paralysis* 'Our thought is not going through a crisis; it is in a state of paralysis; the main reason is the fact that our peoples have not up to the present been able to determine their right to bread and freedom. No thought can flourish under oppression and famine.'[9] Mme Az-Zayyat comes to the conclusion that the impoverishment of Arab thought has aggravated discimination in the midst of one and the same nation. Within the Egyptian nation, for example, there are very different intellectual worlds almost completely isolated from one another. We even find immeasurable contradictions within a single class; this creates an extremely serious situation, for it is impossible to have the homogeneity needed by every class that wants to get the wished-for changes made. For Latifa Az-Aayyat, the cause of this crisis lies in 'the public's lack of critical sense'. There is a very wide gap between a word and its meaning. Public opinion is incapable of distinguishing true from false, right from wrong, public interest from private interest. Another aspect of this crisis is the isolation of culture. Intellectuals are isolated from the people; they are also isolated from each other.

> In consequence we have no cultural and intellectual movement that can go ahead, enrich the public and enrich itself in doing it. All we have is a collection of individual creations due to a few intellectuals. This almost total sterility, this paralysis in the domains of culture and art is a characteristic of the period through which we are living. Worse still, [adds Latifa Az-Zayyat] today's writings, for the reasons given, are empty of any human sense; they express the bankruptcy of artists and writers.

The silence forced upon many of our thinkers, the emigration of others, and the sense of living like an alien in one's own home have steeped our cultural life in gloom. The deep roots of all this are surely to be found in the fact that the movement of Egypt's university community towards freedom was halted by the revolution of 1952, and the stagnation of the current of freedom. The Egyptian university has ceased to play its civilising part. Latifa Az-Zayyat thinks that the *Nahdah* (renaissance) following the revolution of 1919 was stifled by the coalition of local reactionaries with British colonialism in the 30s. But from the fifth to the sixth decade of this century a new renaissance arose, the fruit of the Egyptian national movement of the 40s. According to Latifa Az-Zayyat, these two renaissances are not the result of chance:

> Each of the two was closely bound up with the revolutionary rise of our people, the growing sense of Egyptian identity and the longing to blossom. The liberalism of the 20s was the expression of an awareness of self, of our identity, following a victory over British occupation. The blossoming of the novel, the theatre, and the plastic arts, towards the end of the 50s and the beginning of the 60s was a new expression of this awareness, this feeling of belonging. The measures taken by the

July revolution to speed up the march towards the democratisation
of culture were a great support for this renaissance. However, the flame
of the renaissance did not burn for long. Its flames were quenched by
the revolution itself. I firmly believe that every cultural blossoming
achieved by the Egyptian people was linked with its national struggle
for freedom, and with the extent of success of this struggle.

Latifa Az-Zayyat concludes her statement by affirming that:

> We shall never see a new cultural blossoming except with a new tide of
> liberation and revolution, through a long struggle for liberation and
> progress directed against Israel, symbol of reaction and fanaticism, the
> base of racism and religious segregation. Our war against Israel is not a
> war of frontiers; it is about the very existence of our future civilisation
> Freedom of Arab thought can only come through the awakening of the
> classes to whom the change matters.

Doctor Murad Wahbah, professor of philosophy, under the title: *Arab
thought has stagnated at the stage of revolt* wrote:

> Arab thought, since the end of the 18th Century, has not moved
> steadily forward. It wavers between two stages: revolt and stagnation.
> Revolution is absent. Always, it is still to do. Revolution means the
> radical change of inherited intellectual values. And even when a stand
> was taken and intellectually expressed, it was stifled; and as a result
> Arab thought has been murdered.[10]

How? Murad Wahbah continues:

> The element of cultural blossoming has never been present in the stages
> of modern Arab thought; for the basic requisites for such a blossoming,
> according to a concept which is European, but no less universal for
> that, lie first of all in the liberation of human thought from the yoke
> of all that is arbitrary and alien to reason; even Lutheran reform was
> only an appeal to examine religion freely, whatever the opinion of the
> ecclesiastical powers might be. Certain people will claim that Arab
> thinkers have called for the reform of religion and the liberation of
> reason. But such appeals could not constitute a new era which could
> be called a renaissance. They were only slight shivers which could never
> reach the level of a true blossoming capable of starting a period of
> rebirth and changing a society.

Doctor Murad Wahbah thinks that the absence of a vision of the future
underlies the crisis in Arab thought.

> The vision of the future is not based on the past; the movement of

history begins with the future, not with the past. The future is the main impulse of any movement, cultural, political or economic. The basic question is: What do we want to be? That is a question of the future; but you will notice that the main question asked in the Arab world is: What were we and why should we not be as we have always been? This implies a serious illusion: that movements today should be a reproduction of those of yesterday. Such a conclusion dims every vision of the future, and we should always agree that the future is not a reproduction of the past but a creative action going beyond the past.

Fouad Zakariyyah, professor of philosophy, wrote under the title *We are threatened by emptiness*[11] that 'thought' is not recognised in Arab societies; the Arab thinker lives on the fringe of society and represents no pressure group. One phenomenon of the intellectual crisis in our countries is the fact that 'we do not find in those who make thought their main activity any clear stand on the crises to which thought is exposed.' Fouad Zakariyyah does not blame this fault on the thinkers:

For the chains weighing down Arab thought in all its activities have prevented it from reaching a stage of revolt. The nearer thought comes to discussion on the deep roots of social life, the more the chains tighten. It is impossible to arrive at revolt without risking the roots. Westerners have known this for a long time.

Fouad Zakariyyah adds that the sought-after renaissance can be neither a parallel nor an extension of the European Renaissance. It is enough for Arab reason to 'first begin to think logically about phenomena, leaving behind mythical and legendary modes' and later make its own way towards rebirth; for it cannot reproduce the renaissance of another society, at another time. Fouad Zakariyyah says there is a great intellectual void which, through the most advanced intellectual powers, threatens us with encirclement and isolation. When the Arabs no longer have the source of material strength (oil), we shall be able to see the extent of the danger which will ensue if the intellectual crisis raging today is extended into the future. The author disapproves of the idea that our people would suffer an 'identity crisis'. Our ancient civilisation is in us and around us; present-day progress is human and not only Western. If we wish, we can legitimately share in it without any idea of importation or indebtedness, if we also share in the thought on which this progress is based, associate ourselves with it and not be content to merely enjoy its technological results.

Hussein Munis, editor in chief of the magazine *Al-Hilal,* wondered in July 1977 'Why is Arab thought decadent in every field?' Fathi Radwan, writer and politician, replied: 'This question, although it shows a certain pessimism, is full of good intentions and optimism; for I believe that the Arab thinker is not yet born.' Fathi Radwan then makes a historical survey of the most salient characteristics of Arab thought for a century; he concludes by saying:

In short, Egyptian thought is not yet born, if you want the truth, bitter, hateful and inadmissible though it is. . . . . Both innovators and tradition-alists have done a lot of translating; most of the time they translated well. They have made a lot of adaptations which they have included in their works. Thus they have put their readers in touch with what was happening in this wide world, such as movements of thought, liberation, evolution or extremism. They thought deeply about what they read, heard or saw. They interested their readers by curious points which perhaps incited them to read still more, and to get to know better the relics of the past and the poetry of the present. But they never came out of all this with a well-built intellectual edifice, nor with a global vision of the universe, nor with a new philosophy either. Some of them had undertaken the task of handing down the tradition of piety, others copied present-day thinkers; but none of them have ever gone beyond these limits; and it all had its influence on those who came after, those whose platitudes we deplore.[12]

Is it an exaggeration to say that these five great Egyptian intellectuals who represent the Right, the Centre and the Left, and who belong to different generations, formulate, each according to his own thought or expression, one and the same psychological introduction to a socio-cultural 'case'? Can we not see there a unanimity on the existence of a certain collapse, which one of them calls decadence, another paralysis, the third murder, the fourth emptiness, and the fifth non-existence? And that most of them, when dis-cussing the past, turn towards the lost roots (the dawn of the last century) of questions which cast doubt upon the very existence of the cultural blossoming which existed in the past? Can we not perceive in them the existence of the crisis of a culture which wavers between the legacy of the past and the problems of modernity? Have we not there a thread, very delicate it is true, but none the less present, linking the intellectual problem to that of society? Do we not hear in these vibrations a note of despair that clouds their vision of the future with pessimism? And, finally, does the question of freedom not appear as a common denominator to all five?

There are indeed many points on which they do not agree, on the causes, development and consequences of the problems. But all five are strangely in agreement on the signs and symptoms of these problems. Carried away by their emotions as they face a nightmare scene, they forget their own creations, spread over a period of 30, sometimes 40 years, which still serve as examples to educate generations and form intellectual awareness. Let us bear in mind that they did not think like this ten years earlier, despite the horrible defeat of 1967. Let us bear in mind that a certain victory had been won in 1973 as far as military confrontation was concerned; and finally, let us remember that this explosion of anger took place in 1977, only a few months before the presidential plane flew over occupied Palestine to land at the feet of the Israeli leaders.

The eyes of the 'civilised' world were fixed only on this scene. The civilised world did not see or did not want to see what went before it; it does not want to reflect on what could follow. It is normal in a case like this to be surprised that the 'historic visit' was not the end of a war and the beginning of peace. Only a few realised that this historic visit was no more or less than the consecration of counter-revolution in Egypt. Others knew that it was the final point of what for a moment was called 'the experience of democracy in Egypt'. For only a year after the despairing groans of those Egyptian thinkers accused of pessimism, as though they had foreseen the cataclysm, the President of the Egyptian government, in one of those comedies he has made his own, was submitting to a referendum the murder of reason and the persecution of conscience; which certainly surprised the Western world with its two parts, one a victim, the other an accomplice. For us, there was no surprise, nor was there for those who saw only the collapse, nor for those who had seen Egypt blossom and were present at its downfall. . . those who see revolution in the depths, even though, today, counter-revolution occupies the surface.

III

On the seventh anniversary of the movement of 14th May 1971, while the State of Israel was celebrating the 30th anniversary of its foundation on Palestinian soil, President Sadat made a speech in the Egyptian Parliament in which he drew conclusions from the experience of the past years. This balance sheet enabled him to take some measures about which he was to consult the public a week later (plebiscite of 20th May 1978). As usual, the consultation was rewarded with an almost unanimous 'yes'.

We can summarise these new measures as follows, on the basis of President Sadat's own text:

The law on 'indecency' or 'impropriety' aimed at ending what he called the permissiveness which was rife in Parliament and in the professional associations, in this case that of the lawyers. The President, in fact, had inferred the existence of this permissiveness as a result of two incidents. The first had taken place in Parliament when a deputy had shouted 'Down with the President!' for which the said deputy was relieved of his functions! The second concerns a lawyer who had 'insulted the State and the President of this State'. The Egyptians, unaccustomed to such strange sounding laws, at once understood that it was a matter of 'indecency' with regard to the President of the Republic. It was natural that they should associate such a law with the crime of high treason. So this new law, the first of its kind since the 1952 revolution, will always be associated, in people's memories as well as in legislation, with the President's sadly famous words, addressed to the representatives of the people: 'I am responsible to God, not to you' . . . A responsibility which can only take shape when life is over!

The second decision concerns the reconsideration of the existence of the party of the left led by Khaled Muhyi Ad-Din, a former colleague of President

Sadat on the Revolutionary Council of 1952. The President declared:

> We must reconsider whether we can be democratically associated with
> those people [that is how he designated those of the left], because they
> have infringed the principle of 'social peace'. They constantly repeat
> that the State is moving towards capitalism, that the people are living
> in poverty, which leads to class hatred and incites to class struggle.

The President added that after his speech he was going to meet the First
Secretary of the Central Committee of the Socialist Union and ask him,
according to the law on the organisation of the parties, to take the necessary
measures for a revision of the democracy which the party of the left was
enjoying. He did this. But as the First Secretary did not take the initiative
with regard to the revision, we have a right to advance two hypotheses.
Either this high official, responsible for the application of the law on the
organisation of the parties, found nothing in the conduct of the party of the
left to attract attention or call for reconsideration or punishment; or else
this high official failed in his duty. We have also a right to conclude that the
President was making a very precise accusation against the party of the left;
that they had infringed one of the basic principles of the organisation of the
parties. In other words, the party of the left must have disobeyed one of the
principles of the contract uniting the parties of the State, which involves the
annulment of the contract and consequently the dissolution of the party of
the left. Remember, that 72 hours after the President's speech, the government took the first steps in this direction by confiscating *Al-Ahali*, the organ
of this party. The President had, in fact, reiterated in his speech the assurance
that 'anyone who does not believe in the love of God cannot accept posts in
politics or the media or any other function which exerts or reinforces
influence on the public.' But the President did not always define the means or
the organisation charged with investigating the faith of the citizens. The only
certain fact is that anyone whose unbelief is proven is a second-class citizen.

The third decision concerns thought and information within and without
Egypt. The President links it with the preceding decision, since he declared:
'As the official religion of the State is Islam, we are not prepared to treat
with those who deny religion.' However, this formula is not organically linked
with the accusation which followed it: that some Egyptian writers, within
the country and abroad, opposed the present regime; unless the formula in
question was intended to associate religion with the regime, which would
consequently imply that believing or not believing is the equivalent of
believing or not believing in the regime.

Listeners to this speech were surprised by a slogan coming from the
deputies' benches and interrupting the President several times: 'God is All-
Powerful, it is government by the Koran,' they said — the watchword of the
Muslim Brothers. Speech and watchwords which certainly surprised the
onlookers, especially as, two weeks earlier, the administration of Meniah, in
the south of the capital, had been the victims of a fire, religious in origin,

which was alarmingly like the fires occurring in the Lebanon at the time of
the civil war. Some Muslim Brothers burnt the biggest churches in Meniah.
Young Christians, in their turn, burnt a mosque the following night. The next
day, for the first time in the history of modern Egypt, groups belonging to
both camps began kidnapping operations in the Lebanese style. As though
by chance, an incident — juridical this time, but also the first of its kind —
had just occurred: a tribunal authorised a Christian Egyptian citizen to marry
polygamously, ruling that majority legislation and the State religion allowed
this. Surprise was inevitable at the President's insistence, at this particular
moment, on the Islamic basis of the regime. There was less surprise at his
formal attack against Egyptian intellectuals writing in the press of Arab
capitals or in the Arab press temporarily installed in Paris. The President has
every right to reply to his opponents, though some might wonder whether his
right to order professional associations to exclude these same opponents from
their ranks was well-founded, as professional identity is not acquired or lost
for political reasons, especially as in Egypt membership of a union is a condition of exercising a profession.

Concerning politicians who were members of the new Wafd, the President
decided to consult the people on the right to have a political activity for all
who had been active in the parties before 1952, except members of the
National Party and those of the 'Young Egypt' organisation. Here two points
attract our attention:

President Sadat had decided, as soon as he took supreme responsibility for
the country, to restore political rights suspended in exceptional conditions.
Before re-establishing the permanent Constitution and restructuring the
Socialist Union, before setting up the three tribunals, followed by three, then
four parties, the President had consulted the people about the restoration of
the constitutional State, in which every citizen was to enjoy political liberty.
Since then, and under fire from an unprecedented campaign against the
Nasser government, a series of economic and social laws authorised the
restitution of land to its former owners and the lifting of confiscations on
certain others. It was natural that the Wafd should represent the interests
depending on the new legislation. But this right of representation soon provoked a violent struggle between the centre party supported by Sadat and led
by Mamduh Salem, the Prime Minister, and the new Wafd on the right to
represent the same interests. The Wafd, from the moment of its restoration,
polarised wider social forces than those of the government. The Wafd quickly
gained the confidence of these social strata and thus became a dangerous rival
of the government party. The President's last decision on pre-1952 politicians
was to end this rivalry by banning the Wafd; which certainly reminded
Egyptians of the purge which had preceded the banning of political parties
after the 1952 revolution.

The second point raised by this last decision concerns the exemption which
the President granted to the Young Egypt and National parties. In fact both
of them are known in the history of modern Egypt for their Islamic tendencies;
and one of them at least practised organised terrorism, while in the same

period the Wafd, which is accused today of wanting to turn the clock back to the period before 1952, was incontestably the party of the popular majority.

The last point in the President's speech was not a decision but a direct defence of the social identity of the regime. For the first time in the history of presidential speeches, a President openly took up the defence of a public personality. President Sadat devoted 25 minutes of his speech to the defence of Osman Ahmed Osman, notably declaring that Mr Osman built the Aswan dam, factories and schools, and that the company 'Arab Enterprises' had lent rare currency to the State! 'I have never had to defend myself, because I have never been accused of anything. I say this so that it may be an example to you. . . . From now on, anyone who dares to open his mouth will be severely punished, and through democratic channels!' It remains to explain why the President considers he is defending himself by defending Arab contractors. Nobody alludes to the fact that Mr Osman is chief among Egyptian millionaires, that he is one of the best-provided of Arab industrialists, that his son is the President's son-in-law, and that, under Nasser as at present, Mr Osman has always had his finger in the pie of large-scale Egyptian enterprise. The same defence was uttered, in the same speech, in favour of Muhammad Hamed Mahmud, but without naming him, and for five minutes only. He is in fact the owner of vast tracts of farmland at Ismailia, a Minister and General Secretary of the party in power. This second defence ended with the same warning: 'I tell you for the first and last time, I do not like to have to defend myself!'

The exceptional importance of President Sadat's speech on the occasion of the seventh anniversary of the putsch of May 1971 does not lie in the fact that it constitutes a balance sheet of the years of political experiment from the announcement of Nasser's death to the visit to Jerusalem. It is rather the end of an experiment, and the rather complex recognition that this experiment came to nothing.

President Sadat had begun his experiment with what he called, on 23rd July 1971, 'The Programme for National Action', which was simply a summary of the main Nasser documents, amplified by justification for the putsch. At the time he was in a strong position, based on the watchwords 'democracy and socialism'. In accordance with the theory of the polarisation of political forces, this attracted to the President's side important social elements wanting a radical change, which would make it possible to reclaim occupied territories and restore to the dignity of the individual the right to expand under the authority of constitutional law, so that social progress could arrive at a fair redistribution of resources. This same President, seven years later, took a diametrically opposite position from that which he had declared on first taking power. Worse still, he is now in such a weak position that he is wiping out little by little the staging of his experiment. Democracy is called in question, since the opposition, particularly from the left, is using its peaceful constitutional right to criticise the basic errors committed in the domain of State politics, and does not excuse the President from his responsibility.

National unity is also called in question because the climate of the Islamic *Shari'a* is weighing more and more on the foundations of the regime, so that today we are witnessing a progressive slide towards a theocratic and fanatical society, even though we have had the Lebanese experience almost on our doorstep.

The liberation of the land is no longer talked about except in negotiations under the American aegis, and without any real hope of ever seeing it restored. This withdrawal is symbolically represented by the fact that the President defends only those whom he represents, that is to say the alliance of rich country landowners with stockbrokers in the capital. By his almost definitive liquidation of any thought of democracy or social transformation, President Sadat combines the liabilities of the pre-1952 regime with those of Nasser's government. He also wipes out every positive feature of the two regimes. He passes by and suppresses the problems brought forward by the Egyptian middle class, who have never been able to bring about their own revolution, but only to fall into the historic impasse of counter-revolution in Egypt.

In reality, the seven years of Sadat's presidency are only a stage in the counter-revolution in Egypt, which has deep roots in the history of modern Egypt. Ahmed Orabi's rising against the Khedive in 1882, and the revolt of 1919 under the leadership of Saad Zaghlul against the British occupation, were not revolutions but rather two important stages on the way to the Egyptian revolution, mainly that of the middle class. Similarly the revolution of July 1952 was not 'the' revolution, but also another stage. The present counter-revolution follows the same rule. It is a counter-revolution and not 'the' counter-revolution. It is a stage. And like the revolution of 1952, which began as a *coup d'etat* and later became revolutionary, the counter-revolution in Egypt began as a putsch, the reactionary nature of which was later consolidated. This putsch was not only directed against Nasser's regime, it was aimed especially at the social alliance represented by Nasser. It was directed against the foundations of a coming revolution. The putsch of 14th May 1971 was not against a definite revolution but against the Egyptian revolution that was taking shape.

The history of the counter-revolution is part of the history of the revolution. From both the internal and external factors of the revolution the elements of regression developed as the natural consequence of the birth and development of the Egyptian bourgeoisie. Originally, this bourgeoisie grew out of the commercial sector, supported by a thin layer of the peasantry and a fringe of the civil servant class. Its interests were of necessity enmeshed with those of the big landowners, who have always been the allies of foreign monopolies. Their origins, qualitatively different from those of the Western bourgeoisies, have left their indelible mark on the evolution of the Egyptian middle class. Born under foreign oppression and an autocratic and theocratic regime led by Muhammad Ali, the Egyptian middle class came out of backward social strata, from the point of view of production methods and relations. It was born under the threat of various means of spoliation, to the point where industrial modernisation, for example, was carried out under an alliance with the big landowners. The bases of the cradle which received this newborn child were simply a mixture of land-owning, commercial and industrial interests added to those of the State bureaucratic machine and the presence of foreign troops. A difficult birth. Difficulties have never stopped dogging the Egyptian middle class throughout its revolutionary history and throughout its struggle against occupation, against absolute power, and for national independence and democracy. When we hear that the Wafd, its largest organised representative body, was in power only for seven and a half years – from the 1923 constitution (fruit of the 1919 revolution) – over a period of 30 years, we realise that this middle class never had time to take breath and bring about its revolution. It was always outstripped by the social history of the Egyptian people. Every time it was about to perform a task laid upon it, economic and social reality imposed fresh problems; which constantly led it to compromise with the upper strata of the pseudo-feudal landowners and the upper middle class, to the detriment of the proletariat. Thus, it signed the 1936 treaty with Great Britain. Thus, Mustapha An-Nahhas, leader of the majority, was imposed on King Farouk by the British Embassy at the time of the famous event of 4th February 1942. Thus, the city of Cairo and all the government were burnt on 26th January 1952, to make way for 'the Free Officers in the ashes of this middle class'. Thus the phoenix was reborn to build its nest again on a branch of the old tree.

With all these economic, social and political involutions of the middle class, it was natural that the revolutionary elements of that class should be closely linked with those of the counter-revolution which has always had adequate supporting forces, such as the occupation, the Palace, and town and country landlords and company directors. In fact the germ of corruption is inherent in the middle class itself. The political version of this hypothesis could lie in the division of the Orabi revolution and in all the splits in the party of Saad Zaghlul, the Wafd, which had seen two minority parties emerging from its ranks and turning against it: the Saadists and the Wafdist bloc which became the minority of minorities. Great personalities had also turned against it at various times. The same phenomenon was repeated in the ranks of the July 1952 revolution. In fact the lack of homogeneity in the leadership itself, which was at the root of the banning of the left and the Muslim Brothers is only the objective reflection of the split in this class, pulled two ways, even torn apart between political form and social content, between the ambition to lead society and the state, and the need to develop on the one hand, and on the other, the points of contact with social strata hostile to its revolution even while forming part of its economic fabric. These strata were hostile to it. The middle class too has never been co-operative enough with its real allies. It flew, but when ambition led it to soar, it broke its wings. . . and fell.

This shows to what an extent the drama is one of a class, but it is also the drama of a society, a nation. When a revolution adapts itself to the counter-revolution, sometimes imposing it, it pronounces its own death sentence and that of the others too.

The destiny of the middle class in Egypt did not only influence its own strata, but had an immense impact on the education of the lower middle classes, on the ideology of the peasants, on working class organisations, on the thinking of intellectuals and the conduct of the army. When it achieved an aim, this became a positive addition to the whole nation. When it degenerated, nobody escaped the consequences of its decline.

Is it not strange that a century afterwards the Egyptian bourgeoisie should be faced with the same questions? In reality no decisive answer has been given up to now, outside the field of culture. But over a century new questions could not help being asked, in both cultural and social fields. And neither history nor the future can expect the answer to come from the present middle class in Egypt.

History and the future expect an answer to come from other classes; an answer not only to the old questions but to the new ones as well. That is what makes it difficult to find social forces capable of showing the way to replace contemporary counter-revolution at the level of thought, as well as at the economic, social and political level.

President Sadat, contrary to what some people think, is perfectly aware that the present crisis does not concern him alone and that he is not the only one responsible; it is the result of a long social history and powerful social forces. The President is taking a chance on pulling down the edifice on everyone's head as Samson did. What could the alternative solution be in this case? The Egyptian writer Abbas Mahmud Al-Aqqad often said: 'God only knows whether Lucifer's revolt was revolution or counter-revolution.' He had welcomed the revolution of July 1952, saying that it was a revolution against the 'red' revolution which he feared at the time. So he had to take the side of this revolution which was preventing the other; this he failed to do. Despite the appearance of a military putsch, Nasserism effectively accomplished some of the missions of the revolution feared by Al-Aqqad.

However, if he had lived (he died in 1964) he would certainly have found a reply to his sarcastic question about Lucifer's revolt. Nasser's putsch would have suggested this reply to him: Lucifer's revolt is a revolution and a counter-revolution at the same time.

The fact is that Nasser led the stage of revolution up to the day it failed, 5th June 1967. Sadat, who had accompanied him throughout the first period, is today leading the counter-revolution.

Both are men of the 23rd July 1952, but the drama is that of a whole class. The story is far from ended.

Ghali Shoukri
Paris, 18th May 1978

Notes

1. R. Debray, *La Revolution dans la revolution* (Maspero 1969), p.122.
2. F. Engels, *Allemagne: La contre-revolution* (Editions sociales internationales 1935) pp.76-7.
3. H. Marcuse, *Revolte et Contre-revolution* (Seuil, Paris 1973) p.9.
4. Al-Afif Al-Akhdar, *Al-Thawrah Al-Almaniyya* 1918-1919, *Dar At-Taliah*, (Beirut 1973) p.63.
5. Speech made at Geneva on March 18th 1908 at the celebration of three occasions: the 25th anniversary of Marx's death, the 60th anniversary of the 1848 Revolution and the anniversary of the Paris Commune.
6. Anouar Abd Al-Malik, *La dialectique sociale* (Paris 1972), pp.367-457.
7. Jacques Berque, *La Despossession du Monde* (Paris 1964).
8. *Rose El Youssef,* 11th April 1977.
9. *Ibid.,* 18th April 1977.
10. *Ibid.,* 2nd May 1977.
11. *Ibid.,* 9th May 1977.
12. *Al-Hilal,* September 1977.

PART 1
Sadat Establishes His Control

1. In the Beginning was the Putsch

A Star for the Putsch

President Sadat kept people waiting on two occasions in his life. The two events ended in the turning of a new page in his political history, pages of good fortune in a life full of contradictions and harmony at the same time, but also completely different from that described in his last book, recently published under the title *In Search of an Identity, the Story of my Life*.

The first time that Lieutenant-Colonel Anwar Al-Sadat kept people waiting was the eve of 23rd July 1952. He had missed 'H'-hour, which had been fixed by Abd El-Nasser on a map left at his home a few hours before the *coup d'etat*. At the critical moment Sadat was with his family in a cinema near his house. Not wishing this absence to be misunderstood, he belittled its importance, though he often acknowledged it in his reminiscences on radio and television. Some say that he was late on purpose. They add to the story of the cinema an incident to which Sadat never alludes; so its verification depends on Sadat himself, or on his biographers later. These gossips say that, after the show, the family of the brown-complexioned officer faked a fight with some other people, as a result of which they were all taken to the police station where the presence and the signature of Anwar Al-Sadat, after midnight on 22nd July 1952, were recorded. The story, with its two episodes, one recognised, the other so far controversial, means that Sadat would have liked an alibi in case the *coup d'etat* failed. But discussing intentions without documentary support throws an objective analysis off course. Later that night Lieutenant-Colonel Anwar Al-Sadat went to a place near the headquarters of the General Staff. The dawn of the 23rd of July 1952 was beginning to break. Nasser charged him with two missions: starting from the main cable he was to cut the telephone lines of certain personalities; then he gave him a written declaration to broadcast from Radio Cairo. So the man who was not present at 'H'-hour was the first to announce the *coup d'etat* to the world.

An oddity which often happens in *coups* was that someone was in advance of 'H'-hour. This was General Yusuf Siddiq, the officer with left-wing ideas, who saved the *coup* from certain failure. The leaders of the armed forces, King Farouk's generals, had met in a great hurry at headquarters following a tip-off that 'something' was going to happen that night. Yusuf Siddiq did not know that there had been a leak and that the generals had met to avert a possible *coup d'etat*. But he found in this meeting a unique opportunity to arrest all the generals at one stroke. Without having received orders to do it, and bypassing military discipline, he laid siege to the General Staff head-quarters, occupied the building and so brought off a fine catch. This bold initiative saved the *coup* from a bloody end. It was also the first sign of success. This swift action, which surprised even those in the plot (the soldiers had arrested Colonel Nasser too, because of his rank), was rewarded; Yussuf Siddiq was made a member of the Council of the Revolution, but he resigned in September 1953, and was even arrested at one time for his left-wing opinions. Less than a year later, the same thing happened to Khaled Muhyi Ad-Din, and for the same reasons, though in different circumstances. Thus the man who was absent at 'H'-hour was the first, early in the morning of July 23rd 1952, to announce the news to Egypt, the Arab world and the world in general; while the one who was in advance was thrown out of the ranks a year afterwards. The first was watching a film, the second was risking his life seizing the highest bastion of the former military leadership. But this often happens.

The second time President Sadat was late was the day President Nasser died. He was the last to arrive at the President's house. He was not there during his long death-agony. The President, on that sad evening of 28th September 1970, had not seen him for more than three months. Those near to the President certainly remembered, at that moment, the Sadat who was a member of the Executive Committee and of the Arab Socialist Union, and very much the official Vice-President of the Republic. But the reality was quite different; in fact, on returning from his last visit to Moscow, during the summer of 1970, President Nasser asked his Deputy, who met him at Cairo airport, to 'rest'. Since 'that affair', the Vice-President had ceased to fulfil his functions, even the most formal ones. Rumours were rife on the subject; but the most important was that during his stay in the Soviet Union, Nasser had received a complaint from a citizen against his Vice-President's wife. She had fallen in love with a private house and offered to buy it from the com-plainant, who declined. The Vice-President then sequestrated the property of this private citizen. Although this rumour was the most popular explanation of the eclipse of the Vice-President after the President's return, no one has ever proved it. But it is certain that the private house was returned to its owner together with all his property. Those who do not like rumours prefer to say that President Nasser had decided to dispense with Sadat's services because of political changes that he intended to carry out in accordance with his political thinking at the time. What is certain, is that Nasser gave no written order on the subject of Sadat's 'neutralisation'. Consequently, at the moment of Nasser's death, the Vice-President was constitutionally on the political scene without being there in effect. This constitutional detail, added to other elements, played an important part in Sadat's rise to the presidency of the Republic. This affair reads like a historical *nukta* (joke). Sadat inherited from

Nasser, who died dissatisfied with Sadat but without having eased him out of office.

But the social history of power in Egypt is unsavoury. Sadat, the last to arrive at the dead President's house, was the first to announce his death to the Egyptian people, the Arab world and the world in general. Those who were present at Nasser's last moments, those who were anxious that the transition from Nasser to Sadat should happen peacefully and constitutionally, were tried, imprisoned, or forced to retire, most of them in less than a year, and others within three years. President Sadat's last act in the dead President's room was to kiss his hand before drawing the sheet over his face.

During Nasser's lifetime, Sadat exhibited no inclination to voice any criticism, or even to express the slightest opinion, unless he was asked for it. But on two occasions he ventured to break this rule; he was then a member of the Council of the Revolution and Vice-President. 'The first time,' he said in his speeches in Nasser's style, after he had succeeded to the presidency, 'was when, at the beginning of the *coup d'etat,* we were voting on the future government of the country.' Nasser, according to Sadat, opted for democracy, while he and the majority were on the side of dictatorship. The truth, as far as it can be gathered, is that Yusuf Siddiq, Khaled Muhyi Ad-Din and General Neguib were for liberal democracy; in other words they wanted new parliamentary elections for a new Chamber, after which power would pass into the hands of the majority and the army would return to its barracks. The crisis of March 1954 shows irrefutably that the left-wing officers, with Muhammad Neguib, were for a return to democracy. But it is more plausible to say that this event, often quoted by Sadat, was only an exploration on Nasser's part of the intentions of the others, and that Sadat had imagined beforehand that Nasser would be in favour of dictatorship. Sixteen years after this crisis it is no longer possible to believe that Nasser had thought for a moment of giving power back to civilians or to the former legitimate heirs. So Sadat's opposition and that of his colleagues to Nasser's (democratic) opinion could have its source in two — rather vague — possibilities: Sadat knew Nasser's personality very well, and thus was sure that Nasser, who never said what he was really thinking until he had heard the others, would be in favour of dictatorship, or Sadat had foreseen the future!

The second time Sadat opposed Nasser was on the occasion of the Rogers Plan brought forward by the American Secretary of State to solve the Middle East problem in December 1969. This time too, Sadat thought that Nasser would not dare accept a proposal like this in the middle of the war of attrition being waged by the Egyptian army against the Israeli forces, especially as Egyptian and Arab public opinion was sufficiently well mobilised to reject such a plan. It is also probable that the calculations of the United States and Israel were based on the same assumptions. But Nasser surprised Sadat, Israel, the United States and the whole world by accepting the proposal. Nasser's gamble had paid off; but those who did not know the rules of the game heaped the worst accusations on him; and these were the first to weep for his death.

The paradox really consists of the fact that Sadat, by twice opposing Nasser, without really trying to, got the better of his real opponents, both the right- and left-wingers among the officers. He voted for dictatorship and reached the top. And when Rogers presented his plan, Sadat, almost at the same time, was appointed Vice-President of the Republic. But some people have remarked that despite this title he had no access to the real levers of the executive power. Actually his allegiance to Nasser in his lifetime, and his almost total lack of executive power are only two sides of the same coin: Sadat prefers peaceful ways and an easy life. This is an aspect which deceived everyone who was surprised to see him become the chief man in Egypt. In reality, Sadat had not changed. He simply made the practical application of his ideas on power and responsibility. Even the style for which he is now well known was not alien to him. The tacit agreement between him and Nasser was that he should not take an effective part in the government but should associate himself with all the outward signs of strength. This time they were wrong, but it was the last time, for the man who had learnt better than anyone the meaning of the first presidency in Egypt, and consequently avoided all risk of opposition, accepted no opposition once he had become President, going so far as to overthrow anyone who wished to be associated with him.

As for those who present, or think of the President's personality as that of a gambler. . . he is perhaps the very opposite. He calculates exactly what he can do to take into account every eventuality and every possibility, and to choose his adversary's 'weak' moment so as to tip the balance by his own weight. Since his youth, for example, he has had a leaning towards the Muslim Brothers, but has never belonged to them. And yet it was he who judged them in 1954 and condemned them to life imprisonment and death. Since his youth he has also been sympathetic to the 'Young Egypt' organis- ation with the slogan 'Egypt above all' in the fascist manner, but he never belonged to them either. And yet he joined the group of Aziz Al-Masri Pasha, who was close to the Axis, when Nazi Germany was near to victory at the time of El-Alamein. He was against King Farouk for the same reasons, despite the latter's attempts to reach an agreement with Germany. He has always planned well. He even managed to get himself acquitted when accused of having murdered Amin Uthman, and once he was freed he become reconciled with the King and rejoined the army after having been cashiered.

Because Sadat knows the rules of the game, he always reaches simultan- eous agreement with parties opposed to each other; but he always chooses the one that will carry the greatest weight when he has won his victory. And because he respects the rules of the game, he remains disciplined during the time he needs for his victory, so as to impose his conditions on his adversary. He gets his own back on his former adversary by affecting to resemble him; and he rids himself of his former allies, friends and colleagues. In both cases he cancels out the past by reincarnating it if his adversary was powerful, and putting it out of his mind if he was weak. For example, he has always harboured a dull hatred against King Farouk and the Abdine palace, as he has always hated Jews (as is natural for an anti-semite) and the English. When he became President, one of his first decisions was to take over the Abdine palace as the official seat of the presidency, even though under Nasser it had been turned into a museum. But on the marriage of King Fuad II, the son of King Farouk, Sadat gave him his father's royal sword. He forged links by marriage with old and new pashas; and for his daughters' marriages he gave parties which reminded the Egyptians of the parties given by Farouk, pictures of which they could see in the newspapers. As for the new English, or rather the new emperors of the present day, the Americans, whose plan he had rejected under Nasser, he became their first ally in the region after Israel. And even for Israel, his incredible visit seemed to mean that he was sorry for everything that had happened, but that was no impediment to his declared sympathy for Nazi Germany. For ceremonial occasions he even made his generals wear a uniform strangely like that of the generals of the Third Reich. The goose-step surprised the Egyptians as well as the West Germans themselves, whose prowess in the Second World War he glorified. And yet, during his visit to Israel he laid a wreath before the Memorial to the Jewish victims of Nazism. In reality, Sadat always admires the strongest, whether it is Menachem Begin and Israel, Hitler and Germany, or the United States of America.

So the past still haunts him, whether he puts it out of his mind or whether he reincarnates it, even if he is at the height of power today in Egypt. His joy was limitless when, alighting from the plane at Teheran airport, he opened his arms wide to embrace the Shah. His broad smile certainly hid the incident of Rabat at the congress of Muslim countries, when he had had a fierce altercation, in Persian, with Muhammad Reza Pahlevi. But the Shah, as could be seen in photographs and on the screen, did not respond in the Arab manner; he contented himself with offering his hand in the manner of kings. Sadat then lowered one arm and stretched out the other, and the burst of joy was quenched.

All this notwithstanding, we must emphasise two truths in the life of the Egyptian President; first, of all the figures in the movement of July 23rd, his has always been the best known to the Egyptian people, as he was always the most active in secret or open politics. He has had the greatest share of trials and prison; for that reason he has been constantly followed by the press. Second, Sadat, in the last analysis, has always counted among the young extremist nationalists whose imagination had been set on fire by Nazi ideas and fascist actions. He thus contrived a synthesis of 'Egypt racially superior to all' and 'Islam' as a doctrine of conquest.

Because of the first, Nasser always used him as a facade, from the broadcast of the first declaration to his nomination as Vice-President, taking in the presidency of the Chamber on the way. The second truth created in him a complex which is still with him even though he is President. Sadat is haunted by the ghost of Nasser, or rather by the 'legitimacy' which the latter achieved in 1956, and by his 'heroism'; this heroism is sanctified by two bitter items in the debit balance: the spontaneous and exceptional demonstration by millions of people, on 9th June 1967, to stop him from resigning, and the hysterical demonstration of 28th September 1970, when the news of his death spread.

The two truths combined make a complex of thought and political conduct which became evident as soon as Sadat took power, and up to his visit to Jerusalem. The first characteristic of this type of conduct consists of the mask of democracy hiding the true face of the dictator. On February 4th, 1971, he took the first step towards peace with Israel by reopening the Suez Canal and guaranteeing free passage through it to all countries including the Zionist State, if the Israeli forces would retreat a few kilometres. The questioning of this by Ali Sabri, his former adjutant, after the putsch of 14th May 1971, shows that the President had consulted no one about this serious affair, neither Ali Sabri, nor the government, nor the members of the Supreme Executive Committee, nor Parliament. The same applies to the decision about the dismissal of the Soviet experts, the cease-fire in 1973, the negotiations with Kissinger and the arrangement for the visit to Jerusalem, which led to the resignations of Ismail Fahmi, Minister of Foreign Affairs, and Muhammad Riad, Minister of State for Foreign Affairs. All these fateful decisions, including the union with Libya and later the war against it, were taken by Sadat alone.

Consequently, a second characteristic of this type of conduct consists in a policy of surprise, not initiative; a policy of hiding the thought behind the putsch, and a conspiratorial spirit with all that it implies of a secretive, sly and deceitful disposition. To rely on sound bases, or on anything else outside oneself, is almost non-existent with Sadat. His political conduct is based on the idea of change through individual violence and terrorist shocks. Surprise, even when it is a question of peace, works exactly the same way. The idea of surprise originates in the complete elimination of any participation in decision-making. It is no mere chance that President Sadat was never a member of a party before the revolution, even of parties thinking along his lines or with his tendencies, unlike his comrades who were members of the Muslim Brothers or the Communist Party. Nor is it by chance that rumour has it that he took part in terrorist activities. In fact surprise as a mode of action developed in Sadat parallel to his political development from nationalist extremism to another extremism; this certainly betrays Nazi belief and fascist behaviour. A policy of surprise gives birth to a violent desire to save time by making precipitate changes which give no time for reflection. Thought, for him, is action; and there is no way to turn the tables on the past, except by reducing the present and precipitating the future. Thus, with an hour on the television, on the radio and in the international media, Sadat can transform 18 years of his life in Nasser's shadow into a great blaze of light concentrated on his own image, alighting at Ben-Gurion airport from Aircraft No. One of Air Egypt. Let us not forget that in his youth he wanted to be an actor, but was turned down by the selection committee!

The Origins of the Putsch

The general characteristics of Sadat's personality do not constitute an introduction to his individual part in the putsch of 14th May 1971, despite the
exceptional importance of the role of the individual in Egyptian history in
general and, in particular, in the modern period beginning with Muhammad
Ali. An autocratic regime and a centralist State have always been the most
outstanding characteristics of Egyptian governments from the most distant
times. But the personal character of President Sadat was an important
criterion for the choice made by social forces with an interest in overthrowing
the government preceding his,

Sadat, after Nasser, is not a historical *'nukta'* (joke), even if some people
preferred so to interpret the chance which made him, officially, a Vice-
President (even if only in name) who was disgraced and forced, unofficially,
to retire at the moment of Nasser's death. Sadat as President was not the fruit
of the Egyptians' love for legitimacy, as certain others would like to think.
In reality the official title of Vice-President was a decisive element in the
course of events following Nasser's death. The passive attitude of the
Egyptian population in the face of these events was another factor which
determined their direction.

But the essential, or decisive element was, without a doubt, the July
revolution itself and its development from the defeat of 1967 to Nasser's
death. Sadat, Kamal Ad-Din Hussein, Hussein Ach-Chafei, Abd Al-Moneim
Raouf and Rachad Mihanna represented the extremist Islamic tendencies in
the leadership of Nasser's putsch. Zakariyya Muhyi Ad-Din, Abd Al-Latif,
Al-Bagdadi and Hassan Ibrahim represented the pro-West tendency in the
same leadership. In other words, the lack of homogeneity in the very structure
of Nasser's movement right at the beginning was an unmistakable sign of
adherence to the right. The germs of counter-revolution were thus contained
within the revolution. Both the representatives of the Muslim Brothers,
Mihanna and Abd Al-Raouf, and those of the left, Yusuf Siddiq and Khaled
Muhyi Ad-Din, were eliminated very early so that the revolution could take
a middle way *(wasatiyya)*. But the development of class representation under
Nasser was, during the 60s, to lead the revolution to eliminate the most
powerful representatives of the right; thus Zakariyya Muhyi Ad-Din, Kamal
Ad-Din Hussein and Abd Al-Latif Al-Bagdadi were dismissed one after the
other following the nationalisations of 1961-1962, the Yemen War, the
introduction of economic planning, and the changed relationship with the
United States. But the elimination of the right wing among the officers, up
to 1967, had not suppressed the 'moderate' character of Nasser's regime.
What is more, the very style of government imposed by Nasser prevented him
from taking three great decisions:

(1) To dispense with the remains of the right wing among the historic leaders
of the revolution represented by Sadat and Hussein Ach-Chafei. For him they
were the extension of the historical leadership; a negative extension, but
inoffensive. In addition, they represented the political balance between right

and left in the forces of the bureaucratic petty bourgeoisie in power.

(2) On the evening of 9th June 1967, to pronounce on the radical changes demanded by the Egyptian people who, in a historic scene, supported the defeated leader on condition that he would make far-reaching changes in the crumbling regime. The Egyptian people gave him a free hand. But its 'will' did not go beyond the limits of its own social and historical tradition. Nasser changed nothing essential; he thus lost a historic opportunity. Some say, with regret: 'In reality he did not hold the reins to enable him to exploit this opportunity. He could not go beyond his own powers.' So it was not a simple manoeuvre to have chosen as successor Zakariyya Muhyi Ad-Din in his famous resignation speech. Was there then another point of view about the future? But let us go on with the story. Abd Al-Hakim Amer, the first Vice-President, committed suicide; Chams Balran, minister of the defeat, was put in prison. The latter was tried by Hussein Al-Chafei; and Amer's successor was Sadat. So it was not by chance that this same Egyptian people who had demonstrated in his support against the United States and Israel, flung insults in his face six months later, and in November 1968 threw itself into one of the greatest hostile demonstrations of students and workers that Egypt has known since 1954.

(3) To form a party which could succeed an individual; because all the pseudo-popular organisations under his power were more like secret security organisations. The 'avant-garde organisation' which emerged from the Socialist Arab Union had as its general secretary — the Minister of the Interior! In reality, Nasser had never seriously believed in the formation of a party. His famous phrase 'when I hear the word *organisation,* I draw my sword' is not without meaning. It reflects a hidden fear of democracy and of the people. It also reflects a metaphysical faith in his own union with the people. His decision is democracy itself; his thought is the people, and technical means are the modern substitute for the party in an under-developed country. As for the listening-post, that consists of receiving reports from the security organisations which have always been the best organised party in Nasser's Egypt. Before 1965, Nasser concentrated on economic development plans; after 1967 he concentrated on the reconstruction of the armed forces. But whatever the time, he paid great attention to the organs of security. So it is very probable that he was never seriously concerned with forming a popular party capable of replacing the individual and taking decisions collectively. The absence of a party, even of the principle, that is to say the absence of democracy in a country like Egypt with its liberal traditions which form the basis of the progressive trend, but also with old traditions of dictatorship on which the political minority has always been based — this absence was in itself a right-wing manifestation, pushing the country towards the right after the death of its only leader.

Neither are these three negative elements in Nasser's attitude to the national and social problems of the country, the reflection of simple individual character traits. Their absence reflects the ideological expression of the entire relationship of social forces in Egypt.

The economic collapse in 1965, after the first and only five-year plan, went with a revival of the private sector, especially after the defeat of 1967. This is where we can put our finger on the economic and social aspect of the co-existence of revolution and counter-revolution in Nasser's Egypt.

The year following the end of the development plan (1965-66) saw a drop of 5% in the rate of development of the national income, whereas it had reached 6% during the years of the plan.[1] As a result savings fell by 13.7%; as a natural consequence this led to a deficit in the balance of payments. To combat the risk of inflation, the government's only course was to increase the tax on essential goods and services; this hit the low-paid social strata. Stamp duty increased by 20.7%, other taxes by 4.1%, services by 41.9%, taxes on other products by 121.9%. The influence of these increases on the price of necessities was soon felt; the price of wheat increased by 4%, beans by 2%, maize by 17%, oats by 12.5%, tea by 9.6% and vegetable oils by 4.1%. The same year saw a rise in the cost of living of 10.9% over the preceding year. The origins of the ascendancy of the private sector were seen in investments which rose from E£11.2 million to E£27.8 million. It was also natural that there should be a fall in all sectors of production (equivalent to 0.9%). The average annual income fell from E£68.1 to E£66.6, that is by 2.2%. And the fall in consumption of necessities was 18.4% for rice, 27.7% for lentils, 5.2% for vegetables, 2.3% for kerosene and 9.5% for textiles,[2] which indicates a large drop in spending power in the widest sectors of the population. The following year 1967/1968 saw a further drop in production of 1.8%. The policy of austerity imposed by the government consisted of price increases, indirect taxation and taxes on production. All these measures brought in only E£150 million while the average income continued to fall to E£62.8, equivalent to 5.7%. Consumption of necessities fell by 8.4% for maize, 14.3% for sugar, 10.7% for margarine, 14.5% for oil, 16.7% for kerosene and 20.9% for beans.[3] And whereas during the running of the five-year plan investments had reached E£404 million in the industrial sector, production E£384 million, and the income of industry about E£129 million, the sum of investments in the years 1965/1966 and 1966/67 was E£200 million, the increase in production E£93 million and of the national income about E£13.5 million, 'which means that half the investments realised only a quarter of the increase in production and one tenth of the increase in income.'[4]

The private sector, which was not subject to State control during the years 1963/1964, 1964/1965, 1965/1966, 1966/1967, had a relative increase of its share in the total production. Thus, in the field of textiles the sequence was as follows: 29.3%, 30.8%, and 27.8%. As for the foodstuffs industry, the series of increases in production was 18.5%, 17.7%, 20.5% and 23.6%. In the mechanical industries, the percentage of increase in production was successively 22.3%, 23.8% and 24.1%. Over the four years quoted, the production of the private sector increased by 132.4%, as against 121.1% in the State-controlled public sector considered as a pioneer of the national economy and the foundations of the road to socialism. T.-Th. Chekir illustrates, by an interesting table, the voracity of capitalist development in the very heart of

Nasser's Egypt. This table shows the variable affecting the value added, in the two sectors, private and public, of industrial production when, in the private sector, the number of workers does not exceed 25.

Table 1

Year	Public Sector		Private Sector	
	Value Added	*Its Maximum*	*Value Added*	*Its Max*
1966/67	392	100	38	100
1967/68	428	109	30	79
1968/69	484	124	53	141
1969/70	505	129	93	246

This table brings out the character of exploitation specific to the private sector, on the basis of its share in value added and the rate of development of the latter before, during and after, the defeat of 1967; the increase in value added in the two sectors between the two first and the two last years reached 118% for the public sector and 310% for the private sector.

The Egyptians remember what Nasser, at the time, had called 'the development of the new class', and what Nasser's theorists had pointed out as typical of 'national capitalism, an exploiting force'; the terminology is too general and does not easily lend itself to detailed analysis. This is not simply the 'middle class', nor simply an alliance between the technocracy, the bureaucracy and/or those who benefited from the July 1952 revolution among high Army officers, senior civil servants and company directors. All these people effectively turned the capitalist wheel within the public sector and for the benefit of the private sector. But a higher social strata still was attained by those whose immediate capitalist interests developed side by side with the measures taken by the revolution. In the countryside, the upper strata middle-income farmers accumulated wealth by helping themselves from the co-operatives, which were originally created by the State to help the peasants. In the hands of this class the co-operatives became a source of illicit profits.

Another class, by its economic and political influence, took the place of the former pashas. They monopolised the 'right' to legislate and to profit from the 'services'. Thanks to their financial power they could increase their production by using modern machines to irrigate, cultivate, fertilise, plough, sow and reap. They also possessed very fertile land exempt from the measures of the agricultural plan. They created model stock farms with a very lucrative yield, or orchards, more lucrative still. They were also closely linked with the commercial and import/export sectors.

In the industrial sector as we demonstrated earlier, the private sector enjoyed hegemony over various industrial branches before 1970. But if we look more closely at firms employing ten workers or less, that is to say those which have a larger production and a larger profit, we can perceive the following facts on the basis of the official figures:[5]

1) Number of firms: 144,566 productive units.
2) Number of employees: 285,000 workers (33% of the total industrial labour force).
3) Total production equivalent to: E£142.4 million.
4) Gain in value added: E£56.5 million.

This economic weight can easily be translated into social terms. In fact this class, which makes enormous profits and does not apply the labour laws to its workers, steals their labour in a scandalous way as shown by the relationship of wages to value added in the following table:[6]

Table 2

Sector	Average Annual Wage	Average Value Added In Respect of Capital
Foodstuffs industry, tobacco, drinks	E£44	20.6%
Shoes, clothes and other textile products	E£16	24.4%
Furniture and assembly	E£21	10.5%

We can conclude from Table 2 that a large number of Egyptian workers up to 1970 earned only E£16 a year each, which is equivalent to 133 piastres a month, while the owner of the firm gained as much as 24.4% in value added. The study to which we have referred adds that this sector gained 11% of the value added of the whole of Egyptian industry, while paying only 4.2% of the total wages in the industrial sector.[7] And whereas the share of wages in value added was between 9.3% and 14.8%, the share of this same value going to the owners was between 85.2% and 90.7%.[8] Despite this capitalist growth, benefiting under every criterion, total credit facilities granted to the private sector went from E£167,000 in 1963/1965 to E£5.8 million in 1969/1970, equal to 71.6% of the total credit granted. These facilities worked to the disadvantage of the nationalised sector which 'never stopped selling machines on credit, of which every one went to the private sector', as the then President and Managing Director of the Industrial Bank declared in an article published by the magazine *Misr Al-Muasarah.*[9]

Table 3, published in the same article, gives the total sums taken by the private sector at the expense of the nationalised and co-operative sectors in the accounts of the Industrial Bank.[10]

This proves that capitalist development at this time could count not only on large profits in production units employing 10 workers or less, gained partly because of the very sharp drop in wages despite the increase in value added, but counted particularly on State help, originally intended for the development of Egyptian industry for the social progress of the whole population. Remember, that since then, the emphasis has been laid on the

Table 3

Accounts	Total Facilities	Nationalised Sector		Private Sector		Co-operative Sector	
		Amount	%	Amount	%	Amount	%
1966/67	4.6	3.8	82.6	0.6	12.9	0.2	4.7
1967/68	3.9	2.4	59.8	1.3	34.2	0.2	6.0
1968/69	5.9	1.3	22.2	4.6	76.7	0.06	1.1
1969/70	8.2	2.3	27.8	5.8	71.2	0.08	1.0

Source: *Misr Al-Muasarah,* April 1971.

necessity to encourage the private sector and grant it facilities, even going to the length of tax exemption. It is noteworthy that the lead singers of this refrain were among the pillars of the economic organisation of the State, who were supposed to be guarding the objectives aimed at by various legal enactments, postulating that the national economy would be led by the nationalised sector.

Housing was entrusted to the nationalised sector, so that more houses could be built and let at a moderate rent, thus lightening the burden on those with limited incomes. This project was taken over like Troy with the wooden horse, that is to say, from within. The nationalised sector had recourse to subcontractors from the private sector, granting them supplies to carry out housing projects. This laid the foundations for parasitic middleman services which soon undermined it. This vast movement took place behind the scenes against a background of brokerage operations accompanied by bribes, concealment, forgery and a variety of scandalously illegal acts. The original purpose of the housing plans was put aside, as the parasitic capitalist always prefers equally parasitic projects, like the building of luxurious residences, which drive poor people not only from their own districts but also from their homes. We need only read the following item on the classified advertisements page of *Al-Ahram* of 29th June 1970 to realise the incredible profits to be gained by the alliance of the leaders of the public sector with the subcontractors. 'We are looking for the owner of a well-situated plot of land who would agree to be associated, contributing land only, with the building of a block of flats for later sale. Net profit 80%.' To avoid any misunderstanding, the advertiser gives the amount in letters: 'eighty per cent'! So the aim of housing projects became to sell and not to let, and popular housing estates became mansions and skyscrapers. The following table shows the rate of development of the private sector in the housing field. The figures indicate the current values of investments in millions of Egyptian pounds.[11]

The natural consequence of the taking over of housing projects by the private sector was an aggravation of the housing crisis in the large lower middle class. It even affected the upper classes. Another consequence was the pitiless struggle between landlords and tenants over the interpretation of the laws,

Table 4

1959/60	1964/65	1965/66	1966/67	1967/68	1968/69
73	74.9	76.1	76	113	115.6

and modified laws regulating rents. Key money was always high. Sometimes it was as much as the cost of the land or of building.

Although there was a State monopoly of foreign and wholesale trade, an official report of 1967 tells of 'the existence of a monopoly held by 219 traders on products the price of which is E£130 million a year, bringing an annual profit of about E£25 million.'[12] This social class laid the foundations of the black market. The Minister of Trade at the time declared:

> There is a businessman who is stockpiling motor spare parts worth half a million Egyptian pounds. Another is stockpiling textiles for popular use worth E£120,000. A third is storing electrical equipment worth E£230,000. An article not worth more than 4 piastres is being sold for 40.[13]

This class also invented the 'contraband' system. Responsible officials recognised that, during the years 1967 and 1968, Egypt was flooded with illegally imported products, estimated by experts at the Ministry of Economic Planning at 10 million Egyptian pounds. But the senior customs officer at Cairo says this figure is far below the true one.[14] The following advertisement is sufficient indication of the point this class has reached:

> Expanding company needs an equal partner to represent the Misr Company in dairy and food products (public sector). The representation guarantees a net profit of more than E£600 per month. Contract with the Company against E£8,000 on the representative's account.[15]

In most cases the advertisement is published as a formality demanded by law; but the agreement between the company and the representative is often concluded in advance. From this publication we can see that E£8,000 can bring in a net profit of E£600 per month, that is to say E£7,200 a year, which is roughly equivalent to the capital invested for a year!

As for the import/export sector, we shall give only these brief facts: a tonne of garlic on the markets of Munich, Paris or Rome, costs E£800; in Egypt it costs E£170. Jasmine oil is sold in France for E£900; in Egypt it costs E£500. A tonne of camomile flowers is sold in Germany for E£700; in Egypt it costs E£280. That is what makes import/export so attractive to the parasitic classes of production. Fiddles with import licences became commonplace; their secrets were revealed only by sporadic outbreaks of resounding scandal, like the notorious trial known by the name of the Basyuni Gumua Affair; the inquiry brought out the following points:

1) Defendant No. 20 had obtained a commission of 5% on the sum of E£1,000,000, representing the value of import licences obtained from the Motor Trade Company for Basyuni Gumua. In addition to his 5% commission he had received from the latter the sum of E£15,000 as a small present.[16]
2) One single company in the private sector had obtained a contract for work amounting to E£1.5 million. A person working on behalf of the said Basyuni Gumua was associated with this work for a commission up to 45% of the profits.
3) An official of a public sector company had given away E£10,000 worth of certificates for electrical equipment, for a commission of 15% of the sum invested.
4) Misid Chalabayah, an invoicing clerk at the imports office, having a primary school certificate and a monthly salary of E£7, left his job to work in imports. He picked up a fortune of E£1 million and took possession of a farm of 200 *feddans.*[17]

One year after this scandal the newspapers published news of the arrest of four officials alleged to have taken bribes of E£6,000. For this sum they were alleged to have worked a swindle on import vouchers, thus enabling a businessman to make a profit of E£50,000.[18]

In fact, leaving aside those scandals the odour of which happened to reach the noses of the judges, the State itself had adopted the policy of providing services to the private sector, not through the intermediary of officials of whatever rank, but by the force of law and legislation. On 26th October 1966, *Al-Ahram* announced 'the opening of the export trade to the private sector'. On 25th October 1967 the same paper announced the cancellation of the distinction in favour of the nationalised sector, for the sale of merchandise or exports. On 13th November 1967 the paper in question gave an assurance that the authorities would sweep away all obstacles and guarantee the private sector a good start in the field of exports. On 19th November 1967 guarantee facilities were promised to exporters and producers in the private sector. On 17th December 1967 the private sector was authorised to import machinery and raw materials within a limit of E£1,000 and exempted from authorisation for the transfer of currency. On 5th March 1968 new facilities were announced to 'encourage the export of products of the private sector and the authorisation of exporters to travel in order to maintain contact with their customers'. On 8th May 1968, *Al-Ahram* contained the decisive news 'All Egyptian products can be exported without tax and exempt from authorisation'. On 19th August 1968 it was announced: 'Exporting is open to the private sector, with the offer of raw materials to start with. Indemnity is granted from proceedings to recover a deficit, and exemption from the costs of checking and inspecting the products to be exported.' On 25th November 1968 there was an increase in the quota of sums assigned to the factories of the private sector so that they could import materials necessary for production of E£1,000 to E£5,000 for each factory; they were also exempt from authorisation for this transfer of currency. On 30th November 1968: 'heads of businesses in the private sector asked for authorisation to buy raw materials necessary for production to a value of E£1 million, with exemption from authorisation for the transfer of currency'. On 1st December 1968 'the private sector exports citrus fruits without conditions'. On 12th December 1968 'a fivefold increase in the exports of the private sector before next June' was announced. On 17th April 1969, *Al-Ahram,* again, published: 'This year the private sector will have exported the equivalent of E£10.4 million as against E£4.3 million last year and only E£2 million the year before that.' On 4th September 1969 *Al-Ahram* reported 'the increase of the import threshold without authorisation for transfer of currency to E£3,000 per person'. After that date the limits were widened several times.

Thus revolution and counter-revolution co-exist. However much one may approve or disapprove of these measures, we shall confine outselves to describing the balance of forces in Egyptian society from the middle 60s to 1970 when Nasser died. These social forces, made up of small farmers, rich landowners, industrial capitalists, big businessmen, contractors and stock-brokers, were present and active in society and State before Nasser's sudden death. Their existence is not purely economic and isolated from the social structure of government and people. It is not isolated from the relationships and value of production. Nor is it isolated from the machinery of government and its structure, nor from institutions, thought, conscience and feeling in Egypt. These forces were present in every field and highly active. From the event of *'Al-Manchiyya'* at Alexandria in 1954 when Mahmud Abd Al-Latif, a member of the Muslim Brothers, shot at Nasser, and up to the latter's sudden death, the right, in all its forms, never laid down its arms. There were several attempts to overthrow the regime, by either the army or religious extremists; the most famous of which is that of the Muslim Brothers in the summer of 1965, and not the least famous is that of Abd Al-Hakim Amer after the defeat of 1967. They have never stopped, but it is difficult to count and identify them. Nasser's government was satisfied with eliminating them administratively by means of security organisations, without eliminating their economic, social, political and ideological foundations. Since Nasser himself felt the danger from the right on several occasions, and from what he called 'the new class', without reacting, we can only come to two conclusions: despite his evolution from one stage to another, Nasser, as the representative of a class, was not up to the radical change demanded by the people on 9th June 1967 and in February and November 1968. Besides, Nasser carried within himself the germs of that contradiction which some people call 'the third way'. Consequently, to have kept Anwar Al-Sadat or Hussein Ach-Chafei was not an act of courtesy with regard to history, nor was it a reward for personal allegiance. It is the very incarnation of one of the terms of the contradiction within him.

For all that went before, the political scene, in the absence of a 'hero', was set for a bloody struggle for power, especially as the heroism was of the tragic sort, for objectively, the regime had crumbled on 5th July 1967. The historic greatness of the heroic character had simply postponed the end of the struggle for three years. His absence enabled the dominant social forces governing the true centres of decision-making to make clear their wish to take power. His absence enabled the contradiction between form and content of the regime to come to the surface. Starting from this 'crack' in the social edifice of the State a putsch was necessary for the form to adequately fit the contents. And that is what happened.

The Constitutional Character of the Putsch

Who discovered and chose the other? Was it the social forces mentioned above that chose Sadat as President? Or was it he who chose them as a base for his government?

The record of the peaceful handing over of the powers of the late President to his successor does not answer this question which was asked again, violently, with the events of the 14th of May 1971, seven and a half months after Nasser's death. Today, ten years afterwards, all that happened is like a play which the literary critics call well made, which means that the plot is well planned and constructed, but the play itself rings false.

The President's death itself appears to be the starting point of the putsch, in fact it was the constitutional facade of the putsch. In his lifetime that would have been difficult, despite his personal psychological conflict and despite his struggle against what he called the 'new class'. This developed in him and outside him like an internal disease growing day by day until it defeated him without the shedding of a drop of blood. There will be many who will think later about this dramatic event, which lasted more than two and a half hours from the moment when the President left Cairo airport after seeing off the Prince of Kuwait (the last to leave of the important people at the conference to stop the massacre of Palestinians in this Jordanian September). Nasser was bathed in perspiration until he died in his bed at about 5.45 pm. on the 28th September 1970. These few hours are full of questions to which, up to now, we still have no certain answers.

We know for example that the Soviets had given the President a mobile resuscitation unit equipped with the most modern medical techniques in the world; it was to follow the President like his shadow. Where was it when he was at the airport? Why was it not used as soon as he arrived home? And after the first examination when thrombosis was diagnosed? There were still two and a half hours and perhaps more, during which the medical profession did nothing commensurate with the importance of the President's office. Who is, or who are, responsible?

We could have understood that very complex organisations at the disposal of some foreign circles could have attacked the President in the September massacre; their direct interest in the Middle Eastern struggle was to finish with the Palestinians and Nasser, so that the Salafite forces, Arab and Egyptian, could make a quick end to the developments in the region, in accordance with foreign strategies. One of the most modern methods of murder is where the murderer does not need to kill directly. To know in minute detail the President's state of health, and create the right climate for a deterioration leading to death is quite possible. However, the serious question of Nasser's last hours of life is still unanswered. The least we can say is that these hours betray 'serious negligence', even inviting the supposition that the President was allowed to die. Nobody killed him directly, but at the Cairo Hilton Hotel foreign elements had undertaken to strike 'the sick heart' of Jordania. The internal element undertook to let him die.

These, in short, are deductions which would disintegrate if, one day, someone among those by the deathbed revealed another, more convincing truth. The death certificate, signed by his own doctors immediately after death and broadcast by the media, convinced no one. Two things, however, are certain: (1) Within Egypt there were social forces, the economic and social composition of which has been indicated above, that would profit politically from the President's death by seizing power directly, instead of appointing a third party to govern in his name; (2) The President's death was in itself a perfect instrument for a constitutional putsch.

It is rather strange that five years after Nasser's death, a journalist (Saleh Gawdat) wrote during the visit of the American President Richard Nixon: 'God intervened just in time to save the nation and for President Sadat to take responsibility.' President Sadat himself did not hesitate to express the same idea on several occasions, arguing that it was by Divine Will that he succeeded to the office of President. Despite the farce of the plebiscite, which had counted some heads that later fell, this was an avowal which at least eliminated the people as participants in the struggle of the 'new Mamelukes'.[19] The possibility of an intervention of God or Divine Will can also be eliminated, unless the 'Devout President' permitted himself, as well as his propaganda organisations, to use God as a symbol of the outside forces, Arab and local, who had a prime interest in his rise to power.

So the answer to the question of whether it was Arab and international social forces that brought Sadat to power, or whether it was he who chose them as the basis of his power, cannot be found in the constitutional events following Nasser's death, and following also, the most persistent rumours about the possibility of a return to power of the former members of the Council of the Revolution, or of Zakariyyah Muhyi Ad-Din. President Sadat was not a stranger to the social forces of which we are speaking, nor to their economic training, nor to their Arab and international ramifications, nor to their political ambition. He was one of their founder members. And in Nasser's lifetime he was their fervent defender and their representative in the alliance with Arab conservative circles. So it was obvious that he should be their representative at the summit of the new power structure after Nasser had made the task easier by his death, and by having chosen Sadat as his successor. Proposing the name of Zakariyyah Muhyi Ad-Din as early as this was a clever diversion, helped by the fact that Sadat and Ali Sabri were presented on the day of the President's funeral as two men with cardiac conditions incapable of following the road. Sakariyyah Muhyi Ad-Din has never been the United States's man in Nasser's Egypt. His name had never appeared in the *Washington*

Post lists exposing C.I.A. agents among people in high office in several countries (February 1977). He was never mentioned as having anything to do with the secret antennae of the conservative oil regimes. Zakariyyah Muhyi Ad-Din is an upright citizen with his own convictions about economic development on the Western model. Perhaps he expresses the aspirations of the technocrats of the Egyptian middle class who have nothing against the public sector; on the contrary, they could benefit from it by adapting it more efficiently to modern technology. With this background, Zakariyyah Muhyi Ad-Din can represent the advanced and enlightened right, and not the rich landowners, businessmen and stockbrokers, among the most backward classes and the most eager to leap to power. It is regrettable that this American image of Zakariyyah Muhyi Ad-Din was fixed in the public mind by Nasser himself, juggling with power and decking out his collaborators with poses and political masks, or mentioning the name of Zakariyyah Muhyi Ad-Din as his successor in his resignation speech after the defeat of 1967. The same applies to the rumour about the return of the former Council of the Revolution. It was only a manoeuvre intended to intimidate the people.

Sadat's rise to power after the President's death was inevitable. It complemented the constitutional foundations of the putsch. The bureaucratic lower middle class, Nasser's other face, could not understand this to the full. They did not understand that their survival in power after the implicit downfall of the regime in 1967 was artificial, and depended on the exceptional historical breadth of Nasser's personality; he could scarcely fill the gap for three years. Secondly, they did not understand that their toppling regime received its death warrant the day Nasser died. Consequently, their idea of extending their period in power rested on a fatal political naivety. Thirdly, they did not understand that the State in which they had security, information, the army and the political organisation under their orders was only a 'paper State' according to Nasser's own expression after the defeat. Fourthly, they did not understand that the seat of the highest responsibility in Egypt has always been the mainstream of legitimacy (they had themselves shared in the formulation of the new legitimacy) and that the President, whether loved or hated, has, in the eyes of the Egyptians throughout history, enjoyed the immunity of the master of 'the' decision. Fifthly, they did not understand that their feet were of clay and their house was built on sand, in the sense that the vast majority of the people (who do not represent the new power) had never given them a cover of legitimacy. For all these reasons, their collective resignation on 13th May 1971 came more than seven and a half months too late. Simple political intelligence would have suggested that they resign the very day of the President's death. They paid the full price of their stupidity with the events of the 14th May 1971. The radical forces were not in a situation which would enable them to represent one of the alternatives; Nasserism in general and in its different trends was one of the causes. The forces of the counter-revolution were in the right situation to represent one of the alternatives, and Nasserism with all its contradictions was one of the causes. There was absolutely no room for those who thought they could take Nasser's place. The economic and social truth is that there was no empty space; the exceptional personality was a veil hiding the fact that this space was being filled by opposing forces. They were not 'centres of force' but 'centres of weakness' as Sadat calls them.

The question of who had chosen whom finds its answer in the actions carried out in the seven years since Nasser's death, and since the elimination of the bureaucratic wing of the bourgeoisie which inhibits the movement of these forces. The very man who had rejected the Rogers Plan in Nasser's lifetime, negotiated with Kissinger, received Nixon, and visited Israel. The very man who kissed Nasser's hand after his death and bowed before his photograph in Parliament, holding up the declaration of March 30th 1968 and saying: 'It was his programme; it is mine, and I have nothing to add', abrogated the National Charter and all the other documents and measures known in Egypt for eighteen years. The vicissitudes experienced by the country during the years since Nasser's death prove that nothing was left to chance after the death of the Rai's. The events of 14th May 1971 would not have happened if those who fell that night had realised that the putsch had actually taken place with Nasser's death. These years also furnish proof of a hasty course of action wavering between a facade and a profound reality, and using surprise tactics; a course of action intended to veil the regression behind constitutional legitimacy. In this context Sadat's putsch is not a spontaneous reaction to Nasser's actions; in fact Sadat's acts were always preceded by long-considered plans. And the putsch itself is a good exploit-ation of the great breaches in the house Nasser built, and at the same time a natural extension of the contradiction which developed in the very heart of this house.

Though Sadat, because of his early political leanings (before July 1952) and because of his close connection with internal, Arab and international plans (since he was the General Secretary of the Islamic Congress) is a founder member of the institution of social forces opposed to the revolution, even from within the leadership of this revolution, his personal characteristics, which give his individual ego a very definite type of thought and conduct, are among the elements which gave him the chance to represent these forces at the highest summit of power.

Its Ratification

For all these reasons, I am disinclined to call the events of 14th May 1971 a plot by those who resigned collectively, or by Sadat himself. These events simply ratified the putsch which had taken place peacefully with Nasser's death, a death succeeded three years afterwards by the death of his regime. The President's death solved the contradiction between the existing socio-economic structure and the political power which sheltered behind the reconstruction of the armed forces to wage regular war against Israel again. As those who resigned collectively had not recognised the new realities, it was for these events to take place; the retiring officials were in fact on the fringe of the real putsch. Anyway, by the arrogant manner of their resignation, they speeded up the official ratification of the putsch.

On 4th February 1971, President Sadat made a speech in Parliament [20] in which he presented to Egyptian, Arab and international public opinion an 'initiative', later known by his own name, for solving the Middle East problem. Remember that this same day saw the end of the suspension of the war of attrition by applying the Rogers Plan which Nasser had accepted in order to defy Israel, and especially to lessen the great loss of men resulting from the barrage of missiles along the Canal. Gunnar Yaring, the personal envoy of the Secretary-General of the United Nations in the Middle East, had already appealed to the interested parties for an extension of the cease-fire. President Sadat replied favourably to the appeal, in order, he said, to show respect for international public opinion. He added 'to all the efforts aimed at solving the crisis' a new Egyptian initiative, the practical application of which could serve as a criterion for the wish to apply the decision of the Security Council:

> We demand, during this period of suspension of hostilities, a partial retreat of the Israeli forces on the east bank of the Suez Canal, as the first stage of a calendar which could later be used to carry out the rest of the points in the resolution of the Security Council. If this retreat is carried out during this period, we will be ready to proceed immediately to the dredging of the Canal and its reopening to international shipping for the service of world economy.

Several historical sources for this period tell us that Mr Ali Sabri, then Vice-President of the Republic, some members of the Supreme Executive Committee and a few ministers, had voiced their disagreement with President Sadat on the subject of this initiative when he told them about it. These sources agree in saying that the President of the Republic then appeared convinced of the necessity of adjourning the examination of this initiative, especially as a serious discussion of the 'future battle' had just started in the National Security Council and among the Army leaders.[21] But what actually happened is that the Rai's took everybody by surprise. Remember that this was the new President's political 'style', from the first initiative at the beginning of 1971 to the last — the visit to Jerusalem in November 1977. When the surprise attack is directed not against the enemy but against his own associates, the only possible meaning is that he is arrogating the right of decision to himself alone.

The phenomenon was to be repeated at a faster pace in April 1971, on the proposal for a union between Egypt, Syria and Libya. In reality, when we consider the chain of events for seven years, and how the situation deteriorated to the point of military confrontation between Egyptian and Libyan forces; when we consider the political confrontation between Egyptian and Syrian leaders, resulting in the flag of this union being torn up in several capitals, Egypt's withdrawal from another plan for union with

Libya, that a peaceful Libyan march asking for union was banned from entering Egyptian territory, we cannot but be sure that the difference between President Sadat and his Deputy, the members of the Supreme Executive Committee and the members of the Central Committee of the Arab Socialist Union, did not originate in the faith of the Rai's in Arab unity and the others' lack of faith in this same unity; for this union was never so flouted in history as it was by Sadat. The whole question lies in the fact that Sadat arrogated to himself the right to decide a question of national destiny on his own; and basically that was only the prologue to the ratification of the putsch. To accomplish the union, says Muhammad Hassanein Haykal, will lead to the establishment of new institutions and to new elections; this is what counted, in view of the circumstances, among the reasons which encouraged the President to accomplish this union.[22] This means seizing a constitutional opportunity to make the desired change in the structure of the State in accordance with the social content of the new power. Haykal leaves no room for doubt when he literally affirms this fact on an earlier page:

> The union of these three States implies the establishment of new political institutions; this also implies new elections resulting in a new Parliament and a new Central Committee of the Socialist Union. These two institutions do not at present have a pro-Sadat majority on which the President can count.

Haykal's emphasis on this point is not without significance. But another reason must be added: the President's wish to possess 'the charter of the union' among other means of exerting pressure and displaying his strength in negotiations concerning the Middle East crisis. The reality is that there was never any interruption to the negotiations with the United States through the Egyptian Minister for Foreign Affairs, or with Israel through Gunnar Yaring, the author of the famous report of 8th February 1971 (just four days after the initiative of the Egyptian President), to which Egypt gave a positive reply, and went even further by drawing up in precise detail a settlement including the recognition of the State of Israel, an undertaking to guarantee passage through the Suez Canal to all countries including Israel, a request for an equitable solution to the problem of the 'Palestinian refugees', and the willingness to fix a term for ending the state of war and signing a peace treaty. But Israel rejected Gunnar Yaring's report, or almost so, this report which resembled the Rogers Plan, demanding the enforcement of Resolution 242 of the Security Council; Israel insisted that Arab territory should retreat within 'safe and recognised frontiers', demanded that Egypt should not enter into any alliance hostile to Israel, and that it should forbid any military activity on its territory that might threaten Israel's security.[23]

From Sadat's initiative for the reopening of the Suez Canal, and from the replies of the Egyptian Minister for Foreign Affairs, it emerges that the strategy of the new power was already completed from the beginning of 1971, and that the events of the years since then were only the stages by which it was put into practice, including the stage of the 1973 war. The only thing to change was the 'charter of the union' which Sadat had one day waved over the conference table. It became the charter of separation, serving to carry out the very premature settlement proposal which Israel has since rejected, even after the visit to Israel. For Israel never made any concession with regard to its reply to Yaring.

The decision, taken by Sadat alone, to take the initiative in reopening the Suez Canal, despite the opposition of the National Security Council, and the decision to carry through the plans for union with Syria and Libya, despite the reservations of the Supreme Executive Committee and the Central Committee of the Arab Socialist Union, were only the background to the constitutional changes to come; on the eve of Roger's visit to Cairo (1st May 1971) the President of the Republic had to relieve his Deputy, and his Minister of the Interior, of their functions because of their radical opposition to his opinions. The Minister of Information, the War Minister and others resigned as a sign of protest or of opposition, it does not matter which. But to call all this a plot, whether on the part of the Ministers or of the President, would show a lack of precision. Sadat was also going beyond the limits of plausibility by making this accusation against them and bringing them to trial, not because they did not deserve prison, but because they all in fact deserved it, and their judges too for other reasons. But it appears that the President wanted to make the change within the shelter of the law; it was just at this moment that he undertook to establish the insitutions of the legislature and the executive, in accordance with the social content of the new State.

In his book, *At-Tariq ila Ramadan (The Road to the War of Ramadan)*[24] Muhammad Hassanein Haykal stresses the instruments of the new change that came with the putsch. He relates the events as follows:

(1) Early in the morning of 10th May 1971, the President's daughter arrived at his home with a message from her father asking Haykal to come at once (p.122). He remained at his house until 8.30 p.m. (p.224). When he got back home, the President telephoned him to come back.
(2) Haykal said to the President, in substance: 'The two main people in this situation in which you are involved are General Al-Laythi Nassef, the commander of the Republican Guard, and General Muhammad Ahmad Sadeq, Chief of the General Staff of the armed forces.' Actually the President, when he felt that the opposition was becoming active against him, had a discussion with General Nassef on 11th March 1971. The latter had said that as a soldier he would obey any order coming from the legitimate constitutional power (p.123). During the same night of 10th May, according to Haykal, the President had received Al-Laythi and Nassef several times (p.124).
(3) As for General Sadeq, the President had met him while visiting a military base on May 12th 1971. It is clear that General Sadeq had understood that the wind was shifting; he seized the opportunity of a private conversation to say to the President: 'We understand your situation.' It was quite enough. (p.123)

(4) The President decided to react. He gave orders to relieve Charawi Gumuah of his functions and to appoint Hamduh Salem Minister of the Interior. By chance, the latter was an important member of the quasi-secret avant-garde organisation which was supposed to form the closed circle of the Socialist Union. His particular charge was to direct political activity within the police organisation. His hierarchical superior in the political organisation was Charawi Gumuah himself. So Charawi's right arm was given the task of striking him down.

So it appears that the main instruments of the putsch were the following persons: Haykal, a political element who had declared his opposition to the resigning group even in Nasser's lifetime; he is the mouthpiece of the civilised and enlightened right. He spoke up boldy for the neutralisation of the United States in the Middle Eastern struggle and opposed an alliance with them. Next come Al-Laythi Nassef, Muhammad Sadeq and Mamduh Salem, internal security chiefs and soldiers. But here we have to make a distinction between conspirators and those who carried out the putsch. An instrument can be got rid of; that was the case with General Sadeq, who was dismissed from his post, arraigned, and almost sentenced to prison, but the sentence was suspended. It was also the case with General Nassef who committed suicide, perhaps 'involuntarily' by falling from the window of his London hotel. The same goes for Haykal, who left *Al-Ahram* after having played an important part at the most critical moments for more than two years.

Like instruments, facades also can be eliminated at a convenient moment. The putsch had achieved a master-stroke by choosing the most important covers in the centre, such as Doctor Mahmud Fawzi, and on the left, like Muhammad Abd As-Salam Az Zayyat, Fuad Mursi, Ismail Sabri Abd Allah and others, who formerly occupied the highest posts in the legislature and the executive. They all left office, either because they were dismissed or because they resigned.

But the figures who had an interest in the change did not move an inch. They even made alliances by marriage among their families; this was the case, among others, with the Uthman family, Ahmed Uthman (Company of Arab Contractors), the family of the agronomy engineer Sayyid Mari, who owned large farms, Muhammad Hamid Mahmud, representative of some oil barons, Muhammad Uthman Ismail and Mahmud Abou Wafiyah, the President's son-in-law. These important figures, and others, never resigned and were never dismissed. If minor dissent broke out among them, they could change jobs, but their power remained intact.

As this chapter comes to an end, we must remember that the alternate hiding behind masks and unveiling of the truth had its influence on the international relationships of the new government from the first moments of the ratification of the putsch. It is often repeated, for example, that the Soviet President Podgorny arrived at Cairo towards the end of May 1971 with the outline of a treaty of friendship and co-operation with Egypt. But Haykal relates the truth of the matter without putting too much emphasis on it, perhaps because the context of the passage does not concern Egypto-Soviet relationships. 'Sami Charaf', says Haykal, 'had a mandate to discuss, during his visit to Moscow, two subjects: the preparation of a permanent treaty to put Egypto-Soviet relationships on an official basis, and the creation of a naval academy at Marsa Matruh.[25] This means that this treaty project was not, to begin with, a Soviet suggestion, nor a direct reaction to the measures of 14th May 1971. The treaty was really only a mask for the benefit of international spectators. It was prepared by a pillar of the old regime, and officially signed on May 27th, 1971. It was a superb disguise which Sadat added to another, domestic this time, by giving figurehead posts to a few men of the left. As for the true face of the new government, Haykal unintentionally indicates it as he continues the story of events:

> Naturally the Americans were pleased about the collapse of the college [understand Ali Sabri's group]. But they were puzzled over the swiftness with which a treaty with the Soviets was concluded. Burges, representing American interests in Cairo, met President Sadat before leaving for the United States on June 8th. He gave him a message from President Nixon. This message said that the American President hoped to have further contacts with President Sadat through peaceful diplomatic channels.[26]

The Americans were the first to realise the identity of the new regime.

Notes

1. See Taha Shakir, *Qadaya Al-Taharrur Al-Watani wa Al-thawrah Al-Ishtirakiyyah fi misr,* Dar Al-Farabi (Beirut, undated) p.121.
2. *Ibid.*
3. *Ibid.*
4. *Ibid.*
5. *Al-Magalla Al-Bank Al-Markazi Al-Misri,* Nos. 3 and 4 1969: 'Study on workers and production in small industries'.
6. *Ibid.*
7. Cf. p.40, *op.cit.,* p.168, on the basis of the statistics 1966/1967, which are identical to those of the Central Organisation of Mobilisation and Statistics 1968.
8. *Ibid.*
9. Fuad Mursi, 'Development of the Industrial Bank', *Misr Al-Muasarah,* April 1971.
10. *Ibid.*
11. *Al-Bank Al-Ahli Al-Misri,* Economic Bulletin No. 2, 1971.
12. 'Inquiry: the secrets of the wholesale trade', *Al-Ahram,* 29th October, 1967
13. *Al-Akhbar,* 26th October 1967.
14. *Al-Ahram,* 11th November 1967.
15. *Ibid.,* 8th October 1967.

16. *Ibid.*
17. *Ibid.*, 4th and 6th September 1963.
18. *Ibid.*, 8th November 1964.
19. Among their traditions of warfare, the Egyptian people always took the attitude of spectators in the struggles of the Mamelukes amongst themselves; those same Mamelukes who reigned over them for a long time until Muhammad Ali got rid of them in the famous massacre of 1811. The Egyptians let the Mamelukes finish each other off, and this weakened all the parties and prepared the ground for a real change of power.
20. Speech by the Egyptian President. Complete text published by *Al-Muharrir* (Lebanese newspaper) 25th February 1971.
21. See Fuad Matar, *Nasser's Place in Sadat's Republic.*
22. Muhammad Hassanein Haykal, *At-Tariq ila Ramadan,* (Arab edition, 1975) p.118.
23. Complete text of the Yaring Report and of the Egyptian and Israeli replies in *Al-Balagh* (Lebanese magazine) 4th June 1973.
24. Haykal, *At-Tariq ila Ramadan* (Arab edition) pp. 115-24.
25. *Ibid.*
26. *Ibid.*, p.127.

2. To Recover and Face the Future

A Credible Programme

On 23rd July 1971, in his double capacity as President of the Republic and of the Arab Socialist Union, President Anwar Al-Sadat presented a programme of national action to the second General Congress:

> Nineteen years ago, [he said by way of introduction] our leader Gamal and his comrades, trusting in God and the people, went forth to carry into effect the historic hope that has always helped our heroic nation through its continual struggles. . . the hope of establishing a better life on our good Arab soil, a life of freedom and dignity, liberated from all the chains of exploitation and under-development in their material and moral forms.[1]
>
> The people, [President Sadat went on] who have never recoiled from work and sacrifice, have also protected the revolution from plots from without and sabotage from within. The people have always been the main foundation of every action against the alliance of foreign agents, feudalism, reaction and creeping capitalism. And our economic foundations have been built thanks to their creative efforts and constant work. It was the people who heroically resisted the aggression of 1956 at the time of the battle of Suez; it was the people who, to a man, forcibly and obstinately refused the defeat of June 9th and 10th 1967. And since then they have given all their energy and more for the reconstruction of our armed forces.[2]

Continuing his appraisal of the past, the President added:

> Our Congress is meeting ten years after the declaration of the glorious laws of July, the expression of our free choice, made in full conscious-ness, for the socialist way of development, a road that we must follow to put an end to economic and social under-development and to build a new State based on justice and on the fulfilment of all needs . . . Practical experience over the last ten years [1961-1971] proves that the revolutionary choice of the method of social enlightenment was right.

Two capital facts emerge from this experience: the revolution for national liberation can achieve its aim of liberating the people only by taking the socialist road.[3] What is more, socialism does not mean the repetition of watchwords, but well-directed efforts to return to the people the legitimate rights of which they had been robbed.[4]

The President ended his appraisal of the past by saying:

> Despite the various colonial pressures, which had reached their culmination with Zionist-Imperialist aggression, despite the very active endeavours of external and internal powers hostile to socialism, despite mistakes and insufficiencies, our people have, during the last ten years, achieved results which had not been achieved for decades.[5]

The President then explained the positive balance sheet of the past, with many statistical details. He emphasised that our industrial production during the period 1961/1971 had increased by 107.3%, whereas over a period of 50 years from the beginning of the century, it had increased by only 8%. Investments during this decade reached E£3,254.4 million.

On the political and social plane, the President recalled the overthrow of the alliance of colonialism with a puppet government and feudalism, and the establishment of the alliance led by the working class and the peasantry, who had an interest in revolutionary action and were social forces 'long and unjustly exploited' − at this point the President referred to the National Charter. In addition, democracy was achieved in production by associating the workers with the administrative councils by election, and by giving four-fifths of the seats on the administrative councils of the co-operatives to small farmers. Free education became a reality, and a minimum wage was fixed. Social security covered all the workers and the social services were expanded. 'And we began to adopt a policy of national planning as a scientific method permitting the mobilisation of all national resources and their use in the most rational way.' In the Arab field 'the revolution gave back to Egypt its Arab identity, and enabled it to take its responsibility and play its historic part as the base of the Arab struggle for freedom.' At an international level, the revolution spread its ripples as far as the Third World; 'and Egypt enjoyed precious friendships, whose worth was appreciated in moments of difficulty, and the first of which is the friendship of the people of the Soviet Union.'[6]

The President's report did not gloss over the negative points of the experience:

> Though the five year plan achieved its objectives up to 1965, the ten year plan could not be carried through, especially after the defeat of 1967. The political organisation also failed in its task; and there has been no decrease in the percentage of illiteracy; with the increase in population this stagnation means an increase in the number of uneducated citizens. Services are not always adequate, and salary

increases are not keeping in step with price rises. What is more, the campaign of calling our achievements in question extends to our foreign policy and our adherence to the bloc of countries fighting for their liberation and for the liquidation of colonialism. Doubts have even been cast on our friendship for the heroic Soviet Union. Voices are being raised which call on us to abandon our development and aspirations, to limit the field of the public sector, to settle our disputes with the colonial powers and to open our doors to the investments of their monopolies.[7]

In the light of this detailed report, the President presented his conception of the new State. He promised the citizens that he would speed up the drafting of a permanent constitution which would profit from the lessons of experience, and would first be submitted to the general congress of the Arab Socialist Union, and also to the people. He announced, in addition, the good news that the word 'Egypt' would be used again in the name which would be 'the Arab Republic of Egypt'. Finally, he announced that the public sector would remain the leading sector and that it would always be the citadel of socialist development in the country.[8] Towards the end of his speech he told the intellectuals that it was high time 'to create a general union of writers consisting of men of letters and political, economic and legal writers, and also a union for artists in their various specialities.'[9]

Before we can attempt to foretell the future from the President's programme, we must deal with a few formal points. First, strong and persistent rumours have always cast doubt on the authenticity of the President's writings. It was said that Egyptian journalists wrote his articles and his books for him after the 1952 revolution. But, to render unto Caesar that which is Caesar's, it would be fairer to say that Sadat was never far from being a professional writer, before, during and after the revolution. But for the same reasons, we have to point out that the style of the national action programme is far from the spirit in which President Sadat wrote and expressed himself; the same applies — and this is the most important thing — to the ideas contained in the programme. In fact they are very far from the President's political views throughout his political history. It is more probable, then, that among the leftist thinkers who had co-operated with the President and the new Arab Socialist Union, a working team was formed to draw up this report. It is more probable still that the role of this team was not confined simply to formulation, and that much of their own thought went into it. The thought behind the report does not contradict the President's first step, quite apart from the tactical or strategic nature of this step.

Second, President Sadat, faced with the true, or supposedly true reaction to the putsch of May 14th 1971, presented this programme, which won unanimous approval, as a series of declarations, decisions and measures of a distinctly radical nature. Remember that he began his rule by announcing the creation of the 'Union of Arab Republics' thus consolidating bonds of mutual understanding with Tripoli and Damascus. On 27th May 1971, he signed the treaty of friendship and co-operation with the Soviet Union. He was also careful to put forward, from the very first hours of the putsch, a group formed of some of the most important figures of the leadership of the Egyptian left. Muhammad Abd As-Salam Az-Zayyat was first appointed General Secretary of the Central Committee of the Arab Socialist Union, and then first assistant to the Prime Minister. Ismail Sabri Abd Allah was first nominated assistant to the Minister of Planning, and then became Minister of Planning himself. Fuad Mursi was first controller of the programme of national action on the Central Committee, and then Minister of Food. Abu Seif Yusuf, Member of Parliament, Lutfi Al-Khuli, liaison officer for the Committee of Arab Affairs and the political organisation, Muhammad Al-Khafif, and others among the former communists and independent democrats were appointed to a large number of posts. On 10th June 1971, the President delivered 'the report' which was later known by the date on which it was read in Parliament.

The Programme of National Action appeared, then, in an atmosphere of credibility which reigned over a public deeply interested in the main ideas contained in the programme. We can add to this the allusion, made by the President in his report on 10th June, to the ex-bosses and landowners who had assembled for a crusade of their own, thinking that history would go backwards, and that the hour had struck for the recovery of their possessions. The citizens understood that the programme of 'National Action' was going to block these people and help history to continue on its way. But the reality was quite different. And whatever objective reservations we may have about the 'personal motives', which led some brilliant men of the left to accept the new regime and support it by taking an immediate part in the functioning of its machinery, there is no doubt that this 'backdrop', painted by President Sadat for his first scene, was attractive enough to persuade them to develop the play along the intended lines. The later measures taken by the government proved how mistaken this idea was. The consequence of this mistake was that these great figures gradually left the government, one after the other. But this is another story which we shall tell later. We allude to it simply to emphasise that the 'balance' created and maintained by President Sadat between the putsch of 14th May 1971, and all the decrees, measures and conventions that he put into operation after that date, was overall and in detail no more than a solidly constructed stage set. You could read, on this set, slogans saying that Egypt is Arab, that its people are part of the Arab nation, that socialism is its ineluctable road, that, consequently, the national-ised sector is the driving force of internal development, and that strategic relations with the socialist bloc are the master weapon in our diplomatic arsenal. We have to add to these brilliant slogans and this attractive setting, that the mistakes of the past, especially those concerning the problem of democracy, the regression of economic development and the military defeat, were still in the mind of those national and progressive leaders who agreed to co-operate with the new regime.

With this partial acceptance of the regime by the left and in the light of the Programme of National Action, the second stage expected by everyone was to 'continue the revolution and changes', the watchword spontaneously uttered by the people immediately after Nasser's death.

The Reservations of the Man in the Street

Two days before the end of August 1971, a curious event took place at the ironworks complex of Helwan, the largest suburb to the south of Cairo and also the largest industrial centre with a concentrated working population. The workers had kept the President of the Federation of Trade Unions, Mr. Salah Gharib, a prisoner for a whole night to try to get their claims satisfied. They even shouted in his face: 'You are a tool of the government', which was as much as to accuse him of being an agent of the central power. The local branch committee of the Arab Socialist Union took a negative attitude to the event. It was proved later that some members of this committee were sympathetic to the workers, their actions and their claims, even when the movement turned into a 'collective occupation' of the site. But they did not down tools; the workers elected strike committees to lead the movement which began with 30,000 workers. At the same time, these committees had the task of keeping the factory going so that there would not be a fall in production, and this kind of self-management actually resulted in an increase in production. We should add that the Union committee had the same attitude; none of its members made the slightest attempt to stop the occupation of the factory site; the chairman himself, and a member of the committee, were among the leaders of the movement and among those who encouraged the workers to take the initiative of locking up the President of the Federation of Trade Unions, who was originally there to examine the workers' claims.

What were these claims? To begin with, they were very modest, and their economic form related simply to their own sector. But their political content was directly linked with the events of 'Abu Kabir' and 'Kamchich', about which there were many rumours, despite the distance between these two provincial towns. In fact, the political content was the same, or almost the same, everywhere. The security machine and the remnants of feudalism were taking their revenge on all elements historically known for their resistance to oppression and social injustice. With one difference — it was an army of students that confronted authority at 'Abu Kabir', while the peasants were the victims of governmental oppression at 'Kamchich'.

It was in this climate that the workers of Helwan, united over economic claims which had their political reflections, occupied the factory sites. They were demanding shorter hours, higher wages, a share in decisions regarding production, that is to say effective participation in the running of the factory, and an undertaking by governmental organisations and their members not to interfere in trade union or political elections.

The authorities could find no other solution but to suppress the strike by force. About 3,000 workers were arrested. The news of these arrests reached

Chubra Al-Khaymah (the other big industrial suburb, with long-standing traditions of organised political action), which replied with a huge demonstration. This was violently suppressed by the police, supported by forces from the regular army. A large number of demonstrators were arrested.[10]
The government, wishing to keep a certain balance, took the following measures after an enquiry:
1) Premature retirement of the President of the Organisation of Metallurgical Industries.
2) Premature retirement of the president and managing director of the company, of the manager of the rolling-mill, the advisor to the president and managing director of the company, and the manager of the hot-rolling section.
3) Transfer of the vice-president of the administrative council, the production manager and the personnel manager.
4) Dismissal and retirement of a certain number of workers who took part in the occupation of the site or helped to carry it out.
5) Transfer to other companies of a certain number of workers who took part in the occupation of the site, with warning of dismissal if they took part in any activity aimed at inciting the workers to strike.
6) Dissolution of the branch of the Arab Socialist Union at the Metallurgical Company of Helwan.
7) Dissolution of the Union committee of the Metallurgical Company of Helwan.
   Following on this event, President Sadat made a speech in which he admitted:

> I do not deny the existence of contradictions within the alliance. But we had agreed to solve them peacefully and democratically within the alliance itself, without letting one of the forces of this alliance impose its opinion or its will, since the strength, and the supreme will, belong to the alliance as a whole. . . . I tell you frankly, [he went on] I would have taken other measures, I would have acted differently had I known how the president of the workers' union, who, moreover, was elected by the workers themselves,has been treated. But the Minister of Industry and the Minister of the Interior preferred to solve the problem before submitting it to me. . . Occupation of factories and strikes [he concluded] are not democratic acts. The political organisation and the State authorities cannot allow them. Neither the State nor its government can respond to claims under such coercion.[11]

Less than three months after this speech (11th November 1971) and perhaps for the first time in its history, the city of Cairo was surprised by a taxi-drivers' strike. The strike began at 7 a.m. with a meeting of 200 taxi-drivers at their Union headquarters. They decided to go on strike in protest against the prison sentences on nine drivers who had refused to take on customers. After the beginning of the strike, taxi-drivers began to prevent their colleagues who had not joined the strike from driving in the streets of Cairo and Guizah. But the accounts published by *Al-Ahram* at the time revealed that since the taxi-drivers' elections had given rise to a strong union committee and a strong union, the general intelligence department and the workers' general secretariat of the Arab Socialist Union encouraged a 'movement' which might overthrow the new order.

The authorities intervened as usual, arresting 100 taxi-drivers (*Al-Ahram,* 12th November 1971). A few days later, the number of persons arrested reached 149 (*Al-Ahram,* 15th November 1971). Of these, 92 were kept in prison, then 22 (*Al-Ahram,* 16th November 1971).

Another event, no less widespread in its effects, and no less unusual when set against the traditions of post-revolutionary Egypt, was added to those already mentioned. On the 30th March 1972, workers in the private sector at Choubrah Al-Khaymah barred the way of the motorcade of the Prime Minister, who was going to Chebine Al-Kom (capital of the governorate of Al-Menoufiyyah to the north-west of Cairo). They threw stones at the motorcade, demanding an increase in the minimum wage, limited working hours and the right to sick leave. *Al-Ahram* of 14th April 1972 reported that 76 workers were arrested during this demonstration.

The labour troubles were scarcely over, towards the end of the first year after the putsch, when the students of the Agricultural Institute at Chubrah Al-Khaymah rose in revolt on 1st May 1972. They set fire to the Dean of the Institute's car and some wooden packing cases, and threw stones at the Dean's office windows, protesting against examination regulations and the system of promotion from one class to another. Courses were immediately suspended for two weeks, and 26 students were arrested.[12] The charge against the students in preventive detention contained the following particulars:
1) Assembly with intent to cause an obstruction to traffic, which is a crime against State security.
2) Wilful damage to public property, breakage of windows at the Institute and setting fire to other objects, which constitutes an attack on State security.
3) Wilful damage to private property, setting fire to and destruction of a vehicle belonging to the Dean of the Institute.
4) Resisting authority by throwing stones at the firemen and fire engines and setting fire to two of the engines.

The records of the examination of the accused show that the students had previously occupied the premises of their Institute on two occasions, demanding the abrogation of the *numerus clausus* of the total marks, a condition of entry into the third year, and, consequently, of obtaining the Higher Diploma in agriculture. Students who did not obtain the requisite marks in fact received only a certificate of aptitude.

Al-Ahram of 3rd May 1972 published a news item saying that four first-year students had been arrested and four lecturers questioned. From the examination of the latter it was proved that they had played an important part in inciting internal revolt in the Institute. The next day, the same

newspaper published news of the release of three students who had been
arrested in the course of the events of January 1972, while they were distributing leaflets at Helwan. One was a student of the Faculty of Political
Science at Cairo, the second of the University of Ain-Chams and the third of
the Aeronautical Institute. One of the four students arrested, the paper added,
was the holder of the cup for the best student.[13] On May 8th, 9th and 11th 1972,
Al-Ahram continued to publish the list of charges containing the names of
70 accused to go on trial at Chubrah Al-Khaymah, including 14 students from
the Agricultural Institute. The number of witnesses was 118, including
policemen, bosses and railway officials.[14] President Sadat ordered, on the
occasion of the first anniversary of the putsch, 15th May 1972, that none of
the accused should be proceeded against.

. . . And Cairo Began to Burn

The President's programme, like that of all declared political groups, was in
flagrant contradiction to the strikes, sit-ins and demonstrations with which
these measures were received. The contradiction, between the watchword
given out by the summit of power and the explosive reality of the base, was
obvious. The most conspicuous phenomena of this troubled and eventful
period (1971-1972) were the series of fires; in this year alone there were 28
fires, of which the saddest and most well known was the one at the Opera
House, which was then about to celebrate its centenary. It was built on the
orders of the Khedive Ismail in the very centre of Cairo, and inaugurated with
Verdi's *Aida;* it was the symbol of progress and links with the West. It was
unique in the East, full of history and profoundly significant. The Egyptians
flocked to the square of the same name, grief stricken and stupefied at the
thick smoke enveloping it. Most of those who wept that sad day had never set
foot inside it. And yet mourning was country-wide. No one took any interest
in the inquiry, which came to nothing anyway, and indirectly almost
involved a humble porter who guarded the building and slept there. The
technical report said that faulty earthing of the electrical circuit was responsible for the disaster. But nobody believed the experts' report because the
building was about ten yards away from the headquarters of the fire brigade.
Even rumours, (which often contain a grain of truth) about some official
using fire to cover up a theft, went unheeded. Nor was the man in the street
interested in political rumours imputing responsibility for the fire sometimes
to the Muslim Brothers, sometimes to the communists. The crime was
recorded as being of 'unknown' origin; that did not even give rise to humour-
ous comments, to the *nukta,* the traditional recourse of the ordinary man in
similar circumstances. The ordinary man was not concerned with the unknown
criminal; he was beginning to be anxious about the unknown future; vague
memories of the Cairo fire of 26th January 1952 were rising from the depths
of the collective unconscious. And although the incendiarist was never found,
at least we know what happened a few hours and then a few months after the

fire. The Wafd, under overwhelming popular pressure, had come to power in 1950 despite the opposition of the Palace and the British occupation. The Wafd abrogated the 1936 treaty which it had itself signed with Great Britain; guerillas took up position on the banks of the Canal and in the Ismailia region, where there were massive concentrations of British troops. When Cairo burnt on that sad day, the King dissolved the Wafd government and proclaimed emergency laws. The Egyptian guerilla war was suspended, and six months later the movement of 23rd July 1952 emerged.

The events of 1971 perhaps evoked memories of those of 20 years ago though without any connection being made between them but the people, confronted with the momentous events and forebodings of 1971, suffered great mental anguish. There was a vague feeling that the putsch had been accomplished on May 14th, but that its true face was not yet visible. They scented something in the successive fires, but could not yet quite grasp it. The great classes of the population sensed, more and more strongly, that all Egypt, and not only Cairo, was burning by stages. Their worry was even greater over the burning of the municipal railway workshops near the Central Station than over the fire that destroyed the examination papers at the Al-Funtat Grammar School in old Cairo, near the Nile. But neither the railway nor the Grammar School fire, despite great losses, shook them as did the series of fires directed, one might almost say, against civilisation. First the Opera House was ravaged; a few months later flames licked one of the oldest historic palaces in the Al-Ola's district — that hill famous for its prisons, its mosques and its wars, throughout the history of Islamic Egypt. The shops of the Bayt Al-Wali palace were no incitement to theft by some dishonest assistant before the annual stocktaking. Nor was there any need to burn the mosque next door to the palace if the aim was to cover up the tracks of a crime. The technical report and the criminal investigation found no electric wires or caretaker to blame, and the affair was classified as of unknown origin. But religious and national tension rose among the inhabitants of the old quarter and for most of the citizens it was mingled with stupefaction and grief.

The unknown criminal did not even let people take breath after the stifled horror that met these events, for another catastrophe occurred at Ouna Al-Gabal, an isolated region in Upper Egypt, more precisely in the middle of the desert south of Luxor. There, hills rise steeply, and winding roads lead to caves difficult to enter and to leave, the way in and out of which is shrouded in mystery for everyone except wild beasts and Pharaohs. This place contains a large quantity of archaeological relics, both known and unknown. At Ouna Al-Gabal recent discoveries, sculptures, bas-reliefs, vessels and mummys, made it possible to rewrite a large part of the history of ancient Egypt; they provided the answer to certain specialists' questions, and filled some gaps in the history of the Pharaohs. To steal these finds, there was no need for a fire, which would not even be in the interest of the thieves.

But that is what happened and went on happening like a blind fate against which nothing could be done. Once more the question was not who or how, but why. The question was all the more reasonable because these fires looked like an inescapable fate that could strike anywhere, at any time; people even woke in the morning and asked where the latest fire was. If the devil himself had confessed to being the culprit, they would not have been interested; even if he had told them of his methods of setting on fire, indiscriminately, a theatre, a statue, an examination paper or a fire engine, they would not have been interested. They did not ask who or how. They wanted to know why. They did not bother to call to memory pictures like that of 'Al-Khutt', the ogre of Said, the famous bandit who, from his refuge in an impregnable mountain stronghold, battled against authority for a very long time; or Amin Sulayman, that extraordinary thief of the late 50s who slipped between the fingers of the police by leaping from one house to another and from one street to another; and when he was besieged in a cave in a hill at Helwan (a southern suburb of Cairo), preferred to kill himself rather than be caught. (This was the news item which inspired the novelist Naguib Mahfuz to write his famous novel *The Thief and the Dogs*.) No, the memories of the people did not resurrect these heroes; they were not interested. The real question was not who but why.

The people turned their backs on security service inquiries, technical reports, government rumours about the official who burnt the traces of a theft before the annual stocktaking, or rumours about political schisms sowing trouble among the citizens. These were answers to a question that was not being asked. What they saw was an enlarged picture of the earlier Cairo fire. It was Egypt burning in stages, far and near. It was felt that these fires were political in character, charging the general atmosphere with something mysterious, unknown and inescapable. For all these reasons the question was why. To know the reason sometimes leads to perceiving the consequences.

So when the roof of the Association of the Holy Book at Matariyyah was burnt, people did not wait either for an inquiry or a report. They considered it as a political fire, but at a different level and more serious than earlier fires. This district in north-west Cairo is, in popular tradition, the place where the Virgin Mary took refuge when she left Palestine for Egypt with the Infant Jesus. It is also said that it was here that the Virgin appeared to certain people after the defeat of June 1967; the government, at the time, put up a giant marquee and organised a non-stop festival attended by millions of people who came from all over the country to ask the Virgin Mary to cure them or intercede for them.[15] To set fire to property is deplorable, to set fire to objects belonging to civilisation and to the nation is heart-rending, but to set fire to a religious centre is a catastrophe, especially in a country like Egypt which has always been immune to civil and religious wars. In its modern history, since the revolution of 1919 at least, and probably since the Orabi revolution, Egypt has been moulded by the struggle against the occupying power and for democracy with a secular and modern philosophy. We can add that Egyptian society, from the dawn of history to modern times, possessed the elements of a class society without tribal or professional anomalies. Despite the Ottoman or Mameluke persecution of the Christian minority, all Egyptians have always played their part in the national struggle; the Egyptian Church, since the resistance of the anchorites and the foundation of its convents scattered about the desert, has always been a bastion of knowledge, science, culture and the struggle against the foreign despoiler; that is an idea which all the Christians in Egypt — and even the atheists — have absorbed with their mother's milk. The occupying British often tried unsuccessfully to apply the tactics of divide and rule. They even tried, on the pretext of protecting minorities, to attract the Christians to themselves. An Egyptian priest, Bishop Sergius, replied in 1919 from the pulpit in the Al-Azhar mosque: 'If the liberation of Egypt needs the sacrifice of a million Egyptians, the Christians will be that million'.[16] Between 1919 and 1952 the majority of Egyptian Christians had belonged to the Wafd, a very influential popular party representing the majority of the middle class with its different strata (the term 'Coptic', by the way, is incorrect; it is of Greek origin and means all Egyptians, and not simply a religious group). Many Christians were observed among the leaders and the strongly militant elements of this party. An important minority among the young Christians had, very early, joined organisations and movements of the Egyptian left. Some of them held leading posts; and today they are very numerous among the intellectuals and leaders of rational and progressive thought.

During the whole of Nasser's time, that is to say for 18 years, there was never any question of religious conflict. Even when the nationalisation measures of 1961-1962 affected businesses and companies owned by Christians, the Church and its staunchest members stayed with the President, who opened the great Cathedral of St Mark; earlier the State had made a gift of E£100,000 to found the greatest patriarchate in the East. In fact the nationalisation measures, immediately after their publication, had taken on a national significance, making no distinction between those who benefited and those who suffered. Moreover, free education at every level, including universities and military academies, delighted the vast majority of Egyptian Christians, whose children could get into military academies and universities without 'intermediaries', entirely on the basis of marks obtained in the matriculation examination. The transformation of *Al-Azhar* into a modern university, the optional application of Islamic legislation to the civil rights of non-Muslims, and the creation of civil rights tribunals, had a beneficial effect on the development of national unity and its progress right through from the period of the Wafd, when the struggle was for independence and democracy, to that of Nasser, when the national struggle was aimed at the liberation and progress of land and people. For all these reasons, Nasser's wall had no crevices through which religious conflict could penetrate.

It was, therefore, natural that the Egyptians should be horrified at the confirmation of rumours that a religious building belonging to Christians had been burned. Whether it was an association (which was the truth) or a church, (according to the rumours) the news sped like lightning from Alexandria to Aswan. The Egyptians felt outraged that the unknown incendiarist of progress and civilisation had dared to carry his latest criminal act to the level of religion.

If, earlier, they had vaguely sensed that these fires had a political origin, they were now certain that they were a national catastrophe. The affair might have been classified as of unknown origin, had it not been for the events preceding and following it, and also, had it not been for the fortuitous presence of a few policemen in the vicinity, the confessions of the accused, and the setting up of a parliamentary commission of enquiry under Gamal Al-Utayfi, the parliamentary general secretary. The results of the enquiry, complex and far-reaching, were largely published in the dailies, which enabled the citizens to learn a few facts in the midst of an avalanche of rumours.

One of these facts was that messages and leaflets were put through letter-boxes; on thorough examination most of these were shown to have been printed in some other Middle Eastern country, as the typography and the paper were not of a kind existing in Egypt. It was even revealed that some of these declarations were printed in Canada, Australia or in the United States. The first conclusion that could be drawn was that some groups of emigre Egyptian Christians might not have been entirely ignorant of the affair, as well as a few State organisations and a religious institution, the World Council of Churches. In a style suggesting that they came from within the country, these tracts said that Egyptian Christians were discriminated against at various levels by the people and by the government, in public offices, education, popular representation and legislation. The Christians, said these leaflets, had suffered enough, and demanded to be represented according to their numbers, estimated, in these messages of unknown origin, to be 30% of the Egyptian population, while official statistics give them as only one-sixth. These declarations, sent by post, demanded that a Christian should be appointed to the post of Vice-President of the Republic, that the Council of Ministers should include six Christians and that the Christians should not be excluded from the office of governor and of his deputy, or from the highest offices in the police and the army, that they should be exempt from the application of Islamic law, that the teaching of certain religious subjects should be terminated; that parliamentary elections should be freer and more accurate so that there should be religious representation in Parliament, and that all considerations preventing Christians from occupying posts of responsibility in the judiciary, the universities, the Civil Service and various organisations should be rejected.

The internal security organisations (General Enquiry Service and General Intelligence Office) could have quietly tracked down these messages and discovered their origins, shortly before the fire at the Association of the Holy Book; it would then have been possible to control any attempt at arson; but the opposite happened. Suddenly the distribution of these leaflets ceased.

But one of them bore the name of Pope Chenudah III, the Patriarch of the Coptic Church; its contents were more or less the same as the others. The Egyptian Pope enjoyed, and still enjoys, a great reputation at a national level, due to his personality. A cultured man, a graduate in history, he had worked in religious journalism. He was editor-in-chief of a religious monthly, *Madaris Al-Ahad*. He was also an officer of the Reserve and had taken part in the war; in addition he was a faithful follower of the previous Pope, Kirellus VI, who was considered a saint by all citizens, whatever their religion. The two men were close personal friends. After the death of Kirellus VI, Pope Chenudah was elected Patriarch in an almost national contest; the opposing candidate was Bishop Samuel, a member of the World Council of Churches, which was suspected of certain connections with American politics. That is why the victory of Nazir Gayyid (the Pope's secular name, which he gave up as soon as he became Patriarch) was a cultural and national victory for the Egyptian Church and the Egyptian Holy See. Pope Chenudah's few writings all concern the struggle of Christianity against Israel and Zionism. After his election, Pope Chenudah III continued with his teachings on this problem, publishing, as a former journalist, a weekly article in the daily *Al-Gumhuriyyah* and giving lectures at the offices of the press syndicate. For these reasons people were greatly surprised to read Pope Chenudah's name on a leaflet publicly distributed in the streets of Cairo and other provincial cities, notably Alexandria. The Holy See, the government and the people were even more surprised. It was not a denial on the part of the Papal Palace that was needed. All the rumours and all the facts should have been recorded. Political agility, well trained in this sort of affair, was what was needed.

There were two rumours more striking still, although, or perhaps because, they were contradictory. According to the first, six young Muslims at Alexandria had embraced Christianity. According to the *Shari'a* (Muslim law) these young men would have to be executed by stoning. The rumour also said that the Church of Alexandria had become their refuge and that it was celebrating their conversion. Counter-rumour said that some men of influence with the Supreme Council of Islamic Affairs had seduced some poor Christian girls and forced them to marry Muslims in exchange for protection and shelter. This counter-rumour alluded to secret societies led by a high official and charged with the same kind of activity — violence and kidnapping.

We must remember that in Egypt rumour is like the *nukta* (joke), it spreads like wildfire from the north to the south of the country. A rumour needs only to be whispered to become true. And because of that, it always carries a biased viewpoint, full of feeling for or against its object. And both sides reacted strongly. In this tense atmosphere, there were some unfortunate attacks against a church in Fayyum and another in the Delta.

The Commission of Enquiry had an interview with a representative of the Patriarch who showed them the registers of conversion to the Church covering a period of 25 years. They found just one case — a lady who had changed from Protestantism to the Orthodox Church. There were no cases of Muslim conversions to Christianity. The facts were that the six young Muslims had, against their parents' will, wanted to emigrate. They threatened to do anything to attain their goal, even if it meant abandoning their religion. This threat was never carried out, although they chose to stay for a time at the house of a Christian friend who was an expert on emigration. In any case, this threat could not be carried out, because the Egyptian Church refuses to convert a Muslim who has renounced his religion; which is an intelligent way of sparing people's feelings and consolidating national unity.

It was also revealed that most of the stories about young girls converted to Islam had been greatly exaggerated so as to fan the flames of religious conflict. Every year, about 500 Christians, men and women, are converted to Islam for compelling reasons (marriage, divorce or other material considerations) or simply to escape the rigidity of the laws of the Church. The Commission of Enquiry tried to establish a balance between the reasons leading to religious extremism, Muslim or Christian; it pointed out that the large number of regular publications of the two parties, and the absence of any State control, were some of the reasons for these extremisms. Following the enquiry, every incident was treated separately and locally, in the form of a special record for each case. But rumour took little account of that. It was said that the President of the Republic had refused to receive the Patriarch, and that the Pope, for this reason, had decided to observe a fast. The opposite was also heard, that Pope Chenudah had refused an invitation to the Presidential Palace. Both rumours were nipped in the bud; on two consecutive days the newspapers published the picture of the President receiving the Sheikh of Al-Azhar, then the Patriarch, and the members of the Pontifical Council.

But although the rumours were gradually dissipated, facts did not take their place; accumulated resentment still lingered in people's hearts, and seemed firmly anchored there. The report of the Commission of Enquiry was probably objective and secular; but in the last analysis it went no further than the administrative enquiries which practically always ended by classifying everything as of unknown origin. In cases like that, the accusation was so general as to lose all effectiveness; there was never any attempt at precision and specification. The fire set for religious motives could not resemble the others on the political level. The whole country was profoundly disturbed. The echoes even reach the Libyan President Muammar Al-Qaddafi who was in Cairo some time after the events. In a famous speech at the headquarters of the Arab Socialist Union he said:

> There is nothing Islamic about provoking religious problems between Muslims and Christians in Egypt at this critical time.[17] Islam is innocent of any provocation of this kind, especially at this moment. We, the Council of the Revolution in Libya, believe in the divinity of Islam, which does not only include the followers of Muhammad, but also all who believe in the Apostles. Islam makes no distinction between those who believe in the message of Jesus and those who believe in that of Muhammad. . . True reason demands that all should worship as they wish, at home, in the mosque, in church, no matter where.[18]

He went even further, ending his speech: 'If there is a group of atheists among us, we must protect them rather than persecute them.' These words are not only important because it was Al-Qaddafi who spoke them, they are important for many reasons. The Libyan President was calling, and perhaps is still calling, for an Islamic renaissance. Some rumours made the connection, in one way or another, between this doctrine and the religious conflicts. It was certainly no mere chance that at the National Congress of the Arab Socialist Union in June 1972, a year after its reconstitution, the *ulemas* of Al-Azhar, with the Great Sheikh at their head, were side by side with the Fathers of the Pontifical Council, in the first rank of whom was the Patriarch Chenudah. All followed attentively the President's warning against any religious conflict, and his eulogy addressed to members of both religions. The photographs published next day by all the newspapers as one, put an end to the destructive fires. But only superficially, for later events took an even more serious turn.

Everyone, consciously or unconsciously, turned away from direct and tangible facts. No one studied the leaflets put through the letter-boxes of certain persons. No one examined the rumours and counter-rumours, or the false declaration in the Pope's name. All, deliberately or without ill intention, ignored the need to question in detail those who were arrested at the time of the fires; they were released with a caution as though it were a simple mis-demeanour not punishable by imprisonment. The whole affair was discussed at an 'administrative' level, far removed from political considerations, although it was known, for example, that the Egyptian Church and its followers among the citizens never aspired to be represented in proportion to its numbers in public office; as a body they always wanted secular and democratic repre-sentation. What, then, was the external element responsible for inventing these demands, completely alien to Egyptian Christians who never made any particular religious claims? Traditionally they belong, according to their class, to social strata with conflicting interests. The extremists among them consider themselves as 'the roots of Egypt'. They are extremely angry if they are treated simply as Christians, since this diminishes their importance. So nobody wondered about the foreign element or elements who took it upon themselves to list these claims. And nobody, consequently, wondered about the possibility of Arab or local element or elements in contact with people abroad, preparing the ground within the country. Nor did anyone wonder about elements offering a climate favourable to an organised and carefully directed course of action.

And so the common man's anxiety about the future increased.

In reality, the very foundation of the whole affair lies in the fact that these pustules of religion on the government's skin come from its own internal workers. The putsch of May 14th 1971 did not grow from nothing, but was legitimate fruit of Nasser's regime. In the same way, the religious conflicts were and remain, after Nasser, a result of the heterogeneous formation of the July 1952 revolution. Nasser believed in secularism, others were on the left or the enlightened right. But there were also those who were very near to the thinking of the Muslim Brothers and the Young Muslims. President Sadat was never far from these ideas and feelings; nor was Hussein Ach-Chafei, who later went on to mysticism and dervishism. But in Nasser's time they never had the audacity of Kamal Ad-Din Hussein, who made no attempt to hide his absolute commitment to religious extremism. And he applied this extremism, for ten years, to every opportunity that fell into his hands; his hostility to the Nasser regime reached such a pitch that he had to retire. Some time afterwards he learned about the armed conspiracy of the Muslim Brothers during the summer of 1965; they offered, if successful, to make him President of the Republic. He did not act. He was detained for some months in the former Royal Pavilion of the Pyramids of Gizeh. Sadat and Hussein Ach-Chafei may not have had Kamal Ad-Din Hussein's audacity, but they were no different from him in matters of ideology.

President Sadat was the first to let himself be nicknamed 'the Devout President' and filmed while praying, and to let people see on his forehead the bump caused by long hours in a prostrate position. The constitution which legitimised his regime was the first Egyptian constitution to stipulate that the *Shari'a* should be a main source of legislation, this article coming immediately after the first, which recognises Islam as the official State religion. It was President Sadat himself who arranged things within popular legislative and executive institutions so that the symbols of the left and of democracy should be a mere facade.

One example among many: the man who carried a Russian gun to enable Muhammad Abd As-Salam Az-Zayyat to enter the Ministry of Information on the evening of May 14th 1971, in order to take over from the resigning Minister, Muhammad Fayeq, who had been arrested, was called Muhammad Uthman Ismail. This bodyguard of Zayyat, the citizen with the long progressive and national history, formed, with two confederates, something called the Said Group within the Central Committee of the new Socialist Union. These three men, Muhammad Uthman Ismail, Yusuf Makkadi and Ahmad Abd Al-Akher, had each played a very minor part in carrying out the putsch. They were immediately rewarded by nominations. None of them had ever played the slightest part in Egyptian political life. The very few people who know them would say that one had been accused of complicity in a murder, and another had been prosecuted for several thefts of public money. The newspapers mentioned only the accusation of theft of public money against Yusuf Makkadi. The only thing that could possibly unite people of this sort with others, like Hamed Mahmud (former agent of a Gulf prince promoted to Governor, then to Minister) was blind fanaticism, a marked tendency to be behind the times, total ignorance of the most elementary constituents of the spirit of the times, and vehement animosity against any thought that might have the slightest trace of democracy. These people are still attached to the old tribal traditions of Upper Egypt, which disappeared long ago. They also belong to the class of rich farmers who stubbornly oppose any possible progress. Their thoughts, feelings and actions are dictated by feudal sentiments. One day they went so far as to accuse Tewfiq Al-Hakim and Muhammad Hassanein Haykal of communism, and even to declare that Sadat's adherence to the revolution of July 1952 was pardonable because it was 'the revolution of redress'. This designation of the putsch of 14th May 1971 was started by Musa Sabri, editor-in-chief of the daily *Al-Akhbar* (traditionally on the extreme right) and by Rahman Ach-Charquawi, that writer so well known for his history in the Egyptian left. Later, President Sadat adopted the designation officially; a designation which I think is correct, but only if it refers to 'the revolution against revolution', which was the expression that Abbas Mahmud Al-Aqqad employed in speaking of the revolution of 23rd July 1952.

This group was an organisation within the organisation. It directed the action from within and in the shadows. It was completely different from the group historically linked with the Muslim Brothers, which developed its philosophy in a less fanatical and more modern direction. Notable names in this group are Dr. Abd Al-Aziz Kamel, former Minister of Property in Mortmain and of the affairs of Al-Azhar, who reached the post of Deputy Prime Minister; Dr. Ahmad Kamal Abu Al-Magd, General Secretary for Religious Affairs in the Arab Socialist Union, Minister for Youth and later Minister of Information. But men with these inclinations, like their opponents among the ministers who had been communists, did not stay long in power. Their mission, like that of their opponents, was to save face. As for the Said Group, it was a real action group.

The most serious declaration coming from it at this time was uttered by Muhammad Uthman Ismail at a public meeting of members of the Socialist Union in the governorate of Bani Sweif in Upper Egypt. He repeated it to the executive office of the secretariat in the capital. 'The enemies of Egypt are three; in order of importance: the Christians, then the Communists and finally the Jews.' It was the kind of formula which could easily spread throughout the country. The Egyptians did not know that Muhammad Uthman Ismail was the founder of religious organisations among the youth, and especially in the universities. It was he who supplied these organisations with money and weapons. He made it possible for them to train on the police training-grounds. It was he who defended them when necessary, as happened when a student member of one of these organisations admitted to the police, after wounding a comrade, that he was instructed by the Socialist Union to defend religion and fight against atheism, communism and Nasserism.

Confrontations between religious students and the rest had at the time become a striking phenomenon. It was also clear that a thread held by certain hands in the very heart of the organisation of the putsch, linked the civil and the religious fires. It was clearer still that it was the social forces of the putsch that chose Sadat and not the other way round. For besides the conservative wing of the previous regime represented by Sadat personally in one direction, by the agricultural engineer Sayyid Mari in another direction, and by the millionaire businessman Uthman Ahmad Uthman in a third, the new regime became the host of a new group of landowners and rich farmers of the most reactionary kind. These had had enough wealth to remain substantially untouched by Nasser's measures, and at the first opportunity they did not hesitate to strike the finishing blow to the lower middle class. The opportunity that occurred was threefold: the deterioration of the previous regime since the defeat of 1967, the sudden death of the leader, and finally Sadat's legitimate retention of power to the point when it was believed that the putsch came naturally from the very heart of the former regime, and was not a counter-revolution. This explains Sadat's temporary retention of the expression 'movement of redress', before definitely keeping the name 'revolution of redress', once it was chosen by the social forces interested in counter-change, mentioned above. But these forces, which brought about a qualitative change in the structure of the government, by eliminating the representatives of the bureaucratic lower middle class and retaining those of so-called rational capitalism, drew into their orbit the dregs of the lower middle class, so as to use them as a respectably popular foundation, and so as to have favourable grounds for the fermentation of extremist feeling, thus propagating disorder and terror.

This is a class differing radically from the rabble of which Mao Tse-tung often spoke. It has nothing to do with porters, prostitutes, taxi-drivers and hawkers. It is chiefly made up of those whom the great historian Al-Gabarti designated two centuries ago as *Al-Harafich (es)* The new *Harafiches* (we can also call them white-collar workers) are poor students, graduates out of work, and hard-pressed minor civil servants, young people crushed by the grindstones of despair, disillusionment and suppressed discontent. These are the elements that set fire to Cairo on 26th January 1952, and again 20 years later. They were, and perhaps they still are, the popular foundation of the secret organisation which manoeuvred from the very heart of the regime, and whose plans, once carried out, seem to have been directed against the regime that shelters it. We can perceive here a first glimmer of an answer to the question of why these fires were lit.

At this time, exactly following the enquiry by the parliamentary commission, the 'People's Council' approved the law on national unity, the first open attack on the sovereignty of the law. This law condemns to life imprisonment any person propagating ideas or rumours provoking 'alarm and despondency' among the public or threatening the foundations of the regime. Formerly this was an offence liable for only a two-year prison sentence in extreme cases. After the new law the offence became a crime punishable by death. There is no need to remind anyone that the propagation of ideas or rumours is an accusation for which it is hard to find exact proof. So a sword of Damocles was suspended by the government over the opposition without the new law itself having any connection with the political arson committed by certain members of government secret circles. The criminals were protected and the purpose of the fire was to clear a space for a new building.

An Economically Decisive Year

In the same year, 1971-1972, this new building began to rise on the basis of two serious decisions: the promulgation of the law on foreign and Arab investments (September 1971) and what was called the declaration 'of the decisive year' (the war) with regard to the Israeli enemy. The implementation of this last decision was adjourned. But the two declarations were accompanied by circumstances which revealed that the putsch, in its first stages and from

73

the formal point of view, consisted in encircling the summit of power and alienating it by giving it a false gloss in style: the left takes part in the government, as a sign of friendship and co-operation with the Soviets; a union is sealed with Syria and Libya and the desire is expressed to end, from a military point of view, the differences with the Israeli enemy. From time to time a campaign against the United States is added. We have to add to these semblances two formulas pompously displayed: 'The law is sovereign' and 'The State governs through its institutions'. As for the objective content of the regime, it was moving towards the foundations of its economic basis and its political ideology. The leaders of the putsch did not waste time building up the framework of counter-revolution. The law on investment of foreign and Arab capital, in September 1971, was the economic preamble to the construction of this framework. This law authorised Arab and foreign capital to move in and out of the country, giving precise guarantees against any possibility of confiscation or nationalisation. It even granted them customs and excise privileges extending to exemption from any liability of this type. No field of investment was prescribed for them; they were not deprived of the right to own land. It was natural, in this context, to take Egyptian capital into account. So at the same time decrees were promulgated freeing imports and exports from the restrictions of central planning, from the conditions under which it was possible to do business with foreigners, from conditions regulating prices, the choice of importable or exportable products and the situation of the domestic market.

Nobody seemed to remember that Nasser's Egypt had tried, in 1953, to interest foreign and national capital and to direct it towards productive enterprises, but without subjecting it to political conditions. There was no result. Hence the 'Egyptianisation' measures followed by nationalisations. The latter were intended to prevent under-development, promote economic development and protect national independence. Nor did anyone bother to think that it was a contradiction to speak of war, which imposes a war economy, and to turn in fact towards a liberal economy. The oldest bourgeois democracies in the liberal West have had recourse in war-time to central planning of large sectors of industry and commerce, both internal and external. But though memory, as the saying goes, is useful to believers, it is not at all so to *'kharigites'*. In reality what the heads of the government, the alliance of rich landowners, businessmen, ground landlords, wholesale merchants, technocrats, pillars of bureaucracy and the top brass of the army and security forces were expected to do was to 'support the institution of authority' at national, Arab and international levels, so that this support would lead economically, socially and politically to normal prosperity in these sectors. By 'normal prosperity' we have to understand traditional capitalist development. Up to this period, the laws of the market prevented investors from engaging in just any development, not by limiting land ownership, for example, but by fixing the ratio of supply and demand and reinforcing State control; in addition the State monopolised a large part of the raw material; it determined the circulation of capital and sometimes even its volume. It was, therefore, in the interest of the alliance in power to apply its encirclement method to the economy as it did in the political field. It was necessary, then, to lay siege to the public sector without breaking the old laws; that was why new ones were promulgated. But these laws had also to favour the development of a new social stratum organically bound up with Arab and foreign capital and the political and economic force it represented at international level. In fact, this new social stratum whose 'legitimate' birth was announced by the law on investments, was formed simply from the stockbrokers, managing directors and agents of foreign and Arab banking monopolies, that is to say middlemen between import and export and vice versa. This is at national level. But at the Arab level, capital to be invested came from the oil countries, conservative by preference. At the international level, banks and tourist companies were the second element liable to accept a calculated risk under the protection of the new legal guarantees.

These are the economic measures which led directly to the new structure of the regime. These measures constituted the second qualitative change in the structure of the regime after the putsch. If we consider the elimination of the bureaucratic middle class as the first change, the second is the addition to the alliance of the commercial middle class. Thus the circle of the alliance at the summit is enlarged. The second consequence of this process is perhaps the absence of any truly productive project in the Arab and foreign investment plans; in fact capital arrived very slowly, hesitantly and cautiously; Arab capital was directed towards the hotel business, luxury building, big restaurants and night clubs. American and Western capital was generally directed towards banking. As for import/export, it was limited to importing consumer goods and exporting basic necessities. The third consequence was a sudden rise in prices, but unaccompanied by an equivalent rise in wages, an increase in inflation and unemployment and a sharp drop in the living standards of the middle classes; these phenomena were all influenced by an external factor, namely the inflation crisis of the Western world and the capitalist monetary crisis, not forgetting that the purpose of the capital which came in was to satisfy the greed of the upper middle class. Another, internal factor was the sovereignty of capitalist economic laws and, in particular, the law of supply and demand. In fact, in the field of luxury goods demand was falling and supply was rapidly increasing. As for basic necessities, demand was increasing more and more, while supply was gradually decreasing. This anarchy in the market forced the peasant to sell his crop at the price fixed by the wholesaler and not by the government. The wholesaler imposed his rule on the retailer, and he in his turn tyrannised over the consumers. The fourth consequence was the over-development of commerce to the detriment of nationalised or national industry. A further consequence was an increase in unemployment and undeclared unemployment; production fell, at the mercy of the laws imposed by the market and the consumer. The sixth and most serious consequence, was the impoverishment of the largest strata of the working class, galloping population growth and the progressive fall in the value of the Egyptian pound because of the lack of gold cover. The seventh consequence was a deficit in the balance of payments; the sum of loans from abroad, the short terms for repayment, the accumulation of debts, the increase in interest rates and the progressive decrease in income, discouraged any idea of planning. In their turn, the national income and the average individual income fell. The eighth consequence was a lack of social balance which was catastrophic for values and individual conduct. The law of quick profits imposed its social criteria right across society. The ninth consequence was the progressive drop in the level of services in the fields of health, education and transport. Finally, the tenth was the brain drain and the emigration of labour — all who could find a foothold in a foreign country.

All this happened in record time, as the language of figures, more eloquent than any analysis, tells us.

In this part of our account we shall have recourse to the official statistics given very cautiously, and sometimes even secretly and in very limited copies, by the Central Accounts Office, the Central Prices Office, the Central Office of Mobilisation and Statistics, or other organisations of the various ministries of Planning, Supply and Economy. Among these statistics, we shall use those which illustrate most simply the economic situation during the financial year 1971/1972. We shall do no more than emphasise the signs which indicate the progressive development of the putsch towards a total counter-revolution; these indicators reflect the level of incomes as well as the variables introduced on the classes and on the distribution of property and means of production. Let us look first at tables 5 and 6 in which the Central Prices Office estimates the distribution of the national income in its two forms, absolute and relative.

So the income of the Egyptian family in 1972, according to this table, is E£365 per year. The individual share is E£68. But the Planning Ministry's estimate of this same average is palpably different. In fact the individual share of the national income is as high as E£80 according to the report of the office monitoring the implementation of the plan for 1971/1972.

Hassan Sadeq, in his article 'Differences in income and the standard of living in Egypt', published in *Kitabat Misriyyah,* quoted above, states that the discrepancy between the estimation of the Price Planning Bureau and that of the Ministry of Planning 'is due to the fact that the Prices Bureau indicates, not the national income, but the net national income; the latter comprises the sum of all incomes distributed, while the national product is the sum of income distributed or not during the year'. But before continuing the analysis let us look at Table 6.

These tables indicate that the three categories with the lowest incomes total 2,300,500, that is 34% of all Egyptian families. This fairly high percentage of families obtained only 11% of the national income in 1972. The number of high-income families is 322,000 (4.7% of the total). This category received 22% of the national income in the same year. We may add that only 2,000 families had the maximum income; they got E£77.1 million between them and E£32,000 average per family. If we take into account the figure given in the reports on the application of the plan, for the number of working

Table 5
Distribution of Families and Their Incomes according to the Categories of
Family Incomes in 1972[19]

Categories of Family Incomes: Egyptian £'s	Number of Families: Millions	Total Family Incomes according to Categories: Million of Egyptians £'s per year	Family Income in Egyptian £'s
less than 50	91	2.3	24.809
50	400	24.4	61.000
100	1,814	254.2	140.196
200	1,567	365.4	233.170
300	1,033	338.7	327.871
400	620	265.8	428.000
500	386	205.3	531.587
600	422	277.0	655.799
800	210	181.2	˙864.197
1,000	310	408.7	1,317.758
2,000	10	45.4	4,339.879
10,000 or more	2	77.1	32,429.679
Total	*6,866*	*2,445.3*	*365.100*[20]

Table 6
Percentage of the Distribution of Incomes and Families

Categories of Family Incomes in Egyptian £'s	Number of Families %	Income of Families in each Category in %
Less than 50	1.33	0.09
50	5.83	1.00
100	26.42	10.40
200	22.82	14.94
300	15.04	13.85
400	9.04	10.87
500	5.62	8.40
600	6.15	11.33
800	3.05	7.41
1,000	4.52	16.71
2,000	0.15	1.86
10,000 or more	0.03	3.14
Total	*100.00*	*100.00*[21]

members in each family, which is 1.2, the average income per active member in this top category will be E£30,000 for 1972. If we now compare it with the E£68 or E£80 which are the shares of the individuals in the working-class categories, we shall see that the source of high incomes is not work but property, that it is not production but the parasitism of the middleman, and speculation. These are the two phenomena which developed very rapidly following the promulgation of the law of September 1971 on the investment of foreign and Arab capital, and also following the facilities granted to the national capital, although it never took the option of long-term projects.

This very great discrepancy between the upper bracket of recipients of the national income, the *creme de la creme,* and those who can scarcely pick up the crumbs, the vast majority, is a great crack in the national edifice. It is the rapid impoverishment of the resources of the Egyptian national wealth. It is this contrast that is at the bottom of the new social relationships which are taking the place of the relationships of productive work. It is the beginning of a radical change in the forces and means of production and in the social values arising from them.

We can note the steps of the ladder, from the bottom, extreme poverty, to the top where we find the high incomes; but the contrast between top and bottom is easily grasped when we realise that in the 2,000 category, families can have an annual income as high as E£200,000 mainly acquired by whole-salers and smugglers, while the day labourer's income is no more than E£15 a year. The situation is not much different with regard to certain categories of workers and craftsmen whose annual income is E£23.5, that is to say less than E£3 per month. Anyway, if official figures tell us that 80% of working citizens have an income of E£68 per person per year, and that their total share in the national income is no more than 50%, it means only one thing: the law of impoverishment prevails.

The criterion of individual incomes related to the national income is the one that best epitomises the new economic structure; and so it is the best pointer to the identity of that structure. But we shall pass from the simplest to the most complex, to see more clearly the main features of this economic form as they gradually crystallise.

Let us, then, after explaining family income in general, take some specific samples. Let us take the civil servant, who represents the State bureaucratic machine from top to bottom. The following table (7) shows the cost of his services according to his place on the Civil Service ladder.

Table 7 shows that the posts at the bottom of the ladder constitute 31.4% of the total number. But they cost the State budget only 15.6% of the total cost of the civil service. Posts from the 5th to the 1st grade come to 8.3% of the whole. They cost the general budget 22.4%. That means that the average cost of posts in the three lowest categories is E£124.4 a year; while the average cost of posts in the 1st grade or higher, is E£1,343.8, that is to say, ten times as much. If we add the differences of net salaries (after deductions), the average salary of the civil servant in the lowest grades is E£108 per year or E£9 per month. And when we take into account the number of working

Table 7
Cost of Civil Servants According to their Categories in Public Service and
Public Organisations (Financial Year 1971/1972)[22]

Category	Number of Officials	In %	Total Costs (E£)	In %	Average Costs (E£)
12, 11, 10	338,598	31.4	42,121,720	15.6	124.4
9, 8	397,501	36.9	82,264,870	30.5	207.0
7, 6	250,675	23.2	85,388,960	31.6	340.6
5, 4	63,398	6.4	38,479,500	14.3	554.5
3, 2	20,423	1.9	19,077,420	7.1	934.1
1 and higher	1,915	0.2	2,573,350	1.0	1,348.8
Total	*1,078,510*	*100.0*	*269,905,820*	*100.0*	*250.3*

Table 8
Development of the Ratio of Wages to the National Income[23]

Financial Year	65-66	66-67	67-68	68-69	69-70	70-71	71-72
Ratio wages/ national income	46.1	46.0	47.2	47.3	49.5	46.2	46.3
Ratio profits/ national income	53.9	54.0	52.8	22.8	52.7	50.5	53.8

members in a family, the average share of each individual in the family of this civil servant at the bottom of the ladder is E£2.5 per month. The high-grade civil servant has a net annual salary (after deduction of 33% for superannuation, tax and other stamps) of E£900, to which we have to add allowances and expenses for entertainment and transport, which come to E£70 per month, tax-free. The total net annual salary is thus E£1,740 for a higher civil servant, that is, E£145 per month. On average, the upper level is 16 times the lower.

But let us look at another, more general schema, which shows how the national income is distributed between those who work in production and those who possess property and do not work. It will give us an even clearer view of the sources, legitimate or not, of incomes. Look at Table 8.

This double statistical comparison between the ratios wages/national income and profits/national income between the years 1965/1966 and 1971/1972 shows relatively stable wages: from 46.1% to 46.3% while in the course of these seven years prices increased spontaneously. But profits, in their absolute volume, increased from E£1,145 million in 1965/1966 to E£1,469 million in 1971/1972. The increase is thus E£324 million, the larger part of which accrues to the private sector; not that the latter played an important part in production, but simply that these profits were made by political influence and by the new economic legislation which allowed any limit imposed by the public sector to be exceeded. So the private sector was able to attack the public sector through its profits. Its first step was to take over control of the national economy. The field of property, a basic one, was, as we can reveal, tragically subject to this takeover. Property in the form of land, which covers the greater part of national resources, and imposes a complete style of production on the great majority of the population (about 70%), is a criterion which will enable us to measure the complex economic basis of the regime. Table 9 shows some of the facts:

Table 9
Distribution of Land and Average Income of Owner according to Size of Property[24]

Size of Property (feddan)	Number of Owners as a %	Areas as a %	Average Profits from Rent per Owner in Egyptian £'s
Less than 1	38.7	4.4	11.7
1	20.7	5.7	28.4
2	13.9	6.6	49.2
3	8.0	5.5	70.8
4	4.3	3.9	93.3
5	7.8	11.2	138.2
10	3.7	10.2	282.4
20	2.0	12.7	653.5
50	0.7	9.4	1,486.5
100 or more	0.2	30.4	16,691.7
Total	*100.0*	*100.0*	*103.2*

This table shows us the very wide gap between the big landowners and those at the bottom. The small owners with less than two feddans number 912,000. They represent 59.4% of all owners, but they possess no more than 10.1% of the cultivable land. As for those who own 20 feddans or more, they represent only 2.9%, but they possess 52.5% of the most fertile land. Of these, 2,885, representing 0.2% of all owners, nevertheless possess 30.4% of all cultivable land. The average income from rents per person in this category is E£16,691.

Among the small farmers 583,000 are at the bottom of the ladder; the whole area they possess is only 323,000 feddans, representing 4.4% of the total area. These peasants represent 38.7% of all people owning land. The average area per owner is 0.5 feddans. The average income from rent is E£11.70 per year.[25] Bearing in mind the agricultural workers who own nothing but their labour, the day labourers and seasonal workers, we can thus form a more exact idea of the tragic situation in the Egyptian countryside – a situation in which the constituent factors continued to exist even through the period of agrarian reform; this was manipulated from within for the benefit of the big landowners and other capitalist groups (wholesalers and stock-brokers) and to re-establish almost feudal relationships; to this, we could add the relationships resulting from the emergence of the new category of middlemen, an integral part of landed property and private enterprise.

These relationships, by the nature of things, throw up certain values. We are not interested here in proving that this society of widely differing classes is unsuited to socialist reform. The social regime before the putsch and especially after the defeat of 1967, or more precisely after the end of the five year plan in 1965, was also unsuited to such a transformation; it had exhausted all its chances of bringing it about; in fact the fall of 1967 was objectively the fall of a regime much more than that of a historical character.

Table 10
Distribution of Spending on Consumer Goods according to Categories of Family Budget[26]

Budget Categories	Total of Individuals (Rural and Urban) in each Category		Total of Consumer Spending (Rural and Urban)		Average Share of Individuals
	Number	as %	Number	as %	
Less than 25	45	0.04	881	0.01	19.6
25	706	0.58	18,646	0.30	26.4
50	2,135	1.74	53,906	0.87	25.2
70	4,608	3.75	117,759	1.89	25.6
100	17,071	13.91	508,388	8.18	29.8
150	19,495	15.88	666,069	10.72	34.2
200	16,666	13.58	654,834	10.54	39.3
250	13,527	11.02	587,649	9.46	43.4
300	18,802	15.32	934,789	15.04	49.7
400	16,095	13.11	1,051,500	16.92	65.3
600	6,328	5.16	539,108	8.67	86.2
800	2,673	2.18	303,443	4.38	113.5
1,000 or more	4,575	2.73	778,190	12.52	170.1
Total	*122,726*	*100.00*	*6,215,162*	*100.00*	*55.9*

What interests us is not the gap between the classes, but its proportions and its rate of growth in a country at war, a developing country. This helps us to find a precise explanation for all that happened throughout the year 1971/1972, behind the meticulously built-up left-wing facade covering the most important sectors of power. Confrontations at the bottom, so complex, so far-reaching and with such varied means and ends, tore away many veils, deliberately or accidentally, and brought into the full light of day the true face of the putsch, both its economic basis and its social values. Table 10 takes account of this through the yardstick of levels of consumption.

It is easy to see that the average individual consumption in towns does not exceed about E£50.5 a year (E£4.2 a month); that is the total expenditure on food, clothing, housing and all the other expenses – which means that the standard of living in Egypt is generally at the very bottom of the ladder. If we study details further, we shall see that the average individual consumption of the first category (less than E£25 per year) is E£19.60 a year, which comes to E£1.65 a month. This average rises to E£194.53, that is 9 times more than the lowest average. Individuals belonging to families whose incomes are lower than the general average make up 60% of the members of Egyptian society. And while noting that the five lowest categories represent 20% of the citizens, and that their total consumption does not exceed 11.25% of general consumption, we can also make clear that, in consequence, the three highest categories represent 11% of members of society, and cover 26% of the general expenditure on consumer goods.

These were the economic realities that welcomed, accompanied and developed the law on foreign, Arab and national investments in September 1971. These are the data on which the government of the putsch based itself in order to build up its power, hiding behind the promises of the Programme of National Action presented by Anwar Al-Sadat, President of the Arab Socialist Union, to the General Congress, and approved on July 23rd of the same year, 1971.

So it was natural that the man in the street should be impervious to all the seductions of the new regime, and it was no less natural that he should not agree to be assimilated into this new regime. He was ready to confront it and oppose it. Was it not scandalous to see in every single daily newspaper the photographs of these series of alliances between the families of the President, the agricultural engineer Sayyid Mari and the businessman Uthman Amad Uthman, sealed by the engagements and marriages of their children? Usually the man in the street is delighted at a wedding; but here he must surely look wide-eyed at these pictures and ask himself about the connection between the position of President of the Republic, of the President of the 'People's Council' and of the Minister of Town Planning and Housing. He surely asked himself about the connection between fruit-growing, so dear to the heart of the agricultural engineer-President of Parliament, and the gigantic building projects being carried out by the businessman-minister. Is there a connect-tion, the man in the street wonders, between all that and the hearts of the girls and boys of this trio in power? The engagements were sudden, and announced with a great flourish in the newspapers. And the man in the street thinks of the feasts of the Arabian Nights, remembers those of King Farouk, and sick at heart, wonders what is happening in the world. What is happening to us? What will the future bring?

A Programme Against the National Programme

An ideological reply was needed to the question arising from the contradiction between appearances and tangible reality. The General Secretariat of the Arab

Socialist Union had been radically reshuffled on July 30th 1972. The Assistant First General Secretary for the Affairs of Upper Egypt was Ahmad Abd Al-Akher, and the secretary to the organisation was Muhammad Uthman Ismail (both mentioned above for their religious extremism and the reactionary character of their right-wing thought). As for Drs. Abd Al-Aziz Kamel and Kamal Abu Al-Majd (former Muslim Brothers but also belonging to the enlightened right) the first was secretary for propaganda, the ideological programme and religious affairs, while the second was in charge of the youth sector, which means that the real power fell to the most extreme right wing

The members of the Arab Socialist Union were surprised one day by the presentation of a project called 'Guide to political, ideological and organisational action', which appeared in a very limited number of copies not for general circulation, but for a secret discussion. The seriousness of the ideological project led the monthly *At-Taliah* to publish it[27] so as to submit it to public opinion before reaching the imprimatur stage, which then caused Lutfi Al-Khuli, the editor-in-chief of this magazine and chairman of the Committee for Arab Affairs of the Socialist Union, to resign from his post in that organisation. The most interesting thing is that this 'project' or 'guide' never saw the official light of day. It remained at the project stage in its authors' minds, providing a real exhibit in evidence in the dossier of their ideology, and a reply diametrically opposed to President Sadat's declaration to the People's Council on 10th June 1971, and his programme of national action of 23rd July 1971. In addition, this project radically contradicted all the documents of the revolution, and particularly the National Charter. But to be more exact, this project or guide was the first ideological indication of the putsch; to put it under wraps at the last minute was a tactic aimed not at all at suspending it, but at carrying it out as quietly as possible. How does this guide reveal the identity of the regime of the putsch?

It begins by recognising that the revolution, after putting a stop to colonial hegemony, feudalism and the exploitation inherent in capitalism, indisputably took an important step on the road to fair distribution of the national income. 'But' says the guide, 'this revolution is today threatened by the growing discrepancy between levels of income in the different social categories. The values of our society, inspired by our religious beliefs, condemn the enjoyment by a minority of the nation's goods, while the majority does not receive its due.' With an appearance of self-criticism, the guide asks the leaders to be an example to the people: 'In our daily behaviour towards the people, we must avoid all types of exploitation. We must respect the value of work and respect the workers. We must learn to appreciate manual work. We must value people for their work and their place in society.'

With its admission and its criticism, the guide cuts the ground from under all the statistics it had previously presented and emphasised. It is only a vulgar attempt to win the people's confidence and to get the nation to believe in the official theses, among which one point is to be emphasised: the ideological and political line professed by the regime is rooted in religious texts; the first sentence in this guide states: 'Our vision finds its spiritual dimension in religion and in our belief in the messages from Heaven, sent through Islam, its ideals and its laws.' So, no Arab way for scientific socialism according to the Charter; now we have an Arab socialism 'inspired by the faith of this nation', an Islamic socialism if we can so express it; and an Arab socialism which believes in the basic laws governing the universe and life; 'our traditions and our religions precede all modern thought and prove the existence of these laws; to flout them is to rob our civilisation of its characteristic scientific foundation.' This religious-based socialism consists of the verses from the Koran which the authors of the guide use to support their doctine, and which we often saw pinned to the wall behind the desks of Egyptian capitalists before the revolution: 'We shall not suffer him who has done good deeds to lose his reward.' . . . 'Work! God will see your deeds; so will Muhammad and those who believe in him.' . . . 'Give your neighbour his rights, and to the poor and the traveller'. . . . 'God loves that he who works, works well.' . . . 'Upon their goods a tax is levied, for the beggar and the needy' etc. These verses have their historical worth because they were ideological instruments intended to change an extremely backward society. But they have nothing to do with the use some people make of their 'holy' source by extending them to a completely different society and a completely different period. Worse still, their use in 'modern' cases is rooted in an error and the use of errors which has nothing to do with the Koranic text. For a good deed is not work in the cycle of production. Alms, good grace and charity are not socialism. On this point, the authors of the project-guide did exactly what the big-business pashas in Royalist Egypt used to do: keep the workers down by means of religion, and decorate their offices, their drawing-rooms and even the workshops with such verses. But the capitalists of today are even more backward than those of old, for they do not invest in production; they get their profits from price differences, contraband and the services of the middleman. But on the ideological plane they go much further than those of the past, when they say:

> Immutable truth, its roots deep in history and in divine law, shows that we are right to say that you can do without the doctrines current in the world. We have all that can bring valid scientific solutions to the problems of life and everything humanity needs in the way of values, thought and rationality.

So this Arab or Islamic socialism is valid not only for us, but for the whole world! So one of the basic points of the National Charter, enacted ten years ago, stipulating 'receptiveness to all human experience' becomes inadmissible; because it is too modest for these gentlemen of the new political organisation.

Denying the National Charter was the first step towards denying its social content. The 'guide' rejects the expression 'social classes' and replaces it with 'social levels' and 'social forces'. All that this change can mean is that the existence of the class struggle is no longer recognised. This of necessity leads to considering the ideological structure of the Arab Socialist Union as the bones of a Nazi organisation representing the 'organic unity of the nation' as seen by Hitler and Mussolini, and also by Ahmad Hussein, leader of Young Egypt, and Antoun Saadeh, leader of the Syrian National Party. In the light of these principles, the attitude with regard to property is defined as follows:

> Our socialism makes the difference between property that exploits and property that does not exploit. It forbids the first and authorises the second within the limits prescribed by the law, which translates conscience and the needs of the group as a whole.

This definition completely contradicts the contents of the National Charter referring to the people's possession of the means of production, and the leadership of the public sector over the national economy. To define exploitation by reference to the group conscience without determining either the content of the law or the identity of the group is tantamount to saying that we are a classless society. It is an attempt to free exploitation from any restrictions apart from those dictated by individual conscience and religious principles.

Finally, the project-guide deals with foreign policy. It warns against the great powers which are trying to monopolise the effort for progress and its methods (meaning the Socialist bloc). 'To free the Arab spirit and guarantee its independence in face of international interests and cupidity' means that all the great powers must be considered on an equal footing; which, more precisely, means that the Socialist bloc, and in particular the Soviet Union, are directly under fire.

This is the new political standpoint on which the regime of the putsch based itself in formulating its ideology, going beyond its facade of apparent concern with progress and its nationalist declarations. This guide may not have seen the light of day, but it was not thrown aside for all that. On the contrary, against all speeches and writings of the period, it was immediately put into effect. So we can consider it as a reply to the social and political events occurring between 1971 and 1972, which expressed the general anguish when faced with the future. But let us continue with the facts.

On the 22nd of April President Sadat sent for the Soviet Ambassador to tell him, before telling the Egyptians, that he was going to 'liquidate Ali Sabri'; he added:

> But, I assure you, I intend nothing against the Soviet Union. This is purely and simply an internal affair. If anyone is clever enough to twist what I am going to do into an act hostile to the presence of the Soviet Union in Egypt, you can say that I would be happy for you to strengthen that presence.[28]

But the Soviets must certainly have had detailed information on what had happened in November 1970:

> Kamal Adham, son-in-law and adviser of King Feisal, in charge of

information services, one of the most influential personalities in the kingdom, came to Cairo. During his visit he spoke of the Soviet presence in Egypt and the disturbance this presence was causing to the Americans.[29]

The President promised to 'get the Russians out of the country.'[30] Later it was said that this 'promise' had been the subject of negotiations between William Rogers, American Secretary of State at the time, and President Sadat, on 3rd May 1971; that is to say only 24 hours after the dismissal of Ali Sabri. That, for the Soviets, was a normal introduction to the officialisation of their relationship with the new regime in the form of the well-known treaty of friendship and co-operation. The failure of confidence in the Egyptian authors of the putsch was born of the unhappy contrast between the intentions paraded to the world and the undercurrents of government. At another level, it was the same failure of confidence that arose between the people and the government.

A month later, after the signature of the treaty of friendship, this failure was made worse by the sordid part played by the new regime in the events of 19th July 1971 in the Sudan. The radical military attempt to overthrow the Khartoum government failed, thanks to the effective intervention of the Egyptian army. The decisive 24 hours following the 19th will remain an enigma in the history of this period as long as no one among those at the top decides to disclose its secrets. The retreat of the Sudanese forces stationed on the Canal bank, their removal in giant aircraft under the command of the Defence Minister An-Nemeiri Khaled, the arrest of Babakre An-Nour and Farouk Hamd Allah in Libyan airspace on a British plane coming from London, the mobilisation of the officers and cadets of the military academy in the Sudan, the crash of the Iraqi plane transporting a Sudanese leader close to Saudi airspace. All this was the result of the faultless execution, in record time, of a plan for which nothing had been spared, from the most highly perfected machines to the best-trained experts in this type of operation, none of which would have been at the disposal of any Arab country. Probably the attitude of Malta, which refused to allow the plane carrying the two Sudanese military leaders from London to land, is one of the keys to this enigma. We remember also that the British aircraft handed over its two distinguished passengers without resistance, without making even the slightest protest. It would need historic courage for one of the heroes of these events to speak.

What is interesting in the final analysis is that the putsch of Commandant Hachem Al-Attar would certainly have been able to overthrow the government of Nemeiri, if it had not been for the Egyptian intervention, which was proudly acknowledged by President Sadat: 'The union of Arab countries sealed by the Charter of Tripoli has been born with teeth! We have been able to see this in the Sudan,' he declared on 23rd July 1971 at the National Congress of the Socialist Union. The President also declared, at one of the sessions, that he would not tolerate the existence of a Marxist regime on the southern frontiers of Egypt.

The Soviet Union was thus right to have doubts about the political identity of the man who uttered these words. And the doubts must have moved rapidly towards certitude when the Soviets asked the Egyptian President to intervene personally to put a stop to the bloodbath which was happening in the Sudan, and to save the lives of Ach-Chafi Ahmad Ach-Sheikh and Abd Al-Khaleq Mahjub; one, an intimate friend of Nasser and leader of the workers' movement, enjoyed worldwide popularity; the other was secretary-general of the Sudanese Communist Party. President Sadat actually did contact Nemeiri, but only to make sure that the executions were being carried out. It appears that the Soviets tapped the telephone conversation between Cairo and Khartoum. No further doubt was possible.[31]

This did not, however, prevent the publication of a Soviet-Egyptian declaration on the occasion of the visit to Cairo of Mr Panaborayov, a member of the Politburo. The common declaration strongly condemned the wave of hostility against the communists. It also said that Egypt, building a new life on socialist foundations, would profit from the enriching experiences of the Soviet Union and other socialist countries. This declaration appears to have satisfied the Soviets and President Sadat, but certainly from two different points of view. The Soviets wished to record the official attitudes of the Egyptian President, who on his side resorted to more mystification in his window-dressing.[32]

This mystification was reinforced by a few decisions, declarations and apparent attitudes. When King Hussein suddenly announced 'the project of a united kingdom' on 15th March 1972, with the idea of establishing, under Jordanian control, a self-governing Palestinian regime over the West Bank and all other territories which might be released by Israel, President Sadat turned down the plan. Egypto-Jordanian relations were strained to breaking-point. On March 30th, *Izvestia* wrote that the Jordanian project was 'a divisive act and an attempt to weaken the progressive Arab countries making efforts to end Israeli aggression.'

Another mystifying element was that President Sadat had promised that 1971 would be a decisive year from the military point of view, when the occupation would be dealt with. But the year passed without any decision. It was then that, in an extraordinary session of the National Congress of the Socialist Union, Sadat had to face a barrage of questions on relations with the Soviets, and earlier, in a speech to the nation on 13th January 1972, he had justified the postponement of the showdown with Israel, on the pretext that the mists of the Indo-Pakistani summer (meaning the war between these two Asian countries) had prevented him from dealing with it! At that meeting of the 16th/18th February 1972, he therefore declared:

> I am afraid that these questions are entirely due to the influence of permanent mud-slinging campaigns aimed at altering our relations with the Soviet Union with a view to isolating us and consequently destroying us. Other similar questions have recently been asked,

insinuating that the Soviet Union wants to keep a state of 'neither war nor peace' in the Middle East because this, they say, would be profitable to it and help it to remain permanently in the region.[33] Our relations with the Soviets can be subject to different points of view, but even brothers do not always agree. The Soviet Union has imposed no conditions for its help in clearing away the effects of Israeli aggression. It is the United States who have imposed on us their conditions in advance. But I tell you clearly, no one could impose conditions on Nasser; no one will be able to impose conditions on me. No one will be able to impose conditions on the July revolution. There is also the problem of bases. I tell you clearly, the Soviet Union has no bases in Egyptian ports. I said earlier that I was going to grant some facilities to the Soviet navy in Egyptian ports. This was a gesture of gratitude for its attitude in 1967 when we lost 80% of our arms. What did the Soviet Union do at that time? It established an air bridge and a sea route between Egypt and its own territory. In the space of only four months and without paying or even talking of payment or signing contracts, we already had a first line of defence. Five months after the installation of this line, the Soviet Union came to sign the contract of sale and to say that as a friend of Egypt it was its duty to help us out of our crisis; they offered us 100 million dollars' worth of arms. The Soviet Union has ships in the Mediterranean, and it is in our interest that they should be there to counter-balance the presence of the American Sixth Fleet. Remember the ship *Liberty*[34]. I really think that it is in our interest that there should be a Soviet fleet in the Mediterranean.

Yet another mystifying element: on 5th April 1972, President Sadat called together the Cabinet for an emergency meeting at which he informed his ministers of his decision to break off diplomatic relations with Jordan as a protest against 'the project of a united kingdom' which, according to him, 'would blow the Palestinian cause sky-high, and attack a burning subject, in face of which we cannot allow ourselves to make any concessions.' At this same meeting, Mr Hussein Ach-Chafi, Vice-President of the Republic, expressed his opposition to the postponement of the showdown with Israel. He made another intervention which aroused the President's anger, and which was identical with the subject of a 'note' which the President had received the day before, signed by Abd Al-Latif Al-Baghdadi, Koural Ad-Din Hussein, Ahmad Abduh Ach-Charabasi, Muhammad Isam Ad-Din Hassunah, Abd Al-Khaliq Ach-Chinnawi, Ahmad Kamal Abu Al-Futuh, General Madkur Abu Al-Izz, Dr. Rachouan Fahmi Mahfuz, the engineer Mustapha Khalil and Salah Ad-Disuqi, all former high officials in the executive, legislative and popular sectors. Some of them had in common religious extremism, others hostility to the Nasser period. The note said:

The Soviet Union is giving us help which does not allow us to liberate the land and regain what is due to it; it is high time to outline a policy of national liberation based on Egypt's spiritual and material forces. It is high time to revise a policy which counts too much on the Soviet Union. There is no opposition to the policy of alliance with Satan; but if the alliance is to his advantage, if the ally is not of Satan's stature, it is best to break it.[35]

This note was confidential. The press did not mention it. But the President's reply to his deputy who dared to repeat its contents to the Council of Ministers was very violent.

The Soviets were supposed to be reassured by this parade of friendship on the part of the new regime. But actually they were not at all; for they were following attentively what was going on behind the scenes. In fact, there were some interesting events taking place there, which bore no relationship to what was happening on the political stage in public view. What actually was going on?

Muhammad Hassanein Haykal tells a very strange story under the title 'The Story of Randopoulos'.[36] Randopoulos was a naturalised Greek, he worked in the famous Egyptian vineyard *Jianklis,* south-west of Alexandria. After the nationalisation of the wine-growing company in 1961, Randopoulos, who was 60 years old, was kept on as manager. He had twice been elected to his district council. In 1970 this likeable Egyptian Greek was surprised to see a curious and interesting neighbour moving in next door to the vineyard. An airport had just been built from which Soviet planes took off to monitor the U.S. fleet in the north Mediterranean and defend the Egyptian positions inland to the south, east and west. In September 1971, the house of an American woman official at the United States Embassy was searched by Egyptian agents. The lady was arrested. Tanachi Randopoulos was similarly treated. According to Haykal's information the story is that the C.I.A. had been able to get to Randopoulos by putting pressure on his son who had emigrated to the United States, and through a Miss Swinn whose cover was a post in the visa section of the American Consulate. The Egyptian security organisations, observing contacts between the two people on the one hand and between them and foreign countries on the other hand, succeeded in intercepting three messages in invisible ink containing information on the Soviet airport. The day of the arrest, Randopoulos was in the company of an American personality, enjoying diplomatic immunity, who was immediately freed. Mr Donald Burges, in charge of affairs concerning American nationals resident in Egypt, and Mr Eugene Thron, representative of United States Information Services, flew into a rage. The latter was also sent for by Ahmad Ismail, Director of the Egyptian Information Services and later Minister of Defence. Thron heard some very harsh words about the exaggerated reports of this airport put out by the United States. But on returning home he wrote General Ismail a very frank letter in which he said, notably:

> I should like to assure you that the information we have been able to obtain through the girl did not get to Israel. It was intended only for

the United States, and for their interests. Actually it is information which could also serve Egypt, as it enables the government of the United States to tell Israel how much it is exaggerating when it demands more arms to keep a balance with Egypt's armaments provided by the Soviets. . . I should like you to know, [the letter went on] that the United States and the Soviet Union are in a situation of conflict. There is an operational Soviet base there, and it is natural that we should be interested in what they are doing. . . We were not spying on you.

Haykal comments on the affair: 'The story of Randopoulos was useful, as it revealed a secret communication route between Egypt and the United States.' This route was later to become very important. It began with the President of the Republic in Egypt, passed first through the Egyptian Information Services, then the C.I.A., and finished in the National Security Council with Mr Kissinger, and in the White House. It was to keep this route open that President Sadat agreed to free Miss Swinn. And the result was the isolation of the Ministries of Foreign Affairs in Egypt and the United States, at the time of Rogers, with respect to what was going on behind their backs.

But this was not going on without the Soviets' knowledge. Their technological and other means of transmitting secrets are no less skilful than those of the Americans. They were bound to hear the story of Randopoulos with its preliminaries, its vicissitudes and its consequences.

Nor could they be unacquainted with the daily communiques sent out by General Muhammad Sadeq, whose name the Egyptians heard for the first time during the events of September 1970 in Jordan. General Sadeq played an important part in the putsch of May 1971 and later became Minister of Defence. One day in May 1972, General Sadeq declared:

The Soviets are giving nothing fundamental to our armed forces. The help they are giving us is not enough to liberate Sinai. We have no munitions factories. That is why, if we begin a war, the munitions we have will not last ten days. The Soviet Union asks us to install a naval base at Mara Matruh and another at Az-Zafaran on the Red Sea. . . that is a strange request.

General Sadeq banged on the table with his fist before adding these words, addressed to the officers:

As long as I am Minister of Defence, I will not let the Soviets have even a single base in Egypt; I swear it on my honour as a soldier. If the Soviets go to Matruh and establish a base there, they will never leave it. We have a hard task to dislodge a small country like Israel from Sinai; it will be much worse with the Soviet Union, a great power. The Soviet Union is selling us arms at black market prices. A tank costing 25,000 pounds on the international market is sold to us for 44,000 pounds by the Soviet Union. The Soviets complain a lot about Colonel Khadafi's hostile attitude towards them. We have asked the Libyan President to ease up on hostilities so that they will not serve as a pretext for not letting us have the arms we want. Khadafi was very understanding and even proposed to send a delegation to Moscow. And in fact a delegation led by Commander Jalloud went to Moscow. Their negotiations with Soviet leaders were characterised by a great deal of deviousness. Finally our Libyan brothers sent us the prices proposed by the Soviets. They are twice those of the international market. So the bargain which our Libyan brothers were going to strike on our behalf never came off. The Libyans were going to pay cash. But after studying the prices and the situation, I told them not to sign. And the alternative solution would be to buy the arms we want from the West. On top of the exorbitant prices, the Soviets officially demanded that Egyptian airmen should go to Syria to take charge of the instruction of the Syrian airmen. So the Egyptian frontier could suffer from a lack of airmen. The Soviets give as an excuse the need for unification of air power. The excuse is inadmissible; it is their job. Anyway I should like you to know that no Egyptian airman will leave his country for anywhere else.[37]

The Soviets, then, were aware of the influence of General Sadeq's daily communiques on the armed forces, and their absolute contradiction with the declarations of the President of the Republic. The failure of confidence could only get worse.

The Soviets also realised the development of the special relations between the Egyptian government and that of the Kingdom of Saudi Arabia. So special, that President Sadat, leaving for Moscow on February 2nd 1972, asked General Sadeq to send a message to Prince Sultan, the Saudi Minister of Defence to say that if anything unexpected happened during his visit to Moscow, the Egyptian armed forces should receive their orders from King Feisal.[38] King Feisal himself declared some months later: 'It is no use talking about oil as a means of pressure on the United States. We can triumph only by returning to our faith.'[39] This idea fell on very fertile ground in the person of one of the chief members of the Said Group on the extreme right, Ahmad Abd Al-Akher, the secretary-general of the Central Committee of the Socialist Union. 'We can give up Sinai,' he said, 'but never our faith.' But the most important point is that Richard Nixon, the American President at the time, asked Prince Sultan, the Saudi Defence Minister, to 'tell President Sadat that if the Soviets left Europe the United States would take a serious part in solving the problem of the Middle East.' The Saudi prince replied to the American President that the Egyptian course of action was conscious, objective and comprehensive, 'for they well know that in political matters there are never undying sentiments but constant interests.'[40]

On 6th July 1972, President Sadat again met the Saudi Defence Minister on his return from Washington. That very day President Sadat received an urgent message from the Soviet Union, but for the first time in the history of relations between the two countries, he did not hurry to receive Vinogradov, the Soviet Ambassador Extraordinary. When he received him two days later, the Soviet Ambassador already had an almost perfect idea of what was going on backstage, from the story of Randopoulos to the wave of religious extremism, through the secret negotiations with the United States and the anti-Soviet press campaign. So he was not greatly surprised when President Sadat, on July 8th 1972, in the private house of Al-Qanatir Al-Khayriyyah, turned to him saying: 'I thank the Soviet Union for the help it has given to Egypt through its experts. I would now like to stop the services of these experts with effect from the 17th of July.'

That day, the 8th July, was the true date of the abrogation of the treaty of friendship which had not lasted more than a year and was not officially abrogated until four years later. For some members of the ruling circle it was an occasion for rejoicing, as though it were a festival of national independence. It was also the day when the regime removed the mask. Kissinger could not help saying that what President Sadat had done went beyond all he could have imagined from the point of view of speed, and that it deserved a 'suitable reply' from the United States. If Vinogradov was not surprised, neither was the United States; for the day before his meeting with the Soviet Ambassador, President Sadat received from the United States a message of which the actual text was: 'You can calm down now and do anything you like. But you must always remember that the key to the solution is here.'[41] Haykal, with a knowing wink, notes: 'No one will ever know what went through the President's mind on the 6th of July when he decided to send back the Soviet experts, unless he himself decides to tell us.' And he adds: 'I was quite unable to guess exactly why the President pressed the trigger.'[42] But here there is a paradox; for Haykal's articles, the colloquium of *Al-Ahram,* and the survey carried out by computer on the situation of 'neither war nor peace' were the intellectual preparation for this decision. Brezhnev's letter to President Sadat of the beginning of August 1972, dotted the i's and brought enlightenment about the diplomatic relations between the two countries.

> We cannot [said the Secretary-General of the Soviet Communist Party] remain indifferent to the direction being taken by the Arab Republic of Egypt; for this concerns the common interests of the Soviets and the Arab nations. Perhaps you remember, President, that the leaders of our two countries agreed on the need to strengthen your movement forward, together with that of all progressive forces in the Middle East. We think we have a right to remind you of it, for you have yourself often spoken to us of the recrudescence of reactionary activities within Egypt, and the attempts of the right, directly or indirectly allied with colonialism, to halt Egypt's march along the road to progress and drag it backwards. Where is Egypt going? These forces, internal and external, where are they taking her? What will be the relationships of our countries in the future? These questions worry your friends and encourage your enemies. We hope to have replies to these questions. We hope that you will

answer them frankly.[43]

The Soviet leader received no reply from the Egyptian President. But the whole world had a reply, of a different kind, from the youth of Egypt.

Reply to the Unknown?

The dismissal of the Soviet experts was the first public measure to unmask the real decision-makers in Egypt, who work in the shadows. The idea of this measure appears explicitly in the note of Al-Baghdadi Kamal Ad-Din Hussein and the others, in Haykal's articles, in the *Al-Ahram* colloquium in which a high official in the Foreign Office took part, and in the declarations of the new leaders of the general secretariat of the Socialist Union and members of the National Congress, all of whom acclaimed the measure with great enthusiasm. Egyptian society, asking itself about the reason for the series of fires, religious conflicts, the rise in prices and the wage-freeze, was trying to foresee the future through decrees and new laws: the law on foreign investments, the 'law of national unity' and the decision to send back the Soviets. The first law was accompanied by an attack on the part of parasites against production, which took the form of suppression of the public sector and an increase in consumption through the private sector of domestic and foreign trade. The second law was accompanied by a strong wave of official religious extremism, propagated by the media. The last measure openly showed a hostile attitude to progressive, Nasserian and democratic forces in society.

The fanatically inspired fires were the negative expression of internal struggles in society, but the student movement was, during the whole of the year 1972/1973, a positive reaction against the course of events. In this sense, the student movement of this year is inseparable from that of 1968, rooted in the tradition of student movements throughout the history of modern Egypt, the most striking example of which was that of 1946, when the National Committee of Students and Workers was set up. It is impossible to understand the Egyptian student movement except in this historical context. Not that the movement of 1972/1973 was an identical extension of the past, but because, on the contrary, it drew conclusions from the variables and invariables of the new politics.

On the one hand, the Egyptian student movement has its roots in modern history up to the beginning of the 20th century, and, more precisely, in 1906, the year of the tragic events of Denchiway. Peasants of Denchiway, a village in the governorate of Menoufiyyah, south-west of Cairo, clashed with some British soldiers who were pigeon-shooting. The colonial power immediately set up an exceptional court, erected gibbets in the village square, and executed some young men of Denchiway. It was an unforgettable event. The crime was severely condemned by many personalities of advanced views, including Bernard Shaw. It also gave birth to the Egyptian novel. Mahmud Taher Haqqi wrote *La Vierge de Denchiway* under the influence of *La Vierge de la Lorraine.* It was at that moment that the Egyptian student movement was born, although the National University did not come into being until two years later, and the official university, of Fuad the First, in 1929. In fact, on 22nd October 1906, some well-known Egyptian intellectuals met at the home of Saad Zaghlul (later the leader of the 1919 revolution, and President of the Wafd party) to discuss politics and education in the country. The Englishman, Dunlop, had drawn up a plan to make teaching fit in with a 'cotton farm' Egypt, needing only humble office workers and craftsmen, for whom an elementary education would be enough. Dunlop also concentrated his efforts on the consolidation of religious education against modernist trends. In these conditions nothing could be further from the Government's mind than the creation of a university. For this very same reason, the university was one of the first preoccupations of the Egyptian struggle against colonialism. The meeting at Saad Zaghlul's house ended with a declaration addressed to the nation:

> This year, a trend towards giving life to this aspiration has been born, spontaneously, in public opinion. The nation is finally understanding that the education available to it is incomplete. It ends before the pupil has been able to reach his goal. But beyond this education there is sublime knowledge, immutable truths, new inventions, creative experiences which have occupied and still occupy the thought of great scholars in Europe, and of which only a feeble echo comes through to us. Among these thoughts, some are about existence, some about the social body; others direct research towards languages, literature, philosophy, custom and usage, education and everything concerning man's past as well as his present and future. More serious still . . . we have no teachers to show us the value of Arab work in literature, philosophy and science, or the worth of Arab authors known, studied and venerated by Europeans. All those among us who feel the lack of intellectual training think that our education must progress. Our nation cannot count itself among the advanced countries of the world simply because most people can read and write or because some have access to the knowledge of arts and specialisations like medicine, engineering or law. We need more than that: our young people, having time and aptitude, must be able to raise their intellect and knowledge to the level of the scholars of the great nations.

The whole of Egypt responded to the appeal. For although the country had possessed schools of translation, engineering and medicine since the time of Muhammad Ali, Rifa ah At-Tahtawi and Ali Mubarak, these 'arts', as the declaration stresses, are not culture. It is interesting to note that ever since the Fatimite period *Al-Azhar* has remained a centre of Muslim theological studies. Saad Zaghlul himself studied there before reading law. It is also interesting to note that the sons of the emerging Egyptian aristocracy studied in European universities and then returned to become 'professors'. But this historic declaration reveals some completely new truths. The first is that the 'social forces' responsible for it were chiefly made up of people belonging to a new middle class, with definite ambitions going beyond the civil service or other officialdom for which the Dunlop programme would have trained them. And although they are very devout, practising Muslims, their aspirations are secular and modern, not from the point of view of material achievements in, for example, medicine and engineering, but by 'thought' which 'educates the spirit'. The declaration also puts the stress, in an unprecedented way, on the Golden Age of Arab-Islamic civilisation which took an active part in the European Renaissance, and affirms that it is high time to recover its 'spirit' to defeat backwardness. This declaration, with its advanced point of view, laid the foundation of a far-reaching dialogue between the cultural legacy, the modern period and society. All these meanings were to come to life in the creation of the university.

All Egypt responded to this appeal, and worked actively from 22nd October 1906 to 7th February 1928, the day when the Egyptian university was founded. The University, born into the tradition of the fight for independence, democracy and rebirth, responded to the people by an unbroken devotion to the struggle to spread enlightened, national and rational thought. It was the bastion of the people's conscience by its identity and its contemporaneity. Seventeen years later, in the summer of 1945, the first organisation of the national front was created, made up of students belonging to all political parties ranging from the extreme right, the Muslim Brothers and Young Egypt, to the extreme left, the communist and trotskyite organisations, and taking in the great national bourgeois party, the Wafd. A committee of students belonging to the various political trends had specified in that summer of 1945 that the struggle for independence was not only directed against military and cultural occupation, but also against the local agents of colonialism among businessmen linked by their interests with foreign monopolies. This committee stressed the necessity to form a wide national front to fight for the achievement of these goals.

On 20th December 1945, the minority parties manifested the desire to negotiate with London to revise the treaty of 1936. A month later, the British Government replied that it saw no reason why not, on condition that the same relations between Great Britain and Egypt should continue, that Egypt should sign a treaty of defensive alliance, and that the military bases in Egypt and the Sudan would be maintained. The students' reply was clear: 'No negotiations before evacuation' and 'Evacuation by force'. The committee, formed during the summer of 1945, summoned a congress for 9th February 1946 at the Fuad I University (now the University of Cairo); members of this congress called for the suspension of negotiations, the abrogation of all treaties and pacts signed with the colonial powers, and the immediate evacuation of the British forces. A great demonstration then set out to present these claims to those responsible. On arriving in the middle of the Abbas Bridge (Independence Bridge), the demonstration was surprised by the raising of the bridge and heavy fire from the police. It was a massacre. Many students died,

95

or were shot or drowned. Popular resistance exploded everywhere. Egyptians and Sudanese died at Alexandria, Zaqaziq and Mansurah. There were seven dead and hundreds of wounded. In Cairo the students destroyed the royal banners, and the photograph of the king, flags and photographs put up for King Farouk's anniversary. There were calls for a republic.

The government closed the University. On the 11th of February the students joined the popular demonstrations which, with angry mutterings, were moving towards the royal palace. The struggle against the occupation could no longer be dissociated from the struggle against reaction and the monarchy. The next day, at Alexandria, the students of Farouk University (now the University of Alexandria) met the workers of Karmuz (the most heavily populated district in the second capital). The whole country, from the north to the south, demanded the resignation of the government. They did resign, but worse was to come: Ismail Sidqi Pasha, President of the Federation of Egyptian Industries, boss of bosses of the mixed companies, whose capital came from big landowners and from abroad. The students' preparatory committee decided to elect national committees. On 17th February 1946, in an amphitheatre in the Faculty of Medicine, the constitution of the National Students' Committee was proclaimed. Its charter demanded the evacuation of all territories in the Nile valley (that is to say Egypt and the Sudan) and freedom from economic slavery. It appealed to the workers to form national committees in the working-class quarters and in the unions, and many were created in Cairo and Alexandria. The meeting of the National Students' Committee went on uninterruptedly until the next day, 18th February 1946. It established contact with Alexandria, with the workers of the transport companies and printing works, with the workers of Chubrah al-Khaymah, with the Egyptian Trade Union Congress and with the preparatory committee of the Federation of Trade Unions of the Egyptian Region. On the 18th and 19th February, the National Committee of Students and Workers, a historic weapon in the national struggle, was set up. At the end of its first meeting:

> The trade unions of the region of Egypt, the students of the Egyptian universities, Al-Azhar, institutes of higher education and private and secondary schools had decided that Thursday 21st February 1946 would be a day of general strike for the whole population and a renewal of the sacred national movement in which the whole Egyptian people would gather around its right to total independence and liberty.

The 21st February 1946, was, then, a historic day in the life of Egypt, the Arab world and all nations chained by colonialism. Demonstrations took place in the Opera House square. Again there were demands for the breaking off of negotiations, immediate evacuation, the abrogation of the treaties and the submission of the problem to the Security Council, that is to say the internationalisation of the Egyptian question and the mobilisation of world public opinion, which had not yet fully understood the terrible price of the end of the Second World War. In Qasr An-Nil Square (now At-Tahrir) British forces mowed down tens of demonstrators, crushing them beneath the tracks of their tanks. But the demonstrations spread their ripples over the whole country, both Upper and Lower Egypt. The first national front had just been born. It was the reply to the parties of 1936 which had signed the treaty of compromise; it was the extension of the revolution of 1919, which came to nothing because of the decadence of the generation of pioneers. The specific difference between the two fronts consists in the fact that the National Committee of Students and Workers effectively represented the alliance of popular forces, the workers, the intellectuals and the democratic petty bourgeoisie; these were the social strata which were to occupy the political scene.

However, the British Embassy and the royal palace, in co-operation with Sidqi pasha, succeeded in making the representatives of the Muslim Brothers and Young Egypt withdraw from the front, this was expressed in a split within the National Committee on 4th March when the 21st of February was designated as a day of national mourning. This split did not prevent 250,000 citizens from assembling and organising a resistance movement against the occupying forces, the minority parties and the palace. Nor did it prevent an Arab echo to the events in Egypt. In the Sudan, students and workers organised a vast demonstration in the capital, Khartoum. In Iraq, students and workers supported the struggle of the Egyptian people; then came the massacre of Karubayi at Karkuk, where many workers died. In India, the Air Force and the Navy demonstrated at Bombay against the British occupying forces; there were 35 dead and 500 wounded. The International Union of Students designated February 21st as an international day of struggle against colonialism.

In Egypt, the Sidqi-Buven negotiations could not lead to a pact of defensive alliance. The Khashabah-Kampbel negotiations suffered the same fate. Revolutionary violence spread, taking various forms, assassinations of the occupying forces and their local agents, and of the agents of the palace, setting fire to barracks, etc. The towns and the Citadel were evacuated on the 4th July, the airports of Helwan and Wadi An-Natron in October and December, Cairo and Alexandria in March 1947. In fact, the 21st of February had determined the new direction of the Egyptian revolution, and of the social forces. National independence meant not only the evacuation of the occupying military forces, but also economic and political independence, and social democracy. The petty bourgeoisie, along with the workers, peasants, intellectuals and the soldiers of the regular army, occupied new positions on the social and political scene, long monopolised by the upper middle class and the pseudo-feudal types, who had never carried out the tasks of the national and democratic revolution started by the Orabi rising, aborted in 1919 and abandoned by the 1936 treaty.

Sidqi pasha was perfectly clear: 'We are the white government of a red nation,' he said to the Senate when asking for the promulgation of emergency laws for 'the suppression of communism', later known by his name. He was perfectly consistent, as a representative of the interests of the upper middle class allied with the colonial power, when he asked for the arrest of hundreds of young people, workers and intellectuals, while brandishing the book of verse *Israr* (Insistence) by Kamal Abd Al-Halim. In fact, on 11th July 1946, Sidqi pasha demanded the arrest of intellectuals like Salamah Musa and Muhammad Mandur, the closure of a large number of newspapers and magazines, and the proscription of the associations, unions and clubs which had taken part in the events of 21st February 1946. Twenty-five years later, the world was surprised by the emergence of a student movement which did not continue that of 1968 or reproduce the events of 1946, but was deeply rooted in the history of the Egyptian universities and their tradition of national struggle; a student movement continuing the fight for the goals of the 'movement' after the defeat of 1967.[44]

If we have lingered over certain moments in the history of the student movement in Egypt, it is not to explain its evolution so much as to touch on both what had changed in the popular movement and the conditions surrounding it, and what had not changed which will help us better to understand the new movements and their prospects for the future.

The student movement of the 70s was in no way surprising. It fits perfectly into the historical tradition of the Egyptian university; a tradition which is mainly nationalist and social, for it is against foreign occupation, and against privileged minorities. It is a fundamentally democratic tradition. In this context, and without too much exaggeration, we can say that the Egyptian student movement is a pioneer movement on an international plane. It is also, on another plane, a product of the revolutionary tradition of the Egyptian people. It was the first to represent the people through national committees and regardless of parties. It was the first to ally itself with the working class. From another point of view, the student movement was a resounding answer to the defeat suffered during an exceptional leadership, that of Nasser. It is the product of its time; it incarnates the flame of the *'widjan'* of the Egyptian people.

What has it taken from the past and what has it added? And above all, what is its historical context?

We must first emphasise that the university students in Egypt in the 70s belonged to a generation that was not yet born when land was distributed among the peasants. They were very young when Nasser decided on free education at all levels. They were adolescent when the workers began to share in the running and the profits of their businesses, and on the threshold of young adulthood at the defeat and death of Nasser. But they were aware, perhaps vaguely, that they were 'heirs to the victories', both national and popular, after every surrender, in the past as in the present. Between 1954 and 1968, nothing was heard of them; but when they exploded in February and November 1968, they condemned the Minister of the Interior on a symbolic gallows, they urged Nasser to make the 'declaration of March 30th' which, for the fist time, established the sovereignty of laws and institutions. In this respect Egyptian youth was not isolated from international youth, both Eastern and Western, in 1968. But it had its specificity, for land and democracy were the axes of its struggle. It lapsed into silence in 1969 at the time of the war of attrition, but followed Nasser's coffin in hosts in September 1970. It took no part in the struggle of the 'new Mamelukes' for power in May 1971. But when 'the decisive year' came to an end without confrontation with the enemy, this youth had already traced the outlines of its new movement on the basis of elements from past and present.

As a whole, these young people were the backbone of the wide popular strata of town and country; the product of the working class, peasants, craftsmen, minor officials, small traders and technicians, the children of little men, who could get to university only because of their academic excellence. They also knew that they would be employed immediately after the end of their studies, according to the labour laws, and not through intercessions, chance opportunities and luck. And if the elimination of landed property, the proclamation of the Republic, agrarian reform, nationalisation and the battle of Suez, evacuation of foreign troops and the nationalisation of foreign interests, limitation of land holdings and the nationalisation of capitalist companies, form a relevant panorama of the past for these young people, defeat and prison camps now occupy for them the centre of the picture, with a background of economic deterioration, social troubles and political oppression.

But if we want to know this new generation better, we must distinguish it from its fellows in the rest of the world who also claimed their rights in the East or the West in 1968. The generation of the 60s in the developed world, socialist or capitalist, was the fruit of the great changes in means of production and social forces after the Second World War, the fruit of what we sometimes call *the revolution of science and technology, the second industrial revolution* or *the revolution in communications;* but it also belongs to the period of the beginning of the defeat of traditional colonialism and the transition towards socialism by new revolutionary creativity. The international student movement, particularly in the West, is the fruit of the consumer society; its fight is mainly against 'the institution', whether State or party.

On the other hand, the Egyptian student movement is the fruit of a society of production governed by social relations in the first stages of development, by autocratic power where there is no liberal or popular democracy, and by a social climate full of theocratic prejudices. This movement is also the fruit of an absence of organisation in political life, because of the void left when the legitimacy of all trends was lost after the prohibition of political parties in 1953; some went underground, others broke up and their members joined the only official party. The void was also due to the ineffectiveness of the official party which ended by being nothing but a stage setting. All this could not fail to affect the fate of student unions and youth organisations within the Socialist Union; they were in fact transformed into social clubs, and their members found themselves in prison as soon as they took things seriously.

At least twice, in the middle and at the end of the 50s, the university suffered the same fate as democratic institutions, when repressive measures clamped down on the parties, the press, the judiciary and the unions. In 1954 the Council of the Leadership of the Revolution issued a decree dismissing about 60 university professors, all important figures known for their democratic or left-wing opinions. Most of them were obliged to work for the press or to emigrate, at least provisionally. In 1959, when Nasser's regime attacked the whole of the Egyptian left, the rest of these professors, as well as new figures in university teaching with national or Marxist opinions, were completely eliminated by a period of detention from two to five years. Those dismissed, or partly so, had no right to reinstatement. So the university was emptied of its experts in economics, philosophy, mathematics, literature, etc. In the 40s, people with the highest qualifications from the Sorbonne, Oxford, Cambridge and Princeton had had to leave their jobs. We mention only Muhammad Mandur, Louis Awad, Fuad Mursi, Ismail Sabri Abd Allah, Abd Al-Azim Anis, Mahmud Al-Alim, Abd Ar-Raziq Hassan and Fawzi Mansur. It was to be expected in this case that intellectual leadership should pass from the university to the press all through the 50s and 60s. Teaching programmes during these two decades were subject to an anti-secular and anti-democratic ideology, especially during the periods when Kamal Ad-Din Hussein, known for his extremist religious tendencies, held posts of highest responsibility for education and culture. In order to fill this gap, religious organisations came into being with names like 'Muslim Youth', 'The Youth of Muhammad', 'The Young Muslims', 'The Muslim Brothers', and others. Among teachers and students, political surveillance appeared, with the job of writing secret reports for various security organisations. In situations like this, no one can claim that the university is the mother of the student movement in Egypt. The real mother is the street, to which they belong socially and culturally.

The internal contradiction from which they suffered lay in the fact that, belonging to the street with its workers, peasants and lower middle class, they nevertheless knew the road to the university through the victory of the revolution of July 1952 over colonialism, feudalism and big business, thanks to free education, industrialisation, agrarian reform and many other things, of which they had heard; but when they entered university, they saw only defeat, backwardness and dictatorship.

They were in no way against the institution of the university, or the constitution; they wanted to give it a developed social content. They were in no way against the single-party system; they wanted to create it from nothing, unlike their fellows in the West who were revolting against the rigidity and bureaucracy of organisational and political structures. They are also different from those in the 1946 movement, who mainly belonged to parties and organisations. For all these reasons, the Egyptian student movement of the 70s differed in character from student movements elsewhere. This time they did not represent organisations, they wanted to create them, starting from a democratic vacuum; they wanted to create them for themselves at university level, and for the rest of the population at the social level, by a 'return to democratic traditions' and by creating independent political tribunes.

They did not belong to a definite social class, as in the case of intellectuals;

but nor were they simply a student movement, but the legitimate representatives of society as a whole. In this sense they were neither an echo of the
international student movement, nor a reproduction of the movement of
1964; but a more developed, specific extension of them. A second point
confirming their special characteristics was the continuity of the movement
over a decade, from 1968 to 1977. In this sense, there was no student movement, but a socio-political movement which, despite all the conditions,
could bring forth 'a democratic spirit', a democratic spirit rising again from its
ashes; so that once again the parties enjoyed a relatively official legitimacy.

There is no doubt that this movement was inspired by the international
and national tradition of student movements. Its organisations bore witness
to the influence of the 'national committees' of 1946; their initiative in
establishing contact with the trade unions and professional bodies, and in
arranging congresses open to all students, sometimes going to different places
among the people, was not lacking in the 1946 movement. But the most
salient characteristic, inspired by the tradition of popular struggle in general
and student struggle in particular, lay in peaceful opposition and self-control;
it was their enemies who always had recourse to violence, the most famous
example of which was the fire of 26th January 1952. It was their enemies
who always had recourse to violence, sabotage and blood to prevent them
from reaching their goals. This student movement inherited much from international youth and its failed experiments in cultural revolution; such as wall
newspapers, occupation of sites and public places. But to this human and
national heritage they added an experience of struggle, new and specific.

The Generation of the Revolution Says No

Some people think that the story of the student movement of the 70s begins
with President Sadat's speech of the 13th January 1972. In this speech the
President said that the postponment of the 'decisive year' was a consequence
of the shadows of the Indo-Pakistani war; for it was unthinkable that the
Soviet ally could deal with events in the Far East and the Middle East all at
once! But these historians certainly did not pay attention to the allusion in
this speech to the Palestinian Week organised by the students of the Polytechnic of the University of Cairo, two weeks earlier — towards the end of
December 1971. We have good reasons for believing that it was this Palestinian
Week that inaugurated the rebirth of the student movement in Egypt after the
end of the war of attrition, the Rogers Plan, the massacre of Palestinian
resistance in Jordan, Nasser's death and Sadat's putsch. This Palestinian Week
was the spark that set off the fuse, long before Sadat's speech about the mists
that were preventing war, mists which called forth a chorus of the most
biting *nuktas*. But this speech also contained a precise and clear condemnation of the 'group of sympathisers with the Palestinian revolution' who had
organised the week. In fact the week was Arab; but it was the Egyptians who
sent out the invitations.

Here we must emphasise the prime importance of the rebirth of the move-ment; it was political and cannot be classified as any sort of university activity. It was also Arab, and went beyond local economic and social prob-lems. These two meanings are also loaded with history, from three different angles: Arab feeling in Egypt in modern times, Egypt's relations with the Palestinian cause, and finally, the relations of Sinai with this Palestinian cause in 1956 and 1967. This continuous story tells an important truth that some-times surprises us in the middle of events and is then forgotten. This truth is that Arab Egypt was not born on July 23rd 1952. It was born long before Nasserism. But it is only to Nasser, as representing the new social strata occupying the political scene, that we owe the revelation of the powerlessness of the old regime, with its interests and alliances, to know the Arab identity of Egypt. But this is not to deny the fact that Nasser himself, as a revolut-ionary, came out of the great Arab event of the 40s – the war in Palestine. On the other hand, he belonged to the radical generation in his attachment to the Arab idea, whatever its trends might be, from the extreme right to the extreme left.[45] We have to add to this that the Zionist plan undertook, from 1956 to 1957, to produce irrefutable proof of the Arab spirit of Egypt and its organic bonds with the Palestinian cause. For all these reasons, the Arab character of the rebirth of the student movement in Egypt was a symbol loaded with history, and a direct allusion to the only valid way to discuss Egypt's problems.

Sadat's speech on January 13th 1972 caused the Palestinian Week to rapidly become seven unforgettable weeks in the history of Egypt after the defeat. Two days after the speech, the students fixed a date for discussing the whole situation. The wall newspapers, posters, leaflets etc., by now were scarcely enough. At this meeting, held at the Polytechnic in Cairo, the existence of two opposing trends was noted from the very beginning: one, on the left, opposed the President's policy; the other, on the right, supported it. It was then decided to put off the discussion to the 17th, when the left-wing opposition would have been able to predominate. It demanded the organis-ation of a student militia, with military training, to serve as a rearguard to the regular forces in case of war. It asked for all pacifist initiatives to be halted, notably the President's proposals for the reopening of the Canal and the gradual retreat of the Israeli forces. It asked, especially, that no more should be expected from the Rogers Plan or the intervention of Gunnar Yaring. The members of the congress warned the government that, if they did not receive a clear answer in the following two days, they would occupy the faculty buildings. But the threat was carried out when they learnt that similar meetings were taking place in provincial universities and at Al-Azhar; they then occupied their faculty before the ultimatum had expired. They called a general assembly for Thursday 20th January, where the President of the Republic could reply in person to the questions pending. A National Commit-tee was set up, charged to prepare for the general assembly and receive volun-teers for the armed struggle.

The government replied by taking a few austerity measures, such as forbidding the import of luxury furniture and cars, and said they were ready to train the students for the protection of civilians. In addition, the President decreed political amnesty for 12,000 persons deprived of their civil rights following the nationalisations of 1961/1962. The students refused to respond to the government manoeuvre; the government was still afraid of 'arms in the hands of the people' and 'independent political organisations'. By inviting volunteers for 'civil' protection, they were trying to keep the developing movement under their power. As arranged, the general assembly took place in the evening; about 20,000 students took part. It decided to send representatives to the President of the Republic to ask him to come to the university and reply to the questions asked, which were later known under the name of 'students' document'. The students spent the night in the university building, and the power of the National Committee was still further consolidated, thanks to the presence of representatives from other provincial universities.

It is interesting to note at this point that the government had recourse to a naive piece of duplicity. It faked declarations in its favour from the University of Alexandria, and the next day announced in the press that this same university was being closed. Finally, the general assembly opened again on the 21st January with an audience of about 10,000 students who had spent the night in the university. The next day they prepared leaflets to be distributed in the working-class districts. Some students went to Helwan, where there was a large concentration of working population. Remember, that the students' demands included the liberation of the Helwan workers arrested in 1971. A leader of the student movement declared: 'We are only expressing the wishes of the people. . . We have contacted the workers, for it is they who must lead this movement.'[46] 'The government,' said another, 'hopes that the movement will die in the summer vacation. Only it forgets that the majority of students are rural in origin, and they will tell their families what was done at the university.'[47]

In the morning of Monday the 24th, at 6 o'clock, the police raided the university buildings, arrested 1,500 students, men and women, and attacked others with weapons specially brought for the occasion, such as rubber bullets, truncheons, tear gas bombs, etc. They succeeded in occupying the campus and putting a cordon round the outer walls to prevent entry. The students then went to Al-Tahrir Square in the centre of Cairo, where they held impromptu meetings with the population. Traffic was held up. The police besieged the Square. Orders were given them to attack. The great Square was turned into a battlefield where the people took the side of the students and there was a pitched battle. Blood flowed everywhere, for the armoured cars drove straight into the crowd, carrying off everyone in their way. But the demonstrations did not stop — on the contrary — they adopted a new technique. Gathering in small groups in side-streets, the demonstrators proceeded by surprise attacks. They took over trams and buses to hold short conferences and then escape. But the shouts continued to thunder, demanding democracy and the liberation of those students and workers who had been arrested. Towards the end of the day the Square was again invaded by an

immense crowd of students. Speeches were made. The police charged again
in a vain attempt to clear the area. The government proclaimed the closure of
all universities and colleges of higher education. Despite the winter cold, the
students spent the night in the Square. The townspeople brought them warm
clothing, food and medicines. The next day, January 25th, news from Helwan
told of mounting tension in the iron foundries. 'The women were screaming
with delight at the students and throwing boiling water out of the windows
on to the ranks of policemen drawn up for attack. Restlessness and tension
began to affect the university people who had been sent with the police to
try to calm the students.'[48] That same day the workers of Helwan sent a
message of support to the university students. As night fell, most of the
leaders of the student movement were arrested, as were the workers who had
composed the message of support. The next day, the 26th January, sad
anniversary of the Cairo fire, about 2,000 students were arrested. The government officially asked the universities to send down all who had taken part in
the movement. In addition, they threatened to dismiss all lecturers who were
sympathetic to the students. On 27th January, after President Sadat's speech
given in the Nasser theatre, all except 30 of the students detained were freed,
but most of them refused to leave the prison.

On January 28th, security chiefs started a rumour saying they had
detected a plot to attack Cairo from the four cardinal points: 4,000 students
from the University of Ain Chams were to attack from the north, 4,000
workers from Chubrah Al-Khaymah in the east, 4,000 others from Helwan
in the south, and 10,000 students from the University of Cairo in the west.
No rumour ever provoked so much sarcasm. It is not even worth discussing.
What must be discussed and commented upon is what the students said.

Essentially, they expressed hostility to all 'peaceful solutions' with Israel,
and consequently rejected Resolution 242 of the Security Council, the
Rogers Plan, and Sadat's initiatives. According to them the only solution was
a long war of liberation, and to that end, a nation armed, a war economy, and
a press free from all censorship except information connected with military
secrets. The students' declarations also demanded that the privileges of high
officials should be cancelled, that the cost of mobilisation should be paid by
those with high incomes, that maximum support should be given to the
Palestinian resistance, that Egyptian youth should be allowed to join in it, and
that the Palestinians should have free and independent access to the Egyptian
population. They demanded resistance in Sinai, and that reactionary Arab
regimes should be isolated from all possibility of taking part in order to
avoid any deviation towards bargaining and compromise. They demanded that
relations should be consolidated with national regimes capable of keeping up
the struggle.

It is certain, then, that the movement of January 1972 was able to carry
out certain main tasks such as, for example, the transformation of 'the
national and democratic line', simple ideas discussed by a large popular
movement. But above all, the movement proved the effectiveness of national
leadership democratically emerging from a popular movement and respecting

a clear, realistic programme. It gave the mass of the people the right to oppose, the right to manifest their opposition to the policies of the government. It foiled the conspiracy of silence of the mass media, and made it possible for the Egyptian people to speak to the rest of the Arab peoples and to the peoples of the whole world. It was a bridge facilitating the re-establishment of contacts and bonds of struggle and common destiny between the Arab population in Egypt and in all parts of the Arab nation.[49] But the positive aspects of the first stage of the movement of 1972 were not the only aspects. There were others, less positive, and at least three which caused a series of aggravations.

First of all there was a parallelism between the workers' and the students' movements. There was no point of fusion as there had been in 1946. There were contacts and messages of support, but there were never reciprocal actions and influences blending together all forces to form a front.

Secondly, despite the great political awareness, there was a certain left-wing tendency which made practically no distinction between the Soviet Union and the United States. Exactly like the right wing, this group was doubtful, and wondered, like the government and its generals, whether it was a good thing to support the Socialist countries.

In the third place, despite intense activity and efforts in every direction, there was a weakness at the tactical level which made it impossible to distinguish the line of the government and police from those of the independent right, which meant that the legitimacy of the latter was completely denied.

Finally, there was a lack of knowledge of the strategy of the authorities, so that sometimes the demands appeared to be only an attempt to embarrass the State, as though it could, but did not wish to satisfy these demands.

But there were positive and negative factors making up the main line of the social controversy. And while the student movement expressed national and democratic opposition in embryo, the government and the different social categories expressed their contradictory attitudes by taking up fixed positions with regard to this movement. How did this controversy develop?

On its side, the government constantly used the traditional double weapon, intimidation and seduction. The Cabinet remained in permanent session from the beginning of the events, and, scarcely a week after the President's obfuscating speech, he gave the command 'all for battle', accompanied by some economic austerity measures. He complicated the import procedures for a few luxury products, reduced the Ministries' expenditure on propaganda and public relations, limited the petrol allowance for government vehicles, prohibited the buying of new vehicles for high officials, limited their authorisations to travel abroad to cases of great necessity, and cancelled their material privileges. He also decided to release 3,000 flats surplus to the requirements of the administration, and reduced the number of telephone lines available to each Minister. It must be emphasised that although these measures meant that high officials were incapable of setting an example in war-time, on the other hand they had no fundamental significance. They gave nothing to the people; they imposed no restrictions on the rich. These are the two things on which the students remarked at their meeting of 20th January, when they found out about these decisions in the morning papers. Remember, the movement had seen an important development the day before. The Council of the Students' Union at Al-Azhar organised a meeting attended by the Deputy Dean and representatives of the Arab Socialist Union and the administration of Al-Azhar. In a communique published on January 20th this meeting declared unanimously: 'We sincerely believe that military action is the only road to the liberation of the land. We reject any concessions and any bargaining about the smallest scrap of our Arab land . . . No abandonment of the rights of the Palestinian people, whatever sacrifice it may cost us.' The declaration goes on to describe a war economy as the only solution for a country preparing for a struggle, the necessity of military training for the young, mobilisation of the people and the freedom of the press.

> Arab youth, [it adds] being aware of the American challenge and the declared intention to attack the existence of our nation and support the Israeli enemy, has the duty to undermine all American interests in the Arab nation, and strive actively towards a successful conclusion in all countries fighting for freedom and peace. It is the duty of all of us to expose the American position and let the whole world see it as it is.

This declaration of the University of Al-Azhar, and the meeting from which it emerged, effectively consolidated the student movement and placed the government in a critical situation in respect of Muslim public opinion in Egypt. It was very difficult for the government to accuse Al-Azhar of communism; half a million students of Al-Azhar and its various ramifications throughout the country were constantly repeating: 'The United States is our first enemy; the natural answer is to finish with all American interests in the whole of the Arab nation.'

Remember also, that, during these events, the official Students' Union lost its legitimacy. Wishing to regain lost ground, the same day that the students asked the President of the Republic to come and answer their questions, it also sent a telegram with the same request. The official Union knew in advance that its demand would be satisfied. On 21st January 1971, Mr Sayyid Mari said that the President 'had accepted the invitation of the Students' Union' and that he would meet them in the very near future, in the Nasser theatre in the University of Cairo. Although the acceptance of the invitation had nothing to do with the demand of the movement, the same Sayyid Mari declared in a meeting with representatives of the movement: 'The student movement has been up to the present a purely national movement.' But less than 48 hours later security forces of the central authority invaded the university. The newspapers of January 25th 1972 published a communique of the Minister of the Interior forbidding all demonstrations in the strictest terms. But these same newspapers had a surprise for everybody: the three biggest and most influential professional unions – of the Press, the lawyers and the teachers – declared themselves in sympathy with the movement, and in mutual accord with its opinions on defence and training. 'The student movement', said the communique of the Press Union, 'is an integral part of the 1952 revolution; it is founded on the principal charters of the revolution from the National Charter of 1962 to the Programme of National Action presented by President Sadat on 23rd July 1971, taking in the declaration of March 30th.' It was easily seen that this declaration left out the so-called 'revolution of redress'. What is more, it added that the student movement was a sincere national movement, that the questions it asked concerned the different strata of the population and that they were in perfect accord with the will to face seriously the circumstances of war. There an allusion to the superficial line of the so-called *government of confrontation* could be clearly distinguished. The declaration of the Press Union also took the opportunity to emphasise the need for freedom of the press as well as other democratic freedoms. As for the communique of the lawyers' Union, it stressed the problem of liberation. 'The Arab nation,' it said, 'has only one road, that of armed struggle and the refusal of all contact, direct or indirect, with the American government.' It also condemned 'attempts to shroud with doubt the attitude of the Soviet Union, the faithful friend who has always been with us at the most difficult moments. These sly attempts are aimed at separating the Arab liberation movement from its chief supporting forces, indispensable to its struggle.' The communique demanded 'democracy for the masses and protection for the Palestinian resistance against the plots made against it.'

The declaration of the teachers' Union was directly addressed to the students. 'We give thanks for your cry, and we are answering the call. . . Your revolt is a warning to us all [and] we believe that it comes from pure hearts, concerned for the fate of the nation.'

It was a surprise for everyone, but more particularly for the President of the Republic, who had heard of it before giving his new speech which cancelled out the previous one given 12 days earlier. These declarations told him that the largest classes of intellectuals were lining up without any hesitation on the side of the students. They made it clear that the student movement filled a gap in political organisation from which the country suffered deeply, that the students were the vanguard of the interests of the largest social classes, and that in no way was it simply a student movement. The specific character of that historic moment in Egypt made them the legitimate agents of the national classes without an independent political organisation. In reality, the courage of these Unions not only had a moral basis but came from something much more important. That the press Union had dared to publish this declaration was not the result of adventurism; for if that had been the case how can the fact that *Akhbar Al-Yawm,* a paper known for its hostility to students, published all their declarations and those of their allies be interpreted? We could advance the hypothesis that these professional groups, coming upon this student initiative, took responsibility for political action without evaluating its danger. This liberalism of the Press, in defiance of censorship rules, was doubtless a consequence of strong popular pressure. For the censorship had not yet been raised, and the Press still belonged to the political organisation of the State alone.

These facts were certainly in President Sadat's mind when he made his speech of 25th January 1972 in which he laid great stress on the two principles of *possession by the people of the means of production* and *non-exploitation of man by man.* After this he added: 'The decision to join battle is already made and we shall not go back on it.' But this was only a preamble — we might say a specious one — to what he was going to say later. He set about relating the events of the preceding days, reproaching the students for their 'ignoble pettiness' and insisting on the fact that the number of students to appear before the courts was not more than 30.

At the end of this speech, given in what was called at the time 'the Congress of all the political and Trade Union institutions', some very interesting discussions took place between the official guests (meaning the people admitted by the authorities) and the President of the Republic. But there was no avoiding the paradox; the official representatives of the 'Students' Unions' took up the defence of the majority. This obliged the President to interrupt a speaker twice; he felt himself compelled to make a distinction between the majority and 'an intrusive minority' (meaning the leaders) and then to make clear the difference between 'these agitators' and the 'elected representatives' who 'should not use the language of revolutionaries'. But a student dared to interrupt the President, telling him that the student majority could no longer put up with the way the official representatives were getting to the top of student organisations. He was one of these 'upstarts'. The President of the Republic found nothing to say in reply but that he was going to prohibit all 'illegal' political activity, and that 'time for study was not going to be spent doing anything else.'

But there was another surprise, not less disagreeable. A university professor in the audience got up to say that his son defended the movement 'and what you have derisively called pettiness' in which he himself saw nothing to be derided, but simply a revolt against oppression. 'Our children,' he said, 'are asking questions, and we, their teachers, have no replies to these questions. Consequently we must give them freedom of speech and of criticism so that they can take part in the constructive process.' The President of the Republic could not contain his anger, replying that it was 'indispensible to suppress this student epidemic'. To this an honourable parliamentarian (Ahmad Yunis, later defendant in a financial affair) added that his personal impression was that the movement was not spontaneous. The President of the Republic, in the course of this discussion, called the National Students' Committee 'the national traitors' committee'. But the audience was quite aware that the affair would not end there.

On the 21st of February the engineers' Union joined with the other three unions in support of the students. The communique it published after the presidential speech totally supported the student movement in opposition to the President of the Republic who thought that the movement in general was healthy but the leaders deviationist, the basis correct but the mode of action underhanded. Five days later, during the National Congress of the Socialist Union, the President surprised the country by two decisions: he revived the 'Youth Organisation' (an institution of the Arab Socialist Union at the time of Nasser) and freed all those students who had been detained. The two decisions were given at the end of this session which was held in camera. The applause might have been enthusiastic but for the President's final declaration: he appealed to the top people in the country for 'patience and silence'. But they did not even have the time to think about it; on 18th February 1972 the Press published the record of the meeting. It was learned that the President had revealed 'an Israeli attempt to exploit the student movement'. A Belgian family and a Frenchman had been arrested while distributing leaflets printed in Israel in the name of the 'National Front' in Egypt. The Minister of Justice in his turn stated in a long communique that numerous 'foreign authorities' had taken part in setting off the *fitnah* or 'division' — a term with an overtone of religious intimidation.

Some people tried to collect the threads of the story together so as to understand better; they came to the conclusion that the authorities were repeating the 1968 scenario. They suppressed the student movement when it was peacefully gaining ground; and when the demands were reduced to one — the liberation of those detained — the President, like an affectionate father, surprised everybody by his generous decision, even while attributing mysterious Israeli or communist origins to those students who were freed, as a kind of intimidation. In 1968, when the demonstrations were at their height, a soldier was accused of spying for the Hebrew state. He was executed. Rumour said that the Embassy of Mr Kim Il Sung was printing the students' leaflets. In 1972, the same scenario was repeated, but with different names and circumstances: and the President loosened the chains and asked them, like the father of prodigal sons, to be patient and quiet.

During the whole of February, the Egyptians impatiently followed two affairs; the trial of the Palestinian resistance fighters accused of murdering Wasfi At-Tal in Cairo; and the uninterrupted Israeli missile attack against South Lebanon.

They also followed, but with many more comments and much less patience, the writings of the intellectuals (meaning writers and journalists). Haykal, as usual, was the centre of all eyes. On 28th January 1972, *Al-Ahram* published the Friday editorial with the title 'The problem of this generation'. The introduction in italics said:

> We must distinguish between the problem of a generation and that of 30 or 40 people whom we could call to account for unbridled acts committed knowingly or inadvertently. But in reality there is a general atmosphere without which the errors of 30 or 40 or even 300 or 400 young people would not have ended in general anguish, suffering and the tearing apart of this generation. . . Dialogue between the generations, [it concluded] must take the place of quarrelling; otherwise all is lost.

Haykal was alluding to Nasser's experience and that of Sadat when they were young in the 40s. It was clear that Haykal was trying to show the whole affair as though it were really no more than a conflict between generations. According to him the younger generation had never known the time before the revolution; it had been surprised by the 1967 defeat as much as by the events of May 1971. It would feel as though it were in a state of weightlessness! Actually Haykal was trying to steer a middle course: he defended the right of the young to criticise and the right of the authorities 'to defend themselves against criticism'. Remember that the students had criticised him violently during their demonstrations. This article achieved his rehabilitation for his great democratic qualities! However, his willingness to retain a sense of proportion deprived his publications of their well-known polish. His reservations about youth were revealed by his low-key appreciation of the fact that 30 students had been detained — reservations evident in his next article, entitled 'Signals on a long road' in which he said he did not want to touch on 'mistakes that might be revealed by enquiries into the last student movement'. But Haykal did not touch on the social content of the movement either. At the most he attributed it *to the spirit of the times and to the revolution in means of communication.* For him, it was 'a proof of energy'.

In spite of these vague generalisations, it was at Haykal that Musa Sabri, writing in the left-wing daily *Al-Akhbar,* directly aimed. He alluded to some people's attempt to 'revive' the student movement and be carried away on its waves. He also condemned this movement, arguing that 'the Israeli occupation' made it impossible to exert pressure on 'this righteous and national regime'. Ihsan Abd Al-Quddus, the managing director of the same newspaper, in an article in the January 20th 1972 issue, 'Days that will not suffer obscurity', expressed his great astonishment that the students should ask questions to which the President had already replied. Further, he imputed partisan motives and foreign influences to the student movement. But on the same day that Abd Al-Quddus published his article, the official Students' Union protested against the way certain newspapers had misrepresented events: and that Union, though created by the government, nevertheless declared itself totally in agreement with the demands formulated by the majority of students.[51]

Even Abd Ar-Rahman Ach-Charqawi, the famous left-wing writer, did not reject the ideas put forward by Sabri and Abd Al-Quddus. In his virtually left-wing weekly, he wrote on 24th January 1972:

> What is the meaning of the demands of our university students, expressed with such insolence? They certainly base their claims on their support for the Egyptian revolution; but certain modes of expression could lead to contradiction, and that would be a catastrophe which the "honest" people among them would not wish.

On February 28th 1972, Ach-Charqawi took a step backwards, declaring that in rising, the students, 'did not speak only with their own voice, but with that of the whole nation.' But all the same he affirmed that they were not acting against 'the national authority'. Muhammad Odah, the writer supporting Nasser, pointed out that 'the negligence of popular institutions in not making the students aware of the importance of the Presidential decision to join battle. To penalise those who go astray is a duty, but to train them when young is better.'[52] Odah did not deny the possibility of delinquency; he even stressed the lack of maturity and awareness in young people.

Muhammad Sid Ahmad was the only Marxist writer authorised to comment on these events. He wrote:

> The question posed by the students is preoccupying all the forces of the nation. How are we facing the question of liberation after 1971? We are not discrediting the necessity for political work, but that needs continuous training in its styles and demands. But political work is useless as long as it is not accompanied by the firm will to struggle. The university students are expressing, through their movement, their inborn sense of this necessity; in that they are following a tradition identical to the whole national movement.[53]

Although the expression 'inborn sense' is not an entirely happy one as a description of political awareness in students, Muhammad Sid Ahmad was the only one not to mince words. What is more, he did not take the side of the government in a newspaper with a wide circulation. Though *At-Taliah,* the left-wing monthly, has always supported the students, its impact on public opinion is much more limited than that of the daily and weekly press. Although an authorised publication, *At–Taliah,* because of the accusations it makes, has always been considered by the information services to be a liability.

So the Egyptian Press proved that it was not the total expression of the social movement; on the contrary, it was only the echo, weak or strong, of the government. In that, it was no different from the other institutions of the government, such as the Socialist Union, Parliament, and the Council of Ministers. It was also diametrically opposed to public institutions such as the professional associations and others.

The State succeeded in muzzling the movement to the point where it finally reduced its demands to a single one — the liberation of the detainees. It was now possible to absorb it by doing this and disperse its solid majority by starting false rumours and bringing forward the date of the mid-year vacation. During this vacation, official organisations busied themselves in forming clandestine terrorist groups. By the end of the year these extreme right-wing activities had perceptibly increased. The national committees of the democratic students continued to organise colloquiums and political conferences on the sites of authorised and legitimate student work-camps.

The End of One Period and the Beginning of Another

Before the year 1972 was over, terrorist demonstrations began to act against the peaceful activity of the national students. Elements trained in sabotage and violence broke into meetings, attacking all those assembled there with whips, iron bars, razor blades and penknives. It was a completely new phenomenon. Its purpose was to break up meetings, tear down the wall newspapers and use any means to prevent all action against the regime. It was a bewildering surprise when a student of the Polytechnic of the University of Cairo (arrested on 29th December 1972) admitted in a public congress that he belonged to à secret organisation led by Muhammad Uthman Ismail, deputy secretary of the Socialist Union. The student admitted that he had been sent for on the day after the fire at the church of Al-Khanqah. The deputy secretary of the Socialist Union had asked him to get together the organisation, with a view to attacking the so-called communists 'because they intend to incite the Coptic students to demonstrate' – in the words of Mr Muhammad Ismail, reported by this student.[54] Another secret organisation, Muslim Youth, published a communique in which they revealed that they had also been incited by the government against 'the group of partisans of the Palestinian revolution.' One of their leaders read this communique at a public meeting. 'He asked pardon for everything he had committed against colleagues who represented the most lofty national values.'[55]

Towards the end of the first week of January 1973, the President in a message to Parliament, asked them to form a Commission of Enquiry to carry out on the spot and with all interested parties a vast investigation on the revival of the student movements. This Commission was made up of a few parliamentary pillars of Egyptian reaction. The enquiry lasted 20 days. On 28th January 1973 all the papers published the complete text of the Commission's report. This report, in both thought and manner of formulation, was closer to the government than to the students; but it must be taken into account, precisely in order to estimate the gravity of the situation.

The report stated that from the beginning the events of 1972 were closely connected with those of 1973, to such an extent that they could be considered one single movement. This is true, although the evidence smacks of police methods, as it was acquired not by intellectual means, but by making enquiries about people visiting students in detention and the relationships between them. The authors apparently regret that the doors of university education should be open to a large number of students from poor families. The report does not say so openly, but alludes to it persistently, bringing out the students' needs in the matter of social and health care, food, clothing and medicines. It is as if it were trying to corroborate the theory of hate, which the President used to explain the origins of the social disturbances.

The report blatantly contradicts itself when it records facts which, in themselves, condemn the extremist right-wing religious groups; but when it comes to apportioning blame, it accuses the left-wing trends without reservation.

For the authors of the report, the student movement begins on December 5th 1972 in the Universities of Cairo, Alexandria, Ain Chams, Al-Mansourah and Assiout, and also the University of Al-Azhar and institutes of higher education, both secular and theological. On that day the University administration decided to bring before a Disciplinary Council three students who had disobeyed instructions by putting up on the wall, without permission, articles and drawings making fun of certain symbols of authority. The students hit back with a strong protest against the principle of disciplinary hearings. Two days later, on 7th December 1972, an extended student congress declared that it rejected the orders of the administration and also the University Statute, which it considered to be undemocratic. The members of the congress emphasised the need for fresh Students' Union elections, in order to have a legitimate leadership different from that which they suspected of links with security organisations. These demands were repeated at the meeting of Sunday December 17th and that of Tuesday 19th December 1972. 'The latter,' says the report, 'was followed by a demonstration in favour of religious and national values.' It was then that a 'group of students', which the report does not identify, attacked their opponents. 'One student was stabbed with a penknife on the left side of the lower back.' 'It was said,' the report went on, 'that this followed an argument in which a woman student blasphemed and denied the existence of God.' The least that can be said is that the use of an indefinite pronoun in the report of a Parliamentary Commission suggests a frivolous approach. The authors seems to be confusing fact with rumour. In reality this group of terrorists was trying, by armed violence, to sabotage the peaceful character of the student demonstration. This comes out of the questioning of the student aggressor. It also arises less explicitly from the parliamentary enquiry, which alludes obscurely to aggressive acts committed by armed students against others who were non-violent. It was certainly not by chance that the armed students were supporting the government while the unarmed ones were opposing it. It is also impossible to discover anything remotely credible in the report's conclusion attributing the events to 'a climate favourable to the appearance of an ideological trend represented by the left in all its forms'. It makes no allusion to the fact that violence was the weapon of the right, while peaceful means were those of the left. The report confines itself to recording the facts and describing them as a 'plot'. How? Why? And where?

The report replies to these questions by completely contradicting the conclusion it had drawn in advance.

In fact, at dawn on the 29th of December 1972, the authorities arrested hundreds of students, workers and intellectuals.

> The next day, [said the report] four students went to the office of the University President, asking for permission to hold a meeting in the room set aside for that use. The request was refused, but the students held their meeting on 31st December 1972, as a result of which they decided on a sit-in and a peaceful march to present their claims. Leaving

ɩhe university perimeter, the demonstrators came up against security forces using methods of dispersion. . . tear-gas bombs, truncheons etc.

It was then decided to close the universities.

Remember that this march was going to Parliament to present to the members the claims formulated; claims which had been presented the year before without any reply. Actually the Enquiry Commission's report, in many of its paragraphs, seemed like a mixture of a criminal charge and a police detective's report. The so-called Parliamentary Commission laid most stress on the fact that among the people occupying the site were a few girls, and a woman journalist who was opposed to the Commission of Enquiry and had written urging the demonstrators to continue their action until the detainees were released.

In its blatant misrepresentation of facts, the conclusion of the report emphasised too: 'A few journalists took part in the student events in one way or another; a leaflet written by one of them attacks national unity. The Commission advises that this leaflet should be submitted to the Disciplinary Council of the Arab Socialist Union, in order to decide on a suitable penalty.' This is not an invitation, but an accusation and a denouncement. Do we have to remind readers that the President of the Disciplinary Council of the Socialist Union is that same Mr Muhammad Uthman Ismail, founder of the secret terrorist student organisation?

The Commission based itself quite shamelessly on a police report when it stressed that on 13th January the students distributed a leaflet called 'After the terrorist campaign' demanding the abrogation of the law of national unity, itself an infamous law removing all liberties. On 14th January 1973, the report goes on, the journalist Samir Amin Tadrus was arrested at Cairo airport; he had on him a sum of money in dollars and an envelope containing poems and folk-verses about the recent events.

> The appeal to the students to form "committees for the defence of democracy" is inspired by left-wing ideology. . . Some writers have been encouraged by doctrinaire ideas to step out of our national line at a time when our country is going through difficult circumstances; that naturally sowed trouble in the minds of our youth, as we can see from leaflets and wall newspapers distributed and published within the university. In addition, executive organisations [meaning the police] and political ones [the President of the Republic] have not completely fulfilled their responsibilities towards student activities since January 1972.

In a word, the report demanded even more repression.

On 28th January 1973, this report was submitted to Parliament. It was bitterly criticised, especially by the Secretary-General, Dr. Gamal Al-Utifi (later appointed Minister of Information and Culture, and rapidly superseded because of his relatively enlightened ideas). The criticism was concentrated on the accusations made by this biased and tendentious Parliamentary Commission; there was no need to prove that it had taken sides against a particular group. When the President of the Commission got up to reply to these criticisms, he began his speech with this verse from the Koran: 'Lord! Decide by Truth between us and our people, for Thou art the best of those who decide.' As for the reply itself, it consisted of a few quotations from the speeches of President Sadat.

Through the President's speech to Parliament on 28th December 1972 it was possible to understand the nature of the arrests and exceptional measures used against hundreds of unorganised or scarcely organised elements. Then, on January 31st 1973 in his speech to Parliament, he admitted that the State had been obliged to undertake, at a very early date, what could seem like a defensive war, to avoid a repetition of the crisis of the previous year. The only evidence against the students that the President could offer to the people was the Public Prosecutor's report, which is simply a rehash of the information service reports. The President did exactly the same as the so-called Parliamentary Commission of Enquiry. But it must be emphasised that the court decided on the release of all the accused; a judgement condemned by all those who had followed the line of the security service's tendentious reports. It was also a violent blow to the Presidency, which was supposed to be in authority. The contradiction was more flagrant still when, on several occasions, the courts acquitted the accused and the President refused to ratify the judgement, even using, three times in succession, his right to have a close watch kept on the prisoners; remember that such a watch can be maintained for six months, an inadmissible thing in an institutional republic. But one contradiction more or less does not matter. Let us simply remember that the report on which the President's speech was based had called these events a plot laid by foreign elements. To confirm what he said, the President of the Republic referred to the fact that, when he was arrested, the journalist Samir Amin Tadrus was in possession of revolutionary poems and was on the point of leaving for East Germany. The President's speech did not say whether citizens were forbidden to travel where they wished, especially if they were journalists. The President, in this same speech, thought himself obliged to speak again of the circumstances in which the Soviet advisers were sent back. He reminded his hearers that it was an affair 'between friends'. Later, he again took up his litany on 'the intrusive minority' and 'the healthy majority'; he did not appear to realise that the pashas of the old regime would have adopted exactly the same reasoning with regard to the Free Officers. He ended by reaffirming that the plot was to have been carried out on 1st of January, and the State had found itself compelled to act two or three days before 'J-Day' so as to foil the conspiracy. He warned that there was no liberty without control, that freedom of thought or belief was allowed so long as it did not pass the bounds of the intellect, but that from the moment it went beyond the individual it must be accounted for to the authorities.

It is noteworthy that the President never stopped making speeches for a whole month. On 9th January he granted an interview to the doyen of the Lebanese press; two days later he gave a press conference at Tripoli in Libya; two days later still he made a long speech at the reception for the Lebanese President Frangieh.

On 26th March 1973, he gave a three and a half hour speech to Parliament; the next day he spoke for two hours to the representatives of the press. And in all these speeches and meetings the President made absolutely no reply to the questions asked by the students, intellectuals, workers and others. He took care to stress only the following points:

All the measures and decisions of the organs and institutions of the State were taken after his consent and sometimes on his own initiative. Total confidence reigned between himself and the organs of the State, to such an extent that he had even suggested to Parliament the creation of a new function which could be called a 'Socialist magistrature' in order to protect the people (meaning the government).

The left, he also alleged, is always an echo from abroad and not a genuine Egyptian voice. Consequently it must be sabotaged from within by arguing that there is a national left-wing, and another which is a foreign agent. The people must be induced to rise against it, as it is atheistic. It must be separated from the Nasser tradition because the National Charter is not Marxist, and Nasser was not Marxist, (which is nothing more nor less than a truism).

In reality, the President tried to divide the ranks of the nation after the coup of May 1971. To do this he had recourse to a great deal of demagogy. He talked too much about democracy and did everything against it. For him, only the institutions and the press of the single party are legitimate. Any popular initiative not in agreement with the point of view of the regime is considered as a plot deserving imprisonment, dismissal or transfer. To the President, there is nothing easier: under the sovereignty of the law, detention camps have been effectively set up; and the number of laws authorising arrest has perceptibly increased, to the point where the President has rights which his predecessor never had. Now it is easier to put a stop to the slightest manifestations of freedom in the name of the law.

The President took care to make it clear, though indirectly, that war was inescapable and very near. But he took the precaution of showing that it would be his war, the government's war; that the people had no right to question. Thus he could easily isolate the people, politically and in the matter of information, from the climate of war. Camouflage is a military trick to surprise the enemy; but that cannot possibly be done with the people; which makes this war doubtful before it has even begun. The absence of a war economy, the elimination of any possibility of training the people to bear arms to forestall any surprise, the deprivation of the public of any information about the enemy, all this and more besides cannot be included under the heading of 'deceive the enemy and so take him by surprise', it is rather deceiving the people and taking them by surprise.

The press on the side of the regime did no better. On 14th February 1973, Musa Sabri wrote in the right-wing daily *Al-Akhbar:* 'The only one to profit from this student movement is the enemy who is watching at our gates.' But Abd Ar-Rahman Ach-Charqawi inferred a slightly different meaning: on several occasions he drew attention to what he called the forces of backwardness, meaning the extreme right-wing religious group. On 19th February 1973, inspired by Garaudy's cry: 'silence is no longer possible', Ach-Charqawi wrote: 'Those who try to turn freedom to their profit, to destroy freedom, those who try to impose ideological terrorism, to use knives instead of words, there is only one way to stand up to them. . . we must have even more freedom and even more democracy.'[56] This writer, famous for his left-wing history, was trying to give a new tone to *Rose Al-Youssef* to make it into a voice on the side of the government, but from a distinct and pseudo-progressive point of view. The following week, the same author enunciated some clear ideas on the same subject:

> Any action aimed at spoiling the democratic climate, or distracting attention from the fight for freedom, or putting obstacles in the way of the movement of progress will be a brake on our course. We must deepen our democratic stream and bar the way to the forces of backwardness and denial which are seeking to topple Egypt. The battle in Egypt is a battle for civilisation. The forces of progress will triumph without a doubt; the logic of history will have it so. It is also an imperative need . . . We are facing violent, barbaric attacks.

In fact the author of *Muhammad, prophete de la liberte,* and *Al-Hussein, revolutionnaire et martyr,* and other enlightened theological works, had just joined the battle with the extreme right-wing religious group. In his opinion that was the source of the country's critical situation. He permitted himself this step on the strength of the immediate support he had given to Sadat's putsch. Ach-Charqawi took care to show that Sadat was a very long way from this extreme right. He hoped thus to gain the President's sympathy without that of his executive organisations; an approach rooted in Charqawi's personal confidence in the President's national integrity and in his deep conviction that the President was above everything. A confidence, and a conviction, due to painful memories.

Dr. Ahmad Kamal Abu Al-Magd, Minister for Youth, wrote much earlier, in *Magalla Ach Chabab,* that the crisis was due to two reasons: 'Materialism which rejects religion' and 'the treatment of the social problem from a position of passionate hate, and a method consisting of deepening the contradictions between social classes so as to drive the situation of conflict to the point of explosion.' But it is a strange thing that in this same issue of the magazine of which Mr Abu Al-Magd was the director, a student made the distinction between the movement of 1968 which demanded change, and that of 1972 which had it, explaining it thus: 'The liberation of the land, practical democracy and a steady movement of transformation to socialism.'[57] Another said: 'What the government has done is the absolute opposite.'[58] A third added: 'As a student of Marxism, it is my right to explain it, especially as the economic part of Marxist theory suits our society perfectly.'[59]

At this time there were two events which were deeply irritating to the government: (a) The meeting of the Congress on working-class culture from which emerged the committees for the defence of democracy. This congress adopted the students' demands concerning the rejection of a political settlement of the Middle East problem; (b) Parallel to President Sadat's speeches, the Libyan President Muammar Al-Khadafi declared: 'Egypt is on the threshold of a political settlement. Libya opposes this settlement.'[60]

The final consequence of the rising of 1972 is a very positive fact: it obliged Egyptian public opinion to consider the problem of political organisations independent of those of the government. Nasser's argument on this subject (which was the original sin of the left) was no longer valid.

The Egyptian student movement of the 1970s was different from its origins in the 40s. University students in that period were only representatives or wings of existing parties. As for the new students, with the exception of a small minority belonging to other social strata, they are the pioneers who have given new life to political organisations in Egyptian political life, and made them legitimate.

A serious negative factor must, however, be stressed: the alliance between students and workers in this new movement never attained to the minimum essential foundation — unlike that of 1946 when the front was a veritable incarnation of the alliance of the popular classes. Contacts and attempts at co-ordination between students and workers on the one hand, and students from the working and professional classes on the other, cannot achieve the status of a political front capable of bringing forward a credible programme in practice, because it is based only upon slogans.

It is self-evident that no student movement can reach the greatly desired radical change alone. But the specificity of the movement and the moment in time gave free play to the intellectuals, without the working class being similarly placed.

Faced with the attempt at settlement from above, the quasi-organised movement of the intellectuals provided a reply, *stand firmly on the majority.* This movement can be considered as having been an active and attentive control on the progress of the government from the defeat of 1967, through the putsch between 1970 and 1971 to the war of 1973.

Notes

1. Programme of National Action (Official edition) pp.2 and 3.
2. *Ibid.*
3. *Ibid.*, p.4.
4. *Ibid.*, p.5.
5. *Ibid.*, p.6.

6. *Ibid.*, p.7.
7. *Ibid.*, pp.9, 10.
8. *Ibid.*, p.34.
9. *Ibid.*, p.49.
10. *Al-Hurriyah* (Lebanese magazine) 6th September 1971.
11. *Al-Muharrir* (Lebanese daily), 30th August 1971.
12. *Al-Ahram,* 2nd May 1972.
13. *Ibid.*, 6th May 1972.
14. *Ibid.*, 14th May 1972.
15. See Sadeq Galal Al-Azm's pertinent analysis in his book *Critique de la pensee religieuse,* At-Taliah.
16. See *Tarbiyat Salamah Mussa* (2nd. ed.) Al-Khangi, (Cairo 1958) p.132. The book exists in an English translation by Schumann, University of Amsterdam, Holland.
17. *Al-Akhbar* (Egyptian daily) 9th February 1973.
18. *Ibid.*
19. 'Distribution of incomes per individual', January 1972. Quoted in *Kitabat Misriyyah* No. 3, July 1975, Beirut, p.68.
20. Price Planning Bureau.
21. *Ibid.*
22. *Op. cit.* Budget of the R.A.E. 71/72 quoted in *Kitabat Misriyyah*, p.83.
23. *Ibid.*, p.76.
24. *Ibid.*, p.74.
25. *Ibid.*, p.75.
26. See the statistical appendix to the study *Inflation and Economic Planning in Egypt,* the chapter on family budgets, for information on the four cycles in rural and urban environments, each separately first, then the two together. But we have to take into account the fact that families in their categories differ according to whether they are rural or urban (see Budget of the R.A.E. 71/72, p.87).
27. The complete text appears in *At-Taliah,* October 1972.
28. M.H. Haykal, *At-Tariq ila Ramadan,* p.119.
29. *Ibid.*
30. *Ibid.*
31. *Ibid.*
32. 'Ponamanyov, responsible for information to the C.C. of the U.C.P., a former officer in the Red Army, closely monitored the activities of sympathisers with the Axis. Sadat learned that Ponamanyov always presented him as a Nazi agent, hostile to socialism and wanting to make Egypt a religious country.' Fuad Matar, *La Russie naserienne et l'Egypte Egyptienne, An-Nahar* (Beirut 1972) pp.94-5.
33. It is interesting to mention here the colloquium organised by *Al-Ahram* and published on Friday, 19th May 1972, three days before the Soviet American summit talks in Moscow. Among those taking part were Ismail Fahmi, Under-Secretary of State for Foreign Affairs at the time, and Tahsin Bachir, head of the Press Office at the same Ministry. Fahmi was of the opinion that the Soviet Union and the United States were agreed on maintaining this situation. 'At about this same time a computer was brought in to estimate the amount of advantage that the different countries gained from the status quo. The computer, after

obtaining all the important data, gave 420 points of advantage for Israel, 380 points for the United States and 110 for the Soviet Union.' (Haykal, *op. cit.*, p.149.) The official measure taken by the Minister for Foreign Affairs, with, of course, the approval of the President, was to give long leave to Fahmi and Bachir; two senior civil servants had taken the liberty of expressing personal opinions which relieved the Soviet Union of the acute discomfort felt on reading Haykal's articles which, at the time, were very hostile to the Soviets.

34. An American spy-ship which played an important part during the July 1967 war; it decoded secret Egyptian messages and communicated their contents to Israel.

35. The complete text of this note can be read in the appendix to Fuad Matar's *La place de Nasser dans la Republique de Sadate*.

36. M.H. Haykal, *op.cit.*

37. *Ibid.*, pp.126-7.

38. *Ibid.*, p.143.

39. *Al-Mosawwar* (Egyptian weekly) 3rd August 1972.

40. Fuad Matar, *op. cit.*, p.20.

41. Haykal, *op. cit.*, p.159.

42. *Ibid.*, pp.154-5.

43. Quoted *ibid.*, pp.160-6.

44. This point is studied in detail in the author's thesis in the chapter entitled *La defaite due radicalism egyptienne*.

45. For more details on this point, see Anis Sayeg, *Al-Fikrah Al-Arabiyyah fi misr*, Haykal Al-Gharib (Beirut, 1959); Dugen Quarqui, *Tatawwur Al-Fikrah Al-Arabiyyah fi misr*, Al-Muassasah Al-Arabiyyah Lildirasset Wa An-Nashr (Beirut, 1972); and *Al-Yassar Al-Misri wa Quadiyyat Filistin*, Dar Al-Farabi, (Beirut, 1974).

46. See *Al-Intifadah At-Tullabiyyah fi misr*, January 1972, in *Watha'iq*, Dar Ibn Khaldoun, (Beirut, 1972), p.27.

47. *Ibid.*

48. *Ibid.*, p.31.

49. See *Al-Harakah Al-Wataniyyat Al-Dimuqratiyyah Al-Gadidah fi misr. Tahlil wa watha'iq li magmu'ah min Al-Munadilin Al-Misriyyin*, Dar Ibn Khaldoun (Beirut, no publication date, pp.71-72).

50. *Al-Ahram*, 23rd January 1972.

51. *Al-Akhbar*, 20th January 1972.

52. *Al-Jumhurriyyah*, 29th January 1972.

53. *Al-Ahram*, 20th January 1972.

54. See *Al-Harakat Ad-Dimuqratiyyah Al-Gadidat fi misr*, p.74.

55. *Ibid.*

56. *Rose Al-Youssef*, 19th February 1973.

57. See the magazine *Ach-Chabab*, No.4, 23rd January 1973.

58. *Ibid.*

59. *Ibid.*

60. *Al-Balagh* (Lebanese newspaper) 1st January 1973.

3. Documents for a First Stage: Towards a Global Cultural Revolution

The Prediction of Youth

The movement of young writers towards the end of the 60s was simply a serious preamble to the events of the 70s. The voice of the young people's literary movement was louder than all the other voices to be heard after the defeat. Those in political power at the time made every effort to counteract this phenomenon and to absorb its manifestations of anger. The youth organisation of the Arab Socialist Union mobilised all its material and moral resources to hold the Congress of Az-Zaqaziq which was to assemble a large number of writers from the capital and the provinces. They intended to subject the Minister of the Interior, then at the peak of his glory, to a confrontation which he would never have believed possible. In reality, the assembly was much greater than the expression it could find simply in the youth organisation or even in the Socialist Union. That is why the congress ended with competitions, prize-givings and recommendations that remained a dead letter. The young writers wanted one thing, the government wanted another; exactly as had happened with the student movement in 1968 which came out of the declaration of March 30th, and which also remained a dead letter.

The authorities saw in these movements mere signs of nervousness, with no need for any rethinking of Egyptian life after the defeat. And because they saw only the surface of the problem, they ordered only skin-deep remedies: recuperation or repression; hence the quantitative accumulation of negative factors which was the cause of the qualitative explosion expressed in the movement of January 1972; that is, only three years after the rising during which the students hanged an effigy of Charawi Gumuah, the Minister of the Interior. The problem of the young writers was not the absence of platforms for their work, as official voices would have us believe. Their problem was not to hold high places on committees, newspapers or other glittering positions, as certain worthy masters believed. What is more, their problem had nothing to do with the blue pencil of a terrified official appointed to censorship. It is true that they suffered from publication difficulties, the snobbishness of some old masters and the ignorance of the censor. But these were only the outward signs of a crisis that touched them to the very marrow of their bones. The problem of youth was that of their native land, beaten on the frontier, alienated internally. There was absolutely no question of personal problems; the proof of that is that they overcame the difficulties of the crisis by publishing their works at their own expense, at the price of their sweat and their children's food. And when the censor prevented them from reaching their readers they emigrated.

The problem, then, remained unsolved, because it was that of the nation. Everything contained in the declarations of the student movement was in the mind of these young writers, as well as in their writings, their opinions and their actions. Muhammah Afifi Matar, Abd Al-Hakim Qassan, Amal Dunqul, Ibrahim Aslan, Izzat Amer, Khalil Kulfat, Ibrahim Mansur, Gamal Al-Ghitani, Sabri Hafez, Sami Khachabah, Farouk Abd Al-Qader, Yahya Al-Taher Abd Allah, Sayyid Hegab, Gamil Atiyyah, Muhammad Yusuf Al-Qaid, Mahmud Diyab, Chawqi Khamis and many other writers of this generation express in their writings a violent inner suffering which the short-sighted, the opportunists and those with no contact with the people have considered as 'superfluous pessimism', while this suffering, at different degrees of knowledge and experience, was the suffering of all Egypt, of the captive land, of the conquered people, the wounded country, and the working classes gratuitously crushed.

The special issue of the monthly *At-Taliah,* in September 1969, provided a lively witness that the young writers were in the vanguard of the revolutionary march, calling for changes and acting for its accomplishment. Despite the difficulties of censorship, these testimonies are an extraordinary proof of the sincerity, the frankness and courage of this generation. The prisons of Al-Qaliah and Turah, which had received a large crowd of these young people at the end of 1966, could symbolise the indescribable suffering of dozens of them for having joined actions to words even before the defeat had cast its shadow over the country. It was in October 1966 that I and my comrades, veterans of the struggle, were surprised by these new faces of political writers filling the entrance to the prison. For the old militants that we were, Raouf Nazmi, Ibrahim Fathi, Ghaleb Halasa and myself, prison was not unknown territory. But hope was lit anew in my heart when I saw these young people, Sabri Hafez, Gamal Al-Ghitani, Sayyid Hegab, Salah Isa, Abd Ar-Rahman Al-Abnudi, and others receiving, with great courage, the baptism of detention.

It was in 1966, shortly before the defeat and before the students and workers revolted. In the work of young writers, as in their conduct, there was a prediction that belonged not to the society of defeat but to that of revolt. For though the preceding generations predicted the defeat in one way or another in plays, novels and criticism, despite this, these older generations, and especially the generation of the 40s, were part of the society of the defeat. The important figures in this generation now had leading positions in the shop-window of official culture. They criticised the regime and the authorities violently and loudly. But almost all their criticisms came from a defeatist, not a revolutionary point of view. That is a fundamental difference separating the two generations, even though they sometimes found common ground between them. The generation of the 40s was characterised by the way it fitted into the social background of the new class, which had inherited the privileges of the old middle class without having its traditional form. It produced directors of companies, editors of newspapers and secretaries of state, and these jobs brought them incomes equal to, if not higher than those of the bosses of companies, factories, farms and businesses in the society before July 1961. They were middle class, outwardly and to the very core. They were an integral part of the new class which sprang from the remnants of the former classes when they crumbled, remnants which adapted to the new situation and formed this conglomeration of bureaucrats, technocrats, soldiers and civilians.

The majority of young writers belong to the lowest echelons of the rural and urban lower middle class. Those of the older generation had the same origin; but it was an artificial social leap that took them so near to the new upstarts and so far from the new generation whose attention and courage have not been altered by the profits and rallying cries of circumstance. We can say, then, that the conflict of generations in the literary field is a social conflict and not a conflict between the young and the not so young. Of course there are always exceptions here and there, but they only prove the rule. Among the older generation there is a minority that has not lost the thread of the revolution. In the new one there have been strata that have never been involved with revolutionary thought, or if they have, were not interested in its applications; yet others have gone only a little way along the road. So the sudden attachment of the generation of the 40s to the new class did not completely stem its ideological veins and its inner awareness. Memories of former struggles and, from time to time, feelings of guilt, encouraged some to speak a word of truth!

But their word of truth was always brought up short by the limits of their intellectual and social education. That is why the view of this older generation could only predict defeat without rising above it, while the new literary generation could go further and attempt change, precisely because of its intellectual and social education. The call for the creation of a General Union of Writers was the cornerstone in the attempt to achieve the hoped-for change. The young generation of writers was the most enthusiastic of all intellectuals for the creation of this Union as the most all-embracing democratic expression of the intellectual and artistic movement. For despite the existence of many literary, artistic and journalistic associations, their standard of responsibility worthy of the writer or artist left much to be desired.

So when the watchwords of democracy and sovereignty of the law of May 15th 1971 were renewed, the call went out again for the creation of a Writers' Union. With a few colleagues, I had the honour of taking part in this appeal. It would perhaps be interesting to record here some personal remarks on the circumstances of this appeal and the consequences which resulted from it.

(1) It was the young people who were most active in this attempt at

change. In contrast, our idea was based on the fact that all official and popular organisations of Egyptian intellectuals were only a mass of negative elements the most salient characteristic of which was isolation from living reality. The Committee for Propaganda and Thought, the Society of Men of Letters, the Association of Modern Literature, the Egyptian Literary Society and the Union of Journalists are only forms, different in scope but with the same content: isolation behind the screen of academic work, personal or official, and the lack of candour and courage to face our cultural reality. Most writers of the older generation, motivated by their high positions in State organisations, took care that things should remain as they were, while most young people wanted change.

(2) Open opposition to the creation of the Union took two forms: the first feared that the Union might become identical to those of the countries of the Socialist bloc. Liberty of expression, according to the supporters of this opinion, would not be guaranteed. Dr. Louis Awad was the figurehead of this trend. The second was based on the fact that the Union already existed in the form of the Society of Men of Letters, the administrative council of which consisted of Seleh Gawdat, Abd Al-Aziz Ad-Dasuqi, Ibrahim Al-Wardani, Suheir Al-Qualamawi, Abd Al-Qader Al-Qutt, Abd Ar-Rahman, Ach-Charqawi, Alfred Farag and Tharwat Abazah. Yussuf As-Sebai was the main representative of this trend.

(3) A third current of opposition was expressed by a few veteran progressive militants who recognised the objective necessity to create a general Union which would open its doors to men of letters and to all writers in different branches – political, economic and others. But they made the condition that this Union should fit into the context of the Socialist Union. Dr. Muhammad Al-Khafif and Lutfi Al-Khuli were the main representatives of this trend.

(4) Although most of my colleagues allowed the principle of the third trend, a certain unconcern condemned the project to be put aside until the day when the programme of national action was declared; this contained a clause indicating that it was time for the Arab Socialist Union to consider the idea of creating professional unions for writers and artists. But this clause remained a dead letter. It appears that the difference between the ideas of the two parties on this Union prevented the project being carried out. To our way of thinking, the union was not a fine building or beautiful offices where we could relax, drink coffee and chat about attractive travel projects. For us the Union was not formal competitions and distributions of prizes, smiles and glasses. It was, and still is, a free platform and democratic immunity for the writer. We never thought for a moment that the Union could be a copy of those in the Socialist bloc countries. We knew very well that we were not in a socialist country. We live in a society of underdeveloped and over-active classes; in consequence, contradictory ideological trends, latent or open, confront each other or form alliances according to circumstances. The Union we want must represent all national parties in whose interest it is to take part in the war on the intellectual front against colonialism and Zionism. The most

adequate context for creating this Union would be a general congress of intellectuals combining all their tendencies and all their legitimate contradictions, and allowing them democratic, free and representative elections. The Union should keep its distance from all official reports and be independent of both the Socialist Union and the Ministry of Culture and Information, so as to keep its own personality and not be subject to pressure from executive or 'popular' powers. The Union could represent the power of popular control of the official institutions of culture and information. The formula of independence is not difficult to reconcile with the sources of finance, as is the case with the Magistrature, the University and the Council of State. The General Union of Writers, as we wanted it, would be a rational independent platform with the power to plan, to legislate and to control the application of cultural decisions.

Some months after we had ceased to speak, we realised that the anxiety expressed by young writers was becoming general. It might have disappeared for a time, but it was felt later in the workers' and professional elections and in the parliamentary elections and those of the Socialist Union. This uneasiness showed in the workers' demonstrations and the taxi-drivers' strike. There was no doubt that Egypt was on the boil, and that the extent to which feelings were aroused would certainly end in fighting. It is astonishing that no one, among those whom the student movement in January 1972 took by surprise, tried to analyse impartially the different phenomena in the country during the last months of 1971. If they had done so, they would at least have been spared the shock of surprise. And they would have been able to see in the student movement a forceful expression of the feelings and ideas of other social strata which had preceded the students; they were the feelings and the thoughts of all Egypt.

The writers, and particularly the young ones, were among those who foresaw and expressed the crisis before the students. But there is an important qualitative difference between the student society with its wide public, possible unity, close-knit nature and homogeneous composition, and that of writers and artists; this enables the students to occupy a historically important place in the Egyptian struggle. And this in turn has enabled the writers, and particularly the young ones, to continue their national march forward. Thus they had to live through an extraordinary experience with many mistakes and very few chances of success; yet this experience is worthy to belong to the tradition of our nation's heroic struggles.

Organisation of the Movement

The movement began and ended in ten days; it began on the morning of January 17th, 1972, when information appeared about the student demonstrations, their congresses and their declarations; the end was their demonstration in the street a week later. During these few days the young writers were hunting for news both inside and outside the university. Some were connected to it by their studies, some by friends and relatives, and others by a bond stronger than all the others, that of blood, sweat and tears; it is from this bond that the love of Egypt springs, and it is for this love that one dies. The cafes, *Riche, Laffas, Isaevich* and *The Studio* were the meeting-places for all who were seeking news. Some were happy, others sad or uneasy. But all were wondering: what shall we do? The easiest solution was to draw up a declaration expressing our opinion; for events followed one upon the other with dizzy speed. We wrote a few words saying:

> We, the nation's writers and artists, support the national and democratic fight of the students. We reject all cowardly solutions of the national problem, from the Resolution of the Security Council [November 1967] to any attempt to barter the signature of a peace treaty with Israel for a partial withdrawal from our territory. We support all the demands contained in the declaration of the Supreme National Students' Committee, the authentic leaders of the student movement. We raise our voices to demand the release of the students detained so that they can continue their national struggle. Long live Egypt! Long live the struggle of the Egyptian people!

Our colleagues went to collect signatures in the theatres, the newspaper offices and cinemas. In less than 24 hours they had obtained the signatures of 90 personalities, well-known and less well-known, great and less great, men and women of both left and right. This list of signatories was like the guest-list for a national congress of writers and artists. At this moment, writers and artists of different generations, classes and opinions, all joined together, for perhaps the first time for 20 years, to help to save the nation.

The first step was taken, and now we had to think, and to consider our position. We made no attempt to publish this declaration in the Press like the professional Unions of lawyers, journalists, teachers and engineers. Were we thinking? Were we dreaming? I cannot say. All I know is that I suggested to my colleagues that we should meet to think aloud to the Journalists' Union. The Union Council had published a declaration in *Al-Ahram*. It was a moderate declaration compared to that of the lawyers' Union. This incited a few journalists to write another, bolder one, which was signed by more than 150 journalists, including myself. My suggestion, then, fell on fertile ground. Yusuf As-Sebai had firmly padlocked the *House of Men of Letters* when he felt, or somebody felt for him, that something was going to happen. We made our way to the Union. But as most of us were not members, I went into the office of my friend and former colleague Saad Zaghlul Fuad, elected member of the Council, and against reaction. 'I have with me,' I said, 'friends and colleagues who are asking the Union to allow them to meet publicly and legitimately to discuss the situation all over the country.' 'You are a member of the Union,' he said, 'You have the right to invite whoever you want.' 'No,' I replied, 'I don't want them to be considered as being invited by me. I belong to their group far more than I do to the Union. We would like you to give us a meeting-place. Here is a request which I have signed with them. If you contacted the chairman so that your action would be official. . .' And Saad Zaghlul telephoned Ali Hamdi Al-Gammal and read him the request. Al-Gammal was extremely generous. We got to work.

The affair did not go off without some provocation from a few journalists who were frightened or annoyed; but our resolution was firm. We agreed that the next day we would hold a general assembly to elect a provisional National Committee. On the evening of January 25th, more than 50 writers and artists met to form this committee and complete the brief declaration made two days before. We collected 116 signatures while the President of the Republic was making his speech. The members of the provisional committee were elected: Ahmad Abd Al-Muti Hegazi, Samir Farid, Radwa Achour, Ibrahim Mansour, Faridah Annaccah, Ahmad Al-Khamisi, Abd-Al-Hakim Qasem, Sami Al-Maadawi, Awni Haykal, Raadat Al-Mihi, Sami Abd Al-Baqi, Iz Ad-Din Nagib, Muhammad Hegazi and myself. We had taken care that representation should be in proportion to the number of writers, people working in the cinema and the theatre, and painters. At midnight we telegraphed our declaration to the President of the Republic, the Prime Minister, the First Secretary of the Central Committee of the Arab Socialist Union, and to the President of the National Assembly. We decided to call a general congress of writers and artists on Thursday 27th January in order to elect the permanent national committee and discuss an overall declaration drawn up in outline by the provisional committee, the wording of which was entrusted to a commission. The meeting of this congress was a good opportunity for us to call for the creation of a General Union of writers and artists. Three colleagues prepared different plans for the new declaration. The three plans were passed to the editing committee. But we could see that some were going too far, some were selling us short, and others were trying to keep a balance. However, these plans all stressed the fact that the main contradiction was between the will of the people and American and Zionist colonialism occupying our land, and that the other secondary contradictions, though they were not to be ignored, should not be given more importance than they deserved, so as not to distract us from our real enemy. If the government declared war, the people would ask no more than to carry it out, not improvising, but preparing the country in a revolutionary way for a decisive battle. Despite arguments, the editing committee managed to prepare the following draft declaration.

Draft declaration

*First Congress of Egyptian Writers and Artists
to take place on Thursday 27th January 1972
at the headquarters of the Union of Journalists*

The First Congress of Egyptian Writers and Artists, meeting on Thursday 27th January 1972 at the headquarters of the Union of Journalists in response to the invitation from the provisional National Committee of writers and artists elected on Tuesday 25th January 1972, declares that the student movement begun on 17th January 1972 is a sincere and advanced national movement, that the Supreme National Students' Committee is the genuine expression of the student public, that the demands expressed by this Committee in the document published on Thursday, 20th January 1972 are the demands of the Egyptian people and also our demands, which we could not express for lack of means; that these demands are not in essence opposed to the national political regime existing since 23rd July 1952; that the fact that one category of the national alliance expressed certain demands at a given moment does not constitute a contradiction with the other categories of this alliance, but rather means that it is indispensable to look for forms of alliance that are more democratic and more likely to enable all national forces to express themselves better within the National Front. On the other hand, the Congress declares that to call every popular movement anarchical and unauthentic deprives social strata and classes capable of acting at the level of the people of the means of freely expressing their political opinions.

The Congress, while firmly stressing the absolute necessity of national unity at this decisive stage in the history of our nation, expresses its intense indignation at the accusations of servility, of collaboration with the enemy, and of attempting to divide national unity, which have been brought against the student movement. It also deplores the methods used by the police to suppress the student movement. The Congress believes that the use of such methods was bound to lead to the students leaving the university precincts, to the descent of the cental security forces and to the regrettable events of Monday the 24th and Tuesday the 25th January 1972, while the Israeli imperialist enemy is occupying part of our territory and impeding our march towards progress and socialism.

The Congress demands:

1) The release of all political detainees, and of any student who participated in the demonstrations, and an undertaking not to bring them before the Disciplinary Councils of the University, so that they can continue their studies unimpeded.

2) That all forms of peaceful solution be rejected: Resolution 242, the Rogers Plan in response to the Yaring document; for it is now proved that none of these propositions in any way constitutes an equitable solution to the problem. More than ever we must insist on the principle of not yielding an inch of our territory or of occupied Arab territory. No reconciliation with Israel, no negotiation, no recognition, and no concessions on the legitimate national rights of the Palestinian people.

3) The liquidation of American interests in Egypt, and action towards the same effect in the whole Arab nation, taking up firm positions with regard to all complaisant Arab countries, on the basis of declared opposition to the United States and to the imperialist Israeli enemy.

4) Total support for all the organisations of the Palestinian resistance. Re-opening of their political and information offices. Authorisation

for Egyptians to join the ranks of the resistance. Authorisation for all printed organs of the resistance to enter Egypt. Struggle against every attempt to liquidate the resistance.

5) Insistence on the transformation of the Egyptian economy into a war economy, and to socialism by the consolidation of national unity, equipping ourselves with every possible guarantee of victory against the imperialist Israeli enemy, by taking the following steps: (a) Most public expenditure to be provided by high incomes;(b) A limit to be set to the very great difference between the maximum and minimum wage levels.

6) Total mobilisation of the country for a people's war of long duration; but we must also be watchful and attentive that this mobilisation is not used for terrorist purposes which could attack national unity or the conditions for victory.

7) Lifting of censorship on the press, publications, cinema, radio, and television, except for everything affecting military secrets. These media should cease to be means of justification and degradation and become an effective weapon in the fight against the imperialist and Israeli enemy, and in the fight for progress, freedom and socialism, and to educate people anew to take an active part in the building of their country.

8) Changes in information policy and the present cultural policy towards a policy on information and culture compatible with a war economy and total mobilisation on the home front.

The Congress decides:

a) To consider the student document published on Thursday 20th January 1972 as a basic document for the information of the National Committee of Writers and Artists elected in the course of the present Congress.

b) To entrust to the National Committee of Writers and Artists the task of creating a General Union for writers and artists. The events of the last few days have proved that the absence of such an organisation is an obstacle to the fulfilment by writers and artists of their duties towards the nation.

The First Congress of Egyptian Writers and Artists
(27th January 1972)

We sent invitations to the Congress to most writers and artists, despite the threats and provocations of a few journalists who were alarmed by our actions. One of them threatened to call the police and have us evicted by force. But the little group of young enthusiasts showed courage and perseverance. We had divided ourselves into small groups in order to be present in the Union headquarters 24 hours a day and to continue our work and follow events as they occurred. However, the great majority of us were constantly present. One was writing a poem, another practising calligraphy, a third copying the declaration, a fourth compiling a wall newspaper, while the fifth, sixth and seventh addressed invitations to the Congress, day and night; and we had many volunteers who were not even members of the provisional Committee. There were also among us some of the older generation, equally sincere and enthusiastic: Michael Kamel, Adib Dimitri, Abd Al-Moni Al-Qassas and others. They supported us, tried to solve our problems with the Union, and gave us modest advice. Though some journalists opposed us, others gave us their support.

Up to five in the afternoon everything seemed to be going normally; a few colleagues and myself had already gone to the Book Exhibition to take advantage of its opening to issue the greatest possible number of invitations. It was a chance for us to meet a large number of writers and artists. But what was my surprise when someone whispered to me that the Union had just decided to ban the meeting of the Congress in its building, and there was no other solution but postponement as it was impossible to find another venue in less than two hours. It was obvious that the opposition had purposely left us in peace until the last minute. Guests had already begun to arrive. It was a scene both sad and extraordinary. More than 200 writers and artists were there, ready for action. It was more than we expected. But we had to find excuses. What could we do but tell them the truth? The decision had just been posted up on the Union notice board. People arrived continuously for two hours; we discussed the situation with them and told them that we would postpone the meeting until a later date. Finally we dispersed. Some thought the experiment was over; others decided to start again, but in a different form. Some were overcome by despair; others took up the challenge and went on thinking about the situation, alone or with others. As far as I was concerned, matters could be summarised as follows:

1) If the journalists', lawyers' and teachers' Unions succeeded in publicising their opinions, it was because they had a distinctive material and moral image. What writers and artists lacked was precisely that image, which could be expressed in a general Union. Our first step, which would have to be taken again, was to call for the creation of this Union, a national action supported by our will and above all by the awareness that we could nothing without a platform.

2) If the experiment failed, despite the brilliance of its conception, it was because its dominant characteristic was improvisation, unlike the student movement the context of which showed how precisely it was prepared. Improvisation was, in fact, the main reason for the ephemeral nature of the movement and the complete absence of any intellectual and organisational homogeneity. Only national sentiment provided the centripetal force of the movement, while the 'threat of attack' was the centrifugal force. The work was done in such a way that the criteria of strategy and tactics were confused. Consequently the preparation for the Congress amounted to groping in the dark.

3) Young writers were and always will be the nerve-centre of any serious effort towards a total cultural revolution. The older generations could at best protect or encourage; they are incapable of confrontation or attack.

Nevertheless, and because the university movement expressed the very essence of the stage we were going through as a nation, great men of letters never stopped thinking and reflecting. Dr. Louis Awad's article: 'Report on the Egyptian Question,' was like a political tract. It was redistributed by the students all day in the closed confines of the university. When all hope of holding the Congress was lost, it was natural that Louis Awad, Tewfiq Al-Hakim, Hussein Fawzi, Nagib Mahfuz and Ahmad Baha Ad-Din should try to use their high reputation in support of the student movement and the national movement in general. With this in mind, Louis Awad prepared a draft declaration to be signed by the five authors and published in *Al-Ahram.* Here is the text:

After considering the events and declarations taking place on the occasion of the student movement during January 1972, we came to the following conclusions:

(1) The student movement is basically a national movement of whose integrity there is no doubt. It was born for Egypt and aims only to free Egypt from Israeli occupation and to demand that the whole of Egypt should prepare for the decisive confrontation with the Israeli enemy. If the demands and appeals of the students are tinged with a few errors or deviations in thought or expression, that is due to youthful enthusiasm and impulsiveness or to a lack of political experience, and not to any lack of national integrity.

(2) Without wishing to interfere in the enquiry carried out by the Magistrature, we consider that the presence of about 30 agitators among tens of thousands of Egyptian students by no means explains the unanimity of the young public. To consider this expression of distress about the future of the country as the result of the work of agitators would be to consider the flower of the nation as no better than a flock of sheep. We must interpret the revolt of our children by the existence of real national reasons, authentic objective problems which must be faced openly and courageously without having recourse to repression. Our native country is a possession common to government and governed. And every citizen has the right to be uneasy about the future of his country and to express this unease in a way sufficiently peaceful for it to reach those who hold power.

(3) Although we regret a few verbal excesses within the student movement, we praise the extraordinarily peaceful spirit which the movement has showed. It has been free from violence and sabotage. Here our children are proving that they are of age; and they set an example of respect for law and order and of the true spirit of democracy.

(4) In consequence we appeal to the generosity of the authorities to instruct those responsible for the maintenance of public order to terminate the hearings and to release the detainees. When appreciations and motivations are confused, the requirements of justice must be above the judgements of individuals, and above their capacity to distinguish between just and unjust. We appeal to the government to direct those

responsible for political and social security towards dialogue with our children, the students, instead of repressing and muzzling them. Our children are the treasure and the strength of our country when the day of reckoning comes.

Long live Egypt, freed from usurpers!
Long live the unity of high and low for the liberation of Egypt!
Long live the great Egyptian nation!

Unfortunately, this draft was never published. But in the most striking way the attempt revealed the role of Egyptian intellectuals in the events of their country. Though experience shows that young writers are in the vanguard of the intellectuals' struggle, it also shows, from a different point of view, that the national struggle in Egypt needs all forces capable of 'doing something', whatever their size, their means of expression or their line of thought. The experiment of January 1972 was only a step on the road to a cultural revolution that was already fermenting; all it needed was an organisation capable of assembling and uniting its thought. The Writers' Union was an urgent necessity for the creation of such an organisation.

The Struggle Continues

At about noon on the 9th of July 1972, in the most important streets of Cairo, a procession of about 70 young and not so young people walked sadly along. Some carried placards, or wreaths tied with blue ribbon. It could be read on the placards and on the ribbon that this group was mourning an 'absent friend'.

The absent friend had been murdered 24 hours before when he started up the engine of his car in the underground car park of the block of flats where he lived. This was on a hill on the coast, east of Beirut, at Al-Hazimiyyah. The explosives with which the engine had been carefully primed blew to pieces the man and his niece who were about to drive out. Nothing remained of the victims but a few rags of flesh, but a little card could still be seen on which was clearly written: 'With greetings from Israel.'

The Arab world, and all forces fighting for freedom, peace and progress, was shaken by the ignoble and barbarous murder of the writer and militant Palestinian Ghassan Kanafani. Little Israeli visiting cards also arrived by post in the centre of Beirut. The appearance of these affected the historian Anis Sayegh, who at the time was Director of the Palestinian Research Centre, and the writer and politician Bassam Abou Charif who had replaced Ghassan Kanafani as editor-in-chief of *Al-Hadaf,* the organ of the Popular Front for the Liberation of Palestine. At the beginning of 1973 the criminals even managed to murder in their homes three of the greatest leaders of the P.L.O., Yussuf and Kamal Adwan and Kamal Nasser, in a bloody pirate raid unequalled except by that at Beirut airport in 1968. Terrorist attacks by Israel against the Palestinian resistance formed a preliminary to the armed confrontation between the Lebanese army and the Palestinian resistance in May 1973; this was part of the plan which began in Jordan in September 1970 and did not end with the Lebanese war in 1975-1976 and the occupation of the south of the country in 1978.

In the literature and for the militancy of modern Arabs, Ghassan Kanafani represented the symbol of a whole generation. As the rising of the students in Egypt began with a Palestinian Week, as every one of their declarations emphasised their attentiveness to Palestinian resistance and the bond between the liberation of Sinai and that of Palestine through a common destiny, as all these manifestations implied the Arab nature of Egypt, the death of Ghassan Kanafani was the starting point for the movement of Egyptian intellectuals. The silent procession left the cafe *Riche* near Tal'at Harb Square and went in the direction of the headquarters of the Journalists' Union. The organisers of this symbolic funeral had not asked the permission of the security authorities. There were traffic jams. The police were faced with a *fait accompli.* A dense, silent crowd was forming on the pavements. As soon as we arrived at Abd Al-Khaleq Tharwat Street, near the Lawyers' Union, the men of the secret police were already waiting for us. Yussuf Idris, in the name of all those taking part in the procession, came forward to ask for explanations. They wanted to know the rest of the programme, and Idris replied that we intended to hold a wake. The symbolic funeral in Egypt was to take place at the same time as the real one in Beirut. We also informed the police of our intention to publish our condolences in the newspapers. After four hours of difficult negotiations, the security forces forbade the funeral; the press refused to publish our short declaration. I remember that Dr. Louis Awad asked me to lend him the works of Ghassan Khanafani, of whom only the early *Litterature de la resistance dans les territoires occupe* and *La litterature sionist* were known in Egypt. Louis Awad had a great admiration for the romantic works of the Palestinian writer. He was preparing to review these works in *Al-Ahram,* when the editorial board, without any apparent reason, said they were sorry they could not publish such a study. Later we learnt that the government's position with regard to the Palestinian organisation to which Ghassan Kanafani belonged was at the bottom of this prohibition. We give here the text of our censored declaration:

> After certain of us had showed in a silent procession, our indignation at the barbarous and atrocious murder of the martyred writer Ghassan Kanafani, we, Egyptian writers, intellectuals and artists, solemnly appeal to the writers of the whole world, and to all free and honest men, to take towards the crimes of the Zionists and imperialists the attitude worthy of every civilised man, to express their indignation at this atrocious crime and stand by the side of the Arab intellectuals against the crimes of the neo-Nazis and in defence of human values. The murder of Ghassan Kanafani is only the first step on the road to destroying the moral and human content of the Arab revolution in order to oppress the very soul of the Arab people, to liquidate its forces

and compel it to kneel before the imperialist conquerors, both Israeli
and American. Writers of every land, support us against neo-Nazism.

This declaration was signed by 73 Egyptian writers including Michael Kamel,
Abou Seif Youssouf, Louis Awad, Loutfi Al-Khouli, Muhammad Anis,
Yussuf Idris, Rifaat As-Said, Ibrahim Mansur, Amal Dounqoul, Mourad
Wahba, Selah Isa, Fathi Abd Al-Fattah, Muhammad Odah, Amir Iskandar,
Nagib Sourour, Izzat Amer, Magid Toubia and the painters Muhyi Ad-Din
Al-Labbad, Hassan Sulayman and Mustapha Ramzi.

The faculty members of the universities and institutes of higher education
had published a joint declaration coinciding with the student events. A
summary of this declaration said:

1) We see that the country is not at present in the effective struggle.
When the battle takes place, divisions and schisms will give place to the
uniting of all in one single movement. For the moment it is natural that
opinions should be many and conflicting.

2) It is their very interest in the battle that leads young people to
oppose numerous phenomena which could be considered as not being on
a level of conduct which is indispensable in a society preparing for a
decisive battle. If preparing for the battle implies complacency about
mistakes, that would mean that it is being used to cover mistakes.

3) It is impossible to decide the boundary between uttering an
opinion opposed to the official point of view and what is called
'circulating rumours'. If what people say is enough for them to
be called to account and penalised, most people could be exposed to
such accusations. As for written opinions (wall newspapers, distribution
of declarations), that, in the present circumstances, is a direct consequence of the failure to satisfy a claim dear to the heart of every
intellectual, the raising of the censorship. If freedom of opinion and of
the press were guaranteed, secret or public declarations and tracts
would have no reason for existing.

4) The recent events were set off by the provocative way in which
the press reported the arrest and charging of certain students. Not
content with that, the press also gave a picture of the student movement
which was far from the truth. It even went so far as to make accusations
which we believe to be unfounded. Professors are said to have been
attacked by students. Need we say that this sort of accusation has
always been brought against honest citizens all through our history, and
that of other countries?

5) The student movement from January 1972 to the present must not
be considered in isolation from the general situation throughout the
country with regard to both the problem of liberation and the absence
of democracy.

This declaration, summarised above, was signed by 52 men and women teachers in the various universities and institutes of higher education in Egypt. Among the signatories were deans of faculty and heads of department. The complete text was published in the Lebanese magazine *Al-Balagh* of 19th February 1973. University professors formed an important sector of the opposition movement carried on by intellectuals, despite threats and promises (threats of dismissal and promises of ministerial posts).

The police had arrested the journalist Sapinaz Kazem in January 1973. She had taken part with the students in the occupation of the university buildings. Samir Tadrus, journalist, had been arrested about the same time at Cairo airport. Just before January 1973 the secret police had also arrested more than 400 writers, journalists, workers, students and lawyers among the democratic element. The alliance between the students and the professional classes was more solid than that between students and workers. But the charges against the intellectuals did not hold water; most of them were based on reports from the secret services. That is why the courts ordered their release; but the President of the Republic usually exercised his right to oppose them. Many were kept under surveillance for having demonstrated in support of the students, read a poem, been in possession of resistance literature, given a lecture at the university or organised a meeting in opposition to the journalists', lawyers' or engineers' Unions. Hence, the sudden action of Tewfiq Al-Hakim, Nagib Mahfuz and Louis Awad. In fact they were acting under pressure from the Egyptian intellectuals. On 8th January 1973, in the presence of Yussuf Idris, Ibrahim Mansur and myself, Tewfiq Al-Hakim wrote this declaration, the complete text of which we give here, in view of its exceptional importance.

Declaration of writers and men of letters

Through our feeling of historical responsibility, our confidence in our people, and our esteem for the patriotism of the leader of State, and because we believe in his capacity to lead the country through ways strewn with ambushes, which will need wisdom and perspicacity so that the nation may not lose its way, and may be brought where it can regain its strength and blossom in the affirmation of its identity, we, writers and men of letters, signatories to this declaration, feel that it is our duty to help the institutions of State through the function we fulfil in society, and share in the search for truth about the troubled state shown in today's events.

The nature of the writer and man of letters, through his mission within the nation, is to look beneath the surface and delve into the mind, while the nature of the press is to find out the news, and as far as official organisations are concerned, to seek out the truth on the basis of very precise facts which may be a symptom of an unseen disease or the smoke of a fire hidden beneath the ashes. So it is for us, then, writers and men of letters, to complete the picture and to help to bring to light what is rumbling in the heart and mind of the nation. This we do, not to add to what is done by other institutions, but through fear that the seething in people's mind could be neglected, which could lead to an explosion and its attendant catastrophes. There is no doubt that the country is seething within, and very obviously to those who look for it. Not all people, perhaps, find an explanation for their distress; the simplest, the innocents among the young people, may suggest various reasons without looking too closely; they may repeat them in their conversations or put them into their publications. Explanations, demands and protests may mostly appear superficial, immature or unexplained. But the truth, which cannot be doubted, is that they are all uneasy for some vague reason, and cannot stand this feeling of disorientation much longer. What is the origin of this feeling of distress, trouble and confusion? The most important reason is that they cannot see the road in front of them. To shout, over and over, the word 'battle', to say that battle is the only way, might have been a reply to their questions, and a visible path.

That, doubtless, is the reply the State has tried to give, so as to throw light on the dark road of truth.

But the days are passing. The word 'battle' is becoming a vague term with blurred outlines, the elements of which have still to be analysed. . . . A term repeated a thousand times. From morning till night this word is repeated in every key, in songs and hymns, in speeches and slogans, until it is losing all its force, all its effectiveness, and even all its meaning. Young people can no longer swallow this much-chewed word, but they dare not spit it out either. They are put out of countenance. The road to the future is once more blocked; hence their feeling of distress.

Youth is the most sensitive part of the nation. Young people have more interest in the future than others. But the future they see is dark. They are studying for qualifications, and when they have got them they are flung upon the sands of the frontier. They forget what they have learned and cannot find the enemy with whom they must fight. That, too, is a kind of loss.

Other citizens are in no less difficult a situation. Life is hard, the public services bad; lack, carelessness and complacency are hiding behind the face of war, waiting for war and preparing for war, until it all becomes a vast comedy provoking general anger and disgust. These are only a few elements of today's prevailing mood.

We need a quick solution to this situation. And there is no solution except in truth. Truth and truth alone will put an end to the general perplexity and confusion. The people would like to be convinced of something. To calm and convince them they must be clearly told the truth.

This means that we must reconsider some current practices in the State today, with a view to changing them. It is essential to guarantee freedom of opinion, thought, discussion and explanation, so that light can be shed on everything about which the nation is anxious. This may be done first within institutions, because our present circumstances demand secrecy; but also on condition that the State has no preconceived ideas to impose on those who guide public opinion by their writings, and so force them to become their heralds. The State should be the last to utter opinions, and should not do so without seriously listening to the opinions of free Egypt. Its opinion should be that of the people and their representatives. It is not the place of the State to formulate opinions and watchwords and subsequently impose them on the people.

It is time, in these difficult circumstances, for the State to rid itself of too many burdens, too many responsibilities. It is time to surrender responsibility to the nation.

This is in its interest and to keep its place in history.

This declaration was signed by some of the great writers of Egypt. The name of Tewfiq Al-Hakim was its first claim to consideration. The document was swiftly photocopied so that it could be sent to the Prime Minister, the First Secretary of the Socialist Union, the President of the People's Council (Parliament), the Parliamentary Commission of Enquiry, the heads of the universities, the professional associations, and the press, which was warned not to publish it.

Four Ends for a Journey

The next day, 9th January 1973, the Lebanese daily *Al-Anwar* published the declaration of these Egyptian writers and men of letters on its front page and in full. The paper reproduced 12 names among the 43 signatures, representing the most important writers of different generations and trends (even Tharwat Abaza, the well-known right-wing writer, had signed the declaration). At this time *Al-Anwar* was very close to the Egyptian government. The news was taken up and sent out by the press agencies. This was done fairly quickly for several reasons: first because it had been revealed by a sympathetic paper, and so must be accurate. Secondly, because the declaration was the first opposition coming from writers, led by personalities who could not be called left-wing. Thirdly, because it was published outside Egypt, proving that even 'great writers' could not express themselves freely at home; and finally, because the reservations expressed in this declaration agreed on many points with the students' declaration, and supported them.

The authorities in Egypt raged at the declaration, its authors and the paper that published it. It was natural that Tewfiq Al-Hakim should feel angry and resentful at this evasion of responsibility. It was difficult to dictate the declaration by telephone to Beirut. Our Lebanese colleague Talal Salman, who was on the editorial staff of *Al-Anwar,* was in Cairo at the time of the events, and knew that I was very close to what was happening in Tewfiq Al-Hakim's office, and was actually taking part; so he asked me to do the impossible — to get a copy of the declaration. It really was impossible, as the copies were limited in number, and all were known. My office was near to that of Al-Hakim, so I copied it myself, chose a few signatures and handed it over to Talal Salman. He left my place to go directly to the airport and so managed to be in time for next day's issue. What happened, happened; but the owners of *Al-Anwar* probably did not realise the importance of the declaration until after its publication and the reactions to it in Cairo. This active and patriotic journalist certainly suffered the consequences both from his bosses and Cairo.

On 10th January 1973, President Sadat urgently summoned the newspaper directors. He harshly rebuked them for their 'carelessness'. He took note of the declaration of Tewfiq Al-Hakim (which was what he called it), quoted a few paragraphs and mentioned a few signatures in a way that contained a veiled threat.

On the fourth day, 11th January 1973, Dr. Abd Al-Qader Hatem, Deputy Prime Minister and Minister of Culture and Information, asked Tewfiq Al-Hakim, Nagib Mahfuz and Tharwat Abaza to meet him the next day at 1 p.m. in his office. The three writers told us that they had repeated to the Minister the contents of the declaration, assuring him that they were not responsible for its publication. This joint declaration can never be confirmed or denied unless one of the three decides to change his story.

But the event which followed started more than one interrogation; a McCarthy-like campaign was unleashed against the editor-in-chief of *Al-Ahram* and against Tewfiq Al-Hakim, whom some people accused of communism. The headquarters of the campaign were the offices and organisations of the Socialist Union.

On 4th February 1973, less than a month after the publication of the declaration, the morning papers *(Al-Ahram, Al-Akhbar, Al-Gumhuriyyah)* gave their readers, on the front page, a special article entitled '64 members of the Socialist Union struck off', with the sub-title 'The Disciplinary Committee took the decision after a three-hour meeting.' Printed over three columns, the decision read: 'The Disciplinary Committee of the Socialist Union has decided to strike from their rolls of active member 64 of the members of the political organisation.' The article gave the names of 64 writers and journalists, among them the most brilliant figures of the Egyptian press, belonging to different trends, Nasserist, Marxist and independent democrat. We noticed that the names were given with two and sometimes three patronymns. We learned that Louis Awad was called Louis Hanna Khalil Awad, and Muhammad Odah, Muhammad Abd Al-Fattah Ahmed Odah, and so on. This proved that the list came from the intelligence files of the secret police. One of the most striking paradoxes was that some of the persons struck off were members neither of the Socialist Union nor of the Journalists Union.An explanatory note appended to the list said:

> It is well known that to be struck off the list of active members of
> the Socialist Union results in the member being struck off the rolls of
> every trade union organisation, every administrative council, every unit

of the Socialist Union and every political organisation. It also puts an end to the exercise of every profession requiring active membership of the Socialist Union, as in the case of journalists – this is the application of the statute of the Journalists' Union. A journalist struck off the rolls has not the right to consider himself as carrying on his profession, since that requires that he should first be an active member of the Socialist Union. The press organisation to which he belongs must retire him early. The Disciplinary Committee is in permanent session for the examination of other cases.

The Egyptians, although they had never heard of the Disciplinary Committee of the Socialist Union, realised that this was a strange disciplinary court to which the accused was never summoned, and so was denied his right to defend himself, either in person or through a lawyer. It was something like the courts of the Inquisition in mediaeval Europe, against the judgements of which there was no appeal. The Egyptians certainly thought about the names of the members of this tribunal: Hafez Badawi, President of the People's Council, former President of the tribunal which had endorsed the putsch of May 14th 1971 by condemning the leaders who resigned to death or life sentences, a former provincial lawyer, and a most incompetent versifier, Muhammad Hamed Mahmud, Ahmed Abd Al-Akher, Ahmad Kamal Abou Al-Magd, Youssouf Makkadi and Muhammad Uthman Ismail. The Middle Eastern Press Agency did not forget to add to the report of this measure – a curious one to say the least – a statement by an official spokesman emphasising that the report of the Parliamentary Commission of Enquiry mentioned writers and journalists as manipulators of the recent student movements. Certain among them – still according to the official spokesman – gave the press, and foreign press agencies, false information, and signed lying statements published abroad, with a view to showing the country as shaken by instability and disorder.

On 7th February 1973, a second list of people struck off was published. It contained the names of 15 journalists and writers, men and women. It was followed a little later by a third list which, this time, did not compulsorily retire the victims, but transferred them to the Office of Information, which was simply another way of shunting them into a siding. The three lists together totalled 111 writers and journalists, among the best elements of intellectual, literary, artistic and journalistic work in Egypt, from Ahmad Baha Ad-Din, Louis Awad, Lutfi Al-Khuli, Michael Kamel, Yussuf Idris, Alfred Farag and Muhammad Odah to the youngest generation of novelists, painters, radio announcers and television presenters. It had also been said that a list of university teachers was being prepared. But events went ahead at an insane pace. Egyptians, in both Nasser's and Sadat's time, had become accustomed to the suppression of freedom of speech and expression. From the affair at the university in 1954, when a large number of professors had been dismissed simply by a Decree of the Council of the Revolution; the affair of the Journalists' Union in the same year, when the former lists of active members were cancelled so that new lists would allow a screening operation; the expulsion from their newspapers of the great progressive national figures Muhammad Mandur, Abd Ar-Rahman Al-Khamisi and others, and their transfer to wood, shoe and fish companies; to the arrest or exile of the founders of radio and television in the affair of May 1971; nothing more could surprise the Egyptians. The most recent events were not completely new to them, but,because of their importance and the fact that they happened under the aegis of 'the sovereignty of law', they were no longer bearable. As the State is the head of all press organs, the condemnation of 111 writers could have only one meaning; it was virtually condemning them to death, and at the same time condemning the press to degeneration and Egyptian thought to exile, suicide and madness.

This first stage in the progress of the cultural revolution in Egypt had four consequences. First, the emigration of all the finest national intellectuals and democrats to Beirut, Baghdad, Kuwait, Algiers, Paris or London. Writers, journalists, university people, painters, actors, producers, men, women, young and old, with different doctrines and political opinions,left the country.

Second, on 22nd March 1973 *Al-Ahram* reproduced on its front page a large photograph of President Sadat greeting Tewfiq Al-Hakim. The caption read:

> The President of the Republic received Tewfiq Al-Hakim in company with Dr. Hakim for half an hour, and then had a private conversation with the great man of letters, which lasted an hour and a half, after which Tewfiq Al-Hakim in a statement with the character of a joint declaration, said that the President "was considering the rebuilding of Egypt as a base and support for our military force. This rebuilding will consume all our efforts and make us forget all religious, doctrinal or social differences. All without discredit must take part in the building and the production we need. All must come back into the arms of the Egyptian nation, and build a victorious, civilised and powerful Egypt."

Observers had remarked that Tewfiq Al-Hakim and Nagib Mahfuz had been 'excepted from the measures of the Disciplinary Committee'. But these observations, after the picture in *Al-Ahram,* emphasised the importance of the following facts: It was at this precise moment that the Congress of Arab Writers took place at Tunis. The problem of Egyptian writers had been submitted to the meeting by the Lebanese Writers' Union. It was then that Yussuf As-Sebai, President of the Egyptian delegation, waived this issue of *Al-Ahram* to assure the members of the Congress that everything had returned to normal. On his return, he was appointed Minister of Culture and Information.

Not long after his meeting with the President, Tewfiq brought out of his satchel his famous little book *Le retour a la conscience.* With great shrewdness he first had it typed. Then a few friends (meaning Tharwat Abaza) 'volunteered their services' to duplicate it — as though it were a clandestine tract — before it was published as a book first in Beirut, and then in Cairo. Tewfiq Al-Hakim recognises that he lost his conscience through the whole of Nasser's period, and that this conscience recently came back to him. In this book, he gives the green light to the attack on the Nasserist period in all its aspects, negative and positive, and on the pretext of opening the records.

Since this time, Tewfiq Al-Hakim, Nagib Mahfuz and others have become the writers of the new regime, supporting all its plans for the future. They have divorced themselves completely from the current which they allowed to carry them along for a short time at the beginning of the 70s.

The third consequence was the division of the left; those who had learned their lesson well tried to reconcile their left-wing thought with the government, which was well received by the latter from the first days of the putsch applying the policy of recovery guided from above. Others, who had learnt the lesson equally well, took care to be independent, and not to be puppets, painted, dressed and manipulated by the government.

The fourth consequence was the 'surprise' given by the President about the last week in September 1973, and the surprise of surprises, also given by him, before the end of the first meeting in October of the same year.

These four facts or consequences were to end in a new beginning.

Note

1.　*Al-Ahram,* 21st January 1973.

4. A Substitute for War

It Was Not a Surprise

The leading article of the December 1973 issue of the Egyptian monthly journal *At-Taliah* was about a 'popular view of the October war.' It was an enquiry in the field; the first question was 'Did you expect the battle of the 6th of October and its consequences?' By 'consequences' we must of course understand the military situation so far as it was known at the date of the questionnaire.

The samples chosen in working-class districts replied as follows: 57.2% expected it. 18.20% were surprised. 24.55% expected it but were surprised by the timing. The results for those chosen from a rural environment (farmers and small landowners) were: 52.60% expected it. 26.30% were surprised. 21.10 expected it but were surprised by the timing.

Whatever the reservations about this type of sampling, the replies contained an extra element which the questionnaire was not seeking — the spontaneity of the samples questioned in the interpretation and justification of replies. Those who were not surprised by the war said they were sure of victory. Those who did not expect it were surprised by the victory. Those who were surprised by the timing of the start of the war thought that it was certain to happen, but at a different time and with greater military losses than those which were actually suffered, a difference that certainly surprised them. But everyone questioned said spontaneously *why* war was inescapable.

Those who expected it gave the following justifications:

(a) Egypt, whatever people might say, was constantly rebuilding its military forces.

(b) The situation of the armed forces could not tolerate the status quo indefinitely.

(c) The home situation could no longer tolerate the status quo.

(d) Israel did not want a peaceful solution.

(e) The United States was vacillating and putting no pressure on Israel.

Those who did not expect war gave the following justifications:

(a) They heard day and night that the Soviets had no wish to give us arms.

(b) They were constantly hearing about initiatives for the reopening of the Suez Canal, proposals made by the Secretary-General of the United Nations

and contacts with the United States, which would freeze any military solution.
(c) The home front was disunited.
(d) One respondent among the workers said that what happened was a divine 'miracle'.

Those who were not expecting war at that particular time but expected it some time, justified their reasoning by saying that it was a normal way of proceeding; the political and military leaders had to deceive the enemy. Two respondents in a rural environment added that 'the divine will' stepped in and determined the moment.

All these replies, whatever their source, indicate in one way or the other that the widest sectors of the Egyptian people were neither surprised by the war nor by its direct consequences, for several obvious reasons.

First, the defeat of June 1967 did not break the will to battle of the Egyptian soldier; neither did it break the citizens' will to struggle. The successive waves of unrest between 1968 and 1973 had, as their main basis, 'the recovery of the land'. The programmes proposed by the declarations of the students, intellectuals, workers and the military were only the details of this basis. Remember that Israel, in its psychological war against Egypt, actually said that Sinai was neither regionally nor geographically part of Egyptian territory. Egypt, Israel said, is African and has nothing to do with Asia; the west bank of the Suez Canal is a natural frontier for Egypt.[1] But the Egyptian people were very close to Nasser when he reformed the armed forces between 1967 and 1980. They observed in silence, but with the hope of the conquered, the battles of Ras Al-Uch and Gazirat Chadwan, and the scuttling of the ship *Eilat*. Hope was reborn with the war of attrition which continued uninterrupted and with unslackening pace from March 1969 to 23rd July 1970 — the date when Egypt accepted the Rogers Plan.

> The war of attrition [said Colonel T.N. Dupuy] gave the Egyptian gunners the chance to train. It helped them to discover the capacity of the Soviet SAM ground-to-air missiles, reducing Israeli's superiority in the air; a superiority which, at that time, was unchallenged. It also gave Egyptian morale a much-needed boost; this happened through exchanges of fire with the enemy, and raids carried out by commandos crossing the Canal. . . Professional aptitude [he said] both for planning and execution, qualities thanks to which the crossing was accomplished, could not be better in any other army in the world. The result of this delicate operation by the General Staff, and of the element of surprise, was a remarkable success in crossing the Suez Canal over quite a wide front.

According to the Briton Edgar O. Balance, author of the book *The War of 67,* the Soviet military style, based on a centralised control of thousands of guns, is one of the best styles in the world. There is no doubt that it helped the Egyptians to breach the Barlerv Line.[2] This is an appreciation of the war of attrition written by a foreign professional — the same war which an

Egyptian said had proved the weakness of the Egyptian army, and that the Soviet Union only gave Egypt the means of replying, after the event, to the improved technological might of the Zionist state.[3] But all who knew the strategic importance of the Barlerv Line realised the importance of the war of attrition, which made veritable breaches in this impregnable wall, and forced Israel to pull its forces back 15 km., beyond the Egyptian artillery's range; this was the first sign to herald the October war.[4]

For the Egyptian people, it was no secret that the rebuilding of the Egyptian armed forces, to which Nasser had devoted all his efforts for three years, was almost finished before he died, by a first plan, known later by the code-name Granite Z, the aim of which was to move right up to the passes.[5] We may believe that the J-Day of the battle was not far away at the time when Nasser died. We know now that one problem which set President Sadat against his Deputy and his Ministers who resigned in May 1971 was the fact that he had inherited both the plan of the battle to come and the Rogers Plan. If the latter was only an American manoeuvre to give Israel time to draw breath (Israel in fact had never accepted this proposal), it was also for Egypt a Nasserist manoeuvre, making it possible to advance the barrage of missiles all along the front; this was confirmed by American spy satellites and served Israel as a pretext for failing to adhere to the other clauses of the Plan. The Egyptian leaders were divided into two camps, both Nasserist. One wanted to fight the battle, the other wanted to try for a peaceful solution under the aegis of the United States. However, it was clear that all attempts at a peaceful solution had failed, to such an extent that in speeches before the October war, President Sadat addressed some harsh words to the United States and their President. No less clear was the wound in the heart of the nation that threatened to open as long as the scar of 1967 was not healed, especially as the poison of the occupation was beginning to spread through the economic, social and moral arteries in a way that presaged a real catastrophe.

The performance of the new regime was constantly falling behind the demands of the students, workers and intellectuals, or because of the questions which had not been answered since the arrests of May 1971, the dismissal of the military advisers, the new laws on investment of foreign capital and the suppression of freedom of thought and expression. The gulf between promises and their fulfilment, official programmes and actual legislation, and propaganda and social reality, became deeper and deeper.

The people were calling for war and had made their decision; it could be seen in demonstrations organised far in advance or arising spontaneously. Sometimes consciously and sometimes not, it was the incarnation of a new revolution in which the liberation of the land and of Man went together. But at the same time, President Sadat's State, on the eve of the October war, was enduring the greatest difficulties in its search for some kind of legitimacy, to transform the putsch — confirmed by the events of 1971 — into a stable and recognised government, however much it might be in contradiction to the new revolution dreamed of by the people, and symbolised by the movements and works of the intellectuals. The people were thinking of a war of liberation, like a total cultural revolution. The government was planning to replace this war with. . . another, which would help them to acquire an identity by the baptism of fire and blood.

So there appears to be an essential contradiction, between Nasser's regime, which had accepted the Rogers Plan as a stopgap between the introduction — which might be called the war of attrition — and the as yet unknown contents of a book whose title might be *The liquidation of the after-effects of aggression,* and Sadat's regime, which accepted the plan of the war of October 1973 as an interim measure between his initiative for reopening the Canal in 1971 and his visit to Jerusalem in 1977.

All this does not alter the fact that the war of 1973 was a surprise in another sense and from another angle. In autumn 1967, General Abd Al-Moneim Riyad had said to Nasser: 'It cannot help but be a surprise, for the fact that we are the ones to start the attack is in itself one of the elements of surprise . . . . The enemy will not expect an attack from us.'[6] General Riyad was right. He was one of the greatest soldiers in the history of modern Egypt. Six years later, the Israelis did not accept the truth until about five hours before Yom Kippur, for one of their greatest thinkers thought and acted on the basis of two premises: 1) Trahal is powerful and capable of crushing any Arab movement. 2) The perpetuation of the status qho for 20 or 30 years would permit the creation of new truths and deepen the technological gulf between Arabs and Israel.[7] This was the foundation of the thought and behaviour of Moshe Dayan.

In 1967 commenting on the Khartoum Summit, Dayan had declared: 'The unity which appeared at this summit will not survive long.' We may add, that the strategic enquiry team of the International Institute of Strategic Studies in London studied the Middle East twice in 1972 and, despite the armaments fever, eliminated the likelihood of any military intervention that could change the situation of stalemate.[8] The Soviet-American summit in Moscow in 1973 confirmed this trend. Need we remind readers of what was said about Kissinger's surprise when they wakened him to tell him the news?

Of course experts and historians did not agree on the strategic or tactical identity of the surprise. An American Colonel said: 'The military advantage gained by the effect of surprise is indeed remarkable, but it was not decisive.'[9] The Egyptian generals think that surprise was a strategic factor (international colloquium on the October war). Haykal thinks that the surprise had a strategic and a tactical sense at the same time. By all evidence, the war was not a surprise in the economic, social or political fields in Egypt, but it certainly was, and in the most absolute way, on a military level and on the battlefield.

The Search for an Identity

During and after the war, a vast dialogue had taken place on every level, from the rank and file of citizens, through the intellectuals, to those governing the country. And it can be said that all Egyptians, at home and abroad, affirmed that it really was a 'war of national liberation'.[10] It can also be said that only a few voices, outside Egypt, used the word 'pretence' or something similar. They even went so far as to talk about complicity, especially between the Egyptian and American parties.[11]

Those who thought in this way were strengthened in their convictions by the immediate consequences of the war, and by the preponderant part played by the United States in the affair. The proof lies in the military effects resulting from Egypt's promise to respect the ceasefire; Israel's breaking of the same promise, from the breaching of the Outfall gate, the encirclement of the third army and the city of Suez, and the negotiations of kilometre 101, the Geneva meeting at the Palais des Nations; from Resolution 338 of the Security Council to the first disengagement agreement on the Egyptian front. These are the facts which led some national writers to interpret the war and its consequences as 'the remains of the defeat of June 1967'.[12] But that does not alter the fact that there were earlier writings which could have prevented the October war being described in terms of pretence, complicity with the United States or liberation.[13]

One of the most interesting attitudes to the war was that of President Muammar Al-Khadafi. He said publicly that he was very doubtful about the war, its aims and its consequences, which did not prevent him from quickly sending all the food and medicine stockpiled in Libya. From the first days of the war, he sent two members of the Council of the Revolution to observe events more closely. When the Israelis succeeded in crossing the Canal and making the famous breach, the Libyan President felt that his doubts about the plan of operations 'were well-founded'.[14] Khadafi's reaction to the new situation was clear in his telegram addressed to Sadat:

> I am sending you all we possess in the way of anti-aircraft missiles, and the garrison of Tobruk with them. Orders have been given to a brigade of tanks to go immediately to Cairo. The shops have been emptied. I have learned of your emotion at the content of my proposals, which have been transmitted to you. I had said, quite truthfully, that if the war went against us — and may God preserve us from that — it would be the consequence of the superiority of enemy arms, and not the consequence of our soldiers' incapacity. For the moment it is enough that the Israeli soldier should flee before the Egyptian soldier. This is not only a victory for the Egyptian people, this factor is also very important outside Egypt. For the moment I can imagine nothing else. But I should like, President, to tell you that our people feel a certain embarrassment when they listen to the broadcasts of Radio Cairo about our political participation in the battle, while these same broadcasts exaggerate everything they say about King Feisal's participation. Libya is not mentioned at all. It is regrettable, Sir. But the most important thing is

the will to fight. God be with you! Al-Kadhafi.[15]

The Libyan President was voicing reproaches, but he was also trying to minimise the declarations he made less than 48 hours after the start of the battles. The Israeli advance confirmed what he had foreseen on the military plane. The political consequences only aggravated it on the political plane. We should not forget that Kadhafi was our associate in war and peace, through the arms and soldiers he gave us (the world did not know about the affair of the Mirages until after the war), and because he was one of the Presidents of the Egypt-Syria-Libyan Union, which was almost formalised in constitutional terms between Egypt and Libya just a month before the war. But the Libyan President has never told us the facts which made him utter reservations about the war when it had only just begun, that is, at the moment of the peak of victory of the first two days. Kadhafi repeated the same reservations – at the time of Kissinger's negotiations at Aswan in Spring 1975 – about the second Agreement on Sinai. He even admitted that he had information that the Agreement was going to be made and even worse. But up to now Kadhafi has given away none of his secrets.

However, the documents, or rather the facts, are there to light our way a little.

The first fact is that as told by Muhammad Hassanein Haykal:

> In the evening of 24th October 1972, President Sadat called a meeting of the National Security Council at his home at Guizeh. Fifteen generals commanding brigades and divisions, and Vice-Admiral Abd Ar-Rahnan Fahmi were present. The discussion, part of which was very tense, went on past midnight. The President fervently upheld the principle of limited war. He insisted on his favourite idea, that ten millimetres of land won on the east bank of the Canal would better consolidate his situation in his later political and diplomatic negotiations. Many of the officers were doubtful. Two days later, the President had made his decision. At 4 o'clock in the afternoon, he sent for Saad Ad-Din Al-Chagli, Chief of the General Staff and said to him: 'From this moment on, consider yourself head of the army.' At a quarter to five, he sent his secretary to General Sadeq to tell him that the President was accepting his resignation. Sadeq had never dreamed of resigning. The next day, the Minister for War, his deputy, the head of the Navy, the head of the central military region and the director of the general information bureau were relieved of their functions.[16]

It became clear in the course of the war that there was no problem of armaments. But the official attitude that was assumed to this question, before and after the war, contained a great deal of hostility against the Soviet Union. Haykal mentions a rather important fact on this subject. Some time before the war, the President said to him: 'They [the Soviets] are burying me in new weapons; between December 1972 and June 1973, Egypt received more arms than we had received during the whole of the last two years.'[17] So the constantly paraded difference with the Soviets, which went hand in hand with the fierce campaign against the Nasser regime, did not spring from the socialist State's parsimony in the matter of weapons. This difference was a complete invention, with the object of bringing a second element into the alternative solution to war, and limiting the war, first from a military point of view, and then to eliminate politically our international ally – the Soviet Union.

The two preceding elements fortuitously prepared the ground for the third element, which was the justification of the relationship between President Sadat and the United States. The elimination of Ali Sabri and the others was not, indeed, decided with the representative of American interests, but the fact that it happened precisely at the time when Rogers was to arrive in Cairo could only be an 'invitation' to consolidate the secret contacts with the United States. The same applies to the dismissal of the Soviet military advisers; Kissinger's comment was that if the President had laid his cards on the table, he could have had something in return; but he gave them away for nothing. Which is true. The dismissal of the Soviet advisers was neither a condition nor was it complicity. It was a new invitation addressed to the United States. The substitute for war was a last invitation, but it was accepted at once. Why? In his book *The Need for Choice*,[18] Henry Kissinger says: 'Limited war is based on malicious bargaining which does not go beyond certain limits.' Saad Ad-Din Ibrahim describes the phases of the application of the American Secretary of State's theory in the October war:[19]

a) The call for a ceasefire and the return to the former lines on 6th October 1973 were the first steps.

b) On the third day of the war, between the 8th and 10th October, the United States established their air bridge with Israel for massive military aid.

c) On the fourth day of the war, Kissinger made another proposal for a ceasefire, but this time it was done on the basis of both parties keeping their positions, which meant a partial victory for the Arabs.

d) On 20th October, the Israeli advance on both the Egyptian and Syrian fronts had already reduced the Arab advantage of the first week.

> Kissinger found this a golden opportunity to impose a new ceasefire acceptable by all parties. He took off for Moscow at the invitation of the Secretary General of the Soviet Communist Party, Leonid Brezhnev. In the Soviet capital, the two superpowers reached a plan for an agreement on an end to the fighting. Both presented it to the Security Council where it was accepted.

e) While the adventure of the Outfall gate became a political manifestation more than a strategic breach, Israel realised that the tactical victory might be transformed into a strategic mousetrap where the Israeli forces, besieged on three sides, could be exterminated. Kissinger went to the Middle East; he ran to and fro between Cairo and Tel-Aviv. On 11th November he reached an agreement in principle between Egypt and Israel. On December 21st,

Egyptians and Israelis met for the first time at Geneva. Kissinger had achieved an indisputable success.

But to whose profit?

First of all, to the United States. The Middle East is, as Eisenhower once said, the best piece of real estate in the world.[20] It is no mere chance that he was the author of the project which bears his name and which was intended to fill the gap in the Middle East after the departure of the French, British and Israeli forces from Egypt following the aggression of 1956. It was this same project which was revived with Kissinger's help in 1973, taking into account the changes that had occurred during the previous 15 years.

Saad Ad-Din Ibrahim put forward a theory of American interests in the Middle East, a theory represented by a diagram of a triangle, of which the first side is military and political, the second economic and the third cultural:

> For at the same time as the ships of the American Sixth Fleet were sailing into Egyptian territorial waters to "help" in the dredging of the Canal, the three largest banks in America were asking for authorisation to open branches in Cairo; the American University of Cairo was asking for the sequestration to be lifted so that it could become once more a purely American institution, independent of any intervention or direction coming from the Egyptian national government.[21]

These three moves took place simultaneously a few weeks after the October war. In order to carry out this plan, the United States accepted Sadat's invitation addressed in the form of a substitute for war. Thus was revealed the true identity of the regime, declared in the presidential speech of 16th October 1973, when the war was in full swing, and at the exact moment of Israel's breach of the Outfall gate. The United States responded to the invitation — in its own interests, which Kissinger stated quite frankly: American strategic security in one of the most sensitive regions; a guarantee of oil to the West under American control; driving the Soviets out of Egypt. To attain these objectives, Kissinger had recourse to military blackmail through client States (Israel in the Middle East, Iran in the Arabian Gulf), emphasising the Arab element in the conflicts relating to the Palestinian cause (from the Jordanian September massacre to the Lebanese war). In addition, the Arab military forces were neutralised and frozen (from the second Agreement of Sinai through the Syrian intervention in Lebanon and the Egypto-Libyan war to the Arab interventions in the Horn of Africa). On the economic plane, Egypt was bombarded with promises on Nixon's visit to Cairo on 10th June 1974, but nothing was done. Worse still, the I.M.F. made it a condition of any aid that State subsidies to essential products should be suppressed, which led to the events of 18th and 19th January 1977. And finally, the liquidation of the radicalism which was in the air in the region, especially in the forces of the left in Egypt and in the Arab world in general.

It was also an achievement for Israel, for some conservative Arab regimes and for some Egyptian social strata supporting the regime. It was this achievement of Kissinger's that led, logically, to the second Sinai Agreement, the signature of which encouraged the Israelis to go back on their acceptance of Resolution 242, even in spite of President Sadat's hot haste in his visit to Jerusalem. This same achievement incited the Kingdom of Saudi Arabia to take the lead in the region for four years.[22] It also enabled new social forces which had come into being through the Egyptian government to draw breath again on an international plane, after having been almost encircled; they could now point to the United States as their friend and address the American Secretary of State as 'my dear Henry'!

In Search of Legitimacy

On the social plane the war must be studied in its historical context; but history must link the past with the future. Many things which happened before October 1973 explain the decision taken on the 6th of that month, and what happened afterwards completes the explanation. The Egyptian regime before and after the war was continually searching for its own legitimacy; and there is no doubt that military action immediately gave it that legitimacy, at least enough for it to declare its identity publicly. This sort of legitimacy is exceptional in history in general and in Egyptian history in particular; it even seems to be the exact opposite of the legitimacy acquired by Nasser in the war of 1956.

In their speeches of 16th October 1973, President Sadat and the Israeli Prime Minister Mrs Golda Meir announced, each from their own position, the true nature of the war. Their views were in flat contradiction to the declaration made by Houon Boumedienne to the Soviets on his secret visit to Moscow — which was that the war of 6th October was the first war of total liberation, and the Soviet Union was bound to fulfil all its promises. Kosygin, the Soviet Prime Minister, came to Cairo to study the situation on the spot. But just before his arrival, in the most surprising way, President Sadat brought forward, in his speech to Parliament, a peace plan and a request for a ceasefire. In the course of very intensive negotiations Egypt begged the Soviet Union to intervene and stop the fighting. President Sadat expressed this request in a letter addressed to the Soviet leaders.[23]

In the course of the international colloquium on the October war, General Abd Al-Ghani Al-Gamasi made the following statement: 'The plans for the war of October 1973 were drawn up for a total local war with decisive strategic aims, to upset the balance in the region, to invalidate Israel's theory and destroy the foundations of its strategy.'[24] But the British Brigadier-General Kenneth Hunt declared in the same colloquium, which took place two years after the war:

> The psychological shock caused by the completely unexpected start of the war, was immense for Israel. It caused a deep rift. It showed the value of surprise. But this same shock, from the material and human

point of view, made the value of sure and deep frontiers more precious still in the minds of the Israelis.[25]

Five years after the war of 1973, following the visit to Jerusalem of the President of the largest Arab state, Israel confirmed the point of view of the British military authorities by insisting that the military settlements in Sinai should be retained.

But the most important thing for history about this war is the contradiction between General Al-Gamasi and Haykal. It is true that Gamasi was not the first, nor even the second man in the operations room. It is no less true that Haykal was a civilian; however he was nearer to events, as shown in his book *At-Tariq ila Ramadan.* In it, Haykal tells of an important meeting between himself and the Soviet Ambassador Vinogradov at an evening party during the first week of fighting.

> All day [the ambassador said to him] I have had continual meetings with our military attaches. To tell you the truth, they are not satisfied with the development of the situation. I do not understand why you do not advance towards the passes. That is not only a logical follow-up to the route your army will have to take, but your advance will help to relieve the pressure on the Syrians. . . The Arabs have very little time to get satisfactory results.[26]

The Ambassador added that Brezhnev wanted to know, among other things, 'What were the limits of the goals sought'; for President Sadat, Haykal said, always asserted to the Soviets that this was a limited war,[27] an assertion which, to say the least, contradicted that made by the Algerian President. In spite of everything, the Soviet air bridge, extended to Egypt and Syria, had just been established. Haykal told the President of the discussion he had just had with the Soviet Ambassador. Sadat replied: 'As I said to Hafez Al-Assad, the land is not important, the important thing is to wear down the enemy. I should not like to make the mistake of advancing rapidly simply to gain more ground.' The Minister for War, General Ahmad Ismail, said to Haykal:

> That was precisely my intention [to get to the passes]. Only now we must modify our plans because of the situation on the Syrian front. If the enemy turned and concentrated his attacks on us, we must at any price avoid our forces being spread out in a way that is harmful to us.

From the Egyptian demand for a ceasefire, through Boumedienne's secret visit to Moscow, to the President's speech on 16th October 1973, the Egyptian President appears to have successfully carried off a vast swindle; before the war, he went on in the same way, giving as a pretext the military necessity to deceive the enemy in order to surprise him. With the setting of the stage for this substitute for a war, President Sadat abused everyone's confidence, and went on to the confusion of his own allies, Arab and international. It appears that since then the rift in Egypto-Syrian relations has widened. At the time, President Hafez Al-Assad had written to President Sadat:

> I should have preferred, when the battle was still going on, to have been informed about the proposals which you have just announced to Parliament. Each of us has the right to know the ideas and intentions of the other before learning about them from the radio, since we are associated in a battle for life or death.[28]

The Egyptian President replied to his Syrian colleague with what later became the dominant thought in all his speeches. 'We fought the Israelis until the fifteenth day. Israel was quite alone for the first four days. But during the last six days I was fighting the United States instead of Israel! I tell you quite frankly, I cannot make war on the United States.'[29] Kissinger went one better than this idea of which President Sadat was so fond, saying: 'The United States established the air bridge with Israel after the Soviets had established theirs with the Arab countries concerned.'[30] But we will let Colonel T.N. Dupuy have the last word:

> I felt that our Arab friends were fluctuating strangely in their opinions about the activities of the two great powers during the war. They considered it quite natural that the Soviets should help them, for the Soviet Union, they say, has undertaken to provide them with arms and train them. They are too quick to assert that the Soviet Union had nothing to do with the outbreak of war, because it was planned and carried out by themselves with no outside help. At the same time they condemn American help to Israel, and take it to be active American participation in the war . . . I do not believe, [he adds with a semblance of sarcasm] that anyone could imagine that the Americans were taking part in the fighting. . . In my opinion, that shows a lack of logic and consistency of ideas; it is based on a misunderstanding of the role of the two superpowers.[31]

However that may be, it was President Sadat's misfortune that nobody was convinced by his American argument; it would mean that the Soviet Union and the United States had been waging war against each other for the last 30 years. But unfortunately for Egypt and the Arabs in general, this argument was translated into military terms by what is called 'the breach of the outfall gate', while the reality of that affair is something quite different. The British military expert Edgar O. Balance describes it in the following terms:

> Nothing but a propaganda campaign. . . It brought out the courage and tenacity of the Egyptian officers, N.C.O.'s and men, the great majority of whom, organised in small pockets of resistance, were able to go on holding the positions which the Israelis claimed to have occupied. The

Israelis' disappointment was great when the Third Army refused to throw down its arms and surrender when it was suffering from a lack of munitions, food and water, and despite the systematic pounding and the bombardment with Israeli leaflets to which the infantry was subjected.[32]

The underlying reality of the affair of the breach was effectively brought out in the course of several interviews given by President Sadat to the magazine *Al-Hawadith*. 'It could have been,' said President Sadat, 'one of the Arabs' finest battles, if it had not been for Kissinger's threat of direct American intervention on top of the famous nuclear manoeuvre and the alerting of American forces in every corner of the world'!

The actual military truth is told by Haykal:

> On October 17th 1973, orders were given to the Parachute Division, well-known for its efficiency, to go to the spot and take possession of it. Some parts of this division had already arrived at Israeli intersections, and the General Staff of the division was beginning to co-ordinate operations with units of divers to destroy the bridge when they received orders to retreat and form a front with the neighbouring troops to avoid any sally. The colonel in command of the regiment could not believe that an order like that could come from headquarters. He asked for confirmation. He got it, and in the voice of an officer he knew well. In an attempt to gain time and successfully accomplish his mission, he asked for another confirmation from the commander-in-chief of the armed forces in Cairo. Again he found himself being ordered to loosen the cordon he had already thrown around the Israeli forces. The artillery of the Second Army was under the command of a highly qualified professional, Commander Abd Al-Halim Abu-Ghazala; elements of the Third Army artillery, under the command of a no less capable leader, were already bombarding the enemy bridges and had scored direct hits at several points when both received, in their turn, the order to retreat.[33]

In the light of President Sadat's statements, Haykal's story and the testimony of foreign experts, the importance of the breach of the outfall gate lies in the fact that it clearly determined the real nature of the October war. It was not a real war at all, but a substitute for real war. President Sadat's speech during the first days of this breach was only the identification card. From that point of view we have to forgive those who — among Egyptians and among Arabs — called this war a 'war of total national liberation'. The military achievements of the first days gave it, without any doubt, the appearance of a war of liberation. As for its political content, this was defined by the orders to retreat and the failure to counteract the Israeli breach of the outfall gate, by the negotiations of kilometre 101 and by the signatures recorded at the Palais des Nations at Geneva. For Mr Sadat's regime, to act in this way was to acquire legitimacy on the field of battle, precisely in order to immunise itself against any attempt at a new revolution in Egypt.

The Egyptian army certainly fulfilled its historic role in the war. But a great distance separates the military from the political aspect of the 6th October 1973. A great distance which inflicts on the whole of Egypt an injustice that it does not deserve. The decision, taken by the Arab people of Egypt, to go to war had quite a different aim. There is no need to recall that the Egyptian armed forces were perfectly aware of the popular reasons for this decision — nor that they had nothing to do with President Sadat's political intentions. When they discovered a few indications of these intentions, when they opposed them in word or deed, they exposed themselves to the inescapable fate of all opposition under Mr Sadat's regime. The people and the Egyptian army were responsible for the positive and creative aspect of the first week of the war of October 1973. President Sadat alone is responsible for the equation he took upon himself to create in order to pass from the battlefield to the negotiating table.

President Sadat, the Arab conservatives, the Americans and the Hebrew state could well say that they had won through this war, but they could not at all say that they had won the war. They could use it so that each one of them could carry out his plans, and together they could arrive at the minimum common ground needed for all their plans. This war enabled President Sadat to transform his putsch into a legitimate regime capable of absorbing public anger for a long time, capable also of revealing the economic, social and intellectual foundations of his regime. It enabled the United States to take complete political possession of Middle East oil resources and their transport channels, not only to face the world energy crisis, but also to impose their leadership even more firmly on Western Europe and Japan — who depend on Middle Eastern oil — and to solve their own monetary problems resulting from the deficit in their balance of payments.[34] It enabled Israel to regain the power of strategic initiative; which, at least temporarily, allowed it to deal with, overcome and even exploit its consequences, even to the point of occupying South Lebanon in the spring of 1978, as though the Arab defeat of June 1967 was continuing to bear fruit.

This substitute for a war is at the bottom of all these consequences; though the October war may have momentarily immunised the government against the possibility of being overthrown, and given it legitimacy for a certain time, its consequences for Egypt and its people are surely more durable than personalities and governments.

When, on October 16th 1973, President Sadat's open car made its way through Cairo's main streets towards the People's Council (Parliament), both sides of the streets were lined with those who expected war, those who had been surprised by the moment of its outbreak, and those who did not expect it at all. They were all there to offer an ovation to the new regime. It was the moment of birth of the legitimacy of a putsch which had long sought recognition. During the three difficult years which had preceded this moment and which had begun with the sad and bloody September of 1970, the

Egyptian regime had never ceased to seek this legitimacy, the basic guarantee of its continuity and of a peaceful transition from a society dreaming of revolution to a society living under counter-revolution.

Here we have to follow two adjacent lines in Egypt's social, historical and cultural character. The first is that of the cult of legitimacy, represented in ancient times by the oneness of God and King (Pharaoh); this appeared anew in the revolution of 23rd July 1952, when many people throughout the world found it difficult to understand how the military revolutionaries, up to the very last moment, were saying official farewells to a dethroned king, and how Egypt still remained under the monarchy for a year after the revolution! These two facts, among many others, led those researchers looking into the revolutionary content of the putsch of 23rd July 1952 astray; they had taken it for a putsch confirming – but with new figures – the economic, social and political identity of the old regime. Specialists in constitutional law were at the time pre-occupied by the Regency Council and by the royal document bequeathing the Kingdom to the Crown Prince; a preoccupation which shook the confidence of a great many people and worried those who supported the change, especially as the members of the Regency Council were among the most extremist of the extreme religious right. Lieutenant-Colonel Rachad Mehanna with his thick beard and membership of the Muslim Brothers was the most outstanding figure of this royalist front; the Republic was not proclaimed until June 18th 1953.

The cult of legitimacy as vesting in Egyptians, and not in an individual, is one of their most important national characteristics. For them, it means law, order and peace; it does not imply any idea of dictatorship or tyranny. Law, peace and order epitomise, in the minds of this ancient civilisation, liberty, justice and progress. It is essential to understand these very deep roots if one is to grasp what may appear paradoxical in the conscience and conduct of the Egyptian citizen.

The second line in this specifically Egyptian character is the fact that there has never been a civil war in their history. They may have been against the local sultan, but they united nationally in peaceful action. Their union is total when there is a war of liberation to be waged against an occupying force; then they sacrifice their blood with legendary courage. In fact, with the Egyptians there is no middle way (as some people claim on the basis of geographical illusions). Nor have they any tendency to resignation, as some others think, on the basis of historical illusions about Egyptian psychology. Even when they look on at the struggles of the conquerors among themselves, that does not mean they are passive. They let the antagonists weaken each other, and deal the finishing blow to the survivor.

The idea of the unanimity of the people in war and peace goes back to the importance of the land in the life of the Egyptians, masters of the most ancient agrarian civilisation known to man. The union of God and King in ancient Egyptian doctrines is a reflection, more complex it is true, of the union of man with the land. The legitimacy of the king is the dimension of his bonds with the Absolute, which his land and his subjects know through the

rays of the sun and the waters of the Nile. The legitimacy of the king on earth
is the fruit of his bonds with the earth and with men. The ancient Egyptian
religions, beginning with the revolution of Akhenaton, were simply sociological
expressions of both oneness and multiplicity in the social history of Egypt;
they have always been two interpenetrating aspects of one and the same
essence: peaceful unanimity to change a regime – that is to say, withdraw
legitimacy from it – in order to free the land and its people and offer legitimacy to the one who leads the war, who achieves the victory. It was the
Egyptian people who placed Muhammad Ali on the throne when he made
Egypt independent of the Ottoman Empire; it was they who dethroned King
Farouk, the last descendant of the Alawite dynasty; it was always the people
who conferred or denied legitimacy. It was also the Egyptian people who,
behind the officer Ahmad Orabi, faced the Khedive in the great square of
Abdin. And it was they who supported Gamal Abd An-Nasser in the same
great square. And perhaps it granted legitimacy to him only when he led the
war of 1956.

All these meanings, or their shadows, were certainly in President Sadat's
mind, or at least in his unconscious, as he made his way to Parliament on the
morning of 16th October 1973. He must without any doubt have had the
unshakeable conviction that these people had assembled spontaneously
to offer him that *'bay ah'*, that oath of allegiance for which he had waited
since 1970. His initial legitimacy was based on the fact that he was the deputy
of Gamal Abd An-Nasser and one of the men still in power from the July
revolution. This formal legitimacy was deeply shaken by the measures he had
taken on May 14th 1971 to confirm the putsch following the sudden death
of the leader of the revolution. The new, real legitimacy was more necessary
than the one he had seized for himself, not only the better to consolidate all
the measures taken previously, but also to justify what was to happen later,
and to put the new regime on its feet. But, from the October war, the
Egyptian people understood something which the President did not mean to
say. In his autobiography the President speaks of the troubles of the students
and intellectuals.

> In my speech of 28th September 1973, I declared total amnesty for
> students and journalists. . . I even cancelled the trials where they were
> to appear as the accused, and they were all people of the left. The left-
> wing opposition seized the opportunity to interpret it as the sign of a
> national reconciliation for the purpose of consolidating the home front.
> No one dreamed that it was part of my plan for war.[36]

This was a surprising admission; for in fact the desire for national unity, which
was the basic reason for freezing the 'exceptional measures', according to the
left wing's interpretation, was not taken into account at all by President
Sadat, even though it was the very basis of the unanimity with which the
people granted him legitimacy. But the most surprising thing is the fact that
the amnesty for students and journalists was only part of the plan for war, as

though this amnesty were simply a manoeuvre. In fact the vicissitudes of the war, its military and political consequences, confirmed what the President had said; for with the war, President Sadat made a bargain the like of which has never been seen in history: if he advanced a few kilometres on the east bank of the Suez Canal, it was to make possible the opposite road to that of war, the road to Jerusalem — something which not only the left never dreamed of, but which nobody ever dreamed of at all.

The Non-Victory and the Non-Defeat

The first week of the war of October 1973 played an exceptional part in the life of the Egyptian people and of its leader, thanks to the nation's armed forces. Although the President obtained his longed-for legitimacy, it could not have been what he really wanted; he took the form, that is to say the popular will to liberation, and rejected the content: the unity of people and the land. If President Sadat had been capable of uniting people and the land in a war to free them both, he would surely have outshone all the glory of national heroism in the history of Egypt from Ahmad Orabi to Nasser. But that is a hypothesis without any scientific foundation, for no one can go beyond himself and all those things that, objectively, makes up his personality. That is why, at the moment when, in the glare of the limelight, he tried to offer the land in exchange for his own legitimacy, at the moment when he was trying to capture the people's loyalty, he lost the land itself. He lost it symbolically, by the Israeli counter-movement across to the west of the Canal. He lost it strategically, by the impossibility of obtaining a political gain superior to that obtained by the armed forces when they effectively regained part of the occupied territory. In reality that loss was not only the President's lot, but also that of the people, who lost the gamble of legitimacy; it was also the lot of the army whose victory was besmirched. The military forces of Egypt were surprised to see the Supreme Commander of the Armed Forces offer to the enemy, on the 16th of October, a solution to the conflict other than that of arms, when the armed conflict had not yet reached the conclusion that was its aim. It is true that the leaders of the Egyptian army after the defeat of 1967 did not plan for the liberation of Palestine; but it is also true that they had planned for the liberation of Sinai, at least as far as the Passes. Whatever reservations one may have about the political leanings of some of the military leaders, their aim had never changed. That was the hidden reason behind the successive clashes between these leaders and the President, who hastened to change them. It seems that Ahmed Ismail, now dead, who was Minister for War after Marshal Sadeq, was the only one to know the President's political intention — the decision to pass through, not to liberate. The increasing gap between political and military decisions was at the bottom of the many complications arising with the end of the war and the beginning of diplomatic negotiations. We can summarise them as follows.

The Israeli movement westwards, whatever it might be, put the Egyptian

Third Army into a difficult situation. It also decided the final result of the war – a 'draw'. This was a double wrong: first because the Egyptian armed forces had proven their capacity to liberate Sinai completely, a goal they were prevented from attaining in political, not military terms. The Egyptian armed forces are not equal to those of Israel, they are superior. Second, because the liberation of some kilometres of our territory and the retention of almost all Sinai under continued Israeli occupation cannot be said to be the result of a 'draw', even if there had been no Israeli counter-move. In either case there is no equality.

There is a formula 'neither victory no defeat', a corollary of the formula 'neither war nor peace'; it was in reality only a military preparation for the political idea that the two adversaries were equal, and that in consequence it was possible to meet, negotiate and agree directly, and pass through all the stages of the road in the opposite direction – to Jerusalem. The Egyptian President was true to himself when, at the height of the war, he appealed for negotiation. To go on with the war would inevitably lead to results opposed to all his calculations. The nation, wounded since 1967, was not in a position to see clearly; it could easily believe, while swearing allegiance to its President, that he was addressing the whole world – and not only the enemy – from a position of strength and victory.

The truth was clear to the military; hence all the dramatic changes in leading posts which could have an influence on military thought and strategic planning.[37]

The status quo is simply a theoretical explanation of a non-existent reality, otherwise this situation would have to be called an armistice. What is the meaning of this theoretical euphemism if we are at war with Israel, from the battle of Ras Al-Uch through the scuttling of the vessel *Eilat* and the battle for the island of Chadwan, to the war of attrition? The political truth is defeat, since it was we who declared war without achieving its aims, or the aims of the nation, or those of the military. The only aim achieved was that of the President and the social coalition he represents. This inevitably led to many concessions, going so far as to visit Jerusalem without the slightest change being made in the enemy's position. This series of retreats began, in practice, with the speech of 16th October 1973; but they reached an unbridled rate because of the complications following the breach opened in the west. In the speech it was said:

> We are ready to accept the ceasefire on the basis of an immediate retreat of the Israeli forces from all occupied territory, under international control, to the lines of 5th June 1967 . . . We are ready, immediately after the retreat from all these territories, to attend an international peace conference at the United Nations . . . I will do my best to persuade the representatives of the Palestinian people to take part with us.

The military were surprised by this speech and by the moment when it was uttered, since they knew better than anyone else what was going on, for the new situation arising west of Suez necessitated, not negotiation, but the pursuit of military tasks; the simple soldier in Sinai was no less surprised. And although this offer was not discussed with companions-in-arms on the other fronts, those who called themselves moderates believed that the application of such a programme was achieving some aspirations without abdication and without direct negotiation. But all, without exception, were surprised to see the orator accepting the ceasefire, before Israel's retreat from the occupied territories that had been stipulated by Resolution 338 of the Security Council.

On 9th November 1973, Henry Kissinger, the American Secretary of State, sent Kurt Waldheim, the Secretary-General of the United Nations, a message, telling him that the Egyptian President — in an Army tent pitched at kilometre 101 on the Cairo-Suez road — had just accepted a 6-point agreement. The agreement was signed by Colonel Muhammad Abd-El Ghani Al-Gamasi (Deputy Chief of the General Staff at the time and now Minister for War) and by General Aaron Yariv, at the time Deputy Chief of the General Staff of the Israeli forces. It stipulated:

1) Egypt and Israel agree to respect the ceasefire decided by the Security Council.
2) The two parties agree to begin negotiations immediately to solve the problem of a return to the lines of the ceasefire of 22nd October, under a military disengagement controlled by the United Nations.
3) The town of Suez will receive a daily provision of food, water and medicines, with evacuation of all wounded civilians.
4) No obstacle will be put in the way of the transport of non-military supplies for the East Bank.
5) All Israeli checkpoints on the Cairo-Suez road will be replaced by international checkpoints. Towards the end of the road, near the town of Suez, Israeli officers may take part with United Nations forces in the checking of non-military loads on the bank of the Canal.
6) Immediately after the establishment of international checkpoints on the Cairo-Suez road, the exchange of prisoners of war, including wounded, will begin.[38]

The kilometre 101 meeting, and the 6-point agreement, were a radical backward step even compared to the speech of October 16th, which was already tantamount to an abandonment of the war. The meeting constituted a direct agreement with the enemy on our occupied territories. That was only a sample in miniature of the scenes which were to take place up to the visit to Jerusalem. The bigger the scene, the greater were the concessions on others' rights, rights of which only the interested parties could dispose. On 21st December 1973, the Geneva Conference was inaugurated in the presence of representatives of Egypt, Israel, Jordan, the United States and the Soviet Union. The members present approved the agreement quoted above, which put an end to any comments by President Sadat. So all the cards were put in the hands of the United States.

We have to interpret the evolution of the new Egyptian regime in the light of its attachment to the military agreement concluded with Israel, and its political agreement concluded with the United States. Both are simply two sides of the same coin; we shall see this when we examine more closely the economic, social and political events lived through by Egypt from this substitute for war to the second Sinai Agreement, when the government found a strategic expedient.

Earlier, on 14th June 1974, the Egyptian regime had reached a politically decisive point marked by the visit to Cairo of the American ex-President Richard Nixon. At the end of this visit, a declaration was published under the title:

> **Principles of Relations and Co-operation between Egypt and the United States**
> 1) A just peace means the application of Resolution 242 of the Security Council, taking into consideration the interests of the people of the region and the right to existence of their States.
> 2) Peace can be achieved by negotiations and according to Resolution 338 of the Security Council.
> 3) The two countries must intensify their consultations, consolidate their economic, scientific, technical and touristic co-operation and take steps to achieve peace.
> 4) The two countries consider the meeting of the two Presidents as the first meeting of the Egypto-American Co-operation Committee, 31st May 1974.

The Egyptian and American Ministers for Foreign Affairs were to consult with a view to defining common programmes:

> **Support from the United States for the Egyptian Financial Situation**
> 6) To begin negotiations concerning co-operation on nuclear energy for peaceful ends. Egypt undertakes to give all the guarantees demanded by the United States to prohibit the use of a reactor for military purposes.
> 7) To set up study groups for the deepening of the Suez Canal, the increase of American private investments in Egypt, the increase of Egyptian agricultural production, technological exchanges and scientific research, the development of medical research, and also cultural exchanges.
> 8) To form a common economic council, comprising representatives of the private sector of both countries.
> 9) The United States undertakes to provide the aid necessary for Egyptian economic development.
> 10) To help Egypt to rebuild the Opera House.
> 11) Both countries decide to do everything possible to consolidate the ties of friendship and co-operation in the interest of both countries.[39]

To those who know the customary formulas of official statements, it was clear that the Egypto-American Agreement automatically abrogated the Egypto-Soviet Treaty of Friendship, which had already been abrogated in fact. Article 4 of the latter Treaty stipulates the undertaking of both contracting parties to fight *against imperialism and to liquidate colonialism, totally and finally.* In Article 10 both parties undertake *not to conclude international treaties conflicting with the Treaty.* But in fact it was two years before the Treaty was officially abrogated. The President did not present the plan for abrogating the Egypt-Soviet Treaty of Friendship and Co-operation until March 14th 1976; during this period two extremely serious events were to occur: the outbreak of the Lebanese war on April 13th 1975, and the signing of the second Sinai Agreement on September 12th of the same year.

Was there, concealed in President Sadat's mind, an impeccably worked out scenario, from the Israeli-Arab war to the Lebanese civil war and the second Sinai Agreement? But this question leads to another, even more important: was this substitute for war a prelude to the Lebanese war and the road to Jerusalem?

If we want the strategic meaning of the question to be clear, it must be couched in social, not individual terms. This is so that we can make clear the phenomenon of the reception given to Nixon and that given to Sadat on his return from Israel, whatever might be the exaggerations of the Egyptian media and whatever the number of demonstrators paid or compelled to be present.

The majority of Egyptians do not know even today that on 16th October 1973, that day so charged with meaning, the President of the Republic signed Decree No. 1637 concerning the ratification of the agreement between Egypt and the Federal Republic of Germany on the importation of wheat.[40] Do they know that on 15th November 1973 the President of the Republic ratified Decree No. 1905 concerning the acceptance of two agreements, one loan, the other guarantee, with regard to the project for development and exploitation of a deposit of natural gas at Aboukir; Treaties signed between Egypt and the Kuwait Bank of Arab Economic Development, at Kuwait on July 4th 1973?[41]

In addition, on 26th January 1974, the President of the Republic ratified Decree No. 6 authorising the Minister of Oil and Mineral resources to treat with the Egyptian Oil organisation and the German crude oil import company DEMINEX for prospecting, boring and exploiting oil in the area of the Gulf of Suez.[42] On 30th January 1974, Presidential Decree No. 7 was published, concerning the creation of the Arab Company of Soned Pipelines, consisting of Egypt, Kuwait, Saudi Arabia, Abu Dhabi and Qatar; the articles of this company stipulate that the shareholders should receive the profits of their shares in free currency, that the company should not be subject to the normal laws regulating monetary matters, nor to those regulating limited liability companies, general organisations and companies in the nationalised sector.[43]

On March 17th 1974 Presidential Decree No. 337 was published, concerning the creation of an international Arab organisation for economic co-operation. The specific function of this is to organise, develop and consolidate economic and technical relations with other Arab countries, with technical assistance organisations and international, regional and national financing institutions. Its function is thus to encourage Arab and foreign investments.[44]

All these decrees were crowned in the same year by the global Law No. 43 of 1974 concerning Arab and foreign investment and the free zones. This law grants privileges to Arab and foreign capital in the field of investment banks and business banks, the activities of which are limited to operations carried out in free currency, so long as these banks depend on organisations the headquarters of which are abroad (Para. B of Article 4). Landed properties cannot be alienated so as to be devoted to investment projects (Article 5). According to Article 10: companies benefiting from this law are not subject to Law No. 73 of 1973 concerning the definition of conditions and methods of election of worker representatives on the administrative councils, productive units of the nationalised sector, limited companies, associations and private organisations. These companies are exempted from the laws, statutes and decrees organising imports. Companies benefiting from this law can import without previous authorisation, directly or through a third party, everything they need for their establishment and running: raw materials, machines, tools, spare parts and transport equipment required for their activities. These operations are exempted from submission to decision-making committees. Article 16 stipulates: Without affecting any other more favourable exemption from taxation contained in other laws, the profits of these companies are exempted from all taxes on commercial and industrial profits and supplementary income; their shares are exempt from stamp duty and from duty on transferable assets and their supplements. These exemptions are also applicable to profits reinvested in the same companies.

What is the social and economic significance of these measures and laws? Why were they decided parallel with the military disengagement with Israel and the consolidation of political relations with the United States? What is the connection of all that with the balance of social forces within Egypt?

In Search of an Alternative

Here we have a right to reply implicitly to the question of this substitute for war and to find out whether all these affairs are only scenes from a perfect scenario in the President's mind. Social truth tells us that war was the only way for the putsch, not only to acquire constitutional legitimacy (the unanimity of the people) but also to be able to prepare the substitute regime by laying the foundations on which it was to be built. The military movement towards the east was the only way to its economic and political movement towards the West. That is what I meant when I brought forward the idea of the bargain, brilliantly negotiated by the President when he wished to separate land and men, that is, to loosen the bonds of the Egyptian people with the revolution, or abort the possible revolution by a substitute for war; it was then that Egyptians understood something which the President did not mean to say. It is also what I meant when I brought forward the idea of the union of the land with man in the history of Egyptian civilisation; a union which does not lie in the political geography of Egypt. . . a union of which the elements are indissociable. For Mr Sadat's regime, then, it was impossible to recover the land, even if the attempt at recovery went as far as concluding the second Sinai Agreement. The visit to Jerusalem wrote that word *impossible* in very large letters, and in several languages.

And all this has no part in the President's diligent search or his personal temperament. It was, in the first place, only a representation of the balance of social forces which was disturbed on May 14th 1971 — to the advantage of the new coalition of classes in power. The social content of the new regime, mainly founded on agrarian capitalism and the moneylending sector of mercantile capitalism, demanded definite economic decisions and a strategic transformation in the very structure of the regime. The fact of having eliminated the traditional international ally (the socialist bloc) from the game of peaceful settlement, the fact of persecuting national opposition, is only the political form of what is called economic opening up in an underdeveloped and occupied country. A developed capitalist country, associated with the international capitalist system, can establish balanced relationships with the two great blocs; internally it is freely open to all political forces. Undeveloped capitalism, and its corollary non-productive capitalism, cannot become equal associates with international capitalism; they can only turn in their own orbit. That is why we cannot say that the President's mind contained a scenario in serial form; there were strategic bases for the social coalition represented by the President; and this coalition, on the evening of 14th May 1971, presented a request to join an international system equivalent to the non-aligned bloc. Between 1971 and 1973 it gave the guarantees, assurances and recommendations demanded. The substitute for war was the greatest document thanks to which the regime won an exceptional double legitimacy: the unanimity of the people at home, and its recognition by the West through the intermediary of the United States. The presence of the American State Department, the Pentagon and the White House in the Middle East arena was a material and direct presence, from the end of the war and the first disengagement Agreement to the second Sinai Agreement; this presence was simply an official recognition of the new member of the group of satellites in the American orbit. It was from that moment that there was a scenario, not in the mind of the Egyptian government, but elsewhere. In fact the government was beginning to receive directives from American strategic planning organisations, for a satellite member does not decide, nor take part in the making of decisions. It has only to carry them out.

But though we do not say that the Egyptian regime and its President had a scenario from the beginning, we cannot say either, that American strategy did all the planning and carrying out. The conservative Arab powers were also present in the arena, either by their offers or their obstructions. We can in fact say that our contemporary Arab history is going through a *Saudi* period.[45] This may give a rather exaggerated picture of the Saudi role, and the justification for so calling it may imply, directly or indirectly, some approval of this role, but we cannot neglect the fact that it was the putsch in Egypt which led the conservative Arab powers to play an active and exceptional part. And because exaggeration was master of Egypt's home political situation, the help of the conservative Arab powers could not save either the Egyptian economy or the Egyptian government; their organic alliance with the West could not lead to decisive political outcomes as far as Israel is concerned. That is why the negative reflection of this role was doubled on the Egyptian home front. On the socio-cultural plane, the small groups of the religious extreme right, the promulgation by Parliament of theocratic laws, and the religious conflicts, filled the whole of the home stage. On the political plane, the average Egyptian felt deeply hostile to everything Arab; he could not make the distinction between Arabism and Arab conservatism; the formidable obscurantism of the Egyptian media was there to prevent him from doing so.

Israel, side by side with the Egyptian and Arab conservative forces, also helped to prepare the ground for the American plan, by signing the first military disengagement Agreement on both frontiers, by signing the second Sinai Agreement, and by intervening in the Lebanese war from both a military and political point of view. All these elements gave American strategy the necessary means for practical action to attain two principal aims:

1) To cause Egyptian independence to collapse in order to change the balance of international forces in the Middle East, Africa and some countries of the non-aligned bloc. For Egypt, even when poor and exhausted by its population explosion, is still, as it was two centuries ago, the main key enabling the developing world to get to the raw materials necessary for industrial development, to the maritime shipping routes, and to strategic military positions. For Egypt to abandon the independence of a free country in order to enter the American orbit is the greatest gain for the United States, after the Second World War.[46]

2) To weaken the Soviet presence in the region and replace the Zionist danger by the communist danger; this constitutes an important obstacle to all future radical development; in this way the oil resources will be protected. On the other hand, this will consolidate the legitimate existence of Israel and put the Soviets in a defensive position in other regions.

So a great Egyptian jurist, Dr. Wahid Rafat, could write: 'The Communist danger is threatening the security of the region, and is becoming more serious than the Zionist danger which we have pledged ourselves to fight.'[47] So also, it was possible for the President of the largest Arab country to recognise Israel in Jerusalem itself, without recompense or even the promise of recompense.

This substitute for war, then, was only the military formulation of an economic decision which has been called the economic opening up of Egypt to Western capitalism. It was also a strategic expedient with the second Sinai Agreement. These two points form the alternative long sought by the new regime, which in its turn, represents the alternative long sought by the West.

The only problem which arose from time to time was to find an adequate political formula for both decisions, economic and strategic. If, originally and by definition, a putsch is not carried out by but against democracy, how is it possible to have recourse to it in a case of strategic change? From the beginning there was a latent contradiction between the idea of economic opening up (meaning movement towards a backward satellite capitalist regime) and a liberal political ideology which needs productive capitalism, as is the case in India, Portugal, Spain, Turkey, Japan or the Federal Republic of Germany (despite their specific differences, these are countries full of weak points as a consequence of the Second World War, or of earlier Fascist regimes, or the scarcity of raw materials, or galloping over-population).

This critical situation with regard to internal politics is at the bottom of this curious groping between the formula of multiple platforms within the Socialist Union and the formula of political parties which the regime tried to set up as a background to its own party. But as this latter formula was taken seriously by the Egyptian people, the government hastened to pull up its democratic signboard, suppressed one party and froze another. The President recently declared his intention of creating a new party. Thus, indirectly, he is recognising the illegitimacy of the government party, its bitter failure to solve present problems and its incapacity to face the opposition of the man-in-the-street.

Why did this alternative fail to convince Egyptians despite the impact of the October war? We can always find the answer in the special nature of Egypt — both explicitly and implicitly expressed. In economic terms, prices of consumer goods rose in 1973 beyond all expectations. This inflation reminds us of the situation in 1950-51 just before the revolution of July 1952.[48] This rise was the preamble to the open economy justified by an official study entitled: *The Egyptian Economy in 1973.* 'An exceptional monetary expansion,' says this study, 'which had never been achieved in the past 20 years, and the influence of which was felt in the record price figures, and which has more than doubled the increase of 1972.'[49] This very steep rise in prices was not due only to world inflation; the study already quoted informs us of a fall in agricultural production and consequently in the production of foodstuffs of 2% each with respect to the preceding year, while the population was increasing at a rate of 2.24% per year, which must of necessity lead to a fall in the minimum average individual share in agricultural and food production of 2%. In addition, 'the production of electricity during the year 1973 had fallen by 1% with respect to the preceding year.'[50] This indicates a deterioration in manufacturing and services dependent on the production of electricity. These were the preambles to the open economy which was crowned by non-military foreign debts estimated at about $6 billion for the years 1973-1975.[51] There is no need to recall that in that same year (1975) in September, the second Sinai Agreement, the acme of post-October war diplomacy was concluded.

A Halt on the Road to Jerusalem

Between the war of October 1973 and the visit to Jerusalem in November 1977, the Second Sinai Agreement was, as it were, a principal halt, which led most observers astray; they had thought that the settlement train was going to Geneva. The many readings of this Agreement in different languages forgot to put the Egyptian dots on the Arab 'I's. That is to say, they forgot to take Egypt as the starting point for the understanding of what was happening in Lebanon, and for a general view of the map of the Middle East after the last changes. An agreement is not simply a provisional military treaty between two countries, but rather a precise setting out of ends and means, providing a global view of the alliance of classes dominating the Egyptian government.

It is not simply the fruit of a number of causes, nor is it the result of the addition of several factors. An agreement implies a continous movement in time and space, and not a document enshrined for ever in the museum of history.

The social, political, economic or cultural details may seem a long way from the general background of the Sinai Agreement. But on reflection, we realise the essence of this agreement and its authentic meaning, which is related to the various aspects of our life.

For example: concerning foreign policy, we can given an African case. Let us take the episode of the Egyptian Vice-President's visit to Addis Ababa at the time of the African O.A.U. summit talks about the problem of Angola, voting for or against the seating of the Angolan people's movement, M.P.L.A. This summit was to give the great African leaders the chance to reflect on the future of the former Portuguese colony. And what was the position of Egypt, whose whole past is rich in examples of support given to African liberation movements; Egypt, the friend of Sekou Toure, Nkrumah and Lumumba? Egypt, who one day arrested Tshombe? Mr Husni Mubarek, Vice-President of the Egyptian Republic, rose to say that the three Angolan movements should be associated in a National Government, and that there was no reason to recognise a single one of these three movements separately from the others. He was thus repeating exactly what the United States had said. Mr Mubarek knew perfectly well that two of these three movements were financed by the United States, supported with troops and weapons by the racist government of South Africa, and backed by mercenaries from the four corners of the colonial West. He knew that the C.I.A. was not far from the battlefields, because it was supporting puppet groups with experience, training, money, weapons and even active participation in the struggle. Naturally, when the legitimate government, the government of the people's movement, was victorious, Egypt recognised it, and the Organisation of African Unity accepted Angola as a full member. The United States of America became reconciled to this, at least for a time, through the intermediary of their Secretary of State during his last African tour. Could this have happened before the Sinai Agreement? Indeed not, for in the matter of foreign policy, this Agreement meant that Egyptian decisions depended on those of the United States.

This example came after the Agreement. We can give another, preceding the Salzburg Agreement and having a direct bearing on our national problem. This is the Congress of Kampala, at which the Palestine Liberation Organisation was present, as the political climate was favourable to the taking of a historic decision – to eject Israel from the General Assembly of the United Nations. At Khartoum, just before his arrival at Kampala, President Anwar Al-Sadat declared that he saw no point in ejecting Israel from the international organisation, the decisions of which it is bound to respect. He added that Israel would be very pleased with such a decision, which would free it from all international constraints. Both justifications are wrong. The United Nations has never forced Israel to apply its decisions, from 1948 until today. Besides, Israel had always had its hands free, whether or not it was a member of the international community. Actually, neither Israel, the United States, nor the West in general would have been pleased at the call to eject Israel. They all had recourse to clear declared positions on all the countries in the world, so that the question would not be put to the vote. Since then, and even today, they are all filled with rage at the idea of discussing such a problem. The Congress of Arab countries at Kampala, when it saw Egypt opposing a primary decision in that direction, could come to no decision. Would such a position have been possible in any other climate than that of preparation for the Second Sinai Agreement? Preparations aiming above everything to prove to Israel and the United States the good intentions of Egypt? Such a proof could only end in the subjection of Egyptian decision-making centres to considerations which contradict the foundations of national policy, and its most sensitive areas, which means the Israel-Arab conflict.

At the level of internal politics, we can take a small example which might at first appear irrelevant or futile. I mean the law forbidding Egyptians to drink alcohol in public places. The example is futile, because more than 35 million workers, peasants and people with very low incomes are in no way concerned with such a law. They are satisfied with bitter tea, tobacco or cigarettes, and at the very best, the hookah.

And yet this example has its serious implications. Egypt, the mother of a great civilisation, distinguished among the countries of the Third World and the Arab states for its intellectual refinement, Egypt, which has always had its living traditions to give it the strength of continuity, this Egypt is told that alcohol is a sin in the street but permitted in private. It is told that a woman's song is illicit because her voice is impure; tomorrow she will be told not to leave her home and will be forced once more to wear the veil. Today it is repeated that the world *socialism* is forbidden, because it is not mentioned in the Koran; that a thief's hand must be cut off, and that . . . and that . . . there is no end to the prohibitions and retributions rightly or wrongly imputed to the Muslim religion.

Whether they are right or wrong, the authorities are moving towards the application of Islamic law in a country where a person's faith has never been a matter for questioning, in a country whose children have been struggling for more than a century and a half against theocracy. These same authorities do not include among crimes punishable by decapitation or the loss of a hand, direct, indirect, secret or public prostitution; they do not include organised pillage, bribes, misappropriation of public funds, parasitism on production, back-door brokerage operations, licit and illicit monopolies – all that gets through the so-called *opening-up*. As for alcohol, women's voices, the word socialism and any attacks against the United States, those are impious things, expressly forbidden by the Koran!

What is at the bottom of this alcohol business? It began with the meeting of 38 Deputies under the vault of the People's Council. They decreed that alcohol was illicit for Egyptians, licit for tourists, illicit for citizens in bars, clubs and public festivals, licit for them in houses and bedrooms! Simple people, blinded by the watchword *Infitah* (opening), said this was striking a blow against economic expansion. They took up their pens, worked their calculators and hastened to denounce the evil consequences of such a law on the national economy. Humourists were quick to laugh at the formalistic character of this law, which would compel a provincial from Upper Egypt to put on a hat and ask the barman, in execrable English, for a glass of spirits! A Christian writer, the late Sami Daoud, had the courage to write that the principle of freedom of religion gives the Christian citizen the right to drink alcohol because the Gospels do not forbid it; one of the miracles of Jesus was the changing of water into wine during a wedding, that is to say a public festival. As the good Egyptian proverb says, *every knot has someone to untie it:* the Ministry of Tourism, whose Minister, incidentally, was a Christian, published a statement that the law in question would have no effect on tourism and thus on the national economy, at least from that point of view; the same statement omits to take into account the influence of this law on the black market, inflation and the losses to vineyards and factories making alcoholic drinks, with all the unemployment that goes with it. We are speaking only from the point of view of the government's national economy, without making the slightest allusion to the socio-cultural meaning of such a law, more serious than the law itself – or than alcohol. A hypocrite, a priest and member of the People's Council told a gratuitous lie, saying that the Christian religion forbade alcohol, exactly like Islam. Finally, the People's Council met and unanimously decided to accept the law.

Here it would perhaps be more interesting to underline two historic events. The first took place before the October war, during a meeting of the Presidential Council of the Union of Arab countries. President Muammar Al-Kadhafi asked for the application of Islamic law in the countries of the Union, insisting on this question of alcohol. The second took place after the October war: His Majesty King Feisal made it a condition of Saudi economic aid to Egypt that Islamic law should be applied in such a way that socialism (which is what he called the Egyptian regime) would be eliminated from the economy, from politics, education and instruction; he emphasised – may God have mercy on his soul! – the necessity to change the education programme to an Islamic programme, and also the necessity to forbid alcohol as it was *a defilement and the work of the Devil.*

Despite the basic differences between the reasoning of the two, between Kadhafi's position and that of Feisal, and although Kadhafi did not practise blackmail, the attitude of the Egyptian leaders in both cases was clear on two points.

Firstly, although the percentage of Muslims who drink alcohol is much greater than that of Christians, such a prohibition would give the Egyptian Christians (and there are several million of them) a feeling of injustice, and would be a great affront to their freedom of belief, which does not forbid alcohol.

The second point is the fact that the reputation of Egyptian civilisation would, without any possible doubt, be dimmed by reaction following the serious blow to tourism and its economic effects. On that day, Kadhafi did not lay much stress on this point. As for King Feisal, he dwelt on it for a long time . . . . Even after departing for another world, since Saudi Arabia continues to insist on these conditions for aid to Egypt!

That is the real beginning of the history of the ban on Egyptians drinking alcohol in public places. Saudi Arabia knows perfectly well that our Arab brothers, beginning with Saudi subjects themselves, drink, in Egypt, much more than foreigners, and very much more than the Egyptians. But our Arab brothers, beginning with the Saudi subjects, do not go to cafes, to civilised cultured places, or to cheap little bars. They settle themselves in big hotels, in luxury furnished flats and in the night-clubs of the Street of the Pyramids. In the eyes of Egyptian law, they are foreigners, in no way affected by the prohibition which applies to Egyptians. Saudi Arabia's condition, then, was aimed at the heart of Egypt, as a civilisation, as a society, and as the epitome of the civilised Arab. While President Sadat was saying that the Egyptian debt had reached $8 billion, Saudi Arabia was piling up in American banks the sum of $28 billion for the year 1975 alone. Saudi Arabia offered Egypt only $300 million, and a condition of the offer was the creation of joint projects. The Saudi position with regard to the support of Syria is no better, in spite of the fact that it was the October war, waged by Egypt and Syria together, that was at the root of the rise in oil prices. What then is the reason for this parsimony?

The answer is that the Saudi money-tap is controlled by American levers. The United States succeeded in weakening Egypt from a military and political point of view, thanks to the conclusion of the Sinai Agreement — which pulled Egypt down from being part of the national liberation movement against colonialism to a position of dependence in the orbit of imperialist influence — and they have given Saudi Arabia the task of weakening it culturally, socially and morally. So the Saudi conditions, which seem religious in character, become a form of blackmail, aimed at forcing Egypt towards moral suicide. Egypt, fettered by its economic need, is thus turning backwards and becoming a veritable desert; not a stage-set desert, but a desert, like the desert of Saudi Arabia.

What the groups of Muslim Brothers and the small groups of the religious

extreme right did not succeed in doing for many decades, Saudi Arabia
appears to have done successfully. It is treating a few Egyptian Deputies as
it treated a few Lebanese Deputies, misleading them, urging them to vote to
prohibit Egyptians drinking alcohol in public places. It must be emphasised
once again, that this law in itself does not concern the vast majority of
Egyptians. But it is surely full of meaning for the face of civilised Egypt, for
public freedoms and for the freedom of religion according to the Constitution, which is even more serious. It may not mean much to the Christians
either, but it is an insidious introduction of a religious conflict foreign to
Egypt and the Egyptians. Today a law on alcohol, tomorrow a law on theft,
and so on — a never-ending sequence of Muslim laws which will, in the end,
lead to a religious society like Lebanese society before the massacre. That is
the real aim hidden behind the Saudi intervention, which could be added to
the Sinai Agreement, depending on American influence and the collapse of
the Egyptian economy after the so-called open economy.

By quoting these examples, serious and less serious, I have tried to prove
that the Sinai Agreement is not simply a document confirming the past, nor
a military agreement separating the forces fighting in Sinai, but a movement
continuous in time and space, an agreement which today gives birth to what
was yesterday in embryo. Tomorrow it will bring to birth something which
today is a simple microbe moving inside the body. This Agreement is the
total warrant of a regime coming to the end of an era. It is what we meant
when we spoke of a strategic expedient. That is why it was neither plausible
nor possible to draw up a programme of national action for the Egyptian
people, that is more than a strategy, without taking the Sinai Agreement as
the starting-point, with its different dimensions, dynamic, internal, Arab and
external, and on economic, military, social and cultural planes.

Notes

1. *The Diplomatic World,* July 1973. See also Hamid Rabi, *Al-Harb An-
   Nafsiyyah fi Al-Mantiqah Al-Arabiyyah,* Al-Mu'assassah Al-Arabiyyah
   Lil dirassah wa An-Nachr (Beirut 1974) pp. 75-97, in the chapter entitled
   La propagande sioniste et la defait de Juin. But read especially (pp.78-9)
   how Zionist propaganda makes a special point of reminding Western
   man of the merits of Jewish genius in the West, and saying that
   Christian tradition is only an extension of Hebrew tradition; how it
   transforms the famous European guilt complex into a responsibility
   complex; how it affirms that Europe is the civilisation responsible for
   the development of humanity; which obliges it to act in an energetic
   way so as to reflect its historical greatness and affirm its legitimate
   rights in the region.
2. *An-Nawah Ad-Dawkiyyat fi harb October,* Cairo, 27-31 October 1975,

Vol. I. military section, Idarat Al-Matbuat wa An-Nachr lil Quwwat Al-Musallahah (1976) pp.37-8.

3. Mahmoud Hussein, *Les Arabes au present* (Arabic translation) Dar At-Taliah (Beirut) p.32.

4. See Yasin Al-Hafez, *Al-A'qlaniyyah fi As-Siyassah* (Beirut 1975) p.199.

5. Quoted by Haykal in *Le chemin pour Ramadan.*

6. M.H. Haykal, *op.cit.*, p.48.

7. *Haaretz* of 30th November 1973 quoted in *As-Siraa'ala Ard At-Taswiyah Al-Israi'liyyah,* Dar At-Taliah (Beirut 1978) p.36.

8. Nagi Aluch, *Khata An-Nidal wa At-Taswiyah wa At-Tasfiyat,* Dar At-Taliah (Beirut, 1976) p.27.

9. *An-Nadwah Ad-Dawliyyat li harb October,* Vol. I, p.162.

10. Editorial by Lutfi Al-Khuli, editor-in-chief of *At-Taliah,* November 1973: 'The fourth war in the history of the Arab-Israeli conflict is the first on the road to liberation' (p.13). Those who took part in bringing out this issue followed his example. 'A just war of liberation', says Dr. Fuad Mursi (p.22). 'The war of national liberation has begun', Abd Al-Moneim al-Ghazali (p.23). The same idea was expressed, but in different terms, by Rifa't As-Said (p.47), Abu Seif Yusuf (p.50), Khayri Aziz (p.56) and by Dr. Ismail Sabri Abdallah (p.84). It was this same formula which served as a basis for the colloquium organised by *At-Taliah* on the theme 'The movement for Arab liberation after the 6th of October' (January 1974). Al-Ghazali had said that *the 6th of October marked the rebirth of the movement for Arab liberation.* The same expression was used by Said Khayyal; as for Murad Wahtah, professor of philosophy, he was to use the term 'qualitative change' to designate this date; Fuad Mursi agreed with this.

11. There are no precise texts about this interpretation, but the idea was current in extreme left-wing Arab circles without anyone daring to commit it to paper during the war. And very few dared to do it even when there was no doubt of the political consequences.

12. Elyas Farah, *Techrin Al-Awwal bayna At-Taswiyat wa At-Tahrir,* Dar At-Taliah (Beirut 1974), pp.5-60.

13. Yasin Al-Hafiz, *Al-A'qlaniyyah fi As-Siyassah,* pp.208-9.

14. Haykal, *op. cit.*, p.177.

15. *Ibid.,* p.200.

16. *Ibid.* This episode confirms once more the way in which the President acts with his collaborators: dismissal, arrest or exile for any attempt at opposition. This is what he did with Ali Sabri who, in February 1971, opposed the attempt to reopen the Canal as an alternative solution to war. He had the same attitude in 1972 towards his favourite, the Minister for War. Both were relieved of their functions and brought before the courts; one of them was imprisoned. The same with General Chazli, who was exiled first as Ambassador to London, then to Portugal, for having opposed the official attitude to the breach of the Outfall gate. As for the basis of the President's actions, the early attempts at an alternative solution, and the thesis of limited war, can only lead to one conclusion: the elimination of the war of liberation and a political and military search for a substitute for war.

17. *Ibid.,* p.164.

18. Henry Kissinger, *The Need for Choice*, Ch. IV, Introduction.
19. Saad Ad-Din Ibrahim, *Kissinger et les etapes du conflit au Moyen-Orient*, Dar At-Taliah (Beirut 1975) pp.99, 100,102,104,107.
20. 'The Middle East is the bridge joining Europe, Asia and Africa; on its soil the greatest travellers and traders were born. In every era, conquering armies marched over it, and three international religions have their roots there. Under its surface lies the greatest store of oil known in the world, the black gold on which we depend in this age of the machine.' D. Eisenhower, *The White House Years*, 'Waging Peace, 1956-1961', Doubleday (New York), p.20.
21. Saad Ad-Din Ibrahim, *op. cit.*, p.129.
22. Saad Ad-Din Ibrahim, 'An-Naft Al-Arabi burat al-Ihtimam Al-Alami' in *Ad-Duwal Al-Kubra wa As-Sirah Al-Arabi Al-Israili*. 'The stage of political regression organised by the Egyptian regime, supported by Saudi Arabia, led to serious concessions in the matter of oil; this enabled the big cartels to find their second wind after the chain of restrictions that had been imposed on them at the direct behest of Saudi Arabia and Egypt, and under Saudi-Egyptian pressure.' (p.14). See also: Sadeq Al-Azm, *Siyassah Carter wa munaziru Al-Hiqbah As-Su'udiyyah*, Dar At-Taliah (Beirut 1977).
23. Taher Abd Al-Hakim, *Khatwah khatwah min Al-Udwan ila Ar-Riddat*, Dar Al-Thaoura Al-Iraqiyyah (Baghdad 1967), pp.16-17.
24. *Researches on the colloquium, op. cit.*, p.27.
25. *Ibid.*, Vol. I, p.102.
26. M.H. Haykal, *At-Tariq lla Ramadan* (Arab edition) (Beirut 1975).
27. *Ibid.*, p.98.
28. *Ibid.*, p.209.
29. *Ibid.*, p.215.
30. *Ibid.*, p.216.
31. *Researches on the colloquium*, Vol. I, p.55.
32. *Ibid.*, p.190.
33. Haykal, *op.cit.*, p.212.
34. Tahir Abd Al-Hakim, *Hawla Harb Tichrin wa At-Taswiyah Al-Amir kiyyah*, Al-Muassassah al-Arabiyyah lil dirasat, (Beirut 1974) pp.203ff.
35. See D. Hamid Rabit, *Silah Al-Bitrul wa As-Sirah Al-Arabi Al-Israili*, Al-Muassassah Al-Arabiyyah lil Dirasat, (Beirut 1974), pp.203ff.
36. See Anwar Sadat, *A la recherche d'une identite* (Arabic edition) p.330.
37. In his book *A la recherche d'une identite*, President Sadat accuses all the important Army chiefs, except Marshal Ahmed Ismail, of cracking up, although they had planned and carried out the crossing of the Canal. This presentation of the facts must be corrected by reading three of the most important interviews given by Marshal Saad Ad-Din Al-Chazil, to Samir Karam in the Lebanese magazine *Al-Kifah Al-Arabi*, 3rd July 1978; to Nabil Moghrabi in *Al-Watan Al-Arabi*, July 1978, and to Ibrahim Salamah in *Al-Mustaphal* July 1978; besides the documents presented by Samir Nada in the Iraqi magazine *Alif Ba* on 12th July, and 9th and 26th August 1978.
38. See the Lebanese daily *An-Nahar* of 12th January 1973.
39. See *Al-Ahram*, 15th June 1974.
40. See *Economic Report of the Egyptian National Bank*, Office of

Statistical Research, Volume 27, No. 2, Cairo, 1974, p.179.
41. *Ibid.*, p.160.
42. *Ibid.*
43. *Ibid.*, pp.160-1.
44. *Ibid.*, p.162.
45. On this subject, see the book by Sadeq Galal Al-Azm: *Le politique de Carter et les theoriciens de la periode saoudienne,* Dar At-Talia'h, (Beirut 1977).
46. On this subject read Taher Abd Al-Hakim: *Carter et le reglement au Moyen-Orient,* Dar Ibn Khaldoun (Beirut).
47. Cf. *An-Nahar Al-Arabi wa Ad-Dawli* of 12th October 1978.
48. Introduction to the official report of the Economic Bulletin (Egyptian National Bank, Bureau of Research and Statistics) Vol. 27, No. 3, (Cairo 1974) p.252.
49. *Ibid.*, Vol. 4, p.334.
50. *Ibid.*, pp.341, 344.
51. Article by Adel Hussein, 'La dette exterieure egyptienne, ses dimensions et ses consequences' in *Dirasat Arabiyyah,* June 1978.

PART 2
The Sinai Agreement –
A Strategic Turning-Point

5. Who Will Abrogate the Sinai Agreement?

The Sinai Agreement, concluded between Egypt and Israel in September 1975, is a culminating point in the development of the overall picture representing the attitude of the Egyptian bourgeoisie in regard to the national question which, in turn, represents the reference point for all the standpoints taken — social within the country, national on the Arab question, and external at the international level.

Indeed, taken together, the treaties concluded by Egypt with the West, and more recently with Israel, may present us with the historical context of the nationalism of the Egyptian bourgeoisie, with all that that context can contain by way of stages in the revolutionary progression and stages in the violent setbacks of the so-called liberal democracy. These treaties may clarify for us the metamorphoses which crystallised the internal laws of the historical evolution of modern Egypt, with all its negative and positive impacts on the Arab nation and on international policy.

Let us, at the outset, go back to the fifties and more precisely to 8th October 1951. Mustapha An-Nahhas, the leader of the Wafd, had made his historic declaration. For Egypt, he said, he had signed the 1936 treaty; for Egypt, he abrogated it. Following this resounding speech delivered in Parliament and when he was just about to take the train for Alexandria, the journalists questioned him on the next step. The Government has done its duty, he said; it is now up to the people.

It is now up to the people: this was war conducted by Egyptian resistance fighters against the British troops stationed along the banks of the Suez Canal.

Five years later, and indeed on 26th July 1956, we witness another historic scene: Gamal Abd El-Nasser proclaims the nationalisation of the Suez Canal and, shortly afterwards, unilaterally rescinds the evacuation treaty signed with Great Britain in 1954. The Egyptians resume 'action' on the banks of the Canal.

The abrogation of the 1936 Treaty is accompanied by an upward surge in the resistance movement, ending with the Cairo fire of 26th January 1952, the declaration of a state of emergency and the removal of the Wafdist Government. The abrogation of the 1954 Treaty is accompanied by an upward surge of resistance and the tripartite aggression by Britain, France and Israel against Egypt.

But there is a fundamental difference between 1951 and 1956: whereas the Cairo fire announced the fall of a whole regime, the tripartite aggression represented the birth certificate of the new regime. This difference shows the political significance of the historical evolution of the Egyptian bourgeoisie. The similarity between the attitude of Nahhas Pasha, who had signed and abrogated the 1936 Treaty, and that of Nasser who signed and then abrogated the 1954 Treaty, enables us to put our finger on the content and significance of this trend, in the light of which we are better able to understand this last Sinai Treaty; it may also enable us to distinguish the historical candidate who will undertake the task of abrogating that Treaty.

Let us first of all take a look at the 1936 Treaty and then at that of 1954, so as to appreciate in detail the historical context in which they were first signed, then abrogated, one after the other, by the same persons. Let us try to see whether the trend, a subjective one on the part of the Egyptian bourgeoisie and an objective one on the part of Egypt, can result in the reproduction of the two historical scenes, of 1951 and 1956. Or will the new context prevent any such repetition? In that event, should not 'other forces' be in control of the historical initiative to abrogate the new Treaty, with all its secret and apparent implications, both for the Arabs and internationally, and its political, economic and social implications? These forces could thus assume their responsibility for the future.

The 1936 Treaty was only the delayed political culmination of the 1919 revolution, for the dual struggle against colonialism and for democracy was the main Egyptian political action after the defeat of Orabi, even if the Egyptian social classes were not all agreed regarding the meaning of colonialism and democracy; and this inevitably involved disputes as to the most appropriate methods of struggling for independence and the constitution. The complex alliance, both as to degree and form, between the British occupation, the Palace and the rural aristocracy was one of the important factors which contributed towards the formation of the popular Egyptian opposition, the latter having identified its aims after identifying its enemies. Actually, any act of resistance against the British occupation was also and at the same time resistance to the dictatorship of the throne and the constitutional minorities. It was the middle strata of the young Egyptian bourgeoisie, under the direction of Saad Zaghlul, which succeeded in polarising the widest masses of the peasants, petty officials, artisans, students, the services and the workers for a revolution which was peaceful at the outset, but bloody later on. For the peaceful progress was soon converted into violent confrontations, from the moment when the occupation forces, centralised in the ranks of the police and the army, had recourse to their arms.

The 1919 revolution, immediately following the First World War and the victory of the Allies, was one of the premises for the Arab liberation movement. It was contemporary with similar movements in various parts of the great nation. New social forces throughout the Arab nation had just been emerging on to the political scene; they were hoping to escape from the colonial empire. The victory of the Allies represented for the peoples of the colonies the upward surge of democracy, and the October Revolution provided proof of a realisation which for so long had been considered impossible. But the Egyptian bourgeoisie, like its opposite numbers in the colonised regions, was so weak, backward, and socially involved with the strata of the land-owners that, following its 1919 revolution, it was unable to realise the aims defined by the middle classes or, even more, those taken up by the popular masses, such as the prospect of independence and democracy which had been so longed for by these downtrodden masses. It was able to obtain only the February 1922 Declaration and the 1923 Constitution. Both offered only a fragile independence and a formal democracy, and one which was too restric-ted. But, between 1923 and 1936, Egypt was constantly being subjected to terrorism, violence and dictatorship – the suspension of the Constitution, the dissolution of Parliament, the 1930 constitutional reform which gave the King tyrannical new privileges, the conquest of direct power by the aristocratic minorities, and British control over entries and departures from the country, not only economic but also political and military, etc.

Naturally, the Egyptian people never ceased struggling during all those years. The Wafd party, mainly representing the middle strata of the bourge-oisie, never ceased fighting for independence and democracy. But the economic forces of those social strata represented by the Wafd associated themselves more and more with the landed aristorcracy on the one hand and the foreign monopolies on the other. This left an indelible mark on the Wafd movement. For this reason, the Wafd gradually came nearer to the means and the aims which inspired certain minority parties, so that, at a certain moment, the re-establishment of the 1923 Constitution became an aim in itself, as though times had never changed. Throwing off the restrictions of 28th Feb-ruary 1922 became the peak of hopes, as though the world was no longer moving! In other words, the Wafd movement never went outside the 1919 limits; this could only result in the 1936 treaty, a kind of compromise and objectively a step backwards. In the last resort, the 1936 treaty is only a feeble realisation of the aims of the 1919 revolution or, more precisely, the aims sought by the leaders of the petty bourgeoisie and not those of the popular base. In reality, this falling back on the part of the Egyptian bourge-oisie was only the commencement of the decline in its historical capacity to represent the national aspirations of the Egyptian people.

The first article of the treaty signed on 26th August 1936 stipulated 'the end of the military occupation of Egypt by the forces of His Majesty the King and Emperor'. Great Britain officially recognised the sovereignty of Egypt, accepted the abrogation of foreign privileges and the mixed tribunals. Egypt was thus able to join the League of Nations as a full member. The two treaties of 1899 on the status of the Sudan were also abrogated, and a number of principal posts occupied by British officials, especially in the security organisations, were abolished. But the treaty retained naval bases in Egypt for Great Britain and the stationing of 10,000 ground troops. It also provided certain facilities in regard to passage by air and by land. Furthermore, the British army was entitled to take up its positions in Egypt again in the event

179

of war or the threat of war. In the field of international relations, Egypt was not entitled to conclude agreements in conflict with the clauses of the treaty. Great Britain was entitled to require Egypt to declare a state of emergency and a curfew. The treaty fixed a period of 20 years for the continued presence of British troops, at the end of that time the treaty could be re-examined.

Thus, it was not a 'treason treaty' according to the claim of the national party, but it was also no 'treaty of honour and independence', as claimed by Mustapha An-Nahhas. It was quite simply a compromise treaty. Actually, the economic and social tendency of the middle strata of the Egyptian bourgeoisie had passed from the 1919 revolutionary stage to the stage where it was looking for compromises, such as characterised the 1936 period, and this despite the fact that it had succeeded in re-establishing the Constitution and practically annulling the effects of the 28th February declaration. This is why we say that the 1936 treaty reversed 17 years of popular struggle. In the last resort, the 1936 treaty may be considered as a precursor of the affair of 4th February 1942, when, carried along by the armed colonial power, the Wafd agreed to return to power.

It is, perhaps, useful to recall in this connection the immediate reactions to the conclusion of the treaty. Mr Anthony Eden stated in the House of Commons on 24th November 1936: 'The reason which has led the Government to give up the occupation of Cairo and Alexandria and only to maintain the Canal Zone is that the British forces are fully mechanised; they are therefore easily able to move along the paved roads.' It should be added that the annexes to the treaty made the Egyptian Government responsible for building barracks for the occupation troops, (to their specifications) and also for the provision of a road network, with special characteristics, which would connect Cairo, Alexandria, Port Said, Ismailia, Suez and other towns.[1] Dr. Muhammad Hussein Haykal for his part opposed the military burdens imposed upon Egypt. The same opposition was expressed by Muhammad Mahmud Pasha in a famous declaration: 'These military commitments are contrary to Egypt's independence'.

Abd El-Azim Ramadan weighed up the benefits and disadvantages of the treaty thus:

> It enabled Egypt [he wrote] to enjoy internal independence within the limits permitted by the party struggles in Egypt, under the royalty and and the 1923 Constitution, and within the limits permitted by the sincerity of England, in the application of the clauses of that treaty in the course of the episode of 4th February 1942. This treaty enabled the revolution of 23rd July 1952 to take place without having to fear interference from Great Britain with a view to protecting the throne, which had been under the protection of the colonial power prior to the conclusion of the treaty. It enabled Egypt to enjoy its external independence to the extent of taking up a neutral position during the Korean War in 1950, and to the extent of not recognising Communist China and not having close relations with the Soviet Union. It enabled Egypt to enjoy

the alliance with Great Britain, which helped the latter to win the
Second World War and caused Egypt to be conquered by the Zionist
hordes! The 1936 treaty freed Egypt from a large number of its problems with Great Britain, problems which had incited Saad Zaghlul and
other Egyptian politicans not to reduce their efforts, but rather to concentrate them with a view to obtaining independence. Following the
conclusion of that treaty, Egypt began to realise its Arab affiliations
and its membership of the Arab world. Official thinking then began to
turn towards the Arab world, thereby writing a new page in the history
of modern Egypt.[2]

This 1936 review takes us through a period of 15 years, up to 1951, on
which date this treaty was abrogated by precisely that person who had been
a co-signatory of it; the historical context of these 15 years will enable us to
highlight a number of important factors.

First, this treaty which was also signed by the leaders of the opposition,
represented the maximum which could be achieved by the energy of the
middle classes of the Egyptian bourgeoisie in its struggle with the economic
and political conditions of the regime of that time. Actually, the objective
role of the Egyptian bourgeoisie had not yet, historically, been completed,
even though it had been paralysed and made impotent in the general framework of the existing regime.

Second, the period which followed the signature of the treaty up to the
commencement of the 1950s saw a decisive social transformation in the very
structure of modern Egypt and even within the bourgeoisie; certain new
social forces, which had been politically dispersed during the 1920s, had
crystallised while, during the 1930s and 1940s of this century, sectors of the
working class, the peasants, and the petty bourgeoisie with its various strata,
were no longer content with their role as a popular base for the Wafd party;
they began looking for their own independent path, in participation as equals
in the direction of national and social development. The emergence of these
new social forces, right at the heart of the agricultural and industrial sectors,
furnished new bases for the national revolution by the mere fact of having
shown that political independence and economic independence were only
two faces of the same coin. The National Committee of Students and Workers,
established in 1946, marked the political debut of this new trend emerging on
the socio-political map of Egypt.

Third, the events directly surrounding Egypt exploded the regionalist perspective of Saad Zaghlul Pasha, the author of a famous saying to the effect
that the Arabs would be zero plus zero, plus zero. This prospect had been
effaced to such an extent that the first war of the Egyptian army following
this treaty took place on the territories of Palestine, outside the international
frontiers of Egypt.

Fourth, the period extending from 1936 to 1951 saw decisive historical
transformations at the international level through the victory of the Allies in
the Second World War, through the decline of the two great colonial empires,

the British and the French, through the emergence of the socialist bloc around the Soviet Union, in Eastern Europe and in China, through the growing strength of the national liberation forces in the colonies, and through the commencement of American neo-colonialism.

These new factors, taken together, were superimposed on the political struggle in Egypt during the whole period of the 1940s, which saw a seething in the streets of Egypt such as had never been seen before; the Wafd party itself underwent an objective division which was different from those which had been effected by the great Wafdist personalities throughout its history. Indeed, the Wafd witnessed the emergence from its midst of a wave of radical youth, since known by the name of the Wafdist *avant-garde*. Despite the corruption of the social milieu of the traditional leadership of the Wafd, and despite the collusion of the latter with the great landowners and with the upper strata of the bourgeoisie, the correction of the historical error through the abrogation of the 1936 treaty was the final glorious action of the Egyptian bourgeoisie prior to the revolution of July 1952, when it was able to take advantage of a local and international climate favourable for it to strike its blow, certain that the regime as a whole was in an impasse.

Tareq El-Bechri writes:

> The decision taken by the Wafd to abrogate the treaty of 1936 was an action which went beyond its conventional method of struggle; it acknowledged the arrival of a new stage in the history of the Egyptian national movement, a stage which went beyond the legal method of the peaceful struggle and, by definition, every formula and every framework of that form of struggle. Abrogating the treaty without some other alternative proposed by the colonial power went beyond the Wafd itself and the institution, the leaders of which had accepted the peaceful method of struggle, which was not prepared for this kind of action, by its ideology, its composition or its organisation. This institution was unsuited by its very nature for struggling in any other manner and for taking up arms. By this abrogation, the Wafd carried out its last major act as leader of the national movement. Always known for its hesitancy, in its own history as in that of the country, it carried the national movement forward to a new stage which went beyond the existing regime and its foundations, and even going beyond itself.[3]

This analysis confirms that the popular movement, which shed its blood on the banks of the Canal, was no Wafdist solution. For once Cairo began burning (a desperate attempt on the part of the forces of the counter-revolution) the Wafdist Government fell, and with it democracy. For it was not powerful enough to protect the path it had just opened up towards a just solution of the Egyptian question through the abrogation of the treaty. At the most, it was able to exploit a favourable political climate to correct a historical error, namely the treaty, under pressure from the more progressive wing of the Wafd and under maximum pressure from the street. Thus the

Wafd opened up the way to the solution without, however, being historically suited to putting into effect the solution presented at dawn on 23rd July 1952 — the revolution of Gamal Abd El-Nasser.

The legitimate nature of the old regime thus collapsed in 1951 with the abrogation of the 1936 treaty. The Cairo Fire, on 26th January 1952, was merely a symbol of this disastrous fall. The parties and the organisations, both official and clandestine, for very complicated reasons which we need not go into here, were unable to supply the foundations for a new regime. The armed forces, therefore, had to come and open up a breach in this impasse. In the course of their first three years, they consecrated the fall of the old regime by the proclamation of the Republic on 18th June 1953, by the abrogation of honorary titles and the dissolution of the parties, and they endeavoured, within the scope of this consecration, to obtain the evacuation of the British forces. In other words, the attempt at persuading the British forces to evacuate the Canal actually forms part of the measures aimed at effacing the old regime. This was also the case with the promulgation of the agrarian reform law in September 1953. For, in fact, the three pillars of the old regime were the throne, the occupation forces, and the large landowners. It was, therefore, only possible to topple the regime by removing these three pillars. That is why it is impossible to consider 23rd July 1952 as the date of the birth of the new regime. In fact, it has been demonstrated historically that a period of about five years separates the time when the old regime forfeited its legitimacy in the events of 8th October 1951, at the time of the abrogation of the treaty, and the birth of the legitimacy of the regime of Gamal Abd El-Nasser, at the time of the nationalisation of the Suez Canal, and after the evacuation treaty had been torn up (in 1952). The law on agrarian reform, promulgated in September 1952, was a challenge directed against the upper strata of the rural bourgeoisie; the proclamation of the Republic on 18th June 1953 was a constitutional supplement to the fall of the monarchy; the Nasser-Heid negotiations in 1954, as a result of the evacuation treaty, were a consecration of the fall of the old regime without, however, being a true realisation of national independence.

Nasser's negotiations with Great Britain lasted only 16 days, between 11th and 27th July 1954, and on the last day the treaty was signed with the initials of the partners, which means that the effective negotiations had taken place well before the partners took their places at the formal negotiating table. Ahmed Hamrouch affirms, in the second volume of his book on the July revolution, that the speed with which the agreement was signed was the result of American intervention which, as Zakariyyah Muhyi Ad-Din has assured me, aimed at resolving the problems between the British and the Egyptians with a view to creating a climate suited to associating Egypt with a new Western policy in the region.[4] Anouar Abd El-Malek affirms that the negotiations on the evacuation, between Nasser and the British Ambassador, Sir Ralph Stevenson, had begun in the spring of 1953 and that the aim of the United States was clear — an undertaking by the new regime to adhere to a military arrangement for the collective defence of the Middle East, an arrangement directly associated with the Atlantic Alliance.[5] It is useful to recall, in this connection, that the Egyptian negotiator exerted pressure on the British forces stationed in the Canal Zone through a series of resistance campaigns from January to May 1954, when the attacks were suspended. Great Britain, in the guise of a manifestation of its good intentions, took the initiative of unblocking a sum of £10 million sterling forming part of the amount it owed Egypt. In July, it revealed its evacuation plan subject to leaving behind civil technicians, and the return of the British forces in the event of an Arab country or Turkey suffering aggression. The agreement stipulated the withdrawal of the British forces from the Canal Zone within 20 months at the latest. As far as Great Britain was concerned it officially put an end to the 1936 treaty, together with its commitments. Great Britain recognised the Suez Canal as belonging to Egypt, provided international navigation remained free according to the treaty with Turkey of 29th October 1888. The agreement was signed on 19th October 1954. What then were the reactions?

John Badow, a former American ambassador in Cairo, and R.H. Hold, wrote: 'This treaty, for Great Britain and the West, removed the main obstacle to Egypt's participation in a Middle East defence treaty.'[6]

In his book on Nasser, Jean Lacouture writes: 'Never did the Colonel appear so isolated from the people as on the day when he informed them of the evacuation treaty.' Ahmed Hamrouch writes: 'Between the signature of the treaty with the initials and its ratification, opposition crystallised against this treaty in general and against Nasser in particular.'[7] Anthony Nutting relates in his book that he had borrowed Nasser's pen at the time of signature and had kept it; turning to him, Nasser said jokingly: 'I think you have taken a lot from me in this treaty . . . kindly give me back my pen.' The joke was not devoid of meaning and Nasser must have remembered it when the bullets that were fired at Al-Manchiyyah missed him, when the assassin shouted: 'I want to kill him, he has sold my country!'

But Nasser did not sell his country, and the proof is that he tore up this treaty less than two years later. But it was during those two years that he disappointed the hopes of the West, the old and the new, when he refused with heroic obstinacy to adhere to any military pact with them, while destroying their arms sales monopoly and playing a positive role at the Bandung Conference. Admittedly, the 1954 treaty was in essence a compromise with colonialism, since it authorised British civil technicians to remain on Egyptian territory, and since it provided for the return of the British forces in the event of Turkey suffering aggression. But it was a compromise which involved the evacuation from Egypt of all the British armed forces. It was also a compromise of short duration, which cannot be compared with the time which elapsed between the signature of the 1936 treaty and the date of its abrogation in 1951. And thirdly, it was impossible that this treaty would be the last act in the rapid political development of the Egyptian leadership over less than two years. Finally, the balance of such a compromise should not be abstracted from the context of this stage in the Nasser revolution — a stage in the fall of the old regime.

Thus, the measures taken by the 1952 revolution in its early stages were the incarnation of the ambitions of the national bourgeoisie, i.e. the middle strata of the Egyptian bourgeoisie, without the hegemony of the upper strata of the bourgeoisie and without the liberal traditions in the shadow of which the national bourgeoisie had always struggled. In other words, the representation of classes which had been lost by the Wafd, owing to the infiltration of the rural and banking aristocracy into its own structure, was gained by Nasser around this period. The essential change which had taken place was doubtless the fact that the middle strata of the Egyptian bourgeoisie of 1952, both in their production structure and in their social relationships, had attained a qualitative degree of development which was higher than that which it had known in 1919.

In 1956, Nasser provided the proof that the evacuation treaty was not the peak of hope, but simply a tactical step towards the major aim, namely the nationalisation of the Suez Canal and the Egyptianisation of the foreign banks and companies. It was doubtless not by chance that immediately before (in 1955) the necessary economic organisation had been created and the contract signed for Soviet armaments. Thus, the aim was national independence at the economic level; it was then necessary to protect it militarily and give it political substance through the elections which were to make Nasser President of the Republic. The tripartite Suez aggression was unable to overthrow the new legitimacy born at the moment of nationalisation and war. The Egyptian street had just placed a historical trust in Nasser when it witnessed him tearing up the 1954 treaty, arming the people and leading them to defend the country's independence at the price of blood. From that moment, the equilibrium of the classes was to change; even though the middle strata of the bourgeoisie still occupied the dominant position, they no longer overlapped with the rural aristocracy and the foreign monopolies; indeed, the broad popular base made up of workers, peasants and petty bourgeois became an energetic, active factor, deriving benefit from the changes which had been taking place in the social map in its relations with authority.

It might be said that Nasser, once he had signed the 1954 treaty and until it was abrogated in 1956, from the time of the union with Syria in 1958 up to the national measures taken between 1961 and 1962, was expressing a political trend in the direction of the self-determination of the people, the realisation of the tasks of the national democratic revolution, the exploitation of the national resources for the benefit of the widest strata of the people and the elimination of the traditional role of certain strata of the national bourgeoisie. The economic organisation of the country was evolving in the direction of the nationalisation of a broad sector, a nationalisation which was participating in economic development, the acceleration in the rate of that development and the mobilisation of the new social forces round a charter for national action, through participation in profits, management, and political representation. This was proceeding hand in hand with the modernisation of the means of production and heavy industry, and with the training of technical experts through the proclamation of free education at all levels, including the university.

The breach between Nasser and the West was thus only the equivalent of his breach with colonial dependence. Whereas the democratic struggle at the time of the Wafd signified a struggle against the occupation and for the Constitution at one and the same time, the national struggle in Nasser's time had taken on a deeper significance, namely, the consolidation of regional independence within the framework of the Arab destiny, the international liberation movement, and the socialist bloc. It also signified the social progress of the widest sectors of the people.

From these two points of view, the year 1956 was a decisive one. The abrogation of the 1954 treaty constituted a new historical initiative against which the colonial powers, Zionism, local reaction and forces and the elements of the right in the Nasser regime itself, could not but rise up; these elements, in addition to the numerous errors in regard to democracy, were to pursue the Nasser regime until they inflicted upon it the devastating defeat of 1967.

Objectively, the defeat of June 1967 led to the fall of the regime of the July revolution; but the historical economic leadership exercised by the personality of Nasser (what may be referred to as the role of the individual in history) provided the regime with a respite for three years, which in fact were merely a quantitative prolongation of the years prior to the war. This respite culminated in a tragic end without equal in history: the massacre of the Palestinians in Jordan in September, the sudden death of Nasser, and the struggle, which destroyed the authority of his regime, between the bureaucratic wing of Nasserism that was referred to socially and with much euphemism as the 'new class', and the elements of the right in the regime, which had in their ranks the rich of the countryside, the parasitic elements, both in the nationalised sector and in the private sector, proliferating in the absence of democratic control by the people. On the eve of 15th May 1971, the reactionary coalition between the rich of the countryside and the parasitical elements settled the struggle by a putsch against the Nasser bureaucracy.

Where were the people that night? In the fullness of their trust, they stood by and watched. In fact, the widest sectors of the population had finally lost confidence in the political style of the regime and its non-democratic formula. The people suffered greatly from the cancerous proliferation of the new class whose most serious fault consisted in reducing the rate of economic development after 1965. The spontaneous popular risings between 1968 and 1973 did not result in the organisation of the ranks of the people into a national front capable of changing the regime in the interests of the popular forces. Unconsciously, the population was feeling that the regime had succumbed for some time now and that it was bearing the responsibility for the rise in the forces of the right which had filled the political vacuum.

Since then, there has followed the events of which we are aware (economic, political and military) that once more provided confirmation of the accuracy of the view of the people, even if it was not consciously expressed. For, during the period between 1971 and 1975, the Egyptian authorities, with the impudence of a prostitute, gradually took up the path of the renegades.

The Israeli occupation of Sinai was the stumbling block of the new regime of the putsch, which showed little concern for the other Arab territories which had been occupied, or the Palestine problem. It was thus necessary to remove this obstacle from the path towards a partial solution, so that the power of the putsch could acquire its legitimacy on the ashes of the old regime. Taken as a whole, the measures which followed, from the date of the putsch up to the war of October 1973, constituted the elements of the consecration of the fall of Nasserism at the local, Arab and international levels. For their part, the consequences of the war may be considered as a document for the legitimacy of the putsch, if one may so express oneself.

How did this come about? The policy of economic development led to a gradual 'Lebanonisation' of the structure of Egyptian production and this, by proceeding to create so-called international free trade zones (with the encouragement of the private sector) for imports and exports, without any serious control, by encircling the nationalised sector and liquidating it from the inside, by dismantling the laws of agrarian reform and finally, by directing the economy progressively towards parasitic projects, such as smuggling, brokering and luxury building. The political trend resulted in the destruction of the alliance with the socialist countries and the acceptance of the embrace of the Americans; it led to the alliance with the reactionary Arab countries and the maintenance of the formula of the Arab Socialist Union, while modifying the definition of manual worker and peasant so that the large landowners and businessmen became the pillars of authority in the various sectors, legislative and executive. The policy of ideological development led to an attack on the courts, and on the national, progressive writers, forcing them to emigrate, by criticising them, endeavouring to lead them astray or inviting them to take up their abode in the prison cells from time to time, while at the same time putting into circulation ideas which were chauvinistic, regionalistic, racist and religious; and simultaneously propagating the values of the consumer society.

All these measures consecrated the objective fall of the regime and prepared the ground for the October war, of which the Sinai Agreement, concluded in 1975, constituted the most decisive political consequence; indeed, the spirit of that agreement and its clauses crystallise the Egyptian position in regard to the national question, the Arab problem and international peace.

Though those who controlled the political direction of Egypt many times avowed that that agreement had been concluded with the United States and not with Israel, the preamble to it categorically refutes that assertion. The first line of the agreement reads as follows: 'The Government of the Arab Republic of Egypt and the Government of Israel have agreed on the following points.' On the basis of international law, this sentence does, indeed, constitute official recognition of Israel. Definitely so. Yet perhaps the famous Resolution 242 also implies an approximate recognition. Only there is a nuance, and it is an appreciable one. For whereas this resolution was formulated on the basis of an existing fact, namely the defeat, the explicit recognition of 1975 is based on a different reality, and this is asserted by the Egyptian government itself with considerable pride. But what concerns us, is the fact that this official recognition of Israel by Egypt does not so much represent the consequences of the law, as the political identity of the present Egyptian regime.

The characteristics of this identity might be better clarified by the second clause to this agreement, where 'the two parties undertake not to have recourse to force, threats or military blockade, one against the other.' This is rendered explicit in the third clause: 'The two parties continue scrupulously to respect the ceasefire on land, at sea and in the air, and to abstain from any military or quasi-military action against the other party.' The two clauses are explicit on the hamstringing of the Egyptian armed forces in view of the tergiversation of Israel regarding another withdrawal from Sinai, or in the event of Israeli aggression against any other Arab country — particularly Syria — which had been associated in the war, or against the Palestinian resistance which was holed up in Lebanon. This immobilisation of the Egyptian armed forces is still further confirmed by the clauses contained in the annexes to the agreement, under the heading 'Restrictions relating to Forces and Arms'; according to these restrictions the Egyptian forces authorised to be stationed on the East bank should not exceed 8,000 men, including eight units of infantry, 75 tanks and 72 pieces of artillery, including the heavy *haouns*. But the most serious of the clauses is that concerning the pre-alert system, which gives the United States the right to delegate 200 technicians for its operation, and whose withdrawal can only be effected at the wish of the Americans or of the two partners. Though this figure of 200 appears derisory, and though their status as civil technicians sounds easier on the ear, there is no doubt that this does in fact constitute an American presence whose highly sophisticated instruments of detection have no need of an army for their operation. The presence of such instruments not only prevents the unleashing of a war, but they do, moreover, occupy a strategic position for American espionage directed towards the Middle East. These instruments are connected with those of the bases of the NATO Pact stationed not far away. This is the most modern and the most dangerous type of direct occupation. It concerns not only an occupation of territories in Sinai, but, more seriously, it constitutes a threat to Egyptian national sovereignty, and indeed to the whole of Arab sovereignty, whose territories are thus subjected to radar surveillance covering the frontiers of the Arabian Gulf and Iraq, passing through Jordan, Syria, and Lebanon, where the bases of Palestinian resistance are located.

In the light of the clauses of the agreement and its annexes, we may define the identity of the present Egyptian regime as follows:

1) A change in the movement of the Egyptian armed forces in relation to the questions of national and Arab liberation, and more especially in relation to the Palestinian question.

2) An abandonment of Egyptian sovereignty and independence by direct adhesion to the Western defence system, which itself is a consecration of direct entry into the colonial orbit at the economic level.

3) An abandonment of Egypt's Arab membership, by providing military facilities to the most dangerous instruments of imperialist aggression in our contemporary world.

4) An abandonment of the alliance with the socialist bloc, by ejecting from its southern frontiers all the foundations of mutual security between itself and the Arab liberation movement.

All this constitutes defensive barriers on the part of the reactionary, backward faction of the Egyptian bourgeoisie. The latter would defend its parasitic, ephemeral interests, even if that were to entail dragging the flag of independence through the mud. This is an exceptional retrogressive movement in the historical course of modern Egypt, and one which flouts all the objective laws which are the driving forces of its history. For Egypt's social evolution over the whole of the Nasser period had crystallised a social and economic entity which did not allow of any such withdrawal in the field of the productive forces or social relationships. But the unfamiliar circumstances, from the fall of Nasser's power in 1967 to the disappearance of Nasser himself in 1970 and the May 1971 putsch, opened up this exceptional breach in the historical evolution of Egypt, through which it was possible for the renegade forces to infiltrate. However, the objective contradiction between Egypt's social evolution and the present regime does not allow them any length of life. Millions of workers and peasants, students, technicians and soldiers, trained over 20 years and constituting productive forces and new social relationships, have created a new Egypt which, in the absence of any far-reaching uprooting or sinister civil war, it is impossible to overthrow.

Such relationships between forces, however, cannot find expression at any level in this regime which assembles in its ranks the most reactionary sectors of rural capitalism and the parasitic elements of production. We are not in the presence of the traditional national bourgeoisie which, at one time, had directed the revolution of 1919 and that of 1952 after it. We are in the presence of a capitalism aiming, through its pillage, at an immediate profit, a capitalism which is incapable of resolving a single economic, social or cultural problem, whatever the volume of the foreign loans and investments from which it benefits. It was no surprise, therefore, when Mr. Ahmed Abu Ismail, the Egyptian Minister of Finance, declared that the year 1975 was the worst economic year in the history of modern Egypt. It is not by chance that the rate of economic development is continually declining, and that inflation, the rise in prices, and the disappearance of products, constitute the main characteristics of this impasse. Indeed, Egyptian capitalism is too cowardly to be able to direct production; consequently, it has recourse to the technique of pickpocketing, with consumer goods as its objective. Its economic downfall is thus inevitable, despite the anaesthetising effects of the opening up and the extent of supports provided, which are in fact only the precursory signs of political collapse. Of course, the absence of any popular cohesion in a political organism has also participated in the formation of this breach through which the present authorities have passed. Of course, the political and military alliance with the West will protect the latter against the collapse, for a time. But the degree of tenacity in the attachment of the present regime to colonial protection through the Sinai Agreement and other future agreements, will eventually trigger the capacity of the popular front to organise itself and bring about changes in the very structure of political power. For indeed, the present leadership is historically unsuited to the adoption of a similar position to that taken by the Wafd in 1951 when Nahhas Pasha, in the name of Egypt and on its behalf, abrogated the 1936 treaty; it is also unsuited to taking up a position similar to that taken by Nasser in 1956 when he tore up the 1954 treaty before announcing the nationalisation of the Suez Canal.

The historical errors of the 1936 treaty and of the 1954 agreement were capable of being corrected by the social forces which had committed them. The fact of having brought the British presence to an end in Cairo and Alexandria in 1936, and in the Canal Zone in 1954, was no case of national treason, but a compromise, related to the onerous conditions accepted by the Egyptian negotiator with a view to obtaining the first and second evacuations. But compromises are never capable of being rectified, especially when the social forces themselves direct the trend towards national independence. This is why the Wafd caused the fall of this regime that held together these social forces prior to the abrogation of the treaty. For the same reason, Nasser installed new foundations for his regime when he opened the field to the middle class so that this could change the balance of forces which were stifling it, and doing so by effecting the evacuation, Egyptianisation, and suppression of the large estates, and clipping the wings of the upper strata of the rural bourgeoisie.

If we were now to trace a relationship between the clauses of the Sinai Agreement, those of the 1936 treaty and of the 1954 agreement, without at the same time neglecting the historical and social dimension, we should find confirmation that the military commitments entered into by Egypt in 1936, which were effectively in opposition to the independence of Egypt and its sovereignty over its territories, are of much smaller scope than the military commitments of the Sinai Agreement which, for their part, opened the door to an effective American occupation that did not exist before, as well as to the Israeli occupation. Whereas the 1936 treaty opened the way to the evolution of the armed forces which accompanied the 1952 revolution, and whereas it kept a tight rein on Great Britain in regard to any intervention in our internal affairs (which contributed towards the success of the revolution) the Sinai Agreement presented the most serious obstacles to our armed forces and constitutes a warning to any internal movement whose objective might be to face up to this grave situation. The 1936 treaty made Egypt's membership of the Arab world possible, a membership which was confirmed, moreover, in the course of the 1948 Palestine war, and founded more securely by Nasser in the course of the 1956 war, but the Sinai Agreement caused Egypt to shrink behind its national frontiers which had now been amputated.

It is curious that the present Egyptian leadership should have insisted on repeating its assertions that the Sinai Agreement did not contain any secret clauses, as though the known clauses were not already sufficient to condemn it. In fact, the United States hastened to publish the secret clauses in full, a text which delivers the *coup de grâce* to Egypt as the centre of gravity of the Arab liberation movement.

Under Heading 5 of the document, the text reads: 'The United States will not wait for Israel to begin to apply the agreement before Egypt has put into effect its promise in the agreement to disengage as of January 1974, according to which all Israeli convoys would be able to pass through the Suez Canal.'

Under Heading 12 of the same document, we can read:

> The position of the United States is based on the fact that the Egyptian commitments, in respect of the Egypto-Israeli agreement, are not conditional upon any action or any trend which may take place between any other Arab country and Israel. The Government of the United States considers the agreement valid in itself.

Under Heading 2, according to the text:

> The United States will continue with their present policy in regard to the Palestine Liberation Organisation, in the sense that they will not recognise that organisation, and will not negotiate with it as long as it fails to recognise Israel's right to exist, and as long as it refuses to accept Resolutions 242 and 338 of the Security Council. The Government of the United States will undertake complete consultations and will act in order to reconcile its position and strategy in this matter with the Government of Israel in the course of the Geneva Peace Conference.

It is no longer important now to recall that these texts constitute the best refutation of the official Egyptian declarations; it is not important to state that other clauses grant Israel large quantities of the most sophisticated American military weaponry. We need no longer stress that one of these clauses explicitly stipulates direct American intervention for the protection of Israel's security if threatened either directly or indirectly by the intervention of a 'large state' in the Middle East conflict.

All this is of much less significance if we compare it with the essential content of the Sinai Agreement and its annexes, whether secret or published. For this reflects, in the most precise way, the political identity of the present Egyptian regime. This identity only accelerates the country's engulfment in the traps of colonial influence, and allows the present power no possibility of proceeding to abrogate the Sinai Agreement. Such an act would require the installation of a new internal decor and the emergence of protagonists capable of overthrowing all that has been raised up on a foundation of false legitimacy, and capable of suppressing any treaty contrary to Egypt's independence, its Arab destiny, and its social progress.

Notes

1. Ahmed Hamrouch, *l'Histoire de la révolution du 23 juillet*, Vol. I, p. 92.
2. Abd El-Azim Ramadan, *Tatawuur Al-Haraka Al-Wataniyya Fi Misr Min 1918 lla 1936* (The Evolution of the Nationalist Movement 1918-36).
3. Tareq El-Bechri, *Le mouvement politique en Egypte de 1954 a 1952*, p. 485.
4. Ahmed Hamrouch, *Mugtam'a Gamal Abd El-Nasser*, Al-Muassassat Al-Arabiyyah lil Dirasat wa An-Nachr, Beirut 1975, p. 34.
5. Anouar Abd El-Malek, *Al-Mugtam'a wa Al Gaych*, Dar At-Taliah, Beirut, p. 119.
6. Quoted, Anouar Abd El-Malek, *op. cit.*, p. 120.
7. Ahmed Hamrouch, *op. cit.*, Vol. II.

6. An Anachronistic Capitalism

The second Sinai Agreement concluded between Israel, the United States and Egypt, is not simply a great political and military event but constitutes a strategic turning-point in the history of the present Egyptian regime, its power derived from the putsch, which erupted on the Egyptian scene in May 1971; a turning-point frequently given the date of 1st September 1975 when the agreement was initialled. In reality the strategic turning-point represented by this military agreement is only the consecration of an economic and political turning-point which the Egyptian authority, together with its regime, had already reached under the cover of a remarkable camouflage.

Whereas, in the previous chapter, we concluded that it was impossible for the present leadership to reproduce the historical scenes of Mustapha An-Nahhas and Gamal Abd El-Nasser, for reasons related to the emergence of politically reactionary and economically parasitic social strata, today the search for an alternative solution to the abrogation of the Sinai Agreement of necessity implies that we must seek to create it; it also signifies that we need to define the economic and political terms. And finally, it presupposes the necessity of determining the social forces involved which are capable of assuming such a historic task. Above all, this implies that abrogating the Sinai Agreement is not just a matter of suppressing an agreement between two countries, but changing a regime and replacing one power with another.

In accordance with the law that we have been able to define, and which governs the movement of the Egyptian bourgeoisie, we shall now follow their political and economic progress before and after the war of 1973, and before and after the agreement of September 1975. While doing so, we shall also be able to define the law regulating the social movement opposing the partisans of the withdrawal policy, thereby highlighting the forces which are disposed to rectify the course of history. This will enable us to discover the subjective aptitudes of these forces to recover the fatherland, to recognise the dimensions of the challenge they reveal, and the particulars of the contradictions existing within the ranks of the people and the programme of action for the salvation of Egypt.

I

First, it is necessary to determine the methodological framework which will enable us to analyse the turning-point at which the present Egyptian regime has arrived, in the economic, social and political fields, reflected by the strategical stage of the Sinai Agreement.

The first element within this framework is the fact that the May 1971 putsch appeared initially as a struggle for power within the regime, only to finish up as a counter-revolution directed against the regime. In other words, the putsch began with the political details and ended with the general strategic lines at the legislative and constitutional levels and from the economic and social points of view.

The second element resides in the fact that the putsch, in essence, is an objective result of the Nasser regime. It by no means constitutes an exploit in the usurpation of power. For in reality the representation of classes of the Nasser regime, its political mode of action over 18 years, and its way of thinking, created a climate favourable to the birth of the putsch, based on the backbone of the Nasser authority. This is far from being a climate favourable to the birth of a converse movement, and one more progressive and legitimate.

The third element is the blank cheque given to the Nasser authority by the whole of the Egyptian left wing, and the blank cheque given a second time to the authority of the putsch, albeit perhaps more hesitatingly. But this did not fail to have its repercussions on the progress of the Egyptian social movement and on its political forces.

We shall discuss the first and third elements in the course of our disquisition. The second element calls for the greatest clarification, in order to demonstrate that it is not surprising that matters have reached their present stage, following the disappearance of Nasser and the departure of his friends from power.

The year 1965 may constitute an outstanding point in the history of the Nasser regime, if we disregard any association of thought with what had gone before and any reflections on what followed. It was the year which brought to an end the first five-year plan and saw the culmination of the experience of overall national planning, following the nationalisation measures. It was also the year of the beginning of the decline in rates of development, the second plan never seeing the light of day. There can be no doubt that Ali Sabri, in his book *Cinq années de transformation* records the economic victories the Egyptian people obtained through a struggle such as had never been seen before in history, the effort, generous sacrifice, the nationalisation measures, and the fruits of development. But patient reading of this book will enable us to put our finger on the canker which subsequently became legion and gnawed away at the economic structure of the country between 1965 and 1970. In this sense, the military defeat of 1967 was only the tree hiding the forest. In this sense too, the event of 14th May 1971 only burned up a scarecrow. This cankerworm was living in the capitalist foundations of the nationalised sector, in the fact that these foundations had been submerged under non-scientific qualifications, the fact that it was stated, for example, that this was a non-capitalist development, a non-capitalist path for development, the fact also that a social stratum had been designated as deriving from a non-exploitive capitalism. Ali Sabri writes in this official book that the operations entrusted by the nationalised sector to the subcontractors of the private sector:

> attained a total of E£144 million for each year of the plan, realising a net profit of E£29 million . . . The private sector exploited this situation by increasing the price of the operations which had been entrusted to it, even under the tendering system, which resulted in an increase in the cost of the building operations representing 47% of the formal investments of the plan.

The inevitable consequence was, according to Taha Chaker, structural disequilibrium due to the increase in the relative importance of the service sector to the detriment of the consumer goods sector. That was the main reason for the increase in demand on the consumer goods market, and the inflationary pressures which accompanied the execution of the plan.[1] During the five years of the plan, the share of the product-manufacturing sectors in the whole of global production fell from 70.2% to 68.2%, whereas services increased from 29.8% to 31.8%. The proportionate increase in services and government organisations consists of the difference between 14.6% and 17%, whereas industry's share fell from 42.7% to 42.3%. Also, the saving capacity fell considerably, with the result that consumption, during the five years of the plan, increased by 46.9%. It was normal in these circumstances for the consumer goods industries to take a dominating position alongside the promotion of a certain social stratum and of a poor distribution of the working forces, owing to the proliferation of the administrative services to the detriment of the workers.

Despite all this, the rate of development increased during the years of the plan by 7.2%, according to official statistics which should be viewed with some reserve. But this increase was felt through the struggle against unemployment on the part of the workers and the intellectuals. Between 1964 and 1965, per capita income rose by 19.1%, but the rate of development at the commencement of 1966 began to fall. The rate of increase in national income fell. The government imposed new taxes, in addition to increasing the old ones. Between 1966 and 1967, total production in the product-manufacturing sectors fell by 0.9%. Real per capita income fell to E£62.8 per annum. During the years 1963-66, the private sector saw a fresh upward swing; its share in total production rose to 30.8% for textiles, 23.6% for food products, and 24.1% for the engineering industries. Around this period, the production of the private sector rose by 132.4% compared with 121.1% for the nationalised sector.[2]

Why was progress under the development plan so slow and subsequent regression so rapid?

The answer is simple. The plan was not a global, radical development plan. It was by no means a plan for social transformation in the direction of socialism. From the outset, it was a capitalist plan, based on national state capitalism. The great nationalisations, in their essence, constituted national campaigns for modernisation, independence and sovereignty. The upper strata of the Egyptian bourgeoisie had refused to participate freely in the development. But while the nationalisation campaigns had had an impact on the widest sectors of the population, they also constituted a capitalist transformation in regard to legislation and execution, both from the point of view of economic thought and within the existing political framework. Indeed, the national charter saw the constitution of national state capitalism; the Socialist Union was its political organisation.

Thus, what has been called national capitalism is continuing its campaigns in industry, agriculture, commerce and the building firms. Though planning, development and nationalisation have placed a limit on the accumulation of individual capital, national capitalism has been able to derive benefit from the invisible forms of capitalist development, and has even profited from the decline of the greater bourgeois classes while taking their place in lending and commercial operations. Furthermore, it has been able to integrate new, less capitalistic, strata. But the most important thing is the fact that the economic weight of this capitalism, excused the qualification of exploiter by the charter, has thus succeeded in becoming more acute.

It is thus that what is referred to as the 'new class' has been able to develop. This may be too general a description, but it nevertheless indicates that elements which constituted its foundations arose within the framework of the nationalised administrative and technical sector, and within the frameworks of the political organisation and regime.

At the same time, it is necessary to emphasise the strata of the bourgeoisie at large which escaped the measures taken by the capitalist State and succeeded in channelling their capital into such lawful activities as building, exporting, and direct deals with the nationalised sector and the State apparatus. It suffices to stress in this connection, as has been stated by Dr. Fuad Mursi, 'that the wholesale trade was in the hands of 219 traders with a turnover of E£600 million.'[3]

But to these we can also add two social strata which have always played an important part in the preparation of the climate of recession, without attracting the attention of the Nasser authority and the political organisation; these are the successors of the older classes which, dispersed within the country, were investing in what remained for them by way of close economic relations with the public sector, the apparatus of the State or the cadres of the nationalised sector. The second stratum is what Fuad Mursi refers to as hordes of adventurers, smugglers, masters of the black market, broker barons, white-slavers, night-club owners, furnished apartment landlords, go-betweens, masters of the under-cover market, undeclared moneylenders, and masters of the art of kickbacks, auctions, contract awards and illegal services. These two strata, by infiltration, underhand devices, corruption and terrorism, have had the most serious effect on the drawing up of the unwritten capitalist rules, on the structure of production, on the proliferation of parasites to the detriment of trade, and of consumption to the detriment of industry.

As for agrarian capitalism, it experienced neither pressure nor challenge from the Nasser regime. On the contrary, it found it sympathetic and encouraging. For it had taken the place of the great landowners in its manner of dealing with the peasants, and had very early benefited from the laws on agrarian reform which resulted in the parcelling out of the major companies. It was, therefore, able to invest in State assets even in the matter of credit, co-operation and agrarian modernisation. It bought up enormous areas of land belonging to small landowners who had been unable to stand up to the 'legal' capitalist competition. From the internal market it derived incommensurable profits. Thus, agrarian capitalism profited from the fact that it was never touched by any law, or any legislation during all the years of the revolution. Thus, it benefited from the capitalist laws of agrarian reform and the means for their application.

The coalition, spontaneous at times and intentionally sought after at others, or compulsorily constituted, between the capitalist legislation of Nasser's development and its bureaucratic and police methods of application, aimed at eliminating any direct popular control. This was the coalition constituted by the strata which held the hegemony, of the interior and exterior of Nasser's authority, a coalition made up of its friends and enemies. Economic and social relations became more and more intertwined, while political interests were increasingly being formed between the bureaucracy of the nationalised sector, the entrepreneurs of the private sector and the former members of the military, 'diluted in civil life' according to the expression of Nasser himself, and the remains of the older classes, the brokers and usurers.

This was the Nasser climate, viewed entirely objectively, the climate which favoured the putsch of May 1971. The year 1965 was only the beginning of the end, which arrived in 1967. It was only Nasser's historical stature which delayed its consecration. With his sudden disappearance, the putsch was already born, and it was thus a legitimate putsch, if one may so express oneself. But the fact that its origin was the Nasser regime by no means signifies that there is no need to change it. This is dependent on a 'historical fate'.

II

From the night of the putsch up to the great strategic turning-point, passing through the decisive point, five years were to pass. Between 1965 and 1970, there was a five-year plan, absent from minds and especially from reality. Between 1968 and 1973, there was a student movement, dispersed worker and peasant movements, and also an advanced cultural movement which was halted at the first shot of the October war. These five-year periods are connected together to show in the last resort the burning dialogue between the people and the power, from defeat to war. But they also indicate a possible dialogue within the ranks of the people, from war towards a revolution – a total cultural revolution, which could change the regime, society, the structure of production and its working forces; a revolution which could abrogate the Sinai Agreement, i.e. a strategic turning-point at the moment when it will abruptly do away with the preambles, the consequences and the context of that agreement, which constitute the decisive moment in the history of the putsch.

But first, what is this decisive point? It constitutes the moment of economic transition from national state capitalism to a traditional capitalism, with all its natural complications and its spontaneous prolongations, in the specific conditions of a country such as Egypt, essentially belonging to the underdeveloped and sparsely populated world. This is the moment when global national planning is cancelled so far as modernisation, independence, and centralised development of the structure of production were concerned, and the substitution of these aims by economic liberalism, i.e. by instituting individual enterprise, companies and monopolies, solely for the sake of profit and the accumulation of capital. In this case, modernisation is restricted to merely changing certain means of production, certain aspects of administration and certain consumption products; this clearly did not go so far as modernising the social relations and services of the people. Independence, here, does not go beyond the walls of the factory, in order to achieve national independence. Development, in turn, becomes decentralised and dispersed, as part of the social division of production. The fruits of development go to some classes to the detriment of others, to certain geographical areas to the detriment of others. But it should be noted, in passing, that even these very modest aims, forming part of the decisive economic point of the new regime, have not been realised. And what is worse: the country, with this liberal endeavour, stands at the brink of total bankruptcy, and bankruptcy which may take the form of famine. None of these aims has been realised, neither technical modernisation, nor independence of the individual enterprise, nor even decentralised development. For the specific conditions of Egypt could not permit such objectives.

Certainly, the employers have earned millions, but this was by submitting to the general capitalist rules which are inescapable, whatever the good intentions of those who choose the capitalist road to development. In an underdeveloped country such as Egypt, the commercial sector dominates all the others, and in particular industry; and importing dominates exporting. The parasitic strata dominate the capitalist strata; foreign monopoly dominates the local market. The owner of the Egyptian capitalist enterprise does not even enjoy the right to play the part of the lesser associate; he is only a subordinate. This is the very basis of the decisive economic point, whether or not it has been specifically expressed by the masters of the putsch. This is a transition from the nation state capitalist regime, a regime which plans and struggles against colonialism, to a state capitalist regime moving within the orbit of imperialist influence. This is the point which was inevitably to transform the putsch, through the intervention of the October war, into a new regime, the qualitatively clearest expression of which is to be found in the strategic turning-point of the Sinai Agreement.

It is under these two related watchwords, 'the sovereignty of the law' and 'development', that things happened. Let us recall the declaration of 30th March 1968. This, for the first time, appealed to the 'sovereignty of the law' and to economic development; the latter, in fact, was never far from the Nasser experience in its various stages. There were numerous laws inviting foreign capital to invest. But the watchwords of the 1971 putsch were not based on the meaning contained in the programme of 30th March 1968, or on that contained in the laws on investment promulgated by the Nasser authority. The sovereignty of the law was – and still is – a restriction on the putsch authority, which nevertheless has pursued the practical stifling of all the national and left-wing trends. Let us recall the liquidation of the Committee of Order, the magazine *El-Kateb*, the periodical arrests, the forced emigration of intellectuals, the silence imposed on writers, and the attempts at seduction suffered by the latter to force them to come under the banner of authority. The watchwords of the putsch authority practically opened the doors to the reactionary economic, social and political tendencies, while at the same time restoring the properties which had been sequestrated, rehabilitating persons whose national honour had been impugned, inviting 'white' émigrés to return, and radically changing the policy for the dissemination of news and, at the top of the cultural and information organisations, installing individuals considered trustworthy by the authorities.

The policy of opening up the country under the Nasser authority, which, politically, had gone so far as to accept the Rogers Plan, authorised foreign investment within limits which did not threaten national independence and within a framework of getting economic development going again. As for the opening up which was the aim of the putsch, this began symbolically with expelling the Soviet experts and complicating Egypto-Soviet relations. Economically, it began with Law No. 65 of 1971, concerning Arab investments and free zones, which was amended on 9th June 1974 by a further law, that relating to Arab and foreign investment and the free zones in Egypt.

This was indeed the climax of the 'general principles' proclaimed by Egypt and the United States during the visit of the American President to Cairo. It was also imposed as a condition for the military disengagement. This law contains clauses authorising foreign capital to derive the maximum profit from investment over a very wide field. It authorises it to invest in industry, in mining, in energy; in the tourist industry, transport, housing, the banks, insurance, and in land clearance. In addition, this law provides guarantees and privileges encouraging the investment of foreign capital in Egypt; guarantees and privileges which go far beyond those offered by developing countries bound to American imperialism, such as, for example, Iran.

Among the guarantees supplied by Egyptian law, are the following: It is not permissible to nationalise or confiscate capital invested, and further, it is not permitted to freeze amounts, mortgage them or place them under sequestration by methods other than legal methods (Article 7).

In the event of any dispute regarding the investments and in regard to the application of the previous article, the arrangements may be carried out according to procedures agreed beforehand with the investor and within the scope of current treaties between Egypt and the country of the investor, and also within the scope of settlements of disputes concerning investment between the countries and nationals of those countries, with which Egypt is bound by Law No. 90 of 1971; in the event of this being impossible, the dispute will be submitted to an arbitration committee, etc. (Article 8).

Those companies benefiting under this law are considered as being private companies, quite apart from the legal nature of the national capital which is associated with them. They cannot be subjected to the laws, legal systems and statutes concerning the nationalised sector or those working in it (Article 9).

These enterprises are exempted from the application of the laws relating to the maximum limits on wages, salaries and fees, and they are also exempted from the application of the laws relating to social insurance and retirement, provided the workers in those enterprises enjoy a better system of insurance (Article 11).

Among the other privileges granted to foreign capital, there is also, for the benefit of the companies' profits, exemption from taxes on commercial, industrial and related profits. They are also exempted from the graduated stamps on capital shares and from the taxation of income from transferable securities for a period of 5 years following the first fiscal year after the commencement of production or activities. This same exemption is applied to profits which are reinvested, provided this income is not taxable in the foreign investor's own country or in other countries. It is also possible, by a decree from the Council of Ministers, for the duration of the exemption to be extended according to the nature of the enterprise, its geographical location, and its importance in terms of the economic development of the country (Article 16). Further, the net income and profits of these enterprises are exempted from income tax, and this exemption may be as much as 5% of the value of the capital (Article 17). Similarly, external loans taken up by these enterprises are completely exempted from any duty or tax. This same exemption is applicable to interest on Egyptian loans granted by the Egyptian partners for financing these enterprises (Article 18). At the same time, the law authorises the foreign experts and workers of enterprises benefiting from these measures to transfer abroad part of their wages and fees earned in Egypt provided the proportion does not exceed 50% of their total income (Article 20). The capital invested under these laws may be exported or made available in any other way after approval by the board of directors of the enterprise (Article 21).

The second facet of these laws concerns mixed capital. The law defines this as being capital invested in mixed enterprises in the form of joint stock companies or private limited companies (Article 23).

The third facet concerns the properties of the General Organisation for Foreign and Arab Investment, and the free zones. As regards the fourth facet, this governs the activities and powers of the boards of the free zone.

The privileges and guarantees provided by Egyptian law for foreign capital, and more particularly American capital, are without precedent, even in the laws of countries like Saudi Arabia or pre-revolutionary Iran. The only privilege obtained by Egypt in consideration of this unique law was the sum of $2,000 million paid over by the American government for investment in Egyptian projects, outside the capital invested by American monopolistic enterprises and companies; these investments produced very little effect since, in reality, the American promise was merely political blackmail, a condition for submitting the Egyptian economy to American law.[4]

In her lecture on 'Egypt in the year 2000', at Cairo in December 1974, Dr. Odette Al-Asyuti concluded by saying:

> It is unnecessary to stress once again the need for a stable law consistently applied by the Government; for the 1971 law on direct investment caused little reaction, due to the opposition of the previous policy to the principle of foreign investment. As for the 1974 law, which supplemented the first one, it met with more approval; for the principle of the distinction (and of privilege) was already in existence. In fact, Egypt has to be master of the initiative. For when the local conditions and requirements are known, when the demand of the multinationals is certain and corresponds to the needs of the country, Egypt will have to contact these foreign enterprises to set out its requirements. In a world in which the benefits of the multinationals are considered as a rare commodity, the expanding countries may arouse the interest of such companies. The offer submitted by the Soviet Union to the Fiat Company may serve as a good example of such a philosophy. Though the 1971 and 1974 laws on investment resulted in the creation of the free zone, suitable conditions do not necessarily attract the multinationals, since frequently they incite internal hatred, which cancels out the advantages of exemption from tax. The idea of a free trade zone is not without its attractions, for large external markets are frequently quite near the country, such as those of Western Europe and the Arab countries. Western Europe suffers from a shortage of labour; it imports workers from the Mediterranean region. Consequently, if stress were to be laid on industries requiring a large labour force, Egypt, with its seekers after employment, can supply the industries established in the free zone [with] the labour necessary for the production of products which can be exported to Europe or to other destinations. The only condition is that the cost of the Egyptian labour should be sufficiently low to make up for the cost of transport, storage and exporting from Egypt to Europe.

Thus, Mrs. Al-Asyuti explains in this paper, possibly unintentionally, 'the advantages' of the two laws promulgated in 1971 and 1974 for the foreign monopolies, and not for the Egyptian people; the latter were to 'supply low-priced labour'!

In practice, we are able to record a number of examples of the specific manner whereby the economy was to be opened up; it may be illustrated from the projects for enterprises approved by the administration of the General Organisation for Foreign and Arab Investment Capital on 5th May 1974:[5]

1) A company with Egyptian and Saudi capital for the building of a hotel to replace the one at Semiramis, to be managed by the international *Hotel Intercontinental* chain.

2) A farm for raising sheep and goats with Egyptian and British capital.

3) A shipping company for transporting Egyptian merchandise with Egyptian and American capital.

4) Tourist vessels on the Nile, with Greek capital.

5) A tourist coach company, with Egyptian and Arab capital.

6) A company for tourist transport and services with Arab capital.

7) A discotheque, restaurant and swimming pool, financed by Egyptians with American nationality.

8) A colour photography laboratory with Egyptian and Saudi capital.

9) A factory for the manufacture of leather garments, gloves, bags and belts, with Egyptian and West German capital.

10) A Khan Al-Khalil manufacturing unit with Egyptian and Arab capital.

These are a few samples of entirely non-developing enterprises, for these are projects for consumption by certain well defined social classes, the sole result of which is inflation and higher prices for essential goods. It must also be remembered that these measures were rapidly followed by a tendency to abolish the ceiling on an individual's income. We should add that, at the same time, sub-paragraph 19 of the investment law grants the owners of recent buildings the privilege of not being subject to the law relating to the leasing of residential property.

By virtue of the economic agreement concluded between Egypt and the United States, it is now possible for all Egyptian capital associated with any foreign country to set up banks, where any banking operation is authorised, without any restriction except such as stipulates that the Egyptian share in the capital should not be less than 51% of the capital. It is now possible, and this has already happened, to open branches of foreign banks in Egypt. It is also possible to set up mixed Egyptian and foreign capital banks for investments and business transactions, without any constraints, apart from that of free trading in free foreign exchange in free zones!

Thus the *coup de grâce* was delivered, in the most legal manner, to two fundamental principles of the Charter for National Action, namely the primacy of the nationalised sector and the fact that banks formed part of the public sector. It is unnecessary to recall that sequestrations were reversed as well as the laws governing the parallel foreign exchange markets, thereby rendering smuggling and the black market official.

After commerce, industry and the banks, there only remained agriculture and the land, where capitalism had not been affected during the years of the Nasser revolution — quite the contrary: its foundations had been strengthened.

What profit has agrarian capitalism derived from the economic change brought about by the putsch?

The Council of the Egyptian People, on 24th July 1975, approved the following four pieces of legislation:

1) An increase in the rents of farming properties provided they did not exceed *seven* times the value of the current agrarian tax.

2) The possibility of converting tenant-farming arrangements into sharecropping arrangements.

3) The abrogation of the committees entrusted with the settlement of disputes and their replacement by courts of first instance.

4) The possibility of expelling the tenant in the event of any delay in payment longer than two months following the end of the agricultural year.

These four pieces of legislation are fundamental, but they do not constitute all the laws of the counter-revolution aimed against the poor peasants and small landowners. They supplement the economic counter-revolution which aims at striking down centralised planning and national development as a whole. And, whereas the nationalised sector, as the moving force of the national economy, was liquidated, thanks to the attacks on the legitimacy of the National Charter and the rights established for public ownership, the contents of the agrarian reform, for its part, though it did not go beyond the laws of national capitalism, were also liquidated. Even more, the putsch really wished to be radical in the matter of economic change.

And what was the consequence?

III

So far, we have only considered the preliminaries; we shall reach conclusions only after relating the context. It suffices for the moment to recall what was stated by the Egyptian Minister of Finance who recognised that: 'the year 1975 was the worst economic year in the history of Egypt.' The Minister for the Plan, the great thinker Ibrahim Hilmi Abd Al-Rahman was more precise. He declared that the basic assumptions of the Plan and also the strategy of development and the paths adopted for opening up the economy were leading Egypt towards disaster. As for the Prime Minister, he made a very eloquent statement to the Council of the People on 11th February 1976 on the disastrous situation! The Prime Minister offered a dual solution: austerity at home and a request for aid from 'our Arab brothers'!

This was a tone in serious contradiction with the dreams evoked by the famous visit of Nixon to Egypt in 1974. Why, then, was this free fall inevitable and so crushing? What is the horizon of the experience of the putsch which, after having been exceptionally legitimised by the war, slipped from the breach of the Outfall to take refuge in the tent of kilometer 101, and finally to fall from the precipice (!) of Sinai? How can the power of the putsch survive the decline of its own legitimacy which was born of the October War? What, in time, are the limits for this survival?

Dr. Fuad Mursi introduces his three critical articles on the policy of opening up the economy in these terms: 'Opening up the economy is not simply taking a position in regard to foreign capital. It is also not an incidental policy, or one which is temporary or provisional. It is the very essence of the strategy of the historical period inaugurated by the October war.'[6] The only error in this judicious introduction consists in the fact that this new strategy is dated 'after' the October war. For, objectively, it was born with the 1971 putsch. It then gained its legitimacy by stealing from popular opinion its demand to have recourse to war. The authorities of the putsch endeavoured on several occasions to stifle the popular demand to have recourse to armed struggle in order to recover the occupied territories. The error is perhaps a subjective one; for Dr. Mursi was the Minister of Supply in the putsch government. But he is also a brave man; that is why he resigned and refused to be a mere instrument for applying the law of the jungle. The error could be due to the fact that the appeal for opening up the economy was louder and less discreet afterwards, thanks to the October war.

But this is not the most important aspect. What is much more important is the conclusion drawn by Dr. Fuad Mursi from the application of the theory of opening up the economy:

> The direction adopted for opening up the economy is at present clear [he states]. It is a question of allowing foreign capital to invest private capital, both foreign and local. Everything which earlier had been prohibited is at present permitted. The opening up of the economy means permitting private capital to develop horizontally and vertically without any restriction. In particular, it is a question of permitting local capital to develop and become large-scale capital and enabling it to join up with international capital. Finally, it is a question of permitting international capital to recover its positions of strength right at the heart of the Egyptian economy.

Thus were the prohibitions defined by the National Charter violated. Foreign capital conquered areas which until then had remained solely the responsibility of the nationalised sector. The latter was itself gradually transformed into a private sector by reason of the participation of local private capital and foreign investors, and this strongly influenced the government to finally abandon the development plan and the elimination of any danger to private capital of nationalisation, confiscation, or placing under sequestration. These measures were also accompanied by the end of the State's commitment to the workers, both as regards their participation in management and profits and as regards legislation concerning labour or the production plan. This violation of what had been considered most sacred in the National Charter constituted an ideal climate for the conditions posed by foreign capital and the private sector.

International capitalism, still hides behind local participation in order to reinforce its hold over the satellite economies.[7] It derives profit from the privileged situation enjoyed by local capitalism. But international capitalism returns to impose its hegemony more and more over local capitalism which, in turn, finds in the installation of foreign capital, and its most exorbitant privileges, a historic chance first to enjoy economic influence and then political influence. Accordingly, the promulgation of the laws relating to foreign investment was accompanied by the liquidation of the properties placed under sequestration and by the transfer of commercial mandates to local capitalism. The climate was thus favourable to international, and to local, capitalism. It was within this framework that foreigners were authorised to own farm properties. Still within this framework, the international organisations and companies working in the enterprises for developing the Suez Canal were entirely exempted from any duty or tax on their income, finances, equipment and transactions. The foreign sector is imperceptibly moving forward to become the leading sector in the Egyptian economy, due to its international ties, its internal activities, its financial power, its prospects and its relations with local capitalism, and even with the State and the nationalised sector.

It was thus natural that, following the promulgation of the legislation authorising foreign investment with the widest facilities, a law should also be promulgated for governing commercial mandates. This law restored to agents, individuals, and private companies, their commercial mandates, thereby killing two birds with one stone: encouraging the parasitic sector of commerce, and liquidating the overseas commerce of the nationalised sector, and finally, subjecting imports to the joint plans of the Egyptian agent and foreign exporter, irrespective of the objective requirements of the country as regards essential and strategic goods. The facilities granted to imports, the most important of which is the flight of capital without any transfer of foreign exchange, were skilfully exploited by the professional robbers in order to import luxury products and to export those which were of prime necessity for the people. The door was thrown wide open for imports by adventurers, without any control or condition, and without the State specifying the products to be imported, the exporter, or the currency for the transactions. It is unnecessary to recall that foreign trade was a basic article in the table of the development plan; for the public sector, it constitutes the best way of obtaining scarce foreign exchange, enabling it to avoid deficit financing, loans at high rates of interest, or conditions which pose a threat to national sovereignty. Today, foreign trade is a principal element in the plans of commercial capitalism which, for its part, is the dominant characteristic of the development of the Egyptian bourgeoisie and more particularly the sector of the speculators.

The collapse of the structures of the nationalised sector was, therefore, fatal. Shares were sold by auction, and experts in the private sector took them up. The laws of capitalism, beginning with those concerning profit and loss, supply and demand, and the law relating to capital gains, now constitute the general framework of production with no consideration for the complementarity which should unite the production units; with no consideration for the development of the means and forces of production; and finally with no consideration for the function of production, its role and its beneficiaries. Today, it is no longer regarded as desirable that production should be geared towards providing public services to the people, like health and education. No consideration is given to the need for production to participate in supporting the armed forces which defend national independence. For all these considerations are unable to pass through the spirit of the laws relating to individual, local or foreign investment; they are not taken into account when facilities are granted which objectively serve aims which are contrary to the interests of the nation.

The same also applies to agriculture; this was affected by the counter-revolution through the new agrarian reform, which was essentially capitalist in nature. The future of 3 million small farmers is threatened. They live by tenant-farming 2.5 million feddans, representing 43% of the total cultivated area. Increasing the amount of rent from seven times the old tax to seven times the new is the fastest way of ruining the widest stratum of small farmers. As for the legislation authorising the owner to turn out the farmer if he is late in paying his rent, this is simply to expel hundreds of thousands of small peasants in order for the land to be taken over by the larger cultivators, not to produce the traditional crops providing sustenance for the people (maize, beans, rice and cotton) but to cultivate fruit and vegetables, the profit from which is greater, more rapid and more certain. At the same time, the decision to transform the relations between the owner and the tenant, by converting from tenant-farming to sharecropping, is frankly a return to feudalism. Slavery then becomes the rule, and leasing the exception. Thus agrarian capitalism is able to protect itself from the 'aggression' of the tenant. Disputes in future will be resolved before the courts; problems may be lost in the labyrinths of justice instead of being quickly settled by commissions operating locally. A peasant may die before judgment is pronounced.

The immediate consequences of this economic reversal were catastrophic. They may be summarised as follows:

1) A disastrous deficit in the balance of payments, and therefore deficit financing and the issuing of bank notes without cover.

2) The disappearance of domestic financing of the development plan, while persons with high incomes abstain from saving; this leads to contracting loans from capitalist countries at exorbitant rates of interest. The burden on the popular sectors with limited incomes thus becomes very heavy.

3) The freezing of exports and the impossibility of controlling imports. For Egyptian capitalism has specialised in campaigns of piracy, smuggling, brokering and illegal stocking; and any other action making possible rapid profits and an individual cowardly accumulation of capital. In a very short time, the Egyptian market has become inundated with luxury products and completely deprived of vital necessities. Inflation has been even further accentuated and unemployment is increasing from day to day, for capital is avoiding long-term investment.

4) In the absence of planning, due to competition from the private sector and the dismantling of the nationalised sector with its plans for management,

finance and production, the share of the latter in production fell for the first time by 1.3%.

It was thus not by chance that 1975 was the 'worst year in the history of modern Egypt', according to the Ministers of Finance and Planning, and the Prime Minister; this, despite the opening of the Suez Canal, the prosperity of tourism and Western aid offered (not without interest), from the World Bank and certain European companies. It was not by chance that Egypt, despite its achievements in the October war, arrived at such a catastrophic situation as was never achieved even in 1967, the year of its disastrous defeat.

This economic situation, it must be remembered, was not due to 'the effort necessitated by war'; in fact, the debts caused by this have not yet been repaid. Neither was it as a consequence of the international rise in prices, for this only affected the country indirectly, and solely as a result of debts owing to the capitalist world. Nor was this situation due to the soaring population, for massive emigration was still in full swing, as was the death-rate. And finally, it was not due to Arab parsimony, for the support given by the oil-producing countries decided upon at the Khartoum summit was still in force.

This situation was the normal, albeit very bitter, fruit of the putsch decision to legislate for the counter-revolution, to get away from the national liberation movement and enter the bosom of imperialist influence.

It is regrettable, though to be expected, that the remedy, according to the Prime Minister, should consist of reducing the people to tightening their belts still further, to go begging to their Arab brothers and to trade in Arab blood in Egypt. But, of course, this whole catastrophic economic situation does not preoccupy the minds of those who have opted for a few metres of Sinai in exchange for the integrity of Egypt in its entirety.

This was a political choice which was made from the outset. It could not but end in a strategic choice at the time of the Sinai Agreement. Through that most sacred of doors, that of war, Egypt moved from the Nasser defeat to victory, a defeat via what is referred to militarily as the breach of the Outfall.

It is essential in this connection to take note of the declarations of General Saad Ad-Din Al-Chazli after being transferred from his post as Army Chief of Staff to that of Ambassador in Great Britain. At the time, he had said this:

> An individual, whatever his courage, cannot bring off a victory without arms. In this battle, the arms were 100% Soviet. We cannot forget the benefits given us by the Soviet Union before, during and after the battle. The Soviet Union, prior to the October War, armed the region in a manner which would never have been realised without it. The Soviet Union sent Egypt, Syria, Algeria, Iraq and even the Maghreb a considerable quantity of arms in each convoy. Russian arms, with which even the Warsaw Pact is not supplied, took part in the fighting. The breach effected by the Israeli forces on the west bank of the Canal was not inevitable. But how was it made? . . . The Egyptian command only recognised the importance it merited when it was too late. However, it

207

was possible to clean out this pocket even later. But Kissinger arrived at that moment, bearing a whole host of promises; he succeeded in convincing the political leadership which, for its part, received him with open arms, in the guise of a manifestation of good intentions and with a view to showing that there was no desire to liquidate Israel . . . The political leadership in Egypt went back on the strategy it had been applying earlier. The Egypto-Soviet strategy prior to the War was based on the following assumption: the longer the war is prolonged, the more the enemy will give way. If we had applied that strategy, the breach would never have been made. And even afterwards, it was possible to plug the gap and so still triumph. If we had observed that strategy, we should have been able to avoid the disengagement and the war would have continued.[8]

It must be remembered that General Chazli was speaking as a soldier whom history will not fail to honour. Moreover, he has never been known to have sympathy for the Soviets. This is a man who has never had any political ambitions or canvassed for civil power. He has always been known for his respect for orders and his faithfulness towards the legitimate political leadership. For all these reasons, the reports he gives attain a level of solid truthfulness. His analyses are closer to the historical facts. How then are we to interpret his words, which show no lack of seriousness?

First of all, we can interpret them by the fact that the power of the putsch in Egypt lied to the Egyptian people and international public opinion when it asserted, on various occasions, that the Soviets were shirking the supplying of arms. This was a lie, which was aimed at covering up the first measure hostile to the very essence of the alliance between the Egyptian liberation movement and the socialist bloc, namely the expulsion of the Soviet experts and advisers. Haykal loses himself in the labyrinths of this 'obscure' point only to say in the end that no one can state the factors which led President Sadat to take such a decision. But this 'surprise' was surrounded by a number of dubious circumstances, the most important of which was without doubt the visit of the Saudi Minister of Defence to Washington and Cairo at the time of the presidential decision.[9]

Admittedly, no one at the Pentagon or the White House officially asked Egypt to expel the Soviets, though the American declarations stressing that the Soviet presence in Egypt prevented any settlement of the Arab-Israeli conflict were very numerous; but let that pass. The objective final result of Mr. Sadat's decision revealed the identity of the new power after the latter had eliminated from the game what may be referred to as the Nasser wing. This identity resides above all in the distance the authorities put between them and the liberation movement and the socialist bloc. This deliberate distancing of themselves was the first message the authorities asked the West to decode.

Secondly, we may interpret the words of General Chazli by referring to the successive declarations of President Sadat to the Lebanese magazine, *Al-*

Hawadith, in which he insisted on two matters: the fact that he had sent Mr. Hafiz Ismail to Washington to sound out the United States prior to the October war, to which the polite and diplomatic reply was that Egypt was faced with a choice, either to consider itself as beaten, and in that case to accept the conditions of the defeat; or to act so that the United States could act too. The same thing, or almost the same, was signified in the declarations of the leaders of Western Europe, more particularly in those of the French leaders.

Egypt acted in October. Here is the second point stressed several times by President Sadat in his statements to *Al-Hawadith* between 1974 and 1975. It was possible, he said, for the breach of the Outfall to become the tomb of the Israeli forces. That breach could have been one of the most extraordinary battles of the Arabs; but Dr. Kissinger advised slowing down, or otherwise the United States would intervene. President Sadat, during the last ten days of the war, stated that he had been surprised to find himself waging war against the United States, instead of against Israel! The important point is that the Egyptian political leadership stated that it could not make war on the United States, for which reason it accepted the six points of the first disengagement agreement. This was the famous agreement crowned by the restoration of diplomatic relations between Cairo and Washington and the fabulous visit by President Nixon, accompanied by economic agreements and dreams. 'The declaration of joint principles', signed by the American President during that visit, replaced the Egypto-Soviet friendship treaty which was first put on ice, and then officially attacked. That agreement is thus nothing more than the other facet of the expulsion of the Soviet experts.

In third place, the words of General Chazli may be interpreted in the light of the historic speech in which the supreme head of the Egyptian armed forces declared that he was ready to negotiate for peace even while the area liberated did not exceed a few kilometres and while General Sharon was making his incursion into the west bank of the Canal. For Mr. Sadat, 16th October 1973 was the date of the drawn match which enabled him to conduct his negotiations from a position of strength!

This context may no doubt give the impression that the war was nothing but a farce, but that cannot be true. For the field of battle cannot be a stage on which one acts with thousands of tanks, cannon and aircraft, where thousands of tons of ammunition are manipulated. In fact, the decision to make war was taken on the Egyptian and Arab streets. But it was without doubt no war of liberation from the point of view of the Egyptian political leadership, even if it was for the people and the army. The breach of the Outfall, in reality, represents the distance separating the military decision from the political decision. Similarly, the second Sinai Agreement represents the distance separating the choice of the people from the choice of the authorities.

For the choice of the people, to struggle against Israel was both a national and social choice, aimed at surpassing the 1967 Nasser defeat to achieve a higher stage of national and social liberation, aiming at avoiding falling into the same errors as were previously experienced, whose bureaucratic leaders were now under lock and key, and aiming above all, to give back to Sinai its national independence in the light of a national Arab vision of independence for all the occupied territories, starting with Palestine. This was a choice directed towards achieving a transition of society from national state capitalism to the foundation of a solid socialist base. These are no isolated elements; it is a dialectical movement whose aims and resources mutually affect one another. The uprising of the students, intellectuals, workers and peasants in Egypt between 1968 and 1973 was a decision for war. But the events which occurred between 1971 and 1973 were preparing for a quite different war, the aim of which was to legitimate the power of the putsch and transform it into a regime. The power of the putsch wished to consecrate the sufferings of previous experience by legislating so as the better to consolidate the deviation It wished to exploit the economic, social and political climate of the five years prior to 1970, in order to lay the foundations for a new regime which would be qualitatively different from that which had gone before. But, when it came, the Egyptians waged the October war without paying any attention to the goals of the regime. They waged it with the courage of apostles and the purity of prophets. Shortly afterwards, they realised that they were like a monk who had accomplished his prayers in a brothel. They were astounded at having effectively overcome the Nasser defeat and then finding themselves in a kind of 'defeat-victory' situation. As though, for the authorities, war were a mere pretext for obtaining the legitimacy necessary for transforming themselves into a regime. In reality, this was always as it were a foetus in the womb of the Nasser regime. The war in that case was no longer a war of liberation, but rather a Caesarian operation.

IV

The conflict between the population and the authorities was once more foreseeable. But it was to be delayed for a year.

Once the disengagement had been carried out on the Sinai front, the Egyptian security organisations presented President Sadat with a report which sounded the alarm bell.

At an extraordinary meeting of the national security organisation, Mr. Hafez Ismail, at the time the President's adviser on matters of national security and now Egypt's ambassador in France, said: 'I am in agreement with the descriptive part of this report, but I do not accept the conclusions which it reaches. I note a certain exaggeration in its manner of viewing affairs.'

Hafez Ismail went as Ambassador to the Soviet Union.

The circle of advisers on the content and analysis of this report was enlarged. Some of them, including Mourad Ghaleb, the Minister of Foreign Affairs at the time, said that the task of the security organisations was to give information and that 'advice' fell outside their mandate.

Mourad Ghaleb went as Ambassador to Belgrade.

Less than a year later, the streets of Cairo were invaded by a violent wave

of demonstrations. The authors of the report asked the supreme authorities
to put their plan into effect. They obtained the green light in less than 24
hours and were thus able to arrest more than 1,000 Egyptian citizens in less
than three days!

But what did the report say? The report said that, since the death of
President Nasser, certain organisations and certain political groups were
beginning to be formed, clandestinely in some cases and semi-publicly in
others. Alongside the Arab Socialist Union, an official political organisation,
there were:

1) Nasser organisations, the residues of the avant-garde organisation of the
Socialist Union, in addition to new elements, most of them young, who
believe, particularly following the 15th May, that the new regime has overthrown Nasserism.

2) Communist organisations, gradually joined by elements which had
belonged to the old formations; but massive groups of students and workers
joined as well.

3) A Wafdist organisation with 40 members within the People's Council. This
organisation is dominant at the university. Its partisans posted up four wall
newspapers, one at the faculty of law at Cairo University and three at the
faculty of commerce.

4) The Muslim Brothers, the Islamic Liberation Party and the Muhammad
Youth; these three organisations are independent of one another.

5) Groups not organised into parties; they are to be found within the workers'
unions, the students' unions, among the cadres and particularly among the
journalists, the engineers and the lawyers.

When assessing these organisations, the report makes the following points.
The Nasserites constitute the largest organisation 'of the left', whereas the
Muslim Brothers constitute the strongest among the organisations of the
right. The Communists are fewer in number, but better organised, more united and more influential. There is a certain degree of understanding between
the Communists and the Nasserites which goes as far as co-operation. Very
bitter differences exist between the Muslim Brothers and the Islamic Liberation Party.

The report adds, moreover, that these organisations are not all in agreement regarding the roles of the Soviet Union, the United States and the Arabs,
or on the meaning and forms of democracy. But, apart from a few differences,
they are agreed regarding the need to once again take up the armed struggle.
Finally, the report advises the political leadership to beat 'this organised
minority' before the danger it is causing proliferates.

But the political leadership shelved the report and directed matters as
follows: It declared the economy open to Arab, foreign and, of course,
Egyptian capital. It declared it open to the West in general and to the United
States in particular. It officially abolished censorship of the press; 'but the
security organisations will require to be watchful to the highest degree.'
Capital was directed into the building of hotels, casinos and the manufacture
of cars. The signs of export/import offices appeared in the main streets. The

211

Middle East air space witnessed the passage of the aircraft of Kissinger and Nixon. And the Egyptian press commenced a 'new era'.

This new era began, very early, with the removal of Muhammad Hassanein Haykal from the directorship of *Al-Ahram*. He had warned against throwing oneself into the arms of the United States and depending on the personality of an American President who was threatened with scandal, or a Kissinger whose career could not but be ephemeral. But the official inauguration of this new period was marked by the rehabilitation of the brothers, Ali and Mustapha Amine. The new democracy implied attacking Nasser, the Soviet Union, socialism and all that the July Revolution had achieved for the economy and foreign policy.

The Egyptian left was content to defend Nasser, the July Revolution, the Soviet Union and socialism. The publications, *Rose Al-Youssef, Al-Gumhuriyyah, Al-Kateb* and *At-Taliah*, made their columns available for this purpose. But once the non-clandestine left, trusting in the leadership of President Sadat, began analysing the October war and assessing its political consequences, the new era was also marked by the liquidation of the monthly magazine, *Al-Kateb*.

In fact, the political power was not content with abolishing censorship in order to make what it had been told in the famous report by the security organisations more widely known. President Sadat took the initiative of submitting a project for developing the Socialist Union. For though the abolition of censorship made it possible to know approximately the general 'political' trends of society, the dialogue on the subject of the Socialist Union made it possible to know the 'organisational' intentions of these trends.

Thus, there unfolded in Egypt one of the most violent discussions on the subject of the Socialist Union. The commission charged with hearing and reporting at the People's Council was presided over by Mr. Mahmud Abu Wafigah, related to President Sadat through the marriage of their children. The final report was written by Mr. Sayyid Mari, the President's son-in-law.

Drawn up by the committee for reviewing the trends in the discussions on the subject of the 'project for the development of the Socialist Union', this report underlined the following points:[10]

> Our people assert that the aim of this development is to have more liberty, democracy and effectiveness.
>
> Certain people have asked for the question of the definition of the peasant and the worker to be raised, so that the representation of the workers and peasants can be guaranteed.
>
> One group among those taking part considers that the formula for the Arab Socialist Union has failed in the realisation of the tasks allocated to it, that this formula is no longer adequate in the face of future forecasts, and all this necessitates a search for a replacement formula. This new formula, still according to this group, might consist of a number of parties. This trend is particularly noticeable among the intellectuals, the university representatives, the journalists and the members

of the various professional bodies. It has also been noticeable in the
discussions which have been taking place in the five governorships.

While the majority of the public, according to the manner in which
it has expressed itself during this wide-ranging national debate, puts
aside, at least for the moment, the idea of a proliferation of parties, it
would prefer, for its political system, to have all the positive advantages
of the regime of a plurality of parties, namely the plurality of trends
and tribunes and the existence of an effective opposition.

These are the conclusions of this official report as presented by Mr. Sayyid
Mari, after toning down the appeal by the public and its desire to have a number of parties. It may be noted in this connection that it has not been able to
escape the problem entirely. The President doubtless recalled the wide-ranging
debate which took place following 15th May 1977, when the great majority
were insistent in calling for a plurality of parties. At that same time, the consequences of the policy of opening up the economy involved other very
precise consequences.

At the political level, the 'settlement' was entering a vicious circle inaugurated by the visits of Dr. Kissinger, that faithful friend, and rounded off by
the visit of Mr. Brezhnev. But the Israeli occupation still continued to weigh
down on the Arab territories, including Sinai.

At the economic level, basic necessities had disappeared from the market.
In the course of a single year, prices doubled while wages did not even
increase by a piastre. The country was in danger of general famine while
parasitical investments, of interest only to the upper classes, were flourishing:
buying and selling cars, and importing luxury products, from underwear to
beauty products. Whole blocks were converted into furnished apartments.
But the production of cloth for the mass of the people was becoming increasingly difficult; and the widest sectors of the population were no longer able
to find anything, either housing or medicines or everyday commodities. It
was no longer only the workers, the peasants and the students who were
suffering poverty; other social strata, originally forming part of the bourgeoisie, were suffering too.

Referring to official statistics, the daily *Al-Gumhuriyyah* reported that in
Egypt 219 traders were earning E£25 million a year.[11] *Rose Al-Youssef*
wrote: 'The rental of the Mary-Land casino is more than half a million
whereas the former tenant paid only £30,000 a year.' At the same time, a
night club in Pyramids Road was sold to an Arab trader for E£450,000 compared with E£13,000 the previous year.

Thus the citizen was no longer able even to dream of housing, food, clothing or education. Trading in university books became one of the most monstrous manifestations of economic deviance; this encouraged the poor student
not to learn, but to look for work. And in the calm and silence, the companies
in the nationalised sector were going into liquidation one after the other.
Today, the master of the situation as regards essential commodities is the
private sector.

Murmurs appeared in the press. The political leadership merely said: 'We allow people to express themselves freely, and then it is we who decide.'

Egypt once again witnessed a wave of 'regrettable events', according to the description of the security organisations. In a queue waiting in front of a co-operative selling soap, one man killed another because he had obtained three more pieces of soap than was authorised. In another queue, a man died from a heart attack: he had been given a chicken and a kilogram of meat to last a whole week. In a banal affair in the popular quarter of Sayyeda Zeinab, the police arrested a suspect, and there was a rumour that the defendant died during questioning; the population of the quarter attacked the police station. The seating at a stadium in Cairo collapsed and young men were killed; a bloody confrontation then followed between the police and the public. A private car knocked down a pedestrian in front of the Chebine Al-Kom Works; the population gathered, set fire to all the cars which came past and attacked the police. The authorities' memory no doubt recalled the series of fires which had taken place prior to the October war, a series which was sadly crowned by the fire at the Opera. But the author of these crimes still remains unknown!

For the first time in history, Cairo's drinking water was polluted. The socialist public prosecutor attributed this crime to 'an unknown author'. The humourist, Salah Jahine, commented on the report of the enquiry, and he thereby earned the accusation that he had 'attacked the magistracy'. But the prosecutor, with this accusation, thereby opened a door which had hitherto been tightly closed: a number of people wrote to ask how it was that the socialist public prosecutor could also at the same time be the Minister of Justice. Questions attacking still more serious subjects began to be asked: how can the Minister of Justice couple with his main function the Chairman-ship of the Union of Workers and that of a number of trade unions? How can the Minister of Culture accumulate 11 posts? And above all, how can the President of the Republic also be the President of the Socialist Union, a unique political organisation?

The 'regrettable' events continued and increased, but taking on other forms. By judicial decree, the Board of the Union of Architects was ordered to dissolve itself; a second and third order condemned it for infringing the electoral law, but none of these decisions was put into effect. A section head at the University of Ain-Chams struck a professor with his shoe, because the latter had dared to make certain observations on the corruption which was rife in the university.

These regrettable events were occurring parallel to the sad political vacuum consequent upon the steps taken to find a peaceful solution following the war, and also parallel to the grotesque rise in prices, the fall in wages, and the monstrous wealth being accumulated by the brokers.

One morning the security 'organisations' presented President Sadat with a report under the title, *Project for a Programme of Action of the Popular Forces*. According to these organisations, the authors of this report were 'Communists and Nasserites'. They had contacted one another and agreed on its wording. In particular, this report states:

> Since the cessation of the fighting and as a result of the trends conse-
> quent upon it, we are witnessing a series of rapid, evident manoeuvres
> on the part of the forces involved in this conflict. American imperialism,
> at the head of the forces hostile to our struggle, Israel's fundamental
> support and the protector of the reactionary and counter-revolutionary
> forces within our country, is actively pursuing the realisation of its aims
> which it has never abandoned. The United States, while providing
> Israeli aggression with political, economic and military support, shame-
> lessly appears to play the role of intermediary and to put itself forward
> as the sole arbiter in the conflict. The United States thereby aims at
> making good the consequences of the war. It is endeavouring to contain
> these consequences in its own interests to the detriment of our struggle
> and the sacrifices of our people, and those of Arab brother nations.
>
> The strata of the right belonging to national capitalism and weakly
> tied to the camp of the national revolution are today preparing, with a
> view to guaranteeing their interests, to realise their ambitions, to break
> this already very tenuous bond and take up their stances as regards the
> nation. They are preparing to abandon the flag of national independence,
> to take up the role of lesser partner with imperialist and foreign capital,
> and this, in the framework of an underdeveloped, satellite, capitalist
> State.
>
> The great majority of the popular forces knows its way. It knows
> what it wants and what it must refuse. It refuses to see the problem of
> the plundered land passing along the path of bargaining and separate
> partial solutions. It refuses to see the United States, our enemy, acting
> as arbitrator between Israel and ourselves. It refuses all efforts on the
> part of American imperialism and its agents aiming at using Israeli
> aggression to subject our country to hegemony, to isolate us from the
> Arab nation and to make us abandon our position in the movement of
> the Arab struggle for liberation, progress and unity. The majority of
> our people rejects all attempts by the reaction and the Arab right aimed
> at exploiting the national ties, for their own benefit, and giving the
> movement for solidarity and unity between the Arab countries a reac-
> tionary content opposed to the interests and aspirations of the Arab
> peoples. It rejects the reactionary right-wing tendency towards the
> handing over of our foreign policy, which is moving more and more in
> the direction of compromise and conciliation with the imperialist
> forces, while isolating itself from the forces which are friendly towards
> our people. It rejects the perpetuation of the anti-democratic situations
> of our country under any pretext. It rejects the imperialist and reaction-
> ary attempts aimed at freezing, and the liquidation of, our economic
> and social evolution. It rejects the right-wing line, which it is desired to
> impose upon our economic and social evolution and which would
> merely result in the liquidation of the achievements of our evolution

and the restoration of the positive achievements, both economic and social, of the revolution of 23rd July.

There can be no doubt that a programme uniting all the popular forces into a single front will be able to play a great organising and unifying role. The people's avant-garde might have as its watchword: Let us mobilise the popular forces into a single front capable of directing the struggle for the realisation of the popular programme, a front in which all the national, democratic and revolutionary forces would be represented, and all the trends, all the political and ideological currents, which represent these forces. This front will of course be a front against imperialism, reaction and the powers of the capitalist right wing.

But this front is not necessarily to be considered as being hostile to the present authority; for due to its situation in the struggle for the liberation of the land and the maintenance of national independence, this front has to undertake to uphold any measure taken by the authorities in this direction. But, and still due to its situation, this front has to undertake to oppose, resolutely, any steps taken by the authorities in opposition to a just conception of the national interest.

And finally, conscious of the fact that the only democratic guarantee consists in all classes of the people and its various working strata being represented within the very heart of the State authority in its various organisations, the front of the popular forces is entitled to struggle without respite in order to obtain a national, democratic and popular power in which there would be separate participation for all classes and all strata of our working people; this power should represent the democratic alliance of the social components of our nation.

This secret report was dated August 1974. It is followed by the general aims of the programme submitted to the dialogue between the various political forces in Egypt.[12]

Following upon this document the political power realised that all its safety valves had not succeeded in dissipating the atmosphere favourable to the existence of secret or semi-clandestine organisations. The lifting (a formal one) of censorship, and the vast dialogue on the subject of the development project for the Socialist Union afforded no assistance. The political leadership read again the first report drawn up by those responsible for security. It found indications of developments that were contrary to what it had hoped to find; problems which were believed to have been buried surfaced once again. The affair in 1960 of the death under torture of the militant, Chouhdi Attiyah Ach-Chafei at the Abou Zabal camp, was vindicated; the court awarded E£12,000 to the litigants bringing the case. A book published in Beirut (*Le pieds nus*) denounced the acts of torture resulting in death to which Egyptian militants − both communists and non-communists − were subjected between 1959 and 1964. The security organisations realised that they were not far removed from denunciation, even if circumstances had changed, and that their future existence required that they should regain their prestige in the matter of repression.

Consequently, these organisations prepared new lists of arrests, a preparation which lasted nine months according to the chance admission, made by the Middle East Information Agency, the official mouthpiece of the authorities. A communique from that agency published on 15th January 1975 stated: 'The security organisations, in collaboration with the magistracy, had been following these subversive activities which are undermining national security, for around nine months.' These organisations were thus not occupied with locating the Israeli espionage networks; nor were they tracking down the smuggling networks, the misappropriation of funds, or those speculating in the daily bread of the citizens. They were concerning themselves with those who were struggling for their right to an independent political organisation, those who were defending democracy. Thus, the 'free press', the discussions on the means for developing the Socialist Union, were only a trap set to make people talk. And when they had expressed their opinions, the security organisations took care to record what they said, where they went and who they were.

Events succeeded one another rapidly. The 'settlement' was speeding along a road with no way out; the well-meaning efforts of Dr. Kissinger came to nothing. The dreams about American capital evaporated. The street, the home, the university, the factory and the office were suffocating. Transport, food supplies, medicines, boots and shoes, clothing, school books and housing were running short.

It was in such a climate that Brezhnev's visit took place. With its preambles and its consequences, it seemed just the opposite of the famous visit by Kruschev in 1964, for he arrived at a time when Egypt was just reaching an important stage in the process of the social transformations which had begun with the decrees of July 1962. On the day of Kruschev's arrival there was not a single communist detainee. In contrast, Brezhnev's visit took place at the completion of the social and political transformations which had begun with the disengagement, thereafter turning in a vicious circle.

At the same time a small demonstration occurred at Port Said; it ended up affecting the whole of the country. Thousands of workers demonstrated against the cost of living, and the repression and the impasse into which the problem of the liberation of the occupied territories had been driven. Thousands of students demonstrated against the restraints imposed upon their political activities, against the reactionary teaching programmes, and against those who sold university books.

In reality, these 'regrettable events' were merely a warning, announcing what was bubbling under the social surface. The explosion came on New Year's Day, 1975. It was not organised, but it was charged with every kind of bitterness. This is one of the traditional forms of struggle of the Egyptian people which has always been a conscious one. It has never had any need of 'elements from outside', or remote control. In reality, the 'intruders' (a sacred expression, launched in the first instance by the security organisations, and then used by the political leadership and broadcast by the mass media)

217

were, according to the admission of a well-informed source, only police officers trained in acts of sabotage and the manufacture of trivial slogans. It was they who deliberately destroyed the offices of the French and Libyan airlines, the Soviet library, and dozens of private cars without any discrimination; for it was vital to show that the accusation of sabotage against the people who were demonstrating was true.

These demonstrations against the monstrous increase in prices, the repression of liberties and compromise have always been honest and open in their watchwords as well as in their style of action. They have always been ahead of the clandestine or semi-clandestine organisations. At the time when they erupted, the Nasserites, the communists, and the democrats were endeavouring to find a correct formula for a common struggle for democracy.

But the security organisations were only interested in the demonstrations from the point of view of 'security'; the authorities had no thought for their serious significance; thus the lists became increasingly overloaded with the names of militants for Egypt, Arabism, independence and socialism.

These demonstrations, it needs to be stressed, were never the work of the American intelligence authorities, as was stated by Abd Al-Rahman Al-Charqawi in *Rose Al-Youssef*. They were conducted by the Egyptian people against repression and price rises. In so far as there were one or two deviations, these were due to outside elements cunningly introduced into the ranks of the people. Nor were they the fruit of a plan drawn up by a Nasserite organisation, whether national or of the left. This was a spontaneous uprising expressing the general climate, rather than representing the activity of one or the other of the parties involved.

The remedy adopted by the authorities, namely the arrest of a thousand citizens from among the workers, students and intellectuals, did not succeed in extinguishing the flame. The disease in fact lay in the authorities themselves who had had the idea of filling their organisations with some of the rich inhabitants of the country and parasitic elements such as brokers and agents of foreign companies. This could not, therefore, be a remedy, for the disease consisted in the disastrous cost of living, the absence of democracy and the acceptance of compromise in regard to the problem of the liberation of the land. Nor could the remedy consist of what certain oil kings or princes demanded in order to save Egypt from famine. Similarly, asking the United States to undertake fresh initiatives to save the regime threatened with collapse, could not constitute a solution to Egypt's internal problem.

Thus, the arrest of thousands of citizens and their release, only to be re-arrested, could have only one meaning; this came within an overall programme for a political compromise and for an economic and social liquidation of all that the July Revolution had realised.

Let us recall: on 1st January 1959, the Egyptian security organisations had undertaken one of the largest campaigns of arrests in the history of modern Egypt. The immediate consequence had been the collapse of Egypto-Syrian unity. The long-term consequence had been the defeat of June 1967.

Now, on 2nd and 3rd January 1975, the security organisations undertook the largest campaign of arrests since the death of Nasser. And what was the result? That is the question.

The reply came, in fact, from Mahalla Al-Kubra. It was swift and decisive. For the first time in the history of Egypt, a veritable commune was constituted in the largest industrial city. It was beseiged by the army and eventually frustrated by armed force and imprisonment. This occurred in March 1975 when the comedy of 'checkmating' Kissinger in the negotiations for the agreements on the fate of Sinai was enacted; these agreements were obtained subsequently at the Salzburg summit meeting between the two Presidents, American and Egyptian, and signed in September of that same year.

Actually, Salzburg represents a point of arrival in Egyptian politics. This is where the economic decisions were to be converted into strategy. Between the two, we can locate the point of arrival at the road which began with the putsch and ended by installing a regime which expressed itself militarily by way of the October War and the Breach of the Outfall. But what of the political framework overall of this road which has been so short and so swiftly traversed?

V

There can be no doubt that the bourgeoisie who took over the controls was, in the last resort, that of commercial capitalism and more particularly, its parasitic and speculating sector. The latter constitutes the broadest stratum in the new Egyptian capitalist structure; it is accompanied by strata of bureaucrats and technocrats whose sole capital is their 'function'; and this is closely tied to the cycle of speculative capital and correspondingly far from the material, productive, structure of society. Associated with this sector, to share in the power, is agrarian capitalism, likewise, since 1971, containing new elements with different origins cited by Dr. Fuad Mursi in the latter part of his study as follows:[13]
1) After 1971, the State property holdings were liquidated. The farms held as a result of the land reform were distributed to those holding diplomas from the agronomic institutes. Part was sold, and some 136,000 feddans which had belonged to the Ministry for Property in Mortmain and had been managed by the Agrarian Reform Organisation, were returned to that Ministry, which forthwith put them up for sale.
2) In 1973, it was decided to change the system of co-operative cotton marketing by purchasing direct from the producer, which made possible the return of the brokers and traders to the interior. All this could only benefit the large capitalist cotton producer. Today, the trend is towards the lifting of controls on the marketing of all agricultural products which had formerly been subjected to the same co-operative system.
3) Still in accordance with the law for the liquidation of properties placed under sequestration, the remains of the lands under sequestration were returned to their former owners, the majority of whom were great feudal

overlords. Thus, the reconciliation of agrarian capitalism with the sequels of feudalism was accomplished.

4) The general assembly for legislation, attached to the Council of State, granted every family (who could afford to!) the right to hold more than 50 feddans at any location.

We would add that the agrarian measures rendered service to the upper strata of agrarian capitalism by reducing to nothing the small tenants and proprietors. All these measures enable us the better to appreciate the extent of the class alliance which dominates present Egyptian power. We are here referring to the alliance of the two sectors, the commercial sector and the agrarian.

Face to face with these, we find the middle strata practising small-scale production; these are the peasants and the smaller peasants, the broadest stratum of proprietors, covering more than 3 million people. Their means of production are truly archaic and scarcely suffice for the requirements of the family. At the same time, there are the agricultural workers numbering 4.1 million, who constitute exactly half of the labour force at national level. But it must be noted that 40% of these agricultural workers may be considered as being unemployed, again owing to the archaic nature of agrarian production. For, whereas the agricultural worker produces a value of E£296 per annum, the industrial worker produces a value of E£2,188 over the same period.

It is also necessary to take into consideration the artisans of the urban areas; they are the equivalent of the lesser peasants. In fact, the production of small wares in Egypt dominates a large part of industry; for example, the production of furniture, leatherware and fabrics. It is normal, in this instance, for the artisan to live in an old-fashioned workshop, archaic both as regards the means of production and the quantity of output or profit. This stratum resembles another in the commercial sector, namely that of the retailers.

And finally, in this capitalist sector with its strata, distinct both in quantity and quality, there is the large stratum of civil servants, which like society itself, and capitalism itself, encompasses numerous substrata and interests. We find here the higher authorities who, by their functions in production and by the profits they realise, do not differ from the upper parasitic strata in the commercial sector. We find also the middle strata, whose social origin is, and remains, attached to the small properties, to more humble origins, peasant or petty commercial. We find also those whose situation, in practice, does not differ from that of the working class, despite the difference in the means and functions of production.

As for the Egyptian working class, this comprises 9.5 million workers. In 1973, the number was 8.7 million. In relation to their activities, they might be distributed as follows: 64% in the agrarian and industrial production sectors; 14% in the sectors of commerce and distribution; 22% in the service sectors. The overall figure of workers may be divided into the two sectors: 32% in the nationalised sector and 68% in the private sector. The industrial working class comprises 1.1 million workers representing 12% of the total Egyptian working class.

What is the political form proposed by the new regime to harness the intense social reactions? Owing to the new economic trends the discrepancy between the classes is growing deeper and deeper. The social struggle is becoming increasingly acute and bitter. What then might be an adequate form for controlling this struggle which is now approaching the extreme limits? The inflation index rose by 22 points between 1972 and 1974. The price index for consumer goods rose to 119 in December 1972 and 141.3 in October 1974. The prices of foodstuffs rose 24% over 13 months, despite the fact that the share of income generally allocated to food is already 57% and more for the man in the street. The countryside also saw the same price increases. (We should note in passing that tea, sugar and tobacco are not luxury products.) Rents rose by a minimum of 100%. As regards the maximum, this is known only to the speculators and entrepreneurs in the private sector.

> 9.8% of all citizens consume 44.5% of total consumption, whereas 90.2%, i.e. the overwhelming majority, consume 55.5% of total consumption. Within the first category, 2.3% alone consume 24% of consumption by volume. It is thus not surprising that many families in the middle strata have ceased to take meat, to drink milk or eat eggs. The list of foodstuffs people do without grows longer and longer. It was no surprise when, at the end of an enquiry, it was learned that 99 pupils out of a hundred are underfed or anaemic.[14]

What political form is, then, capable of guaranteeing security in a regime which in the last resort is nothing but one small jungle attached to another larger jungle?

At the outset, it is necessary to underline a number of considerations: Egyptian capitalism, crystallised at the economic and social levels over the last ten years and solidly installed over the last five years, is completely different from Egyptian capitalism prior to 1952. It differs qualitatively from the capitalism which survived the revolution and even persisted during the years of social transformation (1961-1965). Its dominant orientation is commerce and in particular its parasitical aspects. It is irrefutably subject to the foreign monopolies, and this in a society which is underdeveloped and in which the land is occupied.

This speculation capitalism inherited, among other passive factors of the previous regime, the formula of the single political organisation, popularly known as the alliance of the forces of the working classes, an organisation which, even prior to the death of Nasser, proved itself to be incompetent. A fact plainly illustrated by its resounding collapse on the night of 14th May 1971, for it was never more than a paper organisation; but its danger resided in the fact that it prohibited any independent organisation of the various social classes. It was specially designed for a non-democratic power as regards

political practice. And even when that power 'granted' certain rights to the
popular working strata, this was by the 'decision' of the upper hierarchical
echelons without any participation or control on the part of the people.

While demagogic camouflage was a dominant characteristic of the Egyptian
regime after 1952, it became its backbone after 1971, to the extent that,
nowadays, the term 'documents' no longer means anything. If these are able
to serve any purpose, it is merely to enable the research worker to measure
the depth of the abyss separating the dream, with which the mass media and
the legislative institutions cram the minds of the people, from the nightmare
of reality.

In the light of these main considerations, it is possible to specify the political form proposed by the present regime in the following manner:

The present Egyptian bourgeoisie does not have the means to be like the
good old bourgeoisie prior to 1952; that was liberal in the true sense of the
word. Dr. Fuad Mursi, in the latter part of his study, wrote:

> The former great bourgeoisie, had as its basis a capitalism of sharehol-
> ders. It had created industrial and commercial companies and banks.
> Socially, it represented a very thin layer: 62% of all shares were held by
> 9% of all shareholders. The 1961 nationalisation measures only affected
> 7,300 persons. At that time, there were only 4 persons who could be
> considered as millionaires. As for the great new capitalism of today, its
> millionaires can be counted in thousands.[15]

This purely economic truth automatically prevents the realisation of the liberal character of the advanced bourgeoisies, because of the way they are
normally constituted. The bourgeoisie we are concerned with here is depriving
the social struggle of its democratic expression, for this, of necessity, would
apply the brakes to the cancerous proliferation of parasitical capital, its illegal
methods, its abandonment of the tasks of national independence and its
absolute dependence in regard to foreign capital. Liberal democracy in the
case of Egypt today is a sword, not an olive branch. This is why it is rejected
by present Egyptian capitalism, whose characteristics are underdevelopment
and pillage.

For all these reasons, contemporary Egyptian capitalism finds in the formula of the Socialist Union and in the alleged national alliance a golden
inheritance which must not be abandoned as long as it prevents 'the others'
from organising democratically. Let us not forget that it controls, among
others, all the organs of repression. If at times it is a supporter of plurality
and diversity, this is to avoid departing too far from the roots of capitalist
ideology in relation to the free economy. If it is in favour of '*laissez-faire,
laissez-passer*', this is always provided that this is within the framework of the
maintenance of the Socialist Union, and provided that the courts only express
themselves within this framework. For, from its own point of view, whereas
the 'laws' define the worker, the peasant and the national capitalist, the sovereignty of the law lays down the dialogue of the opposing interests in one of

the most modern of political clubs represented by this Socialist Union! But that is not all. Indeed, the plurality of courts also makes it possible to embrace the idea of a plurality of parties; for in the last resort it is the authority of the Council of the People which authorises, or otherwise, the existence of the parties 'proposed'. It suffices in this event to accept 'several' parties expressing all the interests of a single class. For the present authority, these are good ideas, and their implementation can be envisaged after the realisation of total liberation!

In other words, even the deformation of democracy depends entirely on the peaceful settlement of the Middle East crisis, a settlement of which the most illustrious expression is the Sinai Agreement. Here, the demagogic camouflage becomes a cutting weapon. What do the 'documents' say?

Prepared two months prior to the October war, by the General Secretariat of the Socialist Union in collaboration with the permanent committee of the Council of the People, 'the document of the dialogue' states that the event of 15th May 1971 is only a 'movement' of rectification. Later, in 1975, President Sadat stated that this was a revolution. We are entitled to ask: whom are we to believe? But let us leave aside this minor detail; what is important is that this document provides, 'in a manner which does not allow the least doubt to remain', a total commitment in regard to the 'charters of our revolution', and a total commitment 'to protect the socialist and democratic revolutionary achievements realised by our people through the revolution of 23rd July'. But reality contradicts, most scandalously, this commitment; for not only is the ferocious campaign against Nasser and the Nasserite experience in full swing but, at the same time, in all fields, everything is being done to liquidate the applications of the Nasserite experience.

This document, moreover, despite the high quality of its style and formulation, exposes its camouflage when it deals with certain problems:

For example, when it deals with international detente which, as usual, it refers to as 'the international reconciliation'. This reconciliation, it states, 'has enfeebled the United Nations'! In particular, it stresses that it was following the Helsinki Agreement that the United Nations recognised the Palestine Liberation Organisation (P.L.O.) and almost unanimously condemned Zionism as a racialist ideology. The question now, is, are these measures signs of weakness as this document suggests? That is, other than for the United States, Israel and the satellite countries.

For the authors of this document, international reconciliation between the United States and the Soviet Union has been brought about 'to the detriment of the smaller nations'. They are doubtless forgetting that it was during this international detente that Vietnam, Cambodia, Laos and Angola (!) were liberated. The authors of this document consider that it was during the time of international detente that restrictions were lifted on the emigration of the Soviet Jews, whereas the reality was quite the opposite. For the Soviet Union categorically refused to conclude any commercial agreement with the United States conditional upon any clauses whatsoever concerning the Soviet Jews!

And finally, the document 'accuses' the United States of supporting the

Israeli occupation; but later, the same United States is described as a faithful friend. Finally, the document urges the early conclusion of the union with Libya; and shortly afterwards precisely the opposite occurred (the Libyan march for union was halted because the Egyptian forces barricaded the desert road).

After all this, the authors of the document of the dialogue conclude by recalling the 'need for the maintenance of national unity inside the alliance of the forces of the working people'. In reality, that was the fundamental point at which this document aimed to arrive, under the pretext that Egypt was passing through a 'stage of total confrontation', meaning the October war, in the name of which the President submitted to a popular plebiscite another document, which again obtained a unanimous popular 'yes'! And what does this second document say?

This document stresses that the first article of the Constitution stipulates that the economic foundation of the Arab Republic of Egypt is the socialist system, based on justice and satisfaction of requirements in such a manner as to prevent exploitation and reduce difference between classes. It also stresses Article 26, which lays down the right of the workers to take part in management and to share in the profits, Article 37 protecting the agrarian reform measures, and Article 30 laying down support for the nationalised sector, the motive force for progress in all fields and mainly responsible for the development plan. But, it must be emphasised, we have observed that the economic measures taken before and after the October document constitute a swift and unorganised withdrawal in relation to the very contents of the articles of the Constitution. And to crown it all, this document concludes with a quotation from President Sadat:

> We are aware that democracy is not merely texts: it is a daily practice. Democracy is not practised in a vacuum. It requires frameworks through which the trends are defined which concern the country's political, economic and social affairs. The nation has accepted the system of the alliance of the forces of the working people as the framework for its political life. In the battle for construction and progress, we need this concentration more than ever. As a consequence, I reject the fragmentation of national unity under the pretext of forming parties. But I likewise reject the theory of the single party which imposes its will on the people, deprives it of its freedom and takes away from the people the practice of its political liberty. This is why I attach considerable importance to the alliance being a proper framework for national unity within which all forces will be able to express their legitimate interests and their opinions, so that it will be possible to see the trends which enjoy the support of the majority and which should be adopted by the State. The political organisation should be a centre where opposing ideas can fuse and trends crystallise which should truly express what the broadest popular base desires.

Thus the formula of the Socialist Union remains the ideal political form even despite the October war. The document says: 'It is only in this way that we shall remain true to the spirit of that great October'! Which means that any other path which is sought cannot be true to the spirit of October!

In August 1974, President Sadat presented his second document for developing the Socialist Union,[16] the organisation for which everyone had exhausted themselves in a futile effort to develop. For plugging the gaps in this type of problem is useless. A formula of this kind, which has proved its incompetence in practice during all these years, cannot but be based on a false theory. The second document for the development of the Socialist Union is, it would seem, only a last attempt on the part of the authorities to maintain the formula of the single political organisation prior to giving the green light to the plurality of their own parties. The document states: 'The negation of the idea of the single party can only be certain by admitting the plurality of trends within the Socialist Union.' This is an old adage; but the new one was doubtless the appeal to the plurality of 'platforms' within the single organisation. But in the effort at application, the idea has been transformed into a circus or a screen concealing the effective plurality of the parties. In fact, the fate of the multiple tribunes is the same as that of the Socialist Union . . . impossible of realisation; for the President publicly rejected that there should be a Nasserite tribune. As for the communists, we make no mention of them, for they have been systematically imprisoned after being brought before the courts. The reality is that the regime is swinging to and fro like a pendulum, when it is a question of deciding once and for all the definitive political form it would like to adopt; but the political path has been laid out in advance.

Will the authorities hesitate long? In reality, they are still hoping to discover a formula which will install the dictatorship of the dominant class. But they still have recourse to democratic slogans to camouflage their demagogy. The real contradiction not only places the authorities in opposition to the people, but also in contradiction to themselves and the interior; for this is an anachronistic capitalism, incapable of even resolving the urgent problems on the two fronts, economic and social. This is an adventurist capitalism which cannot see further than the end of its nose. That is why it loses its way while endeavouring to organise the country; the sole decisive factor is, without doubt, that this capitalism is dragging the country to the verge of bankruptcy.

For all these reasons, this regime has never possessed the means for resolving its own problems.

In reality, the solution that is capable of saving what still can be saved resides in another solution. The Egyptian programme for struggle against the Sinai Agreement, a strategic turning-point of this renegade regime, states that it is still not too late.

Notes

1. Taha Chaker, *Problèmes de libération nationale et révolution socialiste*, Dar El-Farabi (Beirut), pp. 116-17.
2. *Ibid.*, p. 124.
3. Fuad Mursi, 'l'Hégémonie des rapports de production capitaliste', *At-Taliah*, No. 12, 1975.
4. Harbi Muhammad, 'Lla anya tattagih Misr' in *Al-thawrah* (Iraqi newspaper), 8th July 1974.
5. Hazim Amin Thabit, *Kitabat Misriyyah*, September 1974 (Beirut), pp. 57-9.
6. Fuad Mursi, in *Haza Al-Infitah Al-Iqtissadi*, Dar Al-Thaquafah Al-Gadidah; also in *At-Taliah* (Egyptian journal) No. 10, 1975.
7. *Ibid.*
8. *As-Safir* (Lebanese newspaper) 22nd August 1974.
9. Muhammad Hassanein Haykal, *At-Tariq lla Ramadan*, (Beirut 1975).
10. See *At-Talia'h*, September and October for the full text and a study of the text.
11. *Al-Gumhuriyyah*, 14th November 1974.
12. This report was published by the Beirut magazine *Ach-Chararah*, No. 3, January/March 1975.
13. *At-Taliah*, No. 12, 1975.
14. Fuad Mursi, *op. cit.*
15. *Ibid.*
16. *Al-Ahram*, 9th August 1974.

7. The Left as the Opinion of the Man-in-the-Street

If, for the present Egyptian regime the Sinai Agreement represents a strategic turning-point, in the sense that it marks a culmination as regards economic, social and political affairs, can it be said that the opposing popular forces have also reached a point of no return? Are they seeking for a strategic alternative in order to abrogate that agreement, together with all its implications, namely the liberation of the land, man and society? If the reply is in the affirmative, what then is the Egyptian programme for struggling against the Sinai Agreement, against all its dimensions, local, Arab and international?

There can be no doubt that the Sinai Agreement, the process of which began with the expulsion of the Soviet experts and ended with the abrogation of the Egypto-Soviet Treaty of Friendship and Co-operation, polarised some very distinct social strata; these clearly expressed their unanimity within the People's Council and the Central Committee of the Socialist Union and through the mass media, regarding the stages of this political approach of the authorities at three levels: internal, Arab and external. For this Agreement is not simply a decision taken by the Head of State; its approval by the Ministerial Cabinet was no simple formality. This Agreement was, and still is, an overall political framework complying with the aspirations of social strata somewhat broader than the circle of direct power (although much narrower than the people at large) — strata even smaller than the cross-section of the bourgeoisie in the social structure. Together, these social strata constituted a very clearly defined cross-section, which, immediately following the 1971 putsch, took control of thought, legislation, the executive and information. Though relatively insignificant, this cross-section twice succeeded in concluding agreements on Sinai. The first time was when, under the watchword of 'opening up the economy', it set out along the economic path implicit in that agreement with all that this signified by way of new legislation which, as far as the economy was concerned, constituted a veritable withdrawal when compared with the national Charter. At the social level, this stratum launched the watchword of 'social peace', with the aim of maintaining the structure of the Socialist Union and the formula of the single political organisation. In the political field, it launched the watchword 'revolution of adjustment', which necessitated rectifications in the local position adopted in regard to the forces of the left, to the Palestinian problem, and to that adopted toward the socialist forces and the Soviet Union.

The second time was when it succeeded in convincing the broader strata of the petty bourgeoisie that its policy was correct. We should note that it was able to do this thanks to the mass media, which it still controlled. We would also add that it was able to convince certain Arab groups dazzled by the October war, and certain other Arab groups resembling it and cherishing economic and political dreams. At the international level, it succeeded in attracting the sympathy of some extremists hostile to socialism and the socialist bloc, as well as the sympathy of certain international groups which saw in the October war a suitable outcome of the Middle East crisis. If we admit that this very slender stratum of the Egyptian bourgeoisie succeeded twice over, it is still necessary to write this 'success' in quotation marks, for reasons which will be discussed later. But it must also be admitted that this success was real; for our public must not be deceived, if we wish to have a struggle in order to breach this success. Recognising reality is the first essential step towards changing it. Failing to recognise it is tantamount to delivering oneself up to fatalism.

It must, therefore, be admitted that the putsch authority succeeded in realising its plans. The Agreement on Sinai constitutes their culmination, or rather the best representation, of the various successes achieved in a variety of fields. What then is the reason for this success?

From a certain point of view, this authority is the prolongation of the right-wing virus which had resided in the previous authority. Its strength is not, therefore, of recent origin. Its roots go well back into the Nasserite regime itself. Nasser, for all his historical stature and charismatic strength, was never able to suppress it; and possibly, it is this virus which finished him in 1967, and assassinated him in 1970, converting that assassination into a putsch.

This fringe of authority exploited some real defects in the old regime, and more particularly that relating to the problem of democracy. This authority, once installed, found shortcomings already in existence that needed no modification — shortcomings which reached the very depths. This fringe of authority, under Nasser, participated in errors and in crimes. Later, it did not hesitate to seize the opportunity for exploiting the bloodshed and the sad memories of the Egyptians. It even engaged in trading with the corpses of its adversaries.

Because, in the 1967 defeat, this authority perceived a deep national wound, it succeeded in making the crossing of the Canal towards the east a bridge of gold which enabled it to move from the status of a putsch State to that of a legitimate State. In reality, the October war was a resurrection of the regime. And though the war came under the authority of the people and the army from June 1967 to October 1973, in the practical phase, in the eyes of the present powers, it was only a pass for arriving at the Sinai Agreement in 1975.

This regime succeeded in executing its plans because at the time the Egyptian people lacked any vanguard direction capable of organising popular opposition and exerting pressure to prevent the signature of such an agreement. Never in the modern history of the Egyptian people had such a treaty been concluded. Others, far less serious than the Sinai Agreement, provoked violent upheavals. In reality, the Egyptian people never ceased opposing the measures taken by the counter-revolution. Its spontaneous uprisings bear witness to this. This hostility was even shown at an early stage, in 1968, at the time of the rising of the workers, students, peasants and intellectuals. The problem lies in the fact that its vanguard, whose role is to organise pressure and resistance and prevent degradation, has always been tragically fragmented. Some chose to struggle within the regime; some preferred to manifest their struggle verbally; and still others struggled silently, or outside the country. In fact, these different forms of resistance reflect a grievous division in thinking and a serious waste from the point of view of action. This absence of an organised vanguard of the Egyptian people, which is due to fragmentation, tardiness, or the weakness of its development, was largely responsible for the failure of the spontaneous popular uprisings and authority's thrust toward the execution of its plans and its disregard of the opposition.

The present Egyptian power succeeded in realising its plans because the Arab division, and the shuffling of the Arab cards, reached a catastrophic point following the October war, when Arab kingdoms were directing policy, and liberal regimes had drawn nearer to reactionary ones, so that the minimum threshold for an agreement between most of the Arab national regimes ceased to exist. The political consequences of the October war largely opened the doors for the return to the Arab scene of the oil kingdoms and their emirates, and this enabled them to form communications networks between hesitant wings of certain liberal regimes and international imperialism.

We should add to all this the fact that the international situation was, and still is, tragically lagging behind in relation to the Middle East region; for at the moment when the old and the new capitalisms were falling back from their traditional positions in Asia and Africa, the Arab nation, especially in the Mashreq, still remained attached to a colonial safety belt, both internally and externally. Internally, there is first and foremost our national wound, represented by the Israeli presence, organically bound up with American imperialism. And there are also the regimes rich in raw materials which have long been revolving within the orbit of imperialist influence. For the latter, Israel only represents a religious problem and their main enemy is none other than the Arab liberation movement. Externally, there is the Persian Empire which is stifling the Gulf. There is also the Atlantic Alliance, which, on the verge of our Mediterranean coastline more or less constitutes an American lake, despite Egypt's relations of good neighbourliness with Turkey and Greece. The conflict between the two latter countries in connection with Cyprus is transforming that island into a source of direct threats to our security.

In such conditions, the Soviet Union finds itself in an unenviable historical situation, especially as the main split in the international revolutionary current in this case only benefits the local and international reactionary forces.

Consequently, the possibility of international progressive action becomes acutely restricted; it would be governed in advance by the balance of internal forces in Egypt and in the Arab nation in general.

For all these reasons, the steps taken to conclude the Sinai Agreement succeeded. While the October war gave the putsch of May 1971 an exceptional legitimacy and one which was essentially hostile to the logic of history, and which must be rectified once the subjective conditions and objective situations are ripe, the success of the Sinai Agreement, with its economic and social aspects contained in the military and political agreement, is likewise an exceptional success, hostile to the movement of history, and essential to rectify as soon as possible. Those who are charged with correcting the movement of history by revolutionary means, i.e. abrogating the Sinai Agreement with its various significations, both implicit and explicit, constitute the organised vanguard of the Arab people in Egypt, who are charged with controlling the spontaneous uprisings of the public in the ranks of the struggle capable of realising the historical project, from the point of view of both thought and action. In other words, the Egyptian left, despite the diversity of its social sources and its ideological roots, still remains the sole candidate for saving the revolution from the counter-revolution.

But more precisely, and above all, who are the Egyptian left?

Is this an intellectual group known for its 'communist' activities over the last quarter of a century? Is it these groups of young people attached to Nasserism by their allegiance and revolt over the past ten years?

Are these a few individuals on whom the spotlights have been directed, even after the dissolution of the political organisations in 1965? Or are these a few individuals faithful to the idea of the party, whatever the possibility of creating that party?

Is the Egyptian left a group of active underground militants? Within the framework of the present regime? Or is it a group of militants acting in the open and in the official information organisations? Is it a group acting outside the country's frontiers?

Is the Egyptian left made up of intellectual elements, executives, writers, journalists and artists, or is it made up of elements working in the fields or the factories? Is this the left of action or of thought?

When asking these questions, I am not seeking any overall answer, but only to dissipate some of the confusion enveloping the Egyptian left which, due to so many distortions, has become a mystery to the majority of people. The stereotyped image of the people of the left is a mixture of atheism, blood, and vulgar revolt against the dominant social usages and customs. Various factors have contributed to the formation of this false image, starting with colonial propaganda, first English and then American. To which it is necessary to add the political trends which had recourse to religion to serve their cause, such as for example the Muslim Brothers. This false image has been worked upon also by minds corrupted by collaboration with the West and allegiance to local reaction, notably those responsible for the Akhbar Al-Yom firm. At the same time, the sharp contradictions between the power of

23rd July and the communists were not without influence in distorting the image of the communists — whether deliberately or not is of little consequence today.

There can be no doubt that the historical and social origins of the direction of the Egyptian left, and the climate of repression which manifested itself very early and under successive powers over the whole of modern history, form part of the objective reasons for the manifold political errors and upheavals among the organisations; and this has also played its part in the widespread distortion of the image of the Egyptian left.

Despite falsification and confusion, the image has nevertheless escaped excessive adulteration. For the Egyptian left has always been greater than the particular clandestine organisations and the public figures. It has always been more international than the historical directions, broader than the information vehicles, deeper than the watchwords launched, and greater than the intellectual sectors; it has always been the first to foresee the future. The Egyptian left has been, and still is, a popular movement with its roots deeply implanted in national reality. This movement was at different times represented by clandestine organisations, an authorised newspaper, a trade-union campaign, a students' front or a peasant uprising. For, perfect organisation capable of bringing together the revolutionary population has been, and still is, the Achilles heel in this movement of the people; a movement which, in most cases, was prevented from popularising itself by successive governments over more than half a century, which in turn repressed the left because of their inability to resolve the two central problems in the life of the country, namely the national question and social progress. Crushing popular pressure, albeit unorganised, always directed power towards a choice between repression and slow social reform. It is no chance that the Wafdist avant-garde is a fruit of the Wafd party. Nor is it merely by chance that the authority of 23rd July undertook certain national and progressive measures while hundreds of communists were languishing in gaol.

This means that it is the common man in the street who is the Egyptian left; the changeover never went as far as a radical revolution within the ruling power. In other words, so far, there has never been any organisation capable of embodying the street in order to undertake to change society while changing the power itself. In most countries throughout the world, the street is of necessity leftist; it is the political symbol of the working-class and peasant population and the progressive strata of the petty bourgeoisie; but in most countries it has representatives and organisations, which, with the support of the street itself, carry on a dialogue with the authority in power. As far as the Egyptian street is concerned, it is not merely *to* the left — it *is* the left itself.

How has this come about?

The most powerful secret organisation in the history of modern Egypt is indisputably the organisation of the Muslim Brothers, the party of the extreme right. The largest, non-clandestine party in the history of Egypt has indisputably been the Wafd. The clandestine underground, like the unification of the communist parties, has undergone the bitterest of setbacks. This, too,

231

has been the fate of the non-clandestine Nasserite organisations, from the liberation organisation to the vanguard organisation, including the National Union and the Socialist Union en route.

Let us now consider this assembly of historical facts and endeavour to draw some conclusions. When an organisation is a reactionary one and on the extreme right, it always enjoys cast-iron structure and solid continuity, despite anything to which it may be exposed by way of proceedings and attempts at liquidation. However, it never comes to power, either under a liberal democracy (the Muslim Brothers never obtained a single seat in Parliament during the Wafdist periods), or even when that organisation may have special relations with the political leadership. The Muslim Brothers certainly had such relations with a number of members of the Council of the Revolution of 23rd July.

The Wafd was the largest non-clandestine party which came to power; but it was never a party in the political and organisational sense of the term. Rather, it was a club, whose members were grouped around certain values, beginning with political liberalism, and around certain historical personalities, such as Saad Zaghlul and Mustapha An-Nahhas.

The political organisations which suffered the most atrocious repression, persecution and police infiltration, also experienced fragmentation, dispersion and ravages such as had never been experienced by other organisations. However, they always exerted an intellectual influence and played a political role outside authority, but going beyond their real dimensions. Of themselves, they never have constituted pressures on successive authorities; but owing to their intellectual and political effectiveness within the very heart of society, they disseminated a climate of pressure which was not restricted to the mere fields of culture, letters and the arts. This climate of pressure also extended to national action and social reforms. Though the merit of having polarised the Egyptian population on the national question falls to the Wafd Party, the merit of having polarised the broadest sectors of the Egyptian population on the social question falls without question to the Egyptian Marxists. To this we should add the deep-seated changes brought about by them in the fields of thought, culture, and letters, changes which have had extensions even beyond the regional frontiers of Egypt; they have reached out to the Arab nation as a whole.

The organisations of Nasserite power never succeeded in constituting a real party, despite the membership of thousands of people, and the fact that these were organisations of the authority in power and, at certain times, that power adopted positions and measures in favour of the popular majority. Their failure was due to the absence of the element of free choice. The Egyptian citizen had only one party he could join; that was the radical difference between belonging to the Wafd which was not always in power, and belonging to a power which was omnipresent and never yielded.

What can be derived from these observations? First, that the Egyptian street, from the end of the 1920s up to the beginning of the 1950s, remained Wafdist, whether or not that party was in power; and, from the middle 50s to the middle 60s, it was Nasserite, whether Nasser was victorious or vanquished. But belonging to the Wafd or to Nasserism represents an attachment to an assembly of values, ambitions and personalities, rather than representing an attachment to a party or a political organisation.

We may also state that the street has been neither communist nor 'Muslim Brotherhood', despite the fact that the Egyptian communists represented the best political expression of Egyptian popular aspirations, and that the Muslim Brothers were hidden behind what was most sacred in the life of the great Egyptian majority. Neither the Muslim Brothers nor the communists were able to contain the movement of the Egyptian street in an organised way, because of the excessively rigid nature of the organisation of the former and the fragmented nature of the latter.

But it would be a serious mistake to draw a naive political conclusion from these facts, by assuming that the Egyptian people were moderates, and hostile to any extremism. More serious still is the mistake of placing communists and Muslim Brothers on an equal footing. For the street has never been impartial, and adept at middle paths.

In fact, in our modern history there is a political peculiarity which achieves the force of a law, namely the spontaneity of popular uprisings among Egyptians and that of the popular movement which has always been greater than the organisations and has accordingly escaped control by the parties.

The street was Wafdist, without, for all that, being a member of that party; the active Wafdists themselves did not form a party in the precise meaning of the term. In short, this was an attachment to independence, democracy, the personality of Saad Zaghlul and later than of Mustapha An-Nahhas. This same street was also later Nasserite without, for all that, being a member of the organisation for liberation, the National Union, or the Socialist Union. Those organisations, on the admission even of their leaders, never succeeded in forming a true party. The attachment of the people was thus in the direction of national realisations, rather than the progressive measures and personality of Nasser.

It is now necessary to make a clear distinction between the attitude of the Egyptian street with regard to the Muslim Brothers and with regard to the communists. For, despite the dispersion and division of the Marxist organisations, their influence was by no means negligible; on the contrary, it was an active, and at times decisive influence. It was their ideas which resulted in the birth of the wing referred to as the 'Wafdist avant-garde'. It was their clashes and their meetings with Nasserism which gave rise to the progressive formulations for the decisions and charters of the revolution of 23rd July 1952. It was they who were behind the watchwords of the revolutionary power, and behind numerous measures taken by that power. It may even be said that the transformation toward socialism of a party which embraced fascism — 'Young Egypt' — is not entirely a stranger to their influence.

If the main bloc of the Egyptian people has always maintained its distance from the idea of organising itself politically, this calls for far-reaching reflection. Let us be content here with saying that this phenomenon largely explains the Wafdism of the street at one moment and its Nasserism at another. In reality, this is a symbolic adherence. The great majority of the population has never been organically linked to one or the other of these trends, but attached to the general aims and personalities, even if these aims were merely dreams and promises, or measures effectively taken; even if these personalities were at the summit of their power or had been swallowed up by history. Researchers will no doubt pause before two famous obsequies in our history: those of Mustapha An-Nahhas in 1966 and those of Nasser in 1970. At the time of his death, Mustapha An-Nahhas was already far removed from power, and had been for 15 years; and Nasser had been defeated in a destructive war only three years before he died. Nevertheless, millions of people came to pay their last respects in an atmosphere of inconsolable sorrow.

For, as has already been indicated, the street in Egypt is itself the left; even if it is Wafdist at one moment and Nasserite at another. But in all cases, it does not remain a simple expression; the street is the first source and the first measure which serves to plumb the future. While at times it has been in conflict with this or that organisation of the left, it has always been in radical contradiction with the right and its various organisations. These parties of the left have always found success when they received their directives from the street, when they stopped to listen to the heart of the people, when they saw through the eyes of the people, and when they preserved for the street its position as leader.

It is this street which invents the forms of national and social struggle, which lays the foundations for the political campaign which bears its imprint, and which decides to act or remain passive. But in all cases it cannot ignore the national organisations which already exist, whether they be clandestine or not. And all its actions bear witness to the fact that it is unable to replace them. However, there is a great difference between the phenomenon of the Egyptian street and that of the political organisations in certain Arab countries; the latter are able to mobilise their streets in a specific manner and in accordance with very precise directives. But when the leaders are imprisoned, the base is afflicted with paralysis until such time as other leaders appear. But the Egyptian street is never subject to the phases of the retreat of democracy. It may experience great sadness at the sudden halt which affects its intellectual side, but it never ceases to act and have recourse to pressure, as though nothing had happened. The powers imprisoning the Wafdists or Nasserites reap nothing from repression. For the true problem resides always in these millions of people, and despite the fact that from time to time a few individuals are kidnapped from amongst them, their activities never cease. It is due to a lack of understanding of this phenomenon that the absurd idea arises that popular uprisings are always the work of intruding minorities. The reality, for the repressive authorities, is that the whole nation is an intruding minority.

But even though the Egyptian street is itself the left, it does not replace the left-wing organisations; but it is from them that it derives its spirit and conscience and from what we may call the general climate dispersed within society by the Egyptian Marxists. But it is the inability of governments to provide radical solutions to the national and social questions which historically impels the Egyptian street towards the left; for the backbone of this street consists, at all times, of workers, peasants, students and petty artisans. As for the bourgeoisie of officialdom, with its heavy bureaucratic trappings, the agrarian bourgeoisie with its traditions inherited from feudalism, and the commercial bourgeoisie which has been nurtured in the warm bosom of the foreign monopolies, these constitute the ramparts of the reaction, of despotism and passivity. As for the industrial bourgeoisie, time has never given it an opportunity to reach maturity.

Thus it was with the peasant risings referred to in the popular songs on the life of 'Adham Al-Charqawi', 'Yassin and Bahiyyah' and many another hero. The village of Kamchich, and the death of the militant, Salah Hussein, are merely the framework and the most recent episodes in these heroic epics.

Thus it was with the National Committee of Students and Workers in 1946. The creation of that committee was the work of public opinion on the left, and the culmination of various detachments of the national campaign conducted in the factory and the university by the communists, the Wafdists and many others. In fact, the 'silent majority' in Egypt is not exactly silent.

In order to distinguish what separates the left, (considered as Egyptian public opinion) from barbarism and counter-revolution, it is sufficient to appreciate the difference between the National Committee of Students and Workers in 1946, and the Cairo Fire of 26th January 1952. This distinction becomes all the more striking when we think of the population of the resistance campaign on the banks of the Canal in 1950-51, and that of the crisis of March 1954. This line of demarcation exists even more sharply between collective democratic action, which has been known in Egypt from 1919 to date, and individual assassinations.

If, then, the Egyptian street is far removed from the idea of organisation into parties, it is still further from disorder and sabotage. Historical events have always proved that the adulteration of democratic style by the false interpretation of a demonstration or a strike, or any other form of action undertaken by the people at a revolutionary moment, is only brought about at the hands of the 'dissimulating power'; this is what burns and destroys uselessly in order to distract opinion from its principal line. It is this that endeavours to exploit the opportunity in order to tear the militants from their homes, that always starts the violence; and in these cases it is necessary to defend oneself.

The Egyptian population came out on to the streets on the evening of 9th June 1967, and at the time of the funeral of Abd Al-Monem Riad, and on the death of Nasser — in their millions, without the slightest directive, without committing the least act of sabotage, and at a time when authority was extremely weak. The old democratic traditions have always remained alive among the Egyptian population from the time of the student demonstrations when Ismail Sidqi had the Albas Bridge cleared, thus killing dozens of demonstrators, up to the 1972 demonstrations. The national committees coming from the ranks of the people represented the most glorious traditions in our national history. While the Egyptian street has not been polarised by any party, it is far from being a feather tossed in the wind. It has its own creative campaigns, at the university, in the factory and in the fields.

Even since 1972, the Egyptian street, in the face of renegades whose most significant action is the Sinai Agreement, has never ceased to rise up spontaneously, thereby providing its creative contributions in the fields of thought and action. In order to derive the laws of action opposed to counter-revolution attention is drawn here to the most significant of these uprisings.

The Student Movement

The recent origins of this movement go back to 1968, immediately following the defeat. But in 1972 it was relatively able to crystallise into a coherent, solid, polarising movement, and was thus able to avoid the pitfalls of liberal disorder in relation to thought, and of violence in relation to action. In this it was helped by the direction of the political situation following the death of Nasser.

At the outset, this movement was a simple reaction to the events of the defeat, to the corruption of the military institution of the country, and to the repressive measures taken by the authorities. In 1972, it was almost transformed into a political movement speaking in the name of certain social classes. Change in the archaic teaching programmes, i.e. a specifically student demand, was no longer the main thrust of student activity for change. The anti-democratic status of the universitities, the relations between teachers and students, the relations of the latter with their unions, no longer constituted departure points for the formulation of programmes of change. The problems of national liberation, economic development, social progress, Palestinian resistance and Arab unity became the main preoccupations of this movement. The student movement was no longer isolated in the amphitheatres, but made contact with similar intellectual and professional movements. It organised interaction with intellectual and professional circles through its political clubs, its cultural, literary, artistic and theatrical manifestations. These organisations showed imagination by creating new national committees, information tribunes, wall newspapers, etc.

From the fact that it was able to escape from that bottleneck, the making of demands as a narrow sector in its own interests, and because it was coming closer to being a semi-organised revolutionary vanguard, the student movement was beginning to see its ideological ramifications multiplying, which also implied a plurality of social origins. The movement thus became an indicator of the manifest division, which at national level, opposed the Nasserites and Marxists to the religious and extreme right-wing groups.

From 1972 to 1975, including the year of the war, the Egyptian student movement was exposed to violent currents in its alliances, internal oppositions, position in regard to the regime, and in its relations with the various social forces. For the war, with its very definite political consequences, including the Sinai Agreements, spread confusion among the ranks of the people and the whole of the Arab nation. The student movement did not escape. Very serious mistakes were committed, both with regard to thought and to action.

The most serious of these mistakes lay in the belief that the student movement could replace an organised national movement. There is no tract expressing such an idea, but a political analysis of those in power, or the movement of Egyptian society, an analysis which was undertaken by certain members of this movement, clearly gave an impression of the existence of just such an idea among those who were acting in a politically short-sighted manner. In most cases, and more particularly immediately prior to the civil war, the part played by the students in the direction of the overall national uprising was exaggerated, and this, following the war, reduced the movement to occupying a subordinate position. Admittedly, such a movement has specific features which fit in well with the particular reality of the Egyptian movement for struggle, and there can be no doubt that this movement did take creative initiatives as a result of these specific features. But this active role cannot, qualitatively, go beyond the position occupied by the students in the structure of production. Thus, this role could not be greater than the objective capacity of the students in the process of changing the structure of production. This error of assessment, the exaggeration of the part played by the students, condemned them to relative isolation in relation to the great majority of the population, following the October war.

The second mistake consisted in the common right-wing idea that student action should be restricted to university campuses, those frameworks regarded as legitimate by the regime, and a total submission to the law. According to this idea, student action should content itself with revealing the contradictions between the actions and work of the authorities, and at the same time, as far as possible avoid provoking them and giving them grounds for combatting the movement. Admittedly, there is no tract directly setting out this idea, but the thinking of certain persons, and their political practices, have proved the existence of this 'sectorial and legitimist' vision, and this played a part in still further isolating the movement from its social origins on the one hand, and circumscribing its political aspirations on the other.

A third mistake consisted in the absence of any clear vision in regard to the economic and social identity of the regime. The movement no longer appreciated the class nature of the regime, and this frequently dragged it down to the level of voicing superficial and inconclusive comments on the decisions, speeches or measures of the regime. Since the regime's political countenance was in reality merely a mask, and since political information was frequently contradictory, student political thought was, therefore, often subject to distortion; the very body of the movement was frequently torn by conflicting tendencies, and this did not fail to tip the balance in favour of the movement's right wing.

However, these mistakes, and many others like them, do nothing to detract from the fact that the Egyptian student movement has, since 1972, remained a progressive creation of the popular street in Egypt in the face of the Sinai Agreements before and after the October war. Overall, this movement was no passing phenomenon, no simple demonstration; on the contrary, its continuity constitutes today a popular phenomenon with far-reaching roots. Furthermore, it brought to the political scene a group of young activists whose maturity is constantly on the increase. It was, moreover, a valuable source of examples of struggles extending beyond university frontiers and moving into the relatively broader political frameworks of the Marxist and Nasserite organisations.

It must be added, however, that the declarations of the Egyptian students concerning the nature of the power and identity of the regime contain neither any global class analyses, nor any global analyses of the Sinai Agreements. But if we set aside the intellectual attitude to these two problems — which would be a considerable omission — we shall note that the practical attitudes of the students regarding the Sinai Agreements and their wider implications — such as the official attitudes in regard to the nationalised sector, agrarian reform, the achievements of peasants and workers, the liberation of the land, the Palestinian problem, the mass media, the struggle of the intelligentsia and the assessment of Nasserism — take account of the general characteristics of the class at present wielding power, and also the general content of the Sinai Agreements.

The student movement, since it first appeared, never ceased to surprise; for due to the pre-eminence of the single political organisation of the Nasserite state and its government controlled information media, and to the dated nature of the teaching programmes and educational methods in relation to the life and ideas of the modern world, the absence of organised political activity was total. This movement, it must be emphasised, arose at a time when no relationship existed between the generations of the 1950s and 1960s and the old traditions of militancy experienced by the students of the 1940s and even earlier.

But the surprise was gradually dissipated when it was realised that this positive phenomenon in Egypt's political history was inherent in the Nasserite revolution. For these students were, after all, the sons of workers, peasants and the various sectors of the petty bourgeoisie; those who benefited from free education and were therefore able to go to the universities. They came from the villages and hamlets and the back streets of the towns; at the end of the day or the university year, they went back home to their modest dwellings. The bonds between their social origins and their ambitions have never been severed. Simultaneously, from time to time, they have had what others never had outside the universities, namely an opportunity to learn from democratic and progressive books, artists and journalists, and the developed world. All this was frequently within their reach. There was no lack of books — they were being sold on the pavements. At other times, books were considered as incriminating evidence against their owners who were branded as 'reds'!

But in all cases, the student movement was, and still is, the result of the creativity of the Egyptian street. In one sense, it was its reply to defeat, its uninterrupted protest against the preambles and consequences of the Sinai

Agreements. The student movement is an important factor in the Egyptian peoples' programme for struggle, and constitutes a permanent element in its struggle against the counter-revolution.

The Workers' Movement

This movement set off the first spark of the rising of 1968, and the main nub, made up of the workers at the Helouan factories, also took the initiative for the uprising of 1975. They were followed by those of the two largest industrial cities, Mahalla Al-Kubra (March 1975) and Kafr Ad-Dawwar (March 1976). The period between these two dates was the most significant in the history of the Egyptian working class, a class whose roots reach far down into the emotional subconscious of the Egyptian people, and which has always provided the inspiration for revolutionary achievements. Prior to the movement of 23rd July 1952, this class was the backbone of the famous rising of the 1940s which found its organisational form in the National Committee for Students and Workers in 1946. This, too, provided the first of the martyrs of the democratic opposition in 1952, with the execution of the two national heroes, Khamis and Al-Baqari.

The fruits of the constant struggle of the working class were to mature later. In fact the Nasserite movement was to take important decisions in the 1960s. Measures were thus taken for nationalising the means of production and heavy industry, for modernisation, for increasing the minimum wage and for worker participation in the management and profits of enterprises. Similarly, workers and peasants were to be entitled to 50% in popular and legislative representation at all levels.

To these measures, there should be added the dimension represented by Egyptian labour in the system of national production. This will enable us to appreciate the extent of the economic, social and political part which, historically, the working class has had to assume in the face of the withdrawal represented by the Sinai Agreements, the steps towards which, at all levels, were well thought out by the present regime. For in fact, the liquidation of the nationalised sector, the hegemony of the private sector and more particularly its parasitic wing, the facilities granted to foreign capital to the detriment of the national industry and the achievements of the Egyptian workers, the blows struck against Egypto-Soviet relations and their consequences for industry, both military and non-military, all emanate from the Sinai Agreements and the attack upon the Egyptian working class.

The spontaneous uprising at the beginning of 1975 was merely a stage terminating the movement which began in 1968. But it also heralded a fresh period of struggle. The most important feature of the movement of January 1975 was that it was the workers in the munitions factories who started it. It was they, too, who set off the movement in May 1968. But their new movement was to clash with the settlement plan envisaged by the authorities, the climate for which had already been prepared. For they were making their preparations for resuscitating the Alexandria Declaration, with a view to exerting pressure on the Palestinian resistance, and reaching agreement with the more reactionary Arab circles on the subject of a possible settlement, and carrying on a defamation campaign against the Soviet Union. This went hand in hand with the arrest of a large number of leaders of workers' and students' unions and peasants' co-operatives. Furthermore, elements connected with the police were infiltrated into these organisations with the aim of sabotaging them from inside. However, the movement of 1st January 1975 remains a direct extension of those which had preceded it, the strikes, and the occupation of the factories, Alexandria University and the Port Said House of Culture – and since the funeral of General Ahman Ismail.

Of all these demonstrations, the most decisive was without doubt the initiative of the workers of Mahalla Al-Kubra in March 1975; a strike of such proportions had not been seen in that town since 1947. It should be remembered that this is the very centre of the textile industry; it has the largest workers' complex with 30,000 employees in the nationalised sector (those in the private sector also totalled tens of thousands). Also, the Mahalla factories and companies had, around that time, taken on 5,400 workers who had completed their military service.

At the outset, the Mahalla workers demonstrated in protest against the wages law. They demanded a new and fairer statute which would guarantee the rights to promotion and increased wages of those workers who had completed their military service. They rejected the implementation of the law on employment reform, which laid down the scales of wages and promotions based on diplomas, thereby damaging the interests of production and discounting the experience of the workers. They demanded the introduction of humane means for guaranteeing security of employment and protecting them against occupational diseases, beginning with asthma, which frequently leads to pulmonary complications.

The authorities, for their part, believed that by suppressing the workers and imposing 'yellow' union leaders on them, they could make them forget their legitimate demands – demands which they pretended to ignore – and this incited the workers to strike. On 19th and 20th March 1975, two groups of workers occupied the premises, despite the siege established by the forces of public order round the factory. So far the strike had passed off without any violence or clashes. But on Friday, 21st March, central security forces descended on the town, and inevitably this angered the strikers; additionally, combat aircraft appeared, some flying low and others breaking the sound barrier by way of intimidation. The population believed that the aircraft were bombing the factories and thousands of people went to the defence of their comrades besieged by the police. A great demonstration was organised; private sector workers, the cotton strippers, the tertiary sector workers and the students assembled. Placards written on the spur of the moment, read: 'Nasser left behind a will: the workers on the side of the fedayeen' or 'Nasser said: take care of the workers'. The police were no longer able to control the situation and a few workers entered the houses of the managers. They tore down chandeliers, destroying clothing and luxury foodstuffs. They hung all these signs of wealth on the telegraph poles, alongside rags and black bread.

These tableaux required no comment. The next day, Mustapha Amin wrote in *Akhbar Al-Yom* that the workers at Mahalla were the cause of the breakdown of the Kissinger negotiations!

Inside the factories, the workers created a real workers' commune. The occupation of the premises was effected whilst production went on. Management and technical committees were set up at the same time as supervision and control committees. Ownership of the factory passed into the hands of the workers during these three glorious days. This led to a bloody confrontation with the authorities. There were 50 dead; 2,000 Nasserite, Marxist and trade union militants were arrested. In reality, what had been called the 'breakdown of the Kissinger negotiations' was nothing more than a stage on the path towards the Salzburg summit which culminated in the signing of the Treaty in September of that same year.

But the wave of strikes did not stop. The echoes of the Mahalla commune enjoyed overwhelming support from the textile workers of Mansurah, the workers at the Helouan steel works, and those at the Choubra Al-Khaymah textile factory. Indeed, 30,000 workers at the Choubra Al-Khaymah cable works, and at Alexandria, called a general strike. But the official reports made no mention of this. As usual, the reasons for the strike were economic at the outset; they called for the enforcement of a law on promotion and on wage increases, which had been frozen for years. They called for an increase in the price rise bonus and meals at the works, which had been suspended for some time. The workers at the cable factories had organised their strike down to the last detail. After removing the women and the older members, they formed three teams. One was to supervise the barricades, to protect them against any sabotage by agents of the authorities and prevent any ambiguous action which might serve as a pretext for the central security forces to lead an assault against the works, as had been the case at Mahalla Al-Kubra. The second team was charged with continuing production so as to ensure above average output, and the third was to relieve the other two.

The Governor of Gharbiyyah, when endeavouring to negotiate, was driven out of the factory. The Minister of Labour received no better welcome, despite the presence of the forces of order besieging the factory. The Minister of the Interior, arriving under the protection of the tanks, was carried as far as his car parked outside the factory. In the face of the workers' persistence, the authorities were obliged to tacitly accede to some of the demands. This took place in June 1975. There remained very little time to conclude the Sinai Agreements.

During the months of September and October 1975, the textile workers at Alexandria held conventions every week at the headquarters of the textile union; the latter had more than 70,000 members. In addition to the economic demands, the union called for 'independence of union action, union freedom, and a vote on Law 62 of 1964.' 'The new law', said the members of the congress, 'should be subject to discussion by the base. Control of the elections should be removed from the judiciary in order to guarantee objectivity.' The public transport workers launched forth in their turn. The Prime

Minister came in person; he swore on the honour of the President of the Republic that their demands would be met!

On 29th January 1976, a bloody clash brought the population of Manzalah up against the central security forces following the death under torture of a man who had publicly declared that he was opposed to the regime. The population invaded the police headquarters. There was a massacre. The authorities endeavoured to hush up the scandal by recommending compensation for the victims' families.

Some time afterwards a similar massacre took place at Damiette, where fishermen had opposed the forces of order. But the main 1976 clash took place at Kafr Ad-Dawwar, another large industrial town. There were deaths and arrests, but the slogans hostile to the regime gave the commune of Kafr Ad-Dawwar a new dimension.

The first observation to be made about the movement of the Egyptian working class during its struggle over recent years is, that in the face of the decisions and legislation undermining the legacy of the Nasserite structure of production, the movement put forward economic slogans against the withdrawal, and this proves that it was conscious of the fact that economic demands in such conditions constituted a political platform against the counter-revolution.

The second observation is that this movement, though it may take on certain trade union forms and contain certain political organisations (mainly represented by Nasserites and communists) is overall an independent popular initiative and creative in its modes of action and in its content.

The Intellectuals, the Peasants and the Armed Forces

These groups never hesitated to take part in the courageous national initiative both before and after the signing of the Sinai Agreement. For their part, the intellectuals — writers, men of letters, artists and journalists — made way for this unity of action in their platforms, both legitimate and clandestine, inside and outside the country. They were subjected to imprisonment, famine, enforced exile and a ban on expressing themselves. Doctors, lawyers, engineers and other professional men, in their great majority and through their respective unions, were opposed to this Agreement. But the great part played by the intellectuals was and still is that of making the people conscious and enlightening them. At times their struggle went to the extent of taking positive initiative, becoming as important as that of the students and workers. They founded the Association of Writers of the Future; they pressed for the formation of a democratic union for writers; they organised congresses, published declarations, played an active part in student discussions, in defence of the achievements of the Nasserite revolution, in the opposition shown to many pieces of legislation of the present regime, and in the direct opposition to the Sinai Agreement.

But the dependence of a large number of Egyptian intellectuals on government office increasingly imposed the idea of legitimism and its intricate patterns. To this might be added the fact that the shortcomings of the

Nasserite regime cast many shadows in the eyes of some, so that it became difficult for them to view the present regime clearly. And due to the earlier repressions, the 'liberal folly' became a sickness finding fertile ground in the *'wijdan'* (sensitivity) of the intellectual, who, by his nature, is frequently subject to individualism, isolation and narcissism, and these frequently become a cause of division and disunity. All in all, this resulted in the role of the Egyptian intellectuals in respect to the Sinai Agreement and its various dimensions being a purely ideal one, apart from a few rare exceptions which, in their political content, took no part in the popular initiative in relation to organised thought.

The peasants, from Kamchich to Dekernes, passing by Abou-Kabir en route, rose up against the counter-revolutionary measures, and martyrs fell. For it was they who were the first to be affected by the regression in the application of the agrarian reform laws, by the enlargement of the great landed properties, by the return to influence of the rich of the countryside, and by the hegemony of the pseudo-feudal landlords.

As for the body of the armed forces, they remained profoundly national, for at the time of the October war, they had collected in their ranks a large number of university representatives from the working class, peasant and petty-bourgeois strata, and who, thanks to the Nasserite revolution, had benefited from the right to enjoy free study at military schools. Some time prior to the signature of the Agreement, the military intelligence services arrested more than 100 officers; 43 high-ranking officers were cashiered and a large number of airmen were arrested on the pretext that they were hatching a plot. The truth was quite different: since part of the national trend in the army was dissatisfied with the general lines of the Sinai Agreement, which it had become aware of during Kissinger's tour in March 1975, officers asked that no agreement should be signed before it had been shown to the army. The authorities replied with repression.

In fact, in the history of modern Egypt the intellectuals, peasants and soldiers have always had deeply national traditions and creative initiatives. But the division of the intellectuals into factions, and their liberal 'sensitivity', the crushing of the peasants under pressure from lack of awareness and organisation, and the submission of the soldiers to a strict military hierarchy, made the student and worker initiatives the backbone of the creativity of the popular street in Egypt, and of its spontaneous uprisings in the face of the Sinai Agreement.

These uprisings, however, cannot be compared to those of 1946 when students and workers united in joint action; due to their spontaneity, they were and will continue to be unable to take the place of the organised vanguard. But it is undeniable that they constitute a favourable climate for the birth of its essential elements.

It is not by chance, therefore, that in view of the decision of the authorities to conclude this Agreement the response from the opposing social forces, with all their political trends, was also violent.

Certainly, Egypt had never been without its clandestine organisations, whether under the so-called democratic regime or following the decision to dissolve taken by the communist organisations in 1965. The organisations of the left and right continued to survive in one way or another. But the 1967 defeat, and the death of Nasser followed by the 1971 putsch, caused a re-opening of the question of independent political organisation. The measures taken by the authorities, from the putsch to the Sinai Agreement (taking in the war en route) and at the economic, social, military and political levels, gave this idea a certain legitimacy with public opinion. Even the idea of the promulgation of platforms was, for certain people, synonymous with parties, or at least a step in the direction of the creation of parties. One of the most indomitable reactionaries, the lawyer, Abd Al-Moneim Al-Chourbagi, declared that he was going to form a party and that, if necessary, he would appear before the courts to prove that the Constitution is not against the formation of political parties. The pens of the old reaction exulted. Two members of the former Council of the Revolution, Kamal Ad-Din Hussein and Hussein Al-Chafei, put forward a demand for the re-creation of the association of the Muslim Brothers, under the pretext that as a religious association the law could not prohibit it. In June 1975, the Mecca-based magazine, *Al-Alam Al-Islami*, announced the good news of the reconstitution of the organisation of the Muslim Brothers in Egypt; the policy office was constituted under the direction of Dr. Tawfiq Al-Chawi, a professor at the law faculty at Cairo University. But the leading circles were careful to keep the Socialist Union alive, even if its platforms were to multiply and develop side by side with the organs of repression, the whole representing the ideal form of the party in power.

The Egyptian left, too, did not fail the insistent social appeal for the creation of an independent political organisation. Most of those who had experienced association with the Socialist Union or its avant-garde organisa-tion, those whose hopes had been disappointed, joined the new formations which, during the five years prior to 1975 had gathered into a coherent whole, students, workers, intellectuals, lower-grade civil servants and the professional classes.

The year 1975 saw the culmination of the earlier dialogues between the various trends of the left, and a culmination also of the action of the militants faithful to the idea of an independent political party. The announcement of the reconstitution of the Egyptian Communist Party in July 1975 was the ratification of the popular decision against the decisive measures taken by the classes in power. That remained, and still remains, a historic symbol, for groups of old and new communists were able to unite in the largest organisa-tion of Egyptian communists.

But this in no way gainsays the fact that both before and after the forma-tion of the party, other communist and Nasserite organisations were formed. It must be emphasised here that the constituency of the Nasserite organisa-tions remains the most considerable, even though its organisations are less solid, less homogeneous and less powerful than the Marxist organisations. We would also stress the plurality of ideological trends within all these Nasserite or communist organisations. At times, the militants are Marxist or Nasserite for reasons rooted in the past. Marxists are to be found in the Nasserite core; others borrow the Sadat language. Among the Nasserites, there are those who take up their positions in the Marxist current. In fact, some of them are partisans of one or the other stage in Nasser's evolution. Some remain at the stage of hostility to communism; others find no defect in the Nasser experience, considering it to be perfect and needing no modification. But in every case, the great majority of Egyptian Nasserites never cease to show their hostility towards the present regime under the banner of the charters of revolution and the National Charter in particular. For this reason, they firmly defended those Nasserite achievements under threat, such as the nationalised sector, the rights of the workers, peasants and students, and the defence of the great accomplishments, heavy industry, the Dam, Egypto-Soviet relations, the Arab liberation movement and the Palestinian cause. Thus, they could not avoid opposing the Sinai Agreement with all its implications. But those Egyptian Nasserite documents to which there is access reveal no programme of struggle at political or organisational level, instead they reduce opposition to the level of mere reaction — at times spontaneous — to counter-revolutionary measures against creative revolutionary action. The Nasserites remain the most fervent political stratum in favour of the maintenance of the formula of the Socialist Union as the sole political party; and this constitutes a genuine obstacle to the crystallisation of independent political parties and the formation of a broad democratic front capable of calling a halt to the Sinai Agreement.

As for the Marxists, only some are organised. Those who are, do not share the same point of view and not all are in the same organisation. But it is they who, to differing extents, took the initiative of formulating the programmes of struggle which they claimed would be capable of rectifying the movement of history which the forces of the counter-revolution are endeavouring to turn back.

What then has the left in Egypt to say?

We should at the outset draw a distinction between the non-clandestine and the clandestine left, the one supported by the official mass media and the other finding expression in its clandestine platforms. But this distinction should overlook any ideological or organisational reservations. We shall, then, need to define the points held in common and the differences between the various leftist trends; this will enable us to define the main direction that the programme of the left in Egypt will take.

8. Towards a National Programme of Action

There can be no doubt that an editorial in *At-Taliah*, entitled 'The Sinai Agreement',[1] is almost the sole public commentary expressed in the name of the Egyptian left in opposition to the Sinai Agreement. By 'public', we mean that the opposition had found a means of expressing itself through the official media, and by 'almost the sole' we mean that this editorial was the only one that did not mince its words; there was no question of 'no, but . . .'. The expression of opposition was clear and precise despite any reservation which may be made in regard to the content or formulation.

This courageous editorial raised a storm outside Egypt, quite contrary to what had been anticipated. Some doubted whether the article really expressed the thoughts of the editor-in-chief, whose customary signature was missing on this occasion. Others asked whether it expressed 'only' the author's point of view. In truth, *At-Taliah*'s opposition to the Sinai Agreement, both its form and its substance, did not express only the point of view of the author or the editorial team of that journal. We believe that it adequately and powerfully formulated the opposition of a large sector of the militant Egyptian left wing inside Egypt, namely those groups which had chosen to struggle on the advance lines of the front, but within the framework of legitimacy, and that it would be no exaggeration to say that it represented the attitude of the far from negligible parties of public opinion of the left. It is now necessary for us to underline the following points.

The official left-wing information media represented solely by the monthly journal, *At-Taliah*, is more effective than the clandestine or illegal publications in so far as public awareness is concerned. This effectiveness extends to the bases of the organised parties, and even goes beyond them to reach the broadest strata rising spontaneously among the workers, students, intellectuals, professional classes, lower-grade civil servants and soldiers.

It is not enough to say that, for the regime in power, an official leftist platform constitutes an effective instrument for sublimating anger. A platform of this nature plays an influential role quite independently of the wishes of those manipulating the situation; no mass media are capable of acting as a shock-absorber for objectively justified anger, unless the reasons for that anger are false. But it also has to be added that because it is restricted at the level of thought and even of formulation, the struggle, once declared, is fraught with danger. With time, the expression of opposition establishes a private code between the platform and its readers who need to learn to 'read between the lines'.

Despite these limitations, this official voice of the left was able to establish many progressive cadres among the ranks of the people. It is, therefore, necessary to be wary of lumping together a writer who justifies the regime, another who explains it and a third who dots the 'i's and crosses the 't's for it.

It must be stressed that for a large sector of the public a democratic platform is socially equivalent to an unorganised democratic uprising. This bond of declared political action between a non-clandestine voice and the public must be ever-present in our minds when we analyse the role which may be played by such a voice in opposing measures, especially the most serious, taken by the authorities. Let us not forget either, all those restrictions which limit the action of those writing within the framework of legitimacy; they are always faced with a delicate choice, not between the minimum and the maximum of what may be written, but between writing and explaining a minimum and not writing at all.

For all this, we believe that *At-Taliah*'s editorial was the only, or almost the only, expression of opposition to the Sinai Agreement in the name of an important sector of the Egyptian left in general. The most fundamental aspect of this opposition may be represented by what that editorial said on the subject of the United States:

> It is impossible for the United States to be an impartial party to the extent of locating experts on our territory and between Israel and ourselves. Nor is it possible for it to be an arbitrator between Israel and ourselves in any situation whatsoever.

This statement constitutes a methodological base for questioning the foundations of the Sinai Agreement, the successive stages of which were the ceasefire 'so as not to make war against the United States', according to the statement by President Sadat on the subject of the possibility of liquidating the Israeli-held pocket of the Outfall, the first disengagement agreement with its six points, and finally, acceptance of 'step-by-step' diplomacy crowned by the visit from Nixon and the declaration of Egypto-American co-operation.

This statement of the situation cannot be separated from the overall policy of the *At-Taliah* editorial which clearly said that: 'The step-by-step policy proposed by the United States is not in our interests', contrary to what was stated in the text under the first point. As for the second point, which relates to Articles 1, 2, 3 and 9 of the Agreement, the editorial states:

> There is no need to reflect for very long to see that these articles mean that the agreement requires us not to have recourse to force, though it contains no restriction as regards time. The agreement, therefore, remains in operation until another agreement is concluded; which gives Israel the opportunity for procrastinating indefinitely.

Regarding the third criticism put forward by *At-Taliah*, this relates in general to the particular part allocated by this treaty to the United States and more especially in respect of the early warning system which necessitates an American military presence disguised in civilian clothing; espionage thus becomes legitimate, authorised action on Egypt's territory. In this connection, the editorial made an assessment of the positions taken up by the United States in relation to the Arab-Israeli conflict before and after the Agreement. From these lessons of the recent as well as more distant past, the author concluded that allocating a role such as this to the United States 'does not assist the advancement of the Geneva formula, and consequently does not bring us any nearer the time of overall settlement'. And finally, that: 'The most sacred task now consists of making every effort to reconstitute the national anti-colonial and anti-Zionist line.'

Within the scope of these general lines opposed to the very essence of the Sinai Agreement, we may consider this editorial as representing a broad current of opinion, within both the ranks of the Egyptian left and those of the Egyptian people. But this in no way diminishes the danger of authorised action and the risks of the official voice; all this has cast doubts on the formulation for which *At-Taliah* has borne responsibility. These doubts have perforce gone beyond the form to reach the very substance of the content; the following points will enable us to appreciate this.

The political direction in Egypt, the editorial stated, has not put an end to the war; which is correct from the formal point of view, in the sense that no declaration officially putting an end to the state of war in an independent manner has been signed. But from an objective point of view this is by no means correct. For the first article of this Agreement stipulates that disputes between the two parties shall not lead to armed confrontation, but will be settled by peaceful means. The second stipulates that the two parties undertake not to have recourse to force, to the threat of force or to military blockade. The third stipulates that the two parties will respect the ceasefire on land, at sea and in the air, and that they will abstain from any military or semi-military action against one another. The paradox consists in the fact that although *At-Taliah* did mention these articles, it was only in a footnote. But there should be added to these Article 9, which stipulates that none of the contracting parties is entitled to abrogate the Agreement unilaterally; it remains in force, without any restriction as to time, until replaced by another

This clearly proves that the Egyptian political leadership, and none other, in practice did put an end to the war.

From the foregoing, an extremely serious consequence ensues, namely, an evaluation of the meaning of the ending of the state of war with the Zionist enemy. This will enable us to see clearly the steps taken by the authorities — domestic, Arab, and international — in the economic, political and strategic fields; but it will not enable us to evaluate the political leadership which has undertaken all these steps under the slogans of opening up the economy, the sovereignty of the law and the 'international variables'. For it is hardly possible to separate criticism of the economic measures affecting the nationalised sector and unrestrictedly encouraging the private sector, from the political and strategic measures hostile to the movement for Arab liberation and to the socialist bloc. These measures, in a word, open the doors to the return of imperialist influence in the region. Partial criticism is, therefore, neither possible nor permissible; neither is it possible to refer to quotations from the political leadership made for particular occasions, manoeuvres and tactics. It is not enough to say, as *At-Taliah* has: 'It suffices to listen to what the President stated in connection with the Agreement which, according to him, does not satisfy us, to be convinced that this Agreement, like any other human achievement, is subject to criticism and even to opposition.' It is no longer permissible to be content with explaining a strategy of liberation in the light of the so-called thesis put forward by President Sadat prior to the October war; indeed, he himself had determined its features — autonomous Egyptian force, Arab resources and Soviet support. Referring to the political leadership, in order to cover one's rear or because one is convinced of the correctness of its positions, constitutes a fatal error; if it was possible in the past it cannot be so today, and especially where the Sinai Agreement is concerned; for this Agreement is not like any normal 'human action subject to criticism or opposition'. It is, in fact, a decisive turning-point in the history of modern Egypt, a turning-point brought about by the political leadership in relation to a strategy which speaks of Arab or Soviet support, whereas it is constantly in opposition to both the Arabs and the Soviet Union; and this contradiction is insurmountable so long as this Agreement remains in force.

The Sinai Agreement is, without any doubt, a human action, and no one has claimed that any sacred or satanic dimension is involved; but it is certainly not 'like all human actions', for it constitutes a well defined political and strategic action. In reality, *At-Taliah*'s criticism, by failing to stress the steps taken by the authorities, is accordingly far from just to them. The editorial refers to the political direction which had been taken only in order to suggest what it does not say; as though the Sinai Agreement resembled a project submitted by the State which could be criticised within the limits of legitimacy. In reality, this Agreement casts doubt upon precisely that legitimacy which the authority in power secured thanks to the October war. It is absurd to analyse it as though it was only a minor detail within the overall picture; it must be looked upon as a very specific transition, as a decisive turning-point in the direction taken by the authority. This Agreement is the fruit of the quantitative accumulations of the five years which preceded it. The attitude manifested in the editorial of *At-Taliah* cannot in any way be justified by the fact that it is the only, or almost the only, voice of the left-wing opposition in Egypt. But the criticism put forward by it is not, however, the less positive for all that; it is important to recall in this connection that it represented a very broad section of opinion, not merely of left-wing intellectuals, but above all of progressive public opinion in Egypt.

This editorial is as important as the discussion organised by *At-Taliah* on the Nasserite period, which brought together a large number of progressive Egyptian intellectuals in confrontation with Mr. Tawfiq Al-Hakim. This discussion, which began in December 1974 and ended in June 1975 (that is, prior to the signature of the Sinai Agreement) enables us to appreciate the general nature of the national programme put forward by the left for the realisation of the national democratic revolution of the Egypt of tomorrow. It did not, of course, allow for the Sinai Agreement, simply because that had not then been signed; on the other hand, it is possible to find discussions dealing with the general features of the treaty in its latent state, and this in the light of the successive measures taken by the authorities in the economic, social and political fields. The discussion was held within well defined dimensions. On the agenda, there was not only the Nasserite experience – which was the subject of the most virulent attacks – but, though this was not the main topic, there was also the question of assessing the present and forecasting the future.

If we take the liberty of according scant importance to what, in this discussion, was referred to as 'the paper of Mr. Tawfiq Al-Hakim',[2] – or to its implications – which contained a great deal of political naivety and beating about the bush (for example, he referred to Egypt as being a matter for metaphysics!), it is necessary to briefly consider the proposals put forward by Mr. Khaled Muhyi Ad-Din. Indeed, the latter tried to determine the future of Egypt in terms of the realisation of a strategic aim. The evolution of an Arab society, he said, industrially, agriculturally and culturally, imposes upon Egypt, owing to its situation in the Arab world, the duty to play a pioneer role. Which amounts to saying that Arab unity becomes a basis for the conceptualisation and movement towards the formulation of economic and political relations between Egypt and the Arab world. This involves a vision of the struggle between the two main dangers, namely colonialism and Zionism. By relying on support from the Socialist bloc, Khaled Muhyi Ad-Din rejects liberal democracy; for the latter allows capitalism in Egypt new opportunities for development. But he accepts what he calls 'socialist democracy' or again, 'progressive democracy'; this allows the popular forces, organised into a party, a principal role with, as its basis, a national alliance and a common programme.

Abu Seif Yussef, for his part, adds a detail concerning the significance of the national, democratic and modern state. For him, this is a democracy in which power would be held by the popular masses, mainly the workers, peasants, intellectuals, soldiers, and the capitalist sectors whose interests do not clash with the process of social transformation. Still according to Abu Seif Yussef, the leading role of the working class within this authority will need to be accentuated and to develop.[3] For him, this is a transitional regime preparing the field for the socialist future. Abu Seif Yussef accepts the hypothesis of Khaled Muhyi Ad-Din on the subject of liberalism and the new democracy; this should be at the basis of a new formula for an alliance between the national classes.

As for Mourad Wahbah, he suggests a minimum basis for the progress of the Arab world, namely secularism. He does not think, and in this he stands almost alone, that there is a national capitalism in Egypt. Consequently, he eliminates the idea of an alliance of classes.

Abd Al-Azim Amis, for his part, is more specific when he calls for the creation of a national front uniting the socialist and national parties defending a clear national programme in favour of the workers and peasants. According to him, these parties should represent the true interests of the national classes of the Egyptian people, namely the workers, peasants and the strata with limited incomes among the middle classes.[4] Latifa Az-Zayyat agrees with Abd Al-Azim Amis regarding these definitions; but she stresses the fact that the creation of a national front is bound up with democratic liberties. It is even impossible, she says, to bring about these democratic liberties without the creation of this front; for its founders are the beneficiaries of the democratic liberties.[5]

But the participants in this dialogue were temporarily silenced by what Mr. Fuad Mursi had to say. We are faced, he said, with a problem of the absence of measures capable of ensuring the continuance of the operation for moving towards socialism in our country.

> This is Egypt's problem in the economic and political fields. The fate of the future, its future, have been determined since 1962 by socialism. There is no need to revert to that again. Therefore, if Egypt's future is socialism, the discussion should be directed to considering how we are to resume the road towards socialism.[6]

But Ahmad Abbas Saleh goes back to the starting point in order to sound out the future, an operation which cannot be undertaken without reviewing the existing political organisation, namely the Arab Socialist Union. Probably he surprised some of those taking part in this discussion. The fact is, that for him, the forces of Egyptian reaction, which at the time were endeavouring to upset the balance of power, could not by their very nature undertake any such action. 'I accuse,' he said, 'the Egyptian reaction of endeavouring to overthrow authority.' Ahmad Abbas Saleh advised extending the local political organisation outside Egypt in view of the fact that any change taking place in Egypt directly concerned the whole of the Arab world.[7]

Lutfi Al-Khuli, at the end of the nine sessions of the discussion, put forward five main ideas, the first of which forms part of the programme suggested by the Egyptian left wing expressing the point of view of the progressive national forces of the country:

> These forces are agreed on struggling against imperialism, neo-colonialism, Zionism, economic and social underdevelopment and the general regional situation. These forces have thus indeed made their choice on a very precise basis, namely political and economic liberation, the transition from the stage of underdevelopment to that of progress with the aid of an overall economic and social plan with a socialist orientation, and with the final aim of the elimination of exploitation of man by man, respect for the human being and his independence, and

the encouragement of his creative powers. This programme is also based on action for the achievement of Arab unity in a democratic style and in respect of a content serving the movement of progress of the popular Arab forces.[8]

The forces putting forward this programme are not united; their social and ideological origins are manifold due to their differing realities and circumstances; but these forces extend over a very broad front embracing workers, poor and middle peasants, democratic and progressive intellectuals, soldiers and the productive and enlightened national bourgeoisie.[9]

In the light of the multiplicity of origins of the forces putting forward this programme, it is essential to create a national democratic alliance, an alliance which would not detract from the specific identity of each in the allied group, an alliance which would not take away the independence of each as regards organisation, ideology, platforms, parties and political groups.[10]

This programme comes at a time when the whole problem of the ments already made thanks to the 1952 revolution, while at the same time constituting a continuity in the struggle for the fulfilment of the tasks of the national and democratic revolution.[11]

This progrmme comes at a time when the whole problem of the liberation of the Arab nation and Palestine from the yoke of the Israeli occupation still exists and in a most acute manner. The new map of international relations today is governed by a fresh factor, namely the co-existence of the capitalist world with the socialist bloc, without the struggle between the two being diminished for all that . . . But to this it is necessary to add the revolution of science and technology which has opened up new horizons for man and for progress. Thanks to this scientific progress, man is able to master nature, his own reality and his destiny.[12]

After this preamble, we are entitled to ask: of what does this programme consist? It is made up of three main points: the creation of democracy on the basis of the alliance of all national and progressive forces within the framework of their independent organisations and on the basis of a minimum of agreements relating to an overall plan for the social and economic development of Egyptian society and the liberation of the land militarily and politically. Secondly, both as regards the past and the future, Egypt is an integral part of the Arab nation. It adheres to everything the latter demands, and in particular, it adheres to the claim of the Palestinian right to a fatherland. Thirdly, is the question of an independent foreign policy vis-a-vis the various blocs, but one which allows for the support provided by the strategic wings, beginning with that provided by the Socialist bloc and the liberation movements throughout the world.

The sessions of this discussion took place in June 1975, namely following the preambles to the Sinai Agreement and on the eve of its signature. This public discussion, which brought together a group of the most important leaders of the democratic left, expressed the thinking of a considerable sector of Egyptian intellectuals as well as that of a no less considerable sector representing the public opinion of the left. It also has to be accepted that an admittedly very tenuous bond united this programme put forward by the sector of the left to the method dominating the criticism of *At-Taliah* in regard to the Sinai Agreement. We can, moreover, find this same criticism formulated in the general context of the programme and this will enable us to draw the following conclusions.

The dominant idea is that the left cannot have any future without an independent voice or, frankly speaking, without a party. This is a step forward with profoundly significant implications, whether the authors of this idea meant a recognised party or, indeed, just a party and no more. For the simple fact of arriving at agreement on the need to set up a left-wing party diminishes the importance of knowing whether this party has to be clandestine or openly recognised. This new conviction, one way or another, constitutes self-criticism on the part of those who officially dissolved the left-wing political parties in 1965, and who were present at the discussion. Accordingly, it constitutes a retreat in relation to the idea that the presence of a group, or even of a socialist individual, at the summit of power was sufficient reason to adhere to the single party system or, at best, for adhering to the organisation qualifying as the vanguard of that party. Perhaps this new conviction does not constitute self-criticism or retreat. But it could mean that things have indeed changed since the death of Nasser and the imprisonment of his companions. There can be no doubt, however, that the overall significance of this conviction is that the workers, peasants, soldiers, petty bourgeoisie and revolutionary intellectuals are not represented in the present authority in power; consequently, it is their duty to form their own party or parties in order to exert pressure and thus to confront the authority in power.

The second idea which dominated these discussions is that it is impossible for any single party or clearly determined social stratum to be able to monopolise power. It is, therefore, essential to form a national democratic front comprising the aforementioned popular classes and the national strata of the middle bourgeoisie. At the same time, the suggested programme stresses that parasitic capitalism, the backward rural bourgeoisie, and the upper strata of the bureaucracy cannot be included in the framework for this programme.[13] Because these social classes and strata occupy the present centres of decision-making within the regime, the implicit meaning to be drawn from this programme suggests a fundamental change in the structure of power so that the front envisaged will be able, at the summit of power, to represent the people and the nation during the period of transition to socialism. This was, moreover, repeated on several occasions during the course of these discussions.

Thirdly, another dominant idea in these discussions arises from the maturity of Marxist thinking in Egypt in regard to unity and Arab nationalism. For this current of thought it is no longer a question of economic complementarity, Arab solidarity or other similar expressions; rather it is a question of an

organic entity of which Egypt constitutes the backbone; this implies economic, social, cultural, political and militant significance in regard to the
liberation of the land, the formation of a united, democratic Arab State,
with the aim of ending the state of underdevelopment suffered by the Arab
countries as a whole. The fact that this small group of Egyptian Marxists
should have insisted on the Arab fundamentals of Egypt, widens and deepens
the strategic vision of the popular street in Egypt regarding the tasks and
problems which the present authority is handling, based on regionalistic,
chauvinistic or religious ideas, starting with the Palestinian problem and the
Arab-Israeli conflict, the situation of the reactionary Arab regimes in the
face of the Arab liberation movements, and the relationship of all these
problems to the problem of the alliances in the world of today.

Fourthly, another dominant idea consisted in underlining the problem of
democracy, for this group of left-wing Egyptian intellectuals made a clear
distinction between national democracy and bourgeois liberalism whilst
engaged in surveying the past and attempting an assessment of the future;
this enabled them to avoid a number of errors committed in the past. It also
enabled them to avoid wasting too much time on excessively traditional con-
ceptions of popular democracy; for the specific Egyptian reality requires true
creativity in order to resolve the practical problem of the contradiction
between democracy and socialism. Today, through action and practice, it is
essential for democracy, with its old traditions in human history, to become
the other face of socialism. It is necessary for socialism to become a living,
creative application of democracy, not only in the field of material life, but
also in that of the mind, the conscience, and of values. If we now trace the
link between this important dossier and the criticism voiced by *At-Taliah*
regarding the Sinai Agreement, taking into consideration that similar criticism
was expressed by most of the participants in the discussions, we can easily
observe the absence of any precise definition of the identity of the present
authority in power, even if at times we perceive certain general characteristics
of this identity contained in the analysis of certain economic measures taken
by the authorities. Similarly, this criticism does not enable us to gain any
precise idea of the tasks confronting the Egyptian or Arab militants in respect
of the Sinai Agreement, apart from the very general line calling for unity in
the national anti-colonial and anti-Zionist ranks; but no such line can satisfy
those who are questioning the action to be taken against that Agreement.
Should it be abrogated, or amended, or merely criticised and opposed? And
what are the forces suitable for proceeding to abrogation or rectification?
How is that to be done?

These are questions posed by the authors of the suggested programme, those
who criticised the Sinai Agreement. But what is to be done if the action of the
opposition, from the outset, is limited by the fact that it addresses its criticism
from an authorised platform, and therefore a platform restricted by the authority in power? But it must not be overlooked that both the criticism and the
suggestions contained in the programme have kept alive the hopes of broad
sectors of the population which have remained unorganised in a changing world.

All the same, it must be recognised that this programme, together with the criticism of the Sinai Agreement, constituted a much more advanced contribution than the ideas of the semi-clandestine group of the left bearing the name 'revolutionary current'; this had indeed formulated a declaration, but one that certainly did not contain revolutionary features. Its authors warned against falling into the political mistake of misjudging the ruling Egyptian political leadership; this, they said, 'would cause considerable prejudice to the progress of the Arab struggle, and it would be even more serious than that resulting from the Sinai Agreement'. This group revealed its identity when it stated: 'theoretically, there is a process of revolutionary haggling which can be tolerated; it enables those claiming their rights to prepare to take up the struggle once more and entirely recover what they are claiming.' The Egyptian bourgeoisie, this group stated, considers that this haggling could result in Israel's withdrawal and its return to its proper dimensions; and this will consequently clip Israel's claws and end with the achievement of a just and lasting peace in the region! It also claimed that haggling is in the interests of the Palestinian people as well, for the Palestinians, it would appear, will never be able to achieve what the Egyptian bourgeoisie is aiming for, due both to their weakness and to the international situation which recognises Israel and is opposed to its liquidation.

This declaration then goes on to justify the Sinai Agreement on a basis which is very close to that of the justifications put forward by the authorities in power. This Agreement, say the authors of the declaration, was signed because the Egyptian bourgeoisie was unable any longer to suffer a situation which was neither war nor peace. They maintain most firmly that those who had prepared for the glorious October War, under the direction of Mr. Sadat, will never succumb to the delusion that they will be able to reach a solution to the Arab-Israeli conflict by peaceful means; which means, in other words, that the Egyptian authorities are preparing for a new war if the Israeli enemy continually fails to compromise.

For all these reasons, the authors of this declaration warned against student demonstrations, strikes by the workers, and the spontaneous uprisings of the Egyptian street; all these disturbances, they stated, will end by inciting the front against the authorities in power! 'And it would be a very serious error to consider the signature of this Agreement as a good opportunity for settling accounts with Sadat.' What we need today, said this declaration, is not demonstrations, the aim of which would be to declare opposition and to defame Sadat and the authority in power; what we need is the creation of a popular movement gathering together all the classes of the people under the banner of continuous democracy. The declaration concluded by saying that Sadat's plan for the solution of the Arab-Israeli conflict enjoyed the support of most Egyptians.

We should not have spent so much time on such a declaration emanating from a so-called 'revolutionary current' which, moreover, only embraces a small group of individuals with no influence, if it had not stressed the following facts:

255

1) Today, a person's history of political activity is no longer grounds for a valid distinction between an authentic militant and those who took the liberty of going into early political retirement; for this so-called revolutionary current, though numerically small and carrying little weight, groups together people who were once considered among the champions of the Marxist movement.

2) The Egyptian street, with its spontaneous uprisings and its revolutionary creativity, remains on the left wing of the clandestine organisations; these are organisations which, by their origins, are hostile to the formation of the party or its reconstitution; consequently, all they are able to contribute towards a national front is so many isolated phrases incapable of constituting coherent ideas. This evaluation should not lead us to doubt the sincerity of this current of opinion, but rather should be seen as demonstrating the errors which can be committed by those who fail to listen to the heart-beat of the people.

At the same time, it does not follow that the aberrations of this tired group mean that the recognised current (part of which was represented at the *At-Taliah* symposium) is the candidate incarnating the programme of the Egyptian street. The unassailable truth is that it is impossible to replace the revolutionary vanguard organised and directed by the party. Let us remember that the discussions on the reconstitution of the party took place just at the time when the authorities were preparing to sign the Sinai Agreement. This was no mere coincidence; this concomitance signifies that the people, too, had arrived at a decisive turning-point. In reality, the appeal for the reconstitution of the Egyptian Communist Party is not a simple appeal for the creation of an independent platform, but a courageous initiative for the achievement of the object of the appeal. The first manifesto published by the Central Secretariat is no circumstantial formula made on the occasion of the birth of the party; it is a militant action of prime importance.

What does this first manifesto say?

It states, at the outset, that the authorities in Egypt are challenging the progress of history, are obstinately clutching at a policy of withdrawal and regression in all fields.[14] Regarding the national problem, the authorities in power are supporting the American role in the region by progressively recognising the State of Israel and preparing for co-existence with it. They are not opposed to a partial, separate solution with Israel in exchange for a few kilometres of the Sinai desert. In foreign policy, they are increasingly abandoning the watchword of a strategic alliance with the Soviet Union; their constant preoccupation is to whitewash American imperialism. As for Arab policy, they are increasing their co-operation with the reactionary Arab regimes while progressively dropping their commitments to the Arab national problem. In the social, economic and democratic fields, the manifesto then records the retrogressive measures taken by the authorities in power, resulting from the putsch of 15th May 1971, and concludes that what is happening in Egypt today is the normal and logical outcome of the line pursued by the authorities since taking over control.

The declaration of the Secretariat of the Egyptian Communist Party tends to directly define the class identity of the present powers. The strength of the authorities, this declaration states, is made up of an alliance comprising new social categories arising out of social transformations which took place both before and after the October War. The elements taking part in this alliance are the big capitalists of the building sector, the landowners and capitalists benefiting from the dismantling of the nationalisation policy and the economic reforms, and other elements arising from this alliance, including, notably, the middlemen and agents of the great monopolist companies. The declaration explains that the new forces have conquered the alliance in power following the economic legislation and the measures it introduced; which means that this economic legislation and these economic measures constitute a veritable breach opened up by the authorities themselves to enable these new social categories to leap into the centres of decision. Thus, the class nature of this power centre is a heterogeneous mixture, certain elements of which may even be prepared to go as far as treason in order to preserve their economic interests, while certain others tend to compromise with imperialism in the hope of gaining admission as lesser members. This category is acting thus owing to the dual nature of the bourgeoisie. A third group still believes in the national Nasserite line.

Consequently, the line advocated by the Egyptian Communist Party consists in the struggle for overthrowing, within the present authorities, those collaborating elements which are endeavouring to apply imperialist plans, and for neutralising those elements tending to compromise with imperialism. The report advocates urging and encouraging the national elements and strata represented in the powers that be to resist the defeatist and conciliatory tendencies bearing grist to the mill of the American plan for the region. In the light of this analysis, the task falling to the militants will consist in revealing the defeatist and conciliatory tendencies, and encouraging the attitude of unitary struggle adopted by the revolutionary and national forces at local and Arab levels against the imperialist and American plans and solutions. Accordingly, the report argues, they will need to expose those tendencies aiming at Egypt's abandonment of its responsibilities to the Arab national liberation movement, and to warn against the appeal to overthrow the Egyptian regime, since such an appeal could come only from a certain left-wing adventurism. The progressive militants will also need to defend the achievements made by the workers and peasants, mobilise the population, and stand firm against any aggression toward and any infringement of democratic liberties. They will need to arouse themselves to act for the establishment of an alliance between workers and peasants and the construction of a front of popular forces, while at the same time exploiting the conditions created by the policy of the authorities to extend the social basis of that front. And finally, they must establish the most intimate relationships between the party and the people.[15]

Before going on to evaluate the judgment made by the Egyptian Communist Party on the Sinai Agreement, we should pause for a moment to consider the attitude of the Party to the authority at present in power; for there can be no doubt that this attitude influences the criticism of the Agreement, especially as this report constitutes a veritable political analysis undertaken in July 1975, whereas the criticism of the Agreement was, properly speaking, formulated in September 1975, i.e. two months later. It is accordingly necessary to aim our sights at the ideological structure of the Party's report, so as to highlight the overall attitude of the Egyptian left wing in regard to the Sinai Agreement and the better to appreciate the programme suggested against this Agreement, and finally, take part in the conduct of a democratic dialogue, essential for the thought of the Egyptian Communist Party in its new formula:

(1) To say that what is happening today is the natural, logical outcome of the line pursued by the authorities in power in Egypt since 15th May 1971 is totally contrary to saying that, as a result of the war of October 1973, after the visit of Kissinger to the region, after the signature of the first disengagement agreement, after the adoption of the American solution, and after the opening up of the economy, new social forces allied themselves with the authorities in power in order to orientate its progress. This opposition, we might even say this contradiction, in the analysis of the two stages of 1971 and 1973, is extremely serious. It prevents our understanding the nature of the events of 1971; it separates, or almost separates it, from what has happened since. At the same time, such opposition would mean that the first to be responsible for the consequences of the Sinai Agreement would be those who participated in power after the war of October 1973.

(2) The review, albeit brief, of the reactionary measures, as a whole, taken by the authorities constitutes in essence a criticism of the Nasserite regime. The report of the Egyptian Communist Party warns against the appeal to overthrow the present regime without producing any convincing explanations, apart from stating that such an appeal smacks of left-wing adventurism. Some people might agree with this, but in a different context from that provided by this report, though the latter can only lead the reader to implicitly accept the idea of overthrowing authority. The report does not state against whom the struggle should be conducted. Is it to uphold or to overthrow the regime? Nor do we know whether the popular front proposed will have the task of acting in order to take over power or to consolidate the power at present in authority.

(3) This lack of clarity accurately reflects the authors' absence of a clear understanding of the class nature of the authorities in power. This can be defined as a right wing mentality well known in Egyptian communist circles in the 1960s and which led to the dissolution of the communist organisations in 1965. This is an analysis which is believed to be objective when it makes distinctions between each member of the group in power in order to justify the claim thereafter that it is made up of distinct strata and wings which must not be lumped together as a single entity. Those in power, according to this analysis, comprise strata which are patriotic, others which are collaborators, and still others which hesitate between the other two. Furthermore,

this analysis urges the need to support the patriotic strata, expose the colla-borators and neutralise those who are still hesitating. It seems to us that the supposedly dual nature of the bourgeoisie is rather the character of those who carried out this analysis; for it is only possible to be objective when allowance is made for the specific nature of Egyptian reality, which specific nature con-sists in the fact that the President of the Republic occupies an exceptional position at the centre of power. The prerogatives granted to him by the Constitution are absolute. At one and the same time, he is the President of the sole party and President of the State; this combination of supreme offices, of necessity, involves a centralisation of power; and this considerably reduces the possibilities of manoeuvre and influence within the alliance in power. This alliance is unlike any we have known before; it resembles that of a patriarchal family where the father always has the final word.

It is this 'final word', called 'decision' in political matters, which should be the subject of analysis by Marxists; for a presidential decision, which receives the blessing of the Council of the People, the Central Committee of the Socialist Union and also of the Ministerial Cabinet, is more worthy of analysis than personalities, their history or their hidden intentions. It is this that grants priority to the private or to the public sector, to free education or to the private university, to the distribution of land to the peasants or to the centralisation of ownership among a handful of pashas; in the last resort, this is what determines the choice of proceeding to agreements with the enemy or to a war of liberation, and reveals the class identity of the authorities in power, since this is not the sum total of the members of the government. Nor is the regime the common denominator between the social origins and politi-cal ambitions of those who hold power. The regime, quite simply, is a centre of decision, legislation and execution. The fact that, in the United States, there is a liberal group alongside the President, does nothing to change the monopolistic nature of the American system. The presence of the Labour Party at the summit of power in Great Britain in no way alters the capitalist nature of the British regime. Similarly, the presence of a former Marxist or an ex-Nasserite or even a present Nasserite in the Egyptian regime, in the govern-ment or the Council of the People or the Central Committee of the Socialist Union, adds nothing, or almost nothing, to the class nature of the regime. For it is the decisions emanating from it which define this nature.

Carrying out an objective, pertinent analysis of the decisions of the Egyptian authorities in power from the 1971 putsch up to the 1975 Sinai Agreement is the only way to enable us clearly to see the class identity of this power. And if this analysis leads us to the conclusion that it acts in a direction which is opposed to the interests of the people, the country and the nation as a whole, this does not lead us to call directly for its overthrow; not that it does not deserve to be overthrown, not because a new power might be still more reactionary, but quite simply because the balance of internal forces – Arab and international – that govern the opportunities for change have to be taken into consideration. Nor must this lead us to confuse the minds of militants by nurturing within them a theoretical illusion regarding the plurality of tendencies within the heart of the power centre itself.

These reservations in no way diminish the importance of the opposition of the Egyptian Communist Party to the authorities at present in power. They in no way diminish the importance of its criticism expressed immediately following the signature of the Sinai Agreement; for, unlike the 'revolutionary current', this analysis, made in the secret report, describes the Sinai Agreement as a step along the road to abdication:

> When the Egyptian Communist Party declares its categorical rejection of the Agreement for the disengagement of the Egyptian and Israeli forces, when it condemns, in the content of the Agreement, the abandonment of the national, progressive line, it calls upon the popular forces to express their opposition and record their opinions at meetings of the popular organisations. It also calls on them to reject all manifestations manufactured to uphold the Agreement.
>
> The secret report calls for an intensification of the struggle to force the authorities to change their abdicationist line, to halt the policy of concessions and to abandon the illusions of American solutions, and to associate themselves publicly with any Arab front struggling against Israel.
>
> The party asks the patriotic elements amongst the authorities in power to declare their position, to state their attitude in regard to the abdicationist line, especially as the signature of this Agreement signifies most irrefutably that the collaborating wing in the regime, supported by those who are adept at conciliation at any price, firmly intends to go to the end of the road of regression, both at the domestic Arab level and at the international level.
>
> The Agreement to disengage provides a clear proof that running after the mirages of an American revolution, taking steps to resolve the problems of national liberation based on the good intentions of American imperialism, and independently of the natural allies of the national liberation movements, must of necessity lead us to fall into the clutches of the imperialist plans.
>
> But the Egyptian Communist Party is absolutely certain that the Egyptian people, who have struggled for so long against the imperialist alliances and against doubtful agreements, constitute a great barrier against any abdicationist solution.[16]

After considering these texts, it is not difficult to see that this opposition to the Sinai Agreement constitutes an application of the theoretical lines enunciated in the report of the Central Secretariat of the Egyptian Communist Party. It may be stated in this connection that the formulation here is much more radical and clear than the criticism published by *At-Taliah*; for at least this report comes to the serious conclusion that the collaborating wing, in full agreement with the conciliatory wing, is firmly resolved to go to the end of the road of regression. But this analysis, nevertheless, contains one

weak element: namely, the idea that the authorities in power are composed
of several tendencies; which does not fail to upset, even neutralise the struggle
against the Sinai Agreement whilst simultaneously hoping that the so-called
nationalist current will take a decisive position by breaking with the other
currents of opinion, in order to avoid bearing responsibility for treason
before the judgment of history. The line of struggle against this Agreement,
thus formulated, might be summarised in three points:

> Encourage the people to express their opposition publicly; require the
> patriotic elements which are hesitating to take up a clear, and honest
> position; and finally, have absolute confidence in the people who have
> always done away with doubtful pacts.

If we associate ourselves with the idea that the people should express their
opposition — which they have already done — and if we set aside the osten-
sibly patriotic elements which do not yet appear to have taken up any
position (and we do not believe they are likely to do so since they would
rather appear to have already chosen their camp, contrary to what the
authors of the report believe) we shall be left with only our confidence in the
Egyptian people, whose history is renowned for their rejection of doubtful
treaties. But how is this confidence to be translated politically? What is the
programme for struggle? Is it a matter of relying on an unknown quantity and
on the spontaneous uprisings of the people, as though it were a question of
fate bound up with metaphysics? Or is it a question of supporting and consolidating this confidence through a programme of action, explaining to the
population how to do away with this Agreement without overthrowing the
regime? For the report calls for an intensification of the struggle in order to
force the authorities to abandon their abdicationist line.

One fact of major importance which must be stressed is that the disturbance suffered by the organised militant cadres because of the ideological
confusion regarding the identity of the authorities in power had its repercussions on the whole opposition of the Party to the Sinai Agreement;
inevitably, this also upset the thought and conduct of the popular masses.
The party's ideology and its directives should, instead, have been a compass
to guide them through the storm; their ideologies and directives should have
constituted a framework to control the movement of the popular masses and
direct them towards a firm and valid position. If that is not the historical rôle
of the organised vanguard, what is? Especially in a country like Egypt where
the spontaneous uprising is still in favour of the Party. In fact, the whole of
this confusion is simply the consequence of the conditions of the reconstitution of the Party; for a clear majority of its leading figures belong to the old
school of Egyptian communists known for its right-wing tendencies in its
analysis of the authorities in power. But it is clear that the reconstitution of
the Party, the fact that it represents the largest organised structure of Egyptian communists and public opinion of the left, makes its opposition to the
Sinai Agreement as important as the criticism published by *At-Taliah.*

261

True, other clandestine left wing organisations were constituted both before and after the reconstitution of the new Communist Party. But whatever the extent of these organisations, they can only be described as cells, as a recent and further removed inheritance of left wing tendencies. At the same time, these organisations demonstrate the multiplicity of the currents of Egyptian communism — currents that extend from one extreme to the other, and as often as not dominated by intellectuals.

The furthest to the left among these organisations is without doubt the Communist Party of Egyptian Workers. Between 1970 and 1971 it published a number of studies that postulated some very valid theses from the point of view of method; for example, in one of these studies the following appears:

> The bourgeoisie cannot go to the ultimate end of its own revolution, for it still keeps the remains of the feudal relationships alive, their institutions and their ideology, in order to make use of them with the aim of more efficiently exploiting and controlling. On the other hand, the bourgeoisie never tends to finally liquidate its relationships with the colonialist market. It never ceases to establish fresh relationships with colonialism within the framework of the constant changes in relative strength. For all these reasons, it is on the working class that the task falls of pursuing the bourgeois revolution right to the end. We would stress straight away that the volume and nature of this task do not make of it a strategic task, but rather a tactical task forming part of the onward march for the achievement of the socialist revolution proper.[17]

Apart from the expression, 'bureaucratic bourgeoisie', which requires revising so as the better to describe the Egyptian bourgeoisie in power, the following paragraph, without any doubt contains a scientific forecast:

> The bureaucratic bourgeoisie that constructs a capitalist economy during a period of decline in international capitalism, is faced with fatal contradictions arising from its exploiting nature and expressing its own crisis of development; this is why we should not be surprised when the national reaction tends to make contact with the imperialist blocs. At the end of its political meanderings, in which it is not impossible to negotiate with the enemy, to attack him from time to time or to make excessively sensational declarations against American imperialism, we shall still find this class seeking to ally itself with international colonialism; this is a normal consequence of the development of Egyptian capitalism. We find here a different alliance from the one which had collaboration as its form.[18]

On 13th September 1975, the Communist Party of Egyptian Workers published a detailed declaration under the title, 'Let us resist the abdication of the Egyptian regime in the face of American colonialism and Israel.' This declaration strongly condemns the treasonous agreement concluded to the detriment of the Egyptian people, the Arab nation and the Palestinian people. The October war, it states, changed nothing as regards the reality of the 1967 defeat. The present government is merely the continuance of an uninterrupted abdicationist line. The most serious feature in the present stage is that Arab territories and the Palestinian cause have been abandoned, and that an American presence has been authorised in Sinai. The strategic situation of the struggle consists of taking action in order to overthrow by revolution the power of the Egyptian bourgeoisie. As for the transitional position, it will consist of struggling against the American overlord. The Egyptian people, in this case, must act side by side with the Arab revolutionary forces; for the Sinai Agreement does not merely represent a regional treason, but a treason affecting the whole of the Arab world. This strategy will also have the task of putting the revolutionary forces on their guard against any endeavour to tie them to the Arab 'axis'; for it is essential for them to maintain their independence in the face of the abdicationist regime. 'It is the duty of the Arab revolutionary forces to expose the Egyptian regime to the Egyptian popular masses and to keep the latter informed of all the plots which are being hatched against them so that they will be able to stand together against the catastrophe.'[19]

No one disputes the validity of these general ideas as set out in this declaration. However, it is possible to discern certain points in the general context of the analysis which smack of leftism.

First, the expression, 'bureaucratic bourgeoisie', is very similar to the old expression, 'military bourgeoisie', in that the former latches on to one characteristic of the bourgeoisie to attribute it thereafter to the authorities in power, thereby feigning ignorance of the economic function of this social stratum and its role — parasitic or otherwise — in production. If this is a group which bears major responsibilities in the State apparatus, i.e. in the legislative and executive bodies, if the aim is to draw a distinction between the old and the new capitalism, the description 'bureaucratic' cannot embrace the categories of parasites and middlemen who do not occupy a position in the front rank of the State apparatus; neither does the expression describe the traditional private sector or agrarian capitalism, for which bureaucracy may sometimes be the symbol. Thus, a leftist generalisation contained in the expression, 'bureaucratic bourgeoisie' may, in political practice, result in consequences of a reactionary nature; for the fact of passing over the identity of the class monopolising power implies a lack of clear appreciation of the means for struggling against that class. The expression, 'bureaucratic bourgeoisie', therefore, leads to general confusion regarding the economic, social and political identity of the regime.

The second point concerns the strategic aim of the Communist Party of Egyptian Workers, namely the overthrow of the authorities in power. If we accept that any strategy a priori includes tactical stages, we may then wonder what are the stages of which the sum total, in the longer term, might result in the overthrow of the regime. Will this fall of the present regime come about spontaneously and of its own accord? Or are these social and vanguard forces organised and capable of taking the initiative of overthrowing this regime? In a word, what are the tactical initiatives of these forces? Who are they? And what is their programme? These are questions which have not been answered.

The third point relates to the danger lying in the fact that no distinction is drawn between before and after 15th May 1971. For the analysis by the Communist Party of Egyptian Workers does not give the least impression that there was a putsch in 1971. Its report deals with the acceptance of Resolution 242 of the Security Council and the signature of the Sinai Agreement as forming part of an uninterrupted series, which would mean that there has been no change in the authority in power. This is a leftist confusion which, overall, leads to grave theoretical consequences of a reactionary nature; for to equate the Nasserite power and the present power immediately eliminates from the front of the popular and national alliance very broad sectors of the people who benefited from the nationalisations and the agrarian reforms in the Nasserite period; it also fails to appreciate the presence of the Nasserite masses and the organised Nasserites. This is a leftist logic which sees reality from a one-dimensional viewpoint, exaggerating the strength of its supporters and minimising that of the others. Another paradoxical fact is, that while the analysis apparently fails to appreciate the Nasserite popular masses, it dares to attack the present authority in power in defence of the achievements of the workers and peasants and Egypto-Soviet relations; achievements and relations which, it cannot be forgotten, form part of the actions of the Nasserite power.

Failing to make a clear distinction between before and after 15th May 1971 constitutes one of the most serious errors in the analysis of the Sinai Agreement made by this organisation both in respect of theory and of the day-to-day military action inside and outside Egypt. Ideologically, this analysis simplifies, albeit naively, the movement and development of the authority in power in Egypt. Further, it makes an excessively approximate evaluation of the Nasserite power over 18 years. It passes over the reality of the 1967 defeat and the 1973 war; and this risks exacerbating the Arab and international powers that are hostile to the Sinai Agreement from other points of view, even though still close to Nasserism.

However, there is one positive, brilliant aspect in the analysis by the Communist Party of the Egyptian Workers which must not be neglected; on the contrary, it must be emphasised and an effort must be made to develop it. This is the Arab framework imposed by the Sinai Agreement. For although Egyptian national sovereignty has been deeply affected by this Agreement, because of the military restrictions imposed upon the movement of the Egyptian army, the American presence, and the continuation of a large area of our territory in the Sinai under occupation, the wound suffered by the sovereignty of the Arab nation is no less deep. Indeed, this is not merely a bilateral agreement enabling the enemy the better to exert pressure on the other fronts; nor is it merely a question of bringing to an end the state of war between Egypt and Israel in order to prevent Egypt's possible participation in any defensive action in the face of the Israeli enemy. This Agreement is much more serious than that, for it neglects the Palestinian issue; it offers American strategy a better field for espionage against the Arab world, which constitutes a threat to Arab security generally and more particularly to Palestine. These Arab repercussions from the Sinai Agreement must, more than ever, unite the Egyptian revolutionary forces and the Arab forces into a total organic unity, both strategic and tactical. For it is no longer a question of a common struggle; this is a unique struggle. This is the general sense suggested by the Communist Party of the Egyptian Workers when it underlines the prime importance of the struggle of the Arab revolutionaries against the Sinai Agreement, while enlightening the Arab masses regarding its role and influence on their lives and on their futures. This must inevitably result in a mobilisation of the popular masses for the abolition of this Agreement.

Lastly, we should turn to the current of opinion finding its expression in the bulletin, *At-Tadamun*, published by the Committee for Solidarity with the Egyptian National Democratic Movement in collaboration with the Patriotic Militants in Egypt. It is clear that this is indeed the voice of an independent organisation. An article, signed with the pseudonym, 'Tarek', states: 'We must now draw the only conclusion which is valid, namely that a just militant position ought to aim at barring the way to a Zionist, American, and Arab reactionary settlement, mobilising the popular Arab masses for a total national war of liberation of long duration.'[20] These few lines enable us to put our finger on the key to the only possible solution to the crisis consequent upon this Agreement. For a new Arab war is alone capable of correcting this tragic situation. With the same lucid insight, the author continues:

> The putsch of 15th May 1971 was carried out by forces of the right sympathetic to the United States. That putsch had been prepared as long ago as the 1967 aggression. It was undertaken with the aim of suppressing the national, progressive line in Egypt. Any other interpretation is an illusion inflicting a serious blow to the struggle of the popular masses.[21]

We consider this point of view to be most mature and profound, albeit at times lacking details and failing to represent one political organisation to be as equally important as the others.

These 'messages to the Egyptian militants' take the initiative in tracing the general outlines of a national, democratic and realistic policy and programme which, overall, constitutes a project worthy of discussion that the Egyptian left must undertake. If the author says that our country is passing through the period of continuation of the national, democratic revolution, this in the first instance means that it is necessary to resolve the agrarian problem in the most revolutionary manner, that it is essential to free the occupied territories, and that the agreements which were concluded on the terms of the Zionist enemy and American imperialism must be abrogated. The author continues:

'It would be necessary to liquidate all the aspects and all the bases of the colonialist influences of American imperialism and Arab oil reaction'.[22]

'It will be necessary to liquidate the present reactionary alliance in order to establish the power of the democratic national front in which the working class and its vanguard party will play a dominant role.'[23] The author then goes on to set down a detailed programme which he concludes in these terms:

> Planned organised action, uniting the workers, peasants, students and intellectuals, is alone capable of shaking the other social sectors. It will prevent them interesting themselves only in the problems peculiar to their own groups. It will incite them to act and organise their ranks so as the better to defend themselves. Broad sectors among the intellectuals, which are generally content to observe, will be attracted by organised political action. Among the professional cadres (teachers, university staff, engineers, doctors, lawyers, journalists, etc.), organised currents will be able to crystallise, in order, thereafter, to take the form of a political organisation expressing the positions and interests of those strata in relation to the problems of their groups, and political and national problems. These will be able to be joined by those sectors of the petty bourgeoisie (minor officials, artisans, small-scale producers, etc.) with no ties with foreign capital or with the brokers and speculators. From this mass, immobile as a whole, organised in part, there will be born the national democratic front.

This text is quoted in full, because it shows in a practical way, how to organise the spontaneous movement of left-wing public opinion that is opposed to the counter-revolution. It explains how it is possible to transform the creative urges of the street into a front capable of taking action. These details regarding national action represent a very refined form of theoretical thought when the author writes:

> Action for the construction of the party and also construction of the front of the workers and peasants should be conducted at the same time as action among the allied social strata. For there is a dialectical interaction between the construction of the party and the action among workers and peasants; moreover, this incites the other strata to act politically. The political action among the allied social strata enlarges the field for democratic struggle, which creates a favourable climate for accelerating the rhythm of the construction of the party and of the worker and peasant alliance. The more constant the democratic climate and the better protected the construction of the party and of the alliance, the more the channels will multiply along which the Party will discover and recruit the advanced elements essential for its own flourishing.

This is a summary of the thought of the organised Marxist movements.

266

This is its clandestine action. What observations can we make regarding its tendencies? What are the observations called for by the officially recognised democratic tendency, which also originated in Marxism? What conclusions can we draw regarding the other tendencies, headed by the Nasserite current?

It should be noted, that an Egyptian left-wing party is still in the foetal state; for the reconstitution of the Egyptian Communist Party only represents a nucleus drawing together Marxist militants; for their part the Nasserites have not yet crystallised an organisational structure capable of polarising all their tendencies. The street therefore remains master of the Egyptian struggle, with all that its spontaneity represents in the way of positive and negative at one and the same time. The first negative element consists of the fact that a considerable period of time will be required in order to mature a solution suitable for abrogating the Sinai Agreement and all its strategic, military and political implications. In reality, a call to action which repeats that it is essential to overthrow the authority at present in power will possess no merit nor find any echo among the masses, until the popular front itself is capable of correcting the progress of the country at both theoretical and practical levels; this can be realised on one condition only, namely, provided there is a positive approach by the left to the spontaneous initiatives of the street.

Anyone reflecting on the various political strands of the Marxist left wing will realise that what unites them is just as important as what divides them. This leads us to raise the question of the unification — ideological and organisational — of the Marxist militants on bases other than those of the classic and fragmented condition inherited from the old Egyptian communist movement. The first responsibility in the achievement of this task will fall to the Egyptian Communist Party.

Anyone reflecting also on the various political strands of the Nasserite left wing will realise that what unites it with the rest of the left wing represents decisive factors in the face of the Sinai Agreement with all that it implies by way of retrogression. These elements constitute an objective foundation which may serve as a basis for a point of departure for the assembly of an Egyptian left wing front.

Finally, it remains to be said that the Sinai Agreement is not the end of the road for power in Egypt. It represents a strategic turning-point in relation to the previous regime. The race against time today favours the Egypto-Israeli-American equation. What then, is the agenda for the opposition? But first, what is the general counter-strategy in the face of the counter-revolution?

Notes

1. *At-Taliah*, No. 10, 1975.
2. The dossier of this discussion was published under the title *le Dossier de Nasser entre la gauche égytienne et Tawfiq Al-Hakim*, by the Lebanese

publishers Dar Al-Qadaya (printed by The Commercial Press of *Al-Ahram*), 1975.

3.   *Ibid.*, pp. 64-72; 117-9.
4.   *Ibid.*, p. 152.
5.   *Ibid.*, p. 169.
6.   *Ibid.*, pp. 174-5.
7.   *Ibid.*, pp. 180-1.
8.   *Ibid.*, p. 218.
9.   *Ibid.*, p. 219.
10.   *Ibid.*, p. 429.
11.   *Ibid.*, p. 430.
12.   *Ibid.*, p. 431.
13.   *Ibid.*, p. 430.
14.   *As-Safir* (Lebanese daily paper), 4th April 1975.
15.   See *Awraq Dimuqratiyyah*, Nos. 3 and 4, 1975; for annexures 'Documents of the Egyptian Communist Party'.
16.   These quotations are taken from *Al-Intissar*, a clandestine magazine, and *Awraq Dimuqratiyyah*.
17.   *Nature du pouvoir et problèmes de l'alliance de classes*, the Communist Party of Egyptian Workers (1970-1), pp. 73-4.
18.   *Ibid.*, p. 78.
19.   First issue of *Ach-Chuyu'i Al-Misri*, October 1975, pp. 30-45.
20.   *At-Tadamun*, No. 4, September 1975.
21.   *Ibid.*
22.   *Ibid.*, p. 23.
23.   *Ibid.*, p. 24.

PART 3
The Counter-Revolution
Faces the Crisis

9. The Religious Right Brandishes Its Weapons

The Religious Question and the Revolution

1954 was without doubt the most decisive year in the history of the Nasser revolution. In that year we saw the crystallization of the power struggle, unusual confrontations between workers and intellectuals and the attempted assassination of Gamal Abd El-Nasser. Demonstrators were shouting, 'Down with democracy' and the Chief Justice of the Council of State was attacked. Six important members of the Muslim Brotherhood were executed and 16,000 other members were arrested. The military trials took place under different names: Treason Tribunal, People's Tribunal and Revolutionary Tribunal. Most of the political leaders from the time of Farouk found themselves in the dock. So many events took place that will live for ever in the Egyptian memory because, during that year, the Egyptians were watching and discovering how Egypt was governed and asking themselves what the future would hold.

Most of them, however, will perhaps only remember the most significant days of this year that was so crammed with unique and exceptional events in the modern history of their country. But let us begin at the beginning. Five armed young Christians broke into the Orthodox Coptic Patriarchate which is situated in a small street leading off the main thoroughfare, *Clot Bey.* Under the direction of their leader, a 34-year old advocate named Ibrahim Helal, they overcame the guard and made their way to the residence of Pope Youssab II. It was dawn, between four and five o'clock, and the barely awake Papal Guard offered no resistance. The group had little difficulty in reaching the Patriarch's bedroom.

Even though the history of the Egyptian national church is full of politically involved popes, none of them had ever been woken at gunpoint, and if we consider the fact that Pope Youssab II had never dabbled in politics in any way whatever, we can well imagine that he probably thought he was having a nightmare at that moment. He sat on the edge of his bed and rubbed his eyes incredulously. He may perhaps have thought that thieves had dared break into the sacred quarters![1] His shock was not lessened when the invaders gave him five minutes to dress. Two documents were then presented to him for signature. The first was a formal abdication of the Papal Throne. In the

271

second he was to ask his office and the Christian General Council (*Al-Majlis al-Milli Al-'Am*) to prepare for new elections after revising the legislation in force at the time so that it would be possible for all Egyptian Orthodox Christians to take part in the elections.

After signing the documents Pope Youssab II was led out by the young gunmen; all the priests resident in the papal palace were still asleep. The bewildered guards inside and outside remained immobilised. All telephone lines to the outside world had been cut. A black car was waiting by the outer door. One of the group opened the rear, right-hand door, he got in first and ordered the Pope to follow him and to make room for a third person. As soon as this was done another member of the group took the steering wheel and a fourth sat in the front right-hand seat and asked for the rear blinds to be lowered. The leader of the group gave the order to leave and then made off.

It was about six o'clock. In that quarter shops and cafes are usually open very early, the trams are always overloaded with workers on their way to the factories, and newspaper sellers are trading in the street crowded with travellers from the central railway station.

For three hours no one was aware of this unusual event; not even the guards, who were released soon after the departure of the car, realised what had happened. They did not even try to follow the fifth member of the group who calmly hailed a taxi right in front of them. They did not even bother to take down the registration number or to wake up the priests who were still asleep.

At about 9.00 a.m., Pope Youssab II had already arrived with his 'companions' at the Wadi An-Natrum monastery by Lake Marictis in the desert to the west of Alexandria. The monastic community was surprised to receive a visit from their sovereign pontiff without warning, without an official cortege, unaccompanied by his clerical court and at a time of no religious significance. They were no doubt very surprised by the lay people surrounding the Pope, one of whom announced, 'The Pope is sick. He has come here to rest.' They jumped into the car and drove off, giving no further explanation.

At that same time most of the churches of Cairo and Alexandria, most of the principal Governorates, and the press agencies received a declaration signed by 'The Coptic National Group'. It announced the Pope's abdication and condemned the corruption that was rampant in the church under his rule. It called on the Coptic people to participate strongly in the expected elections. The declaration demanded that the government should not meddle in the internal affairs of the Copts. It finished with the slogan 'The Gospel is our Constitution, Coptic is our language, and to die for Christ is our greatest ambition.'

It was later discovered that the Ministry of Social Affairs had actually granted a licence to the Advocate Ibrahim Helal for the establishment of a religious association which would be named Coptic National Group. It was also learnt that certain members of the Revolutionary Council had sent messages in support or of congratulation, at times of religious festival. Hanging on the wall at the group's headquarters was a framed message addressed to the group and signed 'Anouar Al-Sadat'. Following these events the Ministry of the Interior discovered that after its foundation this group had been intensely active in a way only equalled by the Muslim Brotherhood. The group's slogan appeared to be no more than a copy of that used by the Muslim Brotherhood, 'The Koran is our Constitution. The Prophet is our guide, and death for the glory of God is our greatest ambition.' Like the Muslim Brotherhood, this group was no more than a political organization using religion as a cover. It was an extremist group formed by dissidents from the Association of Sunday Schools which teaches religion to the young. The group had expanded rapidly in all the provinces of Egypt. The Sunday Schools were active and legitimate, i.e. under the official protection of the church. The new group criticized the weakness of the clergy and demanded the teaching of the Coptic language. Without waiting for the satisfaction of their demands, the group set up free classes in Coptic in all the villages and governorates. And so this archaic language began to be taught to an enthusiastic and fanatical youth which considered itself Coptic rather than Egyptian.

At the time of the subsequent court hearings, the Egyptian magistrates gave little importance to the slogan used by this group. However, the call for the practically impossible return to the use of an archaic Egyptian language, the transformation of the Gospel into a constitution — even though it has no legislative character, and dying for Christ long after the age of the martyrs constitutes in the most flagrant way possible an appeal for the creation of an independent Coptic state, separate from the Egyptian state. However, this was not noticed by the churches, by those in power, or by the intellectuals. The Tribunal sentenced Ibrahim Helal and his accomplices to three years imprisonment for the illegal bearing of arms and for having detained a person by force. The penalty is of no importance. However, the justifications for it show a total ignorance of social life in Egypt.

Twenty years later, the same event took place but in the opposite direction. The President of the Republic was almost the victim. This happened in 1974. Three years later one of the mullahs of Al-Azhar was victim of the same type of event. The charges in the legal hearings in these two cases were the same: illegal bearing of arms, arbitrary detention of people, or attempted assassination. And certainly the sentences were always the same: imprisonment or death by hanging. But no one tried to understand what was behind all these incidents. Nobody asked why the extremist groups were being liquidated — whether Christian or Muslim — by imprisonment, exile, or torture. Whether they were rightist militants or democrats, those in power always opposed them politically, using the media and forbidding the opposition to express its point of view, even if it was in agreement with official policy, as was the case with the Muslim Brotherhood.

But let us ask the question in another way: Why was the regime always on the defensive in its struggle against religious terrorism? Why did its organs only act once the extreme theocratic right resorted to actual armed threats, while the State's war against national leftist ideals is 'preventive' and takes place without the left ever having brandished its arms? Nasser ordered executions and imprisonments only when the Muslim Brotherhood tried to assassinate him in 1954 and 1965. Sadat did the same thing; he freed some of them, executed the extremists and imprisoned others at the time of the Military School affair in 1974 and the assassination of Sheikh Muhammad Az-Zahabi in 1977.

Events Leading to the Religious Crisis

In trying to bring together precisely those things that are common to the two regimes, and those in which they differ, we arrive at a definition of the religious crisis that occurred in the 1970s. The crisis was not altogether different from that now ravishing Lebanon; both are in some way or other related to the Near East conflict and to what is called 'peaceful settlement'. But it must be added that the main aspect of the two crises remains the theocratic social systems in both countries and even in all the Arab countries.

Egypt, which has fought for one and a half centuries for secularization and democracy, is acting today as though history had stood still. The truth is that the revolution of July 1952 is responsible, because of its impotence, for failing to solve the problem of democracy. The religious question has always been taboo, not to be tackled, even if it would be to the advantage of religious people themselves. The reason for this is very simple: the great majority of the Revolutionary Council, including the most progressive elements, has always been in contact with the Muslim Brotherhood. Even though Nasser had never been tempted to exploit the religious situation, even though he never claimed Muslim attributes, even though he never finished his speeches with verses from the Koran, the only book he censored in 1957 was *Dieu et l'homme* by Mustapha Mahmud, a materialist writer who had repented and recently been converted to the ideas of the Muslim extremists. The pro-Nasser publishing organizations authorized the publication of masses of politico-religious books. Nasser himself wrote the introduction for an anti-communist book entitled *Le communisme et nous*.

In fact the association of the left with materialist philosophy had long been made in the minds of the middle-class intelligentsia. If that proves 'active ignorance', as Voltaire expressed it, it also proves that the Egyptian left had been particularly interested in the thinking of Lumieres during the 1940s. But the final result of this interest was negative in two respects. The first time was when certain members of the left tried to reconcile science and religion, thus separating themselves from the positive experiences of the modern Arab renaissance from the beginning of the last century until half way through the present one. They tried to modernize Islam, or to make modern civilization Islamic. Such a task would have been understood if undertaken by the religious, but coming from informed social thinkers it could only surprise. The second time was when some of the leaders of the revolution called for a separation between the economic aspect of the renaissance, that of social reform, and materialist thinking. This separation in the minds of the informed Egyptian intelligentsia is one of the main reasons for underdevelopment and progressive decline under the influence of conservative thinking.

Let us add, that for most of the time factors generally considered relevant to tactics are often taken as the bases of strategy. When the Nasser organizations turned to the strength of religion for the attack on communism, they did not think that one day this religious cover would be transformed into an anti-Nasser force.

It was a crisis well understood by the middle classes, from the beginning of the renaissance (the *Nahda*), when the idea of the reconciliation of science with religion, and the legacy of tradition with modern civilisation, was formulated; a manicheism which had to break down in the face of the division between thinking and conduct in matters of civilisation and collective disintegration. One practically throws oneself into the utilization of modern technology but often hesitates to study the cultural consequences. Liberal slogans are coined in matters of constitution and law but they are completely impossible to carry out in practice. The high percentage of illiteracy (more than 85% in 1979) of the total population makes this division even more serious for the Egyptian personality. For a long time men of the left seemed to have escaped this disintegration because of their scientific view of nature and society. The extreme religious right also escaped because of its Muslim or Christian view of the world, but it should be stated that these two groups have always been on the periphery of Egyptian society. The overwhelming majority of the people have never followed either the ideals of the left or the extremist Coptic or Muslim outlook. The regime itself does not escape it. What used to be called 'the non-capitalist road' to development has never been a socialist path, and the immediate consequence of this is the deepening of the divide between economic development and social underdevelopment. Furthermore, the *Nahda,* which had attained high cultural standards during the 1960s went into rapid decline after the defeat of 1967; this collapse was completed by the putsch of 14th May 1971. Egypt's lack of raw materials, the population explosion, the repercussions of the democratic crisis on what was incorrectly called errors in the transition to socialism, the cancerous proliferation of a 'new class' holding key positions in the social structure, and the catastrophic effect of military actions from outside, had all perhaps encouraged the climate of despair and an exaggerated search for solace in religion.

It can be seen that the differences in the attitudes of the two regimes (the present and that immediately preceding it) with respect to religion and its institutions, either Christian or Muslim, can be treated as fundamental elements in our analysis of the events that followed, that accompanied or preceded the Second Sinai Agreement and the Arab battle for the Lebanon.

The course of these events was settled by the Egyptian about-turn at the time of the visit to Jerusalem. Strange to say, this visit was made not just to a country that was racist in origin, foundation, regime and political doctrine, but to its most extreme party in terms of theology and the most terrorist in terms of history. The visit sanctioned the Lebanese civil war and a Lebanese-Palestinian war which took on the character of a religious war, thus hiding the obvious, and also, the secret objectives. It is, therefore, more important to compare the points of difference between the present and preceding regimes than to compare those they have in common. The struggle for secularism and democracy led by informed Egyptians has achieved much on the level of thought but little on the social level. This has enabled the new regime to develop an extreme religious ideology as a bulwark against any possible radicalism within the country. This has also enabled it to have talks with conservative Arab regimes, and also with the racist and religious Israelis. It was not by chance that the present Egyptian regime supported the Lebanese Phalangists at a crucial moment in the Lebanese war. That is the background against which we have to compare the two regimes; we may now proceed with a dialectical analysis of the struggle between the revolution and the counter-revolution.

Nasser, therefore, inherited a society in which the great majority of the people were dominated by the vague idea that there was a definite link between democracy, liberation and national unity. This idea, conscious or otherwise, was a dominant feature in the way Egyptians had felt (*wijdan*) since the revolution of 1919 led by Saad Zaghlul and inherited by the Wafd. The campaign against the British occupation also implied the limitation of autocratic royal authority by the proper use of the Constitution, Parliament and the press. Both campaigns implied secularism. During the struggle against the British occupation, popular pressure also intensified against the dictatorship of the regime and against theocratism. Nasser also inherited a situation deeply opposed to national tradition, in which the Wafd had only been in power for seven and a half years during the 32 years between the revolutions of 1919 and 1952; this meant that, for three-quarters of this historic period, Egypt was subjected to defeatism imposed by foreign occupation, to dictatorship, and to theocracy. This is undeniable, even in the face of apparent signs to the contrary, such as the participation of the Wafd in the 1936 treaty, or its agreement to regain power with the help of British bayonets on 4th February 1942; the assassination of the Prime Minister, Mahmoud Fahmi An-Noukrahi — the Muslim Brotherhood's symbol of its constitutional subordination; the assassination of Hassan Al-Banna himself under the power of a minority government; the tendency of the Green Shirts (Young Egypt) to support the Axis; and the tendency of the Muslim Brotherhood to support Britain during the Second World War, even though both were terrorist organisations of the right.[2] It must be said that these contradictions occurred against a background of no democratic liberty, the dissolution of Parliament, liquidation of the opposition press, arrests of citizens, individual assassinations, interminable dealings with the occupier

following the Sidqi-Buven negotiations (the people said that George V negotiated with George V), application of martial and special laws, revival of
organized religious extremism, arson of churches, and many more things of
this type. All this went against more than twenty-four years of democratic
tradition in Egypt. Nasser therefore inherited two traditions rather than one,
but he was unaware of their significance in the national context. These two
opposed streams — democracy and religion — represent the totality of the
Egyptian social movement. The noise made by the Muslim Brotherhood's
terrorist organizations does not represent the whole of their popular base.
Constitutional minority governments truly represent only a minority of the
people and consequently, the contradiction between the size of minorities,
the duration of their time in power and the meagreness of their popular base,
makes any radical change in the structure of the regime or of society a matter
of democratic choice.

Because of the conditions at its birth, and of the social environment of the
lower middle classes and the ideological background of most of its leaders,
the Nasser administration nationalised democracy according to a formula
which was at variance with the actual socio-historic conditions in Egypt,
where the two aspects of change, social and national, are organically linked,
and where democracy is the essential characteristic of change. Democracy
necessarily supports the progressive movement in developing or recently
liberated countries. The specific character of this link can have nothing in
common with experiences in the East or West if the objectives of the slogan
'Rise up from our condition' are objectively sought. In fact the East, with its
social experience and its single party, should theoretically possess an organiza-
tionally and politically homogeneous structure; but the problems of
democracy arises forcibly in spite of all material achievements. The capitalist
West, with its liberal politics, is theoretically consistent, but in practice,
monopoly transforms itself into disguised dictatorial power. De Gaulle, for
example, was obliged to flirt with the army during the events of May 1968.

The tragic consequences suffered by the Nasser regime are in fact no more
than the fruit of the separation between democracy and the two factors;
social change and national liberation. The defeat of 1967 and the political
defeat which is typified by the putsch of 1971, irrefutably prove that the
artificial separation between democracy and other forces of change was
never an expression, or the specific character, of Egypt. That is why
theocracy was and is one of the most serious wounds suffered by the Nasser
regime when it wanted to reconcile autocracy and secularism. What were the
practical consequences of it?

Thanks to social change, it was possible to proceed with measures that
directly affected the superstructure and infrastructure of society: the
nationalisation of foreign interests, the nationalisation of the higher levels
of local capitalism, the removal of middlemen, restriction of land ownership, starting to build up the nationalised sector in industry and commerce,
the creation of agricultural cooperatives, the modernization of production
by employing modern technology, the construction of the high dam at Aswan

for the production of hydroelectric power, increasing the area of cultivable land, and spreading natural irrigation etc. These were the measures which directly concerned the socio-economic infrastructure. At the same time, free education was given at all levels, including the universities and military schools. Admission to institutions of higher education was restricted to those obtaining distinctions in their school-leaving certificates. This was an important decision on the socio-cultural level.

These measures simultaneously affecting both superstructure and infra-structure, had the effect of mixing economic and social issues on the path to national unity and secularism. The law granted social equality to all citizens. Foreign interests were affected, whatever their religious identity, and also certain interests of the local middle classes were affected irrespective of religious association. The most numerous social classes, having benefited by the redistribution of land, and by industrialization and education, were not made subject to any distinction on the grounds of religion in the eyes of the law. The employment law, for example, guaranteed employment to all graduates whatever their religion. Religious fanaticism could not therefore prevent a graduate from taking his functional position in society.

All this led to a reduction in religious tension. Previously the army and the police had been organizations specifically forbidden to Egyptian Christians. The Military Colleges admitted no more than 3% of Christian students. It was not by chance that such a situation was accompanied by a law, according to which any Egyptian wishing to undertake military studies had to present documents declaring that his parents were landowners or shareholders, as well as a special recommendation by someone of influence.

The Consequences of the Absence of Democracy

The reduction in religious tension achieved by the application of a minimum of social democracy could not nevertheless achieve the radical goal, secularism, because there was no real political democracy.

Illiteracy (75% of the entire population were illiterate) by its nature is the result of the class system. It is also the class system which determines the pattern of education: generally those whose studies stop after primary educa-tion do not belong to the same class as those who stop after completing their secondary education. Both classes are radically different from those who have the chance to enter university and these, in turn, are different from those who are able to study abroad. In reality, the revolution contented itself in giving parcels of land to some peasants and granting to their children the 'right' to higher education though not the means to enable them to partake of it. One wonders how many of the peasant children would be able to com-plete secondary education, given that illiteracy is much greater in the country than in the towns. The revolution did not raise the school-leaving age. It took no action on the politically organised level to combat illiteracy, as was the case in China and in Cuba. In consequence, the illiteracy percentage remained static and, during all the years of the revolution, there was a lowering of teaching standards in the universities. The socio-cultural impact of this on the relationships and values in the villages was zero, in spite of the changes brought about by improvements in production. The patterns and customs of Egyptian peasant life, therefore, did not change in any way; the overwhelming majority of the peasants still remain victims of social misery. But the most serious consequence of this is that the level of awareness has remained very low; it has shown no sign of change. A purely objective reading of the books *La Terre* and *Le Paysan*, by the Egyptian novelist, Abd Al-Rahman Al-Charqawi, can only confirm this social truth. The first is a portrait of the campaign in the 1930s, and the second deals with the same situation 30 years later, i.e. during the 1960s. The reader will detect no difference between the two situations, even though 30 years separate them. It can be said that at the end of these three decades the theocratic society and autocracy still persisted. This situation was pictured by Tawfiq Al-Hakim in his *Journal d'un procureur de campagne* (1933) and by Youssef Al-Haram (*L'Illicite*) in 1959. We should note that these two dates are of social significance in the history of the Egyptian people because they reflect, under two different regimes, a total absence of democracy.

If the free education preached by Taha Hussein and others during the 1940s has been realised, it has not been accompanied by freedom of thought even though, in the 30 years preceding the revolution, the Egyptian university was a centre of intellectual enlightenment. In fact the first dealings between the revolution and the university can only be called 'the massacre of the university'. Sixty professors and lecturers were sacked because they were free-thinkers, democrats or leftists. The university guard was abolished, only to be replaced by the secret police and by anti-democratic regulations. A single political system was imposed on teachers and students, and, more seriously, the political history of the country was completely falsified, as though Egyptians had been born at dawn on 23 July 1952. Even more serious was that conservative programmes and teaching methods were maintained in matters of economics, philosophy and sociology. 'Other' ways of thinking were forbidden; it was only possible to study in line with official thinking. Progressive academics were imprisoned or, at best, shelved. Only schools hostile to the left and to secularism had the authority to teach young minds.

It was not by chance that Kamal Ad-Din Hussein, one of the most powerful members of the Revolutionary Council, one of the best officers outside the ranks of the Muslim Brotherhood, was, for more than ten years, Minister of Education, President of the Universities, Secretary-General of the Teachers Union and President/Director-General of the Higher Council for Arts, Literature and the Social Sciences.

To this should be added that Nasser, during one of his periods of conflict with the Muslim Brotherhood, went one better in religious matters as a tactical move. He took two actions which, seen from outside appear contradictory, whereas in fact they both led to the same result. By government decision, religion became a main subject at all levels of education. The success or otherwise of a student in religious matters determined whether or not he could pass on to the next class, just as was the case in scientific subjects. Al-Azhar became a modern university, but open to any Muslim student who wished to study medicine, technology or agronomics alongside his religious studies. In spite of the apparent contradiction between these two measures they both led to a new religious presence in Egypt. While young students still learnt to practise religious segregation both Muslims and Christians began to attach importance to religion under threat of being held back. The students became progressively more interested in religion in the absence of any proper scientific or secular education. Religious sentiment dominated the sensitive thinking of the young to the detriment of national or patriotic sentiment. As for the Al-Azhar graduates in medicine, engineering and pharmacy, they were neither pure doctors nor pure *'azharians'*. This new mixture had to lead to a religious extremism, deeply hostile to science, except when it came to the making of bombs. It is no surprise that most of the graduates of Al-Azhar University later became members of the Muslim Brotherhood.

Egypt, which at the time of its secular and democratic revolution had a very real separation between religion and the state, now saw itself, under Nasser's leadership, following a line of compromise which enabled the leadership to flirt with both religion and science. This phenomenon is not, however, totally alien to the history of Egyptian thinking; manicheism has been a noticeable feature in the history of religious reform from Rifa'ah At-Tahtawi to Muhammad Abduh. Under Nasser, a line was adopted which extended from Ali Abd-Raziq, author of *L 'islam et les fondements du pouvoir* (1925) to Taha Hussein, author of *La Poesie anteislamique* (1926). Both thinkers were prosecuted and their works were condemned. Judgement and condemnation are thus the expression of the impotence of the young Egyptian middle classes faced with the fear of being accused of atheism. Fear of the occupier and of their allies in the interior at the time of the King led to the search for a compromise on the problem of democracy and national liberation. This had occurred in the atmosphere of the failure of the 1919 revolution. But these tragic events in no way diminished the fact that the constitution created by Ahmad Orabi, leader of the Egyptian revolution against the English (1881-82) had not contained any clause specifying the religion of the State. Neither does it diminish the fact that there was a large opposition to the persecution waged against the ideas of Ali Abd Al-Raziq and Taha Hussein.

But let us return to the revolution in 1952. In fact the Nasser revolution had adopted the manicheist idea of religious reform to achieve middle-class national democracy. Let us remember that the idea of reconciling science with religion had been put forward by enlightened theologians with the aim of modernising Islam, to make research possible and to justify the use of science in various aspects of practical life. But it is in no way admissible coming from revolutionaries seeking harmony between ideas and practice. In reality it is the absence of democracy, the lack of confidence among the people, that brought about the conditions under Nasser whereby the solution of compromise and contradiction was adopted. It was, therefore, decided that the State should have an official religion. The consequence of this was that laws concerning the equality of citizens were applied, but in general terms; distribution of land, education and the right to work were guaranteed to all. But all things not specifically subject to legislation remained governed by the tradition established before the revolution. There was still, as usual, a Christian minister in the Cabinet and ten Christian Deputies in Parliament, as though the non-democratic state granted to a religion things that were not granted by society. In fact this State had never given society the chance to express its opinion; perhaps it would have elected just one Christian Deputy or perhaps 50. Perhaps there would not have been a single Christian suitable to assume the function of minister; perhaps there would have been several of them. The fact remains that nomination always stayed in the hands of the dictatorship and this strengthened, even more, the division between the religions, even though the original intention had been to reduce the tension between them.

Also, the ministries directed by Christians were for the most part marginal. Nomination was one of the main reasons why many Egyptian Christians felt that they were only a minority, not because they had been treated as such, but because they had not been treated as full citizens. The absence of Christians in most of the main positions in state organisations led them to think that they were considered a minority, or separate citizens.

Such was the feeling which, for the first time in the history of the Copts, led to phenomena such as the National Coptic Group which of course failed to create a state within the state but which, even though officially dissolved, still remained in the minds of a large number of young Christians whose only recourse was to turn to emigration to America, Australia and Canada or to enter holy orders. In fact the terrorist activity of the National Coptic Group towards Pope Youssab II in 1954 was not a fairy-tale. Anyone reading newspapers such as *Al-Fida'*, *An-Nil* or *Misr* in that year would note immediately that the religious identity of this extremist group was, at the end of the day, nothing more than a reaction to the absence of democracy and the increasing strength of the Muslim Brotherhood. That is why this bitter polarisation occurred in the ranks of the Egyptian people. The media had presented what happened in 1954 at the pontifical palace as an overturning of power in the ecclesiastical world which, in fact, it had been. But it was also an action against the State, and against the social system based on an agreement with a religious minority and following the military example of the July 1952 revolution.

As for the Muslim Brotherhood, belonging to the religious majority enabled them that same year to take on the State, using the methods of counter-revolution. In the person of Mahmud Abd Ar-Rauf, the Muslim Brotherhood opened fire on Gamal Abd An-Nasser in Al-Manchiyyah Square in Alexandria. That was the fatal consequence of the negative attitude of the

Nasser regime towards democracy. That is what the policy of compromise on religious matters led to: Christian extremism embraces dissidence; Muslim extremism attacks the entire system in an attempt to bring it down.

In spite of the armed attempt[3] by the Muslim Brotherhood, the Nasser regime could not shake off its socio-historic origins nor its cultural identity. 'In the first days of the revolution, General Muhammad Naguib had gone to the tomb of Hassan Al-Banna to bow down and weep.'[4] The revolution then decided to open the case of the assassination of Hassan Al-Banna. Colonel Muhammad At-Tab'i, attorney at the emergency court, delivered a glorious eulogy on the 'Martyr Imam', he demanded capital punishment for his assassins saying, 'The lamented Hassan Al-Banna gave his life for an ideal; an ideal based on reform and aimed at putting an end to the state of occupation, the origin and principal cause of the corruption rampant in our country.' By chance, some time later, the same tribunal had to judge the Muslim Brotherhood, condemning some of them to death and thousands more to prison.

At the height of the attack against the Muslim Brotherhood, Nasser, in the company of several members of the Revolutionary Council and some sympathetic members of the Muslim Brotherhood, had one day visited the tomb of the 'Martyr Imam' to pay him homage.[5]

However, bargaining with religious extremism was of no use. Repression, prison, torture, and even the death penalty, did not prevent the Muslim Brotherhood, 11 years later, from attempting to assassinate Gamal Abd An-Nasser for a second time. The absence of democracy, absence of secularism and fear of the left were always there. In fact, during the Nasser administration, religion had no place in any strategic plan for a new social structure. It was always of transitory use. It was simply a card to be played as a manoeuvre. Certainly the State had never been religious under Nasser but it is also certain that religion was never separated from the State. It was a simple matter to combat religious extremism when it brandished a gun but the Nasser regime was completely incapable of combatting it when it brandished a 'Book' because it never made the vital link between the 'Book' and the 'Gun'. Writings such as *La Barbarie du XXe siecle* by Muhammad Qutb and *Des signes sur un chemin* by his brother Sayyid Qutb who was condemned to death and executed, were issued as state publications under the responsibility of Abd Al-Qader who was Minister of Cultural Affairs and Information at the time. Officially there was no religious sedition under Nasser. The Coptic National Group and the Muslim Brotherhood were dissolved. But the embers were still glowing beneath the ashes.

The defeats were bought at great cost, for it is easy to destroy any positive attainments when there is a total lack of democracy. Democracy is the sole element in the Egyptian situation that can make the link between social change and national liberation. Without political democracy, economic and social democracy can be no more than a reflection of the ideas and ideology of the social class from which sprang the 1952 revolution. The absence of organic links between the three elements of democracy led to the failure of the Economic Development Plan in 1965 and to the military defeat by the enemy in 1967. It was easy to overturn the regime in 1971. The absence of one element had to lead to the progressive breaking down of the other two. But the biggest defeat was that suffered by the lower middle classes who, as part of the political structure in power, saw the left as their enemy. Conditions were just right, therefore, for a putsch to put an end to hesitation, to the advantage of the extreme religious right. In fact religion in the Nasser regime was a precarious balancing force between the right and the left. It is no surprise that the right became victorious, because making use of religion in a political sense always guarantees the success of the most extreme.

The Ideological About-Turn

The putsch of 14th May 1971 began the operation to regain its authority as ideologically against mystification. During that year Muhammad Hassanien Haykal published two articles on 'spiritualism'. The leaders of the Nasser party who had been deposed following the putsch turned to this idea in order to be in contact with and inspired by the mind of Nasser! The two articles tried to present this group as having been only servants of Nasser and completely incapable of taking the least decision or of playing their part in politics in his absence. It also proved, though perhaps not intentionally, that this group clung to mediaeval practices that had nothing in common with science.

That was the first stage of recovery. What happened afterwards is much more important. The new President gave the State the slogan 'Science and Belief'. He was nicknamed the 'Believing President'. He was no longer called Anouar Al-Sadat but Muhammad Anouar Al-Sadat. This is not without significance because, gradually, one began to see girls wearing the white veil in the streets of Cairo as had been the practice at the very birth of Islam and still is in certain Arab countries. Friday prayers in the mosques of the capital and in the provinces became a passionate religious demonstration. The faithful, crowded around the mosques on their prayer mats, obstructed the traffic. Five times a day television and radio programmes were interrupted to broadcast the call to prayer; morning, noon, afternoon, twilight and after sunset. Even Parliament had to interrupt its sessions at the times of prayer. Magazines and newspapers devoted entire pages to religion. People began to talk about substituting the common law with Muslim law (shar'ia), i.e. to cut off the hands of thieves, to stone adulterers, to forbid alcohol, etc. Religious wall newspapers appeared at the universities. Bands of extremists provoked their comrades.

The incident at the Military College in 1974 was the culmination of all this. A group of armed extremists took over the College, killed the caretakers and tried to take control of the College in order to proceed with a military overthrow of the regime. The attempt failed for purely 'technical' reasons. As usual the regime accused the rebels of having attacked religion and of having violated the Koranic verse 'Obey your leaders'. Some *mullahs* of Al-Azhar and other well-known Islamic personalities wrote articles accusing the young rebels of being atheists. Al-Azhar now started a campaign against the rebels. It called on people not to confuse religion with those who exploit it for political purposes. The rebels were presented as a group of neurotics; psychologists and the television cameras showed them as mentally deranged. In the end some of them were condemned to death and others to prison. And there the matter ended, at least officially. The sociologists tried to convince the public that this delinquent minority was seeking revenge against the whole of society because of their own failure in family and university life. The psychopathic personality was the official cause of the problem. The only constitutional solution to the problem was for the regime to create a theocratic state.

Towards a Religious State

In religious matters, the only fundamental difference between Nasserism and the putsch of 1971 was that the former was always torn between total secularism, which presumes democracy, and a deep-seated hostility to democracy, whereas the regime that followed the putsch of 1971 tried to be logical with itself by creating a kind of uniformity with religious ideology. The only problem was that it wanted to use the ideology to prevent others from forming political organizations.

The difference between the two regimes is fundamentally a social one. During the first years after the July 1952 revolution, the political scene in Egypt betrayed the social identity of the revolution, because less than one year after taking power the regime condemned to death two workers' leaders from Kafr Ad-Dawwar for having claimed the right to strike. At that time the private sector was in control of the economic situation. This same revolution, however, only condemned Muslim Brotherhood members to death when they brandished arms against Nasser himself in 1954.

It must be said that the way the revolution developed afterwards was such that it did not turn to religion after the 1967 defeat and neither did it turn to violence, in spite of its immense despair during the big demonstrations in 1968. Nasser issued his 30th March Declaration in which he adopted, and assumed as his own, the results of the wide discussions triggered off by the intelligentsia. The 30th March Declaration called for the establishment of a modern State based on the institutions and sovereignty of the law. It called for science to play its role in finding the solutions to the problems of society. Thus, at least in theory, Nasser had the definitive solution to the problem of social underdevelopment. The new ideology, officially expressed in the National Charter, chose scientific socialism as the medium of social change. The declaration also chose democracy as the type of government. But during the two years before Nasser's death these intentions did not become the subject of legislation; they were not transformed into practical measures. As a whole, they were an intellectual tendency towards modernisation, laicism and renaissance, against a theocracy which extended its roots below the surface of the social classes, within state organisations and in the meandering subsurface of culture. During those two years, Nasser particularly applied himself to the military liberation of territory, always seeking the most rapid solution, whether military or peaceful. Acceptance of Security Council Resolution No. 242 in 1967, and the war of attrition serve as examples. One day in 1967, at a meeting with a group of Marxist intellectuals at Al-Ahram, Nasser opened his remarks with: 'We will not discuss social problems. We will leave those until the liberation.' Several days after this meeting he decided to reduce land holdings from 200 feddans to 50, but the system for representation of classes in the State remained unchanged. In fact the hesitant ideology of compromise remained in place, thus determining the way events were to develop after the defeat.

President Sadat did not come to establish the indispensable link between national liberation, social change and democracy. He took power to remake society and the regime so as to form a new State conforming more closely to his own personal ideology. The President, at the beginning, was strongly influenced by three political parties and three men. The three parties were Al-Watani,[6] Young Egypt and the Muslim Brotherhood. The politicians were Aziz Al-Masri Pasha,[7] Sheikh Hassan Al-Banna[8] and Ahmad Hussein.[9]

Describing his first meeting with Hassan Al-Banna in 1940, Sadat who was just an officer in the army at the time, wrote:

> By chance there are some members of the Muslim Brotherhood among my soldiers. On the day of the Anniversary of the Prophet, someone whispered that an important man was waiting outside who wanted to say a few words to the soldiers on the occasion of the *'Mawlid'*. I asked who it was, and when I learnt that it was Sheikh Hassan Al-Banna, supreme leader of the Muslim Brotherhood, I welcomed him warmly and authorized him to address the soldiers on my behalf. His choice of subject was excellent. His deep understanding of religion was incomparable. His explanations and his elocution were excellent. This man had all the qualities of religious leadership from all points of view. He was also deeply Egyptian, with all that this implies in terms of courtesy, tolerance and simplicity in dealing with people. I had often heard of the Muslim Brotherhood. I thought that they were a religious group whose sole objective was moral reform and the renaissance of Islamic values. But after having listened to Sheikh Hassan Al-Banna I began to change my opinion of this group. This man spoke of the world and of religion in a way that was quite different from that expected from religious people. I admired him greatly. I congratulated him warmly at the end of this talk. We had a short discussion and, as he was leaving, he invited me to attend his Tuesday Lesson which he gave every week after the twilight prayers at the group's headquarters at Helmuyyah Al-Gididah. I attended several lessons and, each time, he joined me for discussions.

> I was impressed by the way in which this group was organized and by the respect in which this man was held, the kind of respect one has for a saint. The Brothers were prepared to prostrate themselves before me simply because their supreme leader had granted me the favour of sitting by him.[10]

As for Aziz Al-Masri, we can read the following:

> I used to admire passionately the character of Aziz Al-Masri. We had much to learn from the experience and leadership of this great warrior. I therefore asked Sheikh Hassan Al-Banna to bring us together. This happened in the same year that I got to know the sheikh. My request was granted. My contacts with Aziz Al-Masri Pasha and Sheikh Hassan Al-Banna were permanent.[11]

Without going into political detail, the common element that drew these three men and their parties together was clearly: Aziz Al-Masri and Ahmed Hussein never disguised their sympathy for nor their relationship with Hitler's Germany; Hassan Al-Banna never disguised his friendly relationship with the representatives of the British occupying power nor with the minority governments; the three men were deeply partial to para-military political organization and to individual assassinations.

The three parties – the Young Egypt Party, the National Party (*Watani*) and the Muslim Brotherhood – believed in a Muslim ideology to unite all Islamic peoples. At the same time they believed in Egyptian regionalism. The National Party, under the leadership of Mustapha Kamel, supported the idea of the Ottoman Caliphate against the Western occupation following the defeat of the Orabi revolution. The Muslim Brotherhood believed, and still believe, in the unity of the Muslim world. To them Arab nationalism is a colonialist idea even though they had collaborated with Great Britain. The Young Egypt Party proclaimed the slogan, 'Egypt above All', while maintaining contact with the Axis.

In other words, autocracy – i.e. the cult of the individual in power, theocracy – i.e. submission of social relationships to a hierarchy, armed terrorism and religious doctrine and, finally, leaning on the most reactionary foreign powers, Nazi Germany and Fascist Italy, as well as collaboration with the British occupier, were the common elements between these three personalities and the parties that they inspired.

Because of his ideology, his political practice and his social origin,[12] President Sadat represents a synthesis of all the elements mentioned above. This enables him to justify his understanding with agricultural capitalism, parasitic capitalism, bureaucracy and his sympathy with the idea of a religious cover for State and society. There lies the root of the crisis; for this regime is opposed to politico-religious organizations that are older and better organized than the regime itself.

The stumbling blocks of the Nasser regime were national liberation, social reform and, what should have been the link between them, democracy. To avoid them, the new regime used the October war as a substitute for a war of liberation, and had recourse to economic measures and to a multiplicity of tribunals. But the substitute war could neither bring about liberation nor an opening up of the economy. A multiplicity of tribunals could not, and cannot, provide the least guarantee of democracy. The present regime, dependent on international capitalism led by the United States, could only make a poor attempt at window-dressing of these issues, because it could in no way hide the fact that it was an autocratic form of government, that its values were based on theocracy, and that these things formed the socio-cultural basis of society.

For these reasons, the kind of religious polarisation known in Egypt in 1954 rapidly returned. The Muslim Brotherhood is not the only party on the scene; other groups exist today – The Youth of Muhammad (*Chabab Muhammad*), the Soldiers of God (under the leadership of Mustapha Churi, leader of *At-Takfir wa Al-Hijrah*), etc. As for the National Coptic Group, it has reappeared but bearing no relationship to the old organization nor using the old slogan; it is no longer against the Church, but under its protection. All this coincided with the very hasty preparations for the Second Sinai Agreement and with the Lebanese war. At the moment that the regime was preparing to conclude its ceasefire treaty with the enemy and when the fighting broke out in Lebanon, the Egyptian paradox appeared as follows: the attempt to bring about a Lebanese-type economy was impossible, but the attempt to bring about a Lebanese-type social conflict was perfectly possible.

Such a change in the economic structure was impossible to achieve. Even if the parasitic elements became much stronger, the basic socio-economic structure in Egypt is both productive and national. Consider the story of agricultural production, consider the fact that Egypt is the first Arab society to have approached the Western level in certain industries in the last half of this century, so forming a social base for local production. Egypt has never been a market for the international monopolies in the true sense of the term. Neither has she been an entrepot society. It is true to say that she had not become a consumer society at the time of the revolution because the revolution itself had blocked this by setting up heavy industry and the nationalised sector. Commercial capitalism, in particular the construction and import/export sectors, had never been masters of the Egyptian economy even though they had a privileged position right from the birth of the Egyptian middle class. For all these reasons, the structure of the Egyptian economy is radically different from that of the Lebanese economy, which is essentially based on commerce, banking, profit, entrepot trade, brokerage, commissions, etc. That is the fundamental reason for the wide social and cultural differences between Egypt and Lebanon. The truth is that the entrepot society has a very attractive external appearance because of the accoutrements of modern society, but beneath this glittering surface lies a torn and fragmented society constantly shaken by tribal and religious conflicts. The 1975 war lifted the mask and revealed the ugly truth proving, once and for all, the impossibility of what is complacently called 'The Lebanese Equation'.[13]

It must be pointed out that Egypt has not suffered the division between outward appearance and inward reality such as occurred in Lebanon. The war in Lebanon proves how impossible it is to continue with such a model. That is why it cannot be reproduced in Egypt. Also, the social history of Lebanon contains elements that have nourished the religious war. Let us remember the events of 1860 and 1958. In fact, what is often called Greater Lebanon, founded in 1920, and what is called The National Charter, established in 1943, had one day or another to face the religious question.[14] Those are the things that do not exist in the social history of the Egyptian people, in its geopolitics or in its demographic composition. The unity of the Nile Valley, the 1,000 year old Central State, cultural access to the ancient, mediaeval and modern worlds, conquests and counter-conquests and an unusual strategic position have made Egypt a relatively stable country in body and spirit. That is why its class structure has always been classical, and national unity a socio-cultural matter. Religious and tribal differences have only been of secondary importance compared with what unites the total Egyptian population. For these reasons it was impossible to make the social conflict in Egypt like that in Lebanon, and also impossible to make the Egyptian economy like that of Lebanon. For a while, however, the attempt seemed possible. At that time, politics dominated historical, social and cultural influences, and held an exceptional place in the social superstructure of the political world, thus having influence on economic and cultural measures. The economy was 'open' during the transition. Social conflict and national liberation were trampled under foot by religious ideology and theocratic activity.

A False Right and Two Authentic Rights

Following the 'substitute war' and at the time of taking economic decisions and strategic decisions, the right in power was besieged by the religious right, more internally consistent, and by the liberal right represented by the rest of the Wafd Party. The religious right had been able to progressively regain its strength, thanks to the protection of the regime. But this protection did not prevent the religious right from openly turning against the regime and declaring that it was more faithful to Islamic principles, and that it had an historic right to represent these principles. The liberal right had developed steadily thanks to the opening up of the economy. It was the first to realise that the liquidation of the July revolution signified a return to the preceding regime, but without restoration. It had recourse to its old symbols in which it was assisted by the historic popularity of the Wadf Party, historic custodian of the right to represent liberalism and the national unity of both Christians and Muslims.

The new regime was certainly surprised by the resurgence of these two phenomena, even though it had engendered them. The putsch had brought about its own counter-revolution; first for itself, secondly for the social classes that had supported it, and thirdly for the Arab and international powers that had helped it. In such a situation, the social base of religious ideology, and that which united the supporters of the free economy, were realised to be much greater than had been thought. Consequently, in spite of the apparent contradiction, these two streams were particularly interested in the counter-revolution. After the Military College affair, the small groups of the extreme religious right had the strength of organized initiative, as shown by the spread of extreme right-wing religious thinking throughout the army. The direct consequence of this infiltration is illustrated by the rumours that were current during the October war, according to which Christian soldiers might have been responsible for the Deversoir breach. This obliged President Sadat to name a Christian officer as hero, at the head of the Second Army, of the liberation of the east of Qantara.

This bloody affair uncovered two inseparable phenomena; numerous young people were abandoning their studies to go underground in the caves and mountains of Upper Egypt. They abandoned their western clothes and adopted those of the Bedouins or the peasants. They even changed their names and broke all contact with society, to enter into a new order where they spent all their time studying the Koran, obeying the orders of their leaders and learning to handle weapons. This phenomenon revealed another: large hidden arms dumps were discovered in Upper Egypt. At Qana more than 30,000 items of armament were captured, including light and heavy arms and, notably, anti-aircraft artillery pieces. At no time during the inquiries conducted into these matters did those responsible see, or want to see, the link between the Military College affair, the young people going under-ground, and the large quantities of arms not normally available to individuals. Those conducting the inquiries only saw the youth as being mad, and the storing of such quantities of arms as illegal.

Henry Kissinger, American Secretary of State, in March 1975 declared the failure of his attempt to bring about a second cease fire agreement. War broke out in Lebanon on 3rd April of that same year. It began in a symbolic but none the less representative manner, for the first bullet was fired by the Phalangists, and the Palestinians were the target. Following that, the Sadat-Ford summit took place in July 1975 at Salzburg, just a few months after the signing of the first ceasefire agreement. But the war in Lebanon continued and the religious bullets were aimed at the heart of the Lebanese nation. What then was the official reaction of the Egyptian regime to these internal and external events?

During a visit to the Suez Canal on the first anniversary of its reopening, President Sadat declared that he did not consider Pierre Gemayel as a traitor and that he had no doubt about his Arab integrity. At the same time, the results of a national census were published in Egypt. This showed that there were 2,300,000 Christians in Egypt. It was hard to see why such a census was undertaken but the media drew attention to this figure by publicising it in an extensive manner. At about that time, Al-Azhar presented a bill to the Council of the People on the control of religious communities. In reality, this was no more than a manoeuvre by the regime in response to internal religious extremism, and to cover the Sinai Agreement which in effect supported the most religious of the Lebanese parties. The regime wanted to be more Muslim than the small Muslim groups in the country, while at the same time being the greatest ally of the Christian Party in Lebanon. These were just two sides of the same coin.

It can be seen that religious action and reaction occurred originally in official circles: the census had been carried out on government initiative, the Bill for the control of religious communities had been presented by Al-Azhar and not by the Muslim Brotherhood. The Christian protest did not come from the Coptic National Group nor even from the Sunday Schools, it came from the priests, bishops, archbishops, patriarchs and finally from the Pontifical palace. It is easy to understand the deep anxiety running through the Egyptian population when one realizes that Al-Azhar represented a section of the people bigger than all the extremist groups put together, and that many more of the Christian faithful supported the Church than were attracted by the extremist Coptic groups. The shaky religious minorities took note of their awesome political situation resulting from the census and the bill on the communities. Even fewer people understood the relationship between the attempt to bring about a Lebanese structure in Egypt and that which took Saudi Arabia as a model. Few people then could see the problem in its correct light; it was not a question of the difference between Christians and Muslims, neither was it a problem about the application of Islamic law (*Shari'a*) in place of the common law, it concerned, and still concerns, the role of Egypt in the Middle East conflict from the Sinai Agreement to the visit to Jerusalem, and also in the Lebanese war.

Gamal Sadeq Al-Marsafawi, legal adviser and President of the Supreme Court of Appeal, broke the silence that he had scrupulously maintained since his nomination in 1972, to declare that the Senior Committee for the Drafting of Laws had completed its study of Bills and that it was now the responsibility of the Ministry of Justice to apply them to Egyptians and non-Egyptians, to Muslims and non-Muslims with respect to the regionality of the laws.[15] Marsafawi's declaration summarized the laws in question: they were, in a more judicial form, the same propositions as those of Al-Azhar. The Law on the Abjuration of the Faith, for example was changed to The Law on the Abandonment of the Muslim Religion. The bill was precise: 'All renegades will be urged to change their minds and to repent; if, 30 days after, the person concerned has not returned to Islam, and if that person persists with his abjuration, he will be condemned to death.'[16] The bill also stated that two witnesses were necessary to attest the abjuration of the faith in order that judgement could be made.

Even though these official ideas were accompanied by an equally official press campaign against the left, atheism, and the extremist Muslim organizations, the Church felt particularly vulnerable under such a law. The leftist thinkers could see that the regime wished to go further than the existing sanctions, to oppose all free thinking and to have the ability to apply the death penalty in cases of activity against the right under the pretext of abjuration of the faith. But intentions are one thing, and non-Muslim reaction another. Mustapha Amin, a writer of the right, expressed his opposition to such a law,[17] but the religious reaction had already occurred and was particularly demonstrated after the ratification of the law by the Council of State and its publication in the Official Gazette.[18]

The most important, Christian, religious Congress for 66 years in the history of Egypt took place on 17th January 1977.[19] The final declaration of this Congress, which however was not published, said:

> It was necessary to gather together in Congress the representatives of the Coptic people with the fathers of the Church to discuss certain general questions of interest to all Copts. The Sovereign Pontiff, Pope Chenouda III, granted us the favour of attending the inaugural session held at the Cathedral of St. Mark on 17th December, 1976.[20] . . . The delegates have studied the matters brought before the Congress. They have reviewed the decisions made at the meeting of the preparatory committee of the Priests of the Coptic Churches in Egypt held on 5th July 1976.[21] . . . All responsible people in the church and of the faithful, take note of two, inseparable, considerations: firstly, the unfailing belief of the eternal Coptic Church in Egypt, sanctified by St. Mark and by innocent martyrs in all generations; secondly, total faithfulness to the country, of which the Copts are the oldest and purest of its races; no people on earth are as attached to their country and to their nationality as are the Copts to Egypt.

The declaration then reviews the subjects discussed: freedom of belief, freedom of religious practice, protection of Coptic marriage and families, equality of opportunity, representation of Copts in parliamentary bodies and caution against extremist religious tendencies. The declaration called for the repeal of the Bill on the Abjuration of the Faith, the idea of applying Muslim law to non-Muslims, repeal of the Ottoman law against the building of churches, elimination of religious requirements in the employment regulations of the public service and, finally, freedom of publication.

This declaration was addressed to the higher levels in the state hierarchy. It deliberately made use of extremist phrases such as 'the Coptic People' and 'the pure Coptic Race'. It should be emphasised that this 'rallying round the Church' does not mean that the assembly was not legitimate and consistent with an attachment to the country. However, the most serious part of this declaration was what were called Executive Recommendations. These asked Christians to undergo a total fast for the three days from 31st January to 2nd February, 1977 and to 'consider the congress in permanent session to monitor the application of its recommendations concerning all matters connected with the Copts'.

Several notes from Copts resident in the United States and in Canada were sent to the President of the Republic; they were dated 11th February 1977. The President of the Council of the People also received a note from Australia dated 9th May 1977. These notes dealt with the same subjects contained in the Alexandria Declaration. Of particular note was a list of questions from the Coptic Church of Melbourne addressed to Sayed Mar'i. 'What is meant,' wrote the authors of this message, 'by articles considering our Holy Gospel as apocryphal?[22] What is meant by articles calling us atheists and *"muchikins"*?[23] [those who ascribe another divinity to God] What is meant by the call for the conquest of atheists and *"muchikins"*?'[24] This note also pointed out the difference between the number of Christian Egyptians in the public service at the time, compared with the situation in the past. To this message was attached a document entitled 'Decisions of the Coptic Congress held at Melbourne, Saturday 25th June 1977 and at Sydney on Sunday 30th July, 1977'. In this document the delegates declared their intention to undergo a total fast, to publish a pamphlet containing Government declarations on the subject of the Muslim Law (translated into several languages), to organize Coptic marches in all the cities of Australia, to contact all the Coptic Churches in America, Europe and Africa to co-ordinate activities and to arrange a meeting for all those with responsibilities in government, radio, and television. Christian activists in Egypt and Australia had no need to make contact with other continents because, in fact, action by other Egyptian Christians living abroad had been triggered off at the same time. One cannot think of good intentions or of spontaneity in these circumstances. Without going too much into details we can say that these activities abroad tried to bring Lebanese Christians abroad together with all other Oriental Christians living abroad. It was all very blatant, but the means are less important than the result: the Sinai Agreement or the Lebanese war.

The international press began to speak of The Coptic Problem. In Paris a magazine was published with the name *Al-Alam Al-Qibti (The Coptic World)*.[25] We cannot fail to draw the parallel from history when, about 1911, an Islamic Congress was held in reaction to the Coptic Congress, following which the nation was in danger of splitting up. The British occupation grasped the opportunity to propose The Law for the Protection of Minorities, a law that was categorically rejected by the Copts themselves.[26] But let us continue. In July 1977, a Congress of Islamic Associations and Groups was held under the patronage of Sheikh Al-Azhar Abd Al-Halim Mahmoud. This Congress was attended by 'All the Islamic Institutions and Associations in Egypt'. The final declaration of the Congress included the following recommendations:

> All legislation and all judgment contrary to Islam is considered false. Muslims must not submit to them; they must contest them and adhere to Divine Law. Their faith is only effective when submitted to this Law and this Law alone.

To demand the application of the Muslim *Shari'a* is the duty of all Muslims. No one has the right to dispute it. We accept no advice concerning moderation or delay in this matter.

To postpone the application of Islamic Law is a sin and a disobedience to God and to His Prophet. The legislature must fulfil its responsibility before God and Man by proceeding with the ratification of Bills proposed to it.

The Congress is very pleased to note the declaration made by the President of the Republic announcing his intention to purge the administration of all atheistic elements.[27] The Congress calls for an acceleration in the application of this decision for the salvation and strengthening of the nation.

The Congress calls on the President of the Republic to order a purging of the information media.

All young people at all levels of education should be provided with religious teaching.

The executive committee of the Congress will remain permanent, in order to monitor the efforts for national unity and for the application of Muslim Law.[28]

In its conclusion, the declaration emphasized that Al-Azhar and all the participating organizations had taken part in the Congress [and here note] as in the case of the Christians, within the framework of legitimacy.

But as these two legitimacies were of a religious nature, if such an expression can be used, the political legitimacy of the regime appeared to be unstably balanced between two right-wing forces, the Muslim and Christian religious right and the secular right represented by the resurgence of the Wafd Party. The former was ideologically more coherent than the regime and the latter more economically coherent and more authentic than the alliance represented by the regime. To make Egypt like either Lebanon on the one hand or Saudi Arabia on the other was therefore a hopeless cause, even if the counter-revolution at one time had thought otherwise.[29]

The Bloody Disillusion

The dream turned into a nightmare a little after midnight on 3rd July 1977. Something had just happened which no one knew about except some members of the family of an 'Azharian' sheikh. The next morning, at about 11 o'clock, the telephone rang in certain people's homes. At the other end of the line a young, calm and monotonous voice tirelessly repeated, 'We are the group that the atheists call *Al-Takfir Wa Al-Hijrah*. We have just kidnapped Dr. Hussein Az-Zahabi who published an article against us on 30th May in the blasphemous newspaper *Al-Akhbar*'. The news rapidly spread throughout the country. President Sadat was not in Egypt; he was somewhere between Rumania, Iran and Saudi Arabia. His Prime Minister, the former police officer

Mamduh Salem and mainstay of the 14th May 1971 putsch, took the initiative and mobilized all the security forces, both secret and public, to search for the kidnapped sheikh. In spite of the size of the operation his forces were not able to find either the man or his kidnappers. Only three days later the body of the victim was discovered. This discovery made it easier to conduct a full-scale search. Hideouts were discovered. The leader of the group, Chukri Ahmad Mustapha, known as the Emir by his followers, was arrested. A wave of arrests swept the entire country from Alexandria in the north to Aswan in the south, passing through all the governorates of the Delta and of Upper Egypt. It was then it was discovered that the group had set up 'principalities' (cells) in each town and village; large quantities of arms and cash were seized.

How did the regime, and society, react to this? What was this group that liked to call itself 'the Chukrists' because of its allegiance and submission to their chief, Chukri Ahmad Mustapha, who called himself the Emir or Prince of the Believers?

The attention of Egyptians was particularly drawn to this event because it was the first political assassination in the country for 30 years. It was entirely different from all the political assassinations committed in the 1940s because for the first time a person had been kidnapped and a ransom had been demanded for his liberation. It was also an individual assassination, different from those carried out on King Farouk's orders or on those of the constitutional minority governments. It did not appear like the activity of the small terrorist groups of the recent past because it was an organized, collective action based upon a ideological and political decision. Finally, the victim was an important person among the mullahs of Al-Azhar.

During the three days of the search the whole Egyptian population held its breath and suffered total confusion; the regime was in a critical condition. The standing of the police underwent a harsh test. A tremor of fear ran through the ranks of the leaders because of rumours concerning a list of persons who might be assassinated. Arresting most of the members of the group in no way changed how they thought about the affair. A vast press campaign was organised in which important personalities from Al-Azhar denounced the extremists. The leader of the Muhammadiyyah fraternity stated that members of *Al-Takfir Wa Al-Hijrah* were suffering from 'psychological complexes.'[30] 'It is not a religious association, it is a group of atheists and destroyers,' said the President of the *Shar'iyyah* Association in the same issue. The President of the group *Chabab Muhammad* (The Youth of The Prophet) said, 'The principles of *Al-Takfir Wa Al-Hijrah* are against the teachings of Islam.' The President of the Association for the Upholding of the Koran stated in the same edition of the same newspaper: 'Islam does not recognise these terrorist barbarians who threaten the safety of society.'[31]

But all of these declarations were exegetical as well as justifying the regime which was now suffering a crisis of identity. It was particularly torn between the religious instructions that it continuously affirmed and the economic reality, i.e. the open situation. Even the legitimacy of Al-Azhar was questioned by this group of extremists. The State itself was firmly accused of atheism. In other words, the more the regime injected Islam into state and society under the external pressure of Saudi Arabia and the internal pressure of the Muslim Brotherhood, the faster it plunged into the turmoil of a religious explosion. Considering Egypt's reputation for freedom of religion and the tolerance in its 1,000 year old culture, it was impossible to submit 8 million Egyptian Christians to Muslim Law.

The regime continued its policy of rushing ahead and, in the face of the extremists, it issued commands that outbid them in extremism. Writers in the pay of the regime described the religious troubles as the result of the lack of faith among the people, the absence of true religious education and propagation of the atheistic ideas of the left. In fact, the Sadat regime was trying to create religious unity and not national unity; for the former enabled him to fight the left. A union between the Church and Al-Azhar under his direction would have enabled him to face atheism and the left, to snatch the ground from under the feet of the deviationist minorities, Christian or Muslim, and to cut down the growing political importance of the left and the Wafdist right. The left, which, at the time of the authorization of political parties appeared to be a nebulous background — a condition which it was not desirable to aggravate — began to influence a significant number of people. Educated Christian and Muslim personalities supported the regime strongly and thus demonstrated their support for a national unity that was social and non-sectarian. As for the Wafd, it succeeded in a very short time in gaining the support of large sections of the Egyptian Christian community, as though the Church saw there a safe refuge from the government party. Historically, since the 1919 revolution, the Wafd was known for its support of a unity between the Cross and the Crescent.

It was natural in those conditions that the average Muslim citizen should listen, if only out of curiosity, to the voice of Chukri Ahmad Mustapha, Emir of the *At-Takfir Wa Al-Hijrah* group. It was also natural that they should find his words of more consequence than those of the regime and Al-Azhar. The name of the group, *Takfir Wa Hijrah*, was a simple slogan summarizing the Chukrists' call for a total condemnation of the State, society and the modern world and for an exposure of its blasphemy. A call for emigration (*hijrah*) was meant to be an invitation stemming from the emigration of the Prophet, a preparation for a total change by force of arms. But none of the attorneys interrogating the accused made the apparently logical connection between the assassination of Sheikh Az-Zahabi and previous occurrences: the Military College Affair, the capture of large munitions and arms dumps, collective emigration to the desert and building up a significant underground, the growth in the activities of the extreme religious right at the universities, etc. None of the attorneys, in spite of the existence of compromising documents, saw the correlation between the ideology of the Chukrist group and the Muslim Brotherhood. Seemingly it was even more unthinkable for them to look back to the history of the end of the 19th Century to discover the social origins of religious extremism.

Let us examine what is said in the writings of Chukri Mustapha who, in his booklet *At-Tawassumat* (*Searching Looks*), grants himself the titles Prince of Believers, Prince of the End of Time and Heir to the Land. The booklet, secretly circulated by the Chukrists, was in the form of a manuscript, so that the blasphemy of printing could be avoided, this being an invention of the *Kuffirs* (atheists). The manuscript declares that the Islamic State must be based on two things: annihilation of the infidels and giving all the land and all that lives upon it to the faithful. 'When the atheists are conquered, when the faithful are purified, then the Religion of God will appear.'[32]

> But, [the manuscript says] it is not possible to establish this State without treading the path traced out by the Prophet of Islam because neither State nor Islam can be established before this emigration. Death of the atheists and the destruction of their State cannot be achieved while the faithful are still living among them. Furthermore, the Prophet requires Muslims to leave the blasphemous land; it is then that the retribution of God will fall upon the infidels.

Mustapha Chukri divided the Holy War into three phases:

> First, the faithful must escape the pitfall of the '*chirk*', of ascribing another divinity to God. He must avoid being tortured by the infidels. He must then spread 'The Knowledge' throughout the land. Finally, the Holy War must be fought to establish the Islamic State.

The subject of the *Jihad* or Holy War is formulated as follows: 'In our time, Egypt is the pagan city which has taken the place of Mecca before Islam. Egypt exports infidelity to the whole Arab world. She makes war on all who fight for the glory of God.'

This group sees Egypt as the starting point for their war but does not see the war as ending there. The Chukrist state will have to extend throughout the world:

> God be praised. He will prepare the land for the group of the just by provoking a war between the two great powers, Russia and America. Each is trying to extend its domination over all the world. The war is inevitable; they will destroy each other. God will thus have prepared the land for the Islamic State and the society that follows the right path. Following the destruction of the two great powers in the Third World War, the forces of the Muslim nation will be about equal in number to those of its enemies. It is then that the true *Jihad* will start.

Such is the central core in the thinking of the group's Emir. Let us see what it actually means, which is different from the false commentaries made by the information media. Is this doctrine really opposed to that of the Muslim Brotherhood? In reality, does this Chukrist group show the slightest difference from that old extremist organisation?

In fact, these words are not entirely new. It was Hassan Al-Banna and not Chukri Mustapha who originally, 30 years ago, addressed his partisans with these words:

> Muslim Brothers, when the time comes that among you are three hundred companies, spiritually strengthened by the faith and by the doctrine, and physically exercised, you will ask me to invade Heaven and Earth with you and to conquer the most violent of the infidels and I will do it by the will of God.[33] [Or again] You will be a formidable enemy of those in power and of those not in power.[34]

That was just a small sample of Sheikh Al-Banna's speeches. Finally, let us add that it was he who invented such expressions as 'The art of death', 'The industry of death':

> The nation that excels in the industry of death, [he would say] believes that the All Powerful grants him an easy life on earth and eternal happiness in heaven. We are corroded by weakness because we love life too much and we hate death. Therefore prepare yourselves for a major action. Seek death and life will be offered to you. . .[35] Put to the sword those who oppose your majority.[36]

What a master! What a disciple! If Chukri Mustapha, agricultural engineer, abandoned life in the world to build up and mobilise armed companies with the intention of establishing an Islamic State and if he was opposed to the Muslim Brotherhood, it was simply because the political manoeuvres within the group had failed to alter the doctrinal structure of the old organization. Chukri Mustapha, therefore, represents the purest form of the ideals of the Muslim Brotherhood. These ideals were originally drawn from such sources as Gamal Ad-Din Al-Afghani[37] in his *Response aux naturistes,* Muhammad Iqbal Al-Bakistani, author of the famous book on Islamic doctrine; Abu Al-A'la Al-Mawdudi, author of *La theorie politique de l'islam;* and finally Rachid Rida, author of *Kalifat ou le grand Imama.* These authors enabled the Muslim Brotherhood to develop the idea that Islam is a religion, a state, a country and a nationality. For them Islam is not only the religion of God but also His state in the world.

The first comment that can be made about these ideas is that they are largely imported and that in reality they do not originate from Egyptian or Arab sources. Even the ideas of Sheikh Rashid Rida were no more than a flagrant distortion of the ideas of his master Muhammad Abdah. Another aspect is that this thinking has religious allegiance as its source of inspiration. It is separated from the heritage of Rifa'ah At-Tahtawi, Muhammad Abdah, Ali Abd Al-Raziq and Taha Hussein. All those called for religious

297

reform, secularism, democracy, modernization and a reopening of research. They were the authors who best expressed the general Arab sensitivity and popular Egyptian feelings in spite of the persecution that most of them suffered in the time of the British occupation, under the monarchy and the feudal-comprador coalition. In fact, extremist Muslim thinking had always been contained within organisations that only became important in certain circumstances, but when liberalism flourished these organisations commanded very little popular support capable of carrying them into power or into parliamentary institutions. This means that the great majority of the Egyptian people have never been inclined to extremism and even less inclined to support a government based on religion.

But the Egyptian people, deeply moved by the assassination of this learned Azharian, wanted to know more about this self-styled Emir. They wanted to know what was behind the dispute between Sheikh Az-Zahabi and this 'Prince of Believers'. How surprised they were to learn that there had been no real dispute! The sheikh had even written that this group aspired to live the religious life at the most sublime level and free from all aspects of immorality. These words are taken from a small book written by Sheikh Az-Zahabi while he was Minister of Property in Mortmain in 1976.[38] We should also note that this man had never been opposed to a certain ideology. In a research paper 'The effects of the restriction of the communities on social stability' presented to the Muslim Fiqh Congress at the Muhammad Ibn Saoud University at Riyad, Sheikh Az-Zahabi had written: 'Muslim societies are now experiencing a rebirth of a hope; the return of Muslims to Divine Law, the return of the blind who miraculously regain their sight, the return of the dead resurrected by Divine Grace.' It was the clear and frank statement of a supporter of the transformation of Egypt — constitutionally and socially — into an Islamic society. One wonders, therefore, what was the contradiction that could have led to the assassination of this man?

That was the big question asked by the majority of Egyptians. The answer was not easy to find, particularly as most of the people had long since lost all confidence in declarations made by religious officials. Since 1954, people had become accustomed to not taking such religious declarations seriously. They had become accustomed to the regime's repetitive campaigns against the Muslim Brotherhood and others. Some even dared to publicly express their opposition to the official point of view. Sayed At-Tawil, Professor at the Faculty of Islamic Studies wrote:

> May our reverend mullahs be careful in making judgements against this group in the name of Islam. They must consider the members objectively in the light of Islam. These young people did not give themselves the name *At-Takfir Wa Al-Hijrah*. The name was given to them in security publications. The name that they chose for themselves is, 'The Call to Islam Group'.[39]

The press also informed the public about the group's training camps, their

way of life in the desert, the wives who followed their husbands and wore
a special habit, similar to those of Christian nuns etc. It was known that the
group was very active in the Universities of Cairo, Alexandria, Ain Chams and
Al-Mansourah. Some members, students of the Faculty of Commerce at the
University of Cairo, had even taken part in religious television broadcasts.
It was also known that some of the group's members lived permanently in the
mosques of Cairo, Guizeh and Abdim and in the Al-Qulali quarter. The
organisation was also present in many villages in Upper Egypt, particularly
at Al-Miniyeh, Assiout and at Guizeh. Printed membership lists were regularly
distributed among the population. The leader of the group was able to leave
the country several times to go to the Yemen, in spite of the warrant for
arrest issued against him following his condemnation in the 1972 hearing.[40]

The Egyptians knew all this and even more. Security publications had
even contained a report following threats received by several dissident
members in which one particularly notes:

> This group is a terrorist, religious organisation which does not hesitate
> to turn to violence to bring other religious associations under its control
> with the aim of changing the regime by force. This organisation is
> effectively an extension of that of Saleh Sariyyah, condemned to death
> following the Military College affair.[41]

For all these reasons the puzzling question of what had led to the assassination of Dr. Hussein Az-Zahabi continued to be asked among the population. The ordinary people were disturbed. They did not understand why the
government and Al-Azhar were opposed to Chukri Mustapha and his group;
neither did they understand the reasons for their reaction. But the tiny
minority who had understood tried to analyse the events and declarations.
Their analysis can be expressed as follows: The action adopted by the regime
against the armed extremist organisations shows that the struggle for power
even within the coalition which holds it is far from over. On the other hand,
certain individuals in the regime, known historically for having set up
religious cadres, have deliberately provoked religious troubles and discredited the left, are associated with the reasons for the presence of such
extremist organisations. But most striking is that the coalition in power,
composed of the rich people from the countryside and the import-export
brokers, had two contradictory ideologies. Agricultural capitalism and
bureaucracy prefer to be cushioned by religion. The parasites, however, prefer
consumer values, pleasures and amusements, and all that is forbidden by
religion. One takes the mosque as its fortress, the other takes the night club.
One is in favour of a Lebanese-type society in Egypt, and the other of a
Saudi-type structure. The power struggle within the ruling coalition is
intimately tied to the Arab powers, which are also torn apart between the
opening up of their economies and the conservatism imposed by religion. The
conservative Arab powers do not form a united and homogeneous front, not
even in a single State. In Egypt, one conservative party supports religious

officials, the information media and some members of parliament; the other supports the extremist organisations; and a third party supports the Wafdist right. The existence of these differing political outlooks within the same power structure at local and the Arab level is not separate from the Middle East conflict or the strategic interests of foreign powers. One local and Arab current of thought favours the creation of small religious States that could form a natural barrier against Israel and thus justify their existence ideologically. Another outlook tries to forestall these particular Arab reactionary forces wanting the creation of small states after the fashion of Israel, and restricts itself instead to the formation of a theocratic society hostile to all radical change. A third stream of thought favours a degree of modernization and liberalism sufficient to bring about a measure of economic prosperity and a show of democracy which would make the regime less vulnerable to the left.

But such an analysis has to come up against the specific differences between the Lebanese, Egyptian and Saudi societies. For example, Egyptians interpreted the ideas of the *At-Takfir Wa Al-Hijrah* group in different ways. Some circles strove for the ratification of the Law on the Abjuration of the Faith, which in turn led to the call by Pope Chenouda III for a general fast. And even though the general tendency was to seek a minimum agreement between Christians and Muslims against the left, the Christians strongly supported the Wafd. Their fast was a new and rather grave phenomenon. Egyptian Muslims living in the United States and Canada held a Congress in Toronto in July 1977 similar to those held by the Christians, the only difference being that the decisions and recommendations were the exact opposite, as though an invisible hand was manipulating the two congresses to consolidate the national division among Egyptians living abroad.

One day a curious event took place in the governorate of Menyah to the south of Cairo. Several young Muslims under cover of night set fire to the principal church. The following night, young Christians burnt the town mosque. The next day, for the first time in its history Egypt saw a scene typical of those in Lebanon: behind improvised barricades looting operations were carried out on the basis of the religion of the victims. This activity, common in the Lebanon, is called 'looting according to identity'. Tension was increased during that same week when the press published a news item dealing at length with these incidents. A civil court had granted a Christian the right to have a second wife. The reasons adduced took into account 'the application of Muslim legislation to non-Muslims living in a State whose official religion is Islam'. The burnings started again. Churches, mosques, Korans and Bibles were burnt from the north to the south of the country. People were attacked. In Upper Egypt alone, 4,000 varied items of armament were captured. The 'Lebanonisation' of Egypt almost collapsed into religious turmoil.

At about the same time, the President of the Republic sent a written message to the Islamic Congress meeting in Toronto. The essence of the message was that naturally Islam was the sole means of saving the world from the fear caused by atheism and all that follows, such as spiritual sickness and demonic tendencies.[42] This hit both Christian and Muslims. For the *At-Takir Wa Al-Hijrah* group could be accused of anything – but atheism!

In fact the President was trying to equate atheism with the left, and this campaign, therefore, produced confusion. The President changed his approach; he almost attacked those who asked too many questions about food and land.

Pope Chenouda III went to the United States where he met President Carter, but nothing is known of what was discussed. All that is known, is that one day, in the presence of the Egyptian Ambassador to the U.S.A., Achraf Ghorbal, the American President made strong remarks about the impossibility of pretending to ignore the religious feelings of 8 million Copts. Achraf Ghorbal understood the meaning of the President's comments.

On 9th November 1977, the President of the Republic addressed the Peoples' Council (Parliament):

> On the 18th and 19th January, [he said] a tiny minority went out into the streets to exploit the population. Several days later, in one of its high power radio transmissions, the Soviet Union declared that these activities were a popular uprising. What were these activities? Arson. They wanted to burn the capital; they wanted to burn and pillage the co-operative, even though we were suffering from inflation and from a crisis in agricultural production. They set fire to cars, even though we have grave problems with public transport. Does this activity constitute for them and their agents a popular uprising? I say No. We will deal with them firmly and strongly. I will not permit any group to impose that which the people do not accept, or to spread atheism among our faithful people – our people in whose veins the faith flows. I will not allow atheism to be imposed. You have already heard me condemn these actions. I have told you and I repeat: You cannot have confidence in those with no religious faith. I say this before you so that it will be recorded in your proceedings: as long as I am there, I will not allow any atheist to occupy a post or any kind of position in any area able to influence public opinion. I am in no way attacking anybody in saying that. But as I have already told you, I, representing the authority, am striving faithfully to accomplish my task and to answer for it one day when God will ask me to give my account. I will never abandon my task, even if I have to go down into the streets. We are a faithful people; the faith is part of our identity. We cannot allow any power whatever to disturb this faith or to mislead our future generations as has been the case in other countries. In this country, no atheist will be able to hold a position where he can influence public opinion.[43]

We recall that it was in this same speech that President Sadat declared for the first time that he was ready to go to Israel. Ten days later President Sadat descended from his aircraft at Lod airport and bowed before the flag of

Israel. The first message of support that he received was signed 'Abd Al-Halim Mahmoud, Rector of Al-Azhar', while the President was still in Jerusalem and the Sheikh himself was in Washington.

Such were the events of 18th and 19th January. It was not the Chukrist group or others that sent the religious personages to the United States and the politician to the Mosque of Al-Aqsa. The presidential aircraft, in 35 minutes, crossed occupied Sinai and a Lebanon in flames. It was an attempt to wipe out 30 years of struggle.

Notes

1. The Egyptian Church is independent. Its Pope still claims the title 'Pope of Alexandria and of the 5,000 of the West' to show his authority over the 5,000 inhabitants of Western Egypt before the Muslim conquest.
2. See *Al-Harakah As-Siyasiyyah fi Misr,* Tare Al-Bichri (Cairo, 1972). and Hassan Al-Banna, *Kayf wa Limaza,* Rifa't Al-Said (Cairo, 1978).
3. *Op. cit.,* p. 59.
4. Muhakamat Al-Thawra, case of Ibrahim Abd Al-Hadi Pasha, p. 179.
5. *Al Gumriyyah*, 13th February 1954.
6. Several parties have the same name in modern Egyptian history. The first grew out of the revolution of Orabi towards the end of the last century. Here we refer to the party led by the young advocate Mustapha Kamel. Founded in 1907, the party became more conservative after the premature death of its founder.
7. 1879–1974. Egyptian officer, adventurer and right-wing politician.
8. 1906–49. Founder of the Muslim Brotherhood in 1928.
9. Founder of the 'Young Egypt' party in 1930, under the slogan 'God, the Country and the King'.
10. Anwar Al-Sadat, *A la recherche d'une identite,* p. 35.
11. *Ibid.*
12. In his book (Sadat, *op. cit.*) one can detect signs of Sadat's social complex from the time of his youth. He quotes the 'pasha' who had given the scornful reply when Sadat's father has asked him to assist his son to gain entry to the Military College. Sadat wrote: 'It was an experience that will exist in my memory for the rest of my life.' But after sequestering his property Sadat saw this same pasha one day and said: 'Do not think that our first meeting has left its mark (p. 27).' Another example: when accused of having collaborated with the Nazis he was imprisoned – 'One day I was surprised to see the gaoler bringing me food and a fine dressing gown. I laid it on the bed, looked at it and touched it. It was a beautiful thing such as is seen at the cinema. I asked the gaoler if the dressing gown really was for me. Reassured, I put it on with pleasure, for even as a lieutenant-colonel in the army, I had never been able to buy such an item (p. 65).' Again, describing the ramparts of the Royal Palace: 'At that time I did not realise that I was involved with my colleagues in the changing of history or that one day I would cross these walls and sit on the same throne as King

Farouk (p. 17).'
13. The Arab novelist Ghada Al-Samman published a very important book, *Beyrouth 1975*. It appeared one month before the war and described in a literary way the socio-cultural determinism of the collapse of such a social system. The second novel, *Les Cauchemars de Beyrouth*, Dar Al-Adab (Beirut 1976) described this predicted collapse.
14. With reference to this, see: *Al-Omiyyah Al-Cha'biyyah fi Lebnan* by Yusef Khattar Al-Hilw, Al-Nagah (Beirut 1955); *Tarikh Lebnan Al-Igtimai*, by Mas'ud Daher, Al-Farabi (Beirut 1974); *Fi usul Lebnan*, by Bichara Marheg, Al-Muassassah Al-Arabiyyah lil Dirasat (Beirut 1974); and *Adwa' Falsafiyyah Ala Sahat Al-Harb Al-Lebnaniyyah*, by Antoine Georges Khury, At-Taliah (Beirut 1978).
15. *Al-Gumhurriyah*, 11th June 1977, p. 42.
16. *Ibid.*
17. In his daily editorial Mustapha Amin wrote: I thank God that this law, approved by the Council of State and condemning renegades to death, was not promulgated 70 years ago, for Quassem Amin in publishing his book, *Liberer la femme*, was accused of abandoning Islam. Ali-Abd Al-Razeq was also accused of apostasy when he published *L'Islam et les bases du gouvernement*. The same can be said of Taher Hussein when he published *De la poesie anteislamique*. Within ten years perhaps a tyrant will take power in Egypt and will consider as renegades all those who criticise him as well as those who demand liberty; all of them could be executed or stoned with sharp stones.
18. *Al-Ahram*, 15th July 1977, p. 43.
19. The first Christian religious congress in the history of Egypt took place at Assiout in 1911. The British occupier had succeeded in provoking religious troubles following the defeat of Orabi and in the nomination of Butros Ghali Pasha, President of the Tribunal of Dinchiwag, who condemned to death a group of peasants for having refused British officers the right to hunt pigeons near their village (1906).
20. Declaration of the Christian Congress, 17th January 1977 (unpublished), p. 44. This was the first time that previous preparatory conferences had been mentioned.
21. *Ibid.*
22. Article in *Al-Ahram*, 12th March 1976, signed Sheikh Hassanein Makhluf.
23. A notice by Sheikh Al-Fahham, in *Al-Ahram*, 22nd October 1976.
24. See article by Muhammad Bissar, *Al-Ahram*, 24th September 1976.
25. Is it not curious that the first issue of *Al-Alam Al-Qibt* (*The Coptic World*) appeared in July 1977, the very month when the religious crisis reached its climax in Egypt? The editorial stated that the magazine aimed to create links between Copts dispersed throughout the world. Astonished commentators noted that the first issue contained messages from three illustrious persons: President Giscard d'Estaing found that the eyes of the Sphinx were 'Not turned towards the past but towards the horizon, waiting for the sun'; Anouar Al-Sadat described the Coptic civilisation as 'tending to consolidate links with French-speaking countries'. Leopold Sedar Senghor found the magazine to be 'the heritage of the ancient Egyptian civilisation'. Georges Al-Rasi wrote in *Al-Destour*, 8th August 1978. 'Is it not natural to ask oneself if a link

exists between the present Coptic movement and the insistent attempts
to create a Lebanese-type religious discrimination in Egypt, particularly
after the emergence of extremist groups like *Al-Takfir wa Al-Hijrah?*'

26. This referred to a bill that, at the time, had even been rejected by the
Copts. Among the important Coptic politicians to have taken part in
this sabre rattling were Wissa Wassef Pasha, Senut Hanna Bey, Wassef
Ghali Pasha, William Makram Ubeid and Bishop Morqus Sergius.

27. President Sadat had made this declaration following the January 1977
uprising.

28. The magazine *Ad-Da'wa*, organ of the Muslim Brotherhood, had just
reappeared. The February 1977 edition stated that Christians were
accepting the application of the Muslim Shari'a.

29. The paradox was, and still is, as follows: according to the 1977 radio-
television statistics, the number of religious talks and programmes
transmitted by official bodies amounted to 32 hours a day. A statistical
study, published by the American University of Cairo in a limited
edition, reports that in that same year 120 religious pages appeared in
the press. Statistics of the National Library show that in that same year
1,035 religious works were published, not counting re-issues of the
Koran. However, the magazine *Ad-Da'wa*, organ of the Muslim Brotherhood, wrote in its August 1977 issue under the title 'To the Minister of
Information, this is the Opinion of the People' that television, by transmitting immoral plays, was making propaganda in favour of marital
infidelity (*sic*), and that the state of science and faith was no more than
just a slogan for the information media. The Islamic Congress demanded
that the President of the Republic purge the information media of 'these
immoralities that wound Muslims'. The Centre for Social Research
reported in a statistical study that the number of night clubs in Pyramids
Road had increased by 375% between 1976 and 1977, that flats used
for prostitution had increased by 1,000% over the same period and that
rapes and kidnapping of girls had increased by 400%.

30. *Al-Ahram,* 8th July 1977.

31. Sheikh Hassanein Makhful, Mufti of Egypt, said that this group were
like 'criminals with no scruples, spreading corruption through the land'.
Muhammad Sallam Makdur, head of the Shari'a section of the Cairo
Faculty of Law, saw them as iniquitous men. Ahmed Chalabi, Director
of the History of Islam section at the Dar Al-Ulum Institute, declared
that such an event was unique in the history of Islam (*Al-Ahram,* 8th
July 1977).

32. See Rif'at As-Said, *Al-Harakat Al-Islamiyyah Min Al-Irtidad . . .* in
Dirasat Arabiyyah, November 1977.

33. See Rif'at As Said: *Al Chukriyun wa gamaat Al-Ikhwan* in *Al-Mustakbal*
(Paris), 27th August 1977.

34. *Ibid.*

35. *Ibid.*

36. *Ibid.*

37. *Ibid.*

38. *Rose Al-Youssef,* No. 2561, 11th July 1977.

39. *Ibid.*

40. *Ibid.*

41. *Ibid*.
42. *Al-Ahram*, 15th July 1977.
43. *Al-Ahram*, 10th July 1977.

10. The Revolution in Suspense

Class Opinion and Alienated Consciousness

The religious conflict took place during 1976 and 1977 and the armed activity of the extreme right was, in spite of the importance it had been given by the mass media, no more than a sparse camouflage hiding the beginnings and consequences of the events of January 1977. As an example of how absurd the fraud had become, the Cairo daily *Al Akhbar* put forward the idea that the *At-Takfir Wa Al-Hijrah* group were communists in disguise who had been responsible for the acts of sabotage on the 18th and 19th January![1] This newspaper therefore reinforced the secret reports of the security services which claimed that the extremist group had been planning an armed overthrow of the regime for two years.[2] In fact the article in *Al-Akhbar* shows how far the regime was caught in its own trap. Expecting that hostility would come only from the left, it was surprised to see it coming from the right as well. But as the regime was so far to the right itself it could only ascribe all sins, whatever their political origin, to the left. Thus the joke, the *nuktah*, of *Al-Akhbar* revealed the state of confusion in which the supporters of the regime found themselves.

The chronic socio-cultural problem suffered by the supporters of the regime was the result of their ignorance of the true facts about the social reality of Egypt. In fact the right could not undertake any action without having recourse to an armed organisation, an organisation which could only have a very limited influence. As for the left, it could accomplish, action, positively or negatively, without recourse to arms or to an armed organisation.

For in Egypt the left is also the man-in-the-street, not just the avant-garde intelligentsia. It is not a left sharing the common notions of the left in other countries. It is not a natural inclination towards the left; it is rather a class struggle tending towards the left; a struggle which can be disassociated from ideological consciousness or from the knowledge of the necessity to organise itself. These people in fact bear arms only in cases of extreme necessity, i.e. when it is a matter of self-defence. That is why action from the left takes the form of spontaneous uprising, which contrasts with action from the right which always takes the form of a plot. The history of Egypt from

the times of the Mamelukes, through the French expedition in Egypt until
the revolution in 1919, proves that popular uprisings have always taken the
form admirably described by Al-Gabarty after the first uprising in Cairo
towards the end of the 18th Century. Gamada Al Ula wrote in *Aga'ib Al-Atar
Fi At-Taragim Wa Al-Akhbar* (*Merveilles des histoires et des biographies*)

> On Sunday 10th, the council met. A list of properties and holdings
> was brought to them. Eight *paransah* were imposed on the largest of
> them, six on the medium sized and three on the smallest. The popula-
> tion assembled with no leaders or guides to direct them. The next day
> it was united and committed to fight. Weapons were unearthed and the
> people went to the house of the High Judge (*Qadi Al-Askar*). There
> were over a thousand of them. The judge, frightened of what might
> happen, bolted and barred his house. Projectiles, stones and pebbles
> rained down on his home.

This picture repeats itself throughout the social history of Egypt. It is
difficult to understand the events of 18th and 19th January without seeing
them in the light of the socio-historic reality of Egypt. Without this the
observer is in danger of seeing only an accumulation of events without logic
and without connection.[3]
All popular uprisings in Egypt are typified by three principal elements:
spontanaeity, specific aims and their peaceful character. No large party could
hope for such spontaneity, to choose its moment, its method of expression,
or the place where it should happen; all these elements are more precisely
realised and more surprising than any that could be achieved by modern technological preparation. The aims are direct because economic demands
dominate everything else. Finally, they have been peaceful because these
movements were always careful not to attack the nation, its territory or its
institutions. By their very nature they were against sabotage and invaders.
They are exploited only by the agents of the invader, or the reactionary
regime, with the intention of smearing them.
Let us now examine this collection of hypotheses in the light of the
findings of several exercises in socio-cultural research conducted during the
1970s. The first of these is an unpublished statistical study conducted by
Muhammad Al-Chazli, researcher for the Ministry of Industry, on three
samples of industrial workers. The first was taken from the workers of the
Light Vehicles Company, the second from the Eastern Tobacco Company
and the third from the Iron and Steel Company. The document consists of
23 mimeographed pages, the first of which bears the words, 'At-Taliah
Magazine, Al-Ahram Organization'. The document's title is *Political, Cultural
and Social Consciousness in a sample of industrial workers in Egypt.* This
sample included 30 workers from each of the companies mentioned above
who completed questionnaires between 1st and 15th January 1972. Each questionnaire included ten items of social background information on each worker
and 55 questions concerning various cultural, political and social subjects.

From the preliminary information it can be seen that four of the 90 workers were under 20 years of age, 26 were between 20 and 30, and 60 were over 30 years of age. Concerning salaries, only four received a salary of less than £12 per month,[4] 61 earned between £12 and £25 per month and 25 earned more than £25 per month. Concerning education: 37 workers had medium level certificates, seven had studied at intermediate level, 36 could read and write well without having obtained diplomas and ten 'knew' how to read and write. The sample included 81 men and 9 women. Seven of the 90 workers were married with no children; 27 were married with between one and three children; 27 had more than three children; and 29 were unmarried. Seven workers received supplementary incomes greater than £60 per year; the remaining 83 had only their salary. Concerning culture, 46 workers had attended only one cultural series and six had attended more than one. As for political training with the Arab Socialist Union or the Organisation of Youth, only eight workers had taken a single course, two had taken more than one course and 31 had taken no course at all. In the area of religious or regional activities, eight workers were members of religious associations and five were members of regional associations. The others (78) did not take part in any activity.

On the question of elections in the company, the questionnaire asked if the subject had a preference in the choice of candidates; 74 replied in the affirmative and 16 said they had no preferences. On the basis of choice, 34 workers said that candidates in elections should understand the problems of workers; 31 thought that they should be of good character, should be frank and possess integrity; 19 said that they should be capable of taking part in public action; 18 thought that they should excel in their work; 13 required that they should be extremely cultured; 13 thought they should be able to sacrifice themselves for others; nine thought that they should be workers, so that it would be easy to relate to them; eight that they should be bold enough to press for the rights of workers; seven that they should be ready to listen to the complaints of the workers; six thought that they should have an independent opinion, and three that they should be 'humble', only one said that the candidate should be free from any influence by the management and, finally, three workers had other criteria.

In answer to a question about whether the worker accepted the presence of engineers, lawyers, chemists and civil servants in the ranks of the General Workers Union, 54 replied in the affirmative and 36 in the negative. On appreciation of workers' experience on the boards of companies, 54 said that it was successful, and 36 said the opposite. Concerning the role of workers in the national struggle, 89 replied that this role consisted in 'increasing production', 'to act as volunteers in the popular and civil defence' and to 'fight when necessary'. One worker only, replied that this role consisted in 'spreading political consciousness among the population'. When asked to state the Egyptian social classes in the order of their importance in production and in the liberation of the land, 75 workers put the working class in first place, then the peasants and finally national capitalists. 11 workers said peasants, workers, and national capitalists. Four said workers, national capitalists and finally peasants. In reply to the question whether the political organisations were, in accordance with the Constitution, composed of 50% workers and peasants, and if the 'representatives' of the workers and peasants fulfilled the required conditions, 18 workers said that the percentage was enforced and correct, while 72 said that it was neither enforced nor correct.

The researcher then asked the workers to name five socialist countries; 35 gave a correct answer. When they were asked to quote five capitalist countries, 50 gave a correct reply. He then asked them if they thought that the United States could be on 'our' side of the conflict with Israel; nine replied in the affirmative and 81 in the negative. In giving reasons for replies to the last question, three among those who had replied in the affirmative said, 'if the Arabs severed their relationship with the United States and used oil against them as a weapon'. Two others said, 'when there was no more American investment in the Middle East'. The last two said, 'if the Russians got out of the area'. Of those who replied in the negative, 42 said, 'because Israel is an American base in the Middle East'; 21 said that abandoning Israel would signify a collapse in America's sphere of influence. 'Because the United States could not be on our side, because we are for socialism', was the reason given by 17 others. 16 workers said, 'our economic interests do not correspond with those of America in the region'. 13 gave the reason for their reply as the influence of Zionism in the United States.

The questionnaire also revealed that 52 workers read a daily newspaper and 38 did not. On the other hand, writers whose works were read were: Muhammad Hassanein Haykal (65 workers), Mousa Sabri (15), Ahmed Baha Ad-Din (13), Ihsan Abd Al-Quddus (12), Muhammad Zaki Abd Al-Qader (11), Ali Hamdi Al-Gammal (6), Hussein Fahmi (5), Muhammad At-Tab'i (4), Lufti Al-Khuli (3), Fikri Abaza (3), Gamal Al-Uteifi (3), Muhammad Udah (2), Klovis Maksud (a Lebanese writer who at the time was living in Egypt and writing for *Al-Ahram*) (1), and each one of a further eight workers said they had read works by Sami Daoud, Mahmud Amin Al-Alim, Mamduh Rida, Abd Ar-Rahman Al-Charqawi, Kamil Zuheiri, Yussouf As-Sibai, Hafiz Mahmud, Butrus Ghali and Hahtim Sadeq, respectively. As for literary or cultural books, 20 said that they did read them and 70 that they did not. For the cinema, 86 workers went to the cinema and 4 had never been. Sixty workers went to the theatre, 30 had never been. Seventy-one said that culture was 'necessary' for all workers; 15 said that it was desirable, and 4 that it had no value. Forty-three workers thought that there was no difference between the productive capacities of men and women workers in the factory, while 47 thought that women workers produced less. In reply to the question about whether home was the natural place for a woman, 23 said 'Yes' and 67 said 'No'. If the worker decided to marry a woman worker, would he recommend a relation or a friend to do the same? In reply to this 51 said 'Yes', and 30 said, 'No'. If he had a daughter of marriageable age, would he find her a husband or would he allow her to continue her studies? Ten preferred marriage and 80 education.

Whatever general reservations there may be about such surveys, what precautions have to be taken not to generalize their significance, what scientific reservations one may have about such a survey, which excluded certain important questions concerning industrial workers in Egypt, we can derive from these answers certain relative truths concerning the socio-cultural situation of the working class in Egypt, this class which participated with the student movement in the events of January 1972, January 1975 and January 1977. The relationship between the social structure and the type of thinking can provide pointers to the type of thinking and conduct occurring at moments of social and historical crisis. The socio-cultural facts in this survey tell us that a catastrophically low standard of living weighs down on this social layer which controls national production. It gives all that it possesses but takes only that which enables it to continue giving. It does not find the time to organize itself (politically and non-union) nor to have a cultural (not class) consciousness. It is deprived of the benefits of production which would allow it to have an independent political existence and a consciousness of its class role in cultural affairs. The ready alternative is a spontaneous acquirement of class consciousness, but this is not to be compared with political or ideological consciousness, for most of the subjects in the sample drew their consciousness from middle-class writers with their various tendencies. They know very little about world politics. They understand their interests as a class and not just as individuals, they understand the interests of the nation as a whole and, when it comes to action, that understanding is far greater than any theoretical consciousness. Because of this, and to avoid any confusion, we can call this type of instinctive consciousness class feeling (*wijdan*).

Public action and moral qualities form normative values. Let us note here that morals are not synonymous with religion but are rather indicators of controlled thinking and behaviour in service, work and the nation. Therefore, the religious associations cannot be considered as centres of attraction.

These statements can be expressed more significantly by a case study conducted by the *At-Tali'ah* group. It concerns Abd At-Tawwab,[5] a 34 year old worker for the cotton-spinning company 'Ad-Delta'. He held a certificate of primary education, was married with three children and earned only £16.5 per month. The editors of *At-Tali'ah* asked him 154 questions concerning almost all aspects of his private and public life. What did citizen Abd At-Tawwab say?

1) He said that the worst days of the month were those on which he drew his pay when he went home without a single piastre in his pocket, because he always owed it to his creditors. He did not eat fruit, and neither did his family. Basic products such as bread, tobacco, maize, beans, cheese and potatoes were all bought on credit. In most cases interest was levied on his credit. He and his family only ate meat once in two months. He did not have a radio and certainly not a television receiver, but he bought the daily newspaper *Al-Akhbar*.

2) He used to know the Koran by heart, but he had forgotten it. He did not

310

read books but he was a member of the Socialist Union. He found that the People's Council did not express the problems of the workers, or the workers' representatives did not represent the workers. He had never thought of offering himself as a candidate in the elections 'because nobody would listen to me . . . Nobody would listen to me if I said that I wanted to solve problems.' 'The Government is always talking . . . but takes no action. Public transport is getting worse. In this country there can be no supporters of poverty.'

3) To him, Israel is a Zionist state. He will never hesitate to carry out his national duty; he is, however, in favour of a partial solution and against 'Arab Unity'; for the Egyptian-Syrian pact had ended in failure. 'The union between Libya, Syria and Egypt is neither correct nor just.' He was against the early warning system in Sinai because, he said, 'We have there a foreign military presence on our territory and in opposition to our armed forces.' He is in favour of a partial solution (he referred to the Sinai Agreement) because it could perhaps improve the internal situation. But he has the firm intention 'to liberate every inch of Egyptian soil,' even at the cost of his life 'because liberation of all parts of the territory will improve the economic situation'.

4) On the subject of opening up the economy he said that he had heard it mentioned but he also believed that foreign investors were not as numerous as stated by the newspapers and the authorities. For him the cost of living had reached an intolerably high level and 'prices must not only be stabilized, they must be reduced.'

5) He said that the United States is our enemy. 'It is they, with Israel, who made war against us in 1967 and 1973.' 'As for the Soviet Union, I do not know the truth. According to latest opinion it was behind the defeat of 1967. The weapons that we had were old and taken from Algeria it seems. But the Russians have built industry for us and created work for our best workmen . . . the High Dam, the Iron and Steel complex at Helouan, the military factories, etc.'

6) If Israel withdrew only from Sinai 'my position as an Egyptian and as an Arab would be not to abandon the fight until the withdrawal from Golan and until the Palestinian people had obtained their rights.'

7) Abd At-Tawwab essentially asked for 'higher wages and lower prices'.

Such were the most important answers given by Abd At-Tawwab, an Egyptian worker on the minimum basic wage in 1976. It is true that any social sample presents problems of generalization. However, Abd At-Tawwab enables the researcher to examine the authentic features of a social type. To compare him with the preceding sample highlights the common denominator of men and women in the sample.

In his commentary on the statements of Abd At-Tawwab, sociologist Sayyed Yarin wonders: 'How can an Egyptian citizen live on a monthly salary of E£16?' But even more tragically he observes: 'Abd At-Tawwab, you are not the poorest of Egyptians.' Murad Wahbah himself grasped the root of the problem: 'A minimum wage and a crisis of social consciousness.'

In spite of the economic nature of things, from the political answers given by Abd At-Tawwab Murad Wahbah clearly sees that the crisis of social consciousness can be ascribed to the duplicity of the information media, the widespread and technically perfect duplicity of which the first serious result is the crisis in language. 'The Arab language is no longer capable of fulfilling its social function in the sense that the words no longer describe the truth of the social reality. The language of citizen Abd At-Tawwab is an example of the lack of contact between words and truth.' Abd At-Tawwab said:

> When I go home I have no money with me because I am already in debt at work. I have to pay them [his creditors] . . . On going into my house people ask me if I have been paid and I say to them, 'Not yet,' even though I already have been. Sometimes my boy would keep asking me to bring home oranges or other fruit. For a couple of days I would tell him that I would bring some. Now he says to me, "Don't ever say you will".

Commenting on this, Murad Wahbah says, 'The words and sentences used by Abd At-Tawwab do not correspond with reality. He used them while knowing that they are false. After a while his son realises the falseness of the words, which is just a symbol of the failure of society.'

The findings of socio-linguistics about language in both the East and the West will confirm these comments, but without the mystification of the media being a natural cause. The same consideration applies to minimum wages. The infrastructure is not isolated, or just a reflection, neither is the superstructure. It is rather the relationship between the two which directly affects the transformation of an individual sample or a social type. Desire and values play an essential role in the formation of partial consciousness, which is of class understanding rather than class opinion. This shows a lack of connection between the economic situation and political vision. The opposite of this is the relative harmony between class situation and class opinion. The paradoxes seen in the answers given by Abd At-Tawwab can only be explained in the light of the separation between social and cultural structure, and in the context of the separation between desire and values. Such conditions are ideal for the creation of ideas of revolt, spontaneous and unorganized, but they also encompass factors which go beyond the simple economic reasons given.

This is again proved in an interview conducted by *At-Taliah*[6] of a 37 year old woman who works as a nurse at the Imbabah Institute of Cardiology. She draws a monthly salary of E£4.75 and works between 8 and 12 hours daily. She is married and has eight children; her husband is a journeyman grinder, earning between 40 and 50 piastres a day — about E£10 per month. £5 of which he keeps for his food, tea and cigarettes, for he does not eat at home. The wife pays £1.75 to rent a room. They never eat meat, but every few months Um Muhammad goes to the abattoirs to buy half a kilo of spleen and gut. The family has no other source of income. They never eat fruit;

the children do not go to school; there is no electricity in their room. She buys only stale bread, and buys clothes on the second-hand market. As a temporary worker she has no right to social security. The family have neither radio nor television; they do not read newspapers and never go to the cinema or the theatre. She has never heard of Yussuf Wahba, Tawfig Al-Hakim, Naguib Mahfuz or Mustapha Amin; but sometimes she hears the singer Abd Al-Halim Hafez on her neighbour's radio.

Um Muhammad asks for a reduction in the price of cloth, paraffin, oil, tea, sugar and meat. She does not know the streets Al-Chawarbi, Soliman Pasha or Kasr An-Nil (the most famous streets in Cairo); but she does know Al-Atabah Al-Khadra (a popular square). She has never heard anyone speak of the open economy or of socialism; neither does she know the name of the Prime Minister nor the Minister of Health. Speaking about Russia, she says: 'It is like Saudi Arabia, they have lots of money and the people work, both men and women.' She knows nothing of such words as socialism, colonialism, capitalism and Arab unity. She has heard that people leave Egypt to go to Palestine, but has never heard about a problem between Palestinians and Israelis, or between Egypt and Israel, or between Syria and Israel. But she knows that the Egyptian army was at war in the month of October 1973 and that, by the grace of God, it gained victory over the people pf Palestine and Al-Arich. As for the United States, she says, 'I don't have anything to do with people when they are speaking. I just get on with my work and that's all.'

She replied in the affirmative to a question aimed at discovering if she was in favour of a law for the protection of women. She was asked: 'Could this law be in agreement with Islam?' She replied, 'And why not? Certainly it would be in agreement.' Asked if she prayed, she said that she did when she had time. Her hope in life was that her children would grow up, the girls would marry and the boys would work . . . that would give her a little rest. When asked what she thought of Nasser, she replied: 'He was good, God had his soul. Life was less expensive; those who had a feddan or two came to own them. Life then was quite different. People ate plenty of bread. People worked and had money and the necessities of life.' She understood the Agricultural Reform, and said that it had changed the life of the country for the better. She believed that returning the nationalized sector to private ownership was a bad thing and that the workers in that sector would have no future. She knew girls in her family who went to university. She was in favour of work for women, after obtaining their qualifications, 'so that they will not be tyrannized by men'.

Latifah Az-Zayyat, critic, novelist and university teacher, summarizes the tragic situation of this woman in a paper entitled 'Alienated Conscious-ness'. It is a matter of awareness, of knowledge, and not of politics; political consciousness is found in her collective ideas on Nasserism, and is not a matter of social awareness based on her ideas of women's work and education. Neither is it an economic awareness which is expressed in her ideas on basic salaries and high prices. Her lack of consciousness or awareness is due not only to her lack of information but to her lack of an overall political view; that is why class opinion becomes the only alternative for this very large class. There is, therefore, no real vision, but in action class opinion is stronger than both religious terrorism and the ideology of slogans.

The sensitivity of this large group is illustrated by the action of 9th June 1967 when millions of people went out to demonstrate their rejection of defeat and their desire to keep Nasser in power. These same people went out to demonstrate, in February and November of 1968 their rejection of the regime's logic in the evaluation of the defeat following the military hearings. These were the millions of people who took part in Nasser's funeral in a historic scene, the like of which had never occurred before. These were the griefstricken people who demonstrated spontaneously and massively, without a hint of sabotage, without leadership, and without recourse to religious slogans. It was their expression of the despair of defeat, and of the death of their leader.

The class feeling of these 8 million industrial and agricultural workers negates the alienation of their consciousness, thanks to the direct link that they have with intellectuals and students. In that, all the details of Egyptian society and Egyptian history are to be found. Egyptian students and intellectuals have an exceptional role in the national movement which outstrips their classic role in the production cycle. For they represent 'organised consciousness' as opposed to alienated consciousness. These are the revolutionary leaders in Egypt since Omar Makram and the first Cairo revolution right up to Ahmad Orabi, Saad Zaghlul and Gamal Abd El-Nasser. They are the mullahs of Al-Azhar, university students, army officers, professionals, engineers, lawyers, journalists, writers and artists. The Egyptian intellectual is not content to play the role traditionally ascribed to him of contestant or rebel in various social and historic environments. Egyptian intellectuals have led the national struggle and, by adding awareness, have brought class feeling to maturity. That which characterizes the Egyptian student movement is its organised political initiative, its continuity and the difference between it and student movements in other parts of the world. The objective coming together of class feeling and organised awareness is the social and historic base linking workers and intellectuals in the history of modern Egypt.

And so the days of 18th and 19th January 1977 were no more than an extension of the alliance between class opinion and the organised awareness of the 1919 revolution and the uprising of 1946. It was a new expression of what occurred on the 9th June 1967 and 28th September 1970; it was the consequence of rapid changes brought about by the leadership of the regime between 1971 and the end of 1976, just three months after the Sinai Agreement and eight and a half months after the start of the war in Lebanon.

Egyptians at the Limits of Patience

What was the actual economic situation in Egypt just before January 1977?

In order to avoid any dispute concerning sources I will use just two in attempting to answer this question: one Western and the other official. The first is the annual *Bulletin on the Middle East* prepared by the research department of the British journal *The Economist*. This research was conducted in 1976, for the 1977 edition, by the *Financial Times* correspondent in Cairo; the report contains 115 pages. In it the author shows nine statistical tables, for which the information was drawn from official Egyptian sources. The report contains the following information:

> The economic results expected by President Sadat were felt much too long after the signing of the Sinai Agreement. Foreign investments did not occur immediately, in spite of the favourable climate brought about by President Sadat's undertaking not to use armed force against Israel for a period of three years. In 1976, the famous projects, such as the nuclear power station promised by Nixon during his visit in 1974, seemed very distant. Having cleared the ground for economic co-operation with Western capitalism, Egypt slowly realised that economic transformation is a long-winded process, the complexities of which had not been considered. (p. 102)
>
> The high cost of aid became a political problem when one considers that the deficit in the balance of payments was approaching E£2,000,000,000. World prices had fallen, but agricultural production had also fallen to the point where agricultural revenue in 1975 was far lower than the cost of imported agricultural products. For the first time in Egypt, agriculture was suffering a grave deficit. (p. 109)
>
> Agreement had been given to free zone projects. By springtime in 1976 more than 100 projects were approved. They amounted to an extraordinary capital of E£854 million ($1,220 million). But these were only paper propositions; more than two-thirds of these projects were to be conducted by oil companies. In 1975 not even E£3.8 million had been spent. The only foreign companies to have arrived in Egypt were oil companies and banks. (p. 110)
>
> One of the clearest points in the financial difficulties of Egypt is the rapid decline of the trade situation. In 1975 imports totalled $2,199 million, while exports were only $874 million. This very grave deficit proved that there was a fundamental weakness in the Egyptian trade situation. (p. 115)
>
> It is possible to name more than 500 millionaires[7] in Egypt since President Sadat came to power. Seeing that most Egyptians earned no more than E£12 per month (approximately $17) it is not surprising to see parliamentarians finding it difficult to contain their anger in the Socialist Union and the People's Council. They have had enough.

The second source is an allegedly false American document produced at the United States Embassy in Athens. A copy of this document was published by the journal *Rose Al-Youssef* in its 21st February 1977 edition. The United

States Embassy in Cairo declared that the document was accurately copied and that it was not aimed at poisoning the relationship between Egypt and America. The declaration of the United States Embassy gave no reasons why anyone should want to circulate such a document; neither did it explain the silence of all American embassies when *Rose Al-Youssef* published the document. It was as though the journal had been tricked into publishing it. *Rose Al-Youssef* had, therefore, done what was required of it; the false document had been knowingly distributed.[8] But what did it actually contain?

It was a report of a 'very confidential' meeting held in Detroit, U.S.A., on 24th March 1976, following the return from Cairo of Mr William Simon, American Treasury Secretary, and a group of American businessmen. The Minister who represented the American government opened the meeting by saying:

> The Egyptian economy is suffering a profound crisis and it is so bad that even an injection of cash will not be able to delay the collapse. The deficit in the balance of payments is now greater than $5 billion per year and everything indicates that this figure will not diminish. Egypt's foreign debts are estimated to be at least $10 billion, if not greater ...
> My colleague, Gerald Parsky, was very optimistic in November 1975 when he thought that it would be possible to establish Goodyear or Ford factories in Egypt. Not one item of these plans has been carried out. Consequently in such a situation, with the exception of a vast oil search operation, no investments in Egypt can be classed as important.

False or not, this report added nothing new to the facts already known and published in the *Bulletin on the Middle East*. But the American government's representative added:

> The leaders of Egypt hope to make Cairo an economic and political centre of the Arab world. The fighting in Beirut pleased them and they supported one of the two contending parties.[9] They were hoping that the troubles in Beirut could launch Cairo. But I tell you that Beirut, Rome and even Washington would have to be destroyed before Cairo could blossom. In fact Cairo is in no way prepared to take over the role of Beirut. Cairo is a crumbling capital; millions live there in misery. There are thousands of unemployed who survive by selling sweets and ball-pens in the crowded streets. Life for the people of Cairo is a merciless battle for survival. They fight to have a seat or have a place to stand in their public transport system. They fight for places in queues outside food shops. Drinking water is a problem. It is not unusual for a flat costing $1,000 a month to be without water or electricity. The telephone service is rudimentary.

There is no question of falsification here. These facts do not reveal any state secrets. But social historians will no doubt make careful comparisons between this American description of Egypt with the writings about Cairo produced by the French Expedition in their *Description de l'Egypt*. It is as though time had stood still for 200 years because, apart from things concerning technical products, the same analysis still applies.

Someone at the meeting put the following question: 'We are selling C.S. 160 aircraft to Egypt. We have also heard that Ford has decided to sell them other arms. How can Cairo pay? Should we not fear that we will suffer the same fate as the Russians?' The Minister replied: 'That is a question to be put to President Ford and to Kissinger. But I suppose that Saudi Arabia will pay the bill for the aircraft sold to Egypt. As for the guarantees that we will not suffer the same fate as the Russians, I know nothing about them. I do not even know if these guarantees exist.' In fact it is this question about guarantees that could justify the 'leaking' or 'falsification' of this document. It is a kind of probe put out to test the Egyptian regime after the Sinai Agreement. There had been a partial rescinding of the Treaty of Friendship between Russia and Egypt. We have here an indirect introduction to the basis of the Egyptian attitude, both to American strategic security and to the regional security of Israel, as shown by the following: 'If we invest in Egypt, with government aid, is it not possible that a new Nasser or an even stronger communist than he will rise up and take the opportunity to seize power and nationalize everything? Has the Ford administration considered that possibility? What guarantees do we have that the American taxpayer would not lose his shirt?'

The U.S. government representative replied: 'The elimination of Soviet influence in Egypt is an incontestable victory for American policy and for the free world in general. The United States should take advantage of this open door to infiltrate Egypt. Are we capable of undertaking this historic action?' But a businessman at the meeting then responded with an even more important question. 'My company invests in Israel, so why invest in Egypt? Our business in Israel is safe, thanks to the Israeli Army. The Egyptians cannot provide this guarantee.' The final question was no less important: 'If we solve the problems in Egypt, in such a way as to guarantee a certain safety for American interests, would this not lead to the destruction of Israel?' The American Minister responded that Israeli circles had come to the same conclusion, but that he supposed this could be a passing jealousy or perhaps a misunderstanding. When these circles understand that anti-communist Egypt is a true ally, they will no longer be jealous. The improvement in political relations between the United States and Egypt and other free Arab countries in no way affects the privileged place of Israel in the Middle East. President Ford gave this assurance to Prime Minister Rabin of Israel and other Israeli leaders: 'There can be no substitute for the role of Israel.'

We can, therefore, see from all this that this document, true or false, is no more than a message addressed to President Sadat, the opposite to what had been supposed by the Egyptian journal; a message that says America knows the real situation in Egypt — the economy is at a zero point with no hope of recovery; the Egyptian Army is incapable of guaranteeing American interests; alliance with Israel and official links with American security strategy are the only means of preventing the collapse of the Egyptian regime.

The third source is the report of a meeting of the People's Council held in 1975, i.e. one year after the promulgation of the law on foreign investments and in the atmosphere of the Second Sinai Agreement which had just been concluded. During the fourth ordinary session, the general report of the budget planning committee for the 1975 financial year, dated 14th December 1974 and signed by Minister Ahmad Abu Ismail, was presented. In the second part entitled, 'Economic and Financial Estimates for the Proposed 1975 Budget' the following appears:

> Investment in agriculture does not exceed 4.3% of the total investment in the 1975 budget. The amount of funds allocated to the Minister of the Interior and Agricultural Reform is lower than in 1974 when the amount of investment totalled E£62 million, investment for the year in question is E£52 million, i.e. a E£10 million difference. If prices continue to increase we can be sure that agricultural investment will be even less. (p. 7)
>
> The 1975 budget allocates an investment of E£27.5 million to the Ministry of Electrical Energy. In 1974 this amount was E£22 million. At first sight there would appear to be an increase in investment in this area. But analysing the 1975 figure we see that this sum is dedicated to items already previously committed to. Because of this, the amount of new investment in 1975 is insignificant. (p. 8) . . . And so we find a shortfall in the amount of money dedicated to investment in the electrification of the country. This organization is therefore unable to complete the projects already started. . . The real meaning of all this is a freezing of projects for electrification of the country. (p. 9)
>
> To dedicate only 3% of the total investment to the Education Services and Sanitary Research is a falling below the strict minimum required to develop these services of which there is a constant need. The insignificance of the investment in education is perhaps due to a common concept according to which education is only a service, and it is consequently more interesting to invest in productive activities which could be directly profitable. (p. 9)
>
> We find a big reduction in the health and sanitary services in the country; better services will not be possible in 1975, medical units in the country remain incomplete and without further development. The country will remain dependent on the big cities, particularly Cairo and Alexandria, for its medical needs. This means a lot of expense and a much increased cost. (p. 10)

The Minister completes his report as follows: 'Reflecting on the different areas of investment quoted and on the investments in different governorates in the country and in the towns, we can see that the countryside has been particularly neglected.' (p. 11) 'The distribution of investment between the urban and rural areas in the 1975 budget is such that the environment in the countryside will not be improved in the slightest way.' (p. 12)

The proceedings of the People's Council meeting, held on 10th May 1975, also agrees with the report made by the Commission of Enquiry into the Iranian Bus Affair, in reply to a question put by Deputy Mahmud Al-Qadi to the Minister of Transport about the truth of the rumour according to which the Government had bought Mercedes buses from Iran at a price that was one-third higher than Iran had charged Sudan and Kuwait at the same time and with the same delivery dates. If the rumour was true, it would mean that the State had paid $10 million more than it should have done. (p. 3) Even though the Bus Contract had not been the most scandalous, it serves as an economic model and symbol of the new open economy. In fact, commissions had become the principal parasitic affliction of production. The alliance between bureaucracy and technocracy is the politico-economic basis of power for the wealthy of the countryside and the interest-charging sections of commercial capitalism.

It was not by chance, therefore, that at this time the first modification of the Nasserite Agricultural Reform was made to the advantage of the big landowners. The minutes of Session 65 (23rd June 1975) register a historical paradox, for most of the members of the People's Council approved the bill for modification, which meant that 50% of the parliamentarians who were supposed to represent the peasants and workers voted against the interests of peasants and workers. Article 33 of Law 178 of the year 1953, in fact, stipulated that the rent on land should be not greater than seven times the value of the land tax: 'The value of the annual rental for an area of cultivable land should not exceed the land tax in force multiplied by seven.' (p. 39) If we consider the enormous increase in the price of land since 1952 we can imagine the real meaning of this modification; the farmer pays a rent which is sometimes ten times greater than the rent he paid before the promulgation of the modification. This modification, being general and not restricted, modifies Article 33D as follows: 'The farmer and the landowner can come to an agreement over changes in rent and sharecropping.' (p. 50) Such a thing was strictly forbidden under the Agricultural Reform Law which had been promulgated for the very purpose of ending feudal relationships. In effect, the new modification of the law meant that the tenant farmer cultivated the land on behalf of the owner as an agricultural worker, rather than as a tenant, for the owner obtained his income directly from the produce of the land. The new modification, in fact, took possible precautions to defend the owners vis-a-vis the small farmers. Article 35 stipulates: 'The owner cannot ask for rented land to be vacated unless the tenant has broken an important clause of the law or the contract. In this case the owner, after having warned the tenant, can ask the appropriate court to cancel the tenancy contract and having the erring party removed.' (p. 51)

The new amendment also includes the following important clause: 'Repeated delays in total or partial payment of rent authorize the owner

to break the tenancy contract and have the tenant expelled with the obligation to reimburse the owner with the total sum due.' (p. 65) This had also
been strictly forbidden under the Agricultural Reform Law, which was
essentially aimed at protecting the farmer from the greed of the landowner.
Under the threat of eviction, the small farmer can only become an agricultural worker relying on his ability to work.

This distraint under the Agricultural Reform Law objectively completes
the counter-revolution accomplished in other areas, for the liquidation of
the small farmers and the general degeneration of the country is paralleled
by the liquidation of the nationalized sector and the degeneration of the
towns. The open economy is no more than the banner of this double
degeneration. Because of this it is natural that crises should arise. Imports
at too high a level, loans, and the reduction in agricultural production, all
lead to the deficit in the balance of payments, to inflation and to unemployment, all of which in turn lead to an instability in the supply of
basic commodities.

The fourth source is the Congress of Egyptian Economists held in Cairo
in April 1978. Dr. Gudah Abd El Khaleq concluded his study on the evolution of the Egyptian economy between 1975 and 1977 by saying that the
new Egyptian capitalism was qualitatively different from that before 1952.
(This is the same conclusion reached by Dr. Fuad Mursi in his book, *Cette
ouverture economique*). Above all, this capitalism is dependent on foreign
capital: 'Egyptian capital is associated with foreign capital in 22 out of 31
investment projects.'

It is also a commercial capitalism: 'Commerce is its basis, profit is its aim,
and production comes third.' But the most serious statement in this study is
that this capitalism is a 'family' capitalism. The capitalist families are the
same families as those who hold the political power. The researcher gave
several examples of family businesses whose owners were ministers, held
important positions in the State organisations, were in partnership with
foreign capitalist interests, and most were involved with import/export
businesses or with the services sector. None of these companies actually
produces anything. Construction works and banking operations come first
for these family businesses. The name 'Osman Ahmed Osman' usually appears
at the head of the list.[10] And so the rich and the powerful are supported,
almost by a single person. One of the consequences of this irregular situation
is that: 'Sadat, who was counting on his policy of openness towards the West
to provide a solution to his economic, military and political problems, found
himself more and more dependent on the United States but without achieving
the hoped for results.'[11] The situation was, therefore, deadlocked. The events
of January 1977 were just a manifestation of this deadlock and of disillusion
after an impossible dream: to make Egypt like Lebanon, or like Saudi Arabia,
for there are limits to Egyptian patience, limits set by the Egyptians themselves.

The Bankrupt Regime

The gap between the feelings of the Egyptian workers and the organised consciousness of the students was bridged day by day as the counter-revolution developed. After the events of January 1975 and the commune of Muhalla Al Kubra that same year, other events occurred with increasing frequency during the year 1976. They were the immediate reactions to changes brought about in the infrastructure and to production output under the new social system. There was no indication of a possible explosion. A popular uprising took place at El Manzala on 29th January 1976; this was followed by other 'deplorable events', as described by the official media at the time. What happened in fact was that the people attacked police stations almost everywhere, at Chubra El Khayama, Sayyda Zeinab, at Darb Al-Ahrmar, and elsewhere.

Workers went on strike at the Nasr car factories, at the Helouan light transport factory, at the Egypt-Helouan cotton-spinning factory, at the Eastern Tobacco Company, at the Naval workshops of Alexandria and Port Said, etc. But the most effective of all these strikes was that of the transport workers in Cairo on 18th and 19th September 1976. It took place 24 hours after the re-election of the President of the Republic. The Students' Socialist Club held a demonstration in front of the People's Council on 25th November 1976. At the same time, demonstrations were held by graduates of the technical schools, physical education schools, the political science faculty, the fine arts faculty and by the residents of the University city of Giza.[12]

In one way all these events were normal; in another they could be seen as an indication of what could happen. In any case, the events of January 1977 cannot be seen as a surprise.

Instead, the surprise came from the regime, and it came in two ways. The first was when, at the beginning of the month, a vast press campaign was launched aimed at assuring the population that salaries would be increased and that if prices did not actually decrease, they would at least stabilise. The second was on the evening of 2nd January when the government declared an increase in the prices of basic necessities.

For the first surprise, the daily newspaper *Al-Ahram* announced on the 1st January 1977 'the stabilisation of all prices in 1977 and an improvement in the conditions of all the workers in the State'. This was a summary of a press release given by Prime Minister Mamduh Salem to the newspaper's financial editor. Under another heading 'Hopes, Forecasts and Possibilities', the Prime Minister said:

> My hopes and forecasts consist in the achievement of the government plan for 1977, which is a part of the five-year plan, and also indicates its success. This part of the plan includes the reform of certain aspects of the economic structure, the alleviation of some of the burdens borne by the population, the overcoming of certain economic difficulties and the achievement of social justice. I believe that we will succeed in increasing both production and exports, in having better control of public spending, in increasing our agricultural production and ensuring

321

adequate supplies of meat and vegetables on the market. We also wish to encourage imports of foodstuffs and popular fabrics. I hope by these successes to stabilise prices. In any case, measures will be taken after the completion of various studies being conducted by the ministries concerned.

The next day the following headlines appeared on the front page of *Al-Ahram*: 'Sadat asks for rapid promulgation of laws on Workers, Housing and Taxes'; 'The President and the political leaders study the means of providing the population with food and clothing'; 'Price Stability for basic necessities in 1977'. On 3rd January 1977 the daily newspaper *Al-Gumhuriyyah* asserted that prices would not increase. On 9th January, *Al-Akhbar* said, in its editorial, that the government was tending towards stabilisation of prices and making it possible for the people to easily obtain products and basic essentials.

The *Al-Akhbar* headline on 10th January 1977 was: 'Sadat asks that the young generation does not bear the burden of sacrifice alone.' On 12th January, Gamal Al-Uteifi, Minister of Information, made the following statement after the meeting of the Council of Ministers: 'Mr. Mamduh Salem has given the Council President Sadat's directives concerning prices of consumer goods and actions to take in order to produce a popular canned meal at moderate price.' On 16th January, *Al-Akhbar* announced 'an important meeting of the parliamentary Misr Party [the party in power] to study the means of stabilising prices of certain basic necessities.'

Egyptians went to bed on the night of 17th January sure, or almost sure, that the government had at last understood them. There was no news the next day. Towards the end of the day, the deputies in the People's Council heard the report of Dr. Abd Al-Moneim Al-Qaysuni, Vice-President for Economic Affairs and President of what was called The Economic Group. He gave an account of the State's financial situation. The Minister of the Plan dealt with the development plan for 1977, and finally, the Minister of Finance gave his budget statement for the new programme. The three successive speeches had an overwhelming effect. For all three converged towards a single point: *increasing* prices by abolition of State aid on basic essentials – from bread, vegetables and everyday commodities like sugar, tea, tobacco and paraffin; all these things were of basic necessity for the average citizen.

Without doubt the citizen did not know what to believe, because the day before he had received an assurance which was now totally reversed by the very same people who had given that assurance.

It was as though the government had deliberately prepared the ground to unleash the inferno, as though it had fixed its deadline. It was natural that at the height of it all the workers and students should stage a peaceful march demanding the resignation of the government. The demonstrators marched under the following slogans:

'They dressed us in jute, now they are taking our money.'
'The government of the centre and the dance of the stomach, a kilo
of meat is on credit.'
'They drink whisky and eat chicken while the people die of starvation.'
'The Zionist is on my land and the secret police at my door.'
'America: take your money away, the Arab people will crush you.'
'Students and workers against the Government of Exploitation.'
'Nasser always said, "Take care of the workers".'

Twelve hours after the peaceful demonstrations, while President Sadat
was still at Aswan, the popular masses suddenly turned to violence. A security
report drawn up by General Ahmad Ruchdi, under state instructions, described the demonstration that was directed against the People's Council
at about 19.30 in the following terms:

> The central police force faced them. They were dispersed but into
> small groups whose ranks were then filled with other people and with
> saboteurs . . . Some of the demonstrators ransacked numerous public
> and private buildings, means of transport, police stations and police
> vans. They attacked hotels and shops. They set fire to some press
> offices.[13]

The next day President Sadat, still at Aswan, started preparing for a
rapid return to the capital. The reports that came to him were contradictory. The official report of the Ministry of the Interior intended for the
citizens was published on Wednesday 19th January 1977 and announced
'a return to normal'. Other reports, however, gave accounts of similar
events occurring at Alexandria in the north and at Giza in the south. But
President Sadat had to assess the situation for himself during his return
flight on the morning of 19th January. His assessment could be made on what
he had seen for himself for, with his own eyes, he could see the people of
Aswan shouting their anger and flinging themselves at the leader of Egypt.
The reports that followed showed an Egypt united in one gigantic demonstration, shaking the land from north to south. The presidential aircraft could
not find a place to land. During two hours of forced flight, the President
received despatches informing him that his home, and the homes of other
important State officials had been attacked. He was advised not to land at
Cairo airport. Alexandria was just as unhospitable. Even the attitude within
the armed forces was unfavourable when he was advised to land at a military
airport. Nobody knew until after the event where the presidential plane
had landed. On the other hand, everyone knew that the landing was accompanied by a number of special measures: an order was given to the central
security forces to open fire on the demonstrators. The left – from the
progressive and unionist National Party to the communists – was accused
of having incited 'schism' and 'dissidence' and the abrogation of all the
decrees concerning price increases. In spite of the 80 or more dead and the

200 wounded,[14] the military governor was obliged to impose a curfew, to ban traffic and, for the first time since 1952, to send the army into the streets.

What, in fact, was happening down on the ground while the President was flying over it and about to take the above measures the moment he landed? The events can briefly be described as follows:

Even though violence had broken out on 18th January 1977, the first day of real violence was without any doubt the 19th January. The regime certainly displayed its intelligence when it described the violence as 'vandalism', which is hated by Egyptians. This expression was also taken up by upright and progressive citizens when they tried to defend the population and reject the accusations made against them; this put them in a defensive position right from the start. Certainly the lumpenproletariat and the extremists had carried out acts of sabotage, but this was an insignificant part of the matter. It is also certain that the people, as a whole, were reacting against the violence demonstrated by the aggressive actions of the security forces, and in reaction to accusations made against a certain political group that it had triggered off these events, as though the rise in prices had not been the main reason, or as though the people were acting like a flock of sheep. Volney (1757–1820) had written years before:

> All that we see and hear of Egypt proves that it is a country of slavery and tyranny . . . It is impossible to have a conversation without hearing reports of civil disturbance, famine, extortion, exaction, torture or putting to death. There is no safety whatever for the people or for their property. The blood of a man is as easily shed as that of a beast.[15]

The problem with historians is that they look only at an isolated moment in the history of a country. The author of the above lines does not mention the revolution of the Bedouins and the Egyptian peasants that occurred throughout the periods of the Mamelukes and the Turks. His book was also written before the two revolts against the French Army in Cairo. Volney did not see the revolutions of Orabi, Saad Zaghlul or, finally, that of Nasser. He would, however, at least have found historical justification for the violence of the Egyptian people on the 18th and 19th January 1977; for this violence gained its legitimacy from the counter-revolution and from violence itself. Th. Dasjardin wrote that the security forces were firing on demonstrators without having genuine reasons for doing so. In fact there was a double outrage, that of bullets and that of hunger. The same author wrote: 'For the first time we were seeing the true poverty of Egypt . . . like that in India and Ethiopia. In 1976 Egypt entered a period of total poverty.' Elsewhere he described the violence of the Egyptian population, which he had seen for himself, in the following terms: 'Small children dressed in dirty *jellabas* rushed out. The soldiers took no notice of them. Suddenly these children began throwing Molotov Cocktails at the armoured cars and then ran away crying. The soldiers opened fire but the children had disappeared.'[16]

The Egyptian people of the Egyptian left cannot be accused of violence, because the violence was produced in the face of bullets, death and famine. The violence was legitimate and peaceful, if we can use such terms.

What form did it take? In the country areas it took the form of the interruption of communications, the taking over of administrative centres and marching on the towns, exactly as had happened during the 1919 revolution, with the difference that in 1977 the number of demonstrators in the Egyptian provinces had much greater impact than had been the case in the 1919 revolution. In the towns the people converged massively on police stations, prefectures, night clubs, big hotels and the second homes of high officials and everything that symbolized social injustice and double standards. They went to the food cooperatives which contained the goods stolen from them by bureaucrats and brokers. They went to the American University in the centre of Cairo. What that represented was obvious. On the other hand, no national university or school was attacked in the slightest way. 'No factory was sabotaged, no machines were destroyed, no small shopkeepers complained. The demonstrators took the carts belonging to hawkers into the side streets to avoid any risk of damage.'[17] When the people organised a trial of the actor Fouad Al-Muhandis on the Abu Al-Al-lla bridge, which separates the smart quarter of Zamalek from the common quarter of Boulaq, the only question put to him was, 'Where did you get that from?', they pointed to his luxurious car (they themselves could not even find a place in a bus). The meaning of all this is that the violence of the people was not simply blind violence, but was aimed against certain very specific symbols. It was not, therefore, sabotage, but a revolt against these symbols.

This revolt meant revolution was in the air, as Lenin expressed it. It found its direction from within itself. It was both the fuse and the bomb; government decisions were no more than the match. In fact this match could ignite at any time and under any pretext, for a revolution in suspense needs no external factor. That is why the accusation against the left, both clandestine and open, and also the left's rejection of the accusation, was sad but true. For there can be no doubt that public opinion gave the left the credit for starting the revolt. On the other hand, there is no doubt that the clandestine and open left were not the main participants in the historic event, for they were very much in decline both before and after this sudden manifestation. It is truly regrettable that the national honour of the Egyptian people was questioned by the regime when it described this uprising as 'an uprising of bandits', an expression used by Sadat and then taken up by all the information media. Moscow and Libya were accused, as though the people of Egypt were not responsible.[18] As if the people needed those who had undertaken their defence in order to defend themselves; as though there had been a crime or a plot, even though all the damage caused by the Egyptian demonstrators during two days could not even be compared with the damage done in half an hour in a country such as Lebanon or Iran. The simple reason for this is that there was no civil war. What was described in the first part of this book as 'positive control' had arrived at the threshold of revolution under the direction of national unity and parallel with the degeneration of the regime.

I should like to mention this unity, which drove the masses of ordinary Egyptian people to react against the regime. The huge scale of the events of January 1977 was due to the fact that they were geographically spread over the whole of Egypt; they occurred at the same time and they all involved the same protest. A superficial look at the history of Egyptians could lead to the error of thinking that these events could have been premeditated. But the actual facts of the matter are clearly seen when it is appreciated that all the various parts of the uprising — from its total geographic spread to the synchronization and slogans — exploded at a time that could not be foreseen by the class and national enemies, even though this uprising registered in the collective consciousness. This is a characteristic that many cannot discern from the history of Egypt, from its mythology, its folklore or its literature; a characteristic of which the effects can be partly seen in the two early works of the Egyptian writer Tawfiq Al-Hakin: *Le Retour de l'aime* and *Les Gens de la Caverne*. There Egypt falls into a long deep sleep, but she never dies, and when she awakens it is 'All together'. Many Arabs, including Egyptians, are not aware of this Egyptian characteristic and therefore, they despair and mistake the sleep of Egypt for death. They notice the moment of awakening only when Egypt itself arises. This is why they can only explain these objective phenomena from a subjective viewpoint.

The reason for the peaceable nature of revolt in Egypt lies in the very subtle awareness shared by all Egyptians that its institutions are a part of themselves as Egyptians. 'They were attacking all that was foreign,' said the author of *Le poudre et le pouvoir*. Even though that is an exaggeration it can, nevertheless, be said that in a sense it is true, for it can be said that to the inflamed conscience, night clubs and police stations are foreign. Egyptians like a night out and 'kicking over the traces' but the Pyramid Street night club has always been the symbol of something else, something linked with foreign occupation. Egyptians respect lawfulness to the point of considering it sacred as long as the State is the symbol of a civilised organisation but, like Jesus Christ, they can break into the innermost sanctuary and, with whip in hand, drive out the merchants saying, 'My house is a house of prayer and you have made it a den of thieves.'

On the 18th and 19th January, the Egyptians only pursued the Pharisees, they did not manage to drive them from the altar.

In all the events described above, those who saw them from the outside, those who observed the Egyptian people, were closer to the reality of things than those who saw only from the inside, as did the regime or the opposition.

The American magazine *Time* said:

> The anger of the peasants and middle classes of Egypt is growing. These represent 90% of the population of 40 million. Their anger is growing because the government never ceases asking them to make sacrifices. These classes live in miserable economic conditions; there is a lack of basic foodstuffs, inflation has reached 37% per year. Those who buy in the private shops have noted that prices there are four times

more expensive than those in the cooperatives. People complain about the very high price of milk, meat and vegetables. Only 10% of the total population are economically comfortable. Under the present regime the rich have become richer, and especially so after the restitution of the wealth that had been sequestered from them while President Nasser was in power. Last week, angry demonstrators went into the streets. The demonstrations were more violent than any had been for 25 years since the expulsion of King Farouk. These explosions were due to the sudden decisions decreed by Abd Al-Moneim Al-Qasuni, President of the Economic Group, to increase prices.[19]

Under the headline 'They have made Egypt into a new India', the French magazine *Le Nouvel Observateur* wrote:

The World Bank and the International Monetary Fund did not expect the waves of anger that swept through Egypt when they recommended that the Egyptian government withdraw its aid from the basic necessities (sugar, rice, tea, fuel, etc.) which are essential for survival. Over five years, prices have increased by 120% while incomes have remained static. The guaranteed minimum wage is E£12. A teacher earns E£20. It is easy to see that misery is spreading rapidly. However, it is this population which, according to the international experts, should bear the burden of correcting the economy of the country. Egypt has passed from a planned economy to a totally open economy, customs restrictions have been removed and private capital enjoys enormous privileges. The result of this new tendency is the growth of a parasitic class living on the importation of luxury goods and on the black market.[20]

Fritz Stern, Professor of History at the American University of Columbia, wrote in the journal *Foreign Affairs*:

Arriving in Cairo several weeks after the demonstrations by the starving in the month of January 1977 following the price increases imposed by the government on basic necessities, it appeared to me that the police had no power, whatever the reasons for this might be, and this obliged the government to call out the army. The continuing violence and the immediate abrogation of the decision that had caused the trouble demonstrate the weakness of the government. This came as a shock to President Sadat. The government made the mistake of blaming the communists.[21]

Le Monde wrote:

The demonstrators think that the government has broken the promises made by the President during November by increasing the prices of a certain number of basic essentials. The Prime Minister therefore made

327

a tragic error, for these products are truly the basic necessities of life. In fact the open economy policy has had contrary effects. The gap between rich and poor has become wider and wider. Only a small minority has gained from this policy while the great majority suffers from poverty and misery.[22]

The British newspaper *The Guardian* wrote: 'It is evident that the police acted blindly on the basis of old lists of suspects; this proves that they do not have much information on the real leaders of the demonstrations, assuming that such spontaneous uprisings can have leaders.'

Such were the testimonies of Western media which cannot be accused of communism. They all agree about the spontaneity of the uprising and its economic causes. These two elements are real but in fact they do not represent all the factors behind the events of January 1977. These testimonies are also important because they contradict the regime's accusation against the left and against the self-defence put up by the left. There was no crime and there had been no plot, but simply an explosion of a repressed population.

The regime adopted a highly violent attitude and also accused the left of having hatched a plot with the assistance of Tripoli and of Moscow. But it did recognise that the decision to increase prices had caused the 'discontent' of the population.

The truth is that the regime, with its type of police policy, was surprised by the scale of the events. It is also true that between the 18th and 19th January the regime went through a period of total exposure; it was only because nobody appeared to fill the vacuum that the regime stayed in place.

Today it is virtually certain that the bloodshed that occurred in Cairo and Alexandria, under the gunfire of the central security forces was the result of a deliberate order. Even though security forces did not have instructions to protect the institutions, they fired heavily on the population. It is, however, also true that the police forces were powerless before the onslaught of a human tide armed only with stones. That is why the curfew was ordered and the army sent on to the streets. It is no longer a secret today that the army accepted these orders on the condition that they would not open fire on the people; a condition that had been immediately accepted.

Because the security organisations had lost the battle and had not foreseen the events and proved incapable of containing them, the only way in which the responsibility could be placed on someone was to have recourse to the old lists of men of the left. Because the Prime Minister, a former police officer, was Minister of the Interior in the putsch of 14th May 1971, the document accusing the left was written by him before being sent to the Attorney General. It was the Attorney General who published the infamous declaration accusing the official left (the Assembly Party) and also the clandestine left (the communists) of having stirred up the troubles. And as President Sadat was openly against the left, he instigated the astonishing plebiscite which voted both for and against democracy by authorising, in February 1977, a multi-party State and increasing the penalty for demonstrations, strikes and secret organisations to hard labour for life. The Egyptians will miss Sidqi Pasha (God rest his soul) whose law for these same offences gave a possible maximum of only ten years imprisonment and a minimum of two years.

The excuse given by the regime for this massacre was the resignation of the Minister of the Interior, former Director of Information on State Security. Several days before the events of 18th and 19th January 1977, he had made a declaration before the People's Council concerning the events in the town of Billa:

> The crimes committed recently, [he said] were characterised by violence. This violence is understood the world over. However, the troubles and the insignificant acts of vandalism occurring in Egypt cannot in any way be considered as relating to the economic and socia. conditions in our country. Police stations were attacked by irresponsible people. On studying the matter we can see that we can regard these people as children and not as responsible people. There is extreme tension among the people. We know that our people's opinion is an expression of discontent. The armed presence of the security forces can only increase the tension.[23]

In fact this analysis was a portent. It does not accuse the left but gives an objective evaluation of the situation. Political decision, however, is another matter. It was to make the political decision more credible that Sayyed Fahmi was made a scapegoat. Al-Qaysuni's offer to resign was rejected. The Prime Minister had never even thought of resigning, even though this solution had been cordially proposed to him. And so began the widespread arrests of Egyptian progressives.

Why?

It was not a mistake by the government but rather a fault inherent to the regime. The protest against the price increases covered another protest directed against the entire regime. President Sadat understood this from the rapid progress of the opposition movement. Mamduh Salem was not just a Prime Minister involved in a tactical error, it was the member of the putsch of 14th May 1971 who was being questioned.

As for Abd Al-Moneim Al-Qaysuni, the Vice-President for Economic Affairs, he was perhaps the only man in perfect accord with the social identity of the new regime. In 1965 he had recommended the same proposals to President Nasser. Nasser categorically rejected them. The expert on a laisser faire economy resigned or, more precisely, was relieved of his functions. But under the new regime, Mr. Qaysuni found it necessary — and he was quite right — to be completely consistent, which implied the withdrawal of state aid for basic necessities. In that he was more sincere and consistent with regard to the regime. He was the best representative of the regime; he did not need to resort to compromise between his official position and effective action. That is why Al-Qaysuni took no part in what was interpreted as the deception of the public about the measures that had to be taken. Like many others, he knew of them even before they had been announced to the general public. He also knew that they would continue to be applied even if in different form. For all these reasons, he signified his refusal to take part in this great game of duplicity by presenting his resignation. For the same reasons the regime refused it, as if by doing so it wished to affirm that its position was the same as his. It is known that Qaysuni repeated this request for his resignation to be accepted when the crisis intensified during 1977. He finally succeeded in leaving the sinking ship.

The regime was surprised that the tribunals set up eventually acquitted the Egyptian left. In none of all the inquiries conducted by the judges, could proof be established against the Nasserites and communists who were accused of having taken part in the events as political organisations. There is no need to point out that individual participation in a demonstration is a very different matter from collective participation. This judicial result did not at all suit the security organisations; it suited the political leadership even less. Even more absurd were the authorisations given for the arrest of people who, at the time, were thought either to be dead or to have been abroad for a very long time. This confusion shows that the courts had had the old files opened but in fact had not looked at them. But even more significant was the evidence given on the witness stand by certain security officials; they could not confirm that the Assembly Party had participated in the demonstrations, as a party. The courts released the detainees; but the President of the Republic applied his veto to stop the release. The security organisations found a solution: the political detainees were brought to 'justice' for affairs having nothing to do with the events of 18th and 19th January. The most famous of these was called the 'affair of the secret organisations'. Because the charges could not be proved the courts had to acquit then one after the other, after months of detention and torture.

These proofs of the innocence of the Egyptian left were certainly not to its real advantage because this acquittal was, in one way, a condemnation of its theoretical and practical position as regards the events. In effect, the theoretical position of the Egyptian Communist Party at the time consisted in an analysis according to which the regime was divided into three vacillating tendencies: nationalism, treason and a zone of indecision between the two. According to this analysis, militant action consisted in supporting the nationalist wing in power, so that traitors would be eliminated and those who were undecided would take sides. Such an analysis made it impossible to proceed from a revolution in a state of suspension and to seize power. Later the Party abandoned the form but not the basis of this analysis by affirming that the dominant party in the regime was the party of treason, especially after the visit to Jerusalem. Under the circumstances, this partial abandonment was futile compared with the wholesale demolition needed for a radical change in the local thinking of communist organisations and the Egyptian Communist Party. Even though calling for the overthrow of the regime remained the basic policy, it did not have a background of struggle neither did it constitute the beginnings of effective action which would make it realistic and possible.

The events of 18th and 19th January did constitute an historical beginning; they announced the objective fall of the regime; they removed its legitimacy obtained by the 1973 war. The regime had no cover. A political initiative organised by the opposition was expected. Nothing happened. In a country such as Egypt, analysis of power does not require a vision embracing all streams of thought, even though they are objectively present in the existing social alliance. On the other hand, the relevance of the analysis is tested against its ability to quantitatively evaluate these currents of opinion in political decision-making. It is decision, and decision alone, which must be the object of the analysis and not the formation of levels of power. In a regime that has no relationship with liberal or popular democracy all decision-making is made by the regime. In the countries of the Third World, and in Egypt in particular, individual power becomes the equivalent of the power of the regime and its ability to make decisions. That is why any explanation tending to make a distinction between the President and the government, or between the President and the security organisations, is no more than a short-term tactic whose consequence is to alienate its supporters, to belittle them from the historic point of view and to enable them only unwillingly to assist in its downfall.

As for those acting within the framework of legitimacy, the National Progressive and Unionist Assembly, they can only be asked to be aware of the radical meaning of legitimacy. And, if the people are the source of regimes, when they withdraw legitimacy from the regime, the legitimate opposition can become the nucleus of a new regime and the bearer of legitimacy.

There can be no doubt that the balance of social forces in Egypt cannot allow the left, with its various tendencies, to be alone in power. But it is this very balance, without the complex historic and social relationship between the forces of revolution and the forces of counter-revolution, that can present an alternative candidate to spearhead the revival. The left is a principal organic part of this alternative. The social alliance holding power, composed of big landowners, technocrats and brokers, by its very nature can only accentuate the necessity of a new alliance, a new alliance which is present in essence in the feeling of the ordinary people but which is not organised as a body. The regime and the opposition collapsed and for many hours Egypt did not have a State. Such a condition is unheard of in our modern history and perhaps never known throughout all Egypt's long past. But these hours were and are laden with consequence.

'The innocence of the left' as regards the rising on 18th and 19th January does not mean that the Muslim Brotherhood can be accused. The individual presence of young people of the extreme religious right is, however, a fact, especially at the night clubs of Pyramids Street. But it is no less certain that the author of *Le poudre et le pouvoir* had been the furthest from the truth of all those who accused the extreme religious right.[24] He was not the only one. The American magazine *Time* aligned itself with him by writing: 'The Muslim Brotherhood bears the responsibility for a great deal of the trouble.'[25] Even though for political reasons the regime had accused the left, while knowing it to be innocent and, for the same reason had not accused the religious right, that should not prevent us from considering that the Muslim Brotherhood had nothing to do with the events of January. For one thing, the mainstream of the Muslim Brotherhood remained faithful to the regime that allowed them freedom of action and the freedom to attack the previous Nasser regime. But the main reason is that these extremist organisations have no relationship with the Egyptian man-in-the-street; they themselves do not even think they do. The bases of such organisations are never apparent from the outside. Their thinking cannot overturn governments or regimes. The most they can do is to brandish their weapons against several individual symbols. By their very organisation they are at the opposite extreme from the ordinary Egyptian. That is the proof that the true Egyptian left is the ordinary Egyptian; they are not against the regime but against the society.

The author of *La poudre et le pouvoir* wanted to blame Libya more than the Muslim Brotherhood. In defending the communists he wrote, 'Sadat was too quick to accuse the left when the nature of the demonstrations was purely Islamic.' At the same time he wondered why the demonstrators were hostile to foreigners 'when Egypt, cradle of civilisation throughout history, has always welcomed them.' He said that Egypt is not a fanatical country and Egyptian Islam itself is free from all extremism. These words may be true, but the context in which they are placed is not, for the demonstrators attacked only the American University and the Soviet Cultural Centre, which were both situated in the centre of the city. Because of the opposite nature of these two institutions it is easy to recognise the social components of the demonstrations, their spontaneity and the psychology that permitted such paradoxes. But the real nature of the revolt can be seen in the slogans carried by the demonstrators. They had nothing to do with Islam; and this again demonstrates the nature of revolt in the history of the Egyptian people.[26] This invalidates the conclusion drawn by Th. Desjardin. In fact the author was simply trying to discern the originators of the demonstrations, to find an answer to the same question that was asked by the police. Social historians will not ask such a question. It was an illusion that Libya could have been the cause of these events, something in any case categorically refuted by the Egyptian police.

Ripe Fruit and a Deferred Harvest

The events of January 1977 showed the incapacity both of the regime and the opposition. And how eloquent Mustapha Amin, leader writer of the right, was when he wrote:[27]

> It is not sufficient to be told that the official Communist Party and the clandestine communists, if they were able to unite, would be so weak that they could not plunder a single street, because we are dealing with an accumulation of errors. The decisions concerning increased prices only spilt the petrol; the saboteurs set it on fire. If then we are looking for those responsible for this fire, it is not sufficient to point out the one who struck the match. We must point, and with both hands, to those who spilt the petrol and prepared the ground for the fire.

With these words, Mustapha Amin took into account the lassitude of the 'civilised' right in relation to the whole situation. It is the right which will find its best political expression in the new Wafd Party. It is the right whose social base is growing more and more, in order to include the considerable sections of the middle class who were bewildered to see some of their number converted to parasitic capitalism and abandoning production. It was a progressive breakdown of the principal feature of the middle class.

In fact, this same right, had imparted the lesson of the 26th January 1952 when Cairo was burnt, when democracy was reduced to a minimum and when the army assumed power. Is it not, therefore, astonishing, that Mustapha Amin, traditional enemy of the Wafd during the 1940s, should welcome the return to the political scene of the new Wafdist leader Fouad Serag Ed-Din Pasha? This symbolic reconciliation shows that the true right had prepared the ground for the parasitic right which was known by its system of rapid pillage. From another point of view the events of January 1977 induced the 'civilised' right to offer itself as a candidate to replace the Sadat regime for Egypt, for conservative Arabs, and for the West.

As for the left, one of the leaders of the clandestine wing declared: 'Our party's policy is not the overthrow of the regime and never has been. Our position with regard to the regime is clear: we fight against the collaborating element within the regime.'[28] And also: 'Our political action consists in representing the widest cross-section of the national and progressive forces . . . and there is no need to recall that the major political or socio-economic problems facing Egypt can only be resolved by a national and popular regime.' To say the least, that is an astonishing analysis, especially as it was put out after the events which proved their inability to contain the historic movement of the Egyptian people, and also, their inability to take the helm and form an alternative capable of taking power. This analysis was also abandoned later by the Egyptian Communist Party when it called for the overthrow of the regime without taking any action to prepare or take part in the preparation of the basis for a new alternative. In fact the popularity of the Wafd proved that it was closer to the structure of the new regime.

But this in no way denies that the militant Egyptian communists, as a whole and through their political and organisational activities, as well as the Nasserites and the Assembly Party, conducted a courageous and successful campaign against repression and on behalf of the masses, which actively helped to unmask the regime both to Egypt and to the outside world. Meanwhile, the ideological crisis remained unsolved. The party of Khaled Muhyi Ad-Din tried to take some initiatives within the framework of legitimacy, which will forever remain in the memory of Egyptians as models of national democratic opposition. To become an alternative, however, remains more difficult for the left than for the informed right; for only legitimacy would give it a freedom of action to match the events. In spite of everything, the experience remains a lesson for the Egyptian left and a key to the still locked doors.

The Egyptian January still continues, even though the 19th of this month ended with an inconsolable let-down. The components are still there; the class feeling among the workers is still alive. The organised consciousness of the students and the intellectuals continues. The interaction of the two to produce the basis for a real change depends on a consciousness that could be politically directed as an opposition in the face of the crisis: in fact the mainstay of Egyptian national unity is the organic link between liberation, development and democracy. The absence of democracy under Nasser was an important reason for the degeneration of economic development after 1965 and the military defeat of 1967. The social history of the putsch of May 1971 is the story of the rejection of these three factors. Objectively, this should lead to the fall of the new regime. But instead of collapsing, it engulfed the country in religious conflict, the threat of famine, and repressive legislation. And all this to disguise its own collapse.

In fact the regime did not fall; for though the fruit was ripe, there was nobody there to harvest it.

Notes

1. *Al-Akhbar*, 8th February 1977.
2. *Rose Al-Youssef*, 11th July 1977.
3. Concerning incomprehension and partiality, read Chapter 2 of *La poudre et le pouvoir* by Thierry Desjardins, Fernand-Nathan (Paris 1977).
4. One Egyptian pound is worth about seven new francs.
5. See *At-Taliah*, January 1976: *Humum Al-Huwatin Abd-At-Tawwab*.
6. *La soucis de Um-Muhammad*, February 1976.
7. The figure is identical to that given by *At-Taliah* in the two previously quoted enquiries.
8. *Rose Al-Youssef* believed that it could cast a slur on Egyptian-American relations and upset the relationship between President Sadat and his administration. Publishing the document, the magazine hoped, would prove that the Americans wished to see the downfall of the 'national' regime. This was its basis for letting it be understood that they were not disassociated from the events of January 1977 so that it could reject the accusations made by the security organisations against the left. In fact *Rose Al-Youssef* wanted to show that the left was not to blame for the revolt against the regime: Messrs Abd Al-Rahman Ach Charqawi and Salah Hafez did not consider that the left was, in reality, the

ordinary people of Egypt.

9. To be more precise, the Egyptian regime never had an agreed tactical position during the Lebanese war. Sometimes it supported the Christian right, at others the Muslim right; but it was always a religious right that it helped in its Middle East manoeuvres. It sent young Egyptian Christians, or at least allowed them to go. Those who survived said that, according to the information they had, they were sent to join the Phalangists as volunteer fighters.

10. See the enquiry published by *Al-Ahali*, 3 May 1978.

11. Ch. Aulas, *Le Monde Diplomatique*, January 1976.

12. See 'The Lessons of the Egyptian January Uprising' by Ahmed Al-Masri in *El-Katib Al-Falestini*, No. 2, April 1978.

13. The text is taken from the Egyptian newspaper *Al-Ahali* of 15th March 1978.

14. This is the official estimate. Mr. Desjardins (*op. cit*) noted 80 dead, 600 wounded and 1,000 arrested (p. 165) but the final estimates according to the international Press were 'more than 300 dead and 1,000 wounded'. It was the worst massacre in the history of modern Egypt. The British Army did not have as many victims in 1919 and Sidqi Pasha, the tyrant, only killed five students during the sadly famous demonstration in his time.

15. Volney, 'Reflexions sur les revolutions des empires'. The text is translated from Arabic and taken from Louis Awad, *l'Histoire de la pensee egyptienne moderne,* Vol. I., Al-Hilal (1969), pp. 71–2.

16. Thierry Desjardins, *op. cit.,* pp. 163, 165 and 179.

17. Ahmad Al-Misri, in *Al-Katib Al-Filistini,* April 1978.

18. Concerning this, Desjardins (*op. cit.*) wrote: 'Top ministers accused Moscow, a thing that was never proven. In no way could communists use slogans such as "Down with the Khedive"!' (p. 166).

19. The text is from *Al-Ahali*, 8th March 1978.

20. *Ibid.*

21. *Ibid.*

22. *Ibid.*

23. *Ibid*., 15th March 1978.

24. Louis Awad, *op. cit*., pp. 155, 160, 161 and 182.

25. *Al-Ahali*, 8th March 1978.

26. Louis Awad (*op. cit.*) wrote: 'Popular revolts in Egypt do not denote any religious ideology. To A.N. Poliac this is due to the fact that the clergy was reactionary and admitted being no more than instruments in the hands of the regime.'

27. *Akhbar Al-Yom*, 22 January 1977.

28. *Feuilles democratiques,* January, No. 7.

11. Democracy Before and After the Counter-Revolution

The Left and Democracy

The problem which divided Egyptian Marxists during the whole Nasser period, and perhaps even before and for some time after, was whether they were dealing with one revolution or two. In more explicit terms according to the strategic perspective of the problem, was it a national and middle-class democratic revolution with the objective of achieving economic and political independence, or was it a socialist revolution with the objective of establishing popular democracy? One group affirmed that the Egyptian middle class had not yet achieved its own revolution and therefore was still at the stage of a national and democratic revolution; another that the middle class had lagged behind in the push for independence. Consequently, the working class and its vanguard wing should steer the revolution towards both national liberation and socialism.

It is evident that the thinking and formulation of this hypothesis were much influenced by Soviet and Chinese models and by Eastern European experiences, rather than representing the conclusions of the specific laws governing social development in Egypt. The long-term consequence of this hypothesis was failure for the upholders of either interpretation. In 1965 they discovered, each from his own viewpoint, 'a special way' towards the development of democracy by the dissolution of their parties and, as individuals, supporting the political organisation of the Nasser regime. Political historians could discuss at length this unusual step taken at that time by the two big communist organisations. But socio-cultural history can enlighten them, thanks to the following five facts:

Firstly, social underdevelopment of colonial peoples had had its effect both on thinking and on society. Marxist thinking did not escape. We can also see this effect in the social components of the Marxist movement (foreign management, lower middle class bases, dominance of the party structure by the intelligentsia, etc.). This influence can also be seen in types of political action: the very wide separation between loose and rigid organisation, between the policy 'all for the workers' and that of, 'the entire people'. In neither case were the peasants considered, even though they formed the majority of the people. It can be seen above all in ways of thinking: theory —

he text — becomes almost sacred, abstraction often attains extremes of obscurantism, and strategic thinking is so weak that short-term tactics totally contradict each other. This element is typical of lower middle class indi- vidualism, which leads to numerous divisions, each having its objective reasons and its justifications by principle.

Secondly the left wing of these organisations saw the Nasser putsch as military fascism (all the Stalinist parties at the time held the same view) while another group welcomed it as something hopeful. But they were all arrested and interned in prisons and concentration camps where many milit- ants died. They suffered this fate because they were considered to be opponents. Let us note in passing that between 1956 and 1958 the new regime nationalised the Suez Canal, the banks and foreign companies. This gave the regime a certain legitimacy, which the Marxist left lacked, and it can be said that Egyptian Marxists were sent to the torture chambers although they were not fundamentally opposed either to the regime or to each other. They even failed to unite in January 1958. This attempted union, however, was the main reason for Nasser's nervousness; to him, it was the sign of a radical and independent opposition to the regime. But this was not the position taken by the Egyptian Marxists with regard to the Egyptian-Syrian Union which was the basis of their arrest. Nevertheless, the sequence of events proved that this position was correct; in other words, the problem of democracy remained the principal feature of the crisis in the regime and of the left.

Thirdly, concentration camps were established hundreds of kilometres away from Cairo or any populated area, and were put under the control of German experts. Between 1959 and 1964 Egyptian Marxists and independent democrats lived in complete isolation from the real daily life of the people. They were, therefore, more isolated than they had been before their arrest. Rare family visits, secret correspondence and radio broadcasts received on home-made transistor sets, were the only means of keeping contact with the outside world. In such conditions, which remind one of Nazism, and because the prisons gradually became transformed into self-contained worlds, negative factors due to social composition and types of political thought and action could only worsen. Long years in prison, where normal life became no more than a vague memory, could only bring about individual and collective des- pair. The cult of the text, of theory isolated from human reality, was a natural development. The taste for abstraction was the only means of think- ing in a cell of two square metres or in a room packed to suffocation with people dying of solitude and torture. Small-groupism, if such a term can be used, in thinking and in organisation, thus becomes the unique result of the swollen ego or the ego reduced to the extreme limit. Thinking crumbles, not only within the group but individually. Individuals change their opinions from one day to the next; organisations split up into small groups and these end by disintegrating or by comprising isolated individuals.

Fourthly, from the end of the 1950s to the middle of the 1960s the prisons of Egypt were thus witness to the worst period in the history of the

337

Egyptian Marxist movement, whose members, under torture, returned to their original position as regards the revolution. They said, therefore, that the State represented the power of monopolies. Let us note here that, thanks to them, figures were used for the first time in Egyptian Marxist analyses. They were, however, used in an exaggerated way to contradict the daily measures taken by the regime, and let us also note that the left had originally dissolved their organisation in order to adhere to the Nasser parliament. It was thus natural that they should end their analyses by calling for the overthrow of the regime. Others took the opposite path, to the point of saying that a socialist group directed the revolution from the top levels of the regime. They began secret negotiations to dissolve the Party; an action the Marxist leader, Mahmud Amin Al-Alem, disapproved of. In fact, in 1958, when he was summoned by Sadat who proposed the dissolution of the party, Al-Alem excused himself saying that it was not within his power to do so. But the party of the left which had declared its policy of the overthrow of the regime, was surprised when, in 1961, this same regime took several radical measures concerning the structure of the Egyptian economy and that same year declared a National Charter, which included several Marxist generalities. Those adhering to the other stream of thought, supporters of socialism within the regime, were surprised when they were not freed, as the said measures presupposed a certain alliance with the Marxists. They kept to their policy while, following the economic measures taken by the regime for independence and development, the first group changed theirs; these strict economic measures had no democratic basis. And so the language of figures did not lead to the development of a political position but rather to its reversal, to reject the policy of overthrowing the regime and instead to support it. Meanwhile, nobody wondered how the new society could be constructed without the strength of the left. Nobody wanted to see that the question put to Mahmud Al-Alem by Sadat meant that the regime was even rejecting the support of the left when talking about an organised and independent parliament.

Let us now consider the socio-economic content of the measures taken in 1961–62. In reality, the nationalisation of the upper levels of the Egyptian middle classes was never a starting point for socialist transformation. The nationalised sector was created to be directed by the alliance between technocracy and bureaucracy with its military and civil wings on behalf of national capitalism, which had reached a new historic stage. These measures could not, therefore, resolve the problem of democracy which, according to their analysis, still remained. The talented effort of certain others was not necessary for the application of these measures; for their social content and their function in the overall structure of production did not require their presence.

Finally, three years after these measures the rapprochement between the two main organisations of the Egyptian Marxist movement had progressively crumbled away. This was an enormous paradox, for common thinking should lead to a common organisation. But the thinking consisted in the recognition of the one-party regime and in accepting the dissolution of any other organisation apart from the official party. The disintegration of the organisations led objectively to the justification of the dissolution of the party by recognition of Nasser's leadership in this historic period. It was a belated recognition. But what was the relationship between the legitimacy of the Nasser leadership and that of democracy? There is a relationship; but the leadership itself being democratic in no way constitutes a Marxist analysis of power and society in Egypt. In any case, when the regime was certain that the dissolution of the party asked by Sadat of Al-Alem was already a fact before being officially decided, it freed the communists on the occasion of Khruschev's visit in May 1964. This means, that as far as the regime was concerned, the liberation was related to an external factor. One year later, the official *Al-Ahram* published on its front page some surprising information in relation to the revolutionary tradition of 1952; the newspaper reported that the two large communist organisations had been disbanded and that their members had been asked to join the Arab Socialist Union. The event is, in fact, unique in the history of the Egyptian communist movement if not in the international communist movement. It occurred after a completely antipodal experience; for in Latin America the Cuban communists had not brought about the revolution, but Castro joined them and became Secretary-General of the Communist Party. Let us remember that the Egyptian event occurred at the end of the one five-year plan (1960–1965) for economic development, after which began the degeneration which ended in the defeat of 1967.

This unanimous decision by Egyptian Marxists to dissolve the only independent party was deeply resented. It made the democratic crisis in Egypt even worse, in spite of the ideological errors of the Egyptian communist organisation. This sudden dissolution implied recognition of Nasser's definition of democracy. It also made it extremely difficult for any attempt to be made to suggest an independent political communist organisation. This dissolution swept away the idea of a communist front, and consequently, was partly responsible for the banning of all opposition. The Egyptian left, and society as a whole, paid very dearly for this historic error because it was through this yawning breach that the counter-revolution entered in 1971. At the time it appeared as though the Egyptian left agreed with dictatorship and the police state.

Even more serious was the error of the main Marxist leaders in Egypt who supported the May 1971 putsch and in so doing publicly associated themselves with the leaders holding executive power (the government), popular power (the General Secretariat of the Socialist Union) and legislative power (parliament). The real tragedy is that some of these leaders initiated a new historical error by confirming the legitimacy of the putsch. Hidden intentions aside, this new error was a very complex condemnation of the first error and of the Nasser regime at the same time. For the main difference between the two regimes, which President Sadat was careful to underline, was precisely 'democracy'. Taking part in the new regime was therefore a recognition of the former regime's absence of democracy. How then could the dissolution of the party be justified? How was it possible to take part in the new government while the 'one-party' of the Nasser regime was still in existence? That was a contradiction that the putschist regime solved when it abandoned the tactic of using the leaders of the left as a facade at the beginning of its regime. To say the least, this was a tragic contradiction, for a certain part of the left, as part of the regime, and perhaps with reservations, took part in the successive attacks against democracy in the ministerial cabinet, in the People's Council, in the Central Committee of the Socialist Union and in the press. What could be more tragic than to see some 'comrades' in the government and others in the dock?

This confusion in the position taken by the Egyptian left with regard to the democratic cause is only a reflection of the simplism and the generalisation of the hypothesis/question: 'One revolution or two? Has, or has not, the middle class achieved the goal of the national democratic revolution?' If the question can be considered relevant to the condition of Russian society just before and after the Revolution, and to Eastern Europe just before and after the Second World War, it does not mean that we can apply the Leninist and Stalinist solutions in the case of Egypt. The answer to this problem, in our case, does not depend on the Nasser problem but on that of democracy, during and after Nasser.

Egypt and Democracy

We have emphasised the position of the left with regard to democracy in order to highlight a purely Marxist truth: the influence of production on thinking as a factor determining the development of social consciousness, rather than vice versa. Thus, inadequate production output has produced thinking incapable of making a pertinent analysis, in spite of the fact that those doing the thinking have a perfect theory for becoming aware. We have also insisted on the specific details of the whole society; this is a Marxist law concerning the general and the specific. However, where there is underdevelopment, some Marxists ignore the specific aspect of this law and concentrate on the general, and consider as a general law all that Marx said about Great Britain, all that Engels said about France, and all that Lenin said about Russia. This is far from being true. Lenin added a Russian application of Marxism to the theory of revolution. In fact, any application necessarily supposes a theoretical creativity; this is intimately connected with experience. It can in no way be universal. Neither Lenin nor Mao formulated the concepts of historical materialism or dialectical materialism, but it is to them that we owe detailed dissertations on state, party and class alliance. They faced these problems in real life, that is in real and specific circumstances. The first and last problem of democracy is the organisation of production in the new society, and we do not believe that Marx and Engels in the Europe of the 19th Century had as their objective dealing with 'Production output' in all societies and in all ages.

That is why the fact that the Marxist left had insisted on the general, without discovering the elements of the specific law is simply a direct consequence of the underdevelopment of production in modern Egypt; it also shows them to be incapable of creativity. We are emphasising this phenomenon because we are firmly convinced that the Egyptian left is in the forefront of the living forces capable of bringing about a change in the social structures of Egypt, for this left has been able to keep going for 60 years. The first Socialist Party was founded in 1918 and the Communist Party in 1920. This left has also created a strong intellectual stream which has crossed the regional frontiers of Egypt. It has made heavy sacrifices: sacrifices that leave a prominent trail through the history of the Egyptian struggle and provide a glimmer of hope to resist whenever obscurity dominates.

Democracy in Egypt has also suffered from other sources, particularly after the bankruptcy of Egyptian liberalism on the eve of the Second World War and with the signing of the 1936 treaty, and even before that. First we must underline several socio-cultural facts in the history of modern Egypt which relate, in one way or another, to the problem of democracy.

The Egyptians were completely crushed during the period of the degeneration of the Islamic State under the Ottoman hegemony. The fellahin, (the Egyptians and the Bedouins, i.e. the Arabs) had no right to work, nor to defend themselves, nor even less to take part in any decisions. The Turks were the masters and the Egyptians were the slaves. During the time of the pharaohs, Egyptians were either masters or slaves; during the Mameluke-Turkish or Turco-Mameluke period all Egyptians were slaves of different types. Historians of the period (from the beginning of the 13th to the end of the 18th Century) are unanimous in saying that there were class constituents in Egyptian society. Only foreign lords had the right to govern, collect taxes and form an army and the forces of law and order. The fellahin and the Bedouins could only cultivate the land without either owning or renting it. They had the right to teach the Koran, to learn to obey their superiors, to serve them in their homes or to practise those trades that only they had the skill to practise, such as mural painting, the decoration of copper, leather and fabrics. The Mameluke period is one of the most brilliant in the history of Islamic architecture. Besides the fellahin there were the '*harafiches*', a kind of lumpenproletariat. Social servitude, therefore, comprised the subjugation of the land and the enslavement of human beings.

The absence of class constituents signifies that at that time there was no Egyptian society in the true sense of the term. Meanwhile, paradoxically, the peasant uprisings had continued to succeed, from the middle of the 13th century until the French Expedition towards the end of the 18th century. Gabarti in his *Merveilles* and Tahtawi in *l'Resume de Paris* gave an account of the republic of Prince Mammam, or Hammam, the sheikh of the Arabs, who had broken away from Upper Egypt against the Wali and the Turkish Sultan in 1736. But this Hammammian State survived only four years before collapsing in 1769. This was the last revolution before the French Expedition. Even though Babarti studied this revolution in detail, the few lines concerning the revolution in Rifa'ah's work are particularly important. Describing the beginnings of French democracy and the relationship between the governor and the governed, Rifa'ah wrote: 'It is impossible for people to be governors and governed at the same time. Therefore, they must choose from among themselves deputies to govern them. This is what happened in Egypt in Hammam's regime. The government of Upper Egypt was thoroughly republican.'[1] These few words signify that subjugated Egypt had, nevertheless, had a type of republican regime before the French revolution.

What is most important for us to note is that, over a period of six centuries of decline, and having no class constituents, Egypt was at the same time aware of a certain revolutionary element. There was a series of revolts, starting with that of 'Hawwarah' (from the same tribe as Sheikh Hammam, leader of the previous revolt), that of 'Bani Salim' under the leadership of Hesn Ad-Din Ibn Tha'lab in 1253, which ended with the declaration of the independence of Upper Egypt, according to At-Tarif of Al-Umari and As-Sulud of Maqrizi. In 1260 there was a revolt of the slaves in Cairo led by the Shi'ite mystic, Al-Kurani. This revolt is also quoted by Maqrizi. Poliac says that it lasted seven years. In his chronicle *Bad'i Az-Zuhur*, Ibn Iyas gave account of a large revolt occurring in Upper Egypt in 1352. The chronicler-historian uses the two terms Al-Urban (Arabs) and Al-fallahin (the fellahin) as synonymous. Ibn Taghribardi, in his *Al-Hawadeth*, gives account of numerous revolts by the fellahin to seize corn in 1299, 1301, 1352, 1381, 1401, 1496, 1502, 1506, 1507, and 1512. These revolts occurred in all the regions of Egypt. As for Ibn Iyas, he described revolts of the *'harafiches'* (bullies) and of the poor, of which the most important were those of 1369, 1449 and 1450. Ibn Taghribardi also wrote of slave revolts, of which the most important was that of 1437 which demanded the distribution of the land.

It appears that the revolt of Al-Arab Hammam was the peak of this socio-historic stream for it polarised most of the recurrent phenomena. It was also able to construct an independent and organised state. The first of these phenomena was the organic alliance between the fellahin and the Bedouins — to use the terms of the period. It was an early sign of the fundamental Arabness of Egypt. It appears to us that there would not have been a revolt without this alliance. The second phenomenon was the freeing of Egypt from the yoke of the Mamelukes i.e. independence in modern terms. The third phenomenon was that it was a peasants' revolt. This appears clearly from the social forces, all of which were attached to the land in one way or another, and is illustrated by the demand for distribution of the land. The fourth phenomenon was the fact that it was a thoroughly republican regime; there were, as expressed by Tahtawi, two Chambers, one for the leading citizens (*machajikh*), the other for the public. These revolts made it possible to obtain partial satisfaction in the form of a *'hogga'*, which some have called a Magna Carta, though this is an overstatement. This document was, in fact, no more than a first basis for a constitutional charter, but in no way could it be elevated to the rank of a social contract. However, this document put forward the idea of a constitution such as appeared much later in the form of a concessional firman after Bonepart's arrival in Egypt. Louis Awad made a relevant remark about this: 'The naivety of Egypt's political leaders and their lack of experience could not be more clearly shown than by the fact that they consider all social contracts or any constitution defining the bases of power to be just a document without the support of a popular political organisation.'[2] Such an organisation had never existed, not even when the Egyptians took part in the removal of the Turkish Wali to put Muhammad Ali in his place. It was another half century before the Egyptians formed the idea of popular political organisation. It was natural that this should occur with the beginnings of a class society in Egypt. Because of this, we may say it was Muhammad Ali who had made himself independent with Egypt, and not the other way round.

According to Bonaparte, the declared intention of the French Expedition was to free Egypt from the Mamelukes and return it to the Egyptians. This did not prevent them from revolting on two occasions. The French left two years later but they left the Egyptians with some idea of democratic government, of a parliament, and a type of constitution. In their previous struggles against the Turks and the Mamelukes, struggles against the invader and the tyrant, the Egyptians added another feature: that of unity. But this is to be expected because tyranny existed in Egypt before the formation of class constituents. Muhammad Ali achieved what Bonaparte could not achieve, he also destroyed what had been achieved by Bonaparte; he put an end to the existence of the Mamelukes, and the Egyptians could thus recover some of their economic and social rights. Muhammad Ali also nullified the taste of politics that the Egyptians had been given during the Expedition. Furthermore, it can be said that the new regime qualitatively changed the output of production to the advantage of the Egyptians. It modernised methods of production; and this prepared the ground for the birth of new social classes. But all this was achieved without giving the people any part to play in political decision or the right to take part in government. In spite of his work, which may be summarised by saying that he was the founder of modern Egypt, Muhammad Ali and his Albanian court were no more than foreigners to the Egyptian way of thinking. This idea is confirmed during the whole decadent period from Abbas I to the Tewfiq Khedive, a period where nothing remained of the modern State; there were only foreigners. At that time the Egyptians understood, in the depths of their hearts, that their enforced absence from the political scene of their own country could lead only to military defeats, economic crises and consequently, to decadence. Democracy is an organic part of Egyptian independence and the social progress of its people. In other words, democracy is connected with national unity and internal development.

Bearing all this in mind, Orabi's revolution (1881–82), even though it was very short-lived, and in spite of its tragic end (the British occupation) is the most representative example of national democratic revolution in the history of modern Egypt. It brought together, consciously and unconsciously, all the elements of Egyptian revolts since the decadence of the Islamic Empire and its fragmentation into small states dominated by the Ottoman Sultanate under the Turkish Caliphate. It was a national revolt; there was no foreign military occupation. Economic decadence, from the collapse of the Muhammad Ali State to the removal of Ismael, consisted in debt and consumer projects which led to the ruin of Egypt to the extent that it was being directed at the highest level by foreigners defending their own interests. We can say, therefore, that the first concern of nationalism at the time was the economic independence of Egypt. The aristocracy had already been created by the land generously granted to several notable Egyptians by Muhammad Ali. The middle class was in the process of formation in commerce, on the land, and in the machinery of the State. An objective concept of the 'Egyptian national interest', independent from the autocratic regime, was in the process of being formed, and partial representation of this view was granted by Ismael on the basis of the constitution and parliament of 1866. This lasted for 13 years except for an interruption of two years. This national interest gained a certain importance towards the seventh decade of the 19th Century (1879). Modifications had just been introduced into the National Statute and the new draft constitution. But the Western creditors were afraid of Egyptian liberalism. They dismissed Ismael and put Tewfiq in power, and he refused to promulgate the constitution and reverted to autocratic power. The contradiction, therefore, between socio-economic development and autocratic power under Muhammad Ali, led to a result that was the opposite of that sought by Muhammad Ali himself: Egypt landed in the lap of Western monopolies. Europe directly intervened in the political affairs of the country which it officially regarded as being under the rule of the Ottoman Sultanate. The independence of Egypt came to an end in 1882 with the British military occupation. This was the consequence of the objective presence of the Egyptian national interest and its lack of political representation under the autocratic regime.

Orabi's revolution broke out to restore the constitution and parliament in spite of, or perhaps because of, the fact that its leadership was principally military. In fact before the formation of the social classes the army was subject to taboo, but under Muhammad Ali it became a sign of developing production. The formation of the army was a sign of the birth of Egyptian society. Given that the Egyptians were the most underprivileged and the most downtrodden before the formation of the army, it is natural that its largest social component was that of the peasantry. They were also the avant garde that was most sensitive to the contradiction between economic and political conditions. They already understood the dreams of Tahtawi that had not been formulated in the time of Muhammad Ali. They were simultaneously peasants and intellectuals.

On 9th September 1881 history records a scene which repeated itself 70 years later in a different way. In the Abdine Palace Square before Khedive Tewfiq, a peasant officer, Ahmad Orabi, demanded in the name of the army and the people, the removal of the government, the formation of a parliament, an increase in the strength of the army and the ratification of the reform laws. The scandalised Khedive replied: 'I inherited the ownership of this land from my ancestors.' Orabi replied: 'Henceforth we will no longer be inherited.'[3] The democratic fruit of this historic dialogue was the constitution of 1882.[4] This was the first constitutional document specifically defining the power structure. It forbade the accumulation of governmental functions to be paid for by parliament (Article 20). It made the government responsible to parliament (Article 36). Parliament had the right to legislate, to examine and modify laws (Article 27). Parliament also had the right to interpret and modify the constitution (Article 48). The budget and taxation were directly under the control of parliament (Articles 45 and 46). The deputy 'represents the entire Egyptian nation and not just his constituency' (Article 8). The deputies had 'complete freedom to put forward their opinions and make decisions, for it is inadmissible that a deputy should be bound by directives or threats' (Article 9). Sessions were public (Article 14). The deputies enjoyed parliamentary immunity (Articles 14, 15 and 16). They had the right to formulate their own rules of procedure.

The constitution of 1882 added to that of 1879 the principle of co-responsibility between ministers. Parliament had the right to authorise treaties with foreign countries or the privileges granted to their nationals (Article 38). The judiciary acquired its independence. But the most important feature was that this constitution made no mention of an official state religion. This was the first and unique formulation in the history of modern Egypt of a true democratic revolution shattering autocratic power by separating religion from the State. This took place in 1882. The West could only oppose it. The British fleet intervened to prevent the constitution from taking effect. In other words since the 1860's, the liberal West twice assassinated Egyptian democracy: by dismissing Ismael after having ratified the constitution of 1879, and by striking at Orabi's revolution after the constitution of 1882. Western forces occupied the country for more than 75 years and left only when forced to do so in 1956. Their tripartite aggression came at the time of the nationalisation of the Suez Canal, i.e. on the occasion of the regaining of the last forfeit made by Egypt in the time of Said and Ismael.

The period from 1882 to 1956 is also the period in which the Western occupation developed from colonialism to neo-colonialism. Throughout this period Egypt was subject to Western military domination. Hardly had the foreign troops left the countries to the east of Egypt (Syria, Lebanon and Palestine) than the Zionist presence was established by methods that were even more subtle than those long practised in Rhodesia and South Africa. The Zionist identity was thus a proof of its original alliance with international capitalism. The facade of its democracy hid the true racialist character. What mattered was the 'protection' of the strategic position of Middle East, the routes used by international monopolies and the potential energy in the Arab oil wells.

As usual, impoverished Egypt was the key to the entire region. Factors governing Egypt from within and without were the following. Autocratic power in Egypt, from 1805 until King Farouk's overthrow in 1952, was allied with the West in all its variants, including its Zionist wing in 1948, by a historical interest opposed to Egyptian democracy. In its rare moments of democracy, the Egyptian people had worked things out in isolation from foreign influence and in co-operation with the widest sections of its governing classes and in the hope of alliance with the Mashreq.

The fact that autocratic power had protected the Egyptian landed aristocracy, and the fact that the West had protected the newly formed middle class attached to commerce, left a historic impression on the Egyptian middle classes at all levels. This is what we have called 'reaction between the forces of revolution and the forces of counter-revolution'. This is clearly seen in the constitutional difference between Sherif Pasha and Orabi. The former supported the 1866 constitution and the latter thought that the 1876 constitution should be modified. In fact the difference was basically 'social' for the constitution of Khedive Ismael (1866) selected candidates for election on a social basis (mayors, sheikhs and leading citizens) while the constitution of 1882 gave the legislative power to the people and did not require any aristocratic title.

This interaction was manifested in the creation of the National Party (*Al-Hizb al-Watani*), the first political party in Egypt. It was not a party in opposition to other parties having different principles and programmes, but an organisation that encompassed the entire social movement.[5] We see this same phenomenon later in the Wafd Party in its development from 1919 to the abrogation of the 1936 treaty. We see the same phenomenon in the appearance of the political organisations of the 1952 revolution in their evolution from 'The organisation of liberation' (*Hayat at-tahrir*) through the National Union into the Arab Socialist Union. To be precise none of these organisations are parties; they are more like political clubs in the way they are organised and even more like the ordinary people in their political content; they gathered the whole of Egypt around a cause or a leader. Consequently they cannot be considered as a 'front'. They were non-controlled and non-organised movements.

These interactions of elements in the Egyptian middle classes had both economic bases and political repercussions. Let us note here that these economic bases, which are called Egyptian feudalism, have never been feudalism in the European sense, for the central state in Egypt has organised irrigation and the cultivation of the land since the dawn of written history, in such a way that the creation of a European-type enclosed feudalism was not possible. Besides this, the big landowners invested the revenue of the land in commerce, personal possessions, construction and industry. The middle classes formed of landowners, factory owners and owners of small businesses in Cairo, were organically linked with big local or foreign capital interests. Some of them were made bankrupt by their many speculations on the Stock Exchange; but others were able to escape ruin either by climbing to the upper levels or by becoming middlemen. Politically this interaction is shown by the sympathy of the regime with both the landed and commercial interests of the aristocracy. This formed an early obstacle to the independence of the middle classes; an independence that, in spite of the size of the 1919 revolution, was not achieved until the Nasser revolution. In other words this independence was gained not through the efforts of a class but through a party.

The Western colonial presence in Egypt for three-quarters of a century after Orabi's revolution and the persistence of autocratic royal power always prevented the middle class from achieving a national democratic revolution. The 1923 constitution, set up by King Fuad following and as a fruit of the 1919 revolution, is a very humble affair compared with Orabi's constitution of 1882. This constitution was suspended in 1928 and during the Second World War (1939–45). It was often flouted, notably in 1924 and 1942. During those periods there were constitutional minority governments. They censored the press, banned public meetings and arrested opponents. The press, and Orabi's demonstrations to Saad Zaghlul and to King Farouk, were the best expressions of opposition.

Egyptian liberalism officially filed for bankruptcy by signing the 1936 treaty. But that did not express the failure of liberalism in itself, nor that of the middle class in itself; it was above all the failure of the interaction, the overlapping which existed in a very complex manner between the forces of revolution and those of counter-revolution. And so the ordinary middle classes were not able to achieve independence, and democracy was not acquired by those other developing classes: the lower middle classes, the peasants, the working class and the intellectuals. Economic liberalism as a constitutional system was only applied at rare moments in our history; but during those rare moments it introduced hope and prepared the way for progress for the entire people. When it was destroyed by the West and the autocratic regime, the Egyptians' struggle became embittered and tenaciously embedded in the national consciousness. The 1936 treaty did not strike a blow at the middle class, neither did the revolution of 1952. On the contrary, the Nasser revolution allowed it for the first time to gain an independent existence, which meant that its role in the realisation of the national democratic revolution remained valid. But the revolution hardly belongs to this class any longer, for the social history of Egypt has continued to flow while it remained stagnant. Egypt has been besieged by colonialisation, autocratic power, and big landowners. The times had changed.

Nasserism and Democracy

It would be an injustice to say that Nasserism comprised a single revolution. There were, in effect, three. It would be no less of an injustice to state that any of them was a complete revolution. We would be untrue to Nasserism and to history if we affirmed that this revolution began as a putsch, because from the economic and social points of view it was a true revolution in the traditional meaning of the term. But from the point of view of its political format, it was a putsch in the accepted understanding of this term.

It was a triple revolution: the period from 1952 to 1956 represents the national revolution, which achieved independence for Egypt, a unique independence of a type not seen for tens of centuries. Seen from this viewpoint, it is more radical than the revolution of Orabi and that of 1919. The object of these last two revolutions was not the removal of the Khedive, or the King, who represented autocratic power. The revolution of 23rd July 1952 removed the last symbols of royal authority three days after it had taken power (26th July 1952). The republic was declared 11 months later (18th June 1953). Thus Gamal Abd El-Nasser was the first independent ruler of Egypt for thousands of years. This was a qualitative transition in the history of the *'Nahda'* because it was accompanied by a battle against the British occupation which culminated in the successful defence of Suez in the winter of 1956. And so the sign was given for getting rid of the two main allied enemies to the renaissance of Egypt: the West and autocracy. I said 'the sign' because on leaving the country eight years earlier the West had established its Zionist extension.

The period 1958 to 1966 represents the revolution of Arab national unity of which Egypt and Syria were the first means. In spite of the separation from Syria in 1961, the military association with the Yemen showed the continuity of Nasser's national revolution. This revolution comprised a qualitative step in the strategic recovery of Egypt's independence by securing the eastern access to the country.

The period 1961 to 1970 comprises the social revolution in spite of the failure of the economic development plan and the growth of the new class. That is where the regime, in the person of its leader, passed from the objective representation of the middle classes to that of a wider social base composed of the ordinary and lower middle classes, the peasants and the workers. It is also a new qualitative period in the history of modern Egypt, in which we see reactions to changes in the Egyptian social scene that occurred in the 1930s and 1940s. The revolution distributed the national wealth more justly. It achieved a social equilibrium militating against any possibility of civil war. Likewise, capitalist development of newly independent countries is impossible in the environment of underdevelopment created by international capitalist production. Economic, and therefore, political dependence on the West is the destiny of countries choosing, knowingly or otherwise, the path of capitalist development.

It is perhaps useful to state here that from a certain point of view the three incomplete revolutions form an entrenchment of the first one, the national revolution, for Arab national unity is Egyptian national unity in a strategic horizontal dimension. The social revolution is the national revolution when considered from the vertical social dimension. From considerations of this type one could say that the three revolutions comprised *the* perfect revolution; but all three were incomplete for one objective reason: the lack of democracy. To say that Nasserism inherited a situation from the distant and recent past would be no more than a partial explanation and cannot be used as an overall justification. Social heritage is neither static nor unidimensional. It has multiple aspects and is dynamic in its interactions. It is, therefore, wrong to blame historic mistakes on either the past alone or on the present alone. In this case the responsibility rests with the historic movement and its principal social forces i.e. those of revolution and counter-revolution.

Democracy was both absent and present in the revolution or revolutions of Nasser, and this simultaneous absence and presence characterise an entire period in the history of Egypt.

It is true that the revolution inherited non-democratic traditions in methods of government. It is also true that it inherited a massive under-development in terms of modern civilisation. But it is true also that it inherited Egypt's continuous tradition of struggle for democracy. The direct results of this struggle can be summarised as follows.

First, the revolution came from the army, the initial line of defence for the established regime. Consequently it was, 'a secret military organisation'; the basic nature was, therefore, absolutely non-democratic because here we are dealing with a pyramidal structure of obedience to orders; and it can be said that, until 1951, there were numerous levels within the organisation. The Constituent Committee of Free Officers was created at about this time; this resembled a central committee. Previously there had been a leader surrounded by his supporters among the officers. The second characteristic was that the committee was formed entirely of officers. The ordinary soldiers had no part to play, for according to the pyramidal structure of command, soldiers, when it comes to action, are considered only as machines automatically carrying out orders. The third characteristic was the almost total secrecy that was necessary in order to guarantee success and safety before the putsch. The clandestine nature signifies isolation, and execution of orders without question. With the exception of Sadat, included in the movement of Nasser's decision and unanimously accepted in 1951, none of these officers were known to have been publicly opposed to the British and the Royalist regime, even though all in one way or another had relationships with Young Egypt, the Muslim Brotherhood and the communist organisation.

These historic origins of the organisation of the Free Officers are also the socio-cultural origins comprising the precise social content, and a certain consciousness, which ensured that the revolution, once successful, was attached to its social base and that it had a particular way of dealing with the question of democracy.

Secondly, the army revolution of 23rd July 1952 came as a substitute for the ordinary Egyptian, and not as the culmination of their role as had been the case in the revolution of Orabi. The main reason for this was the decadence of the parties, starting with the Wafd and their incapability of pro-posing social alternatives to the established regime. Everything was tied up with the interests of big landowners and big merchants who were hostile to changes in ordinary Egyptian life before the Second World War. A second reason was the fragmentation of the avant-garde who were best able to represent the new ideas of the ordinary Egyptian. The avant-garde had been unable to achieve the minimum unity necessary to bring about a change in the political structure. A third reason was the fact that the middle classes always had to take an objective part in the construction of the new society, but the decadence of the Wafd, the lack of ideological cohesion, economic overlapping of the new and old classes, and the historical fear of the left, resulted in the loss of any adequate political representation. From the burning of Cairo on 26th January 1952 until the revolution, Egypt lived in a strange vacuum caused by the imminence of the fall of the regime and the absence of any alternative. The regime no longer governed and the people were incapable of taking power. A new phase of history started when the army filled this vacuum.

Thirdly, this army had returned directly from a war outside the frontiers of Egypt, the first such war since the time of Ismael. It came from Palestine where, with other Arab armies, it had been defeated by the Zionist thrust. Because it is more sensitive than any other organisation to the security of the country, it is natural that when it takes power it should be preoccupied with national sovereignty. From the moment of the Nasser revolution, the concept of national sovereignty became geographically wider than just the unity of the Nile valley.

Fourthly, there is no shame in the fact that the revolution did not have its theory previously worked out. In fact, theoretical creativity would have been preferable to a simple application of the theories of others. Besides, an explanation of the revolution by reference to its actions, both right and wrong, can in no way be considered as an explanation of its theoretical basis. In fact, what are called the Six Principles declared by the revolution prove that they lacked any historic cohesion; the young officers did not possess a very refined consciousness, in contrast to those who took part in Orabi's revolution who had attained a high level of maturity. The tragic part of this comparison is that Orabi's revolution, with his mature officers, ended in defeat, while the immature Nasserists were successful. Needless to say, the Six Principles were not the original programme of the revolution. The fact that they were later lost or forgotten proves that they represented only a minimum level of theoretical agreement among the officers.[6] From the beginning, these general ideas brought about a series of consequences that we can summarise as 'the problem of democracy'.

The first of these consequences was the fact that Egypt returned to a system of constriction of authority. This process began from the very first measures taken by the revolution in a series of practical actions: the constitution of 1933 was abrogated on 10th December 1953 and a provisional constitution was declared. This contained 11 articles, six of which dealt with general principles and the other five with the organisation of the regime. One of these latter articles gave the leaders of the revolution the freedom to undertake any action which to them seemed appropriate for the protection of the revolution, and gave them the liberty to appoint ministers and to dismiss them when they felt that to be necessary. The other two articles authorised the Prime Minister to assume both the legislative and the executive powers. On January 16th 1956 Gamal Abd El-Nasser declared a new constitution that was submitted to plebiscite five months later by the referendum on the President of the Republic. And so, on the basis of a presidential republic, Gamal Abd El-Nasser became Head of State and assumed the responsibility of executive power while retaining the post of Commander-in-Chief of the Army. In 1958, the joint constitution with Syria was abrogated and the President of the Republic decreed a constitution for a transition period. The fourth article of this constitution added that the legislative power devolved upon a National Council, whose members were to be chosen by presidential decree. After the separation in 1961, the President of the Republic remained a primary source of legislation.[7] But a new constitution was declared in 1964, which granted to the National Council or parliament the power to authorise the President of the Republic to promulgate laws.

Concerning judicial power, it is well known that the 23rd July revolution took place under the laws of exception in force since the burning of Cairo on 26th January 1952. In fact, this state of affairs continued until the constitution of 1956 was submitted to plebiscite but it was declared again at the time of the tripartite aggression in October 1956. And though removed in 1954, Law 119 of 1964 granted exceptional powers to the President of the Republic, even in normal times.[8]

In May 1967, acting within the constitution, the National Council, i.e. the parliament, authorised the President of the Republic to promulgate laws. Laws of exception were once again imposed one month later on the outbreak of the June 1967 war.

The second consequence was that the revolution annulled the principle of the existence of parties, since General Neguib had declared the dissolution of all existing political parties on 16th January 1953, after which Law No. 37 of 1953 gorbade all party activity and the formation of any political organisation (para 6). On 23rd January 1953 the Free Officers announced the formation of what was called at the time the Liberation Organisation as a political organ of the revolution whose slogan was: 'We are the organisation of liberation'. On 28th May 1957 the name was changed to the National Union with the slogan 'Union, Order and Work'. This National Union was the political organisation from the time of Egypt's union with Syria until the separation. It is only then that we hear Nasser saying:

> I believe that it is my duty to face with you, courageously and honestly, the mistakes of the past, mistakes that have led to an upsurge of reaction: (1) We made the mistake of compromising with reaction. (2) Then we fell into a serious error: incapability of popular organisation. The consequence was that reaction was able to infiltrate popular organisations and by doing so paralyse revolutionary efficiency by turning it into a simple organisational facade. (3) We have not made sufficient efforts to ensure that the people become aware of their rights.

(4) We have not been able to develop the machinery of State to the level of revolutionary action. (5) Some people, while believing in the revolution, found themselves obliged to adopt a negative attitude to the activity of the popular struggle, or, let us rather say that they could not find a position that enabled them to sincerely participate within the trend of the popular struggle.[9]

In this same speech Nasser said: 'Experience has proved that the mistake in the forming of the National Union was the opening of its doors to the forces of reaction. It is, therefore, necessary to reorganize it.'[10] This assertion not only contains a contradiction, but shows Nasser's insistence upon maintaining the one political organisation and not the party, in spite of the bitter setback it had received. This idea also shows the President's afterthought on class structure and on the capitalist nature of the economy. Nobody can dispute the objective Nasserism of the Egyptian writer Esmat Saif Ad-Daula, who, however, wrote 'The fundamental mistake made by the revolution in its attempts to solve the problems of democracy in Egypt was that it imagined that, on taking power, the hold of capitalism on the regime would come to an end.'[11] This economist-author then gives an account of the laws on the opening up of the economy as they affected local and foreign capitalism in Nasser's time. He wrote: 'Even if a council composed of the biggest capitalists had governed Egypt at the time, it would never have granted such facilities to capitalists and capitalism.'[12] Finally the author concludes that the basic mistake during the first decade of the revolution was the fact that, 'in wishing to break the hold of capitalism on the State, it opted for state capitalism, the worst of systems.'[13]

We are right, however, to ask if Nasser, or Nasserism, learnt from this setback in its experience of political organisation. The answer is 'No', for on the 4th November 1961 preparations were started for the creation of the Arab Socialist Union, from which the members affected by the economic measures taken that year had been eliminated. The Socialist Union was created by Law No. 1 of 1962 with the slogan, 'Liberty, Socialism and Unity', in order that it might become as expressed by Saif Ad-Daula, 'the bureaucratic capitalist ally'. According to this same author, this union was no more than the framework of the alliance and the means of domination by the bureaucrats and parasitic capitalism. The democratic views contained in the charter were completely forgotten. The democratic laws contained in the constitution were also obliterated.

Nasser returned to the appraisal of this experience following the shattering defeat of 1967 and the popular uprising of 1st February 1968. The declaration was made on 30th March: a warning addressed to the new class that had become well established since 1965. In the face of bureaucracy it threatened to create a state of institutions, the sovereignty of the law and the upholding of the formula for alliance between the popular working-class movements, i.e. the single political organisation. It is true that Nasser proceeded with the re-creation of the Arab Socialist Union by means of elections from top to bottom of the organisation, but it is also true that the 30th March declaration remained a dead letter. On 20th January 1965, about five years before his death, Nasser declared: 'We cannot pretend that our generation has accomplished its task while we are not striving for continuity of progress; without this striving all that we would have accomplished could, however great it may be, be changed in a single flash of light and quickly extinguished.'[14] It was as though Nasser was foreseeing the future, but foreseeing also means being aware, and being aware implies a certain responsibility.

The third of these consequences consists in the fact of the replacement of the party or parties by the State itself, to the extent that the Minister of the Interior became the Secretary-General of the Socialist Union. Thus the State became the party and, with its administrative and executive systems, the State became the sole means of political action. Political attachment meant attachment to the State. Political activity was concentrated under the personal direction of leaders of the State and society, and took the form of administrative order. Political relationships gave way to administrative relationships. Leadership was confused with management. Regency was confused with administrative hierarchy. From the organisational point of view, the entire revolution emanated from within the machinery of State. The State became the organised institution of the revolution. And so politics were confused with administration;[15] the machinery of State became political and administrative machinery at one and the same time.[16] All in all, because of these overlappings, the President became a source of legislation. The leader became the institution of sovereignty, he was both the people and the State. At one time Nasser even went as far as extolling what he called 'one single Arab movement'. The State and the people became synonymous where decision and action were concerned. Nasserism, therefore, had no need of a political staff within an organisation; for the organisation was no longer the place where policy was formed, or where decisions were taken, as is always the case in political parties. Neither was it a voice of propaganda to the population. This function had been assumed by the mass media, under the direction of the Minister of Information and by addresses in the mosques which, in most cases, were under the control of the Minister of the Wakf. It was no longer the organisation responsible for sounding public opinion; this task had been assumed by several state organisations; thus the State became the Party.[17]

The fourth of these consequences concerns the press, which found itself in the same situation as the political organisation. The press was controlled by law, as it was impossible to abolish it, as had been the case with the political parties. Newspapers were changed into official administrative units as part of the machinery of State; journalists became civil servants like any others in the administration. They took orders from their superiors, i.e. the Minister of Information or the Information Office Censor. And so the four powers fused into one single power. Thought became synonymous with information; it became the echo of the one voice. The press, like the political organisation, became a huge blanket that covered everybody.

The fifth of these consequences began with an early event of deep significance: the execution by hanging of two workers from the textile factories
of Kafedawar in the south-west of the delta in 1953. The condemned men,
whose names were Khamis and Al Bakari, had claimed the right to strike. The
strange thing is that the private sector, i.e. traditional capitalist production,
was at its peak; nevertheless the revolution, which included among its
principles the ending of capitalist hegemony over the regime, had condemned
the two workers for having claimed the right to set up a democratic relationship between workers and capitalists. This was the same revolution that,
during the crisis of March 1954, was based on a strike and occupation of
premises by public transport workers who were in favour of rejecting the
democratic way. The workers asked the regime not to authorise the creation
of parties. They said they did not want electoral campaigns and some of them
put up placards on which they had written, 'Down with liberty'.[18]

Relationships between the State and the workers' and Professionals'
unions were governed by the fact that all members of a union had first to be
a member of the Arab Socialist Union. The Minister of the Interior was also
Secretary-General of the Socialist Union, and most of the time, the Minister
of Education was the Secretary of the Teachers' Union, the Minister of
Labour Secretary of the Workers' Unions. And so the leadership of the
popular and professional organisations was merged at the highest level.

This overlapping collection of factors and consequences lead us to ask
not if Nasser was a dictator[19] but rather to ask a much more important
question: Did Nasserism, with its defeats before its victories, add a new
dimension to the problem of democracy in Egypt? There can be no doubt
that independence of the national will of the Egyptian people had become
the indispensable condition for any new formula of democracy capable of
organising the strong class relationships within society. The independence of
this will could only be achieved by the elimination of direct foreign forces
(the occupation) and indirect forces (in the economy) as well as the local
basis of these forces (the system of ownership and middlemen).

The second contribution of Nasserism was the fact that Egyptian independence became 'the Arab independence of the Egyptian people' because
the national sovereignty of Egypt could only be realised through Arab
national sovereignty and through the deep and dialectic relationship
between the region and the nation.

Thirdly, independence, or rather the will of Egypt, became that of the
widest sections of the populace taking part in national production in order
to reduce the gap between the forces and the output of production, so that
the social transformation necessary to bring about this closing of the gap
would become an objective complementary action for independence
within the perspective of a renaissance of the whole of society.

Such were the factors of the Nasser revolution. But these negative
factors were extremely grave; the army was transformed from a simple
instrument of change into a model for the construction of the regime and

society; in other words, civil life was militarised. The ideological hypothesis of the leader of the revolution was put into practice in social terms, by the fact that a large number of military people entered civilian life in order to take up posts in the nationalised sector as a reward for the change which they had helped to bring about. They thus became a branch of society with definite interests against further change; and, as they had chosen the role of administrators of production, it was more or less natural that they should be strongly linked to the technocrats on one side and the bureaucrats on the other, as also applied to the relationship between these three elements and middlemen operations. And so the nucleus was formed, which Nasser himself, in 1965 (towards the end of the developmnent plan and the start of the economic decline) called 'the new class having no productive capital'.

This class held all the powers of decision and all the means of execution, and consequently they were not interested in anything to do with control of their activities or with participation in the decision-making process. They could see no advantage in any democratic formula. The one political organisation in which the whole of Egypt was gathered was their class's best means for weakening the social struggle and attempting to put a stop to it. This nucleus, that was assimilated into, yet separated from the regime, blessed the decisions coming from above without participating in them. At the moment of execution they spontaneously separated themselves from the regime. The same thing happened to the press, the rest of the media, the professional workers' unions and all other popular organisations. Total economic liberalism during the first ten years of the revolution did not produce corresponding political liberalism. In the years that followed, economic planning also had no popular democratic consequences. And so the revolution remained an incomplete revolution during these three periods: national, Arab national and social. The national, Arab national and social struggle lacked the basic element: democracy. It is true that it had a moment of theoretical creativity, during which a new democratic formula was worked out for the developing world in order to safeguard independence and renaissance. But the revolution missed its opportunity. It never realised that national or social democracy cannot be achieved without political democracy. For Egypt, the Arabs and the Third World the cost of the absence of this basic principle, which could consolidate the various levels of democracy (the achievement of independence, Arab unity and economic development) was incalculable. We are not referring here to the thousands of Egyptian and Arab martyrs who fell on the battlefield for democracy, or of the thousands who died on the battlefield for the nation. We are speaking of the defeat of Egyptian and Arab independence in 1967; of the defeat of the *Nahda* at the putsch of 1971; of the defeat suffered by the Third World generally for, just as Nasser's Egypt was a model of renaissance for the developing world after the Second World War, it was also the key to its fall in the 1970s.

The Democracy of the Putsch

President Sadat, in a kind of confession, relates that the day after the revolution a split occurred in the revolutionary council. It was over the choice of the type of regime for the future; democracy or dictatorship. Nasser was the only one in favour of democracy, within the framework of liberalism, while the others wanted dictatorship. Nasser resigned and went home. The others changed their minds and Nasser withdrew his resignation.[20]

This took place at the beginning of the revolution. But, several months later, a series of anti-democratic measures were taken which reached their peak in March 1954, and this time the situation was reversed: Nasser and the others turned away from liberalism and the two officers of the left, Khaled Mohyi Ad-Din and Yussef Saddiq, were in favour. The former was exiled to Europe and the latter was imprisoned.[21]

Towards the end of the revolution, between 1964 and 1965, the documents show that Nasser tried to build 'a revolutionary party or a socialist vanguard'. On the night of 14th May 1971, this vanguard party fell at the first attack by the forces of counter-revolution, for Mamduh Salem, Governor of Alexandria, took over the leadership of the Ministry of the Interior. El Laiffi Nassef, leader of the Republican Guard, and General Mohamed Ahmed Saadef, Chief of Staff, and President Sadat himself, were members of the secret party, as this revolutionary party was called. In fact it was a secret party for the people and not for the counter-revolution. The most important members were appointed according to their position in the State hierarchy and not by other criteria. That is why the party fell. Its fall left no echo. It fell in secret just as it had been created in secret.

The significance of these two episodes is that the Nasser revolution during these two stages, the liberal economy and the planned economy, never succeeded in establishing political liberalism during the first period nor a revolutionary party in the second period. The lack of democracy during the period of union with Syria was one of the fundamental causes of the breach which enabled the separation to occur. These two periods prove to us that, although Nasser was liberal in the first period and revolutionary in the second, he was unable to establish either liberalism or a revolutionary party. Personal intentions were not the problem and neither was the temperament of the leader of the revolution; he simply did not take account of the unchanging elements in the Egyptian social situation.[22]

The root of the problem is that the Egyptian middle class seized power during the three stages of the Nasser revolution in reaction to its threatened existence during the three-quarters of a century preceding its independence. The fact that it monopolised the regime was also a reaction against the growth of the popular classes during the 30 years preceding the revolution of 1952. Despite the contradiction between Nasserism and the middle classes on the subject of capitalist development and consequently on the type of regime, all the economic and social interests of the middle classes caused it to take power without considering the fact that this monopoly in a developing society would lead to what is called dictatorship.

This Egyptian middle class revenge against the liberalism of the monarchy, which had held it within the thrall of foreign monopolies and the landed aristocracy, enabled it to become independent to such a degree that it was alone on the scene although this did not enable it to acquire freedom of political movement. The fear of the people held by this class led to nationalisation of democracy along with other economic nationalisations affecting the higher levels of the middle classes, a thing which consolidated its independence without giving it the ability to achieve the *Nahda* which in the changed conditions following the revolution of 1952 could not be one-dimensional in economic terms.

Such was the end of the national democratic revolution in Egypt. The military defeat of 1967 was fatal to it; the constitutional putsch of 1971 was the death blow. There were two possible paths of action: a total cultural revolution which, in the field of economy and political democracy, would repeal in the most radical way possible, all the measures undertaken; or a counter-revolution sanctioning the social and economic fall by complete openness to the foreign monopolies to such a degree that Egypt would once again become a satellite of the big foreign monopolies. The effect of individuals and the regime in some social categories monopolising power favoured the second choice as opposed to cultural revolution.

In reality, Sadat's Egypt did not have a counter revolution against Nasserism as suggested by the events of 14th May 1971. This counter-revolution sanctioned what had already taken place on 5th June 1967, the open declaration of which was blocked by the historic personality of Nasser. At the time, the counter-revolutionary forces were ready to go on the offensive on the 9th June 1967 to such a degree that in several places the walls of the Arab Socialist Union were already covered with photographs of Zukariyyah Ed-Din, appointed by Nasser in his resignation speech to undertake negotiations with the Americans. The action taken by the Egyptian population on the evening of 9th June to prevent Nasser from resigning was a spontaneous rejection of the taking of power by the counter-revolution, with a vague hope for a cultural revolution expressed by the word 'Change' and slogans such as 'Continuity of the Revolution' among others. The population gave a unique chance to the leader of the uncompleted revolution and of the Six Day War defeat in order that he himself could proceed with change. The will of the people was one thing, but they were unable to perceive the objective impossibility of a change brought about by a single person. In fact it was not just that the road from Suez to Cairo was open to the military enemy, but that the road from Alexandria to Aswan was open to the class enemy, the national enemy; this fatal vacuum existed between 1967 and 1971, the year of the revolution and the year of the counter-revolution.

The second truth is that Sadat's Egypt is not an Egyptian counter-revolution but it is well and truly a national counter-revolution against the Arabs in Egypt for, just as Egyptian social history does not contain the least hint of civil war, so domestically inspired counter-revolution is impossible. This is a unique feature of the Egyptian situation. In reality counter-revolutions in Egypt have always been the result of relationships between foreigners and the rootless social classes such as the middlemen.[23] But we should add here that, when this alliance between the foreign and the local (and by local we do not mean national) takes place, it polarises the widest social classes, even those whose strategic interests are contradictory to those of such an alliance. This polarisation succeeds most of the time because of the historic facts connecting revolution and counter-revolution in the political and economic context of Egypt; it has always characterised the birth and development of the Egyptian middle classes and is also the result of this class's failure to understand the technical meaning of the term and its constant desire for a wide political organisation encompassing and absorbing all the contradictions.

There is no doubt that the absence of democracy at the time of the Nasserist revolution, which had control of the levers of liberation and development, cleared the path for counter-revolution in Egypt in the 1970s. Because of this, development became alienated and society changed from a producer to a consumer society. Development, therefore, consisted in the promotion of import/export in the interest of foreign capital and the local middlemen and without any control either by the country or society.

The question we must ask then is, 'Is Egypt capable of achieving democracy under Sadat?'

The theoretical answer is that it is impossible for a putsch to use a force which could turn against itself and which does not accord with its social identity, its political function or its economic goal. Democracy was a missing component during the Nasser revolution. But in the counter-revolution, it constitutes an actual threat. That is why Sadat's putsch could not lead either to middle-class liberalism, popular democracy, or even less to a democratic creativity able to surpass other models in the world without closing in upon itself. Why? For a reason that comes from the very heart of the Egyptian social identity, the fact that democracy is the necessary support for the most progressive advocates of the *Nahda* in society as a whole, and for the productive classes in particular. But there is also another reason. It is that this putsch had to totally liquidate the national revolution where it concerned the liberation of the land in so far as development is concerned. In this case the land becomes simply a regional geographic line. It is no longer part of a whole, that of the Arab nation; and the economy no longer has either roots or nationality. In this case Egyptian capital becomes no more than a satellite of a planet composed of the most powerful and productive group of international monopolies.

Egypt under Sadat has no desire to achieve democracy for neither the international monopolies, nor Zionist capital nor the Egyptian middleman is interested in this democracy. To them democracy is the very antithesis of what they want, not only in its means but also in its ends.

Let us now put forward our theoretical examination of the progress of Egyptian democracy in the Egypt of Sadat during the past eight years. Before proceeding with this examination, however, we must deal with two very important points: The first is that the counter-revolution in Egypt is not a revolt against Nasserism in particular. In fact the counter-revolution against Nasserism is a preventive war against a total revolution — that cultural revolution that could recover the democracy missing from the time of Nasser, and in consequence lead to liberation, to development and to progress in society. If then the counter-revolution is not basically against Nasserism, neither is it an extension of it. The counter-revolution has always exploited the deficiencies of the Nasser revolution. There is, in fact, a large difference between extension and exploitation of an open breach. The only extension that was theoretically possible was radical revolution, but the Nasser administration did nothing of that sort until 1971. The proposition that the counter-revolution was fatal can be examined but it is impossible to consider it to be an extension of the Nasser revolution. During 18 years and in bloody and dearly paid for battles against colonialism, the Nasser revolution proved that it was a national revolution which for many reasons was unable to achieve the democratic revolution. It is therefore impossible to pretend that this revolution produced the counter-revolution, despite the fact that it had prepared the way for the success of the counter-revolution.

The second point is that what has happened during the last eight years is a thorough-going international revolution against the Arabs in Egypt. Egypt in fact is not a market for international investment; she possesses neither energy nor natural resources that can be coveted. Egypt forms the most solid link in the contemporary Arab revolution for reasons related to the fact that it is the key to the two great African and Arab doorways. This strategic situation is supported by a powerful social and cultural significance, for Egypt sets the example. (As for Lebanon, in spite of its situation and its prominence, its socio-economic structure makes it the weak link in the contemporary Arab revolution.)

In reality Nasser wanted to hush up the first stages of the international counter-revolution when it attacked him personally. He thought that the tragedy would be covered up by the summit of September 1970. He did not realise that all he had seen was the prologue of this bloody drama for, by his death, he was announcing the most important act. The Arab seaways, and the strategic situation of the Middle East parallel to the belly of the Soviet Union, have always been areas of traditional colonialist and now renewed imperialist influence. In spite of the contradiction between the two countries, the Egyptian example of independence and development and the Lebanese example of a liberal religious society complement each other in facing Western influence and Zionist racism. After the defeat of 1967, the Palestinian question took the form of the resistance movement in Lebanon. The revolution in Sudan in May 1968 and the revolution in Iraq in July that same year, as well as the revolution of 1st September 1969 in Libya, when considered together make it possible to see the defeat of 1967 as simply a battle lost, as Nasser had said. It was just at that moment that the West decided to strike a strategic blow against the Arabs in Egypt and Lebanon in order to preserve the energy sources, the maritime corridors and the strategic security zone for the United States in the Middle East. It was necessary then to strike at the key or model presented by the resistance in Egypt. It was necessary to strike at the religious liberalism and the Palestinian resistance in Lebanon.

But just as the mobilisation time of the fleet had been accomplished with the Vietnam war, so the local elements in the two countries, Egypt and Lebanon, were to receive orders and carry them out only in a manner appropriate to the conditions in each country. And so in Egypt there was a struggle, a conditional putsch, and in Lebanon there was total war. The concomitance of these two events was in no way a chance occurrence, for the direct strategic target of the international counter-revolution was the Arab nation. In fact Cairo and Beirut were just two elements of a preventative war against a potential cultural revolution.

The Lebanonisation of Egypt?

Two dramatic scenes enacted by the putsch regime during the 1970s draw/ our attention.

The first was when President Sadat decided to destroy the internment camp at Torra, as a symbol of the destruction of the Nasserist internment camps and an end to the exceptional measures. The second was when the Minister of the Interior, accompanied by a group of Egyptian and foreign journalists, witnessed the destruction of tape recordings made by Nasser's secret service of conversations between politicians. At that time nobody paid any attention to the factor common to both these scenes: the symbolic destruction of the Torra prison, situated to the south of Cairo and to the north of the Hellouan suburb, did not in any way signify that the prisons of Egypt were to be converted into gardens, but merely the freeing of the members of the Muslim Brotherhood who had been imprisoned as a result of the trials in 1965 following their attempted assassination of Nasser. Also freed at this time were several Israeli and Egyptian spies as well as the writer Mustafa Amin, condemned to five years' imprisonment in 1965 for intelligence activities with American security organisations. Furthermore the symbolic destruction of the magnetic tapes irrefutably proves that the severity practised by the Nasser security organisations was the lot of almost all democratic and leftist politicians. Let us recall in relation to this that as a result of recordings made by these organisations during a family reunion Lutfi Al-Khuli, the writer of the left, his wife and Mrs Nawal Al-Mahalaui, secretary to Mohammad Hassanein Haykal (until 1970) and her husband, were detained over a period of several months and were not freed until after Nasser's death.

After the fall of the Nasser group in 1971 these two dramatic scenes gave the impression that the new regime had the firm intention of 'Lebanonising' Egypt, i.e. of taking this liberal model as their inspiration in the political life of society. Many Egyptians were satisfied with these moves as many of them had suffered imprisonment during the nationalisation of democracy to the benefit of a certain category of society and not to the benefit of the regime. But these measures were only for the sake of appearances, for their political content indicates a certain Saudi quality, and that was a pointer for the future; while the destruction of the magnetic tapes in the inner court of the Ministry of the Interior was no more than a condemnation of the past and an attempt to conquer the left by reminding it of the bad times it had experienced. It was an invitation to the left to regain its freedom within the framework of the regime and for the left to recognise the situation.

We should add to these two scenes, which nobody took very seriously, the decisions and measures taken from the beginning of the putsch. In fact the initiative presented by Sadat in February 1971 and the Law on Arabo-foreign investment promulgated in September 1971 were inseparable. The first initiative defined the identity of the regime even before it was established in May 1971, while the second underlined its economic character after having got rid of the power of the Nasser group. The first initiative was the first step on the path to open political relations with the West and with Israel. The second was the beginning of the open economy. The plebiscite on the Russian advisers in 1972 marked the beginning of the military opening. Towards the end of 1972 and the beginning of 1973 Egypt began to react by way of protests by students and intellectuals; these were in opposition to the religious troubles. It was in this that the first fruits of the new regime were seen in Law No. 34 of 1972 concerning the protection of national unity. It was noted that Article 8 of this new law emphasised that the Arab Socialist Union was the only political organisation expressing the unity of the popular working force. In previous constitutional documents, including the constitution of the putsch, no mention had been made of the Socialist Union as a sole political organisation. This formula was in opposition to any kind of independent political organisation that could form the basis of opposition to the regime. This article declared: 'Any political organisation existing apart from the Arab Socialist Union or other popular organisation is inadmissable and illegal.' We should recall here that during the uprising of the workers, students and intellectuals, new political organisations had grown out of the professional unions, the students and workers' unions, the national committees, permanent congresses and the self-management of factories.

These were the types of organisations that were independent of the clandestine organisations of the left or the right. The new regime soon recognised the danger of these organisational initiatives which in themselves were a threat to the regime's attempt to regain popular control. To counteract this pressure from the base, the putschist mentality had to practise a legal cover-up for the repression that it imposed. Although the internment camps were destroyed or closed, the prisons remained open and subject to the law. The law can be promulgated at any time, even if it is against basic human rights and the basic principles of the constitution. To the regime, the law is a protection from upheaval. Article 3 of the new law 'condemned to prison all those who create, organise or manage an association, organisation or group other than those covered by the preceding article. All those who take the initiative to inform the police of such organisations will not be subject to this penalty.' Article 4 condemns to imprisonment 'all those who endanger national unity.' Article 5 condemns to imprisonment 'all those who divulge information or spread rumours with the intention of attacking national unity.'

Three main comments may be made concerning this new law. Its clauses are inspired by those added by Ismael Sidki Pasha to Egyptian law during the national struggle against the British occupation and the throne. However, important modifications have been introduced. The law on liberty in the time of the monarchy, the British occupation and the minority governments included in its Article 98, paragraph 1, the penalisation of organisations or groups aimed at establishing hegemony of one class over another or the destruction of a class or the overthrow of the regime by force or terrorism. Paragraph 2 of Article 98 penalises all those who spread rumours in order to change the principles of the constitution on a class basis or to establish the domination of one class over another. It can be seen that the old law was much more liberal than the new one, for it did not condemn the creation of organisations or associations as such. In fact it had been promulgated at a time when the multi-party situation had been recognised by the constitution itself. It did, however, condemn a particular action, 'hegemony of one class over another by means of violence'. The new law mentions something that has no precise constitutional definition: 'the threat against national unity'. What is this national unity and when is it exposed to danger?

The second comment that can be made is drawn from the report of the commission on legislative affairs. The report of the inaugural session of the National Congress on the necessity for the preservation of the national unity states: 'The application of this declaration by the President of the Republic requires the People's Council to meet in an extraordinary session for the examination of the law on national unity.'[12] This means that the President of the Republic alone has the authority to define this unity. It must be added that it was the President himself who had called for the promulgation of such a law following pacifist demands for the application of democracy. Taken as a whole, the paragraphs of this law are anti-democratic, with the exception of one paragraph concerning freedom of belief which, however, adds nothing to the clauses of the constitution.

It should be added that the constitution of the 1971 putsch stipulates in Article 74:

> When danger threatens national unity, the security of the country or prevents the State institutions from accomplishing their constitutional role, the President of the Republic can take rapid measures to meet this danger and within the next 60 days will go to the people with a plebiscite on these measures before putting them into effect.

This text, which is completely foreign to the constitution of 1964 was constructed following the events of May 1971. The legislation on national unity was made on the pretext of the events of 1972. As the Egyptian people had taken seriously the democratic policies pronounced by the regime, the President of the Republic had to have recourse to his constitutional right to promulgate a law that would not even have been recognised in the constitution of 1923. In fact neither the King nor the Prime Minister would, at that time, have been able to approve such a deliberately ambiguous law to enable the President to judge matters according to his own opinion when danger threatened national unity. What it meant was that on the basis of this law students and workers were imprisoned at the same time as Muslim Brotherhood members were freed.

In economic matters, the law of 2nd September 1971 concerning foreign investments in Egypt was rounded out by a series of laws among which the following are particularly important: Law No. 1216 of 1972 concerning the administrative organisation of sequestered property;[25] Law No. 52 of 1972 concerning the liquidation of sequestered property subject to Law No. 150 of 1964;[26] Law No. 53 of 1962 concerning property sequestered before the promulgation of Law No. 34 of 1971.[27] The three laws were promulgated on the same day, the 1st October 1972, by the President of the Republic. We should, however, note that they were not all published in the official gazette on the same date; the last two laws were published 14 days after the first, which is reasonable as the liquidation of sequestered property stipulated by Laws 52 and 53 of 1972 must precede the liquidation of the administrative organisation of property sequestered, as decided by the Law No. 1216. It may be proper that all these laws should have been published on the same day, but it is not proper that they should be published directly by the President of the Republic without recourse to popular plebiscite, as such laws involve national unity in their social content. Let us recall that the sequesters had been imposed on the property of several of the big quasi-feudal landowners which, from the Nasserite point of view, guaranteed valid social transformation. To restore these properties unconditionally does not signify a return to liberalism but rather a disturbance in the balance of forces, an imbalance adopted and recognised by law. Let us also note that the publication of the laws on the legislation concerning sequestered property was accompanied by the strengthening of the power of the socialist Attorney General who had accomplished his unique task during the putsch by bringing the Nasserite group to justice, accusing them of high treason before even starting the enquiry. Having once accomplished his task, the function of the Attorney General became more powerful than the judiciary as though this 'civil' function replaced the military tribunals. The socialist Attorney General had the right to arrest on sight any citizen suspected of being a threat to national unity. This of course has nothing to do with the question of sequestered property, which was his responsibility. In fact those who were arrested on his orders — workers and intellectuals — had never been owners of sequestered property. In short, acting on state security information alone he could, for no other reason, remove the freedom of people. And so, in the name of the law, the socialist Attorney General wielded a power greater than that of the magistrature and greater than that of the courts.

Thus was the liberalism of the putsch born . . . a corpse whose winding sheet had been prepared in advance. In reality the new regime did not abandon the essence of the former constitution, nor its exceptional measures. It even conferred wider powers on the President of the Republic than even the former President had enjoyed. In fact the 1971 constitution stipulates in Article 73 that the President of the Republic is the guardian of the limitation of powers which, in cases of necessity, in exceptional circumstances and on the basis of authorisation by the People's Council with a two-thirds majority, can promulgate Orders-in-Council. Article 112 grants the President of the Republic the right to promulgate laws or to veto them. According to Article 137, the President of the Republic is granted executive power, and consequently has the right to preside over the meetings of the Council of Ministers. Article 147 stipulates: 'If in the absence of the People's Council circumstances require measures that cannot be delayed, the President of the Republic has the right to take steps which have the force of law.' Article 152 grants the President the right to turn to the people and he is himself elected by plebiscite.

This means that the new constitution has not abandoned the Presidential system but has added to it rights which, in practice, make the President the absolute master. On the other hand, at the beginning, the new system preserved the Arab Socialist Union, adding to it the principle that it should be the sole political organisation. It created the post of socialist Attorney General to deal with matters transferred to him by Security and having nothing to do with civil justice. Let us recall that these measures were taken at the same time that a new foreign policy was declared in February 1971 and contested by the Supreme Security Council and the High Executive Committee of the Arab Socialist Union at the time. The President of the Republic ignored this opposition and decided by himself to reopen the Suez Canal after a partial retreat by the Israeli Army. Let us finally recall that these measures were taken within the framework of a domestic policy in support of the private commercial sector and in particular of the group of speculators and parasites on production. Arab and foreign capital were almost begged to support this sector. It was in the framework of this democracy that Muslim Brothers, foreign spies, and Egyptians were imprisoned. Students and workers were imprisoned for the slightest pacific recourse to meetings, or publication of declarations. For certain others a disciplinary committee of the Socialist Arab Union was created. This was also a committee that was unknown in the previous political system. This committee expelled more than 100 artists, writers and journalists from their active membership. Later these same people were expelled from their professional unions which also implied their dismissal from their jobs.

What is the significance of all these paradoxes concerning democracy which deceived the entire world into thinking that it was a liberal move against dictatorship? The Egyptian Marxist thinker Michael Kamel wrote concerning this matter: 'In reality the regime, in proposing its liberal conception of democracy and in the context of the various layers of middle classes representing the social and economic basis of the regime, was undertaking to end the monopoly of power by a single hegemonic category.'[28] This reply is correct in general terms, but it can lend itself to different interpretations concerning the identity of the economic content of the putsch; for to pretend that the various middle-class categories constitute the social base of the regime is too general. For example, agricultural capitalism could rise again but it is the higher levels, those closest to the big landowners, who began to play a more and more significant role. The commercial middle classes could also rise again but it is sections concerned with accruing interest that could be determinant where the taking of political decisions is concerned. If we consider the laws for the rectification of the Agricultural Reform and those conceiving economic development, we will discover that it was the non-productive categories who profited most among the average farmers, small merchants, artisans and lower civil servants. This means that the middle class also suffered together with large sections of the middle classes, the workers and the poor peasants. It is, therefore, true that the whole process of alleged democratisation was a matter of an undertaking by the regime, but it was particularly addressed to Arab and foreign investors and to their inside agents. In fact the regime promised that it would not restrict itself to the category from which it was formed and that it would not exceed the limits imposed by the new social alliance.

This type of liberalism will be very upset after the strategic decision on the October war. In fact this had enabled the social categories whose interests were objectively opposed to those represented by the new regime of the counter-revolution to regroup under its auspices. They were driven by the new thinking that was hostile to the national line and under the influence of their own middle-class ambition. They were also driven by reaction to the Nasser style of power, but above all they were unaware of their own true interests because of their long period of deprivation of political and party activity.[29] On the whole, this analysis by Michael Kamel is true, but it needs developing because social interaction was occurring even within the regime. In fact the September 1971 law concerning foreign investments did not convince foreign investors. The subsequent law of 1974 cleared a lot more ground for them and offered them guarantees, to the detriment of the majority of Egyptians. On the other hand, however, a liberalism depending on a single party and on a socialist Attorney General was not convincing enough to make such an undertaking credible. Later events proved it: in the summer of 1974 the Islamic Liberation Party tried to overthrow the regime by force of arms in an attempt to seize the Military Technical College. This formula with its contradiction between its form and its basis, and between a supposed economic liberalism and an actual disguised dictatorship, could not conceal its troubles. In fact it was a false economic liberalism, for the productive middle class began to suffer from the unpleasant consequences of the middlemen's monopolisation of political power; they were subject to an overseas master. Liberalism, therefore, had no deep roots within society. It was simply a facade that could not be taken seriously; a facade for a highly profit-making dictatorship. In fact economic liberalism in an underdeveloped and recently independent society cannot be achieved by forcing things, and many underdeveloped societies have trodden the path towards dependence even after being liberated. In these conditions economic liberalism becomes an impossible dream.

In fact the crisis of the regime between 1975 and 1977 set it in opposition to both the right and the left. We can discern a logical connection between the development of foreign policy from the Second Sinai Agreement up to the Camp David Agreement. But at the same time we should note the successive breakdown of the various terms of the false democracy. As opposed to any democratic practice aimed at creating the link (absent in Nasser's time) between liberation, development and national unity, the regime had discovered a remedy: it had legalised repression.

Forbidden Thinking

Whatever interpretation can be made about the absence of political democracy under Nasser, there remains an undeniable truth: Nasserism was always frightened of organised thinking capable of expressing itself in organisations that were independent of the State and its administration; but on the other hand the communications media enjoyed a large measure of freedom of thought and expression. Press, radio, television, publishers, theatres, cinemas, and the plastic arts expressed visions and values that were not identified with the regime, its thinking or its consciousness. A few examples must be given to show how these forums appeared as replacements for the parties.

Al-Ahram published the magazine *Assiassa Adoulia* whose chief editor was Boutros Ghali, the present Minister of State for Foreign Affairs and known for his right-wing tendencies. Close by on the sixth floor of the same building, the magazine of the left *At-Taliah* was published by a group of former communists under the leadership of Lutfi Al-Khuli. The daily newspaper *Al-Ahram* itself published articles by Muhammad Heykal, Louis Awad, Naguib Mahfouz, Tewfiq El Hakim, Muhammad Said Ahmed, Lutfi Al-Khuli and Boutros Ghali, each having his own particular political tendency. Admittedly, a certain balance is needed in Egyptian thinking but only on the condition that this balance is wisely controlled — a certain facade is also necessary to give the regime a form of democracy — but this balance is often disturbed, and stones are often aimed at this facade. Nasser himself, in a meeting with the editorial staff of *At-Taliah* in 1969, complained of the attitude taken by this magazine of the left towards the student activities of 1968.

During all the incompleted stages of Nasserism, the polemics never ceased between the newspaper *Al Gumhuriyyah,* the most radical forum: *Al-Ahram* which was distinguished by its moderation; and *Al-Akhbar,* which was the organ of the right. Sometimes events necessitated changes in the management of these press organs to such a point that Khaled Moheddine and Mahmud Amin El Ralem at one time had responsibility for *Akhbar El-Yom;* the writer of the right, Sabri, was transferred to *Al-Gumhuriyyah* for a very brief period; the journalist Husein Abd El Razek of *Al-Gumhuriyyah* was imprisoned for having violently criticised Haykal; and finally Djemal El Kouteifi, legal adviser of *Al-Ahram,* was imprisoned for having dealt with a law that had not yet been published in the official gazette. In the literary field there was a wider margin of liberty. The novelist Naguib Mahfuz was able to publish his most important works from *Les Enfants de notre ruelle* to *Miramar* (and these were novels that frankly and bitterly criticised the regime) without being exposed to the least prejudice. On the contrary, he was promoted within the administration to the highest grade of the bureaucracy. When Al Azhar opposed the publication of the novel *Les Enfants de notre ruelle,* El-Ahram published it as a serial. This was the first novel that enabled Naguib Mahfuz to reach the general public by means of a daily newspaper.[30]

The Muslim researcher Mahmud Chaker, in a series of articles replied to Louis Awad when he began to publish his series of critical articles entitled *En marge de El Ghofran.* Telegrams from religious extremists accusing Louis Awad of the worst kind of racism rained on *Al-Ahram* and the Presidency of the Republic. The extent of threats to kill Awad reached such a degree that (with the authority of the Minister of the Interior), he had to carry a pistol which he did not know how to use. Meanwhile *El-Ahram* continued to publish the series and the magazine, *Al Rissalah,* in opposition to Louis Awad, continued to publish replies without any intervention from the government. During the National Congress of those bodies responsible for drawing up the National Charter and justifying social transformation (1961 to 1962), Khaled published a book entitled, *Au debut, c'etait le verbe.* This book was censored because the author called for the liberation of the left and the right. On learning of the matter, Nasser ordered the immediate release of the book. This same situation repeated itself when Abd El Wahman Al-Charkai had his book, *Muhammad, Apotre de la liberte,* seized by the censor. The administration changed its mind on receipt of a telegram from the author addressed to President Nasser. There was also the famous affair of the poet Nazar Kabani concerning his poen, *En marge du cahier de la defaite.* Certainly none of these examples indicate the existence of democracy, for it was the President himself (when he knew about it) who intervened. But in terms of objective reality it can be stated that during the whole of the period of Nasser's regime only one of Mustafa Mahmud's books was censored and this had been published in the form of articles in the magazine *Rose El-Youssef* between 1956 and 1957, the book of which bore the title *Dieu et l'Homme.*

During the two decades of Nasser's power, the Egyptian theatre became

a kind of parliament, a place for popular demonstrations, violently criticising aspects of negativity, absence, impotence, and of various points of
view. In most cases it was a directly political theatre. It is true that the
authors took the precaution of not implicating the Rai's in the areas of criticism. But this in no way prevented certain works from criticising it. Most of
these works dealt with liberation, development and democracy as a broken
triangle before and after the 1967 defeat.

All this was a Nasserite tradition in the absence of a proper formula for
democratic progress. What, then, did the counter-revolution do under the
banner of liberalism? We can answer this question with the following facts.

After the putsch of 14th May 1971, Egyptian journalists believed that
they were entering a period of professional freedom where the new State
would not practise any hegemony over the press. This was natural because
just one month later they had the chance to form the first union which conducted free elections for its management committee. The candidates of the
democratic left, with all their tendencies, were overwhelmingly successful.
The new management committee represented and backed the journalists'
struggle for democracy. They therefore resumed the struggle for the suppression of censorship, an action that ended in temporary success. Colleagues
who, in the past, had been transferred into non-journalistic institutions
because of their opinions, studies and doctrines, were also able to obtain
a Charter of Honour protecting the freedom of the journalist. This Charter
guaranteed respect for state secrets and protected society as a whole from
defamatory actions. They were able to draw up a new statute capable of
avoiding a repetition of past errors. But as soon as the journalists took the
side of the students, intellectuals and workers during their 1972 uprising, the
new committee immediately ceased to act, for half its members as well as
about 100 other journalists were expelled from the Arab Socialist Union,
which implied their expulsion from their Union and their positions with the
publications that employed them. This massacre took place on 11th February
1973 and was the beginning of the battle between the regime and the press
which had tried to convert the policies of liberalism into tangible reality.

Following the war of October 1973, there were several studies published
demonstrating divergent views of the American role in the peace negotiations.
Among these we can cite the opposition of Muhammad Haykal (Chief Editor
of *Al-Ahram*) to the meeting with the United States, the break with the
Soviet Union, the concessions to Israel and the isolation of Egypt with
respect to the other Arab countries. This opposition which, until that time
at least, had not gone as far as basically challenging the regime, resulted in the
dismissal of Haykal from the editorship of *Al-Ahram*. From that time on he
was forbidden to write for the press. In his place Ali Amin, a writer of the
right, was appointed. Just one week before the October War President Sadat
granted an amnesty to the proscribed journalists. The dismissal of Haykal
implicitly confirmed that the amnesty was on the condition that there would
be no opposition to the Head of State. Some journalists also understood that
they would not be able to write, therefore they turned down this amnesty

and chose to leave the country. The five years that followed the war saw a vast emigration of Egyptian journalists and writers which to this day represents an exceptional event in the Egyptian press.

During the Nasser period, Egyptian writers struggled bitterly for the creation of a union to represent their material and democratic interests and, within a legal framework, protect them from publishers, and state censorship. They were able to gain this right in the national action programme for 1971 and four years later, on 5th July 1975, the government undertook to pass through parliament a law authorising the creation of this union but in a non-democratic way. In fact Articles 29, 30 and 73 of the Statute on this union make it totally dependent on the Ministry of Cultural Affairs, i.e. on the State as well as on the Socialist Union. The democratic writers responded by blocking the application of the law by isolating themselves and refusing to take part in any elections; some tried to establish independent associations. This was the case with the Association of the Writers of Tomorrow. State security information caught up with them and they were interned under the pretext that they had transgressed the law on national unity.

Following the war of October 1973, the dismissal of Haykal and the removal of censorship on the three big dailies, the regime adopted a secret plan in the area of information; this amounted to freezing the activities of writers opposing the authorities by paying their salary while forbidding them to publish. Thus arose the problem of those monthly magazines having a radical Arab nationalist character.

The battle against the progressive national forums began with the affair of the magazine *El-Katib* whose editorial staff was directed by Ahmed Abbas Saleh. Those who worked on this magazine were a group of Arab nationalists and Nasserite Marxist writers. The weakness of this magazine was that, during its final stage, it was published by the Ministry of Foreign Affairs after publication and production had been abandoned by the El-Tahlis Company. Yussef El-Sebai, Minister of Cultural Affairs at the time (Autumn 1974), claimed the right to check the written material before printing it. This was after a study on the consequences of the October War had been published by one of its editors, Salah Haissa. The Minister's demand cast a slur on the abilities of the chief editor and signified the re-establishment of censorship by the back-door. The editorial board of the magazine refused to accede to the request, but the Minister insisted and additionally demanded that he should appoint an editorial director. This meant the appointment of a former officer and four writers in whom the Minister had confidence. He also asked for Salah Haissa to be removed from any position of responsibility in the magazine. Salah Haissa resigned. The board of directors accepted the appointment of four new colleagues but rejected the appointment of the former officer as he was neither writer nor journalist but simply a man in whom the Minister and the security organisations had confidence. The editorial board also turned down any tutelage or control of the magazine by the Minister. Yussef El-Sebai, therefore, had recourse to his rights as President/General

Manager of the organisation that published the magazine, and transformed it into a cultural, political and intellectual forum and a literary magazine directed by an Under-Secretary of State for Cultural Affairs and without the assistance of an editorial board. And so ended the magazine *El-Katib* which for ten years had been known as a forum for Arab nationalism and socialist revolution.[31]

The second affair was that of the monthly magazine *At-Taliah*, which had invited some members of the editorial staff of *Al-Katib* to write something for its pages, starting from the November 1974 issue. Meanwhile, Yussef El-Sebai had left the Ministry of Cultural Affairs to become President/General Manager of *Al-Ahram* which issued the magazine *At-Taliah*. Once again he used his administrative right to suppress the second Egyptian publication of the left, 26 months after the suppression of the first. The scenario was the same. In its February 1977 issue, *At-Taliah* published an editorial entitled, 'Le peuple de janvier entre le Governement et la gauche.' The author, El-Khuli, defended the January uprising and accused the government of being implicated in it by raising the prices of basic necessities. Yussef El-Sebai asked to inspect all written matter before printing. This time however, there was a startling paradox because in the meantime the multi-party situation had been authorised, and such an intervention constituted a meddling in the affairs of the Marxist left forum. Let us recall that none of the managing editors who had controlled *Al-Ahram* – from Haykal to Baha El Din, including Ali Amin and Ehsan Abd El-Kudus – had ever cast aspersions on the independence of the magazine. Sebai's interference was also contrary to the suppression of press censorship and to the legal responsibilities of chief editors. But above all, it was an interference by a member of the party in power in the affairs of another party – the National Progressive and Unionist Assembly – within the framework of which the chief editor of *At-Taliah* operated. Finally, this interference cast a slur on the law, the Press Union and the Journalists' Charter of Honour. These were the moral and material institutions to which the journalists were answerable.

However, El-Sebai insisted. Lufti Al-Khuli asked for his name to be removed from issues which contained articles controlled by El-Sebai who, in turn, considered this request as a resignation and immediately appointed a science editor of *Al-Ahram* as Chief Editor of *At-Taliah*; this placed the editorial board in a delicate situation, especially as this science journalist had political tendencies very close to those of the Muslim Brotherhood. The *At-Taliah* slogan, 'The voice of the militants spreads contemporary revolutionary thinking' was replaced by 'Magazine of the Man and Sciences of the Future'. And so the April 1977 edition began with an editorial entitled 'Science, Faith and Love'. In his editorial, the leader writer included the sentence: 'We believe that science invokes faith.'

But in contrast to *El-Katib*, which belonged to the Ministry of Cultural Affairs, Lufti El-Khuli had rights over *At-Taliah* and he therefore put the affair in the hands of the law. On 14th July 1977, the 14th Chamber of the Primary Court of North Cairo decided in favour of Lutfi El-Khuli and gave him legal responsibility for administration of the magazine, authorised him to continue its publication and to manage it until the litigation was definitively resolved. In support of this ruling, one particularly notes the judge's impartiality in matters of ideological differences and the freedom of opinion guaranteed by the Constitution. But this judgment was of no use because, some time later, the publication licence for *At-Taliah* was withdrawn and thus this Egyptian magazine of the left ceased to appear.

The suppression of these two magazines, which struck at most of the writers of the left, and the emigration of many of them, meant that almost the entire democratic voice of the left in the field of culture and the media ceased to transmit its message to the citizens. A small minority continued to publish in the magazine *Rose El-Yussef* during the time of Abd El-Rahman El-Charkaui, but for very special reasons. A writer respected by the left and popular for his novels and theatre plays, he staked his reputation on the 15th May 1971, when he published his famous article, 'La chute de la barde terroriste' in *Al-Akhbar* and by so doing aligned himself firmly with Sadat's putsch against the Nasserist group, at a time when nobody could foresee the consequences. President Sadat was grateful to him and Charkaui continued to support the policies of the new regime.

At moments of crisis, Charkaui always managed to find a formula to reconcile his support of Sadat and his sympathy for others, because of his good relations with the Russians, the Egyptian left and the Arab progressives. Management of the editing of *Rose El-Yussef* was therefore granted to him, partly as a reward and partly as an attempt by the President to have a left closer to the Presidency, as had been the case during Nasser's time.

For his part, Charkaui kept the balance between his support for the President and his criticism of government administration in such a way that he could guarantee a leftist character to *Rose El-Yussef*. He had thus assumed the role that had been played by the Egyptian Theatre during the Nasser period. He removed the President from all areas of criticism while maintaining criticism of the State. As a consequence of these criticisms, the circulation of *Rose El-Yussef* increased until it exceeded 150,000 copies per week. In reality, the reader was not very interested to see the President described by the chief editor as 'Hero of Democracy in the World'; he was more interested to learn the cultural, social and economic secrets that were the cause of the grave degeneration in the country. It must be said that *Rose El-Yussef* conducted violent campaigns against El Ahzar, the information services controlled by state security, the Ministry of Economy, the Ministry of Higher Education, etc. In all its campaigns, *Rose El-Yussef* spared the President and praised him lavishly to such a degree that it was hostile to the entreaties of the international and Arab progressives.

But one day in 1977, during a speech given at the University of Alexandria, the President gave the editors of this magazine an unpleasant surprise. He said, 'When I scan this magazine I get the impression that Egypt is living in total obscurity. Everything is wrong and corrupt. What does this mean?' Charkaui replied in a practical way by tendering his resignation to the

President. It was accepted during a cordial meeting but he was also appointed to the post of President of the Upper Council of Letters and Arts, with the rank of minister and, on a part-time basis, he was also appointed to *Al-Ahram*. Needless to say, this was not a personal matter but one concerning the policy of the magazine. In fact it was later realised that the Alexandria speech was the beginning of an action aimed at changing *Rose El-Yussef*, with or without the resignation of Charkaui, because an editorial board composed of the most reactionary and faithful supporters of the regime was immediately appointed. The type of criticism that had appeared in *Rose El-Yussef* could no longer be tolerated; and so the reconciliatory policy of this magazine came to an end.

At the same time the extreme religious right published the magazine *Abdawa*, organ of the Muslim Brotherhood, while the left had now no means of expression apart from very feeble ones abroad.

That is why the public rushed to the magazine *El-Ahali* (the organ of the National Progressive and Unionist Assembly party) as soon as its publication was authorised. This magazine quickly picked up the readership of *Rose El-Yussef* in spite of its newness, bad printing and its lack of signed articles for fear of sanctions. After the publication of 16 issues, *El-Ahali* began to suffer problems and intimidation by the security services. Several times the magazine was withdrawn from the market by order of the Attorney General; at one time it had to cease publication. Sometime later it was authorised to reappear, but it was always prevented from reaching the public at the last minute. It was as though it had ceased publication of its own free will. And so there was no forum in the country for the people of the left, the democrats, the nationalists and the Nasserists.

Let us recall that all these events took place at the same time as the flare-up in Lebanon and the crushing of several minor aspects of the burgeoning democracy in certain Arab countries. Let us also recall that President Sadat had sent the writer, Ali Amin, to Beirut to ask President Franjieh to expel Egyptian journalists working in Beirut. The Lebanese President replied that, as Lebanon had been host to Ali Amin for more than nine years, it could also invite other writers. During this period, the writer and journalist Ibrahim Amer died from the wounds he received when the press establishment at which he worked was bombarded. The events in Lebanon became increasingly grave, and Egyptian journalists continued to leave for the West as Beirut had ceased to be a source of information. In another Arab country that had just liquidated its own nascent democratic experience, the Ministry of Information politely asked an Egyptian to leave the country within 24 hours.

Lebanese-based organisations also continued to migrate to Western capitals (especially London and Paris). The coming together between this exiled Arab press and the exiled Egyptian journalists was quite natural. It was as though history was recalling memories of the last century when Djemal El Din-el-Afgali and Mohamed Abdov left Egypt to found *El-Ourwa El-Wuthka* in Paris, and when Syrian and Lebanese writers and journalists fled the Ottoman Sultanates to establish famous newspapers and magazines in Paris. This new phenomenon of a refugee Arab press in Paris and London was entirely due to the lack of freedom in Cairo and Beirut. Naturally then, these press organs dealt essentially with the vicissitudes of the counter-revolution in Egypt, despite the fact that there were no Egyptian newspapers among them, with the exception of the magazine *Al Yassar El-Arabi* which ceased to appear after publishing four editions due to financial difficulties (since January 1979 this magazine has been published in Paris). In fact the counter-revolution in Egypt was also opposed to the Arabs in their most sensitive problems, in spite of the economic opening up which gave them exceptional facilities for investment in Egypt. This is the experience of even the Arab nation which, since the Egyptian political leadership took its lone decision to conclude a separate Peace Treaty at Sinai in 1975 and to sign the Camp David agreement on 17th November 1978, is now under threat. It was therefore natural that these overseas forums should polarise Egyptian opposition writing both inside and outside of Egypt. When the international newspapers sent their correspondents to make enquiries in Cairo, Arab writings – including those of exiled Egyptians – appeared very tame in their analysis compared with the objective articles written by the foreign correspondents.

Egypt and the entire world were surprised on 27th May 1978 when the socialist Attorney General in Cairo summoned 34 writers and journalists from abroad to an interrogation, accusing them of defaming the reputation of Egypt overseas. The socialist Attorney General, with an unparalleled ignorance of the law, threatened to use Interpol to bring these journalists to Cairo if they should refuse his summons. He also threatened to withdraw their passports and thus their nationality. All these threats revealed a scandalous ignorance of international law and of the Egyptian constitution, because Interpol does not deal with affairs concerning withdrawal of passports, nationality or freedom of expression. In Cairo, President Sadat threatened the foreign correspondents – particularly those of the BBC and *Le Monde* and the representatives of the Italian News Agency – with expulsion if they continued to besmirch the reputation of Egypt. None of these journalists worked for organisations that could be accused of sympathy with Marxism or Nasserism, but the situation that they reported in their newspapers and over their radios was in itself a total condemnation of the existing regime. Nothing is stranger than President Sadat's remark to a British correspondent: 'Why do you attack me (and not Egypt) when we have very good relations with Her Majesty the Queen, the Conservative Party and the Labour Party?'

The Italian News Agency correspondent asked him a question about Mohamed Said Ahmed, who was forbidden to leave the country, explaining that Italian people found it difficult to understand why this writer could not go to Italy to receive the prize for his book *Apres le silence des canons* which had been translated into Italian. The President replied: 'This writer insulted Egypt in the Italian newspapers.' This was truly contradictory, because this author's book had been acclaimed by President Sadat immediately after its publication, as it had been acclaimed by the American and

Israeli press. The book was nothing more than a very clever leftist formulation of the preceding and subsequent steps on the path to conciliation with Israel. The writer had published nothing in the Italian press, but he had published an article in *Le Monde Diplomatique* which expressed reservations concerning the President's position on Occupied Jerusalem at a time when the enemy did not appear ready to make concessions.

President Sadat did not forgive the foreign correspondents, or those Egyptian correspondents living abroad, for expressing their opposition to these strategic attitudes in which they confused the personality of Sadat with Egypt itself. And so Haykal, Mohamed Said Ahmed, Salah Issah, Ahmed Fuad Negm, Hussein Fahmi, Farida Anakache and other writers, critics and poets whose voices had been heard internationally, were forbidden to leave the country. They were summoned to be questioned by the socialist Attorney General. He could find no basis for their condemnation in law or the constitution, in spite of his previous declaration in which he accused the writers of high treason. Thus President Sadat declared that the interrogations were being conducted so that the people would know what was going on; in other words to cast a slur on the reputations of these writers by means of the Attorney's declarations and articles published by order of the regime. But even this constituted a conciliatory step under the pressure of international public opinion as expressed by the concern of the world press (with its various political tendencies) on seeing the mask of liberalism slipping to reveal the face of dictatorship beneath. This concern was also expressed in a public protest by a group of British Labour Party MPs, and by French intellectuals and politicians who expressed solidarity with the persecuted Egyptian intellectuals at a congress called by Professor Jacques Berque of the College de France, and in a declaration signed by Charles Bettelheim, Lacouture, Sartre, Rene Dumont, Francois Chatelet, Michel Foucauld, Maurice Caprier, Alain Touraine, Maxine Rodinson and others, among the best representatives of French opinion and consciousness. But this international condemnation of the persecution of thinking and free expression in Egypt did not prevent President Sadat and his organisations from taking measures and strategic decisions concerning the repression of any democratic practice by promulgating a law, unique of its kind, banning atheists from any function in the organisations or the management of the communications media or any other field. The term 'atheist' meant Nasserists, independent democrats and all those opposed to President Sadat.

Kidnapping operations started after this; writers were kidnapped and tortured at secret locations by the secret service. The President used his right to veto on two occasions when the magistrates of the courts ordered the release of prisoners. Others were interned in psychiatric hospitals.[32]

We must now deal with the cultural organisations following the purge of the communications media. The most important examples are the theatre and the cinema which were liquidated, that is in so far as they were organisations dependent on the Ministry of Cultural Affairs whose output formed part of general cultural process. Among these institutions were those, such as the National Theatre, that had been created under the monarchy; these institutions were not information media and neither did they exist to make money. Under Nasser a generation of film producers and men of the theatre had been born, who were free of all financial constraints. Despite the restrictions on democracy in Nasser's time, an intellectual and artistic *Nahda* was in full flight, for the State undertook the expenses of theatrical and film production and covered possible losses, partly for the sake of artistic awareness, partly so that the public at large could benefit from moderate prices and partly for the sake of the work of art itself. The staging, production and the artists' performance were freed from commercial considerations.

Under Sadat, quite opposite measures were taken. He encouraged the private sector and abolished the Ministry of Cultural Affairs during the cabinet reshuffle on 1st October 1978 following the Camp David Agreement. After the disbanding of this Ministry and in support of the private sector, the nationalised sector of the cinema and the theatre was gradually dispersed and, the budget normally allocated to this Ministry was used to support private capital. There was a double result, intellectual and artistic: the best artists left Egypt for other Arab countries, among them were the best playwrights. Others were attracted by the commercial sector, and the level of dramatic and film production in Egypt dropped to a level that the country had never known except during the Second World War. They even considered selling the Egyptian television and theatre organisations to a Saudi millionaire.[33]

This affair was discovered purely by chance when the signing of this strange agreement was being celebrated in a nightclub on Pyramids Street. The Egyptian cinema united and sent a telegram of protest to the President of the Republic. A Cinema Committee of the Upper Council of Fine Arts and Letters did the same. A parliamentary enquiry was conducted by the People's Council, the Minister of Cultural Affairs strongly defended the project and accused international communism of casting aspersions on Egyptian cultural strategy, which was open to both Arab and foreign capital. The actress Nadia Lutfi could not contain herself and interrupted the Minister saying, 'It is hardly worth discussing the matter any more Mr. Minister, you have already sold us.' The actress Magda said that she had nothing to do with international or any other communism, and that she supported national capitalism. The writer Yussef Idrisi declared: 'You have sold the Pyramids, you have sold Boulak; we implore you, do not sell the soul of the country. We want to keep Egyptian arts and thinking free from any foreign hegemony'.

However, the Minister, supported by members of his party, proceeded with the application of the agreement; and so the newspaper *El-Ahali*, organ of the National Progressive Unionist Assembly party, published an article whose headline stirred up the emotions of the Egyptian public: 'We implore you, do not sell Egypt.' The article revealed that the son of the Minister in question was one of the shareholders in the multinational Saudi project to the value of E£250,000; this young man had only just completed his university studies.

All this indicated two things; the frequent practice of corruption at the highest level of the regime in the name of financial gain, and secondly and more seriously, this affair confirmed that foreign monopolies had decided to take over the control and orientation of cultural affairs in Egypt and not content themselves with merely being materially and ideologically corrupt representatives. They had to buy the cultural productive force, they had to liquidate national capitalism which, more than half a century previously, had given birth to the Egyptian cinema with the creation of the Misr par Talhat Harba Bank.[34]

At about the same time a similar scandal occurred. On 6th July 1977 Mrs. Ahmed Fuad published an article in *Al-Ahram* sounding the alarm about an enormous fraud that was in progress. What was it about? Mrs. Fuad wrote:

> Towards the end of 1975, an agreement was made between the Egyptian tourism organisation and a foreign multinational company with a capital of $3.4 million for the undertaking of a project at a cost of up to $950 million. The agreement granted the company the right to exploit an area of 4,000 feddans (1 feddan = 4,200m²) in the zone surrounding the pyramids, as well as the exploitation of 1,100 feddans in the Mediterranean region of Raz el Hikma. According to the agreement, this privilege was valid for 99 years as had been the case for the Isthmus of Suez in Khedive Ismail's time.[35]

Egyptians were surprised when the company began to put the project into operation without any legislative proceedings in the People's Council. The Pyramids area was closed to the public to be divided into small areas for several companies or individuals in the United States with the intention of building villas, hotels, tourist villages, private airports and swimming pools. It was as though this company was no more than a broker whose task was to rent this historic place to various American millionaires over a period of 99 years. It was learnt that highly placed officials in the regime had received payments.

Following this article, a wave of protest united archaeologists, academics and lawyers. The Barristers' Association organised a conference before associating itself with the writer of the article in its legal action against the company and government combined.[36]

If these two projects were not achieved (selling of the cinema and television industry and of the area of the Pyramids) it was due to the national consensus of opinion and popular pressure. However, these two macabre affairs showed that the counter-revolution was ready to sell the very civilisation and soul of Egypt to whoever could pay the price, no matter how the national sovereignty, the legacy of the past, or the thinking soul of Egypt would suffer.

The dialogue of thought and creativity are forbidden in the Egypt of Sadat who authorises any citizen to think as he wishes only as long as this thinking remains within defined limits. Egyptian thought is thus condemned to the state of a monologue such as has never before been known, neither under

Nasser, nor under Farouk.

Even though there was a very limited period of persecution of thought at the university in the time of King Fuad, after a bitter battle, the constitution was later able to reinstate Taha Hussein, author of the critical study on anti-Islamic poetry. Under Nasser, 54 of the best academic intellectuals were expelled in 1954; but this was an isolated incident and Nasser never repeated this type of procedure. As for President Sadat, he addressed the Upper Council of the Universities on 30th January 1977 as follows: 'I ask the teaching staff at the University of Alexandria and all other universities to expel from their ranks all those who collaborate with these groups [those asking for the establishment of true democracy] you know them better than I do, you know them all.'[37] Following this appeal, the Government proceeded with unconstitutional and illegal measures against the freedom of the University. Campaigns were conducted against scientific methods and against the rationalism of university work. Teachers were illegally interrogated on their university practices. Attempts were made to stifle research, to prevent teachers from obtaining the amount of lecture time prescribed by the law, under the pretext of protecting the students from the baneful influence of some of them. Some new teaching appointments were refused because the candidates came from particular universities. Promotions were granted on the basis of allegiance to certain parties. Some university authorities belonged to the party in power and deliberately combined their university function with their political adherence. Defamatory campaigns were conducted against certain colleagues and secret reports were drawn up.[38]

Apart from all this, the university administrations and the media of the party in power conducted violent campaigns against university student life. Students' means of expression were besieged; the student press disappeared, wall newspapers were torn down, students were attacked. The university administration had the new task of rebuilding and directing the student unions in order to remove all democratic content from them. The administration, therefore, became a source of terrorism against the students by means of disciplinary councils aimed at dissuading them from exercising their democratic rights.[39]

The immediate consequence of these terrorist actions was the emigration of leading and other university professors. The religious extremist groups made a clean sweep of university political action.

The Prohibition of Organisations

At the same time as the decrees aimed at transforming thought into a sterile monologue, and following upon those granting facilities to foreign and Arab capital in 1974 and, finally, following the second ceasefire agreement in Sinai in 1975, the regime returned to what it had approved on several occasions by means of the constitution: the National Action Programme of 1971 and the documents concerning the Arab Socialist Union presented by the

President of the Republic in 1974. At the beginning, the regime maintained the formula of the Arab Socialist Union. Later, in the National Unity Law of 1972 it added the formula 'the sole political organisation'. It was unexpectedly trying to dismantle the Union and turn it into a forum. Throughout 1975, eager discussions examined every aspect of this Presidential idea. On the 16th March 1976, Parliament adopted the formula of three forums, one for the left, one for the right and another for the centre. On 11th November the President of the Republic proposed to the People's Council that these three forums be converted into parties.

How could thinking be prohibited at the same time as the creation of independent political organisations was permitted? Is not a party the organisation of a certain way of thinking? Egyptians received these propositions with much reservation. Most of them thought they were a plot woven by both the regime and the opposition, for the proposal came from above. In passing, let us recall that ordinary Egyptians had never stopped organising themselves clandestinely, during both the Nasser and Sadat periods. Also, their democratic organising ability had never ceased over the past ten years. On 1st May 1976 President Sadat declared that the charters of revolution, under the circumstances of the 1962 National Charter and the declaration of 30th March 1968, had the sole purpose of temporarily absorbing the people's anger and that they could not be of permanent character and, under the pretext that they had become out-dated, he decided to do away with them. He considered that they were hardly of any more use, which was true from the putsch's point of view as it wanted to return to a multi-party system. In effect, these documents were a kind of social contract, applied or not applied between the incomplete Nasserist revolution and the people. They were cancelled five years later.

In the historical context of these events, we note that the totality of the laws promulgated since 1972, in the circumstances of the Law on National Unity and the 1978 plebiscite, which was aimed at destroying the last aspects of liberalism, add up in themselves to a constitution opposed to that of 1971, imposed by the regime itself in a tactical situation to salvage the Nasserist and Marxist parties at the beginning of the putsch. But because of the persistence of the people in confronting the regime to the point of revolt, the abandonment of the first constitution and the National Action Programme became necessary. How did this come above?

The answer is by the procedure of the two plebiscites on 10th February 1977 and 21st May 1978. The first concerned what was called at the time The Law for the Protection of Security and the Citizen. The first plebiscite occurred after the spontaneous popular uprising of 18th and 19th January 1977, just ten months before the famous visit to Jerusalem. The first article of this law, agreed to then, stipulated the creation of three parties under the terms of a special law which later had to be promulgated. This law made the creation of a party dependent on the approval of 20 members of parliament. It also required that proposed parties should be identified with national unity, social peace and legitimacy. Article 6, submitted to plebiscite, stipulated that any person participating in a gathering to incite people to revolt or to cause an obstacle in the application of the laws and statutes, and, by extension to prevent government organisations, those of the nationalised sector or the government institutes from conducting their business, should be condemned to hard labour for life. Article 7 condemned any worker who had taken part in a strike, either by previous association or by an agreement aimed at achieving a common end, to hard labour for life. Article 8 condemned to hard labour for life any person having decided to or having taken part in a meeting or an occupation of premises in such a way as to threaten public peace. Article 9 cancelled all previous laws contrary to these provisions. There is no need to say that the contradiction between the authorisation of the multi-party system and the forbidding of demonstrations, strikes or occupation of premises, was scandalous.

In spite of the very severe sentences to which they were exposed, the Egyptians mobilised themselves immediately after the publication of these laws. A student demonstration marched from the University of Cairo to the Parliament. Kamel Hussein, Vice-Governor of Banha and former member of the Revolutionary Council, sent a telegram to the President of the Republic drawing his attention to the fact that the plebiscite was not constitutional. There followed a violent dialogue between the President and the representatives of the Student Unions, on 1st February 1977. A Nasserist student explained the principles of Nasserism in various applications to the President, while drawing his attention to the fact that what was happening in the country was quite contrary to those principles in the field of domestic and foreign policy. The newspapers published this strange dialogue and television broadcast it live. The dialogue was also published in the unofficial bulletin *Democratic Papers* published outside Egypt in their issues 8 and 9 of February and March 1977.

The National Unionist and Progressive Assembly Party published a general political programme (it was also published by Ibn Khaldun) dealing with various problems and the main things troubling the country. There then polarised around the movement the nucleus of a National Democratic Front composed of Marxists, Nasserists, independent democrats and enlightened religious groups. That is why the regime and its party went into battle against all those who belonged to this legitimate party. Members, civil servants and workers were transferred to remote posts. Others, without any authorisation by the magistrature, were arrested; still others were threatened with dismissal from their work or from the university. During two months in the year 1977, the newspaper *Al-Akhbar* published lists of those who had resigned from the party. If any importance is given to these so-called resignations, one notices that in the end they did not even represent 1.5% of the membership of the party.

Besides this, the various levels of the Egyptian middle class felt acutely the need to express themselves on 23rd August 1977, on the occasion of the anniversary of the death of the leaders Saad Zaghlul and Mustafa An-Nahhas. Fuad Salah el Din, former pasha and Secretary-General of the former Wafd

Party, gave a three hour speech at the end of which he announced that the Wafd was preparing to return to political life after the authorisation of the multi-party situation, and he said particularly that the Wafd was in the process of formulating a programme to undertake the legal and constitutional procedures for its renewed formation.

Even though he had violently criticised the system and its symbols, in particular Mamduh Salem who was an officer when Salah El Din was Minister of the Interior, he spared President Sadat. In his speech he insisted on democracy as it had been in the time of liberalism under the monarchy. It was also noted that the Church supported him by sending a delegation to be present at the ceremony which took place at the offices of the Barristers' Association. More than 3,000 people could be counted at the offices, and almost double that number around them. There were not only former Wafdists, but also intellectuals and representatives of the middle class who had suffered from the 'Family monopoly of the regime'. The new Wafd formed an original right in society. It was not a transitory right. It was not a matter of a reunion on the occasion of the commemoration of the death of a leader; this meeting expressed a genuine social force, fully existing and well founded. Following the meeting, tens of thousands of citizens in the capital and in the provinces asked to join the new party. It is certain that the new party was not a creation by the regime. The first point in the Wafd programme concerned the transformation of the Presidential regime into a parliamentary regime by the definition of the Presidential powers, the abrogation of various anti-democratic laws and the repeal of the exceptional measures. The programme also noted the necessity for widening the laws of capitalist investment, and support of the private sector, as well as a greater opening up to the West.

The centre party of the regime was besieged from two sides. The newspaper *Al-Ahali,* organ of the assembly of the left, had become the voice of the popular classes and intellectual radicals. From the other side, the Wafd Party became the authentic voice of the quasi-liberal Egyptian right. It was in this climate, at the beginning of the second week of May 1978, that the President held his plebiscite which was basically aimed at thwarting the revival of both the right and the left. The second paragraph of this law concerning consultation stipulated: 'No person calling for the adoption of a doctrine that is a danger to Divine Law can occupy a position of authority in the State or the nationalised sector or any other function likely to affect public opinion.' Paragraph 3 stipulated that this ban also applied to boards of directors, workers unions, professional unions, local councils and unions and co-operatives. Thus the freedom of the elector was removed. But above all, all individual initiative and freedom of belief were also removed. It is significant that, following the promulgation of this law, an Egyptian court had granted an Egyptian Christian the right to practise polygamy, which is forbidden by the Church but permitted under Muslim law. These two paragraphs, however, were particularly aimed at the left.

The other paragraphs denied all political rights to anyone who had been politically active before the revolution, apart from members of the National

Party and Young Egypt, both parties of the right, the first having a leaning towards religious segregation and the second having flirted with fascism. The day after this referendum, 23rd May 1978, Salah Jahim, the *Al-Ahram* cartoonist published a drawing showing the announcer of 'Songs that you love' saying: 'I am amazed. Why is it that today everyone is saying "Yes, my love, yes"?' By this 'Yes' he was of course alluding not to the song but to the referendum. On 1st June 1978, the British *Daily Mirror* wrote, 'President Sadat is acting like any dictator wanting to penalise political criticism and like any tyrant accusing critics of being enemies of the nation.' It was the university teachers rather than the students who reacted to this second referendum. The University of Alexandria sent a telegram to the President just before the plebiscite asking him to revise the laws that were the subject of the referendum. Once put to a plebiscite he was against any such revision. And so the President organised a meeting with the teaching body at which he heard Mohamed Zaki Achmaui, Vice-President of the University, say: 'It is not the merchant who stocks sugar, maize and tea to sell later at a higher price who suffers from lack of freedom.' Doctor Abd El Malem Kharbuch asked the President to prove his democratic intentions. It was noted that the people who had said 'yes' in the referendum were not the Egyptian people.

The opposition did not occur only in the universities but became more and more apparent among the members of parliament. This is why a group of MPs belonging to the party of the regime on the suggestion of the President asked for the application of certain measures against the recalcitrant members. Parliamentarians were thus relieved of their functions as representatives by forbidding them the right to offer themselves as candidates in the next election, a thing that had not occurred even in the time of the monarchy. Just once, in the reign of King Fuad in 1939, a member of parliament had been relieved of his responsibilities after being accused of the crime of high treason. No parliament, either in Egypt or elsewhere, had known members to be threatened with expulsion for contesting the policies of the ruling party, and to palliate this difficulty President Sadat invented from scratch the so-called law on opposition. At one time it was thought that he was referring to opposition to morality, the village morality about which he was so fervent, but it was soon realised that he was referring to opposition to the person of the President as proved by the following events.

Deputy Kamal Ed-Din Hussein, having protested against the anti-democratic law which was the subject of the first referendum, was relieved of his responsibilities on 14th February 1977, following a demand presented by 252 members of parliament belonging to the ruling party. The Council of State, however, judged that this deputy could stand as a candidate in a subsequent election, a right that was later withdrawn by other means and thus the electorate was deprived of a means of expressing this point of view.

Sheikh Ashur Nasser, Deputy for Karmuz in Alexandria, protested against the vacillation of Said Marei, President of the Council, concerning a written question. Having received no reply to his protest, he took advantage of President Sadat's presence during a session and shouted, 'Down with

President Sadat!' He was expelled by a majority vote of 279, on 28th March 1978. The repetition of these incidents revealed certain elements of which the most important is the complicity of the President of the Republic in being at one and the same time the mouthpiece of the Presidency and of the government.

Deputy Abu El-Izz El Hariri was arrested in Alexandria for having given an electoral speech in his own constituency in 1978. This time it was not a sanction against the crime of attack on the President, but simply a sanction against the Assembly Party of the left whose popularity was rapidly growing. The Nasserist Deputy, Kamel Ahmed, interrupted the President during his speech in Parliament on 30th September 1978 after his return from Washington and the signing of the Camp David Agreement. The President asked to have the deputy thrown out; members of the ruling party picked up their colleague and threw him out.

Following these events, the socialist Attorney General drew up a list of people to be excluded from political activity as a result of the latest referendum. The Wafd Party therefore met and decided to disband itself as a protest against the regime's attitude to democracy. In its turn, the Assembly Party also stopped all activity and said that the attitude of the regime was responsible for this decision.

These two decisions disturbed public opinion both in Egypt and abroad but had no effect on the regime. Happy that the scene had been cleared of hindrances, President Sadat decided to fill the political gap. On 23rd July 1978 he decided himself to form the National Democratic Party. But as the deputies of the ruling centre party, led by Mamduh Salem were also of Sadat's party, they immediately adhered to the President's new party. The scandal was such that even Mustafa Amin, the writer of the right, wrote in *Al-Akhbar* that it was inadmissable that deputies, having been elected by the people, should join the President's party without even knowing its programme, since it had not yet been published. The consequence of this was that Mustafa Amin was eliminated and forbidden to write.

Against Democracy

Democracy in the Nasser period was absent in the political sense of the term and, during the monarchy, democracy was just a liberal decoration for quasi-feudal capitalism. But in President Sadat's time there is a total lack of democracy in the national, economic and social sense for, in fact, the liberalism of this period is nothing more than the middleman for the rich of the country and the administration. In no way can it be considered as true liberalism or a capitalist economy. On the other hand, it is not a matter of a dictator acting for the good of his country; it is nothing less than an autocracy representing the most underdeveloped layer of society and the most dependent on the foreigner. Thus, the regime of Mr Sadat by far exceeds the autocracy of the monarchy and that of Nasser. Under Sadat's regime there is neither the formal liberalism of the monarchy nor the economic development, social progress and national liberation known under Nasser. If formal liberalism took part in the fall of the monarchy, if central autocracy took part in the fall of the Nasser regime, then the total absence of democracy in Sadat's regime removes all legitimacy from it. For the entire nation depends at all levels on a will from outside Egypt and this is the basis of the coming together of the Egyptian middlemen and the Zionist entity in the Middle East and the United States.

These anti-democratic measures in Egypt had serious consequences in several areas. In the field of economics, the national debt of Egypt exceeded $2,000 million for the first time in history.[40] The deficit in the balance of payments reached $1,000 million. Taxes increased by 16%; imports increased by 74.8%, and indirect taxes reached 60%. It was also proved that 35% of all investors were practising fiscal fraud.[41]

As a consequence of this new situation, large sections of the national middle classes preferred to liquidate their productive businesses and jump on the bandwagon of commercial and interest-earning capitalism; between 1975 and 1978 more than 443 medium-sized businesses closed down and more than 895 small companies specialising in the finance of smaller-than-average production businesses also closed down. More than 1,560 craftsmen stopped working.

All this means that, little by little, national production gave way to the import/export sector. Between 1975 and 1976, inflation exceeded 25%. In the same period, prices in the country increased by 16%, and in the towns by 20%.[42] In the same period more than one million workers became unemployed. Let us recall that over that same period the revenue of the Suez Canal, the remittances of Egyptians working abroad and Arab and American aid reached more than $4,000 million. At the same time there was a very noticeable decline in education services, sanitary services, public transport and housing.[43] Nobody now, talks about development; the family triangle Sadat-Ahmed/Osman-Said/Maeri has become the symbol of the alliance between the rich from the countryside, interest-earning capitalism, and the administrative bureaucracy, a triangle totally dependent on foreign monopolies.

In the social area there has been a very noticeable increase in crime, rape, theft and fraud equivalent to seven and a half times the crime rate in 1975. In 1977 alone there were more than 55 big cases of arson. The municipal services of the capital can no longer cope with their task to such a degree that over-full drains block certain main thoroughfares. Drinking water is polluted; public transport is so inefficient that a bus falling into the Nile no longer surprises anyone.

There has been a resurgence of religious conflicts. For example, at Samallout, a town that is 90% Christian, there were confrontations with the extremist group 'Repentance and Emigration' which resulted in 17 dead and several dozen wounded. The priest at the church in the town was killed. One no longer counts the arson attacks on churches and mosques. Police discovered two arms depots, one at the home of a Christian and the other at the home of a Muslim; both contained both heavy and light arms. Let us recall that at the same time a large part of the regular army was demobilised and that arms were stolen from army depots to be sold clandestinely.

In the cultural area, the emigration of brainpower was felt and a single system gripped the cultural and informational scene. Film, theatrical and television production responded more and more to the demands of the market, and teaching and educational programmes were qualitatively transformed to the point where regionalism, chauvinism and racialism constituted a dominant triangle in the official culture.[44]

Notes

1. It is astonishing that this sentence from the 1905 edition of Mustapha Fahimi (pp. 196—7) had been removed from the Ministry of Cultural Affairs edition (pp. 252—2). In the Ministry edition, the text has been cut in such a way that it could not possibly be a printing error.
2. Louis Awad. *Hisroire de la pensee egyptienne moderne*, Vol. 1, p. 64.
3. Salah Issa, *Ath-Thaura Al-Arabiyyah*, (Beirut, 1972).
4. Esmet Saif Ad-Dawla, *Al-Ahzab wa muchkilat Ad-Dimuqratiyyah ti Wisr*, Dar El-Massirah (Beirut, 1977), p. 31.
5. Abbas Mahmud Al-Aqqad, *Abqari Al-Islah Muhammad Abdah*, (Cairo, 1962).
6. In a part of what can be considered as his memoirs, Khaled wrote under the headline, 'The First Pages in the Story of 23 July' in the newspaper *Al-Ahali* of 26 July 1978. This was perhaps the first time that a political organisation contented itself with preparing simply a single document that a new member could read before returning it. Ahmed Fuad and I (i.e. the two members of the left) therefore prepared a draft programme which we submitted to Gamal Abd El-Nasser. He accepted if after making some amendments. The programme was very brief; it was contained in a single page. It insisted on the analysis of the nature of colonisation to which it finally attributed all the sufferings of Egypt. That was the first principle. As for the other points, one could mention the formation of a national front gathering together all the national parties to resist colonisation, to create a powerful national army whose soldiers could be promoted to officer rank, and the achievement of justice or social justice. This clear and precise programme was able to attract many officers of all intellectual and political trends to our movement. Later, after the revolution, this text was used as the basis for the Six Principles.
7. Tarik El-Bichari, *la Democratie et le Nasserisme*, Dar Al-Sakafeh Al-Djedida, (Cairo, 1975), p. 20.
8. *Ibid.*, pp. 20 and 21.
9. Anuar Amer, *Le Pouvoir de Nasser en theorie et en pratique*, (Cairo, 1971). pp. 160 and 161.
10. Esmat Saif Ad-Daula, *Les Partis et le probleme de la democratie en Egypte*, p. 98.

11. *Ibid.*, p. 84.
12. *Ibid.*, p. 89.
13. *Ibid.*, p. 90.
14. *Ibid.*, p. 28.
15. Tarik El-Bichari, *op. cit.*, p. 13.
16. *Ibid.*, p. 31.
17. *Ibid.*, p. 36.
18. *Al-Masri* newspaper, 28 March 1954. For more details about this episode, see *Abd El-Nasser et la crise de mars 1954* by Abd El-Azim Ramadane, Dar Rose Al-Youssef, (Cairo, 1976).
19. Esmar Saif Ad-Dawla, *op. cit.*
20. Esmat Saif Ad-Dawla, *Nasser etait-il un dictateur?* p. 31. Ahmed Hamrouch relates this same episode in a more precise manner because he was a member of the Free Officers. He confirms the authenticity of the episode and adds that Khaled Moheddine and Yusseff Saddiq supported Nasser for democracy.
21. Abd El-Azim Ramadane, *op. cit.*, pp. 158 and 159.
22. In the novel *le Nouveau Caire* by Naguib Mahfouz, someone says, 'All political doctrines, when applied in Egypt, become dictatorships.'
23. This is completely contrary and inapplicable to the Egyptian revolution. International revolution cannot be applied to Egypt despite its openness to international experience and thinking. The Egyptian revolution is essentially the product of internal, social factors.
24. This report is signed by Gamal Al-Oteigi, Head of the Commission. The text is taken from the book, *Les Lois d'exception de l'Etat de la securite des biens sequestres* by Moustafa Kamal Mourib. Dar Al-Fikr Ali-Arabi (Cairo, 1947).
25. Official Gazette, No. 24, 19th October 1972.
26. *Ibid.*, No. 40, 5th October 1972.
27. *Ibid.*
28. Michel Kamel, '*Le Jeu de la democratie et les luttes pour le pouvoir en Egypte*' in *As-Safir* (Lebanese newspaper) 3rd August 1978.
29. *Ibid.*
30. Naguib Mahluz, *Les Enfants de notre ruelle.* This novel treats the confrontation between religion and science as symbolic of the search for social justice between men. It was published in its entirety at Dar Al-Adab (Beirut, 1967).
31. See *La Bataille de El-Katib contre la democratie de la droite egyptienne* in *Al-Sakata* (Iraqi magazine) 5th January 1975.
32. See the message sent by Salah Haissa and published in *Al-Watan Al-Arabi* (Paris) 3rd February 1978.
33. See article by Amir Iskandar, in *Al-Thaoura* (Iraqi daily newspaper) 22nd May 1978.
34. *Ibid.*
35. See Amir Iskandar, *Al-Thawra Al-Iraqiyyah*, 7th May 1978.
36. The papers of this colloquium were released by 'Wahdane' Company for publication and printing in Cairo in 1978.
37. *Al-Ahram*, 31st January 1971.
38. See *la Democratie et les libertes academique dans les universites egyptiennes.*
39. *Ibid.*

40. See *Response a la declaration du gouvernement* made by the National Progressive and Unionist Assembly Party, (Cairo, 1978), p. 18.
41. *Ibid.*, p. 47.
42. *Ibid.*
43. The City of the Dead (the Cairo Cemetery) has become a city for the living. According to latest estimates 500,000 people live in this city where one 'room' is occupied by an average of 10 people.
44. See Amir Iskandar, *la Lutte entre la droite et la gauche dans la domaine de la culture egyptienne* (Beirut, 1978).

12. A Dictatorship in Favour of a Separate Peace

The 'Zionisation' of Egypt

Forty-eight hours before the celebration of the 25th anniversary of the July 1952 revolution, the Egyptian airforce carried out a surprise attack on Libyan territory. In fact it was not a surprise, neither in the moment chosen nor in the large number of planes involved. The correspondent of the *New York Times* in Beirut wrote on 25th July 1977 that what had occurred should have happened in May; 'but the United States asked Sadat to postpone the operation and to undertake it at a later date.'[1]

Let us recall in relation to this that Husni Mubarak, Vice-President of the Republic, accompanied by the Egyptian Chief of Staff, paid a lightning visit to Chad and Sudan between the 9th and 11th July 1977. After this the Chad Ambassador in Cairo declared that the problem between Libya and Chad had been raised during the visit.[2] On 12th July 1977 President Sadat himself had inspected several positions in the Western Sahara.

On the very eve of this operation against a member of the tripartite Arab Union (Egypt, Libya and Syria) that was in force until that moment, Mr Begin announced a new peace plan for the Middle East of which the first stage would be the agreement for a separate peace with Egypt. Mr Dayan, Israeli Minister of Foreign Affairs, declared that as far as he was concerned Israeli peace would only be a tangible reality when Israel and Egypt had a common enemy. He added: 'The only thing capable of guaranteeing a genuine peace between the State is a common strategy for the countries of the region both in time of war and in time of peace. Thus there will be a common enemy and also a common prosperity.'

A great deal was written by way of interpretation of this war. I believe that the degeneration of the relationship between Egypt and Libya is an integral part of the strategic perspective of an alliance with the West and with its Zionist extension in the Middle East. The massive air raid on Libyan territory can be considered in the same way as the Sinai Agreement signed in September 1975. They in fact comprise an affirmative reply to the proposition of Mr Begin and the thinking of Mr Dayan. That is why I consider them to be the first steps towards the visit to Jerusalem. In other words, this lightning war was the beginning of a practical policy, not for the visit to

Jerusalem, but for the creation of a strategic alliance between America, Egypt and Israel in the Middle East.

Here we must go back a little: the analysis according to which the consequences of the defeat of 1967 were formulated in the Khartoum Summit in September of that same year, and which proposed that Resolution 242, was the basic reason for the visit to Jerusalem is far from true.[3] Certainly, it cannot be denied that the years of defeat were behind the three 'Nos' of the Khartoum Summit: No to peace, No to negotiation and No to recognition of Israel. They were also behind the desire to strengthen relationships with the world at large by acceptance of Resolution 242 and the Rogers Plan of 1969. However, local, Arab and international elements should be considered in the following perspective.

The Egyptian people who had revolted in 1964, 1967 and 1968, did not know and perhaps do not know that Nasser was conducting an unceasing fight for democracy within a small circle. Today we understand better that the 30th March 1968 declaration remained a dead letter, for most of his colleagues were against democracy.[4]

On the other hand, we should link these popular uprisings for the application of democracy with the calls for the application of a war economy, the creation of national committees for the battle, and to the very light condemnations of leaders of the defeated army, which had to lead to new procedures. On 12th April 1968, Nasser had said to King Hussein during a meeting behind closed doors:

> The most important subject is not contained in Mr. Yaring's proposition. The main thing is to know if we want to move towards a direct or indirect meeting with the Israelis. It would then be necessary to know the consequences of rejecting such a proposition. I reply for Egypt and I say, 'No, we cannot accept a direct or an indirect meeting, whether at Rhodes or Geneva. We reject such a proposition. Our people want war because they do not accept a peace in this form. I believe that the people have borne enough of all this'.[5]

After accepting the Rogers proposition, Nasser said to a leader of the socialist bloc: 'Israel would like to have negotiations with us, even though they are occupying our territory. To accept such a proposition implies capitulation.'[6] So when we read the declaration according to which Egypt accepts Security Council Resolution No. 242 of 1967 and the Rogers Plan in 1969, we must remind the international community that it is an acceptance as much by the people as by its leadership in recognition of the three 'Nos' of the Khartoum Summit. Let us remember the war of attrition. It proves that the military solution had never been ruled out at the Khartoum Summit. This solution, that was then replaced by a substitute war in 1973, proved on the battlefield itself that it was a possibility.

It is no longer a secret today that the Americans and their friends had, on several occasions in 1967 and 1969, proposed an honourable peace with

Israel to Nasser as the only way in which Sinai could be returned to Egypt. The defeated leader, and this is also no longer a secret, had refused this peace because it constituted a betrayal of the revolution and the strategic dimension of Egyptian security. In fact, President Sadat was completely sincere when he said one day about this refusal: 'Nasser could not accept the invitation to go to Israel because he was too attached to old ideas.'[7] We can summarise the Arab factors after the defeat as follows:

1) The three 'Nos' of Khartoum, accompanied by unconditional financial support from the oil-producing countries.

2) The overthrow of the Abd El Rahman Aref regime in Iraq in July 1968, the overthrow of the Senussis dynasty in Libya in September 1969, and it was not by chance that the generation that had seized power from Mashreq to the Maghreb should support the Palestinian cause, the unity of the Arab national and the nationalisation of oil resources.

3) The summit following the Black September of 1970 proved the existence of a Palestinian rebirth after the defeat and the massacres. This proves that Palestine is the only way to peace in the Middle East.

4) The concrete decisions of the Rabat Summit in 1974 show that the tactical goal sought by the Arab nation can be summarised in four points: (a) Total liberation of all Arab territory occupied since the June 1967 aggression and the rejection of all concessions concerning those territories and national sovereignty; (b) Liberation of Arab Jerusalem and total rejection of any situation casting doubt on the total Arab sovereignty in the Holy City; (c) Respect for the rights of the Palestinian people according to the decisions of the Palestine Liberation Organisation, sole representative of the Palestinian people; (d) The Palestinian cause is the cause of all the Arabs. No Arab party has the right to make concessions on this subject with respect to previous Arab summit resolutions.[8]

On the international level, for the first time in its modern history, the Soviet Union risked sending its military technicians outside the Warsaw Pact area. At the 1974 Rabat Summit, the Lebanese President Franjieh was delegated to speak at the United Nations on the Palestinian problem in the name of the summit. The Palestine Liberation Organisation can be admitted to the international organisation as an observer member. Yasser Arafat made a speech to the United Nations in which one glimpsed both the rifle and the olive branch. On 1st October 1977, the Soviet Union was able to convince the United States to make a common declaration recognising for the first time 'the legitimate rights of the Palestinian people' and calling for the Geneva Conference, where all parties should be represented, including representatives of the Palestinian people, to be convened. President Carter, after Nixon's resignation and Ford's failure, was the first American President to refer to a 'home' for the Palestinians.

Seven weeks after President Carter's declarations, President Sadat boarded the aircraft to fly to Ben Gurion airport and, the day after his arrival, to attend prayers on the occasion of the Bayram feast in the El Aksa mosque in Occupied Jerusalem. After all that, can one still pretend that

Resolution 242 was indirectly the reason for this unfortunate visit?[9] At the same moment that international public opinion was preparing to accept the Geneva Conference, Presidant Sadat packed his bags for his journey to Israel with the firm intention of opening direct negotiations with the political leadership of the Israeli occupation.[10] This carnival did not fail to dazzle international public opinion and few wondered what had happened and what was going to happen. In his memoirs,[11] President Sadat wrote: 'How did this visit take place?' and in reply: 'Two months before this initiative I was surprised to receive a communication from the Egyptian Embassy in Washington telling me of a personal message that had been sent to me by President Carter. At my request it was brought to me by special courier. I read it and I believe that nobody knows what it contained. In the same way I wrote the reply by hand and, having sealed it with sealing wax, gave it to the emissary who had to return it personally to President Carter.'[12] President Sadat added that Carter's message contained the elements that enabled the initiative achieved two months later to be undertaken.[13] Sadat said that the American President's letter provided him with a new path.[14]

Today, whatever circumstances were behind what was published in the *Washington Post* in the middle of 1977 concerning the relationship between President Sadat and the CIA, it is not difficult to see the intervention of this organisation in Middle East events throughout the entire period concerned, either in Egypt or in Lebanon.

In reality, the strategic plan of Tel Aviv and Washington ever since the tripartite aggression of 1956, consisted in finding a new formula for the Israeli-Western alliance, in such a way as to give the Hebrew State the chance of expansion in the Arab Mashreq, and to enable the Shah's empire to extend to the Arab Gulf, and the new American colonialism to impose its hegemony over the entire region from the Maghreb to the Near East. Medium-term strategy consisted in knitting this region together in a series of military alliances equivalent to the Atlantic Alliance, and able to besiege the Soviet Union and the socialist bloc as well as any local radical surprise. The Eisenhower Plan of 1957 was in reality only a tactical application of this strategy. As this plan had not succeeded, the Israeli attack of 1967 became necessary. But, for the United States and Israel, this could only lead to Resolution 242 and the Egypto-Jordanian acceptance of the Rogers Plan. Neither realised the long-term strategy of Tel-Aviv and Washington.

However, the defeat created a favourable climate in which to strive for this goal. Here we must repeat that it is difficult to believe that the events of Black September in 1970 and the death of Nasser were just chance occurrences. What happened afterwards cannot in any way be considered just as a simple succession of events. But neither can we say it was a plot. In fact, it was a strategy that knew how to take advantage of the shift of Palestinian resistance to Lebanon and the death of Nasser as a starting point for the reversal of the situation in Egypt and in Lebanon. It can be considered as an internal counter-revolution in which monopolistic Western capitalism (American and Zionist) acted against the Arab national movement, against the will to unity, independence and radical change.

I repeat, it was not a plot but simply an international swing to the right, and one hostile to the Arabs, which could bring about the American-Israeli strategy not by diplomatic means but by means of the security organisations. It is because of this that there were many surprises and manoeuvres in the Middle East crisis. Among the most spectacular surprises we can quote the visit to Jerusalem, the Camp David resolutions, the Israeli-American discussions and reconciliation, the break with the Soviet Union, changing the concept of a Palestinian 'home' into 'legitimate rights of the Palestinian people', and settling on the idea of an autonomous government in Western Jordan and in Gaza. This kind of action was resorted to by Egypt and Lebanon; it is regrettable that some Egyptians and Lebanese positively contributed to it as a result of their confused attitudes and, at the end of the day, their alliance with Israel. In fact they reacted to this type of action as though it represented something positive and to the strategy as though it were a tactic.

What was asked of Egypt and of Lebanon?

Egypt was asked to liquidate its army, its economy and the cultural legacy of the man-in-the-street. Lebanon was asked to end its Palestinian role as well as its quasi-liberal system. What was being asked of the two countries was in fact one and the same thing. That is why there was a concomitance or parallelism between the two trajectories: that which started with the death of Nasser and was completed at Camp David, and that which started with the massacre of Black September and finished with the war in Lebanon. In fact, Israeli strategy which had practically rejected the partition of Palestine in 1948 is the same strategy that, in practice and in theory, rejected the existence of a Palestinian mini-State in West Jordan and in Gaza in 1978. American strategy which favoured the decolonisation of Egypt in 1956 is the same strategy that favours decolonisation of Sinai in Israel in 1978. American strategy has well and truly taken over from the old colonialism.

The 'Lebanonisation' or 'Saudisation' of Egypt was not being sought, as some believed. What was, and is still being sought, is the colonisation of Egypt. The division of Lebanon is not being sought, simply the liquidation of the Palestinian problem and the quasi-liberal forum that Lebanon is. In the same way Egypt does not want to go back to the time of King Farouk, or the British occupation, or feudalism for, during that period, Egypt was almost liberal, almost independent and almost Arab. Egypt is being asked to leap into the dark, for there is no compromise between Arab Egypt and dependent Egypt. Even Israel is genuine in its rejection of any move in the direction of compromise since its creation until the 1973 war. Israel, with or without Sadat, rejects any strategy other than its own. For this same reason, the United States, alone or representing the whole of the West as in the past, supports Israel, the Zionist empire in the Middle East and the goal of a Western presence in one of the world's most strategic areas.

The Upside-Down Peace

The fact that American-Israeli security organisations were used to implement Western and Zionist strategy only confirms what was proved in Egypt and in Lebanon, the means of operation and the objective conditions; for there was never a social choice by one class or another in Egypt or Lebanon to bring about the counter-revolution in Cairo or Beirut, simply because there was no indigenous counter-revolution in either Egypt or Lebanon. The instrument of counter-revolution cannot therefore pass without leaving its mark on events: the two putsches in Egypt and Lebanon, and Begin's coming to power do not lack coherence. History can only laugh at the Israeli Labour Party, member of the Socialist International, which conducted four wars in 29 years against the Arabs, only to see the leader of the Extremist Religious Alliance, the *Likud*, sign the first peace treaty with an Arab country. In reality, the coming together of the Muslim, Christian and Jewish fascists (i.e. religious racialism) was the first instrument in the realisation of an international strategy against the Arabs.

The fascist repression in Egypt, the preventative war conducted by the Lebanese right-wing extremists and the propagation of racialist ideologies in effect constitute the first steps of a dictatorship heading towards a separate peace and preparing to eliminate the Palestinian resistance. This is just the start of the consolidation of the Israeli empire in the Middle East. The presence of middlemen in the regimes of Egypt and Lebanon is the embodiment of this instrument, even at the top of the Egyptian regime and within the Lebanese political structure. The objective condition was certainly the economic and military fall of the Nasser regime. The international counter-revolution had learnt, in 1952, that following the collapse of regimes in Egypt any kind of force could fill the vacuum because of the absence of any real alternative. And as the armed forces had filled this vacuum for 20 years, thus sowing disorder in the plans of the old and the new colonialism, the vacuum should now be filled again by force, to confirm the fall of Nasserism in such a way that the new regime could be the extension of this fall.

And so the new regime becomes a simple means for the achievement of international counter-revolution and effective power remains outside the country.[15] This is the real meaning of Sadat's putsch in Egypt. It is not a matter of going backwards, it is a leap against the flow of the nation's history. It is not a choice made by a given class, it is a confiscation by force of any choice, whatever its source. It is within this framework that we can understand why the regime has repressed the authentic right of the nation, i.e. the new Wafd.[16] It is also explains the lamentable failure of what for a while was called the centre party, the ruling party.[17]

In fact the Sadat regime is not essentially a local power that must be overturned; it is simply the instrument of the international counter-revolution filling the political vacuum between the fall of Nasserism and the absence of an alternative. Consequently, it has no roots within the national territory.

Its destiny is linked with the power of the counter-revolution existing outside its frontiers. This means that the social infrastructure of Egypt, despite all the legislative variables affecting relations of production, remains basically the same.[18]

This also signifies that any future revolution will not be Nasserist.[19] Thirdly, it signifies that the international factor is no longer secondary as it was in the past.[20]

Finally, it signifies that the Zionisation of Egypt can only be achieved by tearing the economic, military, political, social and cultural roots out of their Egyptian soil, for these new bases must have a solid foundation. Thus can be explained the reluctance of the Hebrew State to conclude a separate peace with Egypt and the United States (they too were not eager to go to Geneva) or to radically end the war in Lebanon, or finally to create a 'home' for the Palestinians. Instruments must have time under the control of the general information services, in order to prepare the land for the building of the new Egypt and the new Lebanon.

Economic Corollary

The prosperity of Lebanon was destroyed by civil war but there was a different situation in Egypt. Law No. 43 of 1974 and modifications to Law No. 42 of 1977 opened the doors of the Egyptian economy to foreign capital controlled by the multinationals. Consequently, the hegemony of these multinational companies was established over the Egyptian economy and this in a framework of Egyptian economic development which could only be dependent.[21]

Law No. 118 of 1975 on the import-export sector came at the same time as the Second Sinai Agreement. Its consequence was the dismantling of State control on foreign trade; the private sector could therefore import the machines, tools and raw materials it wanted.

None of this matters, for the importing of consumer products guaranteed a faster, higher and more certain profit. Just a little while before the visit to Occupied Jerusalem, the Law on Foreign Currency was promulgated (Law No. 97). Not only was this law in opposition to the economic measures of the Nasser regime but it also annulled all control over the bank as practised by Egypt since 1948, i.e. even in the time of the monarchy. The new law granted the right to any person to keep foreign currency, which could be obtained with no legal obligation to declare its origin. In other words, this signifies a cancellation of all control by the Egyptian Central Bank over the operations of foreign banks. It also signifies the impossibility of formulating, and especially of implementing, any policy concerning foreign exchange.[22] But the most serious consequence of these laws is the impossibility of any national planning, even in the sense of traditional capitalism. This law was complemented by three other measures: the authorisation of imports without monetary transfer, the cancellation of commercial agreements with the countries of the East and the Third World.[23] The third measure was the promulgation of Law No. 111 of 1975 concerning the reorganisation of the nationalised sector. This law ended the existence of the public institutions that managed the affairs of the companies under their control. This liquidation was immediately linked with the idea of offering the shares of the companies in the nationalised sector for private sale. In this way the national economy was dismantled.

Ali El Gretli, eminent economist and former Minister of Finance, wrote:

> The widening of facilities granted to the foreign and private sectors will result in an increase in the profits of the import-export sectors, the property business, and in brokers' commissions and in what the press and the ministers call "parasitic" revenues. Above all, the exchequer is incapable of controlling these types of profits, including the riches accumulated by landowners in the town and in certain suburbs that attract foreigners and the rich. Opposition will very rapidly be felt in attempts to reconcile two objectives: freedom of the private and foreign sectors on one side and a fair distribution on the other. There is no doubt that the enlargement of the foreign and private sectors will make the task of planning more difficult than in the past for, if the new policy is successful, that would mean that a large part of the organised activity would be completely outside the bounds of planning.[24]

A statistical study published in the Official Gazette from August 1975 to December 1977 proves that the capitalist sector, which now controls the Egyptian economy, depends completely upon foreign capital and also that the social base of this sector is oligarchic. It is useful to recall here that the economic basis of this sector is an interest-charging commerce having no relationship with productive projects. The immediate consequence of this type of economic activity is an increase in the need for foreign loans, of which a large part is short-term, bearing interests between 12% and 19%.[25]

These measures, taken at the same time as the steps towards a separate peace with Israel, do not express the good intention of Western capitalism as was the case in the time of Said Pasha and Khedive Ismail. What is being sought today in Egypt is its transformation on the economic basis of the Camp David Agreements. The main points of this statement can be discovered in an article by journalist Marie-Christine Aulas in *Le Monde Diplomatique,* October 1978: the fall in the value of the Egyptian Pound was accompanied by an increase in the cost of industrial and agricultural production, which leads to an inequality in competitiveness between the local product and the imported product. Also, the emigration of Egyptian manpower to other Arab countries played its part in increasing the cost of national goods in such a way that small processing industries were obliged to stop production and enter businesses such as tourism, services and other import/export activities. All this led to higher inflation, higher emigration and higher unemployment.[26]

The situation is no better in agricultural matters. Peasants are turning from cotton production to dedicate the bulk of their efforts to more profitable crops. On this point we note that a few years ago a feddan cost between

E£500 and E£800, whereas today it costs more than E£7,000. For practical and rapid profitability, it is preferable to exploit the land in projects that are non-productive in agricultural terms, which is why only 35% of products are exported today. Thus the deficit in the balance of payments reached E£1,215 million in 1977. Still according to Marie-Christine Aulas, Arab aid to Egypt between 1971 and 1973 is estimated at $13,400 million and the Russian loan has never been repaid. This shows that an invisible pit exists which has nothing to do with the national economy but which swallows up most of the aid and the unpaid debts. This pit was discovered during an affair that Marie-Christine Aulas calls 'the Scandal of El Amereia'. According to her, this scandal would have had much more serious consequences than the Pyramids Hill or Egyptian Cinema scandals were it not for a falling out of the thieves involved. The project consisted in creating a textile complex in the Amereia region, close to Alexandria. Its capital was estimated at $1,500 million, split between several multinational companies, several Arab investors and a certain understanding with the Egyptian State. But just as the project was about to be implemented, and the Misr Bank had paid out the equivalent of E£127 million in scarce currency, the Prime Minister suspended the project in June 1978 because 'it did not satisfy a vital economic need.' Furthermore, some 'serious mistakes had been made by high authorities.' Today there is no longer any doubt: corruption, the highest stage of parasitic action, has become the central feature of the new Egyptian economic formula.

It is just this new formula that constitutes the corollary of the peace. Without it neither Israel nor the United States would have agreed to sign the Camp David Agreement, no matter what political concessions were made by President Sadat.

Although the Egyptian middle classes reacted strongly to such scandalous projects, they were nevertheless slow to understand the way in which the country was being turned into an important base of Zionist economy. It was only on the signing of the peace treaty that they discovered that the much sought after economic peace could only be achieved after their own destruction. That is why their reaction was violent, not that they realised their main error: that, in following the mirage of peace enabling them to escape the Nasserist bureaucracy, they fell into the trap of economic dependence.

The Egyptian middle classes were slow to see the logic of the concomitance between the events in Egypt and Lebanon, and between the military and political moves between the ruling regime, the Israeli leadership and the American administration on the one hand and the economic measures and repression of democracy on the other hand.[27] The Egyptian middle classes only became aware of the sinister destiny awaiting them when they read the clauses of the Camp David Agreement. In order better to illustrate the differences between the economic ideas of the Egyptian middle classes and those of the Zionist empire, it will suffice to refer to two studies: that of Dr. Eleazar Scheffer, made in the summer of 1977 at Mr. Begin's request, and that of Mr. Lutfi Abd El Azzim made in the winter of 1978 and published in

El-Ahram (economic section).

The first study says that Israeli military expenditure has risen by a factor of 25 over a period of 21 years (1955–77); it absorbed 15% of the GNP. Peace could reduce this expenditure by $1,000 million, which would increase economic investment in Israel by about 50%. We should note that this study was conducted before the visit to Jerusalem. But we should also note that, after the publication of this study, the Israeli press started talking of the opportunity offered to Tel-Aviv to take the place of Beirut. The author of the study said, 'The profit made by Arab countries in commercial exchange would certainly be less than that made by Israel.' Finally, the author advises 'the development of Israeli industry to meet the needs of the Arab countries.'[28]

The Egyptian study poses several questions. 'What have we done,' says the author, 'for those who are going to be demobilised while the country is suffering from unemployment and an excess of manpower?' A second question concerns the inflation that has increased since the peace because of monetary liquidity in the Egyptian market. Thirdly, there is the matter of the interruption of Arab aid after the peace. The author wonders if those responsible had considered that such support would not go on for ever. He also adds that lack of government control has exposed the Egyptian market to violent attacks. The society had become a consumer society without any consideration of the requirements of development in Egypt. At the end of his study the author writes: 'A large difference exists between the new Arab capital and Hebrew capital, experienced as the latter is in the business of the financial and investment markets. What must be done after the Camp David agreements?' Lufti Abd El Azzin replied:

> We must begin immediately with a reconsideration of the Arab and foreign investment laws; new laws must prevent the infiltration of Arab or Jewish capital in areas that can harm the Egyptian people and economic development. We must consider the possibility of forbidding certain areas of investment to non-Egyptian capitals, whatever their nationality. We are thinking first of all about services, property and commerce. We can open the areas of industrial development to foreign capital but only in full conformity with an industrial five-year plan.

This thinker considered the danger of the open economy only from the moment of the peace with Israel. The Egyptian middle classes who complained of restrictions in Nasser's time today find themselves at grips with Zionist capital. They realise that the opening of relations with Israel signifies the end of their own existence as a productive force, as a market and as an important element in the relations of production. The whole of Egypt is now paying for this delay in realisation by the national middle classes . . . the business must be dealt with.

The Guardian of the Fall

Immediately after the Camp David summit, President Sadat declared that he was going to proceed with a total change in the State. The first step in this change was the elimination of three great personalities who had accompanied his complicated progress from the very beginning — Prime Minister Mamduh Salem, Marshal Abd El Bani El Gamassi and Said Marei, President of the People's Council. Mamduh Salem was the first to fall among those manipulated by the putsch of 14th May 1971. He was the last to be eliminated, for his role that night eight years ago was to ensure the security of the putsch. Afterwards he converted the security agencies into power centres to such a degree that the President could not dismiss him in January 1977. American participation in the reorganisation of the Egyptian security services, especially after the visit to Jerusalem, was one of the most important factors in the changing of the State, as expressed by the President himself. For it was not just a matter of defending the person of prime responsibility, the instruments of repression had to be brought under the direct control of the external power to prevent the creation of any local power centre that could have control over a strategic position.

President Sadat removed Mr. Salem from power when the party he directed was completely discredited by the Egyptian people. The second man, Said Marei, was eliminated, to the great surprise of all observers; he had been promoted to be Adviser to the President before leaving his post as President of the People's Council. Even though he was the President's son's brother-in-law, the elimination of Marei symbolised the expulsion of the last productive sector, i.e. agricultural capitalism, from the ruling political structure.

General Abd El-Ghani El Gamassi, Minister of Defence, and General Mohammed Ali Fahmid, Chief of Staff, represent the very essence of the radical change foreseen by President Sadat. El Gamassi was the symbol of the October 1973 war after the elimination of General Chazli. Only history will reveal to us the role played by the airman Husni Mubarak who suddenly became Vice-President. He was able to lead the battle against Messrs Mamduh Salem and Abd El-Ghani El Gamassi, to the point where he could take over from them and be very close to the American control of the security agencies. This took place while the chemist-officer Arhraf Mahuane, husband of Mula Gamal Abd El-Nasser, became more and more removed from the circles of power in which he had been an eminent personality. In fact Arhraf Mahuane had dominated the Presidency of the Republic since the dismissal of Sami Charaf and his participation in the events of May 1971. Meanwhile, he had infiltrated the environment of oil capital via the Arab arms industry network. There was even talk of several arms deals in which he had been an intermediary which made him, thanks to commissions, one of Egypt's biggest millionaires.

The elimination of El Gamassi therefore implied the start of a total change in the military institution. In fact, even though compromised between Mamduh Salem and Said Marei in the consolidation of the new regime since the signing of the Kilometre 101 Treaty, El Gamassi could in no way take part in the elimination of the national military institution which had existed for more than a century. Nobody yet knows General Gamassi's attitude to the aggression against Libya or the participation of Egypt in the African wars. But it is certain that the Egyptian Minister of Defence had imposed the condition of not firing on the people before authorising the army to go into the streets during the events of 1977. El Gamassi, with Egyptian foreign affairs experts, was one of the main reasons for the failure of the Ismailia summit. The absence of the Minister of Defence from Camp David was no mere chance.

Several days before the departure for Camp David, a four-paragraph report was submitted to El Gamassi. The first paragraph noted the increase in the number of Egyptians working in the international mercenary market after leaving the ranks of the national army. This secret report stated that more than 50 officers had become involved in this kind of business between 1974 and 1978. The second paragraph noted the ever increasing loss of light and medium arms. At the same time, dumps of arms belonging to the Egyptian army were discovered in Upper Egypt. The third paragraph noted the tendency of young officers to go in for business; in fact the new dispensation facilitated this. The fourth paragraph dealt with the Military Technical College which at one time had been the goal of ambitious youth; requests for enrolment in the college were falling by 16% each year.

It is convenient to note here certain other facts that are relevant to those exposed in the secret report. The officers who had taken part in the 1973 war and whose heroism had been recognised had all been transferred to administrative posts. To this must be added the vast and sudden wave of transfers and dismissals which took place without any arrangement between the Presidency of the Republic and the Chief of Staff. Immediately after the signing of the Camp David Agreement, another report was received by the Minister of Defence concerning certain tracts signed by 'The Free Officers' and distributed within certain army units. There was a new tone to these tracts and they contained very important information. They were most widely distributed within the armed forces but they were also found in civilian society. They said, among other things:

> Since the end of 1977, hundreds of American military technicians have arrived in small groups wearing civilian clothes. The officers were surprised by this. Unit leaders were not informed. The task of the American military technicians was not the military training of the army; their task was the elaboration of new plans concerning a new role for the Egyptian army. For no apparent reason they also tried to get to know young officers.
>
> The American military technicians freely discussed, with anyone who so wished, a new strategy for the Egyptian armed forces, not in matters of war but concerning a new role for the Egyptian army in the future as well as its possible role in Arab and African affairs.

At small parties that they organised from time to time, the American military technicians asked many questions about the social origin, cultural interests and personal relationships of each officer.

None of this information was new to Marshal El Gamassi. On the other hand, what was new was the violence of their tone and their progressively increasing distribution. President Sadat, on his return from Camp David, was given this same report by General Kamal Hassan Ali, head of general information. The report added that something was astir within the forces that indicated a serious event. The President instructed the Minister of Defence to find out the size of this movement and its capacity to carry out a military putsch. El Gamassi replied: 'Mr. President, there is no putsch within the army; there is a putsch against the army. The sudden change in Egyptian military strategy over a very short period can cause anxiety in the ranks of the armed forces.'

What Gamassi did not say was that for the first time in the modern history of the Egyptian army, i.e. from Mohamed Ali to Gamal Abd El-Nasser, there were plans to change its national identity. This army had never changed its national strategy, even the British occupation did not prevent it from going to Palestine or from revolting in 1952. Change in the identity of the military institution, so that it resembled the armies of the fascist regimes in Latin America, and so that it would be dependent on the strategy of the Atlantic Alliance, had for the first time come to Egypt. In reality, post-Camp David conditions require a new army, acting according to the new alliances and strategic hostilities. An army is necessary to preserve the situation following the putsch within Egypt and to carry out the international counter-revolution aiming at national liberation movements in the Arab nation and in Africa.

But all these attempts to destroy the military institution are, like the economic endeavour, rather superficial because the Egyptian army, like the society, is, in its infrastructure, proof against all such attempts. This infrastructure is even hostile to such attempts to change things. The 1936 treaty had enabled the children of the lower middle classes to enter the Military College and later become the leaders of the 1952 revolution and, during the Nasser period, children of workers and peasants were able to establish a military society parallel to the infrastructure of Nasserist society, a military society that is indestructible except by means of an unparalleled civil war. That is why the real guardian of the decadence is the Supreme Head of the Armed Forces, i.e. President Sadat himself. In these circumstances the armed militias of the ruling party became the possible alternative to the republican guard, the central security forces and even the army. President Sadat had already started to form this militia a little while before the creation of his party. One might suppose that the specific task of this militia is the protection of persons – but bearing in mind the opposition of the people, nobody can now claim that the ingredients for a civil war do not exist as never before seen in Egyptian history. The new policy towards the army has become alarming to the citizens of both town and country at a time when everything seems new in the history of the country.

Many people feel nonplussed by this double phenomenon: the President of the Republic visits Israel without his Foreign Minister; he returns from Camp David without his Foreign Minister. Also, the preparations for this strange visit were like those for a comedy; an American correspondent interviewed President Sadat and the Israeli Prime Minister. Sadat said that he was ready to go to Israel immediately; the Israeli Premier declared that he was ready to defer his visit to Great Britain in order to receive the Egyptian President. And the visit took place.

In reality it was not difficult to make the link between this double phenomenon and the opposition of the army and the Foreign Ministry to the steps taken by President Sadat and to 'the external power' that had prepared this comedy.

Let us recall that the Egyptian Parliament discussed the subject of the visit only on the very day that the President was to go to Jerusalem. It is no surprise if the two most sensitive parties of the old Egyptian bureaucracy — the military institution and democracy — were dislocated first by the entreaties of the higher levels of hierarchy, then by an interference in actions. The army politically opposed this visit while the Foreign Ministry opposed it for military reasons.

This change in roles was in fact an expression of what has been called 'the secret appendices to the Camp David Agreement'. Among other reasons, these appendices were behind the absence of the Egyptian military element and the dismissal of the diplomatic element. The secret Camp David decisions did not come in the form of appendices as had been the case with the Second Sinai Agreement but in the form of letters exchanged between the parties concerned, and at other times by formulas, sometimes specific and sometimes general, in the very text of the documents. There is no doubt that the most important articles among these decisions are those concerning Occupied Jerusalem and the relationship between Egypt and the Arab countries opposed to Israel in the case of war. These are the decisions that led to a quasi-recognition of Jerusalem as the capital of the Hebrew State, and to a quasi-undertaking by Egypt not to go to war on the side of an Arab country in the future. These are the decisions that strategically signify that Egyptian security no longer needs the support of the East, since a union has been made with the very source of danger. Because of the fact that the expressions 'national character' and 'religious identity' in relation to Palestinine or Arab Jerusalem lose their significance, which formed a constant feature of the history of the region, Arab solidarity in the face of the enemy loses all justification. The Arab Embassies in Cairo closed down one after the other while preparations were being made for the creation of an Israeli Embassy. These are the symbolic facts that can be added to the East's turning towards Libya under the influence of the Egyptian army. This turning in fact hides another more serious one: that of Egypt from its Arab connection, that is, away from its national independence and towards giving its allegiance to the Zionist-American empire. The culmination of these symbolic facts is that the

Egyptian regime congratulates Israel on the occasion of its national celebration. Previously Egypt commemorated the 15th May as the day of the usurpation of Palestine.

We see this same significance in the way in which the Camp David Agreements were received in Egypt. The following points can be made about this:

First, the two declarations published by the National Progressive and Unionist Assembly Party and that made by Mr. Khaled Mohy El Din to Parliament, constitute a clear rejection by the party and its leader of what was called The Peace Initiative. The most important element in these declarations was the explanation of the content of the Camp David Agreements, which for the first time gave Egypt two types of frontier: at a distance of 50km. to the east of the Canal there would be no Egyptian military sovereignty over the Sinai, and even within that space, only one single military unit would be authorised to remain. As for the rest of the country's geographic and military space, it will be filled by United Nations forces and American early warning instruments. This means that even from a formal point of view there is no total national independence. That being so, it is hardly necessary to mention Israel's entreaties, during the drafting in Washington, to be associated with the ownership of the Sinai oil wells and legally to rent a certain area at Sharm El Sheik. There is even less need to speak to the Arab identity in Egypt and its undertaking concerning the independence of West Jordan and the Gaza.

Secondly, President Sadat was not surprised by the position taken by the parties of the left. But surprises did come from elsewhere. Without doubt the first consisted in the note sent by the former members of the party of the revolution, Messrs Zakariyyah Mohyi El Din, Hussein El Chafei, Abd El Latef Bagdadi and Kamal El-Din Hussein. This note arrived at the Presidency at the same time as it arrived at the press, on 1st October 1978. The four historic leaders entirely rejected the Camp David Agreements in their detail, in their military aspects and in their political aspects. The attitude taken by the Muslim Brotherhood was no less surprising. The magazine *Ad-Daawa* published an article rejecting capitulation to the national and religious enemy. The article was signed by Omar El-Telemsani.

But the biggest surprise was, without doubt, the heated discussions that took place within the People's Council which had been specially summoned to approve the President's decisions. These discussions were accompanied by a declaration signed by a group of independent deputies, published the day after the note from the former members of the Revolutionary Council. This declaration was signed by Hilmi Murad, Abd El Moneim Hussein, Talaat Raslan, Ahmed Yussif, Kamel Saad, Karam Izz El-Din, sheikh Salah Abu Ismail, Ali El-Gahi and Ali Salama. The signatories demanded that the government recognise the Israeli claims only on the following three conditions:
a) Total evacuation of the Sinai; b) Reduction in the period of evacuation; c) The submission of all the airports to Egyptian sovereignty.
The declaration also warned of a possible Israeli hegemony over Egypt.
It expressed the signatories' refusal to accept the failure to recognise a return

to an Arab Jerusalem while Israel was giving assurances that the city would remain united and become the official capital of the State of Israel. It also contested the fact that the agreements did not mention the rights of the Palestinian people to self-determination and the establishment of their own State. Finally, it criticised the fact that there had been no consultation with the front-line Arab countries.

As for the note drawn up by the People's Council, and despite the expulsion of Deputy Kamel Ahmed, it did not differ from the declaration made by the independent deputies and the articles of Hilmi Murad published in the newspaper *El Chark al Aousat* on 13th October 1978. These oppositional moves can explain the fact that Said Marei had been adviser to the President before dissolving parliament, modifying the constitution and proceeding to new elections to set up a parliament entirely filled with deputies belonging to the party of the President of the Republic.

In spite of the organisation of popular demonstrations to welcome the President on his return from Camp David, he had to take note that the opposition was ever increasing and included circles that had previously been very close to the regime. He had to realise that his entire regime was deprived of any basis, as it was suspended between external power and internal repression. Sadat felt obliged to 'go into the streets' according to his own expression, to 'face the people directly'.

In parallel with this direct action by the President, the ruling regime started multiple actions to facilitate his task by preparing a cultural and informational background favourable to his move. The cinema and television productions were therefore converted into propaganda aimed at forestalling any possibility of argument and, in order to guard against a dispute in the long term, it was decided to abolish free higher education and the Ministry of Cultural Affairs. Culture and higher education thus suffered the fate of becoming a tiny minority. Even more grave was the decision concerning the change in teaching programmes. At the same time unparalleled facilities were granted to foreign universities and cultural institutions; thus the American University and the Franklin Publications resurfaced. Today the Mobil Oil Company awards prizes and organises literary competitions and the Organisation of Cultural Freedom tries to mobilise the rest of the intellectuals in a vast brainwashing operation on the Egyptian people.

But all this is against history. The building that Sadat is in the process of constructing resembles those being erected by contractors in Egypt today; very elegant erections which, several months after their construction, tumble down completely because of lack of foundations.

All the things going on in Egypt today are no more than scratches which do not touch the depths of the individual and the society. To be sure, these depths are not insensitive to what is happening on the surface, but the interaction between the surface and the depths in no way acts in favour of this regime that is the satellite of a power centre outside the frontiers of the country.

It is true that a void exists between a possible collapse of the regime and the absence of an alternative; but repression will not fill this gap. Because of this the interaction between the variables and the constants in the social history of the Arab Egyptian people will not cease to pave the way towards the *Nahda*.

For the *Nahda* has always risen above the contingencies of the present and the attainments of the past to form a new pattern of revolution in the underdeveloped world. Today Egypt is passing through a period which, only to the short-sighted, appears miraculous.

Notes

1. See *la Demarche de Sadate de Salzbourg a la Knesset,* At-Tadamoun, (1977).
2. *Al-Ahram*, 13th July 1977.
3. See Mustafa El-Hussayni: 'le Destin des initiatives du Sadate' in *Al-Destour* (Lebanese weekly) 13–14 January 1978.
4. See 'Notes secretes de Nasser' in *Al-Destour* published in London, 9th October 1978. Here we read that Nasser, during a meeting on 3rd August 1967 in the presence of Zahariyyah Mohy El-Din, Anuar El-Sadat, Ali-Sabri, Azziz Sidki and Hussein Ach-Chafei, had declared; 'We have two duties to accomplish today, after the defeat: First, we must seek a new regime; and secondly, we must define the main mistakes. I think that we must take action to change the regime that we follow. It contains certain vices. We must change it, if we want to guarantee security and peace in this country, so that opposition is permitted, a genuine opposition and not a mere semblance of one. I am against the one-party system as this leads to dictatorship by certain individuals. If we do not change the present regime, we are heading for an unknown destiny and we cannot know who will take over from us. It is bleak future.'
   Nasser said this just six months before the popular uprising; but the following day he was surprised by the reaction of his colleagues for, without exception and from various ideological and social positions, they all opposed the establishment of genuine democracy. In particular, Zakariyyah Mohyi El-Din said, 'Another party will resurrect the past.' Sadat replied, 'I do not accept the existence of two parties at the same time.' Sidki Suleiman, Prime Minister, said, 'Any person accepting leadership of an opposition party at the present time will certainly be accused of madness.' Ali Sabri said, 'I greatly fear the existence of a second party.'
5. *Ibid.,* chapter 11.
6. *Ibid.,* chapter 7.
7. *Akhbar Al-Yom* (Egyptian daily) 10th December 1977.
8. In reaction to the campaign of mystification conducted by the Egyptian media, the Syrian Government was obliged to distribute a secret document which was published by the Lebanese newspaper *As-Safir* on 30th November 1978.
9. Let us recall with regard to this that Israel had categorically rejected Yaring's note, as it had Sadat when proposing the reopening of the Canal.

We also recall that Begin, as soon as he came to power, returned to the Israeli recognition of Resolution 242 and considered Gaza and Western Jordan as liberated Israeli territories.

10. Some consider that Sadat decided to go to Israel to forestall a military attack that was being prepared. General Chazli dealt with this theory in an article published in *Al-Watan Al-Arabi* in October 1978. According to him, such a theory was unthinkable because of the consequences of the military Sinai Agreement in 1975; the American early warning stations had automatically prevented military action from either side.

11. Sadat, *A la recherche d'une identite.*

12. *Ibid.,* p. 401.

13. *Ibid.,* p. 402.

14. *Ibid..*

15. At a meeting behind closed doors in 1968, President Sadat, warning of a possible American seizure, said in particular: 'Any concession signifies the end of this regime. The people would once again be governed from abroad.' *Al Destour,* 13−14 January 1978.

16. The Wafd decision to disband itself does not mean that the basis of this party had ceased to exist as a political force in society.

17. Let us recall in connection with this that some of the deputies of this party adhered to the Wafd Party the moment it was declared. Others adhered to the Socialist Labour Party led by former minister Ibrahim Chukri. Talking of the changes of mind, Muhammad Hassanein Haykal declared: (*Al-Ahali,* No. 11, 12 April 1978) 'Personally, I cannot determine the nature of the present situation. I cannot tell who represents the centre party, which social section belongs to it or what its commitments are. In fact it only expresses the interests of a certain category after the opening up of the economy. I cannot in any way consider them as a class but merely as categories or groups completely outside the processes of production. They only belong to their own interests and only represent a consumer force. Many of them accumulate riches in Egypt for disposal abroad.'

18. Because the economic and social situation in Egypt, which has been evolving for more than a century, can only be radically changed by burning all the factories and destroying the machinery of State bureaucracy.

19. Its main task will be the creation of democracy as a link between liberation, development and Arab national unity.

20. Cutting the relationship between the internal forces of counter-revolution and its external instruments requires a radical consciousness and a strategic reconsideration of alliances and contradictions with international forces.

21. See Fuad Abd El-Khalek in a research paper presented to the Egyptian Congress of Economists held in Cairo entitled, *les Significations politiques ou l'ouverture economiques dans le cadre des transformations structurelles de l'economie Egyptienne 1971−77.*

22. *Ibid.*

23. See Adel Hussein's account of *Vingt-cinque ans d'etudes analytiques des politiques economiques en Egypte 1952−77.*

24. Fuad Abd El-Khalek, *op-cit.*

25. See Mohammed Fakhri Makki.
26. The number of Egyptian workers that have emigrated is estimated at between 3.5 and 4 million. An official estimate puts the figure at 1,500,000.
27. Read *l'Egypte entre le developpement et le Compromis*, by Ahmed Tabet, *Dar El-Fikr El-Jadid* (Beirut 1976) and *l'Egypte sous Sadate 1970–77*, by Albert Fallahat, El-Farabi (Beirut 1978).
28. Article entitled 'Comment les economistes israeliens et egyptiens envisagent paix' in *Al-Mustakbal*, 7th October 1978.

13. Conclusion: Sociology of the Cultural Revolution

Any treatment of the Egyptian revolution and counter-revolution remains incomplete in as much as the study deals with a single factor: political, economic, social or cultural. This is not because these elements react with each other but because the Egyptian revolution, in all these periods, takes on the overall character of a civilisation, exactly as was the case with the great revolutions of modern history.

The French revolution was not just the revolution of the bourgeois against the nobility, the market against the land, industry against agriculture, the Republic and the Social Contract against the monarchy and slavery. The French revolution did not consist in a simple religious liberation from the power of the Church, it was not just a triumph of scientific discovery — the invention of gunpowder and steam; it was the revolution of the rights of man. This has had its impact on production output, social structures, values and human beliefs. It was in fact a *Nahda* — a revolution of civilisation; this revolution had its roots in the distant history of Europe. We speak of a revolution of civilisation because it has restructured society and government in a way that allows a new spurt in human evolution; it can still serve as a normative criterion in human development.

This was not the case with Cromwell's revolution in Great Britain nor with the American War of Independence; both of these were revolutions in the political and economic sense but, for all that, did not produce the beginnings of a new civilisation in human history.

In a certain context the Soviet revolution resembles the French revolution. Marxism is the fruit of European thinking of the Western industrial middle classes; it is also consequent upon the most refined part of 18th century European encyclopaedic thought. Marx was economist, sociologist and philosopher at the same time. That summarises the synthesis of English economic thinking, French socialism and German philosophy, a synthesis that leads to a knowledge qualitatively different from that of the past. This synthesis enables us to see the quality of the new order of knowledge. We find this same synthesis in Lenin who said that the cell, energy and movement are the basis of Marxist dialectics; this could be an over-simplification, but it does show us the components and various layers of the new knowledge. Marx was a European; so was Lenin. If Marx represents the general, Lenin most adequately represents the particular. The interaction between the general and the particular has produced an entirely new page in the modern history of mankind. It is a page of civilisation in the life of the Soviet peoples who had never been part of the European Renaissance. It also shows that capitalism is not the last word in the history of human creativity, despite the concomitant Soviet underdevelopment or perhaps thanks to it. Because the Lenin experience was a profound representation of the reality of the Russian situation, and because this experience had positively assimilated the ideas of Hegel, Marx and Engels, it was, over a very short period of time, able to comprehend both the Renaissance and the Enlightenment. It was a cultural revolution that was able to restructure society and government in such a way that a new surge forward was possible. The Russian revolution was not a simple agricultural reform or a nationalisation of the means of production, but a new pattern of civilisation radiating a new hope for mankind.

The 'popular democracies' of Eastern Europe are different. Their historic importance is that they have given socialism an international status and, because of this, socialism is no longer confined to a single country. However, these popular democracies are not a conquest of a new civilisation in human history. In spite of the shortcomings of the development of Western capitalist experience since the last century, and in spite of the short-comings of the Soviet socialist pattern of development beginning with Stalinism, both of them formed the European way of human civilisation until the end of the Second World War. Although taking contradictory paths, both speak in the name of mankind.

Following the Second World War, two great events occurred which had a profound influence for the saving of civilisation from the consequences of war. The first took place in the Far East, in China. The second occurred in the Middle East, in Egypt. And so for the first time Europe was no longer the originator of a new civilising action. The Egyptian and Chinese revolutions brought new and previously unthought of factors into the fields of politics and economics.

Mao Tse-tung gave birth to the Chinese cultural revolution with the slogan, 'Let one hundred flowers blossom'. This drew its inspiration from European Marxism, but it also had its own deep roots in the Chinese cultural legacy. From this point of view, it can be said that it was a Leninist revolution but, outside the synthesis of the general and the particular, the Chinese cultural revolution has no relationship with Leninism nor with the Soviet pattern. On the contrary, it is intimately linked with Asian production methods and, in passing, we can say that this is the fundamental reason behind the Sino-Soviet antagonism.

However, it is a sad paradox: this pioneer Asian example has fallen into the same path of errors previously followed by the European example. The cultural revolution is producing a revolution against culture and against democracy. It is beyond the Chinese character to build up a new revolution based on Stalinism and Trotskyism: the cult of the individual and the permanence of the international revolution. The cult of Mao and of his Little Red

Book came to an end after his death. Internationalism is banished from Chinese foreign policy which unconditionally supports all the counter-revolutions in the world from the Egypt of Sadat to the Iran of the Shah. Understanding between China and the U.S.A. or Saudi Arabia is the current coin. China, which criticised and still criticises the Soviet Union in terms of the right of each country to follow its own socialist path, today tries to impose its own.

The Chinese Revolution of 1949 is, however, still a vigilant example arousing millions of men. It remains the model revolution for peasants; it shows them the role they must play in new world perspective after the Second World War.

Egypt belongs to one of the oldest civilisations in the world, but it also belongs to an Asian world that has seen most of the great civilisations of history: the Assyrian, Mesopotamian and Phoenician as well as the great religious civilisations of Judaism, Christianity and Islam.

The relationships between Egypt and these civilisations have always resulted in new syntheses. Whether Moses was Jewish or Egyptian, there can be no doubt that he was the founder of a Hebrew pattern of civilisation and that he was, at least, educated in the court of the Pharaoh. If we believe what Elliot Smith said in his book, *The Evolution of Civilisation* and what Henry Brested wrote in *The Dawn of Consciousness* we will be led to accept that the earliest versions of 'The Song of Songs', 'Proverbs' and the 'Wisdom of Solomon' were Egyptian. This is not just a matter of retrospective dating in isolation from socio-cultural history, these texts should be included in the socio-cultural history of Egypt; I would point out the revolution of Akhnaton, which unified the gods in heaven and raised the people to the level of participation. This pre-dating must also be connected with the events that took place on the frontier between Egypt and Sinai as related in the Book of Exodus.

We must be careful to avoid confusing the symbolic with the actual when reading the ancient books. However, the fact remains that the Jews of the ancient world were, for a certain period, prisoners in Egypt and by means of guile and finance they were able to reach the highest levels of society, very close to the Egyptian rulers. A struggle took place between them and the Egyptians which ended in them leaving the country after having acquired a written example of Egyptian knowledge. However, the one god of Akhnaton was more developed than the Hebrew Yahweh. From the Exodus onwards, the Jews were to retain a historic hatred and a cultural inferiority complex. This complex remained with them throughout the Diaspora to have an impact, even 2,000 years later, on the map of the region in modern times. In ancient times Rameses II responded by securing the Eastern access to Egypt, strongly symbolising thereby the very essence of the future struggle, for Egypt, whether conqueror or conquered in the Sinai Desert, cannot recognise independence within a simple regional frontier. This is a constant problem to be found again and again in the various episodes of Egyptian history.

Relationships between Egypt and the Mediterranean are different. Alexander the Great conquered Egypt, and in this we note the constant attitude of the West towards the region. From Alexander to Bonaparte there was no fundamental change in the West's attitude to Egypt in particular and to the whole area in general. Egypt was and still is the strategic key to the East. However, the Greek and French occupations are the two most highly developed masks hiding the ugly face of occupation in the history of Egypt. Conquest is always the same, but the type of civilisation influences the relationships between conquerors and conquered. Because of this, the very content of civilisation can sometimes change. Thus, before the arrival of the Ptolemys in Egypt, Herodotus, Democritus, Pythagoras and Plato had already made the pilgrimage to the cradle of human civilisation. Egypt learnt much from them, as is shown in its sculpture and theatre. Today nobody contests the fact that ancient Greek influenced hieroglyphic writing to such a degree that the Coptic alphabet of today contains seven of its letters. The Greek writing on the Rosetta stone enabled Champollion to decipher the famous inscription. Finally, the fruit of all this was Hellenic Egypt and not Egypt itself, a Greek colony as seen in the University of Alexandria, the greatest university of ancient wisdom. But it should be noted that, from a certain point a view, Hellenic Egypt was an Egyptian period in history after the fall of the Egyptian State.

Bonaparte, like Alexander, came from a background of renaissance to a decadent Egypt. Before the French expedition, Egypt had been under the Turkish Mameluke yoke, but that expedition with its scholars, its printing and its French liberalism was, in spite of its colonialism, a beneficial shock. Among the results of this shock we can quote the awakening of modern Egypt, preparing itself for the first *Nahda* of Muhammed Ali and Tahtawi. During the three years of occupation, the French gave the Egyptians an awareness of the general principles of the modern State; they discovered the ancient languages of Egypt and they produced that historic work that is the description of Egypt. Such were the main nuclei on the way to the modern civilisation whose bases were laid down by Muhammad Ali with the independence of Egypt, the establishment of the modern State, and the action led by his son, Ibrahim, towards the East, that is towards the last Arab-speaking regions. The *Code Napoleon,* French culture and constitution, are signs that still persist today despite the very brief French period in Egypt. One can also say that there are many similarities between Ancient Greece — the light of antiquity — and the France of the Revolution in modern times. The form of Egypt's relationships with these two enlightened cultures also indicates the identity of the Egyptian civilisation and way in which its modern history has developed.

The same thing did not occur in Egypt under the Roman or British occupations. The Coptic calendar starts with the Year of the Martyrs. The Roman Emperor, under the pretext of resisting the new religion, Christianity, killed 400,000 Egyptians. When Constantine made the political decision to become a Christian, Egypt made its Orthodox Christianity an Egyptian

Christianity in order to remain independent from Rome. Coptic Egypt fought a bitter battle against the Holy Roman Empire. It was saved by the Muslim conquest which gave it independence and enabled it to launch into its third renaissance after the two previous ones — the Hellenic and the Christian.

Cultural openness and national independence remain the dominant features in Egyptian cultural development in the face of foreign invasion, internal tyranny or a regional problem. Egypt received Christianity as a new vision of Egyptian origins. The visit of the Infant Jesus and His Mother, according to the Gospel, does not differ fundamentally from the visit of Moses across the Nile according to the Old Testament. Both symbolise the paternity of ancient Egypt over the two greatest spiritual doctrines in the history of humanity. However, there is a basic difference: the Jews came into Egypt and left it without converting the Nile Valley to Judaism; whereas Jesus and His Mother returned alone and made Egypt Christian. This brings to mind the tragedy of Osiris, the god of fertility. It is as though Christianity in Egypt was reviving the ancient monotheism of Akhnaton and the trinity of Isis-Osiris-Horus.

For the Egyptians, Christianity was a weapon with which to fight Rome. Its doctrinal independence from Rome represented the independence of Egypt from Rome. This is what gave the Coptic Church, from its foundation, its character of national struggle against repression and foreign invasion. Even the idea of the Desert Monasteries is an invention inscribed in the spirit of resistance and in the will to save the knowledge.

The British occupation, like the Roman Empire, in a certain way differs from both the French expedition and Hellenic Egypt. Both left no trace on Egypt except for the Year of the Martyrs and the Roman Theatre at Alexandria, where people used to enjoy watching the massacre of the faithful by the lions.

But, in the end, both sides of the coin have to be considered: the cultural West, Hellenic or French; as well as the obscurantist West, Roman or British, represent an identical strategic view of the position of Egypt. Egypt, master-key to the entire region, had to be appropriated. To do this, Egypt had to be prevented from achieving its national independence by possible alliance with all that surrounded it from the Mashreq to the Maghreb. In modern times this independence was achieved on two occasions: the first, during the 19th century, thanks to Muhammad Ali and his son Ibrahim Pasha in what has been called the Arab Empire; the second, during the second part of the 20th century, thanks to Nasser in what has been called Arab Nationalism and Unity.

While the collapse of the State of Muhammad Ali underlined certain constants in the socio-cultural history of Egypt, the Nasserist period of the *Nahda* brought certain changes to the economic and political history of the region.

The constants add to the variables; they are modified but never suppressed by them. The fundamental constants of Egypt assert themselves across its geo-politics: a stable, agricultural and united civilisation in the Nile Valley achieved by Menes; a central State controlling irrigation, ruled by a god-king; cultural openness to the world through conquest and counter-conquest, giving an Egyptian character to all the civilisations coming from outside; geographic extension of the regional frontiers with each renaissance; shrivelling with defeat or decadence; revolution surpassing simple generosity, and, finally, persistent anxiety from the East across Sinai. This anxiety has never disappeared, not even after the disappearance of the Jews. To this must be added the worry coming from the West, a worry that also has never gone, despite the fall of the Roman Empire and the failure of the French expedition. Egypt, coveted by several, watched the rivals liquidate each other. These constants are inseparable from the popular uprisings conducted under religious symbols of national unity (Al Azhar and the Coptic Church).

With Muhammad Ali and Ibrahim Pasha, new constants were formed: modernisation by modern technology, Arabisation in the imperial sense, militarism in the sense of an assimilation of the order of the army with that of society. At the same time the State proceeds with agricultural reform and takes possession of the land. It starts a vast movement of education in order to provide itself with the staff for the bureaucratic machinery of an autocratic system. The Egyptian clergy are removed from the government. At the same time it undertakes very delicate manoeuvres aimed at establishing a balance between its relationships with the East and the West. In the progress from renaissance to decadence we can note the gap between the modernisation of thinking, the State, society and the autocratic regime. By way of example, the French heritage brought by Tahtawi has nothing to do with either Muhammad Ali, and even less with the society that had not yet given birth to its middle classes, for what the Governor was seeking was simply a modernisation of the means of production while rejecting the new relations of production that are intimately tied to the phenomenon of modernisation. What was sought was a force enabling the independence of Egypt to be guaranteed without even creating this independence within the country. That is why the fall of Muhammad Ali brought about the fall of Tahtawi's thinking. There is a basic dilemma between modern thinking and the modern State. It can, therefore, be said that the reasons for the failure of the first attempt at modernisation were inherent in the attempt itself. Half a century later, when General Ahmed Orabi tried to pluck out this inherent weakness, the West settled things with their own contradictions by the British occupation in 1882.

Despite the defeat of Orabi's revolution, it gave birth to the Egyptian social classes. Modern Egyptian society could have a clear structure because of the birth of the landed aristocracy, the commercial middle classes and even the intellectual civil servants, students and artisans, that is, the principal components of what were later called the lower middle classes. Thanks to this new structure of society, the second renaissance was able to arise, that of Muhammad Abduh, Mahmud Sami, Al-Barudi and Abdalla Al-Nadim. There was no longer a division between culture and revolution. The mullahs no longer had the same role that they had in the past. The intellectuals had a new role to play in the leadership of the revolution. They opened the way for a synthesis between the historic legacy and modern times. And as the Egyptian middle classes were born in the struggle against colonialism and internal tyranny, the evacuation, the constitution, as well as the social contract with the Governor, became the means of development and, because of these conditions which accompanied its origins, the Egyptian middle classes will always suffer the worst of these things in revolution and counter-revolution, in the field of the fruits of production and the machinery of the regime.

The 1919 revolution adds nothing to the constants based on the revolution of Orabi. The intellectuals acquired an important role and, under the occupation, the military avant-garde were absent. The revolution crumbled with the treaty of 1936 and this break was confirmed on 4th February 1942, when the Wafd returned to power guarded by British tanks. Thus, between 1919 and 1952, Egyptian liberalism disappeared. However, the lower middle classes continued to increase between the two wars. A relative development was experienced by the working class. The interests of national capitalism were defined. The development of the role of the intellectuals achieved the level of importance experienced in the 1940s. The social class structure at this period expressed a radical contradiction in the whole of the regime. In practice this had declined before the collapse in 1952. Of all the constants of this period we note particularly the unity between the workers and the intellectuals, the relative absence of the role of the peasants, and the predominance of the role of the city. One also notes the development of the left and of the extreme right. But while the right was well organised, the left was fragmented due to subjective reasons and external factors, among which we can include the effect of lower middle class mentality. It is revealing to note in connection with this that the earliest blow suffered by the first Egyptian Communist Party was led by Saad Zaghlul in 1924. The intellectuals were at the beginning of the development of a consciousness of the left, but they were also the origin of the lack of united revolutionary organisation and of the separation between town and country. That is why the ordinary Egyptian became the left. This left, although deprived of the basic elements of organisation, is today capable of overcoming the failure of the regime and the absence of an alternative. Because of this lack of organisation it is natural that the military institution should regain its avant garde role in the presence of change. This is what occurred 70 years after the revolution of Orabi, when Nasser took power in 1952. But we see in all these events the fact that democracy has always supported the most progressive tendencies, with the support of the popular classes and thanks to their cultural revolution. In the face of such a current, the monarchy allied to the British occupation could only resort to sabotage by burning the city of Cairo on 26th January 1956; but this alliance did not last more than six months.

During that period the key change was of the failure of the Arabs in Palestine and the birth of the Zionist entity as a State, thus forming the two biggest dangers for Egypt: the West of Rome, the Crusades, colonialism; and the Jews with their historic hate arising again after 2,000 years. To bind Egypt and separate it from its natural world is the double goal of the unique agreement between the West and Zionism. Much is said about the development of international capitalism and its relationship with Zionism, as well as oil and shipping lanes in the Middle East. This is true, but the root of the problem is the international counter-revolution. Because of the end of colonial empires after the Second World War, the Zionist entity was able momentarily to take the place of Europe in the region.

Suddenly, the Egyptian middle classes realised the danger. That is why Cairo became the seat of the League of Arab States. King Farouk sent his army into Palestine. True, Britain participated in founding the League of Arab States. But the most significant thing is that monarchic Egypt allied to British colonialism recognised the danger that threatened it from the East; in Palestine it was equally significant that Egypt, even before obtaining its own independence, became a unifying Arab centre at the very moment that independence took off in the Mashreq, in Syria and in Lebanon.

It will take time for history to place the Egyptian revolution in its correct place despite its negative factors. For the West, and for its Zionist extension, it represents the possibility of a historic nightmare. But on a lower scale, for the Egyptians as well as for the Arabs, it represents the possibility of the realisation of a historic dream. The 18 years of the Egyptian revolution indicate only one thing, the possibility for both Egypt and the Arabs of the realisation of a specific pattern of development on the basis of a cultural legacy, having no relationship with the riches of oil resources, in order to link up with the current of a modern civilisation.

The West, as well as its Zionist extension in the Middle East, understood the meaning of the Egyptian revolution of 1952. Those who were blinded by the military display of the young officers did not grasp Orabi's movement: they gave importance only to the Syrian putsches in the Mashreq and the military adventures in Latin America. Because of this they were slow to understand what was happening beneath the surface in these regions. The same mistake was made by those who gave too much importance to changes of regime, and legislation concerning economic matters. They all forgot to consider the Arab, international and Egyptian variables and constants.

It was because of these errors that the neo-colonialist United States attempted to harvest the fruit of the former colonialism by trying to establish an Eisenhower Plan in 1957 and a so-called Baghdad Pact which collapsed on the 14th July 1958 with the regime of Nuri El-Said.

From the Western point of view, the Egyptian revolution came, not to apply the Six Principles declared by the officers, but to radically change the progress of the region as well as the dominant pattern of international relationships. Four years later it was no longer the Egyptian revolution but the Arab revolution, the African revolution; it became a pioneer example for what was later called the Third World.

It is not just the sum of the variables and the constants comprising the

Egyptian situation, but it was an historic movement where the traditional broke out on the surface of the modern. Those who did not recognise it at the proper time made the mistake of seeing only the uniforms of the officers. Thus they misunderstood the pioneer role of the national military institution in Egyptian history; they also forgot the inability of the national democratic front to provide a coherent structure. In the diversity of the officers' tendencies they saw only the formation of a single group.

The reality is that the revolution was bigger than its leadership. Its role was greater than its thinking. The tragic difference between cultural assets and effective practice is an illustration of the path taken by the revolution that eventually led on to the counter-revolution.

The revolution, consciously or not, had inherited the variables and constants formulated by geo-politics. It rebuilt the State of Muhammad Ali. It thus rebuilt an Arab and modern Egypt enjoying military power. It tried to find a breach in the balance of international forces in order to progress. It tried to reduce the gap between culture and revolution, an attempt that failed to reach the stage, however, of a union between culture and revolution. It achieved independence, it established the constitution, without solving the problem of democracy and without ending the interaction between the forces of revolution and of counter-revolution. After its subjective collapse following the defeat of 1967, the students and workers faced it and experienced their unity in 1968. It imitated both Saad Zaghlul and his enemies at the same time by striking at the forces of the left, but it nevertheless ended the role of the religious institution in the leadership of the processes of change. It ended the faltering liberalism of the preceding regime but set up another balance which, in the absence of a democratic formula, guaranteed minimum social justice to workers, peasants and soldiers. It was very generous to the ordinary classes, the lower middle classes.

It faced two challenges, the Western and the Zionist. It is in this that it takes on its true dimension, when it brings Egypt out of the ranks of basic underdeveloped colonies in Africa and the Middle East to that of an example of renaissance in a possible new world. All this constitutes a threat to imperialist and Zionist strategy. We should add the support that it gave to the revolutions in the Yemen and in Algeria. Let us bear in mind that it was during this progress that Sudan, Kuwait, South Yemen and the Gulf obtained their independence. The Nasser revolution became a solid base threatening an international system. It was not, therefore, by chance that the separation from Syria came at the same time as the 1961 decisions concerning development based on state capitalism, which would take the place of the private sector fleeing from the burden of development. Neither is it by chance that the war in the Yemen lasted until the eve of the 1967 war. The international dimension played a decisive role in the fall of Nasser, and of his example adopted by Nkrumah in Ghana and Sukarno in Indonesia. The Third World began to be a force threatening international equilibrium. We are not referring to Nasser himself or his experience, but such were the perspectives of the success of this revolution.

Nasserism opened the door to hope, a hope that had to be smothered before it became a reality. The strength of the counter-revolution was proportional to the size of the hope. The historical legacy of this revolution had to be liquidated. Its possible achievements also had to be blocked. The attack was not then just on a Nasserist experience but also on Muhammad Ali, Ibrahim Pasha, Ahmed Orabi, Mustapha Kamel, Muhammad Said, Saad Zaghlul, Mustapha An-Nahhas and Gamal Abd El-Nasser. The counter-revolution assimilated the legacy of Abbas I, of Said, of Tewfiq and of all the tyrants from Zewar to Ismail Sidqi including Muhammad Mahmud. In fact, the present counter-revolution in Egypt is not a single link in the chain of counter-revolution in Egyptian history. It is the faithful local reflection of the international counter-revolution. It does not aim at uprooting Nasserism but aims at putting an end to the very idea of a revolution. If Nasserism had been just a revolution and not *The* revolution, it nevertheless showed the signs of the Arab revolution: the synthesis of national independence, liberation and social progress. Nasser's virtue was that he discovered the organic relationship of this trilogy. His fault was the fact that he neither wanted nor was able to follow his discovery through to the end. He was conquered by the internal rather than the external dragon.

The creation of a great Arab nation extending from the Atlantic to the Gulf is impossible in our time without a new sharing of riches, and without new relationships in the structures of production. This implies that it will necessarily be a socialist nation of one type or another. The successive nationalisations of the country's riches, from the Suez Canal to oil, were an incontestable sign.

Nevertheless, it is impossible to create an Arab nation, even of various regional units, without a new definition of social and cultural structures; which implies that in one way or another it will be both democratic and secular. This possibility can only endanger the Zionist entity.

The creation of an Arab Nation to inherit the oldest traditions of the renaissance implies a potential of generosity. Its Eastern Christianity, its enlightened Islam and its scientific potential that are today scattered over the world imply that this model of civilisation will impose not only the diversity of the examples, but will be a pioneer pattern for a larger area than that which today includes the 140 million Arabs.

For all these reasons, the spectre of this nation is a nightmare in the memory of the West and a wound for Zionism.

Because Egypt remains the key to both the *Nahda* and to the decadence of this Arab nation, she remains the target for destruction by the external dragon. To do this a new fact of life is imposed on the whole region: the preponderance of the role of the international factor in the national and regional movement. These relationships with the 'internal dragon' become more and more organic.

What do we mean by 'dragon'?

It is not just a matter of what has been called the new class; it is rather the general atmosphere created by the autocratic regime on the cultural, political, social and economic levels. It is also the constant interaction between the forces of revolution and counter-revolution at the various levels, which built the road towards union with the two historic enemies. However, the alliance between the internal and external elements of counter-revolution does not embrace the specific Egyptian social character. That is why it is an exception doomed to disappear.

Whatever contrasts there may be between this pattern of civilisation and that of the West, it nevertheless constitutes a new contribution to world peace, which today is tortured by the phenomenon of polarisation, terrorised by the very delicate balance of atomic weapons, while sliding towards the phenomenon of total preoccupation with material consumption. This new pattern has presented the basis of a possible rapprochement between the developed and developing nations in order to bring about human peace.

In trying to put an end to this pattern, the counter-revolution has aggravated the anxiety, sufferings and contradictions of this world. By the success of the counter-revolution in Egypt, the whole world returns to the between-wars victories. The morbid hunger of the industrial West devours the underdeveloped, and the gap between the developed and underdeveloped world becomes more and more pronounced. The Western world should reconsider the future in the light of hope and civilisation. It must, therefore, take into consideration the fact that the counter-revolution in Egypt is not a permanent feature. To consider it so would be seen by future Western generations as a historical error every bit as serious as the impact made by the Crusades on the Arab mind. If the West looks a little further than the end of its nose, it will find itself diametrically opposed to the counter-revolution in Egypt. If it supports it, it will betray its cultural legacy and its future.

There is no Egyptian sacrifice for the Arabs. Egypt was wholly concerned in the last four wars and in all the others of the last 30 centuries. The Arab allegiance of modern Egypt is not a metaphysical doctrine but a historic movement summarising strategic security, development and culture. The fact that Egypt leads the Arab world is not a concession made by the Arabs, it is more the result of the social and cultural prominence of Egypt. There is no way in which this centre that represents Egypt could move elsewhere. The counter-revolution in Egypt has never been in the interests of the Arabs, whatever their ideological or economic viewpoints. Because of this, progressive Arabs should realise that they are in firing range of the Egyptian counter-revolution which cannot fail to affect them in one way or another. If some of them believed that Zionist occupation, first of Palestine and then of Sinai and Golan did not concern them, they must now, before it is too late, understand that the counter-revolution within Egypt is also to be found within their own frontiers.

Conservative Arabs, on the other hand, must realise that the privileges granted them by the counter-revolution in Egypt cannot be compared with what can be brought about in the future. Oil, the price of which has increased thanks to the war, will not have the same value as in times of artificially high prices. In this context, it is not surprising that the important role of Saudi Arabia came to an end with the visit of the Egyptian President to Israel. This very modest political expression is closely connected to less modest consequences in the economic domain. The alliance between Zionist capitalism and Egyptian parasitic capitalism represents a lever to control the whole military and economic direction in the Middle East and Africa. The conservative Arab powers are not in this case dependent on American strategy, but they are subject to the will of the Israeli-Egyptian gendarmerie. To this must be added that the longevity of the counter-revolution in Egypt does not guarantee the longevity of oil. To be sure, the Arab conservatives are inseparable from the counter-revolution in Egypt. However, these same conservatives can also be threatened by a world counter-revolution because, whatever else they may be, they are still Arabs, be they of the right, left or centre.

In fact the entire Arab nation, in this struggle for existence and for the future, is today invited not to make war against Israel but to give unconditional support to the action directed against the counter-revolution in Egypt before it becomes an established fact on the map of the region, and before it is internationally recognised.

The task of putting an end to this counter-revolution falls directly upon the Egyptian revolution.

This revolution will not only have to assimilate the constants and variables of the *Nahda* in Egyptian history, it will also have to assimilate the variables and constants of decadence.

Among the first constants of decadence, we mention the lengths of the obscurantist periods. Let us recall that 40 years separate the end of the State of Muhammad Ali from the revolution of Orabi; 38 years separate Orabi's defeat from the 1919 revolution and 16 years passed between the 1936 treaty and the 1952 revolution. This means that the rhythm of progress accelerates from one period to the next. This phenomenon is not unfamiliar since the great step forward in the means of communication that the world has known since the end of the Second War. If the suspended revolution of the 18th and 19th January 1977 had not lacked organisation, leadership and pertinent analysis, it would certainly have ended the counter-revolution only six years after its birth.

Among the constants of the counter-revolution, we also mention the objective failure of the regime and the absence of an alternative at the same time. The negative consequences of that are the lowering of public morale by spontaneous uprisings of very short duration and by acts of sabotage; all of which leads the popular masses to despair.

Among the constants of the decadence, we mention, in third place, the fragmentation in the ranks of the revolution while the alliance between the forces of counter-revolution does not cease to consolidate. That is why democratic dialogue, and the alliance of a very wide front, form the only possible climate for the creation of a minimum of organised national unity capable of taking power. Finally, we mention among these constants the interaction between the revolution and the counter-revolution itself, which is not to the advantage of the latter only. For the *Nahda* itself is inherent in the heart of the decadence. The great work of Ali Mubarak, the Tewfiqian plans, were achieved at the time of the fall of Muhammad Ali. The creation of the Egyptian opera and the arrival of the Egyptian army in the Sudan occurred in the time of Khedive Ismail. New forms of Egyptian literature, starting with the novel, began in the shadows of Orabi's defeat.

The first fruits of the fourth renaissance were felt during the 1940s – just after the 1936 treaty and during the war years. The Nasserist generation bore its best fruit in the realm of thinking during the past ten years. The uprisings of the workers, students and intellectuals between 1968 and 1977 were shattering responses to the defeat and the failure under Nasser and Sadat. At the same time, the popular movement found new ways to counter the decisions of the regime: national committees, wall newspapers, workers' communes, self-management of factories, creation of the Assembly Party, creative action by intellectuals in exile shaking the regime and its reputation. In fact the decadence of a regime does not signify the decadence of Egypt. It only signifies that the renaissance is in a state of latency. Today we find ourselves on the threshold of the sixth renaissance in the history of modern Egypt which goes back some 200 years.

It is also a renaissance that is assimilating the variables of the decadence just as it has assimilated its constants. The first of these variables is the fact that the Egyptian revolution will be able to end the interaction between the forces of revolution and counter-revolution only by going beyond the too general, too confused slogan 'achievement of the tasks of the democratic national revolution', by which is meant the middle-class revolution. Time has had its effect on this middle class and on Egyptian society as a whole. The question 'one revolution or two?' that had split the left is no longer current, because the revolution for the popular masses is total cultural revolution; that alone which would realise the promise of Orabi and the dream of Nasser. It is not a matter of a simple transfer of power. It is the passing of society to a new realisable pattern. This revolution has to fill the gap separating the revolution from the counter-revolution, the spiritual content of the revolution from the reality of the people. It must come down definitively in favour of secularism and the destruction of every last bastion of autocratic power, in order to achieve the democracy of development and liberation.

The pattern must be capable of solving the false problem that opposes democracy to social change. In this pattern, dialogue will take place between the superstructure and the infrastructure. The question posed in the past, 'which task for which class?', will no longer be pertinent. No longer will one ask which class should control such and such a stage. The undeniable truth is that underdevelopment and the absence of democratic traditions have left their mark on all classes and on all ways of thinking, the consequence of which has been that the middle classes have sold out on the independence of capital; and the working class has, over a long period, neglected the necessity of an independent political organisation. As for the peasants, they were completely ignored, and the intellectuals were exiles in their own country.

The armed forces have kept out of politics. However, the slogan, 'the national and democratic revolution' will remain valid, but it must also signify an Arab nationalism. The liberalisation of the market will be accompanied by the liberation of the land. Democracy will not be a liberal equivalent of *laissez faire, laissez passer*, nor the socialist equivalent of the principle 'whose democracy against whose dictatorship?'

The new democracy will make use of all the means of liberty and its manifestations on the path to progress and civilisation.

Socialism will be the first item on its agenda. In other words, socialism will not be a class theory simply in economic matters but a theory of progress for the whole of the people and for the establishment of a new society. The debts contracted by Egypt from the time of the Khedive Ismail until Sadat prove that they are not the economic solution to the Egyptian crisis and that this solution can only come from within by a new and radical distribution of riches. There is no national wealth without national production. Because of this, the socialism of the total cultural revolution will uproot all the obstacles to production and to development, beginning with the parasitic economic system and finishing with the liquidation of the underdeveloped consumer society. It will put an end to social slavery on the land, in the factory and in the services: the economic content of this socialism is close to the utilisation of the means used by the Chinese revolution. This mass of peasants will transform themselves into a productive force, the land will not be overworked. The enormous unemployment, hunger, crime and emigration will all be able to be converted into considerable wealth.

In view of the limited resources, it is not possible to achieve this transformation without adopting a new definition of social ownership in a way which profoundly surpasses that practised by Muhammad Ali and by Nasser. Sharing the possibility of limited resources among a population in constant development requires a more radical revolutionary creativity than all the examples that have existed in the past. A radical action as large and profound as this will impose a democratic creativity of the same dimensions; if this is not so, the only alternative will be a police state repeating the same story in the name of socialism.

Democratic creativity is the historic challenge on the threshold of the next cultural revolution in Egypt. This challange is the way in which shape will be given to this democratic socialism such that it will not be solely economic or social; it will be the democracy of creation and initiative on the individual and community levels. A democracy in theory and in application. This formula will arise from the depths of the revolutionary forces and their historic movement. In this perspective it is of little use to go over the classic definitions of the notion of the front and the lists of its activities as seen in the Western socialist or capitalist examples. The spontaneity of the popular uprisings preceding the creation of the National Committees in the universities, the workers' communes at Mehalla, Al Kubra and Kafr Ad-Dawwar, the self-management practised in the factories of Helouan and Chubra Al-Kahyma, and the aborted experience of cooperative systems will have to develop the relationship between centralisation of power and decentralisation of production; this will enable the rebuilding of the State according to the needs of society and the initiative of the people, and not according to geographic shape or the historic tradition.

For example, it is not possible for the peasants, who form more than 60% of the Egyptian population, to be separated from the town in matters of social and cultural structure. It is illogical that students and intellectuals should take the initiative in direct political action in the name of other social classes while, day after day, the gap between intellectual work and manual work decreases. The intellectuals of Egypt are not on the margins of the social classes. They are the non-democratic machinery of development, by this I mean that they have an exceptional role in the very structure of production. That is why the new historic bloc, to borrow first the expression of Gramsci and then of Garaudy, in Egypt is this very active force formed of a rural majority, student and worker unity, and the exceptional role of the pioneers, intellectuals and the army.

The Egyptian armed forces will play an exceptional role in the total cultural revolution, but in a different way from that played in 1952. This role will be closer to that which they took during the revolution of Orabi (1881–82) taking into consideration the changes that have occurred over the century. Their principal task will be the liberation of the land beyond Sinai towards the east. This is not a purely military task, but a matter of the development of national consciousness in such a way that the Arab national dimension should also be taken into consideration against the consequences of the counter-revolution. The Sinai was not occupied in 1948 when the Egyptian Army went to Palestine. The past 30 years confirm the strategic sense of this leadership taken by the Egyptian army, even after the occupation of Sinai in 1967, even after the evacuation by the Israeli forces and its demilitarisation in 1978. War beyond the regional frontiers will be the zero hour of the cultural revolution accomplished within the frontiers. The strategic achievement of the armed forces will not consist in the taking of power, but will be the military representation of the national dimension, for Egyptian nationalism will expand to contain the last inch of Arab territory. It is at that moment that Egyptian nationalism will be called Arab nationalism. The Egyptian armed forces will form the vanguard of the cultural revolution by the achievement of the national task.

The popular masses will themselves be the revolution at the moment the vacuum created by the downfall of the regime and the absence of an alternative is filled. It is these masses that will form the link between the various traditions of the 1919 revolution, the 1940s and all the uprisings. that occurred between 1968 and 1977, and this will give shape to a new power structure. And so the vicious circle of the traditional manichaeism of Egyptian middle-class thinking, from Tahtawi to Taha Hussein, from Muhammad Abdu to Khaled Muhammad Khaled, will be broken.

The military institution and the religious institution will no longer be in a position to seek power. The task of the former will be to seek cultural identity in the extension of the regional frontiers towards the Arab national frontiers. It will carry the banner of the new cultural awareness to every last corner where Arabic is spoken, as expressed by Ibrahim Pasha more than one and a half centuries ago. The task of the latter will be to seek the means of driving the merchants from the temple. Thus will conscience remove the robes of clericalism, and the veil of theocracy will fall for all to see the nudity of the values sold on the international slave market. The religious institution will here accomplish a fundamental role in freeing conscience of the burden of centuries of decadence and illusion, making man the slave of the master's interests and not the interests of God. The power of the cultural revolution will not be subject to institutions; it will be the power of revolutionary thinking and action, capable neither of a return to Nasserism, nor to the realisation of the national democratic revolution in its confused traditional conception; it will be a power capable of creating an independent cultural model for the renaissance of modern Egypt.

Because the events that have occurred in Egypt during the past eight years do not constitute an Egyptian counter-revolution but an international revolution against the Arabs in Egypt, as was the case in Lebanon and against the Palestinian resistance, the cultural revolution in Egypt will be total. The international character of the counter-revolution signifies that its internal reflection — the ruling regime — must and can collapse, because its economic, social and cultural roots are not deep in Egyptian soil. The parasites of production have always been the most cowardly people and the first to flee. The parasitic colonies constitute a foreign body in the Egyptian economy, which has always been based on a true production because of its geographic situation, its history and social evolution. The Egyptian middlemen are a continuing phenomenon, but they are the weakest phenomenon in the economic history of Egypt. To 'Lebanonise' or 'Saudise' Egypt is an impossible task.

As the counter-revolution in Egypt is against the Arabs, Egyptian nationalism today faces a historic challenge that Nasser had faced without following through to the end. Nasser will always remain the pioneer of the practical and positive response to the Arab character of Egypt. But the *via media* (*Wasatiya*) in theory and in practice was the basis of the union with Syria and its later breakdown. In ideological terms it is this *via media* which formed the policy of Egyptian patriotism and Arab nationalism. But the historic model, candidate for the realisation of the Arab national unity of Egypt, has yet to be achieved. However, the experiences of unity, aborted as they were by the absence of democracy and development on our side, and by the presence of colonialism and Zionism on the Western side, still have valuable significance for the unity of Arab Egypt at a time when Egyptian patriotism will be synonymous with Arab nationalism. That is why the Egyptian total cultural revolution will consist in the liberation of Palestine and of the Zionist entity, and in the embodiment of the unity of the Arab nation. In this perspective war becomes a means of revolution in a dialectic action accompanying the fall of the regime within the framework of a

421

strategic view of the future. The overthrow of the present Egyptian regime and war will achieve the Arab national unity of Egypt in the face of the international counter-revolution conducted against the Arabs. In a new period these two actions constitute a social, and not only a military or political action. Politics, like military action, are not the means that can enable this social action to take on its true dimension in the process of changing the underdeveloped structures (means of production, relations of production, religious, tribal and Bedouin formations and values, etc). The cultural revolution in Egypt will necessarily include the local, national, Arab and social dimensions. The first two form the framework of the last, which is the principal content of the revolution.

As the counter-revolution in Egypt is international, it is important that the cultural revolution should take into consideration the international factor, in the sense of firm and independent alliances with all those human powers having a strategic interest in the *Nahda* of Egypt and of the Arabs; I mean those powers that envisage a future of human civilisation and of peace in one of the most sensitive regions of the world today.

Finally, the above picture is neither a programme nor the general lines of the future Egypto-Arab revolution, but neither is it a utopia. It is a plausible conclusion among several probabilities coming from this country which is called 'the Mother of the World' by some and 'Mother of Miracles' by others. Egypt has always occupied the world throughout the ages, for she is the key to the ancient, mediaeval and modern world, whether in times of renaissance or in times of decadence. At times she sleeps so long that some think she is dead, but she is always awakened at an unforeseen moment, and not by Zarka Al-Yamama, nor by computers. She has never given up her secret. This book is not a password, but an invitation to do it again. When Egypt awakes, she will not forgive those who were silent or those who spoke words equivalent to silence, for these have hindered her awakening.

Despite all the sorrows, she is awakening. History is not an error, although historical error is possible. There is no historic determinism without will and without awareness. They alone can correct history.

14. Postscript

The Congress of Isolation

On May 8th 1979, an exceptional event took place at Fez, a Moroccan town with a deep-rooted history of Islam: the Congress of Foreign Ministers of the Islamic countries was meeting, and the Egyptian delegation was not there.

Ten years earlier, another Islamic Congress, a summit meeting, had been held at Rabat, the capital of Morocco. The Egyptian delegation was, as it happened, led by Anwar Al-Sadat; Nasser, for one reason or another, was unable to come. An incident had occurred between the future Egyptian President and the Shah of Iran.

Sadat attracted the attention of the rulers of about 40 Islamic States by his passionate defence of Islam and Muslims, of Jerusalem, Palestine, and movements of national liberation all over the world.

It is obvious that the prestige of Egypt and Nasser made the members of the Congress pay great attention to the words of this representative. But Sadat's personal prestige as General Secretary of the Islamic Congress of Cairo since its foundation, was another reason for this impact.

Ten years later: an absolute reversal of the situation. Sadat had become President of the Arab Republic of Egypt, and could not send his Foreign Minister to the Congress at Fez. Several Arab and Muslim countries, and also the P.L.O., demanded that Egypt should be suspended from participating as a member because of its attitude towards Islam, Muslims, Jerusalem and Palestine.

Sadat, after his visit to Israel on 19th November 1977, had concluded (on March 27th 1979) his separate treaty with the Hebrew State. The Shah, who had then just been deposed, had found refuge only in Egypt, where Sadat suggested he should settle. This change of situation was neither senti-mental nor surprising; the Arab summit held at Rabat in 1974 had been firmly opposed to the American plans following the war of October 1973. The P.L.O. had been expressly recognised as the only legitimate representa-tive of the Palestinian people, and it was decided that no Arab party had the right to go back on this undertaking. At the time this was aimed at Jordan and its former project of a 'United Arab Kingdom.'

The secret decisions taken at the Rabat Summit also defined the other aspect of this undertaking: 'the total liberation of the Arab territories occupied at the time of the aggression of June 1967 and the safeguarding of Arab sovereignty over all occupied parts, together with the liberation of Jerusalem and total rejection of any situation which could injure Arab sovereignty over this sacred city.'

The Summit had also defined concerted Arab action as 'rejection of any attempt at a partial political compromise, by reason of the united Arab character of the cause' and 'establishment of a plan which would isolate Israel politically and economically on the international scene.' So at the opening of the Congress of Fez, King Hassan II had to remind the meeting that no one had the right to claim to have a unilateral solution to the Arab question, nor to represent the Palestinian people, who are not an insignificant population.

Egypt stayed away, to avoid having to face such accusations, especially coming from a country like Morocco. But these accusations could only be uttered by Morocco, because it was on Moroccan territory that the decisions had been made which Egypt was contesting in their entirety. These questions had to be raised within the Congress, especially by virtue of its order of the day: Jerusalem and Palestine. Morocco was chosen because it is a country where Arabism is synonymous with Islam. Finally, the decisions of the Islamic Congress fitted into the national context of the Iranian revolution which once more attracted the attention of the world to Islam as a force going beyond that of oil and the strategic importance of the region. It was no mere chance that Egypt did not recognise the new Iranian regime until the Iranian people made their decision and the new Republic decided to break off relations with the Egyptian government. Egypt realised, therefore, the impossibility of taking part in the Congress, all the more so as Morocco also had broken off diplomatic relations with Cairo two weeks earlier.

The Impasse Within Egypt

In view of all these circumstances, the King of Morocco was obliged to make a speech stigmatising Egyptian policy.

In addition, President Sadat, in his speech of 1st May 1979, took violent exception to all the Arab leaders, since the Arab world as a whole had condemned his policies. Sadat seemed surprised by this foreign opposition in which the Arab-Islamic world was joined by the non-aligned bloc and (though more timidly) a few European countries.

But what was the situation in Egypt even after the Sadat-Begin-Carter agreement?

Neither the Egyptian left nor the extremist religious groups had shown themselves capable of overthrowing Sadat. The only alternative presenting itself lay in the formation of a democratic national front in which the Egyptian middle class would be represented in proportion to its economic power within society. This class, ill-used by the dominant classes of parasites

living off the national economy (import-export merchants, foreign monopolies . . .) and other related classes expressed their political will through the
reappearance of the Wafd Party on the political scene, and the foundation of
a new, less important party under the name of the National Front. The
originator of this front was Mahmud Al-Qadi, ex-deputy and professor of the
Faculty of Architecture.

But President Sadat, involved to the point of no return in his relations
with Israel and the United States, and his isolation within the Arab world,
could not let democracy develop even though he had promised it to the
Egyptian people. Exploiting the social destitution of the Egyptian people,
Sadat used the watchwords of 'peace' and 'the opening up of the economy'
as means of repression. The real power of decision-making was concentrated
and all real opposition forbidden. This policy was compulsorily ratified by
referendum — that dictatorial invention of the leaders of the Third World
which reduces human thought and experience to one word, 'yes' or 'no',
concealing the true situation and forcing the result if there seems to be a need.
Thus, for example, elections for the President of the Republic do not allow
a choice between two candidates, but simply acceptance or rejection of one
single candidate.

President Sadat, who knows very well the weak points in Egyptian society,
had to have recourse to a referendum at two decisive moments in 1979:
the first time concerning the separate peace treaty with Israel, concluded on
26th May of the same year, and the second time to liquidate the political
forces of the opposition by altering the constitution and the law on political
parties so as to eliminate the very existence of the opposition.

Illiteracy (affecting 80% of a population estimated at 45 million) reducing
the effectiveness of the mass media and the official press, and the ubiquitous
presence of the police, had of course something to do with the results: an
overwhelming 'yes' on both occasions.

If, in a democratic country, we can distinguish between the political
majority and the political minority by observing the position of the different
organisations and parties of which they consist, Sadat's Egypt is obviously
not such a country. This is illustrated by the following account of Egyptian
political bodies opposed to the Peace Treaty.

The Muslim Brothers, in their monthly organ *Ad-Daawa,* stigmatise the
Israeli-Egyptian treaty through their leader writer Omar El-Telemsani and in
the name of Islam. Their issue for June 1979, under the title 'The voice to
save Jerusalem', asserts: 'The Muslims will never let Jerusalem go, even if the
whole world supported the Jews in their position' and 'if it is true that
Palestine is the cause of the Arabs, it is above all the cause of the Arab and
non-Arab Muslims'.

The Wafdists on several occasions have revealed their opposition to the
separate treaty and to the anti-democratic regime, despite the dissolution of
their party and even though they are on the side of a liberal economy and
were against the Nasser regime.

The Independents: an alliance of old and new politicians and deputies.

The government forbade them the press conference which was to be held in the precincts of Parliament to debate the separate treaty. Instead they published a communique against the treaty because it attacked Egyptian sovereignty over Sinai, the Palestinians' right to set up an independent State, and the rights of the Arab countries, partners in the four preceding wars.

The Nasserists uniting all trends: that represented by the National Progressive and Unionist Assembly party and that expressed by the review *23rd July* published in London (organ of a new organisation born in exile, The Socialist Vanguard) and finally, the mass of people not organised in parties who express themselves by the publication of books and newspaper articles.

The historic leaders of the revolution of July 1952: Zakariyyah Mohyi Ad-Din, Hussein Al-Chafei, Kamal Ad-Din Hussein and Abd El-Latif Al-Bagdadi; two of them belong to the religious trend and the two others are close to the liberal trend. But they are all opposed to the treaty and have vigorously denounced it in a communique distributed to all press agencies as an attack on national sovereignty and the rights of Palestinians, leading to the isolation of Egypt within the Arab world.

The Marxists, notably those of the Egyptian Communist Party, but also those belonging to the National Assembly led by Khaled Mohyi Ad Din and non-party writers whose influence is not negligible, by virtue of their many publications both at home and abroad.

All political forces have rejected Sadat's treaty with Israel and the United States; and despite the contradictions existing between them, they still form the most faithful political expression of Egyptian society in its different economic, social and cultural fields.

This does not mean that President Sadat represents only himself; on the contrary, he represents the interests of the social strata which have profited in the past and are continuing to accumulate profits in the present. They are the same people who make laws in the country to perpetuate their position in the future. But these strata represent only a very limited social sphere; their strength lies in their increasing monopolisation of all positions of authority, with initial help from the regime; which says much about the socio-historical meaning of the latter.

These social strata use a double form of demagogy: on the one hand they exploit the gaps in Nasser's past regime, and on the other they promise the people the false prosperity and democracy which the 'dream industry' dangles permanently before their eyes. This demagogy began on the 14th of May 1971 (the date when Sadat came to power) with the appearance of a recovery which rapidly turned into repression.

And so, although President Sadat and his group of leaders represent objectively only a small minority, and despite an opposition which represents the overwhelming majority of society, the ruling class has been able to dominate the masses by demagogy and manipulation, and the oppressive machinery of the State has managed to obtain their 'consent' to the peace treaty and its promoter.

The fact that the opposition and the mass of the people were so evidently out of step can be explained by two factors: the history of latent or manifest repression by the government on the one hand, and the seductive promise of a prosperous tomorrow on the other hand. All the media were mobilised to organise this unparalleled brainwashing campaign.

There is no doubt that the serious mistakes made by certain of the Arab countries and others, the responsibility for which rests on the Egyptian opposition, may have helped Sadat in the face of public opinion. But we cannot say that they had any decisive effect on the relationship between the opposition and the masses.

It was surely the repressive nature of the regime and its demagogy which were the main reasons for the Egyptian masses and the true representatives of their interests falling out of step.

There can be no vacuum in politics. Sadat filled it. At the summit of power, he led a party similar to the Socialist Union of Nasser's time, made up of deputies, ministers, governors, police chiefs etc., in other words the whole of the administration. In a few days and by magic, thousands of people joined a party with no programme, no ideology and no political history.

A strange electoral campaign followed during the month of May 1979; addressing the Egyptian people, the President asked them to throw out all the opposition candidates. This was the opposition whose activity he was, purely and simply, to forbid from the end of the month.

If there ever was a caricature of democracy, this was it. The father of the Egyptian family, as he likes to call himself, the 'guarantor of the constitution' threatens, suppresses and forbids, sure of his power, all legal opposition in the pure style of the puppet regimes with which the Third World swarms.

Just before the elections, the forces of law and order had arrested deputies belonging to the dissolved Parliament who were accused of spying for a foreign state (Bulgaria!). This crime is punishable by death or life imprisonment, as it comes under the heading of high treason; two weeks later they were released for lack of proof.

The real aim of the operation was of course to prevent them from taking part in the elections and to injure their reputation with the electors. Their indictment appeared on the front pages of all the Egyptian papers, while their release, once the electoral campaign was over, went off in silence.

But that was only one of the methods used to control the electoral process and its results. Thus for example, a magistrate called Mumtaz Nassar, a candidate in the governorate of Assyout in the south, was only elected thanks to men armed with machine-guns supervising the polls. Unarmed candidates had no hope of controlling the course of the elections. The ballot-boxes were already full of voting slips before the elections had even begun. Consequently, no opposition candidate could possibly win. Those who did get through in spite of everything were declared beaten even though their names had appeared in the press among those elected: Khaled Mohyi Ad-Din and Kamal Ad-Din Hussein among others. But President Sadat had already appointed and organised an 'official opposition' formed from two parties, the Liberal Socialists whose president was not elected, and the Socialist Action whose president miraculously got in. Both parties, of course, are supporting the President and his peace treaty.

To have won the elections in these conditions is not a true victory for the President's party, the National Democratic Party, which has not even become a real party. For the day Sadat relinquishes power there will be no more party, just as Nasser's death brought with it the death of the Socialist Union.

But the main problem is still that of the chasm separating the Egyptian masses from their true representatives ranging from the extreme right to the extreme left. As long as this opposition, split vertically and horizontally, is not transformed into a wide national and democratic front, as long as it is not rooted effectively in the people, Egypt, isolated in the Arab and the Islamic world and among national liberation movements, will still face the threat of transformation into a dictatorial regime like the dictatorships of Latin America and certain African states.

If the democratic alternative is in an impasse, it is not alone; the impasse is that of the Egyptian people who – slowly perhaps – will expose the mirage of 'peace' and of 'national sovereignty' over Sinai. But they will first have suffered the consequences of Sadat's denial of Egypt's position as one of the Arab nations and its isolation within the Islamic world. There is always time, of course, to change the road along which Egypt is now moving, and the ten lost years will not have been a dead loss; the reality of Egypt has been plumbed to its very depths.

The population explosion will go on its crazy way (one child born every 15 seconds), there will be less and less moderation in price rises in an economy characterised by unemployment, inflation, a permanent deficit in the balance of payments, the accumulation of debts, the absence of a development plan, the deterioration of agricultural and industrial production, the immoderate recourse to imported consumer goods. The rest of the world, suffering from shortage of fuel and food and from unemployment, can be of no real help. In this situation the designated victim is the Egyptian people, threatened with a state of famine which will never be solved by emigration and foreign debts.

But the impasse is also that of the Egyptian Government, incapable of keeping its promises and already facing new situations in the country. In May 1979 the security services discovered two caches of light and medium arms and seized more than 32,000 weapons. In the same month, President Sadat could not visit the *Mohafazat* of *Al-Mina* because of the deterioration of the security situation which had become uncontrollable. Some weeks earlier, in the south of the Nile Valley, at Assyout, there had been an armed controntation of Christians and Muslims, despite all the helpful efforts of the Sheikh of Al-Azhar and the Patriarch of the Coptic Church.

The regime is in an impasse also, because of its total dependence on foreigners, who are not likely to let their interests sink into the waters of the

Nile. When the machinery of government no longer functions autonomously, an outside force, whatever its interests, can interfere in its functioning, albeit only to a partial and limited extent. In a country like Egypt (without oil, without a profitable market, without weight and without influence in the Arab world since its isolation), the foreign power can do no more than provide spare parts for the machinery of government, which it will abandon if the need arises, having taken all it could from it.

And, as we have already said, there is an impasse for the national and democratic forces, on account of their ideological, social and economic contradictions preventing their organisational unification, and also on account of the violent repression they are suffering and which inhibits their action among the masses; on account, finally, of the changes that have occurred in Egypt, in the Arab world and in the Near East. The weakness of this opposition lies in its very composition. Certain of its constituent parts limit their opposition to Sadat as a person, while embracing his regime. Others base their ideas on a tribal conception of revenge more suitable to a fight between two ancient clans. Yet others, without any social programme, keep their gaze religiously fixed on Jerusalem and see the Palestinian question from a racist point of view. As for those forces which have a more global conception of the national and social question, although objectively they represent the interests of the popular majority, they lack social position, and the State machinery and the government's demagogy have succeeded in falsifying the image of their thought in the minds of a majority of the citizens.

Finally, there is the impasse of the armed forces, restructured and re-armed with the idea of playing a new part, that of a regional police force, previously the role of the Shah's Iran. Hence the inflation of the military budget at the very time when the government had propagated the idea that military spending was one of the reasons for the country's economic crisis. The Egyptian officer is more interested in what is going on outside the frontiers than in the frontiers themselves, which is the logic of the prosperity of the *marchand a valise* (fly-by-night hawker) who has become director of an import-export firm. This does not prevent the rising discontent with Libya, the reality of the 'sovereignty' in Sinai, and, very probably, the rise in the cost of living.

Many officers have been dismissed or arrested, and some even executed for trying to form an organisation within the armed forces. Nevertheless, the present-day Egyptian army, which is no longer that of Nasser, without being a 'royal army' is still in the process of formation and reconstruction; so it is difficult to foresee what its role might be in the course of events to come.

Because of all this, Egypt will, for a long time, be at the meeting-point of several roads, from which military adventure or bloody anarchy — religious or social — is not completely excluded. Nor can we exclude economic destruction parallel to a conflict between several forces. Even 'change for the better' is a risky undertaking, so difficult will it be to get rid of the snags created and established by present political practice. But events, with all

429

their negative consequences, are inescapable, and so is the arrival of the people and of outside forces at the final stage of impasse.

When promises give place to despair, and dreams to nightmares, when no solution shows on the horizon, Egypt becomes a country where surprises are born. It will certainly not be a repetition of the revolution of 23rd July 1952, nor the events of the 18th and 19th January 1977. It might even be a new 'Sadat' arriving and finding the same impasse, until the moment when the real solution comes to light, even though its birth-pangs may be agonising.

The Impasse in the Arab World

Since Nasser's death, the Arabs have had to face what might be called the Egyptian impasse. Most of them, however, did not realise this Egyptian impasse until March 26th 1979. Most governments had even considered Sadat's rise to power as a positive element; others simply bowed to the *fait accompli* or managed to save themselves.

However, all political and economic indications show that the counter-revolution had been on its way ever since February 1971, the date of the reopening of the Suez Canal, which led to the signature of the treaty evacuating Sinai in 1979.

The policy known as 'an open economy' was carried on side by side with the dropping of Egypt's international alliances. These two policies, domestic and foreign, were gladly welcomed by most Arab governments. The Egyptian opposition was all the more weakened because this support for Sadat wiped out by its financial largesse (i.e. Arab aid) the losses of an economy in shreds, and shored up a policy which, consciously or unconsciously, opened the way to the conclusion of a separate peace with Israel.

The great shock given to the Arabs by Sadat's visit to Jerusalem certainly was surprising. Does it not mean that they had shared in a policy the end of which they did not know?

In fact, the primitive anti-communism developed together with the alliance with the United States, and an exaggerated fear of the Soviet danger, had encouraged certain Arab countries to go along with Egypt's present policy, the logical result of which was the visit to Occupied Jerusalem. Why the surprise, then? And why was the surprise repeated with the signing of the Camp David Agreements in November 1978? Does that not mean that these Arab countries were still, in spite of everything, anxious to safeguard the Egyptian regime? And will the signature of the Treaty which came as a third surprise put an end to their position? This continuous chain of surprises, which which we do not want to think of as a political comedy, means that the Arabs lack strategic vision concerning their vital problems. Quite different from the Egyptian President, who has shown in this field a perfect knowledge of the strategy he is elaborating and executing. So by carrying on a policy of 'sufficient unto the day' the Arab regimes empirically regarded the Egyptian President's initiatives in isolation from one another, thus not seeing the bonds which necessarily joined them together.

The same attitude characterises their relationships with the United States; they claim to believe in a 'disinterested and impartial' attitude on the part of the Americans to the Israeli-Arab conflict. Despite the United States insistence for 30 years on the fact that the security of Israel is an integral part of American security, they received with delight Carter's declaration at the time of the American presidential elections that he was bearing in mind the necessity of creating a 'national home' for the Palestinians. But they soon forgot that once he was elected, the new President quickly insisted that Israel's security demanded 'two sorts of frontiers: one geographical, and the other connected with the security of Israel'; that was the first time an American President had agreed that Israel should not be enclosed in precise geographical frontiers. Did he not sign a communique with the Soviet Union (in October 1978) fixing the Geneva Conference as an adequate occasion to debate and find a solution for the crisis of the Near East, and did he not, one month later, go back on this joint declaration, following President Sadat's visit to Israel, thus setting aside the role of the United Nations, the Soviet Union, the Arabs and the Palestinians in the 'pursuit of peace'?

But the Arab regimes' lack of strategy does not mean that they are not part of the strategies of others, carried out in the interests of those others, most often in contradiction with the Arabs' national interests.

That is why the reactions of the Arab countries to Egyptian policies, taking the form of 'surprises', do not mean complete lack of awareness, but rather express a pragmatic awareness which seeks to ally patriotism and dependence on foreigners, a privileged relationship with the United States and also with the Palestinian revolution, that is to say, in the long run, Israel and Palestine.

It was in this sense that the majority of Arab regimes shared in the policy of the Egyptian President and found themselves actually accomplices in his final surprise. The only difference existing between them and Sadat is that the latter was consistent with himself when he placed them at one stroke in the present impasse – the choice between pragmatic knowledge and a real change of strategy.

At the Arab Summit in Baghdad, held after the signing of the Camp David Agreements, the radicals, in the minority, were able to win the day against the 'American peace'. A few hours after the Congress had closed, however, the *Washington Post* claimed that the summit talks had failed and that Sadat's followers had succeeded in blocking any decision against the 'peace'. But the American paper had to retract the next day, saying that it had not 'expected the defeat of the moderates'.

In reality things went differently. The moderates, after Sadat refused to receive their delegation, succeeded in bringing the Congress to the minimum level possible. The decisions made were suspended until the day of the signature of the treaty, and then a Congress of Ministers of Foreign Affairs and Finance met to recommend their implementation. This 'minimum level' did not express the hard line of Damascus, Algiers, Baghdad, Tripoli or Aden, but the position of those countries which are richest and most closely linked with the United States, as they once were (and perhaps soon will be again) with Egypt. The decisions taken are not in fact very far from the pragmatic inclinations of these regimes, which are seeking at any price a compromise between mutually exclusive alternatives — rejecting any definite break with the separate treaty, on the one hand, as long as close links still exist between most Arabs and the United States: and, on the other hand, taking up an absolutely definite position against the peace treaty, as a result of which the moderate Arab regimes are risking the fall of the Egyptian regime, which would in consequence threaten their own regimes which, in many ways they resemble.

We must also make it clear that for the regimes called moderate the minimum level at which the conference stopped comes from a certain internal political necessity. If the support they gave President Sadat before he signed the treaty was, for governments horror-stricken by the prospect of radical change in the region, an act of self-reinforcement, the position with regard to the treaty itself is different.

The man-in-the-street in Saudi Arabia, or other Arab countries, can tolerate close connections with the United States and accept the economic and political aid showered on the Egyptian Government during the preceding years. But this man-in-the-street, deeply Arab and Muslim, may well become much less tolerant when he hears the Iranian Muslim, Ayatollah Khomeini, condemning the separate treaty and the breaking off relations with Sadat's regime, and calling for a Holy War (*Jihad*) for the liberation of Palestine and Jerusalem.

It is true that an absolute ruler is not very interested in the opinions of his people, but it is also true that there were some indications of opposition in Saudi Arabia after the Baghdad Summit. It is true that a ruler can never go beyond a certain limit with impunity, despite his absolutism, when the nation feels that national sovereignty or sacred beliefs are being attacked. It is certain that a number of Arab rulers, feeling their thrones totter at the Baghdad Summit, were obliged to accept a minimum level of action as a middle way between Sadat's policy and the attitude of their people. It must be said that the campaign orchestrated by the Zionist and American media against Saudi Arabia, the Hashemite Kingdom and the Gulf States was the first of its kind; now there was the discovery of a plot in Saudi Arabia or other Arab countries, now there was some king or prince who was very ill or even dying; they even went as fas as threats of military intervention to occupy the oil wells.

As for President Sadat, he succeeded for the first time in exhausting all his reserves of insults, abuse and counter-accusations which the Saudis were hearing for the first time from the head of a State which, as it happened, was the one they had helped the most.

The Saudis reacted to this campaign by a series of unusual measures; they published, for the first time, lists showing the financial aid given to the

Egyptian President — $17 billion. In their press, Saudi journalists were able
to write articles of a rare violence, the tone of which sometimes came very
close (the irony of history!) to revolutionary phraseology. But this campaign
soon developed in a way that perverted it in Saudi Arabia and in other Arab
countries: the Egyptian *people* became the target of attacks at the same time
as President Sadat and his regime. It was even possible to read, in some Arab
and Western capitals, anti-Egyptian articles enough to make the people of
Egypt rally round their President. It might almost have been an elaborate
plan to divert a political struggle against the Egyptian regime by transforming
it into a fight between the Arabs of Egypt and the other Arabs. The fact
is that the blockade of Egypt poses problems radically different from those
posed by the blockade of the Hebrew State. First of all, the Egyptian people
are Arabs; and besides, two million Egyptian nationals work in Arab
countries, as university professors and school-teachers, doctors, nurses,
restaurant workers and building workers — to say nothing of the unemployed
or refugees. Their situation is all the more critical because their families in
Egypt live on what they remit to them, and it is not possible to foresee the
decisions which President Sadat will make with regard to these workers
abroad.

A large number of Egyptians have been badly treated in Arab countries,
considered as Sadat's agents and forced to pay for the treaty with their
dignity. Certain Arab countries have even thought of repatriating these
workers to their native country; this, in perfect accord with the anti-Arab
chauvinism which was developing in Egypt.

The Solution

The Arab impasse took concrete form — after the signing of the separate
treaty — in a series of bloody confrontations; the conflict between the two
Yemens which cost them, among other things, the lives of their heads of
state, an aerial combat between Syria and Israel, the permanent tension on
the Iraq-Iran frontier, the tension between Algeria and Morocco in the
Sahara, the massacre of Alep in Syria, perpetrated by Muslim integrationists,
and Israeli aggression, which became systematic in South Lebanon.

All this happened as though this series of events were completing the
Egypt-Israeli-American treaty, forcing the Arabs to occupy themselves with
their own internal problems, so as to allow free rein to the Egypt-Israeli
negotiations. Because of this, the faint hope, born of the Baghdad Summit,
that it might be possible for the Arabs to hold Sadat's enterprise in check,
gave way to despair.

The challenge which Egypt issued to the Arabs rests on the inability of
the latter to find an alternative solution. It was basically a false challenge,
because Sadat had not offered the Arabs a solution which they could have
opposed. He simply adopted the Israeli attitude which the Arabs had been
rejecting for 30 years. As such, the challenge is not new; it is the one issued

by the Zionists and their supporters as far back as 1948.

The only new element is Egypt's alignment with the Israelis and Americans, causing the Arabs to lose an important part of their strategic weight, without changing the nature of their conflict with Israel, and consequently their rejection, despite defeats, of the imperialist solution. However, the new change in the balance of forces must bring with it a radical revision of the objective analysis of the situation so that the solution may be on the same level as the event.

A false challenge then, but a real challenge in so far as the Arabs could not work out an effective alternative to Sadat's answer; a reply capable of giving positive concrete form to the Arabs' rejection: to regain their rights, beginning with those of the Palestinian people.

The strategic alternative in a struggle for national liberation is not limited to a choice between war and negotiation, as this choice is subject to the relative strengths of the parties involved which decide the setting up of true peace. The example of Vietnam is a model of the use of these two ways simultaneously, but we must not forget that the solution was in that case, above all, liberation and national unification between North and South.

In the same way there will be no other choice for the Arabs in the face of Zionist invasion but national liberation and national unity. But an effective strategy will not come out of this choice until the day when Arabs can unite around a common minimum level which has nothing to do with the one that came out of the Baghdad Summit; that is to say the uncertainty as to whether the Israeli project is nothing less than the establishment of a true world power, not limited to the geographical territory already acquired or to be acquired, but going far beyond it on an economic and political level. In this sense the Israeli Zionists would be looking for a military and strategic 'living space' which would stretch beyond the Nile and the Euphrates and reach out to the centres of Africa and Asia and to the Atlantic and Indian Oceans. The Arabs would then have no choice but to submit to an economic, political and military guardianship (Egypt has already left this road open).

This Zionist project, although it has found concrete form in an independent State will, of course, continue to be an integral part of the Western imperialist plans made under the aegis of the United States.

It cannot be asserted that there is total coincidence between the interests of Zionism and those of Western imperialism (it even happens that contradictions appear within American, German and French society — between the centres of power and the Jewish lobby). But on the other hand, it can be said that in the Near East this correspondence of interests is inescapable because of oil wealth, strategic position and the sea-routes.

There is another essential to be recognised for the elaboration of a common Arab strategy: the Arabs are the first people at whom the American-Zionist plans are aimed. All the Arabs! Men and land. It is an essential element of the Zionist living space. No illusion of 'privileged relations' with the United States, no fear of the common communist danger, no 'deep-rooted friendship with the West' will make any difference, any more than they saved the Shah of Iran or any other African, Asian or Latin American potentate abandoned by the Americans. The Western plans are, right down to the foundations, opposed to the existence of a genuine Arab identity and not only to the radical Arab regimes.

It must be understood, besides, that the object of the treaty was not only to detach Egypt from the Arab nation. For this nation has already split into numerous entities. It is not simply a question of the isolation of Egypt, but an active attempt to perpetuate the splitting apart of the Arabs, for which Egypt has been strategically acquired, but beginning with the amputation of Palestine as stipulated by the treaty.

It must be understood that there is no half-way house between being an Arab Egypt and an Israeli Egypt. Up to the present Egypt's independence and social progress have been consistent only with its belonging to the Arab nation. In the same way, in its new 'Israeli' phase, the country of the Nile cannot be confined in an isolating neutrality; on the contrary it is driven to play the part of a junior partner to Israel and the U.S.A. in their project to found a new Israeli-Western great power in Afro-Asia.

In fact the Egyptianisation of Egypt by its de-Arabisation is only a chauvinist illusion meant to veil its submission to Zionist plans. Opposition to the treaty signed with Israel can only mean the fall of the regime which is trying to drag Egypt along in the wake of Israel. Just as the liberation of Palestine means the destruction of the Zionist entity, the liberation of Egypt signifies its recovery from Zionist domination: these are the two faces of the same reality: overthrow the regime, liberate the country. An economic and political blockade by the Arabs against Egypt is not sufficient to win such a battle, especially as it does not extend to the real master of Sadat's policy, Western imperialism. Only Arab unity, by paralysing the Zionist plans to perpetuate the splitting of the Arab world, by neutralising the deeper meaning of Egypt's detachment from its Arab nature, will be able to provide an effective reply which will deprive the Israeli plans of all their breadth.

In the general context of such an analysis of Arab strategy unified against Sadat and the Zionist plans, four political conditions are necessary:
1) A close alliance with the international camp whose interests are objectively against the treaty, whatever ideological, economic or illusory differences may separate certain Arab regimes from the socialist camp.
2) Consolidation of the bonds between the Palestinian Resistance and the Egyptian opposition, considering this axis as the long-term base for Arab action. The axis will also act as a magnet to the Arab masses disappointed in their government.
3) A basic structural change in Arab policy with regard to energy for the industrialised West, a reconsideration of the policy of development and relations with the productive forces, cultural restructuring, revision of social relationships: all factors necessary to provide a solid base for the national struggle. The present structure built on dependence on Western monopolies can only impose a reduplication of policies concerned with the national question, and consequently bring with it an empirical practice which does violence to

strategy, leading to catastrophe (the fate of South Lebanon all through 1977, and especially 1978 and 1979, is a typical example of such a policy).

4) Active participation of the Arab masses at the centres of decision-making, without which no change in outdated social structures is possible. The absence of democracy, as the most progressive contemporary Arab experiences have shown, goes back to the absence of the necessary link between national liberation and development. In this case everything gained, however historic it may be, can disappear, as these same experiences have proved. No being, even a genius, can exert a beneficial guardianship. At the present day, more than at any other time, one law for all, one constitution, free parties and a free press, conditions for the initiative of the whole population, are more important than anything else, because they condition everything else and decide the result of the struggle. The real choice is between democratic power or foreign domination.

The International Impasse and its Prospects

The course of future events in the Near East will emphasise the dimensions of the international impasse resulting from the separate treaty between Egypt and Israel, beginning with the weapon of oil and ending – simply – with weapons.

The danger of fresh military provocations by Egypt against Libya is still with us. It is not simply a border conflict but a situation with many consequences, as more than 250,000 Egyptians work in Libya. The Soviets are present both on the Egyptian-Libyan frontier and in Libyan ports – Libya is capable of military retaliation. And in the present situation Libya enjoys Arab support because of official Arab hostility against Egypt. Colonel Gadhafi's Arab tour (end of June and beginning of July) could smooth out the apprehensions of certain Arab governments with regard to the Libyan regime; finally, the deterioration of relations between the United States and Libya following America's refusal to sell civilian aircraft to Tripoli, and the Libyan threat to cut off its oil to Washington, could well give the Egyptian aggression quite another meaning. Sadat's regime thus has to exert greater prudence, though the risk of conflict cannot be entirely removed.

An Israeli coup against the Syrian army in the Lebanon or in Syria itself is very probable. Faced with the isolation of the signatories of the treaty, Israel has no choice. The weakest link is the Lebanon, and it was not by chance that the Israeli Prime Minister asked the Lebanon to sign a new treaty with him. The part played by the agent of Israel, Saad Haddad, to whom the Jewish State handed over a frontier strip of Lebanese territory, is part of the Israeli plans, which impose a difficult choice on the Lebanese: either the unity and integrity of the Lebanon under Israeli hegemony, or the dismantling of the Lebanon. In either case the price demanded is the liquidation of Palestinian Resistance and the accentuation of the pressure on Syria.

In a situation already so complicated, a sentence of the Saudi Oil Minister emphasised the weakness of the Western world: a desperate revolutionary act could sink two oil tankers in the Straits of Hormuz, suddenly cutting off oil to the Western world. The present energy crisis rampant in the West could be the subject of a 'children's game' and become transformed into a drama.

The Iraqi President, Saddat Hussein, took a different tone when he threatened to burn all the oil wells in the region if any foreign power tried to occupy them.

The French position, more or less shared by the nine Common Market countries, about the energy crisis, is shown to be more capable of grasping the importance of the Middle Eastern 'powder-barrel' than that which came out of the Japanese-American Summit in Tokyo.

But beyond these differences, the Western impasse concerning the Israeli-Egyptian treaty is still complete. It is not limited to having to face the possibility that the Arabs will use the weapons of oil or money. Its basis is still the necessity to radically revise the Western analysis of the Middle East, not only in the present but also in the future; because though the creation of Israel answers the ambition of the Western world to have a bridgehead in the middle of the Arab region, and also provides the moral solution to the West's attack of conscience with regard to the Jews, it must be understood that the founding of an Israeli power in the Middle East will break all bridges between Arabs and the West, and, in time, replace the attack of conscience about the Jews with a new attack of conscience about the Palestinians.

What is called the 'peace' treaty is not ending the wars in the Middle East, and is not beginning a period of genuine world peace. The Egyptian people should ask themselves why all Arabs, moderate and radical, reject the Egypto-Israeli treaty, and this same question should be put, just as sharply, to the Western world. Not because the West is being threatened, but because there is a risk that a profound state of imbalance in the peace of the world and its development will occur in one of the most sensitive regions of the world.

The founding of an Israeli power can bring hope to the West – but only in the short term – a hope without a future, for a profound analysis of the development of Egypt and the other Arab countries should not encourage the West to place any bets on forces foreign to the area, forces which will remain subject to developments which cannot yet be seen, whatever the weight of the *fait accompli* may be.

The situation of the Egyptian regime is like a hollow tree in danger of being uprooted by the first squall. The 'line of life' of the Egyptian opposition, weak though it may seem at present, is developing in the opposite direction to the regime's 'line of life'. The day when the latter falls will see a change in the whole region and not only in Egypt.

But if the situation in the Middle East is moving more and more swiftly towards an acute crisis, the contrary winds of the Western world are not blowing towards optimism despite the positions of France and the European Economic Community, basically tactical positions which have no place in a strategic view of the future of the West and the world. The victory of the right wing in several European countries, parallel to the revival of fascist groups and the retreat of liberal and radical forces are black marks in relations between the Arabs and the West. The objective alliance between this European retreat and the most aggressive sectors of the U.S.A. and Israel may well encourage military adventures undertaken with the battle-cry of the protection of the West and its industrial development.

The immediate consequences of this situation would bring humanity to the brink of the abyss. It is unthinkable that the SALT II agreements could withstand such an upheaval, and the least Mediterranean region nearest to the West is in danger of being turned into a veritable volcano.

We can no longer rely on the principles of justice, equality and liberty, or on the Rights of Man, for these are the desperate stakes of the authors of an uneasy peace treaty. It is on this treaty — which they will sign amongst themselves — that all will depend. Whether the road it follows will, or will not necessarily lead to war, it alone is capable of leading to an effective peace.

Appendices

Appendix A: The National Question

The First Initiative by Sadat

On February 4th 1971, President Sadat made a speech to the People's Council in which he presented to Arab and international public opinion the initiative for the solution of the Middle East crisis, which later bore his name.

Here is the text:

(1) The United Arab Republic considers itself responsible for the liberation of the land occupied after the aggression of 1967. It is a great responsibility for which we have acted politically, economically, militarily and diplomatically; and we shall continue to offer every sacrifice, whatever the price. A nation is first of all responsible for its own freedom within international law. No one can ask of it or impose on it an undertaking contrary to this responsibility. Every nation has the freedom or the duty to act in the face of the problems confronting it.

(2) But while respecting this great responsibility, we shall reply to the appeal of the Secretary-General of the United Nations, and we are deciding to cease fire for a period of 30 days which will end on March 7th next. The Secretary-General of the United Nations, and the international community, must realise that effective progress has been achieved with regard to the problem. We think it is essential that the Security Council should make themselves acquainted, before the end of this period, with the Secretary-General's report on the progress made. Although we know that Israel, helped by the United States and unconditionally supported, will not budge from its present attitude, we pray God that experience will bring the proof to fight these doubts.

(3) We will share in all efforts to solve the crisis, and we consider this the expression of our wish to apply the resolution of the Security Council.

We ask that, during this period of ceasefire, the Israeli forces on the east bank of the Suez Canal should make a partial retreat, as the first stage of a timetable which could finally be used for the carrying out of the resolutions of the Security Council.

If this is done during the said period, we will be ready to carry out immediately the dredging of the Suez Canal with a view to reopening it for international shipping and the service of the international economy.

439

We think that with our initiative we can help Ambassador Yaring's efforts to pass from the verbal stage to the classic procedures for putting into effect the resolution of the Security Council. Our actions will have their influence on the interests of all countries whose economies have been affected by the closing of the Suez Canal, resulting from Israeli aggression and terrorism.

Cairo, 4th February 1971.

Text of Note from the United Arab Republic (U.A.R.) sent to Ambassador Yaring by the Egyptian Ministry for Foreign Affairs

The U.A.R. has stated clearly that it agreed, on the basis of reciprocity, to fulfil all duties incumbent upon it according to Resolution 242 of the Security Council, in order to reach a peaceful solution in the Middle East, and that on the same basis, Israel should fulfil all its undertakings resulting from the said resolution.

In reference to your note of 10th February 1971, the U.A.R. undertakes to respect an obligation consisting of the following elements:

1) Suspension of all military action.
2) Respect and recognition by both parties of the sovereignty of the other and of its territorial integrity.
3) Respect and recognition by both parties of the right of the other to live within safe and recognised frontiers.
4) Both parties undertake to watch that their territory does not become a source or starting-point for military or hostile actions directed against the inhabitants of the other party.
5) Each of the two parties undertakes not to interfere in the internal affairs of the other.

The U.A.R. on its side undertakes to:

6) Guarantee freedom of navigation in the Suez Canal according to the Treaty of Constantinople of 1888.
7) Guarantee freedom of navigation and passage according to the principles of international law.
8) It agrees to the presence of a United Nations force to guarantee peace at Sharm El Sheik.
9) To ensure a peaceful solution to the problems of the Middle East and to guarantee the territorial integrity of each of the States of the region, the U.A.R. accepts: (a) the establishment of demilitarised zones extending equal distances within the frontiers of each of the two parties: (b) the creation of a United Nations Peacekeeping Force, in which the four permanent members of the Security Council will take part.

Israel should undertake to apply all the provisions of Resolution 242 of the Security Council. Israel should respect an undertaking containing the following elements:

1) The retreat of its military forces from Sinai and the Gaza Strip;
2) Find a fair solution to the question of refugees according to the resolutions of the United Nations Organisation;
3) Suspend all military action;
4) Respect and recognition, on a basis of reciprocity, of the territorial unity and political independence of the other;
5) Each of the two parties respects and recognises the right of the other to a secure life within stable and recognised frontiers;

6) Both parties are responsible for making every effort to ensure that its territory will not be a source or starting-point for military or aggressive actions against the inhabitants, citizens or property of the other;

7) Each of the two parties undertakes not to interfere in the internal; affairs of the other;

8) To guarantee a peaceful solution to the problems of the Middle East and to maintain the territorial sovereignty of all the States of the region, Israel should accept: (a) the creation of demilitarised zones extending for equal distances within the frontiers of both parties; (b) the creation of a United Nations Peacekeeping Force in which the four permanent members of the Security Council take part.

If Israel undertakes to respect the preceding clauses, the U.A.R. will be ready to conclude a peace treaty with Israel containing all the undertakings mentioned and explained in Resolution 242 of the Security Council.

The U.A.R. considers that it is impossible to establish a just and lasting peace if the Security Council's resolution is not totally applied and as long as the forces do not retreat from the territories they occupied on 5th June 1967.

Sadat's Peace Proposals during the War

On 16th October 1973, that is to say ten days after the outbreak of war, and almost at the first moment of the opening of the breach of the outfall gate, President Sadat made a speech to the People's Council in which he addressed a public message to the American President Nixon, containing a peace plan of which this is the text:

1) We must fight honestly and we fight to free our territories occupied by Israel in 1967 and to find ways of restoring and respecting the legitimate rights of the Palestinian people. In this context, we respect the resolution of the United Nations, the General Assembly and the Security Council.

2) We are quite ready to call a ceasefire, on condition that the Israeli forces retreat from all occupied territories immediately and under international control towards the lines held before 5th June 1967.

3) We are ready immediately after the retreat from all these territories to go to a peace conference at the United Nations, and I shall do my best to convince my comrades among the Arab leaders responsible for the struggle against the enemy. I shall do my best to convince the representatives of the Palestinian people of the same thing, so that we can all take part, with the international community, in laying the foundations of peace in the region, built on respect for the legitimate rights of all the peoples of the region.

4) At this precise moment, we are ready to take the necessary action for the reopening of the Suez Canal to international shipping, so that it can resume its role in the prosperity of the whole world. I gave orders to the President of of the Suez Canal Organisation to proceed with these clearing operations on the day after the liberation of the east bank of the Canal. The work has already begun.

5) We are not prepared to accept vague promises or ambiguous words that can be interpreted in various ways. We do not want to waste any more time. Cairo, 16th October 1973.

The Camp David Agreements

What is reproduced here is the second document constituting a basis for work towards a peace treaty between Egypt and Israel. This text has been distributed in Arabic by the Middle East Agency, an official Egyptian agency. It reads as follows:

Israel and Egypt agree, in order to achieve peace, to negotiate in good faith, with the aim of signing a peace treaty within three months of the signature of this outline agreement.

Both parties have agreed on the fact that negotiations will be carried out under the aegis of the United Nations, in one or more places on which both parties will agree.

All principles of Resolution 242 of the United Nations are to be applied to resolve the differences between Egypt and Israel.

Unless there is another agreement between both parties, a peace treaty will be put into execution in a period of two to three years from the date of signature of the peace treaty.

Both parties have expressed agreement on the following matters:

1) Egypt has total sovereignty up to the frontiers internationally recognised between Egypt and the British mandate in Palestine.

2) The retreat of the Israeli armed forces from Sinai.

3) The airports evacuated by the Israelis near El Arrich Rafah, Ras El Nagb and Sharm El Sheik will be used for civilian purposes only, including commercial use by all countries.

4) Rights of passage for Israeli ships through the Gulf of Suez and the Suez Canal on the basis of the Treaty of Constantinople of 1888, applicable to all countries. The Straits of Tiran and of the Gulf of Aqaba are considered international waterways open to shipping and air traffic without obstacles.

5) Building of a road between Sinai and Jordan near Eilat with guaranteed free passage for Egypt and Jordan. The military forces will be concentrated in the following manner:

(a) A single Egyptian unit, motorised or not, may take up position in a region situated about 50 km. east of the Gulf of Suez and the Canal.

(b) The forces of the United Nations and the police to be armed with light weapons, and only for carrying out the usual police tasks, within the region west of the international frontiers and the Gulf of Aqaba, extending over a width from 20 to 40 km.

(c) Israeli military forces not exceeding four companies of the territorial army, and observers from the United Nations forces, may be stationed 3 km. to the east of the international frontiers.

6) Units of border guards not exceeding three companies may be attached to the civil police for the purpose of maintaining order in those areas not stated above. The precise establishment of the frontiers will be carried out according to the decisions made at the peace talks.

7) It is possible to install two pre-alert centres to guarantee that the clauses of the Agreement are respected, and to station forces in a part of the zone in Sinai towards the interior over a distance of 20 km. and also in the Sharm El Sheik region to guarantee passage through the Gulf of Tiran. These forces cannot be withdrawn without the consent of the Security Council, and with the agreement of the Peace Treaty, and after the provisional withdrawal, normal relations will be established between Egypt and Israel, including total

recognition of the latter.

8) Creation of diplomatic, economic and cultural relations, and raising of the blockade on the free movement of products and persons, and mutual protection of citizens according to the law.

Washington, 18th September 1978.

Appendix B: The Religious Question

Complete Text of the Proposed Law Presented by Al Azhar to the Egyptian People's Council

Part I: General Considerations Common to the Application of All Penalties
Article 1: This refers to penalties prescribed by law and concerning the crimes mentioned in this law.
Article 2: For a penalty to be applied to the delinquent, he must have reached the age of 17 or his majority, or he must have had the intention of committing the offence without necessity or without an excuse recognised by the law.
Article 3: The offences to which the penalties are applied must be recognised at least once before a judicial authority by the testimony of two men, or, in case of necessity, by the testimony of one man and two women, or four women.
Article 4: Additional penalties are applicable if the legal proof stipulated by law is lacking, but the judge has the firm conviction that the accused has committed another crime punishable by other laws than this.
Article 5: If the crimes are connected or successive, the accused may be punished in the following way:

1) If the crimes are multiple and equal in seriousness, one single penalty is applicable.

2) If the penalties are of the same kind, but different in degree, the strongest penalty is applicable.

3) If the penalties are of different kinds, they must all be applied.

4) Capital punishment overrides all other penalties.

5) The penalties prescribed by this law cannot be suspended, modified, reduced or annulled.

6) Every penalty, before being applied, must be submitted to the court of appeal. The penalty is applicable only after the judgement of this court.

7) Amputation of the hand must be carried out between the joint and the forearm. The foot must be cut in the middle of the instep in order to leave enough to enable the convicted person to walk.

8) With the exception of the death penalty and stoning, the other punishments are applicable only after the convicted person has been subjected to a medical examination and it has been proved that the carrying out of the punishment does not involve risk to the convicted person's life. Flogging must be carried out with a whip of medium size, without knots and without multiple tails. The convicted person must be stripped and beaten with moderation. The blows must fall all over the body, avoiding sensitive and

intimate parts. A woman is flogged without being undressed. The blows must fall on the back and shoulders.

9) The penalty of stoning is deferred when the convicted woman is pregnant, whether the pregnancy is the result of adultery or not. After the confinement, the penalty is deferred for two years. If someone undertakes to feed the baby, the penalty is immediate. The penalty of flogging is applicable to women, at the end of the post-natal period, if the sentenced woman is in good health and runs no risk of physical deterioration. If she is weak, the penalty is applicable only when she has recovered her health.

10) Acts punished by this law are considered as crimes.

Part 2: Penalties for Theft
Article 12: Theft as punished by this law is any act consisting of the appropriation of goods or money belonging to a third party, where there is no doubt to whom it belongs, and at the request of the victim, whether it is public or private property. To be considered as stolen money, it must be equivalent to an Islamic dinar weighing 4.45 grammes of pure gold.
In this case, the thief is punished in the following way:

1) Amputation of the right hand after the first theft.

2) Amputation of the left foot on recurrence.

3) If the offence is repeated more than twice, the convicted person is sentences to imprisonment until he has declared repentance.
Article 14: The preceding penalties cannot be applied in the following cases:

1) If the theft is committed in a public place, a place of work, or any other place where the accused is allowed to enter.

2) If the theft is committed between marriage partners or between members of the same family.

3) If the owner of the goods is unknown.

4) If the perpetrator of the theft is recognised as a creditor of the victim, and if the sum appropriated is equivalent to the debt or exceeds it, but the difference does not amount to the equivalent of 4.45 g. of pure gold.

5) If the product of the theft is fruit on trees, gathered, and if the accused had consumed it before leaving the property.

6) If the accused had accomplices.

7) If the goods are restored after the theft and before the penalty is carried out.

8) If the perpetrators of the crime were several in number, and the share of each did not exceed the Muslim dinar, unless the stolen object could not have been stolen unless several took part.

Part 3: Penalties for Banditry and Acts of Violence
Article 15: The penalty for acts of violence can be applied in the two following cases:

1) Aggression against the goods, honour or bodies of others.

2) Blocking the way of passers-by for the purpose of causing alarm.

3) In the two above cases, the penalty is not applicable unless the accused has used a weapon or some other instrument to inflict physical or mental harm.
Article 16: Anyone committing this crime or these crimes is punished in the following way:

1) By capital punishment if he had himself killed someone after successfully or unsuccessfully appropriating goods.

2) By the amputation of the right hand and left foot, or by imprisonment, if he had committed violence against goods, a man or his person, but without that violence going as far as murder or rape.

3) By imprisonment if he has simply barred the way for the purpose of causing alarm.

4) By imprisonment until he repents, if the accused has not killed someone.

Article 17: The penalty is cancelled if the accused declares his repentance:

1) The penalty is cancelled if the accused repents and abandons his action before being arrested, or by informing the public authorities before the crime is discovered by other means.

2) The cancellation of this penalty does not imply the non-application of other penalties for other crimes.

Article 18: Impediments to the application of penalties:

1) If the delinquent declares his repentance in accordance with paragraph 1 of the previous article. In this case the presiding magistrate must enquire into the affair and discover some way of cancelling the application of the penalty.

2) If the magistrate's enquiry reveals other crimes or offences, the affair is transferred to a competent court.

3) If the enquiry does not reveal other crimes or offences, and if the accused declares his repentance, the affair is shelved.

Article 19: In addition to the general considerations contained in this law, concerning the application of penalties, the two crimes of theft and banditry must be proved by a material and irrefutable proof. The victim is considered as a witness only in the case of an act of banditry.

The restitution of goods does not constitute a reason for the cancellation of the application of the penalty.

Part 4: Considerations concerning the Application of the Penalty for Adultery
Article 20:

a) A punishable act of adultery is fornication between men and women who have no legal relationship.

b) Pederasty comes under penalties concerning adultery.

Article 21: The crime of adultery is proved:

1) By a confession before the judicial authority on condition that the confession is not modified before the pronouncement of the final judgement.

2) By the testimony of four men of full age. In cases of necessity concerning witnesses, the alternatives contained in Article 2 can be applied.

All this, of course, on condition that there is not the slightest doubt which could lead to the non-application of the penalty.

Article 22: Persons of full age, men or women, convicted of adultery are sentenced to death by stoning.

Part 5: Penalties for Drunkenness
Article 23: Any intoxicating liquid, in large or small amounts, is considered as an alcoholic drink.

Article 24: The drinking of alcohol, its industrial production and distribution, are considered a punishable crime.

1) Anyone guilty of this crime is liable to flogging with 40 strokes.

2) Any person in a state of drunkenness in a public place is sentenced to 40 strokes of the whip.

3) In every case the alcohol is confiscated.

Part 6: Penalties for Slander
Article 25:

1) Any explicit accusation of adultery or pederasty against progeny or kin is considered as slander.

2) The crime of slander is accomplished by explicit spoken words, in writing, by insinuation the meaning of which is clear, or by expressive pictures.

Article 26: The person slandered must:

1) Be free from all vice, whether he is male or female.

2) Have really suffered the slander.

Article 27: Anyone uttering slander is sentenced to 80 strokes of the whip. His testimony is valid only after the certainty of his repentance has been established.

Article 28: The application of the penalty for slander is cancelled for the following facts:

1) Proof of the truth of the accusation.

2) Recognition by the slandered person himself of the object of the slander.

3) Censure.

Article 29:

a) Proceedings on slander can be begun only at the request of the slandered person himself.

b) The complaint of slander is impugned when the plaintiff is the son of the person uttering the slander.

Part 7: Penalties for Apostasy
Article 30: An apostate is any Muslim having abjured Islam, whether or not he has embraced another religion.

Article 31: The crime of apostasy is accomplished by:

1) Explicit spoken words or a definite act, showing apostasy.

2) Abjuration of the principles of Islam.

3) Derision expressed in words or actions with regard to a prophet, an apostle or a saint, or the Koran.

Article 32:

1) The repentance of the apostate: this is achieved when he goes back on his abjuration.

2) This repentance is admitted only from someone who has committed apostasy more than twice.

Article 33: Anyone who abjures Islam, his religion, and when all hope of repentance is lost, is condemned to death; the convicted person has a period of 60 days to repent.

Article 34:

a) The conduct of the apostate is considered and effective before the declaration of abjuration. All goods are restored after the declaration of repentance.

b) If the renegade is killed or dies before declaring his repentance, all the actions he has ever done are considered and effective, and all his goods are transmittable to his Muslim heirs.

c) All the actions of the apostate are null and void. His goods are transferrable to public funds.

Resolutions of the Congress of the Fathers of the Church, the Church Council and the Representatives of the Coptic People Meeting at Alexandria on 17th January 1977

Introduction

Following an invitation from the Council of the Clergy of Alexandria, there was the meeting of the Fathers of the Coptic Churches, presidents and members of Coptic associations, archbishops, members of the Council of Churches, representatives of the different sectors of the Coptic people in institutions of higher education, doctors, lawyers, accountants, engineers, businessmen, and workers in government administration and the nationalised sector.

This Congress met in the form of a conference of representatives of the Coptic people of Alexandria to consider general questions concerning the Copts. His Holiness Pope Chenoudah III was present at the first meeting which took place on 17th December 1976 in St Mark's Cathedral.

Everyone, pastors and congregations, took into consideration two inseparable facts:

1) Unshakeable faith in the eternal Coptic Church in Egypt, sanctified by the Apostle Mark and by the martyrs sacrificed in the course of succeeding generations.

2) Total loyalty to our native country of which the Copts are the oldest stock, to the point where it can be said that no people in the world is so attached to its land and its nationality.

Statement of General Coptic Questions

(1) Freedom of belief: Freedom of belief means that everyone is free to embrace the religious doctrine in which he believes, without suffering pain or prejudice because of his belief.

However, some tendencies towards removing the freedom of Christian belief have been spreading recently. They have been followed by some official authorities such as the police, civil administration and legal officials, concerning certain cases of conversion to Islam on the one hand, and other cases defined as acts of apostasy with regard to Islam on the other hand.

As for the case of conversion to Islam, we are considering with great anxiety these trends expressed in various religious and social circles, attacking Christianity to the point of calling this religion pagan, which shows a misappreciation of the tradition by which Christian religious authorities are informed of requests by Christians to be converted to Islam.

As for what has been called the abjuration of Islam, the official authorities refuse to recognise conversion to Christianity, and worse still, they reject a Christian's return to his own religion. These authorities refuse to take note of such situations in documents, records, identity cards and passports. The faithful who have returned to Christianity, their first religion, are the object of persecution in their family life by the separation of married couples and of fathers and sons under the pretext of disciplinary punishment.

All these trends are in conflict with the freedom of belief declared in the Charter of the Rights of Man and in the Constitution of 1971 and all the other Constitutions since the dawn of independence. According to them, the State guarantees freedom of belief and makes no racial, linguistic or religious distinction.

The Egyptian legislator himself, at the time of the promulgation of the inheritance law of 1943, refused to take into consideration the laws of the *Shari'a* concerning apostasy, because 'they were full of religious spirit contrary to the Constitution'.

The Council of State, for its part, had asserted that 'the penalties for apostasy can only be in contradiction with the spirit of freedom of belief'. *(2) The freedom of religious cults:* Religious doctrine consists of faith and practice. Praying together, and the ceremony of prayer in church, are basic elements of the Christian faith. It is sad to note that Christians are coming up against difficulties, restrictions, complications and even prejudices going as far as aggression, during the building of churches which are there only for the worship of God.

There is no need to recall that the building of new churches is not in any way anything to boast about. There is no budget for this purpose, and the churches are built from gifts from the Coptic people. On this subject we must remember the increase in the population of Egypt. Today there are more than 7,000,000 Christians in Egypt, hence the need to build new churches.

Although this is clear to our leaders, building and repair of churches can only be carried out by special authorisation and in limited numbers. Such authorisations are always subject to restrictions and difficulties much greater than those imposed by the State on places of entertainment and other public places. The Copts are still suffering from restrictive laws which go back to very ancient times. They are still suffering from an administrative decision of 1943 brought in by a government known in history for its injustice and tyranny. After much endeavour, decrees by the President of the Republic authorised the building of a few churches. This could not be done, and the government authorities know it. Churches already in existence were the object, in major cities, towns and villages, of aggressive acts and vandalism preventing the faithful from saying their prayers. Faced with the regrettable events which have occurred continuously for some years, we resent the lack of means of protection which could put an end to such aggression. Such acts affect the liberty of the Church, but they also affect the dignity of the State and the reputation of the Church throughout the world.

The Commission of Enquiry formed by the People's Council submitted to this Council in November 1973 a report on this whole situation, following which, Law No. 34 of 1972, on the protection of national unity, was promulgated. But in spite of the recommendations of the Commission of Enquiry, restrictions and obstacles have still been put in the way of the building of churches.

All this is happening on the soil of our beloved Egypt, sanctified by the visit of Jesus Christ and Mary, Mother of Light for 20 centuries. *(3) Application of Islamic law:* It is clear that, today in Egypt, there is a strong trend towards considering the Muslim *Shari'a* as the only source of the laws to be applied in the country. Writings and speeches of the supporters of this trend in both official circles and the popular domain show that it is certainly the Muslim *Shari'a* that they mean. They base the need for such an application on the religious doctrine which says that the *Shari'a* is divine law, and that no creature must disobey it.

For its supporters, then, there is no question of the rules and laws of the Muslim *Fiqh*. The Egyptian legislator took it as the source of earthly laws. He even often gave it priority over other Egyptian judicial techniques and applications.

The question today is to take all the considerations of the Muslim *Shari'a*, both globally and in detail, on the basis of their purely religious character, that is to say on the basis of the Koran and the Sunnah.

This opinion is not completely new; we find its roots in 1948, when it was officially declared to Parliament by Mr Hassan Al-Hudayb. (At the time he was adviser to the Appeal Court before taking up the leadership of the Muslim Brothers, thus succeeding Mr. Hassan El Banna). In fact he had said: 'I have an opinion about the question as a whole and not only civil law. This opinion, for me, is a doctrine which does not change, and I pray I may go to meet God without having changed it. My doctrine consists in the fact that all our country, all our life must be based in the Koran, meaning also, of course, the Sunnah of the Prophet, since to obey the Prophet is to obey God . . . .' (Record of the session of the Civil Legislative Committee, which took place at the Senate on May 30th 1948.)

If, then, the question was formulated in this way on the day of its birth in 1948 and on the day of its resurrection in 1976, and if it was founded on a basis of pure religion, the result is that any point of view the Coptic citizens may have about the application of the Muslim *Shari'a* is ruled out of court. Here the doctrine concerns only the Muslims, and takes no account of the other doctrines and other religions in Egypt.

The Resolutions of the Congress

(1) Freedom of belief: We demand that freedom of belief should be guaranteed to Christians and that all government orders and *fatwas* attacking this sacred liberty should be abrogated, especially those concerning the possibility of the Christian returning to his religion, a return which is unjustly considered an apostasy with regard to Islam.

(2) Freedom of worship: We demand that all restrictions already made should be abrogated, including the administrative decree issued by an Under-Secretary in the Ministry of the Interior in a tyrannical period, a decree containing ten restrictions on the building of churches. We ask the security organisations to play their part firmly so that the practice of religion may be protected in the churches, especially those in the villages; their protection can be provided either in the context of preventive action or control and condemnation of any activity which is aggressive or prejudicial (to the citizens).

(3) Concerning the application of Islamic law as demanded by Muslim extremists and by trends that are no less extremist and alien to genuine Egyptian society. We declare that we reject such an application vis-a-vis Christians in Egypt. We consider that any attempt in that direction, aiming

at constraint under cover of legislation or discipline, implies something very serious: the compulsion of Christians to submit to a doctrine other than their own, which constitutes a serious violation of the most sacred right of man: the right to freedom of conviction.

(4) Legislation on personal status: We demand that a legislative modification should be made with all speed to Law No. 462 of 1955, so that is clearly stipulated that the law to be applied in the case of the separation of Christian married couples is that under which the contract was signed, leaving out of account any change which may subsequently occur; this is to protect the family and put an end to all speculation on matters of religion.

(5) Lack of equality of opportunity: We demand that an official supreme committee for national unity should be formed, with all the required qualities of objectivity and with all the necessary powers to investigate in order to decide on complaints about discrimination in appointments and promotions in the civil service and the nationalised sector. These steps are absolutely essential before the issue of administrative orders which are to correct situations and give everyone his due. These steps are also necessary before laying clear and precise foundations for the guarantee of objectivity in the matter of appointment and promotion and to overcome any tendency to prejudice. Appointments and promotions must be made on the basis of performance and the reports arising from regular inspections. All administrative authorities deviating from these rules should be firmly penalised so that equality can be guaranteed in the public interest.

(6) The representation of Christians in parliamentary institutions: We demand that a change should be made so that Christians may be guaranteed true representation on the People's Council and on local councils. Such representation must correspond to the effective numbers of the citizens in such a way that the unity of the two elements of the nation is really achieved.

(7) Extremist religious tendencies: We demand that the government authorities concerned in the State should intervene to put an end to these trends in order to maintain national unity. We demand that university administrations take adequate measures to cleanse university circles of all parasites so that the universities may devote themselves to their true mission as happens in all the universities of the civilised world.

(8) Freedom of publication: We demand that the censorship, implicit and explicit, on Christian writings and publications should be lifted. We demand that a limit be set to atheistic writings defaming the Christian religion and its doctrines. We demand that the programmes of historical and literary instruction in the various schools and universities should include the study of the Christian period in Egyptian history, a period which extends over six centuries before the Muslim conquest.

Recommendations to be Carried Out

In the light of what has gone before, and in order to help find means of satisfying the preceding demands, to strengthen love between our fellows, peace and national unity, to ensure understanding and union between the two elements of the nation, in the interests of Egypt for ever, of our pure and united soul, of our thought free from party interest, and in a spirit of peace, sincerity and purity before God and man, we make this declaration:

(1) We call for a total fast in the Church from 31st January to 2nd

February 1977, to raise our thoughts to God, the Maker of all good things, so that He will grant to His people unity of heart, to the fatherland peace and tranquillity, and to the leaders of the country wisdom, success and rationality to liberate every inch of our territory and to herald an era of liberty and happiness for all the children of the eternal fatherland through the divine promise: 'Blessed be the people of Egypt.'

(2) We pass these resolutions and demands to His Holiness Pope Chenoudah III, Pope of the Church of Alexandria, Patriarch of the Church of St Mark, Supreme Chief of the Holy Council and the Council of Christian Churches of Egypt, so that he can take measures for the fulfilment of the Coptic demands.

(3) We present a copy of these resolutions and recommendations to the President of the Republic, to the Prime Minister, to the Secretary-General of the Socialist Union and to the President of the People's Council so that action may be taken by the constitutional and legal means open to the legislative and executive powers to fulfil the desires of the children of the Coptic people.

(4) We consider the Congress in permanent session in order continuously to follow what is being achieved among these recommendations and resolutions concerning all general questions involving the Copts.
Eternal glory of God. Amen.

Appendix C: The Democratic Question

Text of the Law for the Protection of the Security of the Country and its Citizens

Article 1: The freedom to form political parties is assured in accordance with the law on the creation of parties from the moment of its promulgation by the legislative power.

Article 2: Clandestine organisations, hostile to the social system or military in character, are forbidden by the Constitution. Any person having taken part in or called for the creation of such organisations will be condemned to penal servitude or to penal servitude for life.

Article 3: Public property belongs to the people. Collective and private property is protected by the Constitution. Any person having taken part in an assembly for the purpose of sabotaging or damaging public, collective or private property, will be condemned to penal servitude for life. The same punishment is applied to the instigators of such actions.

Article 4: Taxes and participation in public expenditure are a duty (of every citizen) according to law. Peasants owning three feddans or less, and incomes not exceeding E£500 a year are totally exempt.

Article 5: Every citizen, in the coming three months, must present a declaration of capital, of whatever variety it may be and wherever it may be. This declaration includes the goods of the person in question, his wife, and his children, if under age. Capital and goods will be recorded in the tax return book of each citizen. Fraud or false declarations will be punished by penal servitude. The crime of fraud will also involve the loss of the right to work in the public service, and also the loss of civil rights.

Article 6: Any person having taken part in an assembly appealing to the population to oppose the application of the laws and statutes with the intention of influencing the course of constitutional power, or with the intention of preventing the functioning of government institutions, the nationalised or private sectors, and educational institutions, whether by force or by threats, will be condemned to penal servitude. The same punishment will be applied to the instigators of the assembly, even if they do not take part in it.

Article 7: All workers having undertaken strike action with the intention of achieving a common aim will be condemned to penal servitude for life if such a strike constitutes a threat to the national economy.

Article 8: Any person having prepared an assembly or an occupation of buildings in such a way as to threaten a breach of the peace ...

Article 9: All rules and statutes opposed to the above laws are abrogated.

Article 10: These laws are applicable from the moment of their publication.

Article 11: In accordance with Article 74 of the Constitution, this law must be submitted to a popular vote in the week following its publication. I sign it in the presence of the people.

The President of the Republic
People's Council
Cairo, 3rd February 1977.

The Law Known as the Law of the Home Front and Social Peace

This draft law consists of 13 articles of which the first forbids any propaganda against the basic principles of the revolution of 23rd July, and all propaganda in favour of doctrines in opposition to the system of democratic socialism.

Article 2 forbids anyone who has been proved by the investigations of the socialist Attorney General to be guilty of propagating ideas threatening divine law, to occupy any high state position in the nationalised sector, or influencing public opinion, or in the management of general companies or press institutions. Article 2 adds that the socialist Attorney General must present his report to the Prime Minister or to the Supreme Press Council, according to the case, to ask for the transfer of those who fall under paragraph 1 of this law to functions which have no bearing on the direction or influencing of public opinion.

Article 3, approved, stipulates: 'Any person propagating ideas or doctrines abjuring divine law is incapable of being a member of the administrative council of trade unions or professional associations, or of local unions and congresses, or of co-operatives.'

Article 4 forbids membership of political parties and all other political activity to all persons having taken part in the corruption of public life before the revolution of 1952, either by the occupation of ministerial posts, by membership of political parties in power before 1952, or by taking part in the leadership of the said parties, with the exception of the nationalist party (*Watani*) and the Young Egypt Party.

Article 5 indicates that the prohibitions contained in the preceding article also apply to persons condemned by the revolutionary tribunal following Case No. 1 of 1971 concerning persons who had formed centres of power after the revolution of 23rd July 1952. These prohibitions also apply to all those who were condemned in cases illegally affecting the individual liberty of citizens, and their private lives, or injuring citizens morally or physically.

They apply, finally, to all who have been condemned in affairs attacking the security of the government, either from within the country or abroad, with the exception of rehabilitated persons.

Article 6 authorises the commission indicated in Article 8 of the Law No. 40 of 1977 to prevent whomsoever it wishes from belonging to political parties or carrying on political activities if, following the investigation held by the socialist Attorney General, it is proved that the accused person really has committed acts likely to corrupt public life in the country and put at risk either national unity or social peace.

Article 7 stipulates that Articles 4, 5, and 6 can be waived and not applied to persons rehabilitated, exceptionally, after the said laws have come into force.

Article 8 is an assurance that the press belongs to the people. It guarantees freedom of publication within the limits of the Charter of Honour and the laws governing the press and publications.

Article 9 defines the penalties applicable to any journalist publishing or broadcasting within the country or abroad information likely to injure the national interest, corrupt public life or put at risk national unity and social peace.

Article 10 indicates that, to preserve the higher interests of the nation, any person or political party infringing the principles of the system of democratic socialism, or the spiritual and religious values of society, and any party leader committing acts likely to threaten social life or national unity will be laid under interdiction.

Article 11 indicates the responsibility of the socialist Attorney General for ensuring social peace and protecting the social system. Article 12 gives the socialist Attorney General the duty to inform Parliament of all the measures he takes according to law within seven days following his decision; the socialist Attorney General is required subsequently to present a complete report on the measures and the decisions taken.

Article 13 states that anyone contravening Articles 4, 5, 6 and 10 will be condemned to a period of imprisonment of at least three months, and a fine from E£300 to E£3,000.

Article 14 abrogates all other laws opposed to this one.

Article 15 orders the publication of this law in the *Official Gazette;* it will come into force immediately on publication.

This law was issued by the Legislative Committee of the People's Council on 31st May 1978.

Update, 1981

Update, 1981

Camp David and the 'Peace' Treaty

All the phenomena, events, resolutions, laws and changes which have occurred in Egypt in the course of the last ten years together constitute a decisive reaction against the period of Nasser, and, consequently, against all the policies and objectives which have governed the Middle East for 18 years. Of course, we cannot carry this argument to the point of exaggeration and say that the Middle East was a stable region during Nasser's time. The region had experienced two wars between the Arabs and Israel, followed by the Egyptian war of attrition. It had also experienced a series of coups, insurrections, revolutions and counter-revolutions. None of this was in the least stable. But what is certain is that the instability of Nasser's time reflected the Arabs' dominant national ambition for independence, unity and self-liberation. In short, this instability implied an unaccustomed ferment moving towards the achievement of the real objectives vis-a-vis Arab territory – and, in response, the foreign imperialist forces and the reactionary Arab governments did their utmost, in a concerted effort, to prevent their achievement.

The reaction since against Nasser's domestic policy in every field has been at the same time a reaction against his Arab and international policy. The result was a new instability in the Middle East, despite the peace treaty between Egypt and the Israeli State. It could even be said that this treaty actually heralds the start of the most appalling, bloody upheavals in the history of the region, with all their attendant risk of threats to peace and international security and horrible dangers.

There is no doubt that, by getting Sadat to sign the peace treaty, American imperialism and the Zionist State have won a strategic victory, and deprived the Arab nation of two resolves which were an integral part of its patriotic and national sovereignty: the first, the Egyptian resolve to wage war; the second, the Arab resolve to achieve national unity. After the usurpation of the right of free choice with regard to these two resolves, the liberation and unification of the Arab territories became more difficult than ever.

And from another point of view, this treaty did not lead to any sort of stability, either at home or outside Egypt, or, in fact, in the Middle East anywhere. Quite the contrary! The Lebanese war, which has shed so much blood for six years, is enough on its own to give an idea of the true nature of the new instability.

Before introducing this 'new arrival' − the Egypt-Israeli-American treaty − we must look at Nasser's so-called policy of instability, in order to see more clearly what its end would have been − peace or war − if it had been able to continue and develop.

On the home front, Nasser's policy was aimed at a balance between the warring social classes, so as to allow free rein to an independent economy and to fulfil the tasks of modern industrialisation, a possible start to agricultural planning, the improvement of the social services and, above all, the firm-rooted establishment of the national culture.

Despite the efforts of the semi-feudal landowners and the big capitalists, local and foreign, to disturb or even to check the process of national rebirth, Nasser worked resolutely for the progress of the people as a whole, in a context that would shelter them from serious class tensions. In the same way, he led the glorious combat of Suez. After five years he confronted Egyptian capitalism and quickened the movement towards large-scale nationalisations. In a word, political and economic independence was the main pivot of Nasser's time.

But this confrontation was not only internal, but external also: neither colonialism nor Israel were any more favourable to this independence and social progress than Arab and local reactionaries. For this reason, in the face of the will of the Egyptian people and the Arab nation, foreign, Zionist and reactionary Arab forces endeavoured to foment real instability. In 1956, Great Britain, France and Israel organised the invasion of Egypt. In 1958, the Iraqis revolted against the Baghdad Pact, drawn up by colonialism as a solid barrier against the rising forces of the revolution. In 1962, after eight years of fierce and bloody resistance, the revolution triumphed in Algeria. This was also the time when Kuwait, South Yemen and the other Gulf countries won their independence. Revolution was imminent in North Yemen. It was in these circumstances that Israel, in open conspiracy with the Americans, attacked Egypt and Syria in 1967. After this, the Palestinian resistance succeeded in making a transformation within the Palestinian people: from being a nation of refugees, they became revolutionaries. The Libyan Revolution broke out in 1969. A year later came the carnage of Black September and the death of Nasser.

This is what Western literature calls 'Nasserist instability'. It was certainly instability for colonialism, Zionism and reaction. It was a tumultuous upheaval in the ranks of these three enemies. But, on the other hand, it was stability from the point of view of the objectives of the Arab people. It was stability from the point of view of world peace.

It may be true that to rectify wrong situations does not in itself constitute stability, it implies nevertheless the preliminary levelling necessary for the building of true stability. Thus, Nasser's policy on the home front was reflected in a number of principles which also governed his actions in the

Arab and international field.

In the forefront of these principles, in the Arab field, is a profound faith in Arab unity to which Nasser tried for three years (1958—62) to give concrete form in the union between Egypt and Syria. The effective achievement of unity may have turned out to be impossible, but the 'unity of positions' in face of the common national enemy was a fact. Nasser often had to bow to the evidence that the 'unity of objectives' was hard to conceive of because of the class imbalance well-known among Arab regimes. He left the people of these nations to do as they thought best. But he showed no indulgence with regard to the 'unity of positions' in face of the immediate national enemy — Israel. As an army man who had taken part in the war of 1948 on Palestinian soil, he knew that this Western dagger thrust into Arab flesh was there only to separate Egypt from the rest of the Arab world, and to raise an obstacle between the eastern and the western parts of the Arab world by the establishment of local colonialism. It was for this reason that the strategic security of Egypt was the compass which guided his actions in favour of the liberation of Palestine. As soon as he came to power, and especially after Israel's first armed attack, against the Gaza Strip in 1955, he understood that Israel's aggressive expansionism had no limits, and that, consequently, it would never tolerate the establishment in Egypt of an advanced social pattern, supported by a patriotic army, going from strength to strength.

The second of these principles, on the international plane, was a deep conviction as to the merits of positive neutrality, created at the Bandung Conference in 1955 by Nasser, Nehru and Tito — a neutrality based on the rule: 'to be the friends of those who want to be our friends', starting from a position of patriotic independence. Nasser never regarded the great powers of the contemporary world as on the same footing. He could appreciate attitudes supporting Arab rights, and denounce those who supported the enemies of these rights.

In his distinction between friends and enemies, Nasser showed himself to be a real Egyptian patriot, deeply devoted to the interests of the whole nation and its genuine objectives, just as he showed himself to be an Arab nationalist, passionately attached to the soil of this nation and just as devoted to its genuine objectives. He treated his friends as equals, not hesitating, if need be, to declare himself publicly in disagreement with them. He never made mistakes in distinguishing categorically between a friend and an enemy (or the friend of an enemy).

The third of these principles, applying both on the Arab and the international plane, was that oil is 'a national source of energy'. If certain rulers chose to squander a large part of it for purposes not in conformity with the interests of their people, it was for the   people themselves to decide the question. But as far as the cause of Palestine was concerned, no one had the right not to use this fuel for the good of the cause — the Palestinian cause being an Egyptian cause as well as an Arab one.

These are the principles on which Nasser fought colonialism, Zionism and

Arab reaction, right up to his death. And it is against these same principles that the Sadat regime in Egypt turned, applying principles radically and totally opposed to them: the signature of a treaty of alignment with the United States; the signature ratifying the return of the Palestinians to refugee camps. All this is equivalent to a complete reversal of Nasser's former policies and the acceptance, without reservation, of all the ingredients of the American-Israeli 'peace'.

Before examining the effects of this 'peace', two remarks must be made here. The first concerns the delicate balance between the social and political procedures of this reversal. The laws opening the way to economic dependence on the West, approved 'in the name of a free economy', follow a course parallel to the stages of political dependence on the United States and Israel, these latter justified 'in the name of peace'. The second remark concerns the delicate balance between all that has happened in the course of the last decade in Egypt, and what is still happening there, and all the conflicts that have broken out in the Middle East, particularly in the Lebanon.

What we mean by the first remark is that the change of regime in Egypt and the modification of the economic, social and cultural structure of the Nasserist system which followed, had a decisive influence on Egypt's political orientation, Arab and international.

What we mean by the second remark is that, just as under Nasser Egypt was the centre of numerous insurrections and the source of innumerable difficulties for colonialism and Israel, under Sadat it is still the centre of disturbances, just as numerous and more dangerous still for peace in the Middle East and security in the world. It is a fact that (in the past, at present and for the future) Egypt possesses historical, geographical, demographic and cultural characteristics which make it an essential source of real influence, positive or negative, in the region.

These two remarks certainly deserve deep thought on the part of anyone interested in the question of peace in this sensitive part of the world, particularly its peoples and its philosophers. No change can possibly take place in present-day Egyptian policies if the policy-makers themselves do not change. No modification in present events in the Middle East can occur as long as Egypt's abstentionism lasts.

Let us then examine the extent of the dangers inherent in this reaction against Nasser's policies. Just after the death of its historic leader, it seemed that we could have every hope of Egypt's development. But what is the state of 'stability' within the country today?

According to information from the U.N. specialised agencies, and particularly according to the statistics of Unesco, we find that:

* Except for the years 1973–74, Egypt has been the scene of many popular insurrections, the most notable of which was that of 18th and 19th January 1977.
* In the course of the last ten years, 65 religious incidents have occurred in various parts of Egypt. The result has been 376 victims (76 dead and 300

injured) and twelve churches burnt, including the oldest church in the country.

* The only progress recorded for Egypt is in the crime rate, which has been at a record level for ten years, with a 300% increase in crimes committed with firearms.
* 3,400 children reported missing each year.
* During this same period, 17,000 political prisoners have been detained in state prisons.
* 123,000 different weapons have been discovered in secret arms caches.

Such are the realities of the 'social peace' emblazoned in the mass media controlled by Sadat.

As far as the situation outside Egypt is concerned, the following facts can be established.

First, the war in the Lebanon, declared in 1975 but actually prepared for from 1973 onwards. Observers note on this subject that each time Egypt takes a step in the direction of the United States and Israel, the Lebanese War is intensified. In fact, the Second Sinai Agreement was signed in 1975, already looking forward to the separate peace soon to be concluded. In 1977, when Sadat visited Occupied Jerusalem, Israel was preparing for the occupation of South Lebanon which took place shortly afterwards. In 1978, after the signing of the Camp David Agreements, Israel encouraged the stationing of its allies (the Lebanese Christian militia) in the border areas. In 1979, once the Treaty of Washington was signed, the maverick officer Saad-Haddad intensified his aggression against South Lebanon. In 1980, after the first step towards normalisation, the Zionist State carried out a violent campaign against the Palestinians in the interior of the occupied territories. Finally, on the occasion of the second anniversary of normalisation in 1981, Israel carried out a raid against the Iraqi nuclear power station, after a 'peace meeting' between Sadat and Begin.

In fact, after Egypt's isolation, Israel became an internal element in the Lebanese War, in view of its alliance with the Lebanese religious faction aligned internationally much like Sadat's regime. Assured of the neutrality of the Egyptian army in the conflict, Israel could act freely, first attacking the Lebanese *Bakaa*, then threatening Syria and Libya, and finally attacking Iraq.

Secondly, by this isolation of Egypt on ideological grounds, Sadat's regime encouraged religious and racist movements, splitting apart the patriotic unity of the Egyptian people and tearing up the bonds between the different Arab countries, as had already happened with Algeria and Syria. And because the Zionist foundations of the State of Israel are religious, the justification of Sadat's regime for the isolation of Egypt is in perfect agreement with Zionist thought, which consists of fomenting chauvinistic agitation all over the Near East with a view to creating religious quasi-states capable of preventing the Arab world from progressing towards its national unity. This ideological alliance has given rise to a fascist position in which repression and blood are the only language prevailing, thus impeding the establishment of a democratic climate capable of solving the problem of ethnic and religious minorities, as well as other social problems.

Third, with a view to strengthening the alliance between the Egyptian and Israeli regimes on one side and the United States on the other, on 23rd July 1977 Sadat's regime launched an attack on the frontiers of the Libyan Jamahyria, shortly before Sadat's visit to occupied Jerusalem. It is clear that Sadat's intention was to affirm that the page of the July 1952 revolution and its strategic alliances had been turned for good and all, and that the guns formerly trained on the eastern frontier are henceforth trained on the western frontier — thereby overturning a quarter of a century of Egyptian history.

Having given up its adherence to the Arab nation, Egypt is now acting as a strategic base for Israel and the United States — especially since the implementation of the Egyptian-Sudanese project aimed at transforming the Nile Valley into a strategic barrier separating the Arab East from the Maghreb and attacking the African liberation movement. The Egyptian armed forces, whom Sadat had refused to allow to take part in the A.D.F. in the Lebanon 'as long as there was an inch of occupied ground in Sinai', took part, paradoxically, in a war in Zaire, in the heart of Africa, even though Sinai was still occupied. These same forces also gave the present Sudanese regime the protection of thousands of Egyptian soldiers and officers.

A further fact is that, in keeping with its strategy of monopolising the natural resources and occupying the strategic positions in the region, the United States urged the Egyptian Government not only to concede to them strategic facilities for their manoeuvres and permanent military bases, but also to intervene with the Sudan, Somalia and Oman to persuade them to offer the same facilities. The pretexts used for this purpose, such as 'the protection of the Gulf' or 'the danger of Soviet infiltration' have been justly refuted by all Arabs.

The direct consequence of this policy was to heighten the tension in the Gulf area more than ever, especially in the principal oil areas: the war between Iraq and Iran, the internal conflicts in Saudi Arabia, the war between the two Yemens, the recent *coup d'etat* in Turkey and the partition of Cyprus are all 'fruits' of the American offensive against the Middle East — from Nixon, through Ford and Carter, to Reagan. This offensive was considerably accentuated by the reversal of Egyptian policies and the strategic alliance between the regimes of Sadat and Begin, a fascist alliance faithful to American plans.

Finally, the antagonism that exists between the Arab countries is simply a logical consequence of Egyptian abstentionism. In the absence of any leadership capable of initiating the rebirth of the nation, oil has become the centre of leadership and influence, and at the same time an explosive factor, since these essential reserves are under the control of regimes which in principle are favourable to American plans. Consequently, civil wars in these countries and inter-Arab wars on the one hand, and the contradiction between alliance with the United States and cries for the liberation of Palestine on the other, have become the inescapable fate of the Arab world.

In the meantime, explosions continue to occur today, as they did yesterday and will tomorrow. They threaten the peoples of the region, which is effectively caught up in the nuclear phase of the arms race, a race which is surely a serious threat to world peace and security.

Why?

In a word: Because abstentionism in Egypt is a clear renunciation of Nasser's policy (patriotic independence, social progress on the home front, social unity, Arab solidarity, non-alignment with the great powers in foreign policy); and because the problem of the Near East has never been the problem of Sinai or the Sudan, but that of the Arab people of Palestine, that is to say the Arab-Israeli conflict. This conflict has not been solved by Sadat's reaction against Nasser's policy. On the contrary, it has grown to such a size and such a depth that no repression, either from the Arab rulers or from the Israeli or American military machine, will be capable of shaking the will of the Arab nations.

The 'non-stability' of Nasser's time was indeed legitimate, since it was preparing for true stability. As for the reversal of Nasser's policy, it has aggravated the situation and is still aggravating it, while the heartfelt aspiration towards real stability is gradually giving place to despair. The reason is simple: it lies in the fact that Nasser did not create the social struggle in Egypt or in any other Arab country; that is why, by coming down on the side of justice, he came down on the side of true social stability. Nasser did not create foreign hegemony; that is why, by coming down on the side of independence, he came down on the side of effective national stability. What is more, Nasser did not create war – hot or cold – between the great powers, that is why his positive neutrality was a position only for the international forces favourable to the Arab cause. And before that, Nasser did not create either Israel or Egypt's national identity. But he was convinced that the plans of the West – from the Crusades to the founding of Israel – were aimed only at the isolation of Egypt from the rest of the Arab world, so as to weaken it and pillage Arab wealth. That is why he worked for his country's future and its position as an organic part of the Arab nation.

If Nasser's standpoint did not bring stability to colonialism, Zionism or Arab reactionaries, that of Sadat, aligned with Western plans instead of fighting them, does not give stability to a single one of the parties concerned. On the contrary, it has only multipled the contradictions between Egypt and the Arab countries. These fresh contradictions in the Near East are likely to have immeasurable consequences, unless there is still time to pull Egypt out of its abstentionism.

There is a great difference between the damage caused by accidents that can happen to a train going the right way and the damage that could be caused to a train going the wrong way; in the latter case it is not only the driver who is risking his life, but all the passengers.

After the reaction against Nasser's policy, the Near East is the image of a train going the wrong way, and heading straight for the nuclear abyss.

September 1981: The Mass Arrests
'I ask permission from no one. I take my own decisions.'
'Democracy has sharper teeth than any dictatorship.'

These are the opening and closing sentences of Sadat's speech on 5 September 1981. The first was intended as a denial that he had received orders from the U.S., or had been given the green light by Reagan and Begin before implementing the recent measures.

The second was a way of dropping the figleaf of democracy and revealing his regime for what it really is, a form of repression with 'sharper teeth than any dictatorship'. Indeed, Sufi Abu Jahleb, President of the so-called Popular Assembly who introduced Sadat's speech, called the new measures a second revolution, going even further than the rectifications of May 1971.

So what is happening in Egypt? What is going to happen there and elsewhere in the Arab world?

It would be totally wrong to assume that the whole business is simply a massive campaign for repression. After all, Sadat and his regime have been oppressors throughout the last ten years. What has happened, and is still happening, calls for a much broader approach to the question.

To begin with, one must look at events both inside and outside Egypt, and to grasp the connection between the two.

It was clear that during the recent Israeli elections, Western Europe was banking on a victory for Peres, the Labour Party leader, whilst the U.S. and the Egyptian regime were banking on Begin's re-election.

Sadat met Begin in Sharm El Sheikh, just before the Israeli raid on the Iraqi nuclear reactor. This, of course, is not to suggest that the Israeli Prime Minister warned Sadat that he was about to send his planes against Iraq. What really surprised Sadat, however, was not so much Israel's aggression as the tremendous popular reaction it evoked in Egypt. The Egyptians now realized that Israel was acting without any restraint whatsoever, and was taking advantage of the officially recognized separate peace with Egypt to strike out at will against all the other Arab countries. The official media were forced to issue strong condemnations of the Israeli action, and hundreds of Egyptians gathered outside the headquarters of the Workers' Party, the party which Sadat himself had designated as the Party of the Loyal Opposition when it approved the Camp David Agreements. For the first time, the crowd was openly chanting anti-Sadat slogans and calling for his overthrow.

In recent months, the rank and file of the Workers' Party had brought pressure to bear on its leadership, forcing it to move away from its initial position and to become a political organization hostile to a separate peace and normalization. The party journal *Al Shaab*, notably the pieces contributed by Helmi Murad, Fathi Radwan and Ibrahim Shoukri, had become a thorn in the regime's flesh.

A few days later the popular masses came together in a major rally organized by the Patriotic Progressive Unionist Party. Once again the people were clamouring for Sadat's downfall. Under such conditions it is clear that *Al Shaab* was no longer simply the organ of the Worker's Party. It had become the voice of the entire Egyptian patriotic opposition. The paper was now serving as a platform for the increasingly accusatory open letters addressed to the President by Fuad Siraj al Din, the leader of the Wafd, and Mahmud Al Kadhi, leader of the Patriotic Front, used the newspaper's columns to describe scandals beside which Watergate itself seems pale in comparison. Several prominent Nasserists and communists also contributed, reflecting the anger of the entire people.

Furthermore, the vast rallies organized by the Workers' Party, the Patriotic Progressive Union and by the Lawyers' Trade Union, attracted the support of eminent personalities from a variety of different political tendencies, personalities such as Abdel Aziz Churbaji, Muhammad Hassanein Haykal, Fathi Radhwan and Khaled Mohieddine.

The communiques put out by these patriotic coalitions were signed by figures right across the political spectrum, including prominent Islamic personalities, such as Hassan Al-Banna, Sedki Suleyman, Aziz Sedki, Kamel Al Din Hussein and Abdellatif Baghdadi. The Lawyers' Union was indefatigable. Despite threats and attempts to buy them off, its members remained unanimously supportive of its council's opposition to the regime's policies. They burnt the Israeli flag and called for the overthrow of Sadat. Eventually, Sadat was forced to have a law passed in Parliament to dissolve the nominated council of the Lawyers' Union, a body which numbered amongst its ranks such prominent people as Nabil Hilali, an illustrious revolutionary militant imprisoned these last 6 months, Ahmed Nasser, a Wafd leader, and Ahmed Khawaja, a notable Nasserist, as well as many other patriots, democrats and members of the Workers' Party. Many observers were convinced that the various patriotic tendencies had achieved a high level of co-ordination; certainly nobody seemed to have any qualms about expressing their dissatisfaction with the regime.

Meanwhile, the negotiations on the autonomy of the West Bank had come to a complete standstill, and many Zionists were demanding that the Jewish colonies in Sinai be preserved. Events were taking a spectacular turn. Israel's savage attack on Beirut incensed everybody, and few welcomed the U.S. sponsored idea of a 'multinational force in Sinai', simply a pretext for American troops to relieve the Israelis and continue the occupation in another guise. In response, the Egyptian regime actively sponsored one of the most disgusting civil conflicts in the country's history. Fires raged in the Masarra Church in Chubra and in the Al Zawya Al Hamra quarter.

In the midst of all this, the U.S. conducted a crazily aggressive venture into into the Gulf of Syrte, violating the territorial waters of the Libyan Arab Jamahyriya, thereby triggering off the first ever aerial dogfight between U.S. war planes and those of an Arab country.

Such was the background to the recent vast campaign of repression mounted against the principal Egyptian political figures of this half-century.

About 150 years ago, a decisive event took place in Egyptian history. Muhammad Ali invited more than 500 Mamelukes to a reception in the famous Alkalaa (citadel) and massacred them to the last man, thereby succeeding where Napoleon had failed, and achieving a monopoly of power in Egypt. For eight years, Sadat has employed a similar subterfuge, inviting Egyptians to a reception, with 'democracy' on the menu; then, on the evening of 2 September 1981, he eliminated 533 prominent personalities of the Egyptian opposition. A few days later the figure had reached 1,500 and then stabilized at around 5,000 civilians. There are also some 50 army officers languishing in the regime's gaols, and 40,000 citizens under house arrest.

The arrests were aimed at the entire patriotic opposition, from the far right to the far left, and did not spare the various centre groupings, notably numerous pseudo-neutral friends and ex-allies of Sadat and America. Several senior priests of the Coptic and Coptic Orthodox Churches were also arrested. Furthermore, the State refused to recognize the nomination of Pope Chenouda III as Patriarch of Alexandria, an event quite unprecedented in Egyptian history.

So what does this sudden sandstorm in Egyptian affairs really mean? Simply that the regime had to react against the growing popular unrest. The sheer scale of dissent in Egypt and the very real possibility of a vast democratic popular front had proved that, despite months of brain-washing by the media, the Egyptian man in the street had at last seen through all the lies about the peace, prosperity and democracy which the treaty of reconciliation was supposed to ensure.

The political leaders had set aside their ideological and other quarrels and had managed to coordinate their actions with those of the ordinary Egyptian. Indeed, this coordination now appears to be firmly established and has reached a point of no return, at least as far as opposition to the regime is concerned. Throughout all this, the C.I.A. was keeping its masters fully informed of what was happening and was beginning to search for possible alternatives to Sadat.

Once Sadat had given away all his trumps, it soon emerged that he would never be able to deliver what he had promised, namely Palestinian autonomy. The alternative proposal put forward by King Fahd of Saudi Arabia was then wheeled in as a substitute and a way of arabizing Camp David. But this new Arab formula, Camp David II as it were, was more in need of camouflage than of any reorientation of Egyptian policy. Although the Saudi proposal did not succeed in attracting U.S. or Israeli support, it did polarize West European interests, and thereby presented Washington and Tel Aviv with a *fait accompli*. Also, the Saudis are constantly warning the U.S. that the only alternative to their proposal is an eventual seizure of power by the extremists.

The U.S. was also looking for a new formula. Indeed, the Americans were fairly explicit in discussing the matter. During a series of public lectures in the famous 'Yort' amphitheatre of the American University of Cairo, Professor Malcolm Com-Kyr, President of the Berkeley Institute for Middle East Studies, and one of the national security apparatus's top advisers on

Egyptian affairs, indicated seven possible new scenarios that Sadat could adopt. The main ones were:
1) He could step down in favour of a replacement from within the regime.
2) The Patriotic Opposition Front might take power.
3) There could be a military coup.

Leaving aside the second possibility, since it would hardly suit the Americans, and given the difficulty of the third – unless the U.S. provided direct support – the first scheme was likely to be favoured. As the Senegalese experience has shown, now that Leopold Senghor has resigned the Presidency in order to dedicate himself to looking after Western interests within the framework of his Party and the Socialist International, this new American formula seems very well suited to America's aims; the charade of the official hand-over of Sinai in April 1982 would provide a suitable opportunity to implement it.

It thus seemed probable that, in order to forestall a military coup, Sadat would announce his resignation in a blaze of publicity. Having accomplished his historic mission, he would be free to concentrate on serving the international interests of the U.S. and Israel in Africa and the Middle East. A new figure, someone more acceptable to the so-called Arab moderates, would then emerge and continue the effort to arabize Camp David. This is only one scenario amongst many possibilities, of course.

Yet it remains clear that the new massacre in the Citadel, especially the sheer scale of the operation, reflects the weakness rather than the strength of the regime. A series of unprecedented events highlighted the fact that the entire Egyptian population is opposed to the regime. The latter has responded by marshalling practically every political and religious representative of any significance, purging the media, not only of those who oppose the regime without daring to give voice to the dissent, but also of any hesitant supporters and undecided allies it might have. The universities and colleges have been similarly treated: the motto of the day seems to be 'he who is not with me is against me.'

At present it seems that only the American intelligence services stand between Sadat and the anger of the Egyptian people. The scale of the operation which has temporarily stifled a national uprising also reflects the advanced stage reached in the preparations for a major offensive by the U.S., Israel and Sadat, somewhere in the Arab world.

I hope we will not allow ourselves to be taken completely by surprise, as we were by the bombing of the Iraqi reactor, the raid into the Gulf of Syrte and the continuing devastation of Southern Lebanon.

Events in Egypt affect the whole Arab world. Sadat's new mass round-up of the opposition is not simply a vast campaign of repression against the Egyptian patriotic opposition, it is also part of the groundwork for a fullscale political and military campaign against the bases of resistance to the arabization of Camp David. Any radical change in Egypt would upset all the American and Israeli plans for the conflict in the Middle East.

Egypt was on the verge of precisely such a change. It was apparent to all and sundry that the regime had failed on every count. Its economic, social and political programmes were in shambles, it was totally isolated and powe less to cope with the mounting wave of famine. Denominational conflict at home, provocation of the Jamahyriya and the massive military presence in the Sudan were proving fruitless. The regime could only resort to a sawing away at the body and soul of the Arab nation, an operation which may well turn out to be the dramatic prologue to the downfall of the regime and end of an era.

Ghali Shoukri
October 1981.